Mapping the mind

A growing number of researchers now claim that many cognitive abilities are specialized to handle specific types of information. Psychologists with concerns ranging from animal learning to emergent theories of mind and folk biology, cognitive scientists exploring problem solving and expertise, anthropologists working with color terms and folk taxonomies, psycholinguists investigating auditory perception, and philosophers examining reasoning schemata have concluded – often independently – that humans simply could not learn what they do in a purely domain-neutral fashion. In this important volume bringing together different traditions of research, the contributors examine a number of theoretical questions, including the nature of domain-guided knowledge transfer, the biological and evolutionary nature of domain-specific skills, and the implications of a domain-specific perspective for education.

Mapping the mind

Domain specificity in cognition and culture

Edited by

LAWRENCE A. HIRSCHFELD
University of Michigan

SUSAN A. GELMAN
University of Michigan

CAMBRIDGE
UNIVERSITY PRESS

mc

Published by the Press Syndicate of the University of Cambridge
The Pitt Building, Trumpington Street, Cambridge CB2 1RP
40 West 20th Street, New York, NY 10011-4211, USA
10 Stamford Road, Oakleigh, Melbourne 3166, Australia

First published 1994

Printed in the United States of America

Library of Congress Cataloging-in-Publication Data
Mapping the mind / edited by Lawrence A. Hirschfeld, Susan A. Gelman.
     p.   cm.
  Includes index.
  ISBN 0-521-41966-2. - ISBN 0-521-42993-5 (pbk.)
   1. Human information processing. 2. Schemas (Psychology)
3. Cognition and culture. I. Hirschfeld, Lawrence A. II. Gelman,
Susan A.
BF444.M36   1994
153 - dc20
                                   93-3812
                                     CIP

A catalog record for this book is available from the British Library.

ISBN 0-521-41966-2 hardback
ISBN 0-521-42993-5 paperback

To Adam, Bruno, Stephanie, and Tessa

Contents

vii

Contributors

Scott Atran
Centre de recherche en
  épistémologie appliquée
Ecole Polytechnique/CNRS
Paris, France

Pascal Boyer
Department of Anthropology
Cambridge University
Cambridge, England

Kimberly Brenneman
Department of Psychology
University of California
Los Angeles, California

Alfonso Caramazza
Department of Psychology
Dartmouth College
Hanover, New Hampshire

Susan Carey
Department of Brain and Cognitive
  Sciences
Massachusetts Institute of
  Technology
Cambridge, Massachusetts

John D. Coley
Department of Psychology
Northwestern University
Evanston, Illinois

Leda Cosmides
Department of Psychology
University of California, Santa
  Barbara
Santa Barbara, California

Rochel Gelman
Department of Psychology
University of California, Los
  Angeles
Los Angeles, California

Susan A. Gelman
Department of Psychology
University of Michigan
Ann Arbor, Michigan

Alison Gopnik
Department of Psychology
University of California, Berkeley
Berkeley, California

Gail M. Gottfried
Department of Psychology
University of Michigan
Ann Arbor, Michigan

Paul L. Harris
Department of Experimental
  Psychology
Oxford University
Oxford, England

ix

Argye Hillis
Department of Cognitive Science
Johns Hopkins University
Baltimore, Maryland

Lawrence A. Hirschfeld
Department of Anthropology,
    School of Social Work, and
    Research Center for Group
    Dynamics, Institute for Social
    Research
University of Michigan
Ann Arbor, Michigan

Frank C. Keil
Department of Psychology
Cornell University
Ithaca, New York

Elwyn C. Leek
Department of Cognitive Science
Johns Hopkins University
Baltimore, Maryland

Alan M. Leslie
MRC Cognitive Development Unit
London, England, and
Center for Cognitive Science
Rutgers University
Piscataway, New Jersey

Michele Miozzo
Department of Psychology
Dartmouth College
Hanover, New Hampshire

Ann James Premack
Laboratoire Psycho-Biologie de
    l'Enfant
CNRS
Paris, France

David Premack
Laboratoire Psycho-Biologie de
    l'Enfant
CNRS
Paris, France

Lauren B. Resnick
Learning Research and
    Development Center
University of Pittsburgh
Pittsburgh, Pennsylvania

Tamar Shilony
School of Education
Tel Aviv University
Tel Aviv, Israel

Elizabeth Spelke
Psychology Department
Cornell University
Ithaca, New York

Dan Sperber
Centre de recherche en
    épistémologie appliquée
Ecole Polytechnique/CNRS
Paris, France

Sidney Strauss
School of Education
Tel Aviv University
Tel Aviv, Israel

John Tooby
Department of Anthropology
Biological Wing
University of California, Santa
Barbara
Santa Barbara, California

Stella Vosniadou
Department of Education
University of Athens
Athens, Greece, and
    Center for the Study of Reading
University of Illinois
Champaign, Illinois

Henry M. Wellman
Center for Human Growth and
    Development
University of Michigan
Ann Arbor, Michigan

Anna Wierzbicka
Department of Linguistics
Australian National University
Canberra, Australia

Preface

This volume presents research and theoretical discussion on domain specificity in human thought. "Domain specificity" is the idea that all concepts are not equal, and that the structure of knowledge is different in important ways across distinct content areas. The notion of domain specificity has received much attention in recent years, but surprisingly it has not yet been given a unified treatment. A sense of how widely this concept has been discussed can be seen by viewing the range of disciplines represented in this volume: philosophy, psycholinguistics, linguistics, cultural anthropology, biological anthropology, developmental psychology, cognitive neuroscience, and education. We hope that the volume will thus be of interest to scholars in a broad range of disciplines.

The present volume is based on a conference, "Cultural Knowledge and Domain Specificity," held in Ann Arbor, Michigan, October 13–16, 1990. The conference was an attempt to discover if the notion of domain specificity could be discussed profitably (even intelligibly!) across disciplinary lines. Most important, we had the strong hope and belief that knowing more about other traditions could be valuable in informing our own local interests. In preparation for the conference, participants distributed their papers well in advance. Accordingly, we requested attendees to devote little time to formal presentations so that we could focus on discussions, both formal among the entire group and informal among participants over coffee breaks and on walks around campus. We were delighted to discover that we had in fact a lot to say to one another. We believe that this is evident in the chapters that follow.

An editorial committee, composed of Dan Sperber, Rochel Gelman, Scott Atran, Larry Hirschfeld, and Susan Gelman, met several times over the following year, planning the structure of the book. The committee drafted a position paper, distributed to the authors shortly after the conference, outlining a number of critical issues raised at the conference. (We have incorporated some of the points raised in the introduction, though all infelicities are of course our own.) The guidance and effort of Sperber, R. Gelman, and Atran were tremendous; in some sense they should be considered coeditors.

A number of institutions were invaluable in enabling us to carry out this endeavor. For their generous support, both financial and moral, we thank the McDonnell Foundation for two grants, one to support the conference, the other to support the preparation of this volume; Centre de la recherche en épistémologie appliquée (CREA), Centre national de la recherche scientifique (CNRS); the Office of the Vice President for Research at the University of Michigan; the Center for Human Growth and Development at the University of Michigan; and the Departments of Anthropology and Psychology in the College of Literature, Science, and the Arts, University of Michigan.

We are grateful to all conference participants, including Annette Karmiloff-Smith, Jacques Mehler, Rick Shweder, and Doug Medin, who were unable to prepare chapters for this volume. We also thank Marilyn Shatz for leading the discussion on Domains in Language. John Bruer, Michael Witunski, and Marvin Parnes provided encouragement and support from the inception of the project.

A number of people were instrumental in bringing the conference and the book to completion. Without their help this would not have been done. A special thanks to John Coley, for his adept handling of all the conference logistics. Heidi Schweingruber has provided invaluable editorial assistance. Thanks also to Frances Kuo, Chuck Kalish, Gail Gottfried, Grant Gutheil, Andrea Backscheider, and Scott Terrill of the Oxford Conference Center in Ann Arbor for helping to make the conference go smoothly. We are grateful to Nancy Gelman for suggesting the work of Joseph Cornell as a cover photo, and to Mrs. Edwin Bergman for allowing us to reproduce the piece. Finally, we thank Cambridge University Press and Julia Hough for their help in all phases of the book's preparation.

Part I

Overview

1 Toward a topography of mind: An introduction to domain specificity

Lawrence A. Hirschfeld and Susan A. Gelman

Over the past decades, a major challenge to a widely accepted view of the human mind has developed across several disciplines. According to a long predominant view, human beings are endowed with a general set of reasoning abilities that they bring to bear on any cognitive task, whatever its specific content. Thus, many have argued, a common set of processes apply to all thought, whether it involves solving mathematical problems, learning natural languages, calculating the meaning of kinship terms, or categorizing disease concepts. In contrast to this view, a growing number of researchers have concluded that many cognitive abilities are specialized to handle specific types of information. In short, much of human cognition is domain-specific.

The notion of domain specificity is not new. Indeed, intriguing (although brief) hints of domain specificity emerge in the epistemologies of Descartes and Kant and in the psychologies of Thorndike, Vygotsky, and de Groot. For example, in *Mind in Society*, Vygotsky argues that

> the mind is not a complex network of *general* capabilities such as observation, attention, memory, judgment, and so forth, but a set of specific capabilities, each of which is, to some extent, independent of others and is developed independently. Learning is more than the acquisition of the ability to think; it is the acquisition of many specialized abilities for thinking about a variety of things. Learning does not alter our overall ability to focus attention but rather develops various abilities to focus attention on a variety of things. (1978: 83)

Still, in recent years, increased and detailed attention has turned toward the question of domain specificity. Psychologists with concerns ranging from animal learning to emergent theories of mind and body, cognitivists exploring problem solving and expertise, anthropologists working with color terms and

We thank the other members of the editorial committee – Scott Atran, Rochel Gelman, and Dan Sperber – for their help in preparing this introduction. We also thank Alison Gopnik, Gail Gottfried, Bruce Mannheim, Doug Medin, Ed Smith, and Ann Stoler for their helpful comments.

folk taxonomies, psycholinguists investigating auditory perception, and philosophers and others examining reasoning schemata have concluded – often independently – that humans simply could not come to know what they do know in a purely domain-neutral fashion. A major purpose of *Mapping the Mind: Domain Specificity in Cognition and Culture* is to convey the wealth of current research that has resulted from this multidisciplinary exploration.

This introduction will orient readers to a domain specificity perspective. It is divided into three sections. In the first section, we examine work antecedent to the domain perspective drawn from a number of fields. By doing so we hope to give a broad sense of the intellectual traditions from which domain specificity has emerged. Throughout we will highlight the conclusion that the mind is less an all-purpose problem solver than a collection of enduring and independent subsystems designed to perform circumscribed tasks. This common conviction aside, it is important to keep in mind that a domain perspective is not the achievement of a coordinated body of research, unified in a common challenge. Domain researchers have reached some shared conclusions while asking quite diverse questions. In the second section we draw from this multidisciplinary work a common notion of what a domain is. It is important to stress that our intention in this section is to characterize rather than define what a domain is. Finally, in the third section we consider questions that arise by looking at ways in which domain researchers differ in their approaches and conclusions.

It is essential to note, given the diversity of interests and backgrounds of researchers in domain specificity, that conclusions about the nature and scope of the domain specificity approach are not reducible to differences in the traditions from which researchers have engaged the question. Rather, both the major lines of contention *and* commonality evident in these chapters are largely independent of academic discipline or research methodology. We believe that this is one of the most encouraging aspects of domain research, one that provides broad and exciting possibilities for future research directions.

In the introduction we want to raise a number of ideas about domains and issues about their natures. We hope in doing this to motivate the questions that the volume's chapters address: For example, does all domain knowledge reflect the operation of innate devices, or under what conditions might domain-specific knowledge be transferred, or whether initial conceptual organization evolves, is elaborated, or is supplanted in development. In effect, we see our task in this chapter as rendering such questions sensible across disciplines and traditions.

The roots of domain specificity

In this section we review the intellectual antecedents of the contemporary domain perspective. Our goal is twofold. First, we want to indicate the research and theory that have been crucial to the evolution of a domain approach. Although the authors of some of this work may well not be advocates of a domain-specific perspective, their work has nonetheless been critically important to the development of the approach. Second, we review this work with an eye toward building a characterization, if not a definition, of what a domain is and what a domain is not.

Several traditions have converged on a domain perspective. All attempt to solve the central problem of domain specificity, namely, how do humans come to have the wealth of knowledge that they do? These traditions have their roots in the following: (1) Chomsky's theory of natural language grammar; (2) modular approaches to knowledge (particularly vision and auditory speech processing); (3) constraints on induction; (4) philosophical insights into the most intricate knowledge structures created by humans (theories); (5) the learning, memory, and problem solving of our best learners (experts); (6) and the wisdom gained from a comparative perspective (animal, evolutionary, and cross-cultural studies).

Chomsky's theory of natural language grammar

We start with Chomsky's theory of language for two reasons. First, it has special historical interest: Virtually all subsequent domain-specific accounts bear the imprint of Chomsky's arguments about cognitive architecture. Although previous researchers recognized the need for conceiving thought in terms of discrete mental functions, Chomsky elaborated the first modern, sustained, and general account of domain specificity. It would be hard to overestimate the importance that his views have had in forming a broad-ranging domain-specific perspective. Although none of this volume's contributions directly treats natural language grammar, all grapple with issues raised in Chomsky's work.

The second reason for beginning with this theory is the clarity of its claims. Perhaps because it remains controversial, the notion that the language faculty represents a unique mental organ is probably the most widely known domain-specific argument. This attention is well deserved: The study of natural language processing is the arena in which the domain challenge has most continuously and explicitly unfolded. Although not all scholars are convinced that syntax *must* be described in domain-specific terms, the research from which this claim is derived provides an apt and excellent illustration of one domain perspective.

Current Chomskian linguistic theory distinguishes the principles of language structure at the core of the language faculty from language-specific rules derived from these principles. According to this model, (1) understanding a sentence involves assigning it a structural description in terms of abstract categories; (2) operations on sentences necessarily involve interpreting sentences in terms of this abstract phrase structure; (3) this abstract phrase structure cannot be inferred from surface properties of utterances (such as the linear order of words in the sentence).

For example, consider how a grammatically well-formed question is derived from the following two sentences (the example is drawn from Chomsky, 1980a; see also 1988):

(1)   The man is here. – Is the man here?
        The man will leave. – Will the man leave?

Chomsky suggests that two hypotheses fit these data. The first hypothesis for forming an interrogative from a declarative sentence is the *structure independent hypothesis* (H₁). According to this hypothesis, the speaker processes the sentence from beginning to end, word by word. When the speaker reaches the first occurrence of a class of words, say a verb such as *is* or *will*, he or she transposes this word to the beginning of the sentence. The alternative, *structure dependent* hypothesis (H₂), is the same as the first "but select[s] the first occurrence of *is*, *will*, etc., following the *first noun phrase of the declarative*" (Chomsky 1980a, emphasis added).

The (first structure independent) hypothesis is less complex in that it relies on superficial features of sequential order rather than requiring speakers to interpret utterances with respect to components of their constituent phrase structure, that is, "the first noun phrase." If the mind prefers "simpler" solutions – that is, is guided by a sensitivity to mental economy – we would expect to find language organized by principles captured with the structure independent hypothesis rather than the more abstract and language-specific structure dependent hypothesis.

The issue is resolved, Chomsky argues, by looking at the different predictions the two hypotheses make for similar sentences and their associated questions. First, on the structure dependent hypothesis the following movements are predicted:

(2)   The man who is here is tall. – Is the man who is here tall?
        The man who is tall will leave. – Will the man who is tall leave?

In contrast, the structure independent hypothesis, in which movements are calculated over surface properties of the sentence (such as word order), predicts a pattern that is not only ungrammatical, but also never encountered:

(3)   Is the man who here is tall?
        Is the man who tall will leave?

The structure dependent claim, accordingly, more adequately captures the linguistic facts.

The crucial question, Chomsky observes, is how children come to know that structure dependence governs such operations but structure independence does not. It is not, he contends, that the language learner accepts the first hypothesis and then is forced to reject it on the basis of data such as (2). No child is taught the relevant facts. Children make many errors in language learning, but none such as (3), prior to appropriate training or evidence. A person might go through much or all of his life without ever having been exposed to relevant evidence, but he will nevertheless unerringly employ H_2, never H_1, on the first relevant occasions. . . . We cannot, it seems, explain the preference for H_2 on grounds of communicative efficiency or the like. Nor do there appear to be relevant analogies of other than the most superficial and uninformative sort in other cognitive domains. If humans were differently designed, they would acquire a grammar that incorporates H_1, and would be none the worse for that. (Chomsky, 1980a: 40)

Chomsky concludes that the mind is *modular* – "consisting of separate systems [i.e., the language faculty, visual system, facial recognition module, etc.] with their own properties" (Chomsky, 1988: 161). The modular claim has three components: First, the principles that determine the properties of the language faculty are unlike the principles that determine the properties of other domains of thought. Second, these principles reflect our unique biological endowment. Third, these peculiar properties of language cannot be attributed to the operation of a general learning mechanism. Linguistic principles such as structure dependence cannot be inferred from the general language environment alone. Yet children's language development is guided by these principles.

As we observed above, this claim is not uncontroversial. For example, a number of researchers have suggested that the young child's task of inferring the structural properties of language is made easier because adults simplify the language that learners are presented with (Snow, 1972; Furrow & Nelson, 1984, 1986). Cross-cultural work, however, indicates that such simplifications are not a universal feature of the language learning environment (Ochs & Schieffelin, 1984; Pye, 1986). Other studies find that properties of child-directed speech do not correlate with the ease of language learning (e.g., Gleitman, Newport, & Gleitman, 1984; Hoff-Ginsberg & Shatz, 1982). Nonetheless, language acquisition appears to be quite stable and regular across diverse cultural and linguistic environments (Slobin, 1985). The conclusion Chomsky and others have reached is that the child has an innate capacity to learn languages, thus filtering "the input data through an emerging system of rules of grammar" (Gleitman, 1986: 7).

Other evidence lends support to Chomsky's theory. For instance, language learning appears to be stable and regular across significant variation in language *learners* as well as language *learning environments*. Curtiss (1982) has shown that severe disturbances in cognitive capacity do not necessarily result in disrupted language capacity (see also Cromer, 1988). Language development continues to unfold in the typical, predictable sequence for learners who are blind (Landau & Gleitman, 1985) and so have very different sensory experience from sighted children, and for those who are deaf and acquiring language in a different sensory modality (see studies of sign language, such as ASL; Klima & Bellugi, 1979; Newport & Meier, 1985; Petitto, 1988). Even deaf children who, in their first few years of life, have had little exposure to spoken language and no exposure to sign language, invent "words" and two- or three-word "sentences" (Goldin-Meadow, 1982). These results do not imply that the environment has no effect. For example, delaying exposure to language until later in life can have consequences ranging from moderate to severe (Newport, 1991; Curtiss, 1977). Nonetheless, it is striking that learners manage to construct language systems across a wide array of circumstances.

Modular approaches to cognition

As we observed, Chomsky and others maintain that these findings provide compelling evidence for the claim that the mind is modular, comprising a number of distinct (though interacting) systems (the language faculty, the visual system, a module for facial recognition), each of which is characterized by its own structural principles (1980b, 1988). Clearly this claim is related to the notion that thought is domain-specific, the idea that many cognitive abilities are specialized to handle specific types of information.

Chomsky, however, has also suggested that the mind is modular in a somewhat different way, giving rise to a set of proposals about cognitive architecture stressing the organization and contribution of each of the system's subcomponents rather than the system's overall characteristics. Thus, in other more technical writings, Chomsky has described "modules of grammar" (e.g., the lexicon, syntax, bounding theory, government theory, case theory, etc.) (1988: 135). Here the notion of modularity appears to be tied to specific subcomponents or subsystems of the language faculty rather than to the modular uniqueness of the language faculty itself. The grammar, in the traditional sense, is located at the intersection of these distinct modules.

It is not clear whether these two notions of modularity are to be distinguished, and if so how to interpret the relationship between them. One possibility is that modules are nested, that is, the language faculty is a separate module that in turn consists of distinct component operations or modules. Another interpretation – supported indirectly by the fact that Chomsky speaks of the language faculty *as* a module to nonlinguists but speaks of the language faculty *as consisting of* modules to linguists – is that the mind is, strictly speaking, modular with respect only to these second-level component modules. The language faculty itself would accordingly be a more vaguely defined construct resulting from the operation of these modules, but one that in itself is not modular in the sense of being defined in terms of a distinct set of principles.[1]

Modular accounts of other cognitive competencies more often resemble the second modular interpretation of Chomsky's position than the first. Thus, for example, although the visual and auditory systems are often compared with the language faculty as contrasting modules (Chomsky, 1988, 1980b; Fodor, 1983), detailed accounts of these systems typically analyze their structure in terms of a set of component modular operations, each of which accounts for only part of the overall system's functional output. Thus, descriptions of such systems adhere to what Marr (1982) called the *principle of modular design*, "the idea that a large computation [such as vision] can be split up and implemented as a collection of parts that are as nearly independent of one another as the overall task allows" (p. 102).

Marr's own theory of vision is a clearly elaborated example of this sort of modular explanation. The theory's principal goal is to understand how it is that we see stable and identifiable images in spite of great variation and "noise" in the input. For example, although we perceive colors, shapes, and sizes as constant, the stimulus information available to the visual system is not sufficiently constrained to permit us to infer constancy without additional interpretation. Areas of unequal shading (which makes some areas of a single color appear darker than others), the possibility of object movement (which makes the same object appear smaller or larger depending on whether it is moving toward or away from the viewer), or partial occlusion (which obscures large parts of objects that are nonetheless perceived as a single whole) mean that visual information alone often underdetermines our perception of color, shape, and size constancy.

To explain such judgments, Marr puts forward a computational theory of vision that analyzes the perception of shape, size, and motion into representations constructed from a set of specific algorithms. These algorithms transform representations by means of *modular* devices that detect edges, apparent motion, surface texture, and the like. Vision, the process of *seeing*, involves the coordination of these atomic visual modules into a coherent whole.

Other modular devices seem to control auditory processing. A considerable body of research emerging from the Haskins Laboratory under Alvin Liberman provides a computational theory of auditory processing. Central to this work is the demonstration that the phonetic analysis of speech involves mechanisms different from those that affect the perceptual analysis of auditory nonspeech (Mattingly, Liberman, Syrdal, & Halwes, 1971; Liberman & Mattingly, 1989).

Drawing on this empirical work in vision and speech processing, in *Modularity of Mind*, Fodor (1983) offers the first general discussion of the implications of modularity for a wide set of domains. Fodor lists a number of candidate modules, including color perception, analysis of shape, analysis of three-dimensional spatial relations, recognition of faces, and recognition of voices.

Fodor's model involves a functional cognitive taxonomy that distinguishes between input systems or modules (which produce knowledge about the world, such as edge detectors) and transducers (which compile information *from* the world, such as perceptual organs). Input systems, in turn, are distinguished from central processors that take information from the input systems, in a format appropriate for the central processors, and use this information to mediate higher functions, such as the fixation of belief.

Thus, according to Fodor's modular view, knowledge of the different aspects of the world is mentally represented in distinct formats. Perception accordingly involves not only interpretation, but an interpretation that is constrained by the format under which particular world knowledge is represented. In other words, input systems are not simply conduits for perceptual encodings of information; they are mental modules that "deliver representations that are most naturally interpreted as characterizing the arrangement of *things in the world*. Input analyzers are thus inference-performing systems" (1983: 42).

Modular views of cognition represent a major challenge to predominant, domain-general approaches found in psychology, linguistics, philosophy, and anthropology. As such, they have important implications for any domain-specific perspective. Yet modular and domain-specific approaches also contrast in significant ways. The principal difference is the former's emphasis on specificity in functional cognitive architecture and the latter's focus on specialization for specific types of knowledge. In the following three sections we consider the direct intellectual antecedents to domain specificity. The work we examine, rather than focusing on cognitive architecture (a modular issue), is concerned with the mental activities that operate on that architecture. We turn first to the issue of constraints on representations.

Constraints

An appeal to constraints begins with the problem of induction. As Rochel Gelman phrased it (1990: 3), "How is it that our young attend to inputs that will support the development of concepts they share with their elders?" She raises two significant difficulties with developing the appropriate concepts: Experience is inadequate in that many of the critical concepts children need to learn never appear; it is "pluripotential" in that it is logically open to many alternative construals. As R. Gelman points out, "the indeterminacy or inadequacy of experience and the pluripotentiality of experience ... are central to current discussions of the acquisition of syntax (Landau & Gleitman, 1985; Wexler & Culicover, 1980), visual perception (Marr, 1982; Ullman, 1980), the nature of concepts (Armstrong, Gleitman, & Gleitman, 1983; Medin & Wattenmaker, 1987), and the learning of word meaning (Macnamara, 1982; Quine, 1960)" (pp. 3–4).

The inadequacy and pluripotentiality of experience are implicit in many accounts of learning, including Quine's treatment of word meaning acquisition (1960) and Peirce's discussion of hypothesis generation in science (1960). For the child to learn word meanings without constraints is akin to an alien trying to discover the laws of nature by examining the facts listed in the Census Report. Both would be doomed to positing thousands upon thousands of meaningless hypotheses. The child might wonder whether "rabbit" refers to a certain patch of color, or the positioning of a limb; the alien may wonder whether there is a meaningful causal relation between the number of babies born in Cancun and the height of women in Brazil whose names start with "Z." If left unconstrained, induction would yield meaningful knowledge only rarely (if at all), and even then only by chance.

One promising response to the induction puzzle is to suggest that there are constraints on the form development takes. Constraints are restrictions on the kinds of knowledge structures that the learner typically uses (Keil, 1981: 198). With constraints, the induction problem is simplified because the learner need not consider every possible reading of the input. For example, regarding the acquisition of word meanings, Markman (1989) suggests that children first assume that nouns refer to whole objects that are taxonomically related (the *taxonomic* and *whole object* constraints). These constraints would exclude from consideration meanings for *rabbit* such as "white fur" or "things that hop [including pogo sticks and wallabees]." Keil (1981) also proposes domain-specific constraints on number concepts, deductive reasoning, ontological knowledge, and natural language syntax.

All theorists acknowledge the need for constraints of some sort. Even traditional learning theorists propose constraints on learning (e.g., perceptual constraints; contiguity). Disagreement remains as to the importance of constraints, how much focus they deserve, and on how best to characterize their nature (see Behrend, 1990; Nelson, 1988).

Keil points out that constraints could be in the learner or outside the learner. Even focusing just on those in the learner, Keil observes that there are still strong disagreements about whether they are innate or acquired, probabilistic or absolute, regarding process or structure, domain-specific or domain-general, and so forth. Thus, a constraints view need not be domain-specific. For example, in an ingenious argument, Newport (1990) suggests that there are domain-general information-processing constraints on attention that help children acquire language. Other theorists are agnostic as to whether the constraints they propose are domain-specific (e.g., Markman, 1989).

However, in the present context, the suggestion of domain-specific constraints is of particular interest. Indeed, there may be a natural affinity between constraints and domain specificity. If constraints are appealing because they make the induction problem easier, then domain-specific constraints are all the more appealing because they make the induction problem all the more easy (Keil, 1981). The argument is that

it is necessary to grant infants and/or young children domain-specific organizing structures that direct attention to the data that bear on the concepts and facts relevant to a particular cognitive domain. The thesis is that the mind brings domain-specific organizing principles to bear on the assimilation and structuring of facts and concepts, that learners can narrow the range of possible interpretations of the environment because they have implicit assumptions that guide their search for relevant data. (R. Gelman, 1990)

There appears to be a rich array of such constraints. Spelke (1990) proposes a variety of constraints on object perception that seem to be operating from early infancy. R. Gelman (1990) provides support for constraints on early numeric understanding (specifically, principles for counting) and causal understanding of animate and inanimate movement. She refers to these constraints as "skeletal principles" because they are the framework on which developing knowledge depends and grows. Brown (1990) shows evidence for constraints on interpretations of causal relations, and argues that such constraints guide the kinds of analogical transfer subjects find easy or difficult.

The flourishing of a constraints perspective and the wealth of evidence being amassed on domain-specific constraints do not lead to convergence on what is meant by "domain." As Keil points out (1990: 139):

The notion of domain varies considerably across researchers. In some cases, . . . the domains cover very broad areas of cognitive competency such as the representation of space or physical objects. In other cases, the domains may be locally circumscribed bodies of expertise. The critical common factor in all cases is that domain specific constraints are predicated on specific sorts of knowledge types and do not blindly constrain any possible input to learning.

Theories

Another sense of domain specificity arises from considering everyday knowledge as falling into folk or commonsense theories. Theories are by nature domain-specific. A theory of biology cannot be applied to the phenomena of physics. Theories make different ontological commitments (biologists appeal to species and DNA; physicists appeal to quarks and masses). They put forth domain-specific causal laws (e.g., gravity does not affect mental states; biological processes such as growth or respiration cannot be applied to force dynamics). So, if human thought is in important ways analogous to scientific theories, then it should be organized separately for distinct domains.

The claim that there are theories is a controversial and substantive one. Theories are not in principle required for getting around the world. It is possible to form biological categories without the benefit of theories, as when pigeons classify birds and trees (Herrnstein, 1979) or humans form groupings of the biological world (Atran, 1990, this volume). It is possible to respond to others' mental states by simply reflecting on one's own (Harris, this volume).

Moreover, at first blush the claim that everyday knowledge is theory laden may seem implausible. If "theory" means "scientific theory," then it is certainly not the case that everyday knowledge is organized into theories. It is clear that few of us have the detailed, explicit, formal understanding that PhD biologists or physicists have. We rarely, if ever, conduct scientific experiments to test our everyday hypotheses. We often lack conscious awareness of those principles that we do understand implicitly. Consider, for example, how subjects reason about physical laws regarding motion and velocity. Kaiser, Proffitt, and Anderson (1985) found that subjects implicitly know the correct natural trajectory of an object in motion, but perform badly when asked to judge the naturalness of static representations of the same events.

However, a commonsense or folk theory is not the same as a scientific theory. This point has been made by Karmiloff-Smith and Inhelder (1975), Murphy and Medin (1985), Carey (1985), Keil (this volume), Gopnik and Wellman (this volume), and others. Instead, everyday thought may be theory-like in its resistance to counterevidence, ontological commitments, attention to domain-specific causal principles, and coherence of beliefs. We sketch out some examples of these properties in the following sections.

The argument that ordinary knowledge can be likened to commonsense theories is rooted in several distinct strands of research. Karmiloff-Smith and Inhelder (1975), in an important demonstrational study, showed that children construct hypotheses (akin to miniature theories-in-action) that are resistant to counterevidence. They gave children a series of blocks to balance on a fulcrum. Some were symmetrical and thus balanced in the center, but others were asymmetrical, either visibly so (e.g., having an extra, visible weight at one end) or invisibly so (e.g., having a hidden weight at one end). Many of the children at first used trial and error to balance the blocks. They were fairly successful on the task, because they were approaching the task strictly as empiricists. However, as the session continued some children formed the explicit hypothesis that the blocks balanced in the middle, and so started making errors that they did not make previously. Children had particular difficulty with the invisibly asymmetric blocks. Some of the children, after repeated attempts, finally abandoned the blocks that would not balance in the middle, reporting that they were impossible to balance. This demonstration suggests the importance of theoretical beliefs in organizing input.

Another set of demonstrations of theorylike beliefs in ordinary thought emerges from examining semantics and categorization. Murphy and Medin (1985) propose that theories are needed to account for the insufficiencies of similarity as a construct. On a similarity view, word meanings and categories are constructed on the basis of similarity of members to one another, whether these similarities are computed in terms of prototypes, feature lists, or similarity to exemplars (Smith & Medin, 1981). However, Murphy and Medin (1985) note (following Goodman, 1972) the problems with a pure similarity view.

To give an intuitive example, if you see someone jump into a swimming pool with all his clothes on, you may classify him as a "drunk" even though nothing about him or his actions specifically resembles drunks you have seen in the past. Rather, your interpretation of his behavior in that context leads to a series of inferences about the likely causes of his actions, and so yields the classification. More generally, as Goodman points out, similarity is insufficiently constrained to solve the problem of classification or induction. Depending on what counts as a feature, any two objects could have indefinitely many features in common (e.g., a lawnmower and hummingbird both weigh less than 200 pounds, less than 201 pounds, less than 202 pounds . . .). Thus, we need constraints on what counts as a feature and how to weight features, and these constraints come from our theories.

Three examples here suffice. One is taken from a series of items constructed by Rips (1989). Subjects were told about hypothetical circular objects 3 inches in diameter, and were asked to rate them on four dimensions: similarity to pizzas, similarity to quarters, likelihood of being a pizza, likelihood of being a quarter. Rips discovered that similarity judgments and categorization judgments diverged. The object was judged more similar to a quarter than a pizza, but more likely to be a pizza than a quarter. Theoretical beliefs about the possible features of pizzas and quarters yielded the classification, but a general similarity metric did not (see also Medin & Shoben, 1988).

The second example is from Keil (1989). He told children stories, for example about a skunk that was surgically altered to resemble a raccoon but still had the parents and internal structure of a skunk. By approximately the second grade, children reported that the animal was still a skunk, despite its outward appearances. They did not do so for artifacts, such as a coffeepot altered to resemble a birdfeeder. Again, a theoretical grasp of species seems to be driving children's answers. It is striking that this understanding emerges so early. Gelman and Wellman (1991) have similar findings with children as young as preschool age.

The third example is from Putnam (1970) (see also Kripke, 1972, and Schwartz, 1979, for related arguments). He proposes a series of thought experiments. For example, what is required for something to be a lemon? Is it the yellow color, tart taste, thick peel, etc.? He argues that, in the final analysis, none of these features is critical. We treat all the properties associated with lemons as corrigible – that is, potentially disconfirmable. We appeal to experts to know for certain which are the lemons and which are not – and even the experts may ultimately prove to be wrong. This example differs somewhat from the other two. In particular, it emphasizes the corrigibility of "theoretical" properties. Nevertheless, the point again is that semantics are tied into theories, which themselves are open to change.

These examples illustrate some of the benefits of proposing folk theories. However, many questions remain. How many theories are there? Is there a small and manageable set, or can their number be multiplied endlessly? How coherent are everyday beliefs, and do they cohere enough to constitute a theory? How do new theories grow out of old ones? Why posit theories instead of other, related structures (such as constraints)? More extended statements of commonsense knowledge as theorylike can be found in the present volume, in discussions of theories of mind (Wellman & Gopnik; Harris), of biology (Keil; Gelman, Coley, & Gottfried; Atran, taking a critical view), and of physics or material kind (Carey & Spelke). The characterization is far from settled, and more substantive issues continue to be discussed.

Expertise

The claim that expertise carves out domains begins with the following observation. With enough practice at a task, whether that task is the game of chess or the gathering of factual knowledge about dinosaurs, an ordinary person begins to look extraordinary. With sufficient experience, a person attains amazing feats of memory (Chase & Ericsson, 1981), reorganizes knowledge into complex hierarchical systems and develops rich networks of causally related information (Chi, Hutchinson, & Robin, 1989), and can hold in mind an impressive array of possibilities (e.g., expert chess players considering many more chess pieces than novices) (Chase & Simon, 1973). These abilities are so striking that they can even erase the usual developmental finding of adults outperforming children. Chi has found that children who are chess experts have better memory for the positioning of chessboard pieces than adults who are chess novices.

Just as important, these abilities cannot be explained as individual differences in the starting point of the experts, nor as generalized, cross-domain effects. The same individual who is remarkable on the chessboard shows mundane performance on tasks outside the skill domain. For example, the chess expert's memory for a string of digits is quite ordinary, even though the expert's memory for positions of chess pieces on a chessboard is far above what the novice can do. The expertise is so focused in scope that it does not even extend to memory for chess pieces placed randomly on the board. It seems, then, that these abilities are domain-specific, at least in some sense of "domain."

The notion of skill domains identified by expertise is distinct from any of the other senses of domain we have reviewed. There has been no appeal to innate modular structures, innate constraints, or the importance of evolutionary forces. In part this is because it is unlikely that we have innate structures dedicated to the acquisition of chess or go. It may be that skill domains such as chess or go, though themselves artificial and invented, draw on other kinds of cognitive abilities that can be explained in terms of modules or evolutionary constraints. For example, aspects of visual pattern recognition are presumably hardwired into our visual perceptual system, and appear to be an important component of these kinds of board games. Thus, it may be impossible to be an expert in chess if you do not have excellent visual memory.

Nonetheless, the abilities honed for chess do not generalize to other tasks relying on visual pattern recognition. Thus, it seems unlikely that the domains here can be reconceptualized as broader than what they appear to be. In other words, a chess expert really does seem to be an expert in chess, not an expert in visual pattern recognition.

Expertise effects are unlikely to result from innate evolutionary constraints, for the same reasons discussed above. They also cannot always be explained in terms of causal belief systems, as in naive theories (again, consider that chess, although a rule-governed system, is not a theory and is not corrigible). Rather, these domains appear to result from hours of intensive practice.

Consideration of expertise-driven skill domains poses an interesting challenge to other notions of domain specificity. First, it challenges us to consider what can count as a domain. From the perspective of Chomsky, Fodor, and their followers, it has been assumed that domains constitute large and important chunks of cognition – language, perception, mathematics, music. Yet from the expertise literature it is clear that at least in one sense domains can include invented and small corners of experience. Even if we were to reconcile these perspectives by saying that different theorists are dealing with very different senses of domain, we are left with the reminder that the notion of domain needs some constraints if it is to be meaningful. In other words, how can chess be excluded as a domain, excluded from the perspective of theorists who would like to claim that it is not? The challenge, then, is to decide what is not a domain, and why.

A second point is that the effects of expertise demonstrate the far-reaching influences of intensive experience. It reminds us to take seriously the nature of experience, and not to dismiss its potential influence. It becomes all the more important to explicate and understand how experience interacts with more internal mechanisms at the focus of attention (such as constraints).

Comparative perspectives

Animal studies. It is apparent from the work already reviewed that much research relevant to the domain-specificity perspective is comparative in the sense that it contrasts children's states of understanding with adult ones. A particularly critical issue is the extent to which the external world underdetermines children's knowledge. Human children, of course, are not the only animals that learn, and therefore are not the only animals to encounter the problem of how to limit inductions. Like those working on human conceptual development, researchers in animal learning have also framed this question in terms of *constraints*. Constraints, however, are often interpreted as limitations on general abilities, in the sense that constraints modify and sharpen a unitary learning device.

An emphasis on constraints, thus, may seem appropriate when viewed from a human developmental perspective, where children can be seen as having a (less developed) subset of capacities that adults have. From a broader comparative perspective – say, a cross-species or cross-cultural one – constraints make less sense as a way of characterizing domain specificity (Gallistel, Brown, Carey, Gelman, & Keil, 1991). A species-specific adaptation, for example, is not a "constrained" version of an adaptation made by another species. Thus, it does not make sense to say that bats have a subset of human sensory equipment; the sonar-based mental images of the world that bats construct may produce representations of equivalent richness to those humans build through vision, but they are fundamentally different in terms of the capacities employed (Dawkins, 1987).

The claim that much of conceptual development is best understood as a succession of theories about the world raises a similar issue. Rozin and Schull point out that the notion of constraint is unfortunate not only because it overly emphasizes the idea of limitation, but because it has come to "stand for the study of specialized psychological processes" (1988: 506). Thus, unlike studies of human conceptual development, where the differences between a domain-specific and domain-general interpretation may be more difficult to document, research in animal learning has increasingly stressed that learning may be possible only in the context of species-specific mechanisms.

This point is dramatically evident from Garcia's work on animal aversion training. According to the domain-general view that has long predominated in comparative psychology, inferential skills are homogeneous. Problem solving across tasks in different content areas involves the same principles. From a stimulus-response framework this translates into the principle of equipotentiality, the prediction that differences in strength of association between a stimulus and a response are attributable to conditions of pairing (contiguity, duration, etc.) and independent of the nature of the reinforcer. Garcia and Koelling (1966) conducted a study that confronted this prediction directly. They showed that when rats were given electric shocks and these shocks paired with either a visual or taste stimulus, the rats subsequently avoided only the visual stimulus. In contrast, when the experimenters poisoned the rats and paired the poisoning with the same visual and taste stimuli, the rats avoided the flavored water but not the visual stimulus. How rats paired stimulus with response thus depended on the nature of the relation between stimulus and response, undermining the equipotentiality assumption.

Furthermore, the poisoned rats developed an aversion to the new taste stimulus in spite of the fact that there was a delay between ingesting the poison and its effects. This finding also challenges the contiguity assumption. Thus, rats' pairing of stimuli seems to be governed by a constraint: If poisoned, seek the cause in something ingested. From the perspective of stimulus-response psychology this sort of guided hypothesis was unthinkable. From the perspective of contemporary research on the evolution of domain-specific mechanisms, however, such a pairing is both sensible and predictable. It makes good evolutionary sense to select for a cognitive mechanism that teaches the species to avoid poisonous, spoiled, or unripe foods, even if they are eaten considerably before the onset of symptoms.

Students of animal cognition and evolution have stressed the need to interpret cognitive and other adaptive mechanisms in domain-specific terms (Rozin & Schull, 1988; Cosmides & Tooby, 1989). The range of behaviors covered by this approach is quite broad. Cosmides (1989), for example, suggests that conditions of social exchange have selected for certain reasoning schemata, including the one underlying the selection task. Symons (1979) and Langlois and Roggman (1990) have argued that notions of physical attractiveness may be governed by innate mechanisms. Gallistel (1990) reviews the considerable literature on animal systems of navigation, dead reckoning, and temporality, arguing that they reflect similarly specialized, domain-specific mechanisms.

Researchers in animal and evolutionary studies have detailed the importance of viewing learning (specifically what Marler, 1991, has called "an instinct to learn") in domain-specific terms. Several researchers have argued that learning could hardly proceed without domain-specific devices (Cosmides & Tooby, this volume, 1989; Gallistel et al., 1991; Symons, 1979). The reason, as Symons notes (1979: 20), is that learning is not a general ability to modify behavior. Rather it is a set of predispositions that a species has developed to resolve specific problems encountered during the course of evolutionary history. Garcia's demonstration that rats will adopt certain aversions and not others showed that some things are more easily learned, and evolutionary constraints help explicate what those things are.

Cross-cultural studies. The cognitive perspective that emerged in anthropology at the end of the 1950s put forward a program of research aimed at describing cultural competencies on the model of rules of grammar. It was widely agreed that all word meanings in all languages and in all conceptual domains would involve semantic representations in a single general format, namely, one in which elementary semantic features were simply combined: no domain-specific structural idiosyncrasies were envisaged. But as with animal learning studies, the cultural comparative perspective in fact uncovered empirical regularities that proved particularly difficult to interpret in a domain-general light. Moreover, these regularities would almost undoubtedly have escaped discovery in the absence of cross-cultural work.

Color terms. It had long been noted that different languages segment the color spectrum in dramatically different ways. Some languages, for example, appear to have only two color terms, linguistically distinguishing only light from dark chroma. Other languages, like English, have a rich and varied color vocabulary. Given the prevailing doctrine of linguistic relativity, the almost universally accepted interpretation of these data was that language differences reflected differences in the way color was experienced as well as named.

In 1969, Berlin and Kay directly confronted this view of color classification. By analyzing color terms in 98 languages, Berlin and Kay computed that there are 11 basic color terms.[2] There are 2,048 possible ways to combine these 11 basic terms into sets of two or more (black/white, red/blue, white/ green/yellow, ...). Strikingly, Berlin and Kay found that only 22 combinations were actually used. Moreover, the order in which basic color words enter a language is also patterned. If a language has only two terms they are invariably black or white; if three terms they are black, white, and red; if five they are black, white, red, green, and yellow, etc.

$$\begin{bmatrix} \text{white} \\ \text{black} \end{bmatrix} > [\text{red}] > \begin{bmatrix} \text{green} \\ \text{yellow} \end{bmatrix} > [\text{blue}] > [\text{brown}] > \begin{bmatrix} \text{purple} \\ \text{pink} \\ \text{orange} \\ \text{gray} \end{bmatrix}$$

They and subsequent researchers also found that although the boundaries of color terms vary, the focal point of each basic color (that point, e.g., in the array of reds that is the reddest of red) is largely the same across languages. Heider and Oliver (1972), working with Dani tribesmen in New Guinea whose language has only two basic color terms, provided experimental cross-cultural evidence that memory for color as well as the naming of colors is also largely independent of color vocabulary.[3]

Reviewing these and other cross-cultural data, Sperber (1974) proposed a domain-specific approach in semantics and in anthropology. He speculated that the organization of the color lexicon (which Kay & McDaniel, 1978, later argued was tied to specific properties of the visual pathway) was unlikely to be duplicated in other conceptual domains. He evoked the case of kinship terminology where Lounsbury (1964) had proposed a semantic formalism whose application was clearly limited to kinship, and he concluded that there must be "specific devices linked to particular semantic domains" (1974: 502).[4] In an extension of this work, Hirschfeld (1986, 1989) reanalyzed studies of both children and adults' kinship semantics in terms of a domain-specific device for understanding the social world.

Folk biology. A similar pattern, of cross-cultural uniformity in a content area that previously had been assumed to vary widely, was uncovered by Berlin's work on systems of folk biological classification. In a series of studies, Berlin and his associates (1972; 1978; Berlin, Breedlove, & Raven, 1966, 1973, 1974) showed that in spite of significant variation in the plants and animals that any local population encounters, and in spite of the fact that many of these plants and animals lack any cultural salience for any given local population, there is striking consistency in the way humans everywhere classify the world of living things. The basic principles of classification of biological kinds are extremely stable over significant differences in learning environment and exposure. In several publications, including this volume, Atran proposes that these principles must be understood in terms of a domain-specific device for categorizing the biological sphere. He argues that folk biology is uniquely organized in at least two ways: first, that a presumption of underlying essence applies to all living things, and second, that a strict taxonomic hierarchy spans all and only living kinds (1990). Although Atran draws on evidence from a number of disciplines, his cognitive interpretation of the history of natural science is a particularly interesting contribution that has prompted anthropologists to review conclusions about the nature of folk taxonomies (Brown, 1992).

Symbolic representations. Knowledge of biological diversity is a cultural domain closely linked with survival. Not surprisingly, anthropologists working with preliterate populations living in small-scale communities report that biological classifications are the focus of a great deal of attention and interest (Berlin, 1978). But anthropologists have also observed that the biological world is often as much the object of symbolic attention as pragmatic interest (Bulmer, 1967; Rosaldo, 1972; Tambiah, 1969). The impetus to interpret the world symbolically, in fact, is an ubiquitous cultural feature. The predominant view in anthropology has been that symbolism is a kind of language provided by the culture and that symbols get their meanings by metonymic and metaphorical associations. The underlying psychology, usually left implicit, is a mixture of associationism and content-neutral learning mechanisms that allow the internalization of whatever the culture provides.

In a major rethinking of the anthropology of symbolism, Sperber (1975a) argued that symbols are not signs in that they do not figure in codelike structures and do not have paraphrasable meanings. Rather, Sperber proposes that the true cognitive role of symbolic beliefs is to focus attention and to evoke representations from memory. He depicted symbolic representations as metarepresentations of hard-to-process beliefs (such as the not-fully-interpretable notion of the Trinity, in which three is one). Sperber stresses the role such metarepresentations play in communication and culture. He further links such representations with the relative availability of domain-specific competencies. Thus he attempted to explain the rich symbolism of smells by the discrepancy between a powerful perceptual module and the poverty of conceptual tools for the domain. He also argued that the cultural symbolic exploitation of animal representations, a much discussed topic in cultural anthropology, was based more on the domain-specific character of zoological taxonomies than on the symbolic "codes" in terms of which such beliefs have typically been interpreted (Sperber, 1975b). Boyer (1990; this volume) extends this insight by examining how religious representations may also be shaped by domain-specific principles even if there is no domain of religious beliefs. Hirschfeld's chapter also explores the extent that domain-specific competence for living kind classification shapes beliefs about the human realm.

Domains, a characterization

Is it possible, given this survey, to extract what researchers mean when they talk of domain specificity? In spite of the wealth of research, curiously we lack an explicit and well-articulated account of what a domain is. It is easier to think of examples of a domain than to give a definition of one. Physical entities and processes, substances, living kinds, numbers, artifacts, mental states, social types, and supernatural phenomena are all candidate domains. Which of these, if any, are cognitive domains is a question not for general science but for anthropology and psychology: The supernatural may be a domain for human minds though it is not one for science; the cognitive domain of physical phenomena may be quite different from that of physics.

Are there features common to all domains? Our review, though brief, allows us to identify areas of accord, often implicit, in much domain-relevant research. The following we take to be a fairly uncontroversial characterization:

A domain is a body of knowledge that identifies and interprets a class of phenomena assumed to share certain properties and to be of a distinct and general type. A domain functions as a stable response to a set of recurring and complex problems faced by the organism. This response involves difficult-to-access perceptual, encoding, retrieval, and inferential processes dedicated to that solution.

Let us consider each part of this characterization in turn.

Domains as guides to partitioning the world. Most accounts converge on a view that domains function conceptually to identify phenomena belonging to a single general kind, even when these phenomena fall under several concepts. For example, living kinds can be classified in a number of different ways, ranging from foodstuffs to zoo animals. The psychological correlates of competing classifications and their internal structures have significant effects on the way many common categories for living things are sorted, recalled, and recognized (Rosch, Mervis, Gray, Johnson, & Boyes-Braem, 1976). Yet in spite of these competing ways of classifying living things, some beliefs about living kinds are typically early emerging, consistent, and effortlessly acquired. Domain competency facilitates this by focusing attention on a specific domain rather than general knowledge (Chi et al., 1989).

Domains as explanatory frames. Most researchers would also accept that a domain competence systematically links recognized kinds to restricted classes of properties. Thus a cognitive domain is a class of phenomena that share among themselves, but not with other kinds, a number of relevant properties. Though virtually all domains seem to make reference to causal or otherwise model-derived connections, there is considerable variation across domains in how flexible these connections are.[5]

It is not necessary, for example, that all and only members of a given domain share a property. It is a recognized property of humans – recognized through the agency of a naive psychology – that human beings behave in association with their beliefs, whereas artifacts do not. Still, we have little trouble accepting that there are humans who do not have beliefs (e.g., people in deep comas) or humans who do not recognize that others have beliefs (e.g., autistic individuals) or artifacts that are most sensibly dealt with as if they had beliefs (e.g., a chess playing computer). In other domains (say, auditory processing of speech), there may be substantially less flexibility in the degree to which domain properties (say, categorical perception of speech) span domain members.

Domains as functional and widely distributed devices. It is generally accepted among domain researchers that domain competencies are a restricted set of the cognitive skills the organism may develop. Domains of knowledge represent widely shared adaptations targeting recurring problems that an organism faces. Cases where the adaptive aspect of the domain has been challenged, as with the language faculty, have been much debated recently (Pinker & Bloom, 1990). Domains are also generally seen as highly (though not universally) shared among members of a species, not idiosyncratic solutions to individual problems.

Even if a domain skill is unevenly distributed within a population, it must be a solution to a repeatedly encountered problem. To the extent that chess is a domain, the development of perceptual strategies for analyzing chess positions arises *because* chess masters frequently encounter chess problems. Nonmasters do not have a less developed domain of chess; they lack such a domain skill. This relationship between frequency of encounter and domain skill, however, is complex. Some domain skills may appear to be closely tied to differences in the learning environment even if the *underlying domain competence* does *not* depend on environmental conditions.

The ability to develop and understand mathematics may be rooted in some fairly specific cognitive mechanisms, which human beings are innately endowed with. But if so, many cultures do not require that people use this ability. Nor is it occasioned by every environment. Mathematics does not spontaneously arise irrespective of social context, but seems to require a richer and more sustained sequence of experience and instruction in order to flourish than, say, basic grammatical knowledge, color perception or appreciation of living kinds. (Atran, 1988: 8)

Such mathematical skills, involving a formal language of mathematics, are distinct from other, universally emerging arithmetic competencies such as those principles underlying counting and cardinal enumeration (R. Gelman & Brenneman, this volume; R. Gelman & Gallistel, 1978).

Domains as dedicated mechanisms. Domain-specific processing is typically seen as independent of will and accessible to consciousness only with difficulty (if at all). This property is easily evident in domains such as color perception or phonetic interpretation, cases in which some innate mechanism is difficult to doubt. But it is also apparent when an innate mechanism seems less likely, as, for instance, in what some consider a marginal case of domain specificity, like chess. Chess masters differ from chess novices in their visual-perception processing of chess information, not in logical-deductive thinking or memory processes (Chase & Simon, 1973). Accordingly, domain operations generally involve focused, constrained, and involuntary perceptual, conceptual, or inferential processes.

What domains are not. Domains can be characterized by what they are not as well as what they are. In this regard it is useful to contrast domains with other mental structures with which they are potentially confuseable. These include semantic fields, schemata and scripts, prototypes, and analogies. What all of these structures (including domains) share is that they are ways of achieving conceptual interconnectedness and mental economy. However, domains differ from each in important respects as well. Unlike *semantic fields*, domains are not contingent on language (cf. Wierzbicka, this volume). In fact, evidence of the robustness of a domain phenomenon is sometimes supplied by the fact that the effects of domain-specific knowledge organization occur in the absence of lexical indices (as, e.g., in the case of focal color categories [Heider, 1972] or covert folk biological taxa [Berlin, 1974]). In contrast to *scripts* and *schema*, domain structures involve expectations about the model-derived connections between domain elements. In a restaurant script, payment follows service by a convention that the script itself cannot account for. Another way in which conceptual interconnectedness is achieved is via *prototypes*. According to a widely held position, categories are not built around defining features but around central members or prototypes. Because prototypes are described as consisting of collections of correlated attributes, they contribute to underlying conceptual interconnectedness. The particular category structure found in prototypes, however, applies to a wide range of phenomena; hence, domain competencies cross-cut them. Thus, prototypes could apply to any domain. (Conversely, they may not truly characterize any domain. Lakoff, 1987, suggests that prototypes are effects, reflecting other kinds of conceptual structure.) Finally, *analogical transfers* contribute to conceptual interconnectedness and mental economy. Analogical transfer may in fact represent a means for integrating domain knowledge across domains (Brown, 1989; Hirschfeld, this volume). But unlike domain structures, transfers can be both idiosyncratic and not functional.

In addition to these ways of producing conceptual interconnectedness that are clearly not domainlike, there are several means for accomplishing conceptual interconnectedness that domains may not be. These include the notions of *category* and *motoric competencies*. Our characterization of domain stressed the expectation that there is some specific "formal" or "syntactic" property of the mental representations pertaining to a given domain that accounts for their distinctive cognitive role. Unfortunately, this does not exclude arrays that we would hesitate to call domains. For example, single concepts have distinctive semantic and formal properties, yet we would not call single concepts domains. Similarly, pairs of concepts like male or female, key and lock, or hot and cold are too narrow to be domains although they fit most of our criteria. Note also that our characterization does not exclude strictly motoric competencies such as riding a bicycle, which many may not find a compelling example of domain-specific skills.

Domain differences

Clearly, a principled way of defining what a domain is continues to elude us. Many of the chapters in this volume put forward solutions to this question. And other chapters take issue with these proffered solutions. For this reason, in the present introduction we have tried to *characterize* rather than *define* domains. We have highlighted several qualities of domains, particularly their functional and semantic features. In the rest of this chapter we explore four suggestions for more closely defining domains and their consequences. These are: domains (1) as innate mechanisms, (2) as distinct ways of acquiring knowledge, (3) as reflections of specific relations between the world and our knowledge of it, (4) and as the product of a distinct research orientation.

Are all domains innate modules? One proposal for defining domains is to restrict candidate domains to sets of computationally relevant concepts that are the product of innate mechanisms or innately guided learning systems. Even if this proposal is adopted, significant issues remain unresolved. For example, Fodor's modular hypothesis sees domains in terms of discrete sub-systems, each tied to a specific perceptual channel. Other biologically oriented approaches, including Atran's claims about biological beliefs (this volume) or Leslie's contention about theory of mind (this volume), construe domains in terms of much larger competencies implicating numerous perceptual modalities. It is thus not evident that their positions and Fodor's would pick out the same candidate domains. Chomsky (1986) similarly argues that viewing the language module as an input system is too narrow.

Can domains be defined by their mode of acquisition? Domains may be defined in terms of the specific pattern of learning associated with them. Keil (1990) and Atran and Sperber (1991) argue that candidate domains may be identifiable with respect to their mode of acquisition. Many domain skills are acquired with ease by virtually all members of the species. A broad consensus has emerged that the language faculty is a universally distributed and rapidly acquired cognitive system whose acquisition depends on an innately guided learning device. Other domains seem to be considerably less widely distributed, acquired only with great effort, and appear to be outside the scope of any innately dedicated program of learning. Chess mastery, for example, is an unevenly distributed cognitive ability that requires determined and often formal training to acquire. Even within a single domain there may be considerable variation. Many aspects of naive biology emerge spontaneously across quite different learning environments (Boster, 1988). Yet, some biological knowledge appears to be sensitive to differences in expertise, such as the degree to which elements within a content area are seen as causally interconnected (Chi et al., 1989). Inagaki (1990a) suggests that familiarity with a domain increases not only the amount of factual knowledge children have but also their conceptual organization of the domain.

To what extent can domains be defined by their relationship to the external world? Some domains appear to carve the world at its joints. When we think of domains, we think of ranges of phenomena comparable to the ranges of facts that are the subject matter of the different sciences. Naive linguistics, biology, psychology, physics, mathematics, cosmology, and so forth, have all been proposed as domains. It is tempting to go from this observation to a view that some causal link exists between the structure of empirical sciences and domain competencies (Carey, 1985). Domains, on this view, would *necessarily* be comparable in size to the subject matter of the different sciences. Is there reason to believe that we are unduly influenced by the way scientific disciplines partition the universe?

Yes. For example, some domains not so much carve nature at its joints as they create such joints. Color terminology and perception, for example, reflect discrete categories of the mind imposed on a continuous natural phenomenon. In processing speech we automatically ignore variations between the representations of what we take to be the same sounds across speakers and within the utterances a single speaker produces. Yet, when attending to the same human voice singing we just as automatically are sensitive to variations in pitch. In short, color and speech perception are less discoveries about nature than interpretations of it. By the same token, a fairly extensive literature documents domainlike competencies that span contrived phenomena not typically associated with a unique science or discipline – ranging from chess to chicken sexing (Biederman & Shiffrar, 1987) to reading x-rays (Lesgold, Rubinson, Feltovich, Glaser, Klopfer, & Wang, 1988) – whereas others encompass phenomena that lack scientific validity or correspondence (for example, race, magic, or the supernatural).

The degree to which a domain is dependent on the world is complex and variable. Some domains (e.g., naive biology and physics) may be less closely linked to our scientific understandings of the world than is sometimes appreciated. Some changes in scientific understanding quite rapidly become part of commonsense. Thus, whales are widely understood to be mammals, not fish, even by children. Examples of this sort prompted Putnam (1975) to speak of a linguistic division of labor, in which science is seen as determining the meaning of natural kind terms. But changes in the validity of a given scientific or formal description do not always alter our commitment to the commonsense conceptualization of that phenomenon (see Resnick, this volume; Strauss & Shilony, this volume). Anthropologists, for example, have shown that the notion *tree* is central to our understanding of the plant world (Witkowski, Brown, & Chase, 1981). Nonetheless, tree does not represent an interesting evolutionary line and is therefore not a concept in modern systematics. But unlike instances where our commonsense knowledge is altered by scientific discovery (e.g., in the reclassification of whales as mammals), the concept of tree maintains its conceptual salience in the face of scientific challenge. This appears to be true even for experts. Botanists in everyday contexts continue to hold the commonsense notion of tree (Atran, 1990).

Interestingly, discovering the incorrigibility of some commonsense concepts may be less an inference from *new* data than a function of having adopted a domain perspective. For example, the regularity in systems of folk biological classification, and particularly the close correspondence between these systems and formal systematics in biology, is not a new discovery. Ernst Mayr (1949) documented close parallels between nonliterate Papuan folk biology and formal systematics. However, these parallels were interpreted as evidence for the scientific validity of the species concept rather than as evidence of a shared cognitive mechanism for conceptualizing living kinds (Diamond, 1966). In other words, it was assumed that a close correspondence between common-sense and science reflected regularities in the world external to cognition, rather than indicating a set of shared cognitive dispositions. As several of the chapters in this volume suggest, the empirical and structural parallels between folk beliefs and science are indeed informative; but from the perspective of understanding mental domains, these parallels are more pertinent to the cognitive than the other sciences.

Does the question asked make a difference? It is possible that the research question posed may have profound impact on the candidate domains we discover. It may not, in short, be possible to distinguish between the research interest that prompted a set of data and what those data can be interpreted as supporting. A case in point may be the relation between a competence associated with a given domain and the knowledge represented in that domain. Keil (1981) makes a similar point regarding approaches to developmental change, when he distinguishes between theories that are knowledge based from those that are competence based. Keil's concern is with constraints, but his observation can be extended to a discussion of how to approach domains. In broad terms, knowledge-based research sees domains as being derived from knowledge structures, whereas competence-based research focuses more on how differing states of knowledge are derived from distinct competencies. The strongest versions of each of these are, respectively, expertise studies and modular approaches.

The competence-based view lays emphasis on the domain-specific principles of organization that shape the sorts of knowledge to which the organism attends and the kinds of knowledge structures the organism develops (see Gallistel et al., 1991). A central concern of the competence-based researcher is how attention is guided toward a circumscribed set of observations, not only during development but also during mature processing. Knowledge-based studies, in contrast, focus more on the consequences of holding domain knowledge than on the principles that underlie its acquisition (see Shantz, 1989; Chase & Simon, 1973; de Groot, 1966). The principal question posed in this work is what impact does domain knowledge have on subsequent processing? Given a certain level of knowledge integration, what are the implications for thought?

Accordingly, the two viewpoints could be seen simply as different perspectives on the same phenomenon, in which somewhat distinct emphases are applied. Knowledge- and competence-based approaches would accordingly be slightly different points of view on a single issue, namely, the relationship between knowledge of something and the competence underlying that knowledge. The two orientations, however, can also be seen as different levels of analysis, yielding quite different kinds of generalizations. Keil, for example, argues that the knowledge-based approach does not provide a principled way of "distinguishing what is merely a change in a knowledge base from what is a change in computational and representational machinery" (1981: 204). Knowing that a cognitive skill changes with experience thus does not permit us to decide whether that change is best described in knowledge- or competence-based terms. By the same token, knowing that a knowledge-based hypothesis accounts for a set of observations does not permit us to conclude that a competence-based vantage would construe the observations as coming from a bounded type.

Consider, for example, the problem of deciding whether a change in the way knowledge is represented reflects a change in domain competence. There appears to be a domain of dinosaur knowledge for which some children develop a special expertise. Thus Chi and her associates (1989) have shown that increased knowledge about dinosaurs leads to an enriched network of causally linked beliefs. Generally, the conceptual effects of such causal networks appear to be quite limited, in the sense that they do not readily transfer to closely allied content areas (Inagaki, 1990b). From a competence-based perspective, however, dinosaur knowledge is not so much a domain as a subset of another domain, namely, living things. What are the implications of this?

One implication is that knowledge-based claims may not commit the researcher to a particular opinion on questions like "What is a domain?" "What are domain boundaries?" or "How are domains implicated in the learning process?" Discovering the relationship between domain-specific and other sorts of knowledge is presumably dependent on determining what is and what is not domain knowledge, and by extension what is and what is not a domain. Thus, like the contrast between domain-general and domain-specific perspectives, knowledge-based and competence-based views may differ in terms of the kinds of generalizations that each can enlist, particularly about domains.

Conclusion

In this introduction we have sketched out several distinct intellectual traditions that have contributed to the view that human cognition can be fruitfully considered domain-specific. Clearly, the approach seems to us extremely promising. Still, a series of difficult questions remain: What is a domain? How many domains are there? Do they concern processes, representations, or both? Do we have conscious access to domains? Can domains change over time, and if so, how? Do the changes that occur in childhood differ in important ways from those changes in domain knowledge that take place after maturity? Does conceptual change occur because of or in spite of domains? Do domains "communicate" among themselves, and if so how? We leave these issues for the reader to consider. We believe the contributions that follow provide ample food for thought.

The remainder of the volume draws out the implications of these and other questions. We have arranged the contributions into five parts aimed at highlighting some relevant commonalities and contrasts. We do not suggest by this that the parts are self-contained. Indeed, there are many additional links that can be made across sections (e.g., the chapters by Sperber, Keil, and Gelman, Coley, & Gottfried, which are all in different sections, propose an interestingly similar view of how it is that several domains share certain underlying principles). The organization of chapters that we chose, however, is meant to accent the shared comparative perspective – be it historical, biological, developmental or cultural – that all contributions have adopted.

The second part, "The Origins of Domain Knowledge: Biology and Evolution," includes chapters by Dan Sperber, Alfonso Caramazza, Argye Hillis, Elwyn Leek, and Michele Miozzo, and Leda Cosmides and John Tooby. Together these pieces suggest that a domain-specific mental architecture is an inevitable consequence of human biological history and neurostructure. Although all domains may not be innate, these combined chapters strongly argue that some, perhaps much, of domain knowledge must be.

Part III, "The Origins of Domain Knowledge: Conceptual Approaches," includes chapters by Alan Leslie, David and Ann James Premack, Susan Carey and Elizabeth Spelke, Lawrence Hirschfeld, and Frank Keil. Stressing the importance of developmental research in unpacking the nature and scope of domain competencies, these chapters explore the organism's initial conceptual states and their elaborations in infancy and early childhood.

The fourth part considers the question, "Are Domains Theories?" The complexity and richness of the knowledge in any given domain has frequently evoked a comparison with scientific theories. In this section, the "theory-theory" question is explored in two domains: Focusing on early beliefs about the mind and mental states, the chapters by Alison Gopnik and Henry Wellman and by Paul Harris take contrasting positions on the issue. Scott Atran and Susan Gelman, John Coley, and Gail Gottfried then consider the "theory-theory" with regard to biological concepts.

In the fifth part, "Domains across Cultures and Languages," chapters by Rochel Gelman and Kimberly Brenneman, Pascal Boyer, Stella Vosniadou and by Anna Wierzbicka consider whether cultural variation in domain knowledge is a problem for domain specificity. Boyer's and Vosniadou's chapters explore the interesting possibility that domain-specific mechanisms shape the development of nondomain knowledge.

Finally, we end with "Implications for Education," with chapters by Sidney Strauss and Tamar Shilony, in which theory of mind research is used as a basis for exploring teachers' intuitive theories of learning, and Lauren Resnick, in which a domain perspective is integrated with the recently advanced notion of situated cognition.

Notes

1. In a manner analogous to the way language as a social phenomenon ("a shared property of a community" defined in terms of "obscure sociopolitical and normative factors") is built out of language as an individual phenomenon ("a system represented in the mind/brain of a particular individual") (Chomsky, 1988: 36–37).
2. Berlin and Kay (1969: 5–6) defined as basic those color terms that (among other properties): (1) are monolexemic (so that the meaning of the term is not predictable from the meaning of its parts), (2) apply to a broad range of phenomena (thus excluding *blond*, a term that applies only to hair), and (3) are psychologically salient for all speakers (thus excluding the color of something with which only a few individuals are familiar).
3. The domain of color remains a contested one. Berlin and Kay's conclusions regarding linguistic relativity have been tempered by Kay and Kempton (1984) and challenged by Lucy and Shweder (1988) and Lakoff (1987). Yet even if there is significant cross-linguistic relativity in basic color terms, the principles organizing the color lexicon are everywhere specific to the conceptual and perceptual domain of color.
4. Specifically, Lounsbury's proposal argued that the kinship lexicon must be analyzed in terms of core or focal meanings and reduction rules from which other meanings could be derived.
5. As we pointed out, in many domains these connections are clearly seen as causal (Leslie, this volume). Members of a particular living kind, for example, are assumed to share an underlying essence that causes the regularities in outward appearance that help us identify category members (Atran, 1990; Keil, this volume). But the outward appearance is not the shared property since modifying that appearance (by painting out the spots on a leopard) does not change category

membership. In other domains these implications are less clearly causal, but nonetheless not arbitrary. Current linguistic theory proposes that links between the abstract categories of phrase structure grammars are controlled by a few principles (Projection Principle, Bounding Principle, Binding Theory, Case Theory, etc.) that "explain" the surface features of utterances in the way underlying essences (on folk theories) or DNA (on scientific ones) explain the outward appearance of living things, namely, in terms of model-derived connections.

References

Armstrong, S. L., Gleitman, L. R., & Gleitman, H. (1983). What some concepts might not be. *Cognition, 13,* 263–308.

Atran, S. (1988). Basic conceptual domains. *Mind & Language, 3,* 7–16.

Atran, S. (1990). *Cognitive foundations of natural history.* New York: Cambridge University Press.

Atran, S., & Sperber, D. (1991). Learning without teaching: Its place in culture. In L. Landsmann (Ed.), *Culture, schooling, and psychological development* (pp. 39–55). Norwood, NJ: Ablex Publishing.

Behrend, D. A. (1990). Constraints and development: A reply to Nelson (1988). *Cognitive Development, 5,* 313–330.

Berlin, B. (1972). Speculations on the growth of ethnobotanical nomenclature. *Language & Society, 1,* 63–98.

Berlin, B. (1974). Further notes on covert categories. *American Anthropologist, 76,* 327–331.

Berlin, B. (1978). Ethnobiological classification. In E. Rosch & B. Lloyd (Eds.), *Cognition and categorization.* Hillsdale, NJ: Erlbaum.

Berlin, B., Breedlove, D., & Raven, P. (1966). Folk taxonomies and biological classification. *Science, 154,* 273–275.

Berlin, B., Breedlove, D., & Raven, P. (1973). General principles of classification and nomenclature in folk biology. *American Anthropologist, 75,* 214–242.

Berlin, B., Breedlove, D., & Raven, P. (1974). *Principles of Tzeltal plant classification.* New York: Academic Press.

Berlin, B., & Kay, P. (1969). *Basic color terms: Their universality and growth.* Berkeley: University of California Press.

Biederman, I., & Shiffrar, M. M. (1987). Sexing day-old chicks: A case study and expert systems analysis of a difficult perceptual-learning task. *Journal of Experimental Psychology: Learning, Memory, and Cognition, 13,* 640–645.

Boster, J. (1988). Natural sources of internal category structure: Typicality, familiarity, and similarity of birds. *Memory & Cognition, 16*(3), 258–270.

Boyer, P. (1990). *Tradition as truth and communication.* New York: Cambridge University Press.

Brown, A. (1989). Analogical learning and transfer: What develops? In S. Vosniadou & A. Ortony (Eds.), *Similarity and analogical reasoning* (pp. 369–412). New York: Cambridge University Press.

Brown, A. L. (1990). Domain-specific principles affect learning and transfer in children. *Cognitive Science, 14,* 107–133.

Brown, C. (1992). Cognition and common sense. *American Ethnologist, 19,* 367–374.

Bulmer, R. (1967). Why is the cassowary not a bird? *Man, 2,* 5–25.

Carey, S. (1985). *Conceptual change in childhood.* Cambridge, MA: MIT Press.

Chase, W., & Simon, H. (1973). The mind's eye in chess. In W. Chase (Ed.), *Visual information processing.* New York: Academic Press.

Chase, W. G., & Ericsson, K. A. (1981). Skilled memory. In J. R. Anderson (Ed.), *Cognitive skills and their acquisition.* Hillsdale, NJ: Erlbaum.

Chi, M., Hutchinson, J., & Robin, A. (1989). How inferences about novel domain-related concepts can be constrained by structured knowledge. *Merrill-Palmer Quarterly, 35,* 27–62.

Chomsky, N. (1980a). On cognitive structures and their development: A reply to Piaget. In M. Piattelli-Palmarini (Ed.), *Language and learning: The debate between Jean Piaget and Noam Chomsky* (pp. 35–54). Cambridge: Harvard University Press.

Chomsky, N. (1980b). *Rules and representations.* New York: Columbia University Press.

Chomsky, N. (1986). *Knowledge of language: Its nature, origin, and use.* New York: Praeger.

Chomsky, N. (1988). *Language and problems of knowledge.* Cambridge, MA: MIT Press.

Cosmides, L. (1989). The logic of social exchange: Has natural selection shaped how humans reason? Studies with the Wason selection task. *Cognition, 31,* 187–276.

Cosmides, L., & Tooby, J. (1989). Evolutionary psychology and the generation of culture. Part II: A computational theory of social exchange. *Ethology & Sociobiology, 10,* 51–97.

Cromer, R. F. (1988). The cognition hypothesis revisited. In R. S. Kessel (Ed.), *The development of language and language researchers: Essays in honor of Roger Brown* (pp. 223–248). Hillsdale, NJ: Erlbaum.

Curtiss, S. (1977). *Genie: A psycholinguistic study of a modern-day "wild child."* New York: Academic Press.

Curtiss, S. (1982). Developmental dissociation of language and cognition. In L. K. Obler & L. Menn (Eds.), *Exceptional language and linguistics* (pp. 285–312). New York: Academic Press.

Dawkins, R. (1987). *The blind watchmaker.* New York: Norton.

de Groot, A. (1966). Perception and memory versus thought: Some old ideas and recent findings. In B. Kleinmuntz (Ed.), *Problem solving: Research, method, and theory* (pp. 19–51). New York: John Wiley.

Diamond, J. (1966). Zoological classification system of a primitive people. *Science, 151,* 1102–1104.

Fodor, J. (1983). *Modularity of mind.* Cambridge, MA: MIT Press.

Furrow, D., & Nelson, K. (1984). Environmental correlates of individual differences in language acquisition. *Journal of Child Language, 11,* 523–534.

Furrow, D., & Nelson, K. (1986). A further look at the motherese hypothesis: A reply to Gleitman, Newport, & Gleitman. *Journal of Child Language, 13,* 163–176.

Gallistel, C. (1990). *The organization of learning.* Cambridge, MA: MIT Press.

Gallistel, C., Brown, A., Carey, S., Gelman, R., & Keil, F. (1991). Lessons from animal learning for the study of human development. In S. Carey & R. Gelman (Eds.), *The epigenesis of mind: Essays on biology and cognition.* Hillsdale, NJ: Erlbaum.

Garcia, J., & Koelling, R. (1966). Relation of cue to consequence in avoidance learning. *Psychonomics Science, 4,* 123–124.

Gelman, R. (1990). First principles organize attention to and learning about relevant data: Number and the animate–inanimate distinction as examples. *Cognitive Science, 14,* 79–106.

Gelman, R., & Gallistel, C. (1978). *The child's understanding of number.* Cambridge: Harvard University Press.

Gelman, S. A., & Wellman, H. M. (1991). Insides and essences: Early understandings of the nonobvious. *Cognition, 38,* 213–244.

Gleitman, L., Newport, E., & Gleitman, H. (1984). The current status of the motherese hypothesis. *Journal of Child Language, 11,* 43–79.

Gleitman, L. (1986). Biological disposition to learn language. In W. Demopoulos & A. Marras (Eds.), *Language learning and concept acquisition: Foundational issues* (pp. 3–28). Norwood, NJ: Ablex Publishing.

Goldin-Meadow, S. (1982). The resilience of recursion: A study of a communication system developed without a conventional language model. In E. Wanner & L. R. Gleitman (Eds.), *Language acquisition: The state of the art* (pp. 51–77). Cambridge: Cambridge University Press.

Goodman, N. (1972). Seven strictures on similarity. In N. Goodman (Ed.), *Problems and projects* (pp. 437–447). Indianapolis: Bobbs-Merrill.

Heider, E. (1972). Universals in color naming and memory. *Journal of Experimental Psychology, 93,* 10–20.

Heider, E., & Oliver, D. (1972). The structure of the color space in naming and memory for two languages. *Cognitive Psychology, 3,* 337–354.

Herrnstein, R. J. (1979). Acquisition, generalization, and discrimination reversal of a natural concept. *Journal of Experimental Psychology: Animal Behavior Processes, 5,* 116–129.

Hirschfeld, L. (1986). Kinship and cognition: Genealogy and the meaning of kinship terms. *Current Anthropology, 27,* 217–242.

Hirschfeld, L. (1989). Rethinking the acquisition of kinship terms. *International Journal of Behavioral Development, 12*(4), 541–568.

Hoff-Ginsberg, E., & Shatz, M. (1982). Linguistic input and the child's acquisition of language. *Psychological Bulletin, 92,* 2–26.

Inagaki, K. (1990a). Young children's everyday biology as the basis for learning school biology. *The Bulletin of the Faculty of Education, Chiba University, 38,* 177–184.

Inagaki, K. (1990b). The effects of raising animals on children's biological knowledge. *British Journal of Developmental Psychology, 8,* 119–129.

Kaiser, M. K., Proffitt, D. R., & Anderson, K. (1985). Judgments of natural and anomalous trajectories in the presence and absence of motion. *Journal of Experimental Psychology: Learning, Memory, & Cognition, 11*(1–4), 795–803.

Karmiloff-Smith, A., & Inhelder, B. (1975). If you want to get ahead, get a theory. *Cognition, 3,* 195–211.

Kay, P., & Kempton, W. (1984). What is the Sapir–Whorf hypothesis? *American Anthropologist, 86,* 65–79.

Kay, P., & McDaniel, C. (1978). The linguistic significance of the meanings of basic color terms. *Language, 54,* 610–646.

Keil, F. (1981). Constraints on knowledge and cognitive development. *Psychological Review, 88*(3), 197–227.

Keil, F. C. (1989). *Concepts, kinds, and cognitive development.* Cambridge, MA: MIT Press.

Keil, F. (1990). Constraints on constraints: Surveying the epigenetic landscape. *Cognitive Science, 14,* 135–168.

Klima, E., & Bellugi, U. (1979). *The signs of language.* Cambridge, MA: Harvard University Press.

Kripke, S. (1972). *Naming and necessity.* Cambridge, MA: Harvard University Press.

Lakoff, G. (1987). *Women, fire, and dangerous things.* Chicago: University of Chicago Press.

Landau, B., & Gleitman, L. (1985). *Language and experience.* Cambridge, MA: Harvard University Press.

Langlois, J., & Roggman, L. (1990). Attractive faces are only average. *Psychological Science, 1*(2), 115–121.

Lesgold, A. M., Rubinson, H., Feltovich, P., Glaser, R., Klopfer, D., & Wang, Y. (1988). Expertise in a complex skill: Diagnosing x-ray pictures. In M. Chi, R. Glaser, & M. Farr (Eds.), *The nature of expertise.* Hillsdale, NJ: Erlbaum.

Liberman, A., & Mattingly, I. (1989). A specialization for speech perception. *Science, 243,* 489–494.

Lounsbury, F. (1964). A formal account of the Crow and Omaha-type kinship terminologies. In W. Goodenough (Ed.), *Explorations in cultural anthropology.* New York: McGraw-Hill.

Lucy, J., & Shweder, R. (1988). The effect of incidental conversation on memory for focal colors. *American Anthropologist, 90,* 923–931.

Macnamara, J. (1982). *Names for things: A study of human learning.* Cambridge, MA: MIT Press/Bradford Books.

Markman, E. M. (1989). *Categorization and naming in children: Problems of induction.* Cambridge, MA: MIT Press.

Marler, P. (1991). The instinct to learn. In S. Carey & R. Gelman (Eds.), *The epigenesis of mind: Essays on biology and cognition.* Hillsdale, NJ: Erlbaum.

Marr, D. (1982). *Vision.* New York: W. H. Freeman.

Mattingly, I., Liberman, A., Syrdal, A., & Halwes, T. (1971). Discrimination in speech and nonspeech modes. *Cognitive Psychology, 2,* 131–157.

Mayr, E. (1949). *List of New Guinea birds.* New York: American Museum of Natural History.

Medin, D. L., & Shoben, E. J. (1988). Context and structure in conceptual combination. *Cognitive Psychology, 20,* 158–190.

Medin, D. L., & Wattenmaker, W. D. (1987). Category cohesiveness, theories, and cognitive archeology. In U. Neisser (Ed.), *Concepts and conceptual development: Ecological and intellectual factors in categorization* (pp. 25–62). New York: Cambridge University Press.

Murphy, G. L., & Medin, D. L. (1985). The role of theories in conceptual coherence. *Psychological Review, 92,* 289–316.

Nelson, K. (1988). Constraints on word learning? *Cognitive Development, 3,* 221–246.

Newport, E. L. (1990). Maturational constraints on language learning. *Cognitive Science, 14,* 11–28.

Newport, E. L. (1991). Contrasting concepts of the critical period for language. In S. Carey & R. Gelman (Eds.), *The epigenesis of mind: Essays on biology and cognition* (pp. 111–130). Hillsdale, NJ: Erlbaum.

Newport, E. L., & Meier, R. P. (1985). Acquisition of American Sign Language. In D. I. Slobin (Ed.), *The cross-linguistic study of language acquisition, Vol. 1* (pp. 881–938). Hillsdale, NJ: Erlbaum.

Ochs, E., & Schieffelin, B. (1984). Language acquisition and socialization: Three developmental stories and their implications. In R. Shweder and R. LeVine (Eds.), *Culture theory: Essays on mind, self, and emotion* (pp. 276–320). New York: Cambridge University Press.

Peirce, C. S. (1960). *Collected papers of Charles Sanders Peirce* (C. Hartshorne & P. Weiss, Eds.) (4th ed., Vols. 1 & 2). Cambridge, MA: Harvard University Press.

Pettito, L. A. (1988). "Language" in the prelinguistic child. In R. S. Kessel (Ed.), *The development of language and language researchers: Essays in honor of Roger Brown* (pp. 187–221). Hillsdale, NJ: Erlbaum.

Pinker, S., & Bloom, P. (1990). Natural language and natural selection. *Behavioral and Brain Sciences, 13*, 707–784.

Putnam, H. (1970). Is semantics possible? In H. E. Kiefer & M. K. Munitz (Eds.), *Language, belief, and metaphysics* (pp. 50–63). Albany, NY: State University of New York Press.

Putnam, H. (1975). The meaning of "meaning." In H. Putnam (Ed.), *Mind, language, and reality: Philosophical papers, Vol. 2.* New York: Cambridge University Press.

Pye, C. (1986). Quiché Mayan speech to children. *Journal of Child Language, 13*, 85–100.

Quine, W. V. O. (1960). *Word and object.* Cambridge, MA: MIT Press.

Rips, L. J. (1989). Similarity, typicality, and categorization. In S. Vosniadou & A. Ortony (Eds.), *Similarity and analogical reasoning* (pp. 21–59). New York: Cambridge University Press.

Rosaldo, M. (1972). Metaphor and folk classification. *Southwestern Journal of Anthropology, 28*, 83–99.

Rosch, E., Mervis, C., Gray, W., Johnson, D., & Boyes-Braem, P. (1976). Basic objects in natural categories. *Cognitive Psychology, 8*, 382–439.

Rozin, P., & Schull, J. (1988). The adaptive-evolutionary point of view in experimental psychology. In R. Atkinson, R. Herrnstein, G. Lindzey, & R. Luce (Eds.), *Steven's handbook of experimental psychology.* New York: John Wiley & Sons.

Schwartz, S. P. (1979). Natural kind terms. *Cognition, 7*, 301–315.

Shantz, C. (Ed.). (1989). *Merrill-Palmer Quarterly, 35*(1).

Slobin, D. (1985). *The crosslinguistic study of language acquisition.* Hillsdale, NJ: Erlbaum.

Smith, E. E., & Medin, D. L. (1981). *Categories and concepts.* Cambridge, MA: Harvard University Press.

Snow, C. (1972). Mothers' speech to children learning language. *Child Development, 43*, 549–565.

Spelke, E. S. (1990). Principles of object perception. *Cognitive Science, 14*, 29–56.

Sperber, D. (1974). Contre certains a priori anthropologiques. In E. Morin & M. Piatelli-Palmarini (Eds.), *L'Unité de l'homme* (pp. 491–512). Paris: Le Seuil.

Sperber, D. (1975a). Pourquoi les animaux parfaits, les hybrides et les monstres sont-ils bon à penser symboliquement? *L'Homme, 15*(2), 5–24.

Sperber, D. (1975b). *Rethinking symbolism.* New York: Cambridge University Press.

Symons, D. (1979). *The evolution of human sexuality.* New York: Oxford University Press.

Tambiah, S. (1969). Animals are good to think and good to prohibit. *Ethnology, 8*(4), 422–459.

Ullman, S. (1980). Against direct perception. *Behavioral and Brain Sciences, 3,* 373–415.

Vygotsky, L. (1978). *Mind in society.* Cambridge: Harvard University Press.

Wexler, K., & Culicover, P. W. (1980). *Formal principles of language acquisition.* Cambridge, MA: MIT Press.

Witkowski, S., Brown, C., & Chase, P. (1981). Where do trees come from? *Man, 16,* 1–14.

Part II

**The origins of domain knowledge:
Biology and evolution**

2   The modularity of thought and the epidemiology of representations

Dan Sperber

Ten years ago, Jerry Fodor published *The Modularity of Mind*, a book that received much well-deserved attention. His target was the then-dominant view according to which there are no important discontinuities between perceptual processes and conceptual processes. Information flows freely, "up" and "down," between these two kinds of processes, and beliefs inform perception as much as they are informed by it. Against this view, Fodor argued that perceptual processes (and also linguistic decoding) are carried out by specialized, rather rigid mechanisms. These "modules" each have their own proprietary data base, and do not draw on information produced by conceptual processes.

Although this was probably not intended and has not been much noticed, "modularity of mind" was a paradoxical title, for, according to Fodor, modularity is to be found only at the periphery of the mind, in its input systems.[1] In its center and bulk, Fodor's mind is decidedly *non*modular. Conceptual processes – that is, thought proper – are presented as a big holistic lump lacking joints at which to carve. Controversies have focused on the thesis that perceptual and linguistic decoding processes are modular, much more than on the alleged nonmodularity of thought.[2]

In this chapter, I have two aims. The first is to defend the view that thought processes might be modular too (what Fodor [1987: 27] calls "modularity theory gone mad" – oh well!). Let me however echo Fodor and say that, "when I speak of a cognitive system as modular, I shall . . . always mean 'to some interesting extent' " (Fodor, 1983: 37). My second aim is to articulate a modular view of human thought with the naturalistic view of human culture that I have been developing under the label "epidemiology of representations" (Sperber, 1985b). These aims are closely related: Cultural diversity has always been taken to show how plastic the human mind is, whereas the

I thank Lawrence Hirschfeld, Pierre Jacob, and Deirdre Wilson for their useful comments on an earlier version of this paper.

modularity of thought thesis seems to deny that plasticity. I want to show how, contrary to the received view, organisms endowed with truly modular minds might engender truly diverse cultures.

Two commonsense arguments against the modularity of thought

Abstractly and roughly at least, the distinction between perceptual and conceptual processes is clear: Perceptual processes have, as input, information provided by sensory receptors and, as output, a conceptual representation categorizing the object perceived. Conceptual processes have conceptual representations both as input and as output. Thus seeing a cloud and thinking "here is a cloud" is a perceptual process. Inferring from this perception "it might rain" is a conceptual process.

The rough idea of modularity is also clear: A cognitive module is a genetically specified computational device in the mind/brain (henceforth: the mind) that works pretty much on its own on inputs pertaining to some specific cognitive domain and provided by other parts of the nervous systems (e.g., sensory receptors or other modules). Given such notions, the view that perceptual processes might be modular is indeed quite plausible, as argued by Fodor. On the other hand, there are two main commonsense arguments (and several more technical ones) that lead one to expect conceptual thought processes not to be modular.

The first commonsense argument against the modularity of thought has to do with integration of information. The conceptual level is the level at which information from different input modules, each presumably linked to some sensory modality, gets integrated into a modality-independent medium: A dog can be seen, heard, smelled, touched, and talked about: The percepts are different; the concept is the same. As Fodor points out,

the general form of the argument goes back at least to Aristotle: the representations that input systems deliver have to interface somewhere, and the computational mechanisms that affect the interface must ipso facto have access to information from more than one cognitive domain. (Fodor, 1983: 101–102)

The second commonsense argument against the modularity of thought has to do with cultural diversity and novelty. An adult human's conceptual processes range over an indefinite variety of domains, including party politics, baseball history, motorcycle maintenance, Zen Bhuddism, French cuisine, Italian opera, chess playing, stamp collecting, and Fodor's chosen example, modern science. The appearance of many of these domains in human cognition is very recent and not relevantly correlated with changes in the human genome. Many of these domains vary dramatically in content from one culture to another, or are not found at all in many cultures. In such conditions, it would be absurd to assume that there is an ad hoc genetically specified preparedness for these culturally developed conceptual domains.

These two commonsense arguments are so compelling that Fodor's more technical considerations (having to do with "isotropy," illusions, rationality, etc.) look like mere nails in the coffin of a dead idea. My goal will be to shake the commonsense picture and to suggest that the challenge of articulating conceptual integration, cultural diversity, and modularity may be met and turns out to be a source of psychological and anthropological insights.

Notice, to begin with, that both the informational integration argument and the cultural diversity argument are quite compatible with *partial* modularity at the conceptual level.

True, it would be functionally self-defeating to reproduce at the conceptual level the same domain partition found at the perceptual level, and have a different conceptual module treat separately the output of each perceptual module. No integration whatsoever would take place, and the dog seen and the dog heard could never be one and the very same mastiff Goliath. But who says conceptual domains have to match perceptual domains? Why not envisage, at the conceptual level, a wholly different, more or less orthogonal domain partition, with domain-specific conceptual mechanisms, each getting their inputs from several input mechanisms? For instance, all the conceptual outputs of perceptual modules that contain the concept MASTIFF might be fed into a specialized module (say a domain-specific inferential device handling living-kind concepts), which takes care (inter alia) of Goliath qua mastiff. Similarly, all the conceptual outputs of input modules that contain the concept THREE might be fed into a specialized module, which handles inference about numbers, and so forth. In this way, information from different input devices might get genuinely integrated, though not into a single conceptual system, but into several such systems.

Of course, if you have, say, a prudential rule that tells you to run away when you encounter more than two bellicose dogs, you would not really be satisfied to be informed by the living-kinds module that the category BELLICOSE DOG is instantiated in your environment, and by the numerical module that there are more than two of something. Some further, at least partial, integration had better take place. It might even be argued – though *that* is by no means obvious – that a plausible model of human cognition should allow for *full* integration of all conceptual information at some level. Either way, partial or full integration might take place further up the line, among the outputs of conceptual rather than of perceptual modules. Conceptual integration is not incompatible with at least some conceptual modularity.

Similarly, the conceptual diversity argument implies that some conceptual domains (chess, etc.) could not be modular. It certainly does not imply that none of them could be. Thus, in spite of superficial variations, living-kind classification exhibits strong commonalities across cultures (see Berlin, 1978) in a manner that does suggest the presence of a domain-specific cognitive module (see Atran, 1987, 1990).

The thesis that some central thought processes might be modular gets support from a wealth of recent work (well illustrated in the present volume) tending to show that many basic conceptual thought processes, found in every culture and in every fully developed human, are governed by domain-specific competences. For instance, it is argued that people's ordinary understanding of the movements of an inert solid object, of the appearance of an organism, or of the actions of a person are based on three distinct mental mechanisms: a naive physics, a naive biology, and a naive psychology (see for instance Atran, 1987; Keil, 1989; Leslie, 1987, 1988; Spelke, 1988, and their contributions to this volume – see Carey, 1985, for a dissenting view). It is argued moreover that these mechanisms, at least in rudimentary form, are part of the equipment that makes acquisition of knowledge possible, rather than being acquired competences.

Accepting as a possibility some degree of modularity in conceptual systems is innocuous enough. Jerry Fodor himself recently considered favorably the view that "intentional folk psychology is, essentially, an innate, *modularized* database" (Fodor, 1992: 284 – italics added) without suggesting that he was thereby departing from his former views on modularity. But what about the possibility of *massive* modularity at the conceptual level? Do the two common-sense arguments, integration and diversity, really rule it out?

Modularity and evolution

If modularity is a genuine natural property, then what it consists of is a matter of discovery, not stipulation. Fodor himself discusses a number of characteristic and diagnostic features of modularity. Modules, he argues, are "domain-specific, innately specified, hardwired, autonomous" (1983: 36). Their operations are mandatory (p. 52) and fast (p. 61); they are "informationally encapsulated" (p. 64), that is, the only background information available to them is that found in their proprietary data base. Modules are "associated with fixed neural architecture" (p. 98). Fodor discusses still other features that are not essential to the present discussion.

There is one feature of modularity that is implied by Fodor's description, but that he does not mention or discuss. If, as Fodor argues, a module is innately specified, hardwired, and autonomous, then it follows that *a cognitive module is an evolved mechanism with a distinct phylogenetic history*. This is a characteristic, but hardly a diagnostic feature, because we know close to nothing about the actual evolution of cognitive modules. But I have been convinced by Leda Cosmides and John Tooby (see Cosmides, 1989; Cosmides & Tooby, 1987; Tooby & Cosmides, 1989, 1992, this volume)[3] that we know enough about evolution on the one hand and cognition on the other to come up with well-motivated (though, of course, tentative) assumptions as to when to expect modularity, what properties to expect of modules, and even what modules to expect. This section of the chapter owes much to their ideas.

Fodor himself does mention evolutionary considerations, but only in passing.

He maintains that, phylogenetically, modular input systems should have preceded nonmodular central systems:

Cognitive evolution would thus have been in the direction of gradually freeing certain sorts of problem-solving systems from the constraints under which input analyzers labor – hence of producing, as a relatively late achievement, the comparatively domain-free inferential capacities which apparently mediate the higher flights of cognition. (Fodor, 1983: 43)

Let us spell out some of the implications of Fodor's evolutionary suggestion. At an early stage of cognitive evolution we should find modular sensory input analyzers directly connected to modular motor controllers. There is no level yet where information from several perceptual processes would be integrated by a conceptual process. Then there emerges a conceptual device, that is, an inferential device that is not itself directly linked to sensory receptors. This conceptual device accepts input from two or more perceptual devices, constructs new representations warranted by these inputs, and transmits information to motor control mechanisms.

Initially, of course, this conceptual device is just another module: It is specialized, innately wired, fast, automatic, and so forth. Then, so the story should go, it grows and becomes less specialized, possibly it merges with other similar conceptual devices, to the point where it is a single big conceptual system, able to process all the outputs of all the perceptual modules, and able to manage all the conceptual information available to the organism. This true central system cannot, in performing a given cognitive task, activate all the data accessible to it, or exploit all of its many procedures. Automaticity and speed are no longer possible. Indeed, if the central system automatically did what it is capable of doing, this would trigger a computational explosion with no end in sight.[4]

An evolutionary account of the emergence of a conceptual module in a mind that had known only perceptual processes is simple enough to imagine. Its demodularization would be much harder to explain.

A toy example might go like this: Organisms of a certain species, call them "protorgs," are threatened by a danger of a certain kind. This danger (the approach of elephants that might trample the orgs, as it might be) is signaled by the co-occurrence of a noise N and soil vibrations V. Protorgs have an acoustic perception module that detects instances of N and a vibration-perception module that detects instances of V. The detection either of N by one perceptual module, or of V by the other activates an appropriate flight procedure. Fine, except that when N occurs alone, or when V occurs alone, it so happens that there is no danger. So protorgs end up with a lot of "false positives," uselessly running away, and thus wasting energy and resources.

Some descendants of the protorgs, call them "orgs," have evolved another mental device: a conceptual inference mechanism. The perceptual modules no longer directly activate their flight procedure. Rather their relevant outputs, that is, the identification of noise N and that of vibrations V, go to the new device. This conceptual mechanism acts essentially as an AND-gate: When, and only when both N and V have been perceptually identified, does the conceptual mechanism get into a state that can be said to represent the presence of danger, and it is this state that activates the appropriate flight procedure.

Orgs, so the story goes, competed successfully with protorgs for food resources, and that is why you won't find protorgs around.

The orgs' conceptual mechanism, though not an *input* module, is nevertheless a clear case of a module: It is a domain-specific problem solver; it is fast, informationally encapsulated, associated with fixed neural architecture, and so forth. Of course, it is a tiny module, but nothing stops us from imagining it becoming larger: Instead of accepting just two bits of information from two simple perceptual modules, the conceptual module could come to handle more from more sources, and to control more than a single motor procedure, but still be domain-specific, automatic, fast, and so on.

At this juncture, we have two diverging evolutionary scenarios on offer. According to the scenario suggested by Fodor, the conceptual module should evolve toward less domain specificity, less informational encapsulation, less speed, and so on. In other words, it would become less and less modular, possibly merge with other demodularized devices, and end up like the kind of central system with which Fodor believes we are endowed ("Quineian," "isotropic," etc.). There are two gaps in this scenario. The first gap has to do with mental mechanisms and is highlighted by Fodor himself in his "First Law of the Nonexistence of Cognitive Science." This law says in substance that the mechanisms of nonmodular thought processes are too complex to be understood. So, just accept that there are such mechanisms and don't ask how they work.

The second gap in Fodor's scenario has to do with the evolutionary process itself that is supposed to bring about the development of such a mysterious mechanism. No doubt, it might be advantageous to trade a few domain-specific inferential micromodules for an advanced all-purpose macrointelligence, if there is any such thing. For instance, superorgs endowed with general intelligence might develop technologies to eradicate the danger once and for all instead of having to flee again and again. But evolution does not offer such starkly contrasted choices. The available alternatives at any one time are all small departures from the existing state. Selection, the main force driving evolution, is near-sighted (whereas the other forces, genetic drift, etc., are blind). An immediately advantageous alternative is likely to be selected from the narrow available range, and this may bar the path to highly advantageous long-term outcomes. A demodularization scenario is implausible for this very reason.

Suppose indeed the conceptual danger analyzer is modified in some mutant orgs, not in the direction of performing better at its special task, but in that of less domain specificity. The modified conceptual device processes not just information relevant to the orgs' immediate chances of escape, but also information about innocuous features of the dangerous situation, and about a variety of innocuous situations exhibiting these further features; the device draws inferences not just of an urgent practical kind, but also of a more theoretical character. When danger is detected, the new, less modular system does not automatically trigger flight behavior, and when it does, it does so more slowly – automaticity and speed go with modularity – but it has interesting thoughts that are filed in memory for the future . . . if there is any future for mutant orgs endowed with this partly demodularized device.

Of course, speed and automaticity are particularly important for danger analyzers, and less so for other plausible modules, for instance, modules governing the choice of sexual partners. However, the general point remains: Evolved cognitive modules are likely to be answers to specific, usually environmental problems. Loosening the domain of a module will bring about, not greater flexibility, but greater slack in the organism's response to the problem. To the extent that evolution goes toward improving a species' biological endowments, then we should generally expect improvements in the manner in which existing modules perform their task, emergence of new modules to handle other problems, but not demodularization.

True, it is possible to conceive of situations in which the marginal demodularization of a conceptual device might be advantageous, or at least not detrimental, in spite of the loss of speed and reliability involved. Imagine, for instance, that the danger the conceptual module was initially selected to analyze has vanished from the environment; then the module is not adapted any more and a despecialization would do no harm. On the other hand why should it do any good? Such odd possibilities fall quite short of suggesting a positive account of the manner in which, to repeat Fodor's words, "cognitive evolution would . . . have been in the direction of gradually freeing certain sorts of problem-solving systems from the constraints under which input analyzers labor." It is not that this claim could not be right, but it is poorly supported. In fact the only motivation for it seems to be the wish to integrate the belief that human thought processes are nonmodular in some evolutionary perspective, however vague. Better officialize the explanatory gap with a "Second Law of the Nonexistence of Cognitive Science," according to which the forces that have driven cognitive evolution can never be identified.[5] Just accept that cognitive evolution occurred (and resulted in the demodularization of thought) and don't ask how.

Instead of starting from an avowedly enigmatic view of homo sapiens's thought processes and concluding that their past evolution is an unfathomable mystery, one might start from evolutionary considerations plausible in their own right and wonder what kind of cognitive organization these might lead one to expect in a species of which we know that it relies heavily on its cognitive abilities for its survival. This yields our second scenario.

As already suggested, it is reasonable to expect conceptual modules to gain in complexity, fine-grainedness, and inferential sophistication *in the performance of their function*. As with any biological device, the function of a module may vary over time, but there is no reason to expect new functions to be systematically more general than old ones. It is reasonable, on the other hand, to expect new conceptual modules to appear in response to different kinds of problems or opportunities. Thus more and more modules should accumulate.

Because cognitive modules are each the result of a different phylogenetic history, there is no reason to expect them all to be built on the same general pattern and elegantly interconnected. Though most if not all conceptual modules are inferential devices, the inferential procedures that they use may be quite diverse. Therefore, from a modular point of view, it is unreasonable to ask what is the general form of human inference (logical rules, pragmatic schemas, mental models, etc.) as is generally done in the literature on human reasoning (see Manktelow & Over, 1990, for a recent review).

The "domains" of modules may vary in character and in size: There is no reason to expect domain-specific modules to handle each a domain of comparable size. In particular there is no reason to exclude micromodules the domain of which is the size of a concept rather than that of a semantic field. In fact, I will argue that many human concepts are individually modular. Because conceptual modules are likely to be many, their interconnections and their connections with perceptual and motor control modules may be quite diverse too. As argued by Andy Clark (1987, 1990), we had better think of the mind as kludge, with sundry bits and components added at different times, and interconnected in ways that would make an engineer cringe.

Modularity and conceptual integration

The input to the first conceptual modules to have appeared in cognitive evolution must have come from the perceptual modules. However, once some conceptual modules were in place, their output could serve as input to other conceptual modules.

Suppose the orgs can communicate among themselves by means of a small repertoire of vocal signals. Suppose further that the optimal interpretation of some of these signals is sensitive to contextual factors. For instance, an ambiguous danger signal indicates the presence of a snake when emitted by an org on a tree, and approaching elephants when emitted by an org on the ground. Identifying the signals and the relevant contextual information is done by perceptual modules. The relevant output of these perceptual modules is processed by an ad hoc conceptual module that interprets the ambiguous signals. Now, it would be a significant improvement if the conceptual module specialized in inferring the approach of elephants would accept as input not only perceptual information on specific noises and soil vibrations but also interpretations of the relevant signals emitted by other orgs. If so, this danger-inferring conceptual module would receive input not just from perceptual modules but also from another conceptual module, the context-sensitive signal interpreter.

In the human case, it is generally taken for granted that domain-specific abilities can handle not just primary information belonging to their domain and provided by perception but also verbally or picturally communicated information. Thus experiments on the development of zoological knowledge use as material, not actual animals, but pictures or verbal descriptions. Though this practice deserves more discussion than it usually gets, it may well be sound. If so, its being sound is itself quite remarkable.

Then too, some conceptual modules might get *all* of their input from other conceptual modules. Imagine for instance that an org emits a danger signal only when two conditions are fulfilled: It must have inferred the presence of a danger on the one hand, and that of friendly orgs at risk on the other hand. Both inferences are performed by conceptual modules. If so, then the conceptual module that decides whether or not to emit the danger signal gets all of its input from other conceptual modules, and none from perceptual ones.

We are now envisaging a complex network of conceptual modules: Some conceptual modules get all of their input from perceptual modules, other modules get at least some of their input from conceptual modules, and so forth. Every information may get combined with many others across or within levels and in various ways (though overall conceptual integration seems excluded). What would be the behavior of an organism endowed with such complex modular thought processes? Surely, we don't know. Would it behave in a flexible manner like humans do? Its responses could at least be extremely fine-grained. Is there more to flexibility than this fine-grainedness? "Flexibility" is a metaphor without a clear literal interpretation, and therefore it is hard to tell. Still, when we think of flexibility in the human case, we particularly have in mind the ability to learn from experience. Can a fully modular system learn?

Imprinting is a very simple form of modular learning. What, for instance, do orgs know about one another? If orgs are nonlearning animals, they might be merely endowed with a conspecific detector and detectors for some properties of other orgs such as sex or age, but they might otherwise be unable to detect any single individual as such, not even, say, their own mothers. Or, if they are very primitive learners, they might have a mother-detector module that will be "initialized" (i.e., have its parameters fixed or its empty slots filled) once and for all by the newborn org's first encounter with a large moving creature in its immediate vicinity (hopefully its real mum). As a result of this encounter the initialized module becomes a detector for the particular individual who caused the imprinting.

If they are slightly more sophisticated learners, orgs may have the capacity to construct several detectors for different individual conspecifics. They might have a template module quite similar to a mother-detector, except that it can be "initialized" several times, each time projecting a differently initialized copy of itself that is specialized for the identification of a different individual. Would the initialized copies of the template module be modules too? I don't see why not. The only major difference is that these numerous projected modules seem less likely to be hardwired than a single mother-detector module.[6] Otherwise, both kinds of modules get initialized and operate in exactly the same manner. Of our more sophisticated orgs, we would want to say, then, that they had a modular domain-specific ability to represent mentally conspecific individuals, an ability resulting in the generation of micro-modules for each represented individual.

Consider in this light the human domain-specific ability to categorize living kinds. One possibility is that there is an initial template module for living-kind concepts that gets initialized many times, producing each time a new micromodule corresponding to one living-kind concept (the dog module, the cat module, the goldfish module, etc.).

Thinking of such concepts as modules may take some getting used to, I admit. Let me help: Concepts are domain-specific (obviously), they have a proprietary data-basis (the encyclopedic information filed under the concept), and they are autonomous computational devices (they work, I will argue, on representations in which the right concept occurs, just as digestive enzymes work on food in which the right molecule occurs). When, on top of all that, concepts are partly genetically specified (via some domain-specific conceptual template), they are modular at least to some interesting extent, no?

The template–copy relationship might sometimes involve more levels. A general living-kind-categorization metatemplate could project, not directly concepts, but other, more specific templates for different domains of living kinds. For instance, a fundamental parameter to be fixed might concern the contrast between self-propelled and non-self-propelled objects (Premack, 1990), yielding two templates, one for zoological concepts and another one for botanical concepts.

Another possibility still is that the initial metatemplate has three types of features: (1) fixed features that characterize living kinds in general, for instance, it might be an unalterable part of any living-kind concept that the kind is taken to have an underlying essence (Atran, 1987; Gelman & Coley, 1991; Gelman & Markman, 1986, 1987; Keil, 1989; Medin & Ortony, 1989); (2) parameters with default values that can be altered in copies of the template, for instance, "self-propelled" and "non-human" might be revisable features of the initial template; (3) empty slots for information about individual kinds. If so, then, the default-value template could serve as such for nonhuman animal concepts. To use the template for plant concepts, or to include humans in a taxonomy of animals would involve changing a default value of the initial template.

How is the flow of information among modules actually governed? Is there a regulating device? Is it a pandemonium? A market economy? Many types of models can be entertained. Here is a simple possibility.

The output of perceptual and conceptual modules is in the form of conceptual representations. Perceptual modules categorize distal stimuli and must each have therefore the conceptual repertoire needed for the output categorizations of which they are capable. Conceptual modules may infer new output categorizations from the input conceptual representations they process; they must have an input and an output conceptual repertoire to do so. Let us assume that modules accept as input any conceptual representation in which a concept belonging to their input repertoire occurs. In particular single-concept micromodules process all and only representations where their very own concept occurs. These micromodules generate transformations of the input representation by replacing the concept with some inferentially warranted expansion of it. They are otherwise blind to the other conceptual properties of the representations they process (in the manner of the "calculate" procedure in some word processor, which scans the text but "sees" only numbers and mathematical signs). Generally, the presence of specific concepts in a representation determines what modules will be activated and what inferential processes will take place (see Sperber & Wilson, 1986, chap. 2).

A key feature of modularity in Fodor's description is informational encapsulation: A full-fledged module uses a limited data base and is not able to take advantage of information relevant to its task if that information is in some other data base. Central processes on the other hand are not so constrained: They are characterized, on the contrary, by free flow of information. Thus beliefs about Camembert cheese might play a role in forming conclusions about quarks, even though they hardly belong to the same conceptual domain. This is a fact, and I wouldn't dream of denying it. What does it imply regarding the modularity of conceptual processes? It implies that one particular modular picture cannot be right: Imagine a single layer of a few large mutually unconnected modules; then an information treated by one module won't find its way to another. If, on the other hand, the output of one conceptual module can serve as input to another one, modules can each be informationally encapsulated while chains of inference can take a conceptual premise from one module to the next and therefore integrate the contribution of each in some final conclusion. A holistic effect need not be the outcome of a holistic procedure.

Once a certain level of complexity in modular conceptual thought is reached, modules can emerge whose function it is to handle problems raised, not externally by the environment, but internally by the workings of the mind itself. One problem that a rich modular system of the kind we are envisaging would encounter as surely as Fodor's nonmodular central processes is the risk of computational explosion.

Assume that a device would have emerged, the function of which is to put up on the board, so to speak, some limited information for actual processing.

Call this device "attention." Think of it as a temporary buffer. Only representations stored in that buffer are processed (by the modules whose input conditions they satisfy), and they are processed only as long as they stay in the buffer. There is, so to speak, competition among representations for attention. The competition tends to work out so as to maximize cognitive efficiency, that is, it tends to select for a place in the buffer, and thus for inferential processing, the most relevant information available at the time. There is a much longer story to be told: read *Relevance* (Sperber & Wilson, 1986).

Attention is of course not domain-specific. On the other hand it is a clear adaptation to an internal processing problem: the problem encountered by any cognitive system able to identify much more information perceptually than it can fully process conceptually. Such a system must be endowed with a means of selecting the information to be conceptually processed. Relevance-guided attention is such a means. Whether or not it should be called a module does not really matter: Attention fits snugly into a modular picture of thought.

I don't expect these speculations to be convincing – I am only half convinced myself, though I will be a bit more by the end of this chapter – but I hope they are intelligible. If so, this means that one can imagine a richly modular conceptual system that integrates information in so many partial ways that it is not obvious any more that we, human beings, genuinely integrate it in any fuller way. The argument against the modularity of thought based on the alleged impossibility of modular integration should lose at least its immediate commonsense appeal.

Actual and proper domains of modules

Modules are domain-specific, and many, possibly most domains of modern human thought are too novel and too variable to be the specific domain of a genetically specified module. This second commonsense argument against the modularity of thought is reinforced by adaptationist considerations: In many domains, cultural expertise is hard to see as a biological adaptation. This is true not just of new domains such as chess, but also of old domains such as music. Expertise in these domains is unlikely therefore to be based on an ad hoc evolved mechanism. Of course, one can always try to concoct some story showing that, say, musical competence is a biological adaptation. However, merely assuming the adaptive character of a trait without a plausible demonstration is an all too typical misuse of the evolutionary approach.

Let me try an altogether different line. An adaptation is, generally, an adaptation to given environmental conditions. If you look at an adaptive feature just by itself, inside the organism, and forget altogether what you know about the environment and its history, you cannot tell what its function is, what it is an adaptation to. The function of a giraffe's long neck is to help it eat from trees, but in another environment – make it on another planet to free your imagination – the function of an identical body part on an identical organism could be to allow the animal to see farther, or to avoid breathing foul air near the ground, or to fool giant predators into believing that its flesh was poisonous.

A very similar point – or, arguably, a special application of the very same point – has been at the center of major recent debates in the philosophy of language and mind between "individualists" and "externalists." Individualists hold that the content of a concept is in the head of the thinker, or, in other terms, that a conceptual content is an intrinsic property of the thinker's brain state. Externalists maintain – rightly, I believe – that the same brain state that realizes a given concept might realize a different concept in another environment, just as internally identical biological features might have different functions.[7]

The content of a concept is not an intrinsic but a relational property[8] of the neural realizer of that concept, and is contingent upon the environment and the history (including the phylogenetic prehistory) of that neural object. This extends straightforwardly to the case of domain-specific modules. A domain is semantically defined, that is, by a concept under which objects in the domain are supposed to fall. The domain of a module is therefore not a property of its internal structure (whether described in neurological or in computational terms).

There is no way a specialized cognitive module might pick its domain just in virtue of its internal structure, or even in virtue of its connections to other cognitive modules. All that the internal structure provides is, to borrow an apt phrase from Frank Keil (this volume), a *mode of construal*, a disposition to organize information in a certain manner and to perform computations of a certain form. A cognitive module also has structural relations to other mental devices with which it interacts. This determines in particular its *input conditions*: through which other devices the information must come, and how it must be categorized by these other devices. But, as long as one remains within the mind and ignores the connections of perceptual modules with the environment, knowledge of the brain-internal connections of a specialized cognitive module does not determine its domain.

Pace Keil, the fact that the mode of construal afforded by a mental module might fit many domains does *not* make the module any less domain-specific, just as the fact that my key might fit many locks does not make it any less the key to my door. The mode of construal and the domain, just like my key and my lock, have a long common history. How, then, do interactions with the environment over time determine the domain of a cognitive module? To answer this question, we had better distinguish between the *actual* and the *proper* domain of a module.

The *actual domain* of a conceptual module is all the information in the organism's environment that may (once processed by perceptual modules, and possibly by other conceptual modules) satisfy the module's input conditions. Its *proper domain* is all the information that it is the module's biological function to process. Very roughly, the function of a biological device is a class of effects of that device that contributes to making the device a stable feature of an enduring species. The function of a module is to process a specific range of information in a specific manner. That processing contributes to the reproductive success of the organism. The range of information that it is the function of a module to process constitutes its proper domain. What a module actually processes is information found in its actual domain, whether or not it also belongs to its proper domain.

Back to the orgs. The characteristic danger that initially threatened them was being trampled by elephants. Thanks to a module, the orgs reacted selectively to various signs normally produced, in their environment, by approaching elephants. Of course, approaching elephants were sometimes missed, and other, unrelated and innocuous events did sometimes activate the module. But even though the module failed to pick out all and only approaching elephants, we describe its function as having been to do just that (rather than doing what it actually did). Why? Because it is its relative success at that task that explains its having been a stable feature of an enduring species. Even though they were not exactly coextensive, the actual domain of the module overlapped well enough with the approaching-elephants domain. Only the latter, however, was the proper domain of the module.

Many generations later, elephants had vanished from the orgs' habitat, while hippopotamuses had multiplied, and now *they* trampled absent-minded orgs. The same module that had reacted to most approaching elephants and a few sundry events now reacted to most approaching hippos and a few sundry events. Had the module's proper domain become that of approaching hippos? Yes, and for the same reasons as before: Its relative success at reacting to approaching hippos explains why this module remained a stable feature of an enduring species.[9]

Today, however, hippopotamuses too have vanished and there is a railway passing through the orgs' territory. Because orgs don't go near the rails, trains are no danger. However the same module that had reacted selectively to approaching elephants and then to approaching hippos now reacts to approaching trains (and produces a useless panic in the orgs). The *actual* domain of the module includes mostly approaching trains. Has its *proper* domain therefore become that of approaching trains? The answer should be "no" this time: Reacting to trains is what it does, but it is not its function. The module's reacting to trains does not explain its remaining a stable feature of the species. In fact, if the module and the species survive, it is in spite of this marginally harmful effect.[10]

Still, an animal psychologist studying the orgs today might well come to the conclusion that they have a domain-specific ability to react to trains. She might wonder how they have developed such an ability given that trains have been introduced in the area too recently to allow the emergence of a specific biological adaptation (the adaptive value of which would be mysterious anyhow). The truth, of course, is that the earlier proper domains of the module, approaching elephants and then hippos, are now empty, that its actual domain is, by accident, roughly coextensive with the set of approaching trains, and that the explanation of this accident is the fact that the input conditions of the module, which had been positively selected in a different environment, happen to be satisfied by trains and hardly anything else in the orgs' present environment.

Enough of toy examples. In the real world, you are not likely to get elephants neatly replaced by hippos and hippos by trains, and to have each kind in turn satisfying the input conditions of some specialized module. Natural environments, and therefore cognitive functions, are relatively stable. Small shifts of cognitive function are more likely to occur than radical changes. When major changes occur in the environment, for instance as the result of a natural cataclysm, some cognitive functions are just likely to be lost: If elephants go, so does the function of your erstwhile elephant-detector. If a module loses its function, or equivalently if its proper domain becomes empty, then it is unlikely that its actual domain will be neatly filled by objects all falling under a single category, such as passing trains. More probably, the range of stimuli causing the module to react will end up being such an awful medley as to discourage any temptation to describe the actual domain of the module in terms of a specific category. Actual domains are usually not conceptual domains.

Cultural domains and the epidemiology of representations

Most animals get only highly predictable kinds of information from their conspecifics, and not much of it at that. They depend therefore on the rest of the environment for their scant intellectual kicks. Humans are special. They are naturally massive producers, transmitters, and consumers of information. They get a considerable amount and variety of information from fellow humans, and they even produce and store some for their own private consumption. As a result, I will argue, the actual domain of human cognitive modules is likely to have become much larger than their proper domain. Moreover these actual domains, far from being uncategorizable chaos, are likely to be partly organized and categorized by humans themselves. So much so, I will argue, that we should distinguish the *cultural domains* of modules from both their proper and actual domains.

Just a quick illustration before I give a more systematic sketch and a couple of more serious examples: Here is the infant in her cradle, endowed with a domain-specific, modular, naive physics. The proper domain of that module is a range of physical events that typically occur in nature, and the understanding of which is crucial to the organism's later survival. Presumably, other primates are endowed with a similar module. The naive physics module of the infant chimp (and of the infant Pleistocene homo not-yet-sapiens) reacts to the odd fruit or twig falling, to the banana peel being thrown away, to occasional effects of the infant's own movement, and it may be challenged by the irregular fall of a leaf. Our human infant's module, on the other hand, is stimulated not just by physical events happening incidentally, but also by an "activity center" fixed to the side of her cradle, a musical merry-go-round just above her head, balls bounced by elder siblings, moving pictures on a television screen, and a variety of educational toys devised to stimulate her native interest in physical processes.

What makes the human case special? Humans change their own environment at a rhythm that natural selection cannot follow, so that many genetically specified traits of the human organism are likely to be adaptations to features of the environment that have ceased to exist or have greatly changed. This may be true not just of adaptations to the nonhuman environment, but also of adaptations to earlier stages of the hominid social environment.

In particular, the actual domain *of any* human cognitive module is unlikely to be even approximately coextensive with its proper domain. The actual domain of any human cognitive module is sure, on the contrary, to include a large amount of cultural information that meets its input conditions. This results neither from accident, nor from design. It results from a process of social distribution of information.

Humans not only construct individually *mental* representations of information, but they also produce information for one another in the form of *public* representations (e.g., utterances, written texts, pictures), or in the form of other informative behaviors and artifacts. Most communicated information, though, is communicated to one person or a few people on a particular occasion, and that is the end of it. Sometimes, however, addressees of a first act of communication communicate the information received to other addressees who communicate it in turn to others, and so on. This process of repeated transmission may go on to the point where we have a chain of mental and public representations both causally linked and similar in content – similar in content because of their causal links – instantiated throughout a human population. Traditions and rumors spread in this particular manner. Other types of representations may be distributed by causal chains of a different form (e.g., through imitation with or without instruction, or through broadcast communication). All such causally linked, widely distributed representations are what we have in mind when we speak of culture.

I have argued (Sperber, 1985b, 1990a, 1992) that to explain culture is to explain why some representations become widely distributed: A naturalistic science of culture should be an *epidemiology of representations*. It should explain why some representations are more successful – more contagious – than others.[11]

In this epidemiological perspective, all the information that humans introduce into their common environment can be seen as competing[12] for private and public space and time, that is, for attention, internal memory, transmission, and external storage. Many factors affect the chances of some information being successful and reaching a wide and lasting level of distribution, of being stabilized in a culture. Some of these factors are psychological, others are ecological. Most of these factors are relatively local, others are quite general. The most general psychological factor affecting the distribution of information is its compatibility and fit with human cognitive organization.

In particular, relevant information, the relevance of which is relatively independent from the immediate context, is *ceteris paribus*, more likely to reach a cultural level of distribution: Relevance provides the motivation both for storing and for transmitting the information, and independence from an immediate context means that relevance will be maintained in spite of changes of local circumstances, that is, it will be maintained on a social scale. Relevance is, however, always relative to a context; independence from the immediate context means relevance in a wider context of stable beliefs and expectations. On a modular view of conceptual processes, these beliefs, which are stable across a population, are those that play a central role in the modular organization and processing of knowledge. Thus information that either enriches or contradicts these basic modular beliefs stands a greater chance of cultural success.

I have argued (Sperber, 1975, 1980, 1985b) that beliefs that violate head-on module-based expectations (e.g., beliefs in supernatural beings capable of action at a distance, ubiquity, metamorphosis, etc.) thereby gain a salience and relevance that contribute to their cultural robustness. Pascal Boyer (1990) has rightly stressed that these violations of intuitive expectations in the description of supernatural beings are in fact few and take place against a background of satisfied modular expectations. Kelly and Keil (1985) have shown that cultural exploitation of representations of metamorphoses are closely constrained by domain-based conceptual structure. Generally speaking, we should expect culturally successful information essentially to resemble that found in some proper domain, and at the same time to exhibit sufficient originality so as to avoid mere redundancy.

A cognitive module stimulates in every culture the production and distribution of a wide array of information that meets its input conditions. This information, being artifactually produced or organized by the people themselves, is from the start conceptualized and therefore belongs to conceptual domains that I propose to call the module's *cultural domain(s)*. In other terms, cultural transmission causes, in the actual domain of any cognitive module, a proliferation of parasitic information that mimics the module's proper domain.

Let me first illustrate this epidemiological approach with speculations on a nonconceptual case, that of music. This is intended to be an example of a way of thinking suggested by the epidemiological approach rather than a serious scientific hypothesis, which I would not have the competence to develop.

Imagine that the ability and propensity to pay attention to, and analyze certain complex sound patterns became a factor of reproductive success for a long enough period in human prehistory. The sound patterns would have been discriminable by pitch variation and rhythm. What sounds would have exhibited such patterns? The possibility that springs to mind is human vocal communicative sounds. It need not be the sounds of homo sapiens speech, though. One may imagine a human ancestor with much poorer articulatory abilities and relying more than modern humans do on rhythm and pitch for the production of vocal signals. In such conditions, a specialized cognitive module with the required disposition might well have evolved.

This module would have had to combine the necessary discriminative ability with a motivational force to cause individuals to attend to the relevant sound patterns. The motivation would have to be on the hedonistic side: pleasure and hopeful expectation rather than pain and fear. Suppose that the relevant sound pattern co-occurred with noise from which it was hard to discriminate. The human ancestor's vocal abilities may have been quite poor, and the intended sound pattern may have been embedded in a stream of parasitic sounds (a bit like when you speak with a sore throat, a cold, and food in your mouth). Then the motivational component of the module should have been tuned so that detecting a low level of the property suffices to procure a significant reward.

The proper domain of the module we are imagining is the acoustic properties of early human vocal communications. It could be that this proper domain is now empty: Another adaptation, the improved modern human vocal tract, may have rendered it obsolete. Or it may be that the relevant acoustic properties still play a role in modern human speech (in tonal languages in particular) so that the module is still functional. The sounds that the module analyzes thereby causing pleasure to the organism of which it is a part – that is, the sounds meeting the module's input conditions – are not often found in nature (with the obvious exception of bird songs). However, such sounds can be artificially produced. And they have been, providing this module with a particularly rich cultural domain: music. The relevant acoustic pattern of music is much more detectable and delectable than that of any sound in the module's proper domain. The reward mechanism, which was naturally tuned for a hard-to-discriminate input, is now being stimulated to a degree that makes the whole experience utterly addictive.

The idea is, then, that humans have created a cultural domain, music, which is parasitic on a cognitive module, the proper domain of which pre-existed music and had nothing to do with it. The existence of this cognitive module has favored the spreading, stabilization, and progressive diversification and growth of a repertoire meeting its input conditions: First pleasing sounds were serendipitously discovered, then sound patterns were deliberately produced and became music proper. These bits of culture compete for mental and public space and time, and ultimately for the chance to stimulate the module in question in as many individuals as possible for as long as possible. In this competition, some pieces of music do well, at least for a time, whereas others are selected out, and thus music, and musical competence, evolve.

In the case of music, the cultural domain of the module is much more developed and salient than its proper domain, assuming that it still has a proper domain. So much so that it is the existence of the cultural domain and the domain-specificity of the competences it manifestly evokes that justifies looking, in the present or in the past, for a proper domain that is not imme-diately manifest.

In other cases, the existence of a proper domain is at least as immediately manifest as that of a cultural one. Consider zoological knowledge. The exist-ence of a domain-specific competence in the matter is not hard to admit, if the general idea of domain specificity is accepted at all. One way to think of it, as I have suggested, is to suppose that humans have a modular template for constructing concepts of animals. The biological function of this module is to provide humans with ways of categorizing animals they may encounter in their environment and of organizing the information they may gather about them. The proper domain of this modular ability is the living local fauna. What happens however is that you end up, thanks to cultural input, con-structing many more animal concepts than there are animals with which you will ever interact. If you are a twentieth-century Westerner, you may, for instance, have a well-stocked cultural subdomain of dinosaurs. You may be a dinosaur expert. In another culture you might have been a dragon expert.

This invasion of the actual domain of a conceptual module by cultural information occurs irrespective of the size of the module. Consider a micro-module such as the concept of a particular animal, say the rat. Again, you are likely to have fixed, in the data base of that module, culturally trans-mitted information about rats, whether of a folkloristic or of a scientific char-acter, that goes well beyond the proper domain of that micromodule, that is, well beyond information derivable from, and relevant to, interactions with rats (though, of course, it may be of use for your interactions with other human beings, e.g., by providing a data base exploitable in metaphorical communication).

On the macromodular side of things, accept for the sake of this discussion that the modular template on which zoological concepts are constructed is itself an initialized version (maybe the default version) of a more abstract living-kinds metatemplate. That metatemplate is initialized in other ways for other domains (e.g., botany), projecting several domain-specific templates, as I have suggested here. What determines a new initialization is the presence of information that (1) meets the general input conditions specified in the metatemplate, but (2) does not meet the more specific conditions found in the already initialized templates. That information need not be in the proper domain of the metatemplate module. In other words, the metatemplate might get initialized in a manner that fits no proper domain at all but only a cultural domain. A cultural domain that springs to mind in this context is that of representations of supernatural beings (see Boyer, 1990, 1993, this volume). But there may also be less apparent cases.

Consider in this light the problem raised by Hirschfeld (this volume; see also Hirschfeld, 1988, 1993). Children are disposed to categorize humans into "racial" groups conceived in an essentialist manner. Do children possess a domain-specific competence for such categorization? In other terms, are humans naturally disposed to racism? In order to avoid such an unappealing conclusion, it has been suggested (Atran, 1990; Boyer, 1990) that children transfer to the social sphere a competence that they have first developed for living kinds, and that they do so in order to make sense of the regularities in human appearance (e.g., skin color) that they have observed. However, Hirschfeld's experimental evidence shows that racial categorization develops without initially drawing on perceptually relevant input. This strongly suggests that there is a domain-specific competence for racial classification.

What the epidemiological approach adds is the suggestion that racial classification might result from an ad hoc template derived from the living-kinds metatemplate, through an initialization triggered by a cultural input. Indeed, recent experiments suggest that, in certain conditions, the mere encounter with a nominal label used to designate a living thing is enough to tilt the child's categorization of that thing toward an essentialist construal (Davidson & Gelman, 1990; Gelman & Coley, 1991; Markman, 1990; Markman & Hutchinson, 1984). It is quite possible then that being presented with nominal labels for otherwise undefined and undescribed humans is enough (given an appropriate context) to activate the initialization of the ad hoc template. If so, then perception of differences among humans is indeed not the triggering factor.

There is, as Hirschfeld suggested, a genetically specified competence that determines racial classification without importing its models from another concrete domain. However, the underlying competence need not have racial classification as its proper domain. Racial classification may be a mere cultural domain, based on an underlying competence that does not have any proper domain. The initialization of an ad hoc template for racial classification could well be the effect of parasitic, cultural input information on the higher-level learning module the function of which is to generate ad hoc templates for genuine living-kind domains such as zoology and botany. If this hypothesis is correct – mind you, I am not claiming that it is, merely that it may be – then no racist disposition has been selected *for* (Sober, 1984) in humans. However the dispositions that have been selected for make humans all too easily susceptible to racism given minimal, innocuous-looking cultural input.

The relationship between the proper and the cultural domains of the same module is not one of transfer. The module itself does not have a preference between the two kinds of domains, and indeed is blind to a distinction that is grounded in ecology and history.

Even when an evolutionary and epidemiological perspective is adopted, the distinction between the proper and the cultural domain of a module is not always easy to draw. Proper and cultural domains may overlap. Moreover, because cultural domains are things of this world, it can be a function of a module to handle a cultural domain, which ipso facto becomes a proper domain.

Note that the very existence of a cultural domain is an effect of the existence of a module. Therefore, initially at least, a module cannot be an adaptation to its own cultural domain. It must have been selected because of a preexisting proper domain. In principle, it might *become* a function of the module to handle its own cultural domain. This would be so when the ability of the module to handle its cultural domain contributed to its remaining a stable feature of an enduring species. The only clear case of an adaptation of a module to its own effects is that of the linguistic faculty. The linguistic faculty in its initial form cannot have been an adaptation to a public language that could not exist without it. On the other hand it seems hard to doubt that language has become the proper domain of the language faculty.[13]

If there are modular abilities to engage in specific forms of social interaction (as claimed by Cosmides, 1989), then, as in the case of the language faculty, the cultural domains of these abilities should at least overlap with their proper one. Another interesting issue in this context is the relationship between numerosity – the proper domain of a cognitive module – and numeracy, an obvious cultural domain dependent on language (see Dehaene, 1992; Gallistel & Gelman, 1992; Gelman & Gallistel, 1978). In general, however, there is no reason to expect the production and maintenance of cultural domains to be a biological function of all, or even most, human cognitive modules.

If this approach is correct, it has important implications for the study of domain specificity in human cognition. In particular it evaporates, I believe, the cultural diversity argument against the modularity of thought. For even if thought were wholly modular, we should nevertheless find many cultural domains, varying from culture to culture, and whose contents are such that it would be preposterous to assume that they are the proper domain of an evolved module. The cultural idiosyncrasy and lack of relevance to biological fitness of a cognitive domain leaves entirely open the possibility that it might be a domain of a genetically specified module: its cultural domain.

Metarepresentational abilities and cultural explosion

If you are still not satisfied that human thought could be modular through and through, if you feel that there is more integration taking place than I have allowed for so far, if you can think of domains of thought that don't fit with any plausible module, well then we agree. It is not just that beliefs about Camembert cheese might play a role in forming conclusions about quarks, it is that we have no trouble at all entertaining and understanding a conceptual representation in which Camembert and quarks occur simultaneously. You have just proved the point by understanding the previous sentence.

Anyhow, with or without Camembert, beliefs about quarks are hard to fit into a modular picture. Surely, they don't belong to the actual domain of naive physics; similarly, beliefs about chromosomes don't belong to the actual domains of naive biology, beliefs about lycanthropy don't belong to the actual domain of folk zoology, beliefs about the Holy Trinity or about cellular automata seem wholly removed from any module.

Is this to say that there is a whole range of extramodular beliefs, of which many religious or scientific beliefs would be prime examples? Not really. We have not yet exhausted the resources of the modular approach.

Humans have the ability to form mental representations of mental representations; in other words, they have a metarepresentational ability. This ability is so particular, both in terms of its domain and of its computational requirements that anybody willing to contemplate the modularity of thought thesis will be willing to see it as modular. Even Fodor does (Fodor, 1992). The metarepresentational module[14] is a special conceptual module, however, a second-order one, so to speak. Whereas other conceptual modules process concepts and representations of things, typically of things perceived, the metarepresentational module processes concepts of concepts and representations of representations.

The actual domain of the metarepresentational module is clear enough: It is the set of all representations of which the organism is capable of inferring or otherwise apprehending the existence and content. But what could be the proper domain of that module? Much current work (e.g., Astington et al., 1989) assumes that the function of the ability to form and process metarepresentations is to provide humans with a naive psychology. In other terms, the module is a "theory of mind module" (Leslie, this volume), and its proper domain is made of the beliefs, desires, and intentions that cause human behavior. This is indeed highly plausible. The ability to understand and categorize behavior, not as mere bodily movements, but in terms of underlying mental states, is an essential adaptation for organisms that must cooperate and compete with one another in a great variety of ways.

Once you have mental states in your ontology, and the ability to attribute mental states to others, there is but a short step, or no step at all, to your having desires about these mental states – desiring that she should believe this, desiring that he should desire that – and to forming intentions to alter the mental states of others. Human communication is both a way to satisfy such metarepresentational desires, and an exploitation of the metarepresentational abilities of one's audience. As suggested by Grice (1957) and developed by Deirdre Wilson and myself (1986), a communicator, by means of her communicative behavior, is deliberately and overtly helping her addressee to infer the content of the mental representation she wants him to adopt (Sperber & Wilson, 1986).

Communication is, of course, radically facilitated by the emergence of a public language. A public language is rooted in another module, the language faculty. We claim, however, that the very development of a public language is not the cause, but an effect of the development of communication made possible by the metarepresentational module.

As a result of the development of communication, and particularly of linguistic communication, the actual domain of the metarepresentational module is teeming with representations made manifest by communicative behaviors: intentions of communicators and contents communicated. Most representations about which there is some interesting epidemiological story to be told are communicated in this manner and therefore enter people's minds via the metarepresentational module.

As already suggested, many of the contents communicated may find their way to the relevant modules: What you are told about cats is integrated with what you see of cats, in virtue of the fact that the representation communicated contains the concept CAT. But now you have the information in two modes: as a representation of cats, handled by a first-order conceptual module, and as a representation of a representation of cats, handled by the second-order metarepresentational module. That module knows nothing about cats but it may know something about semantic relationships among representations; it may have some ability to evaluate the validity of an inference, the evidential value of some information, the relative plausibility of two contradictory beliefs, and so forth. It may also evaluate a belief, not on the basis of its content, but on the basis of the reliability of its source. The metarepresentational module may therefore form or accept beliefs about cats for reasons that have nothing to do with the kind of intuitive knowledge that the CAT module (or whatever first-order module handles cats) delivers.

An organism endowed with perceptual and first-order conceptual modules has beliefs delivered by these modules, but has no beliefs about beliefs, either its own or those of others, and no reflexive attitude to them. The vocabulary of its beliefs is limited to the output vocabulary of its modules, and it cannot conceive or adopt a new concept nor criticize or reject old ones. An organism also endowed with a metarepresentational module can represent concepts and beliefs qua concepts and beliefs, evaluate them critically, and accept them or reject them on metarepresentational grounds. It may form representations of concepts and of beliefs pertaining to all conceptual domains, of a kind that the modules specialized in those domains might be unable to form on their own, or even to incorporate. In doing so, however, the better endowed organism is merely using its metarepresentational module within the module's own domain, that is, representations.

Humans, with their outstanding metarepresentational abilities, may thus have beliefs pertaining to the same conceptual domain rooted in two quite different modules: The first-order module specialized in that conceptual domain, or the second-order metarepresentational module, specialized in representations. These are, however, two different kinds of beliefs, "intuitive beliefs" rooted in first-order modules, and "reflective beliefs" rooted in the metarepresentational module (see Sperber, 1985a, chap. 2, 1985b, 1990a). Reflective beliefs may contain concepts (e.g., "quarks," "Trinity") that do not belong in the repertoire of any module, and that are therefore available to humans only reflectively, via the beliefs or theories in which they are embedded. The beliefs and concepts that vary most from culture to culture (and that often seem unintelligible or irrational from another culture's perspective) are typically reflective beliefs and the concepts they introduce.

Reflective beliefs can be counterintuitive (more exactly, they can be counterintuitive with respect to our intuitions about their subject matter, while, at the same time, our metarepresentational reasons for accepting them are intuitively compelling). This is relevant to the most interesting of Fodor's technical arguments against the modularity of central processes. The informational encapsulation and mandatory character of perceptual modules is evidenced, Fodor points out, by the persistence of perceptual illusions, even when we are apprised of their illusory character. There is, he argues, nothing equivalent at the conceptual level. True, perceptual illusions have the feel, the vividness of perceptual experiences, that you won't find at the conceptual level. But what you do find is that we may give up a belief and still feel its intuitive force, and feel also the counterintuitive character of the belief we adopt in its stead.

You may believe with total faith in the Holy Trinity, and yet be aware of the intuitive force of the idea that a father and son cannot be one and the same. You may understand why black holes cannot be seen, and yet feel the intuitive force of the idea that a big solid, indeed dense object cannot but be visible. The case of naive versus modern physics provides many other blatant examples.[15] What happens, I suggest, is that the naive physics module remains largely unpenetrated by the ideas of modern physics, and keeps delivering the same intuitions, even when they are not believed any more (or at least not reflectively believed).

More generally the recognition of the metarepresentational module, of the duality of beliefs that it makes possible, and of the gateway it provides for cultural contagion, plugs a major gap in the modular picture of mind I have been trying to outline. The mind is here pictured as involving three tiers: a single thick layer of input modules, just as Fodor says, then a complex network of first-order conceptual modules of all kinds, and then a second-order metarepresentational module. Originally, this metarepresentational module is not very different from the other conceptual modules, but it allows the development of communication and triggers a cultural explosion of such magnitude that its actual domain is blown up and ends up hosting a multitude of cultural representations belonging to several cultural domains.

This is how you can have a truly modular mind playing a major causal role in the generation of true cultural diversity.

Notes

1. Fodor also mentions the possibility that output, i.e., motor systems might be modular too. I assume that it is so, but will not discuss the issue here.
2. Howard Gardner's *Frames of Mind* (1983) defends a modular theory of central processes with a concern that I share for the cultural aspect of the issue. My approach is otherwise quite different from his.
3. See also Barkow (1989), Barkow, Cosmides, & Tooby (1992), Brown (1991), Rozin (1976), Rozin & Schull (1988), and Symons (1979).
4. This is, of course, the "frame problem," the very existence of which Fodor (1987) sees as indissolubly linked to the nonmodularity and to the rationality of thought. The frame problem, qua psychological problem, is being overestimated. Two psychological hypotheses allow us to reduce it to something tractable. First the modularity of thought hypothesis, as pointed out by Tooby & Cosmides (1992) considerably reduces the range of data and procedures that may be invoked in any given conceptual task. Second, the hypothesis that cognitive processes tend to maximize relevance (Sperber & Wilson, 1986) radically narrows down the actual search space for any conceptual task.
5. The point cannot just be that the forces that have driven cognitive evolution cannot be identified for certain; that much is trivially true. The claim must be that these forces cannot be even tentatively and reasonably identified, unlike the forces that have driven the evolution of, say, organs of locomotion. See Piatelli-Palmarini (1989) and Stich (1990) for clever but unconvincing arguments in favor of this Second Law.
6. Note that if apparent lack of hardwiring was an obstacle to acknowledging modularity, this would be an obstacle in the case of Fodor's linguistic input modules too. Take the case of a bilingual. Surely she has two modules, one for each language. Both result from fixing parameters and filling a lexicon in a template module, the language acquisition device. However we should be reluctant to imagine that there were (at least) two hardwired templates in place, waiting to be initialized. Hence, at least one of the initialized templates results from a projection of the initial structure onto new sites.
7. Burge (1979) and Putnam (1975) offered the initial arguments for externalism (I myself am convinced by Putnam's arguments but not by Burge's). For a sophisticated discussion, see Recanati (1993).
8. Arguably, content is a biological function in an extended sense – see Dretske (1988), Millikan (1984), and Papineau (1987). My views have been influenced by Millikan's.
9. There are of course conceptual problems here (see Dennett, 1987; Fodor, 1988). It could be argued, for instance, that the module's proper domain was neither elephants nor hippos, but something else, say, "approaching big animals that might trample orgs." If so, we would want to say that its proper domain had *not*

changed with the passing of the elephants and the coming of the hippos. I side with Dennett in doubting that much of substance hinges on which of these descriptions we choose: The overall explanation remains exactly the same.

10. That is why it would be a mistake to say that the function of a device is to react to whatever might satisfy its input conditions and to equate its actual and proper domains. Though there may be doubt about the correct assignment of the proper domain of some device (see note 9), the distinction between actual and proper domains is as solid as that between effect and function.

11. Comparable evolutionary or epidemiological views of culture have been put forward by Boyd and Richerson (1985), Cavalli-Sforza and Feldman (1981), Dawkins (1976), and myself (in addition to some very different evolutionary approaches by many others). The epidemiology of representations that I have been advocating differs from other approaches (1) by stressing the importance of individual cognitive mechanisms in the overall explanation of culture, and (2) by arguing that information is transformed every time it is transmitted to such an extent that an analogy with biological reproduction or replication is inappropriate. See also Tooby and Cosmides (1992) for important new developments in this area.

12. Here, as in talk of representations competing for attention, the term "competition" is only a vivid metaphor. Of course, no intention or disposition to compete is implied. What is meant is that, out of all the representations present in a human group at a given time, some, at one extreme, will spread and last, whereas, at the opposite extreme, others will occur only very briefly and very locally. This is not a random process, and it is assumed that properties of the information itself play a causal role in determining its wide or narrow distribution.

13. See Pinker and Bloom (1990) and my contribution to the discussion of their paper (Sperber 1990b).

14. The capacity to form and process metarepresentations could be instantiated not in a single, but in several distinct modules, each, say, metarepresenting a different domain or type of representations. For lack of space and compelling arguments, I will ignore this genuine possibility.

15. And a wealth of subtler examples have been analyzed in a proper cognitive perspective by Atran (1990).

References

Astington, J. W., Harris, P., & Olson, D. (1989). *Developing theories of mind.* New York: Cambridge University Press.

Atran, S. (1987). Ordinary constraints on the semantics of living kinds. *Mind & Language, 2*(1), 27–63.

Atran, S. (1990). *Cognitive foundations of natural history.* New York: Cambridge University Press.

Barkow, J. H. (1989). *Darwin, sex and status: Biological approaches to mind and culture.* Toronto: University of Toronto Press.

Barkow, J., Cosmides, L., & Tooby, J. (Eds.). (1992). *The adapted mind: Evolutionary psychology and the generation of culture.* New York: Oxford University Press.

Berlin, B. (1978). Ethnobiological classification. In E. Rosch & B. Lloyd (Eds.), *Cognition and categorization.* Hillsdale, NJ: Erlbaum.

Boyd, Robert, & Richerson, Peter J. (1985). *Culture and the evolutionary process.* Chicago: The University of Chicago Press.

Boyer, P. (1990). *Tradition as truth and communication.* New York: Cambridge University Press.

Boyer, P. (1993). *The naturalness of religious ideas.* Berkeley: University of California Press.

Brown, D. (1991). *Human universals.* New York: McGraw-Hill.

Burge, T. (1979). Individualism and the mental. *Midwest Studies in Philosophy, 5,* 73–122.

Carey, S. (1985). *Conceptual development in childhood.* Cambridge, MA: MIT Press.

Cavalli-Sforza, L. L., & Feldman, M. W. (1981). *Cultural transmission and evolution: A quantitative approach.* Princeton: Princeton University Press.

Clark, A. (1987). The kludge in the machine. *Mind and Language, 2*(4), 277–300.

Clark, A. (1990). *Microcognition: Philosophy, cognitive science, and parallel distributed processing.* Cambridge, MA: MIT Press.

Cosmides, L. (1989). The logic of social exchange: Has natural selection shaped how humans reason? Studies with the Wason selection task. *Cognition, 31,* 187–276.

Cosmides, L., & Tooby, J. (1987). From evolution to behavior: Evolutionary psychology as the missing link. In J. Dupré (Ed.), *The latest on the best: Essays on evolution and optimality.* Cambridge, MA: MIT Press.

Davidson, N. S., & Gelman, S. (1990). Induction from novel categories: The role of language and conceptual structure. *Cognitive Development, 5,* 121–152.

Dawkins, Richard. (1976). *The selfish gene.* Oxford: Oxford University Press.

Dehaene, S. (1992). Varieties of numerical abilities. *Cognition, 44*(1–2), 1–42.

Dennett, D. (1987). *The intentional stance.* Cambridge, MA: MIT Press.

Dretske, F. (1988). *Explaining behavior.* Cambridge, MA: MIT Press.

Fodor, J. (1983). *The modularity of mind.* Cambridge, MA: MIT Press.

Fodor, J. (1987). Modules, frames, fridgeons, sleeping dogs, and the music of the spheres. In J. Garfield (Ed.), *Modularity in knowledge representation and natural-language understanding* (pp. 26–36). Cambridge, MA: MIT Press.

Fodor, J. (1988). *Psychosemantics.* Cambridge, MA: MIT Press.

Fodor, J. (1992). A theory of the child's theory of mind. *Cognition, 44,* 283–296.

Gallistel, C. R., and Gelman, R. (1992). Preverbal and verbal counting and computation. *Cognition, 44*(1–2), 43–74.

Gardner, H. (1983). *Frames of mind: The theory of multiple intelligences.* New York: Basic Books.

Gelman, R., & Gallistel, C. R. (1978). *The child's understanding of number.* Cambridge, MA: Harvard University Press.

Gelman, S., & Coley, J. D. (1991). The acquisition of natural kind terms. In S. Gelman & J. Byrnes (Eds.), *Perspectives on language and thought.* New York: Cambridge University Press.

Gelman, S., & Markman, E. (1986). Categories and induction in young children. *Cognition, 23,* 183–209.

Gelman, S., & Markman, E. (1987). Young children's inductions from natural kinds: The role of categories and appearances. *Child Development, 58,* 1532–1541.

Grice, H. P. (1957). Meaning. *Philosophical Review, 66,* 377–388.

Hirschfeld, L. (1988). On acquiring social categories: Cognitive development and anthropological wisdom. *Man, 23*, 611–638.

Hirschfeld, L. (1993). Discovering social difference: The role of appearance in the
development of racial awareness. *Cognitive Psychology, 25*, 317–350.

Kelly, M., & Keil, F. C. (1985). The more things change . . .: Metamorphoses and
conceptual development. *Cognitive Science, 9*, 403–416.

Keil, F. C. (1989). *Concepts, kinds, and cognitive development*. Cambridge, MA:
Bradford Books/MIT Press.

Leslie, A. (1987). Pretense and representation: The origins of "theory of mind."
Psychological Review, 94, 412–426.

Leslie, A. (1988). The necessity of illusion: Perception and thought in infancy. In
L. Weiskrantz (Ed.), *Thought without language*. Oxford: Clarendon Press.

Manktelow, K., & Over, D. (1990). *Inference and understanding: A philosophical and
psychological perspective*. London: Routledge.

Markman, E. M. (1990). The whole-object, taxonomic, and mutual exclusivity assumptions as initial constraints on word meanings. In S. Gelman & J. Byrnes
(Eds.), *Perspectives on language and thought*. New York: Cambridge University Press.

Markman, E. M., & Hutchinson, J. E. (1984). Children's sensitivity to constraints on
word meaning: Taxonomic versus thematic relations. *Cognitive Psychology,
16*, 1–27.

Medin, D., & Ortony, A. (1989). Psychological essentialism. In S. Vosniadou &
A. Ortony (Eds.), *Similarity and analogical reasoning*. Cambridge: Cambridge University Press.

Millikan, R. G. (1984). *Language, thought, and other biological categories*. Cambridge,
MA: MIT Press.

Papineau, D. (1987). *Reality and representation*. Oxford: Blackwell.

Piatelli-Palmarini, M. (1989). Evolution, selection and cognition: From "learning" to
parameter setting in biology and the study of language. *Cognition, 31*, 1–44.

Pinker, S., & Bloom, P. (1990). Natural language and natural selection. *Behavioral and
Brain Sciences, 13*(4), 703–784.

Premack, D. (1990). The infant's theory of self-propelled objects. *Cognition, 36*, 1–16.

Premack, D., & Woodruff, G. (1978). Does the chimpanzee have a theory of mind?
Behavioral and Brain Sciences, 1(4), 515–526.

Putnam, H. (1975). The meaning of "meaning." In *Mind, language and reality:
Philosophical papers, volume II*. Cambridge: Cambridge University Press.

Recanati, F. (1993). *Direct reference, meaning and thought*. Oxford: Blackwell.

Rozin, P. (1976). The evolution of intelligence and access to the cognitive unconscious. In J. M. Sprague & A. N. Epstein (Eds.), *Progress in psychobiology
and physiological psychology*. New York: Academic Press.

Rozin, P., & Schull, J. (1988). The adaptive-evolutionary point of view in experimen-
tal psychology. In R. Atkinson, R. Herrnstein, G. Lindzey, & R. Luce (Eds.),
Steven's handbook of experimental psychology. New York: John Wiley &
Sons.

Sober, E. (1984). *The nature of selection*. Cambridge, MA: MIT Press.

Spelke, E. S. (1988). The origins of physical knowledge. In L. Weiskrantz (Ed.),
Thought without language. Oxford: Clarendon Press.

Sperber, D. (1975). *Rethinking symbolism*. Cambridge: Cambridge University Press.

Sperber, D. (1980). Is symbolic thought prerational? In Mary Foster & Stanley Brandes (Eds.), *Symbol as sense*. New York: Academic Press.

Sperber, D. (1985a). *On anthropological knowledge*. New York: Cambridge University Press.

Sperber, D. (1985b). Anthropology and psychology: Towards an epidemiology of representations (The Malinowski Memorial Lecture 1984). *Man* (N.S.) *20*, 73–89.

Sperber, D. (1990a). The epidemiology of beliefs. In C. Fraser & G. Gaskell (Eds.), *The social psychological study of widespread beliefs*. Oxford: Clarendon Press.

Sperber, D. (1990b). The evolution of the language faculty: A paradox and its solution. *Behavioral and Brain Sciences*, *13*(4), 756–758.

Sperber, D. (1992). Culture and matter. In J.-C. Gardin & C. S. Peebles (Eds.), *Representations in archeology*. Bloomington: Indiana University Press.

Sperber, D., & Wilson, D. (1986). *Relevance: Communication and cognition*. Oxford: Blackwell.

Stich, S. (1990). *The fragmentation of reason*. Cambridge, MA: MIT Press.

Symons, D. (1979). *The evolution of human sexuality*. New York: Oxford University Press.

Tooby, J., & Cosmides, L. (1989). Evolutionary psychology and the generation of culture, Part I: Theoretical considerations. *Ethology & Sociobiology*, *10*, 29–49.

Tooby, J., & Cosmides, L. (1992). The psychological foundations of culture. In J. Barkow, L. Cosmides, & J. Tooby (Eds.), *The adapted mind: Evolutionary psychology and the generation of culture*. New York: Oxford University Press.

3   The organization of lexical knowledge in the brain: Evidence from category- and modality-specific deficits

Alfonso Caramazza, Argye Hillis, Elwyn C. Leek, and Michele Miozzo

How is lexical knowledge organized in the brain? Are semantic distinctions among, for example, animals, vegetables, furniture, and musical instruments or grammatical distinctions among nouns, verbs, and adjectives reflected in the organization of lexical knowledge in the brain? In this chapter we argue that evidence from the analysis of the performance of brain-damaged subjects provides the basis for far-reaching speculations, not only about the functional organization of lexical knowledge, but also about the relation between lexical knowledge and the brain. Specifically, we review evidence suggesting that distinctions among different aspects of lexical knowledge – for example, lexical form and semantic and grammatical categories – are most likely subserved by distinct neuroanatomical structures. The evidence takes the form of selective impairments affecting restricted domains of knowledge – semantic and grammatical categories. The fractionation of lexical knowledge seemingly along the boundaries of semantic and grammatical categories offers the intriguing possibility that the organization of lexical knowledge in the brain honors these categorical distinctions.

Category-specific deficits: Semantic categories

In several reports it has been documented that brain damage can cause selective impairments of specific semantic categories. The reports of category-specific deficits have included the selective impairment of abstract or concrete nouns (e.g., Warrington, 1975; 1981), proper names (e.g., McKenna & Warrington, 1980; Semenza & Zettin, 1988; Lucchelli & De Renzi, 1992),

The preparation of this chapter and the research reported here was supported in part by NIH grants NS22201, NS19330, and DC00366, and by a grant from the McDonnell-Pew Program in Cognitive Neuroscience.

body parts (e.g., Dennis, 1976), and geographical names (McKenna & Warrington, 1978). In addition, in an important series of papers Warrington and her collaborators (Warrington & Shallice, 1984; Warrington & McCarthy, 1987; see also Pietrini, Nertempi, Vaglia, Revello, Pinna, & Ferro-Milone, 1988; Sartori & Job, 1988; Silveri & Gainotti, 1988; Farah, Hammond, Metha, & Ratcliff, 1989; Young, Newcombe, Hellawell, & DeHaan, 1989; Hillis & Caramazza, 1991) have claimed that the category of living things may be selectively damaged in the face of relative sparing of nonliving things. Thus, for example, Warrington and Shallice (1984) presented a detailed description of two post-herpes encephalitis patients who showed a category-specific impairment for living things that was apparent in several tasks. In a picture-naming task, one of the two patients (JBR), although able to name correctly 90% of nonliving things, could correctly name only 6% of living things. In a word definition task, JBR produced appropriate descriptions for the names of nonliving things but in most cases failed to provide appropriate definitions for the names of living things. Thus, when asked to define the word *compass*[1] he responded: "tool for telling direction you are going"; but he was unable to describe living things like parrot, snail, and daffodil.

The claim that brain damage can lead to category-specific impairments invites the hypothesis that the organization of semantic knowledge in the brain honors these categorical distinctions. To quote Warrington and McCarthy (1987), "It is possible that the patterns of fractionation which are observed reflect the topographical or physiological organization of neural systems that are involved in knowledge processing" (p. 1292). However, the original reports of category-specific deficits by Warrington and her collaborators have been criticized on methodological grounds (Riddoch & Humphreys, 1987; Funnell & Sheridan, 1992; and Stewart, Parkin, & Hunkin, 1992). It has been suggested that the living and nonliving categories may differ in their degree of processing difficulty or familiarity. If this were the case, it could be argued that the observed category-specific deficits for living things are solely the result of relative difficulties in processing different classes of items, and that, therefore, such observations do not provide a genuine empirical basis for speculation about the functional organization of semantic knowledge. In support of the latter thesis, Stewart et al. (1992) reported that their patient's selective deficit in naming pictures of living things relative to nonliving things disappeared when the visual familiarity, visual complexity, and name frequency of the stimuli were matched across categories. Similarly, Funnell and Sheridan (1992) showed that an apparent selective impairment for living things in picture naming was no longer present when the familiarity of living and nonliving things was matched across categories. They concluded that a selective deficit for living things may, in fact, reflect only relative differences in the familiarity of the exemplars of these categories.

If the criticisms of Funnell and Sheridan (1992), Stewart et al. (1992), and Riddoch and Humphreys (1987) were to stand, then speculation about the categorical organization of semantic knowledge in the brain based on the occurrence of category-specific deficits would be undermined. However, it would seem that although not all putative cases of selective impairment of living things constitute true category-specific effects, neither is it the case that all such cases can be explained away by appeal to familiarity or processing difficulty differences between categories. In the first place, the dismissal of semantic category-specific dissociations on the basis of relative task difficulty between categories does not readily account for the occurrence of selective deficits for nonliving things – the category hypothesized by Funnell and Sheridan (1992) to be easier in terms of relative familiarity. Although putative cases of category-specific impairment have been reported more frequently for living than nonliving things, there are also a few reports of the opposite pattern of performance – a selective deficit for nonliving things in the face of preserved ability to name or recognize living things (Warrington & McCarthy, 1983; Hillis & Caramazza, 1991; Sacchett & Humphreys, 1992). Second, Sartori, Miozzo, and Job (in press) have shown that a category-specific impairment for living things can still emerge when the factors that Funnell and Sheridan (1992) and Stewart et al. (1992) claim to be responsible for the categorical effect are controlled. Third, as will be shown in detail in this chapter, there is a report of two patients who show complementary patterns of performance across the same stimulus materials. This pattern of results cannot be explained as arising from systematic differences in task difficulty across stimuli.

One of the most striking sources of evidence for the existence of category-specific deficits in brain-damaged patients is the report of two patients showing a double dissociation of semantic categories on the same stimulus materials (Hillis & Caramazza, 1991). The two patients, JJ and PS, showed contrasting selective impairment and sparing of the categories of animals and artifacts. PS was reported to be selectively impaired for animals but not artifacts across a variety of tasks, whereas JJ showed the reverse pattern – a selective deficit for artifacts relative to animals.

At the time of testing, JJ was a 67-year-old former executive of a large corporation who had suffered brain damage as the result of a stroke. A CT scan showed damage in the left temporal lobe and the left basal ganglia. He was severely impaired in all language tasks. His speech was fluent and grammatical but showed frequent circumlocutions and semantic paraphasias. Comprehension of spoken and written language was severely impaired. During routine clinical testing, prior to any therapeutic intervention, it was noticed that the patient retained a remarkable ability to name animals although he was severely impaired in naming objects in other categories.

PS was a 45-year-old president of a small contracting business who sustained brain damage from a severe blow to the head. A CT scan two years post injury revealed a large area of damage to the left temporal lobe and smaller areas of damage to the right temporal and frontal lobes. His speech was normal except for some difficulty in retrieving the name of words in

Table 3.1. *JJ and PS's percentage of correct oral naming across categories over 7 test sessions*

	(Number of stimuli)	Test sessions						
		1	2	3	4	5	6	7
JJ								
All Animals	(46)	91	85	72	80	76	74	92
Non-Animals	(98)	12	14	14	11	12	7	17
PS								
All Animals	(46)	39	39	39	41	37	48	72
Vegetables	(12)	25	25	25	25	33	33	42
All Other	(86)	88	91	91	92	94	93	95

certain categories (see below). Comprehension was also good except for words in the categories he could not name. His primary difficulties were in reading and writing. In this case, it was noticed during routine clinical testing that the patient had surprisingly severe difficulty in naming animals but not in naming objects in other semantic categories.

The two patients were asked to name orally a set of pictures representing objects in the following semantic categories: land animals, water animals, birds, vegetables, fruits, other foods, body parts, clothing, transportation, and furniture. Contrasting category-specific effects were observed for the two patients, as may be seen in Figure 3.1: PS was severely impaired in naming animals (and vegetables) but not artifacts whereas JJ was impaired in every category but animals. In picture naming the patients' errors were principally semantic substitutions or paraphasias (e.g., JJ produced the error *boat* —> "motorcycle," and PS produced the error *seal* —> "mouse"). The two patients' patterns of performance over 7 test sessions are shown in Table 3.1, where they may be seen to remain highly stable over sessions. Furthermore, the category-specific naming deficits persisted 7 months later when the patients' performance had shown considerable improvement (see Figure 3.1). The same types of errors – semantic paraphasias – were made by the two patients throughout.

The two patients' category-specific deficits were not restricted to oral naming but also extended to written naming, word/picture verification, and word definition tasks. The set of items used in the oral naming task was also used in the latter tasks. The same category effects were obtained in these tasks. In the written naming task, PS correctly wrote the names of animals 35% of the time but correctly wrote the names of other categories (excluding vegetables) 77% of the time; JJ, by contrast, correctly wrote the names of animals 70% of the time but correctly wrote the names of other categories only 15% of the time. In this task, too, the patients' errors mainly consisted of semantic

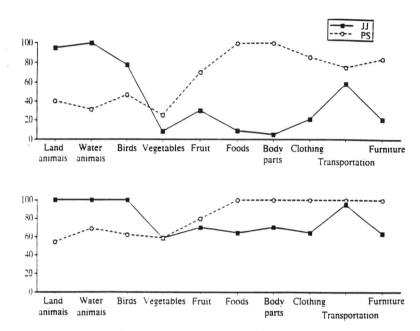

Figure 3.1. JJ and PS's percent correct oral naming as a function of category at 6 months post-onset (top graph) and 13 months post-onset (bottom graph).

paraphasias (in addition to spelling errors: e.g., JJ wrote *shirt* —> "coate" and PS wrote *shark* —> "waile").

The same types of category-specific effects as those obtained in the naming tasks were also obtained in the word/picture verification task: PS made more errors with the animal than the artifact categories whereas JJ had the opposite pattern of difficulty. Here too, the patients' errors involved confusions between semantically related stimuli (e.g., accepting the word *pea* as the name for a picture of a beet).

The patients also showed category-specific effects in a word definition task. JJ was able to give detailed, accurate definitions for animals but not for words in the other semantic categories. Thus, he defined *lion* as "A large animal, about 4 feet tall, maybe taller at the shoulders; it has a long body and very large paws, and stands on all four legs. It has a monstrous head with which it growls; and it has a mane – a large body of hair. It lives in Africa." And, he defined *heron* as "This bird has a long neck and legs. It lives near water. Stands in the water . . . very tall – maybe about six feet. Not brown, but white and blue perhaps." However, when asked to define *bench* he said "A device you sit on, about 12 inches high with four legs. It revolves you around while sitting. Can be made of metal or wood." And, he had great difficulty defining *apricot*: "I don't remember. I've heard of it. It's a fruit, but

I don't remember which one. That's strange. I suppose that it's sweet." The reverse pattern of difficulty was observed for PS. Thus, for example, he defined heron as "A fish" but gave a quite descriptive response for *ottoman*, defining it as "A chair without a back that you put your feet on."

The results we have reviewed indicate that PS and JJ show contrasting selective deficits involving specific semantic categories: PS showed a pervasive deficit in processing animal terms, whereas JJ showed a pervasive deficit in processing all categories tested except for animals. Finally, it is worth emphasizing that the category-specific difficulties encountered by the two patients cannot be attributed to premorbid differences in their degree of familiarity with the animal category (such that PS's selective difficulty with animals might be attributed to his unfamiliarity with this semantic category, and JJ's selective sparing of the animal category being the result of his special expertise with the category). Thus, it is interesting to note that PS had a special interest in animals: He liked to watch documentaries about animals, he hunted, and he visited wildlife reservations. Conversely, JJ claimed to have no special interest in animals.

The existence of apparently nonartifactual selective impairments to living and nonliving things suggests that these categorical distinctions are reflected in the organization of semantic knowledge in the brain. We are thus led to ask whether the "folk taxonomic" categories – for example, living/nonliving, fruits, musical instruments, and so forth – that have been used to capture the category-specific effects reported in the recent literature actually represent the organizing principle of semantic knowledge in the brain or whether the categorical effects observed reflect some other principle of semantic organization. Thus, for example, it might turn out that the observed categorical effects represent emergent properties of a more basic organizational principle of semantic knowledge than taxonomic categories.

One possibility first suggested by Warrington and Shallice (1984) and Warrington and McCarthy (1987) is that categorical distinctions are not a first-order principle in the organization of semantic knowledge, but instead arise as a consequence of the way in which conceptual representations are mapped across an underlying semantic structure (Warrington & Shallice, 1984; Warrington & McCarthy, 1987; see also Caramazza, Hillis, Rapp, & Romani, 1990). On this view, categorical distinctions arise because semantically similar concepts (i.e., members of the same semantic category) will be represented by similar underlying primitives (e.g., capable of self-initiated movement, edible, having internal organs, and so forth). Thus, category-specific deficits may "emerge" following damage to a subset of primitives that support the representation of a particular group (or category) of semantically related concepts.

In one specific version of the emergent categories hypotheses, Warrington and Shallice (1984) proposed a semantic organization based on a system of "modality-specific" components, each representing knowledge acquired in the context of particular sensory/motor channels. To account for the apparent dissociation of living and nonliving things following brain damage, they postulated that these categories may differ in the extent to which each is defined in terms of underlying visual and functional semantic knowledge. According to this "sensory-functional hypothesis," living things would be defined primarily in terms of their visual attributes, whereas nonliving things would be defined primarily in terms of functional information. On this hypothesis, a category-specific deficit for living things would be the result of selective damage to a visual semantic subsystem and a category-specific deficit for nonliving things would be the result of selective damage to a functional semantic (verbal) subsystem.

Although the hypothesized distinction between visual and functional semantic subsystems might be "sufficient" to account for the observed dissociations between living and nonliving categories, this proposal fails to account for other relevant observations about category-specific deficits that cut across the living/nonliving distinction. For example, patient JJ (Hillis & Caramazza, 1991), whose object naming performance is shown in Figure 3.1, showed a selective preservation of animals and objects of transportation. That is, the category-specific deficit in this patient does not honor the living/nonliving distinction – animals dissociated from fruits and vegetables and objects of transportation dissociated from other artifacts.

Such further fractionations of semantic categories seem to be the rule rather than the exception. Warrington and Shallice (1984) documented that their patient, JBR (noted earlier), was impaired in identifying living things as well as gemstones and fabrics. Warrington and McCarthy (1987) reported a patient (YOT) who showed a deficit for artifacts except for large outdoor objects such as an airplane, bridge, train and ship; and Yamadori and Albert (1973) reported a patient with an apparent selective impairment for "indoor objects" (e.g., lamp, chair, and table). An equally strange – though not uncommon – pattern is the co-occurrence of a deficit for living things and musical instruments (Warrington & Shallice, 1984; Silveri & Gainotti, 1988). Although these cases document instances of seemingly strange associations of category-specific deficits, Hart, Berndt, and Caramazza (1985) have reported a patient who showed a particularly fine-grained selective impairment that, as in the case of JJ (Hillis & Caramazza, 1991), violates the living/nonliving distinction. Their patient, MD, was shown to have a category-specific impairment for fruits and vegetables but not animals.

At the time of testing, MD was a 34-year-old college graduate who worked as a systems analyst. As the result of a cerebrovascular accident he suffered damage to the left frontal lobe and the basal ganglia. His only residual difficulty appeared to be a mild naming deficit that was particularly marked for the categories of fruits and vegetables. Table 3.2 summarizes the relevant results obtained in various tasks. He not only had difficulty naming visually presented instances of fruits and vegetables, but he also had difficulty naming these objects when they were presented in the tactile modality or when given

Table 3.2. *MD's percentage of correct responses across categories and different tasks*

Task	Fruits	Vegetables	Other categories
Picture naming	62 (48)	63 (59)	97 (269)
Tactile naming	46 (13)	52 (21)	92 (12)
Picture classification	87 (24)	74 (23)	93 (28)
	Fruits & vegetables		Other categories
Naming to verbal definition	20 (10)		100 (10)

Note: Number of stimuli in each task is shown in parentheses.

a verbal definition. His ability to categorize instances of fruits and vegetables into their appropriate categories was impaired as was his ability to generate instances of the two categories. Thus, for example, he generated four vegetable names as instances of the category fruits. MD's impairment in naming fruits and vegetables occurred in the context of no discernible difficulty in other categories including vehicles, tools, animals, clothing, colors, and body parts.

The existence of such fine-grained fractionations of semantic categories that cut across the living/nonliving distinction would seem to undermine the sensory-functional explanation of category-specific deficits. However, Warrington and McCarthy (1987) have attempted to extend the sensory-functional hypothesis to accommodate fine-grained deficits, such as that observed by Hart et al. (1985) for fruits and vegetables. They suggested that fine-grained category-specific deficits may arise "not only as a consequence of different weighting values between information from each of the major sensory/motor modalities, but also as a consequence of different weighting values on more specialized channels within each modality" (p. 1291). For example, they postulate that within the visual modality, specialized channels for color and shape processing may form specific subcomponents across which finer-grained visually based semantic representations might be mapped. To quote an example from Warrington and McCarthy (1987):

The differentiation of two vegetables (e.g., cabbage and cauliflower) or two fruits (e.g., blackberry and raspberry) can be compared with the differentiation of a closely related category, namely 2 flowers (e.g., a tulip and a carnation). In the former instance, visual information clearly has a high weighting. In addition, within the visual channels, *colour* rather than *shape*, is the critical attribute. For flowers, visual information is once again the dominant sensory channel but *shape* rather than *colour* information is crucial. (p. 1291, italics in text)

Thus, in this view, impairment to the visual semantic subsystem affecting specifically the subregion representing color would result in a deficit for those categories of knowledge that are distinguished primarily by color (in this case, fruits and vegetables). Though interesting, the proposed solution to deal with the recalcitrant dissociations has little empirical or theoretical justification.

It is not clear why fruits and vegetables should be represented primarily in terms of color, as Warrington and McCarthy (1987) seem to suggest, because most fruits and vegetables can be distinguished on the basis of shape alone, such as would be the case for banana, pear, grape, pineapple, carrot, artichoke, celery, and so forth. Although it does not seem improbable that, for example, a lemon and a lime may be differentiated primarily on the basis of color, other instances, such as lemon and banana, may be differentiated primarily in terms of shape, texture, taste, or smell. In any case, it seems that the shapes of most fruits and vegetables are sufficiently distinct to support unique identification from shape alone. The control subjects we have tested have performed flawlessly in naming fruits and vegetables when the stimuli were black and white drawings; they also performed flawlessly when naming from blindfolded tactile exploration. Furthermore, some members of the contrasting category given as an example by Warrington and McCarthy – flowers – differ from each other primarily on the basis of color (e.g., daisy and black-eyed susan), just as other instances are distinguished on the basis of shape (e.g., rose and tulip). Thus, it is not in the least obvious that the categories within living things that have been shown to dissociate in conditions of brain damage differ in appreciable ways in terms of the importance of shape or color in distinguishing among their members – neither is it the case that the categories within nonliving things that have been shown to dissociate differ in obvious ways from other categories in terms of their functional or perceptual attributes.

Ultimately, however, the important question is whether or not the proposal of differential weightings of specific perceptual and functional attributes within the living and nonliving categories can account for the observed pattern of performance in the reported cases of category-specific naming deficits. That is, for the hypothesis of Warrington and McCarthy (1987) to be viable as an account of MD's performance, for example, it would have to identify the type(s) of information that, if unavailable to MD, would account for his pattern of performance. In fact, the possibility of impaired availability of color information (as suggested by Warrington and McCarthy) cannot account for MD's errors; not only did he show a preserved ability in processing color information (e.g., naming colors) but, as already noted, he was severely impaired in naming fruits and vegetables in a blindfolded, tactile naming task – he named correctly only 6 of 13 fruits and 11 of 21 vegetables that normal subjects have no difficulty naming. Hence, the proposal that category-specific deficits in semantic knowledge reflect deficits to subregions of sensory/functional channels that are specialized for particular sensory attributes does not seem to account for the observed pattern of performance.

In this section we have argued that (at least some of) the category-specific deficits that have been reported are not merely methodological artifacts. In addition, we have shown that these category-specific effects may involve highly restricted semantic categories such as animals, vegetables, or musical instruments, and not just the more general categories living versus nonliving things. Furthermore, we have argued that such fine-grained dissociations within the living and nonliving categories pose a major challenge to the sensory/functional hypothesis of category-specific deficits. The appeal of the sensory/functional hypothesis is that there is independent neurophysiological and neuropsychological evidence (e.g., from ablation of circumscribed brain regions in monkeys) that particular brain regions are specialized for particular sensory attributes such as color, shape, depth, and movement (see Kandel, 1991, for review). It is not implausible to extrapolate from this evidence to the idea that there may be *association* areas of the brain that would be specialized for the more abstract representation of perceptual (semantic) information and other areas that would be specialized for the representation of functional attributes. Selective damage to either of the latter regions would, then, account for category-specific effects in naming and other lexical processing tasks. The sensory/functional hypothesis is a powerful alternative to the view that semantic information is organized in the brain along "folk taxonomic" lines (e.g., transportation, furniture) or to the view that brain regions are specialized for semantic predicates or primitives (e.g., "breathes," which would affect the animal category, or "capable of motion," which would affect the animal and transportation categories) that are not simply reducible to a sensory/functional distinction. However, the evidence we have reviewed would seem to suggest that the organization of semantic knowledge is much more richly articulated than the simple sensory/functional distinction. Thus, we are hard put to identify specific forms of organization of sensory or functional attributes, which if damaged, would explain, for example, impaired processing of musical instruments, animals and vegetables, but not items of transportation (Warrington & Shallice, 1984), or preserved processing of animals and transportation but not vegetables or instruments (as in patient JJ, late in his recovery).

Although we have not completely ruled out the possibility that deficits circumscribed to specific semantic categories reflect damage to specific sensory/functional channels specialized for particular sensory attributes, there is one type of category-specific deficit – selective impairment of specific grammatical categories of words (e.g., nouns vs. verbs) – that defies an explanation of this sort. Below we review evidence that indicates the production of nouns and verbs can be differentially affected by brain damage and that this selectivity cannot be attributed to differences in the degree of difficulty, frequency of production, or degree of concreteness.

Category-specific deficits: Grammatical categories

Perhaps the strongest evidence for categorical distinctions in the representation of language in the brain comes not from the study of selective deficits of semantic categories but from dissociations in processing words of different grammatical classes. One such dissociation is that between function (closed class) and content (open class) words (e.g., Andreewsky & Seron, 1975; Gardner & Zurif, 1975; Caramazza, Berndt, & Hart, 1981). The other major dissociation that has been recorded is that between nouns and verbs: Brain-damaged patients may be selectively impaired in processing either nouns or verbs (e.g., Miceli, Silveri, Villa, & Caramazza, 1984; McCarthy & Warrington, 1985; Zingeser & Berndt, 1988). More recently, Caramazza and Hillis (1991) have reported patterns of performances from two patients, SJD and HW, which provide evidence that grammatical class effects can also be modality specific. That is, the impairment may concern a specific grammatical class – for example, verbs – in only one modality of output – either written or spoken production.

At the time of the investigation SJD was a 44-year-old right-handed woman who had earned a master's degree in library science and was employed as a librarian. She had become aphasic 4 years earlier as a consequence of a stroke in the fronto-parietal region. There were no concomitant physical limitations. Her speech was fluent and grammatical, although she tended to speak in rather short sentences (with a variety of syntactical forms) and occasionally made suffix errors in spontaneous speech (e.g., *I say it's lying* —> "I say it's lied"). She complained of persisting deficits in only two areas: writing and retaining phone numbers or citations given verbally long enough to use them (e.g., to dial the number or to look up the citation). Her auditory short-term memory was limited (digit span of 3, compared to a visual digit span of 7), and her comprehension was impaired for spoken but not written sentences with complex syntax (e.g., *The man whom the woman was following was smoking a cigarette*). Comprehension of individual spoken words, for all grammatical classes of words, was above the average for age-matched controls, as tested by the Peabody Picture Vocabulary Test (PPVT, Dunn & Dunn, 1981). Her writing showed a striking omission of verbs (which she replaced with blanks, indicating that she was aware of the omission, but unable to retrieve the appropriate written verb). To illustrate, she wrote, "They———for pizza and turkey" (which she read aloud as, "They ask for pizza and turkey") and wrote, "We———at Champs" (read aloud as, "We ate at Champs").

HW was a 64-year-old (at the time of testing) retired saleslady who had completed 1 year of college. She had suffered two strokes involving the left parietal and occipital regions 2 $^{1}/_{2}$ years prior to testing. Her speech was fluent and grammatical, except for frequent interruptions due to word finding difficulties (e.g., in response to a picture of a woman eating an egg, she said, "The man, no, the woman is eating a . . . what should I say? It looks very good, whatever you call it. She seems to be enjoying it very much. I like it, too, but I shouldn't eat it. Maybe you would like to have some, too. It's . . . [she wrote, "egg"])". As in the case of SJD, HW's comprehension was intact for

Table 3.3. *HW and SJD's percentage of total errors and percentage of errors classified as semantic*

	(Number of stimuli)	HW % total errors	% semantic errors	SJD % total errors	% semantic errors
Spoken output					
Reading	(296)	53	73	2	0
Naming	(60)	63	81	2	0
Written output					
Dictation	(296)	0	0	13	64
Naming	(60)	0	0	50	100

spoken and written single words, as tested by the PPVT, but she had trouble understanding grammatically complex sentences without contextual cues.

In detailed studies of lexical processing, both patients made semantic errors in only one modality of output, independently of the type of input. Thus, HW made errors in oral reading (47% correct) and picture naming (37% correct) but, ignoring spelling errors (e.g., *moose* —> "mosse"), she did not make any errors in writing to dictation or written naming; whereas SJD, ignoring pronunciation and morphological errors (e.g., *sleeve* —> "sleeves"), made virtually no errors in oral reading and naming but made errors in writing to dictation (13% errors) and written naming (50% errors). Her better performance in spelling to dictation compared to written naming is attributable to her partially spared use of sublexical mechanisms for converting sound to print (phonology to orthography), as demonstrated by her ability to write some nonwords that are not homophonic to real words (e.g., *hannee*). Despite her occasional success in using sublexical conversion in spelling, most of her errors in oral production were semantic errors. Similarly, when HW failed, she, too, usually produced semantic errors (see Table 3.3).

Of greater relevance for us here is the fact that the two patients' difficulties were not homogeneous across grammatical categories. Thus, HW's difficulties in orally producing words were much more severe for verbs than for nouns (22% vs. 56% correct), and SJD's difficulties in writing words were more severe for verbs than for nouns (70% vs. 99% correct).

This grammatical effect could not be attributed to item-specific differences in the two categories because the effect persisted when the stimuli were homonyms. Thus, when the patients were asked to read and write the same word, which could function as a noun or a verb in different contexts – for example, the word *check* or the word *watch* functioning as a noun or a verb – the grammatical class effect was still present. The effect was demonstrated in the following way. The patients were asked to read orally or to write the single word *check*, for example, in sentence contexts that disambiguated its

Table 3.4. *HW and SJD's percentage of correct oral and written production of homonyms in sentence context*

	(Number of stimuli)	HW Oral reading	Writing	SJD Oral reading	Writing
A					
Nouns	(50)	88	98	100	98
Verbs	(50)	46	96	100	56
B					
Nouns	(20)	95	95	100	100
Verbs	(20)	40	95	100	85

Note: (A) Noun and verb forms; (B) subset of stimuli in which the verb form is more frequent than the noun form

grammatical role. Thus, in the two following sentences (1) *Please sign the check* and (2) *Please check the time*, the same word *check* has the grammatical function of a noun in the first case, and that of a verb in the second. The patients were presented, on separate occasions, with the two kinds of sentences, (1) and (2), and they were asked to write the single word *check* in the appropriate blank space for each of the two sentences. Similarly, they were required to read aloud the single word *check* after having read silently, on separate occasions, each of the two sentence contexts that served to disambiguate the homonym's grammatical role.

As may be seen in Table 3.4, HW wrote the noun and verb forms of a word equally well, but orally produced the verb form correctly much less often than the noun form. For example, she could read "strike" in *The workers went on strike*, but not in *You strike a match to light a candle*. By contrast, SJD wrote verb forms correctly much less often than noun forms, although in oral reading tasks both the noun and verb forms were produced without error. The patient's greater difficulty for verbs was not the result of a frequency effect because the same pattern was obtained even when the verb form of a homonym pair is more frequent than the noun form (see Table 3.4). Furthermore, the distinction between nouns and verbs cannot be due to the fact that nouns are more concrete than verbs, because neither patient showed a significant effect of concreteness in their oral reading performance.

Further evidence for the dissociability of nouns from verbs at the level of lexical form is provided by another stroke patient, EBA, who shows the opposite effect of grammatical word class; her oral naming (of the same stimuli used in studies with HW and SJD) is strikingly more accurate for verbs than for nouns (Hillis & Caramazza, in preparation). EBA is significantly more accurate in producing the verb form of homonyms than the noun form in response to definitions of the words. For example, in response to *bowl* defined as "A dish you use to eat soup or cereal" she said, "can"; but in response to *bowl* defined as "What you do when you roll a ball down an alley to hit pins" she correctly named "bowl." EBA's grammatical class effect cannot be attributed to a selective difficulty in processing concrete words because she was equally impaired in reading and naming abstract and concrete nouns of the same length and frequency. As found for HW, EBA's difference in naming nouns versus verbs is restricted to spoken production.

The double dissociation between nouns and verbs in naming accuracy, with the same sets of stimuli, by HW as compared to EBA, provides evidence that nouns and verbs are represented in the brain in such a way that processing of the phonological representation of one class for spoken output can be impaired, whereas processing of the phonological representation for the other class is spared. In other words, stored information about the pronunciation of words for production – representations in the phonological output lexicon – must be organized in the brain by grammatical class. Furthermore, the observation that the impaired processing of a single grammatical word class can be restricted either to the phonological output lexicon (as demonstrated in HW's performance) or the orthographic output lexicon (as demonstrated by SJD's performance) provides support for the hypothesis that orthographic and phonological information about each of these word classes is represented in distinct neural structures.

Finally, the finding that access to the lexical phonological or orthographic representations of homonyms (such as match – for which the meaning of the verb form and noun form are unrelated) can be selectively disrupted for use as nouns (as demonstrated by EBA) or for use as verbs (as demonstrated by HW and SJD) indicates that grammatical word class information is represented separately and redundantly in the phonological and orthographic output lexicons, in such a way that each class of words may be selectively affected by damage to the brain. This seemingly nonparsimonious organization of linguistic knowledge in the brain may, in fact, constitute a highly efficient way of organizing lexical information. If lexical knowledge is represented in morphologically decomposed form (Miceli & Caramazza, 1988; Badecker & Caramazza, 1991) – that is, if the entries in the phonological and orthographic lexicons consist of independent representations of "stems" and the affixes they may accept (e.g., the stem **like** represented independently of the affixes **-s, -ing,** and **-ed,** for the production of "likes," "liking," and "liked"), then the grammatical class of the stem (e.g., verb, adjective, noun) would have to be specified at the point where it is needed – the phonological and orthographic lexical stores. In this way, the seeming inefficiency in storage would result in an advantage in computational efficiency.

In summary, what the results from HW, SJD, and EBA suggest is that there are distinct neural mechanisms dedicated to the processing of different grammatical classes of words. And, unlike the various distinctions between semantic categories of knowledge, which may conceivably be attributed to selective impairments of mechanisms devoted to specific sensory attributes (Warrington & McCarthy, 1987), it is doubtful that a similar case can be made for the representation of different grammatical categories. Although one might conceive, for example, that the conceptual representations of certain types of nouns (e.g., donkey, tree, or cabbage) or verbs (e.g., run, lift, or cough) may be related in some way to specific sensory or motor attributes, it is difficult to apply the same reasoning to concepts denoted by abstract nouns (e.g., belief, mercy) and verbs (e.g., learn, listen, achieve), which dissociated in the same manner and to the same degree as concrete nouns and verbs in our patients.

Conclusions

The results we have summarized here have interesting implications for theories of the representation of language processing mechanisms in the brain. They would suggest that there are distinct neural mechanisms dedicated to the processing of different classes of words – whether specified in terms of grammatical class or in terms of shared semantic features. To be sure, the types of conclusions that may be reached about brain/cognitive mechanism relationships from the study of brain-damaged subjects are limited by the fact that we are dealing with experiments of nature in which the size and type of brain lesion is beyond experimental control. Indeed, stable, clear deficits emerge only following relatively large brain lesions, making it impossible to provide a detailed map of the relationship between brain structures and cognitive mechanisms. Nonetheless, such studies provide the basis for biologically motivated theories of language processing in that hypothesized distinctions about lexical knowledge, for example, receive support from neurally based dissociations. Thus, although at this time we do not know which specific neural structures/processes subserve the categorical organization of lexical knowledge, we cannot escape the conclusion that some such organization is directly represented in the brain.

Note

1. We use the following notation to indicate stimuli and responses: Stimuli are given in italics; responses are placed in quotation marks.

References

Andreewsky, E., & Seron, X. (1975). Implicit processing of grammatical rules in a classical case of agrammatism. *Cortex, 11*, 379–390.

Badecker, W., & Caramazza, A. (1991). Morphological composition in the lexical output system. *Cognitive Neuropsychology, 8*, 335–367.

Caramazza, A., Berndt, R. S., & Hart, J. (1981). "Agrammatic" reading. In F. J.

Pirozzolo & M. C. Wittrock (Eds.), *Neuropsychological and cognitive processing in reading.* New York: Academic Press.

Caramazza, A., & Hillis, A. E. (1991). Lexical organization of nouns and verbs in the brain. *Nature, 349,* 788–790.

Caramazza, A., Hillis, A. E., Rapp, B., & Romani, C. (1990). The multiple semantics hypothesis: Multiple confusion? *Cognitive Neuropsychology, 7,* 161–189.

Dennis, M. (1976). Dissociating naming and locating of body parts after left anterior temporal lobe resection: An experimental case study. *Brain and Language, 3,* 147–163.

Dunn, L. M., & Dunn, L. M. (1981). *Peabody Picture Vocabulary Test-revised.* Circle Pines, MN: American Guidance Service.

Farah, M. J., Hammond, K. H., Metha, Z., & Ratcliff, G. (1989). Category-specificity and modality-specificity in semantic memory. *Neuropsychologia, 27,* 193–200.

Funnell, E., & Sheridan, J. (1992). Categories of knowledge? Unfamiliar aspects of living and nonliving things. *Cognitive Neuropsychology, 9,* 135–153.

Gardner, H., & Zurif, E. (1975). *Bee,* but not *be:* Oral reading of single words in aphasia and alexia. *Neuropsychologia, 13,* 181–190.

Hart, J., Berndt, R. S., & Caramazza, A. (1985). Category-specific naming deficit following cerebral infarction. *Nature, 316,* 439–440.

Hillis, A. E., & Caramazza, A. (1991). Category-specific naming and comprehension impairment: A double dissociation. *Brain, 114,* 2081–2094.

Hillis, A. E. & Caramazza, A. (in preparation). Double dissociation between nouns and verbs in input and output.

Kandel, E. (1991). Perception of motion, depth, and form. In E. Kandel, J. Schwartz, T. Jessel (Eds.), *Principles of neuroscience.* New York: Elsevier, pp. 440–465.

Lucchelli, F., & De Renzi, E. (1992). Proper name anomia. *Cortex, 28,* 221–230.

McCarthy, R., & Warrington, E. K. (1985). Category-specificity in an agrammatic patient: The relative impairment of verb retrieval and comprehension. *Neuropsychologia, 23,* 709–727.

McKenna, P., & Warrington, E. K. (1978). Category-specific naming preservation: A single case study. *Journal of Neurology, Neurosurgery, and Psychiatry, 41,* 571–574.

McKenna, P., & Warrington, E. K. (1980). Testing for nominal dysphasia. *Journal of Neurology, Neurosurgery, and Psychiatry, 43,* 781–788.

Miceli, G., & Caramazza, A. (1988). Dissociation of inflectional and derivational morphology. *Brain & Language, 35*(1), 24–65.

Miceli, G., Silveri, M. C., Villa, G., & Caramazza, A. (1984). On the basis for agrammatic's difficulty in producing main verbs. *Cortex, 20,* 207–220.

Pietrini, V., Nertempi, P., Vaglia, A., Revello, M. G., Pinna, V., & Ferro-Milone, F. (1988). Recovery from herpes simplex encephalitis: Selective impairment of specific semantic categories with neuroradiological correlation. *Journal of Neurology, Neurosurgery, and Psychiatry, 51,* 1284–1293.

Riddoch, M. J., & Humphreys, G. W. (1987). Visual objects processing in optic aphasia: A case of semantic access agnosia. *Cognitive Neuropsychology, 4,* 131–185.

Sartori, G., & Job, R. (1988). The oyster with four legs: A neuropsychological study on the interaction of visual and semantic information. *Cognitive Neuropsychology, 5,* 105–132.

Sartori, G., Miozzo, M., & Job, R. (in press). Category-specific naming impairment? Yes. *Quarterly Journal of Experimental Psychology*.

Sacchett, C., & Humphreys, G. W. (1992). Calling a squirrel a squirrel but a canoe a wigwam: A category-specific deficit for artifactual objects and body parts. *Cognitive Neuropsychology, 9*, 73–86.

Semenza, C., & Zettin, M. (1988). Generating proper names: A case of selective inability. *Cognitive Neuropsychology, 5*, 711–721.

Silveri, M. C., & Gainotti, G. (1988). Interaction between vision and language in category-specific semantic impairment. *Cognitive Neuropsychology, 5*, 677–709.

Stewart, F., Parkin, A. J., & Hunkin, N. M. (1992). Naming impairments following recovery from herpes simplex encephalitis: Category-specific? *Quarterly Journal of Experimental Psychology, 44A*, 261–284.

Warrington, E. K. (1975). The selective impairment of semantic memory. *Quarterly Journal of Experimental Psychology, 27*, 635–657.

Warrington, E. K. (1981). Concrete word dyslexia. *British Journal of Psychology, 72*, 175–196.

Warrington, E. K., & McCarthy, R. (1983). Category-specific access dysphasia. *Brain, 106*, 859–878.

Warrington, E. K., & McCarthy, R. A. (1987). Categories of knowledge: Further fractionations and an attempted integration. *Brain, 110*, 1273–1296.

Warrington, E. K., & Shallice, T. (1984). Category-specific semantic impairments. *Brain, 107*, 829–854.

Yamadori, A., & Albert, M. L. (1973). Word category aphasia. *Cortex, 9*, 112–125.

Young, A., Newcombe, F., Hellawell, D., & DeHaan, E. (1989). Implicit access to semantic information. *Brain and Language, 11*, 186–209.

Zingeser, L. B., & Berndt, R. S. (1988). Retrieval of nouns and verbs in agrammatism and anomia. *Brain and Language, 39*, 14–32.

4 Origins of domain specificity: The evolution of functional organization

Leda Cosmides and John Tooby

By establishing that domain-specific machinery is necessary to explain human cognitive performance, psychologists who advocate modular or domain-specific approaches have found themselves in an unanticipated situation. Metaphorically speaking, it is as if they had laboriously built a road up one side of a nearly impassable mountain range into unexplored terrain, only to find themselves met at the top by a foreign road construction crew – evolutionary functionalist researchers – who had been building a road upward to the same destination from the far side of the mountains. Quite unexpectedly, cognitive psychologists find their field intimately connected to a whole new intellectual landscape that had previously seemed remote, unfamiliar, and all but irrelevant. Yet the proliferating connections tying together the cognitive and evolutionary communities promise to transform both fields, with each supplying necessary principles, methods, and a species of rigor that the other lacks. Although the sudden conjunction of these two communities has led to the customary level of mutual misunderstanding, the long-run significance of these developments is unmistakable. From this emerging integrated perspective, the domain-specific mechanisms or modules cognitive psychologists have been studying can be readily recognized for what they are – evolved adaptations, produced by the evolutionary process acting on our hunter-gatherer ancestors (Cosmides & Tooby, 1987).

Natural selection and ancestral environments

Viewed from a more encompassing scientific framework, the confluence of these two research communities seems inevitable (Tooby & Cosmides, 1992). The human brain did not fall out of the sky, an inscrutable artifact of unknown origin, and there is no longer any sensible reason for studying it in ignorance of the causal processes that constructed it. Rather, the reliably developing cognitive mechanisms that collectively constitute the architecture of the human mind acquired their particular functional organization through the process of evolution. The evolutionary history leading to modern humans consisted of a step-by-step succession of designs modified across millions of generations, with two independent forces – chance and natural selection – governing at every point whether each new modification would be incorporated into our species-typical cognitive architecture.

Although chance plays a delimited role in evolution and explains the existence and distribution of many simple and trivial properties, one thing cannot be plausibly explained as the product of chance processes: complex functional design (Williams, 1966; Dawkins, 1986; Pinker & Bloom, 1990; Tooby & Cosmides, 1990a, 1990b). Random walks do not systematically build intricate and improbably functional arrangements such as the visual system, the language faculty, or motor control. The only known explanation for the existence of complex functional design in organic systems is natural selection. Therefore, the existence of any complexly functional species-typical cognitive mechanisms must be related to the cumulative operation of selection (Dawkins, 1986; Pinker & Bloom, 1990). Necessarily, then, the design or functional organization of the mechanisms present in our cognitive architecture reflects the principles and logic of natural selection. Thus, cognitive psychologists, like physiologists, are usually studying adaptations and their effects, and they can find a productive new analytic tool in a carefully reasoned adaptationist approach (e.g., Cosmides, 1989; Cosmides & Tooby, 1989, 1992; Freyd, 1987; Gallistel, 1990; Gigerenzer & Hug, in press; Jackendoff, 1992; Leslie, 1987, 1988; Marr, 1982; Pinker & Bloom, 1990; Ramachadran, 1990; Rozin, 1976; Sherry & Schacter, 1987; Shepard, 1981, 1984, 1987a, 1987b; Shiffrar & Freyd, 1990; Staddon, 1988).

Natural selection operates through the testing of alternative designs through repeated encounters with evolutionarily recurrent situations (long-enduring adaptive problems). In our evolutionary history, design changes that enhanced their own propagation relative to alternative designs were selected for – that is, they caused their own successive spread until they became universal, species-typical features of our evolved architecture.[1] The systematic contribution of a design to its own propagation was the exclusive criterion, aside from chance, that determined which design changes became incorporated into our psychological architecture and which were excluded. Cognitive psychologists need to recognize that in explaining or exploring the reliably developing organization of a cognitive mechanism, the *function* of a design refers solely to how it contributed to its own propagation in ancestral environments. It does not refer to any of the various intuitive or folk definitions of function such as "contributing to the attainment of the individual's goals," "contributing to one's well-being," or "contributing to society." These other kinds of utility may or may not exist as side-effects of a given evolved design, but they can play no role in explaining how such designs came into existence or why they have the organization that they do. The fact that sexual jealousy, for example, may not contribute to any individual's well-being or to any positive social good is irrelevant in explaining why the cognitive mechanisms that reliably produce it under certain limited conditions became part of our species-typical psychological architecture (Daly, Wilson, & Weghorst, 1982; see Tooby & Cosmides, 1990a, for a cognitive-functionalist analysis of emotions).

Evolution is a historical process, not a foresightful one. The evolved design of modern organisms was caused by events in the past without regard to the problems of the present. Natural selection is not a teleological process capable of foreseeing the future and planning ahead for it. Our evolved mechanisms were constructed and adjusted in response to the statistical composite of situations actually encountered by our species during its evolutionary history (Symons, 1992; Tooby & Cosmides, 1990a). These mechanisms were not designed to deal with modern circumstances that are evolutionarily unprecedented. By the same token, they cannot have been designed to solve all potential problems under all possible circumstances either, because our species did not encounter all problems under all circumstances. For humans, the situations our ancestors encountered as Pleistocene hunter-gatherers define the array of adaptive problems our cognitive mechanisms were *designed* to solve, although these do not, of course, exhaust the range of problems they are capable of solving. These mechanisms should be well-engineered for solving this ancestral array of problems – and not necessarily any more inclusive class.

For these reasons, there is no warrant for thinking that selection would have favored cognitive mechanisms that are well-engineered for solving classes of problems beyond those encountered by Pleistocene hunter-gatherers. The widespread prejudice among cognitive psychologists for theories positing evolved architectures that consist of nothing but general-purpose problem-solvers is therefore unjustified. The fact that a mechanism can sometimes solve novel modern problems can play no role in explaining how that mechanism came to have the design it does, because natural selection had no crystal ball. The fact that our evolved mechanisms sometimes operate successfully in changed modern circumstances is a purely secondary consequence of their Pleistocene-forged design. Moreover, well-engineered performance should be evident only under conditions that mimic relevant aspects of the ancestral environments in which these mechanisms were designed to operate.

In short, the statistically recurrent conditions encountered during hominid evolutionary history constituted a series of adaptive problems. These conditions selected for a set of cognitive mechanisms that were capable of solving the associated adaptive problems. An adaptive problem can be defined as an evolutionarily recurrent problem whose solution promoted reproduction, however long or indirect the chain of causation by which it did so. Thus, although enhanced lifetime reproduction of self or kin was the ultimate functional product of adaptations, their proximate functional product need not have been closely associated with reproduction per se. A hominid life history of successfully achieved reproduction (including kin reproduction) required accomplishing the entire tributary network of preconditions and facilitations to reproduction in complex ecological and social environments. This entailed, of course, distinct families of specialized information gathering, inference, and decision making for our hominid ancestors. For this reason, humans are equipped with a diverse range of adaptations designed to perform a wide variety of tasks, from solicitation of assistance from one's parents, to language acquisition, to modeling the spatial distribution of local objects, to coalition formation and cooperation, to the deduction of intentions on the basis of facial expressions, to avoiding incest, to allocating effort between activities, to the interpretation of threats, to mate selection, to object recognition.

When abstracted from their ancestral hunter-gatherer contexts, such varied competences may seem (or be) disconnected from modern reproduction, and the operation of our cognitive architectures may appear instead to be a haphazard expression of activities of no particular evolutionary significance or patterning. This is an illusion produced by considering the operation of our psychological designs in isolation from their natural ancestral environments and without having developed task analyses – what Marr called computational theories – of the adaptive problems our mechanisms evolved to solve (Marr, 1982). An understanding of the nature of the problems to be solved and a model of the detailed structure of these ancestral contexts makes functional sense of the otherwise puzzling design features of our problem-solving mechanisms (for an example of such functional clarification, see Profet, 1992, on pregnancy sickness as an adaptation to the teratogenic effects of toxins present in plant foods in hunter-gatherer diets).

Of course, the design of our mechanisms should reflect the structure of the adaptive problems our ancestors faced only to the extent that natural selection is an effective process. Is it one? Evolutionary biologists since Darwin have been aware that selection does not produce perfect designs (Darwin, 1859; Williams, 1966; Dawkins, 1976, 1982; for a recent convert from the position that organisms are optimally designed to the traditional adaptationist position, see Lewontin, 1967 vs. 1978). Still, because natural selection is a hill-climbing process that tends to choose the best of the variant designs that actually appear, and because of the immense numbers of alternatives that appear over the vast expanse of evolutionary time, natural selection tends to cause the accumulation of increasingly and impressively functional designs. The eye and visual system are collections of cognitive adaptations that are well-engineered products of the evolutionary process, and although they may not be "perfect" or "optimal" – however these somewhat vague concepts may be interpreted – they are better at vision than any human-engineered system yet developed.

In consequence, not only is natural selection the only explanation for the functional organization of our cognitive mechanisms, but these mechanisms can be expected to be relatively well-engineered for solving ancestral adaptive problems. Two related questions arise when one assesses particular hypotheses about our cognitive architecture. The first is a learnability (or solvability) question: What kind of mechanisms are capable of solving the adaptive problems our ancestors are known to have faced and regularly solved – domain-general mechanisms or domain-specific ones? The second is an evolvability question: If there is an adaptive problem that can be solved either by a domain-general or a domain-specific mechanism, which design is the better engineering solution and, therefore, the design more likely to have been selected for?

What's wrong with domain-general mechanisms: An evolutionary perspective

Evolutionary biology provides a series of reasons why it is implausible and unparsimonious to assume that the human mind is an equipotential, general-purpose machine (Cosmides & Tooby, 1987; Tooby & Cosmides, 1992).

In the first place, the more important the adaptive problem, the more intensely natural selection specializes and improves the performance of the mechanism for solving it. This is because different adaptive problems often require different solutions, and different solutions can, in most cases, be implemented only by different, functionally distinct mechanisms. Speed, reliability, and efficiency can be engineered into specialized mechanisms because there is no need to engineer a compromise between competing task demands. Competing task demands can, however, be handled by separate, specialized systems. This accounts for the pervasive empirical finding that natural selection tends to produce functionally distinct adaptive specializations, such as a heart to pump blood, a liver to detoxify poisons, an immune system to defeat infections. As a rule, when two adaptive problems have solutions that are incompatible or simply different, a single general solution will be inferior to two specialized solutions. In such cases, a jack of all trades is necessarily a master of none, because generality can be achieved only by sacrificing effectiveness. Consequently, domain-specific cognitive mechanisms, with design features that exploit the stable structural features of evolutionarily recurring situations, can be expected to systematically outperform (and hence preclude or replace) more general mechanisms that fail to exploit these features.

The alarm calls of vervet monkeys illustrate this point clearly. Vervets have three major predators: leopards, eagles, and snakes. Each of these predators requires different evasive action: climbing a tree (leopard), looking up in the air or diving straight into the bushes (eagle), or standing on hind legs and looking into the grass (snake). Accordingly, vervets have evolved cognitive mechanisms that produce (and respond to) a different alarm call for each of these three predators (Cheney & Seyfarth, 1990). A single, general-purpose alarm call (and response system) would be less effective because the recipients of the call would not know which of the three different and incompatible evasive actions to take.

Simply to survive and reproduce, our Pleistocene ancestors had to be good at solving an enormously broad array of adaptive problems – problems that would defeat any modern artificial intelligence system. A small sampling includes foraging for food, navigating, selecting a mate, parenting, engaging in social exchange, dealing with aggressive threat, avoiding pathogenic contamination, avoiding predators, avoiding naturally occuring plant toxins, avoiding incest, and so on. A woman who used the same taste preference mechanisms in choosing a mate that she used to choose nutritious foods would choose a very strange mate indeed, and such a design would rapidly select itself out. These different adaptive problems are frequently incommensurate: They cannot, in principle, be solved by the same mechanism (Sherry & Schacter, 1987). Even a restricted consideration of hunter-gatherer tasks suggests that it is unlikely that any single general computational system could solve them all under ancestral conditions. (Indeed, it is difficult to imagine a domain-general computational system that could solve *any* of them.)

For this reason, the human mind can be expected to include a number of functionally distinct cognitive adaptive specializations (for discussion, see Chomsky, 1980; Cosmides & Tooby, 1987; Rozin, 1976; Rozin & Kalat, 1971; Sherry & Schacter, 1987; Tooby & Cosmides, 1992). Both empirically and theoretically, there is no more reason to expect any two cognitive mechanisms to be alike than to expect the eye and the spleen, or the pancreas and the pituitary to be alike. The argument frequently made by advocates of domain-general mechanisms – that a hypothetical and yet-to-be-described general problem-solving design would solve a larger class of unencountered or rarely encountered problems – is irrelevant: What governs the course of evolution and, therefore, the design of the human mind, is the statistical distribution of past situations that our ancestors actually encountered over evolutionary time.

In fact, we think the case can be put even more strongly. It is not simply a matter of plausibility, of efficiency, or of evolution being more likely to have produced a better system. Even simple learnability analyses show that *it is in principle impossible for a human psychology that contained nothing but domain-general mechanisms to have evolved, because such a system cannot consistently behave adaptively: It cannot solve the problems that must have been solved in ancestral environments for us to be here today.* A small number of domain-general mechanisms are inadequate in principle to account for adaptive behavior. We have developed this argument in detail elsewhere (Cosmides & Tooby, 1987; Tooby & Cosmides, 1992), so we won't belabor it here. Instead, we will summarize a few of the relevant points.

First, the ground rules for the argument:

1. To be a viable hypothesis about human cognitive architecture, the proposed design must in principle be able to solve its target problem. At a

minimum, any proposed cognitive architecture had to produce minimally adaptive behavior in ancestral environments – we know this because we are here today. Just as a hypothesized set of cognitive mechanisms underlying language must be able to account for the facts of human linguistic behavior, so too must any hypothetical domain-general cognitive architecture solve all the problems that were necessary to survival and reproduction in the Pleistocene. If it can be shown that there are essential adaptive problems that humans must have been able to solve in order to have propagated, and that domain-general mechanisms cannot solve them, then the domain-general hypothesis fails. We think there are a number of such problems, including inclusive fitness regulation, nutritional regulation, incest avoidance, sexual jealousy, predator avoidance – at a minimum, any kind of information-processing problem that involves motivation, and many others as well.

2. Because we know that the human mind evolved primarily by natural selection, hypotheses about the design of the mind gain or lose plausibility depending on whether the proposed design would have enhanced functionality under ancestral conditions – in biological terminology, whether it produced an increase in "fit" behavior. Evolutionary biology suggests that there is no principled reason for parsimony to be a design criterion for the mind, particularly when it conflicts with increased functionality. Enhanced functionality is the only criterion to which natural selection responds. (Equally, there is no reason why chance evolutionary processes would create cognitive architectures that operate according to simple, general, parsimonious principles either.)

A domain-general psychological architecture cannot guide behavior in ways that promote fitness for at least three related reasons:

1. What counts as fit behavior differs from domain to domain, so there is no domain-general criterion of success or failure that correlates with fitness.
2. Adaptive courses of action can be neither deduced nor learned by general criteria, because they depend on statistical relationships between features of the environment, behavior, and fitness that emerge over many generations and are, therefore, not observable during a single lifetime.
3. Combinatorial explosion paralyzes any truly domain-general system when encountering real-world complexity.

Reason 1: The definition of error is domain-dependent. For a domain-general system to learn what to do, it must have some criterion of success and failure; trial-and-error learning requires some definition of error. But there is no domain-independent criterion of success or failure that is correlated with fitness. This is because what counts as fit behavior differs markedly from domain to domain. For example, suppose our hypothetical domain-general learning mechanism guiding an ancestral hunter-gatherer somehow inferred that sexual intercourse is a necessary condition for producing offspring. Should the individual, then, have sex at every opportunity? In fact, such a design would rapidly be selected out. There are large fitness costs associated with incest, to pick only a single kind of sexual error. Given a potential partner with a physique, personality, or resources that would normally elicit sexual desire, the information that the potential partner is a family member must inhibit sexual impulses. Now suppose that this equipotential psyche had somehow learned that avoiding sex with kin had positive fitness consequences. How then should it generalize this knowledge about kin to other domains of human activity? Should one, for instance, avoid any interaction with kin? This would be a mistake; selectively avoiding sex with kin has positive fitness consequences, but selectively avoiding helping kin has negative fitness consequences. With relatives as with so many other things, what counts as adaptive error differs from domain to domain. In the sexual domain, error = sex with kin. In the helping domain, error = not helping kin given the appropriate envelope of circumstances. In cooperative exchanges, error = being cheated, which is paying a cost without receiving the benefit to which this entitles you. When a lion is looking for lunch, error = offering yourself as an appetizer. Because what counts as the wrong thing to do differs from domain to domain, there must be as many domain-specific cognitive mechanisms as there are domains in which the definitions of successful behavioral outcomes are incommensurate. This simple point has been underappreciated because of the traditional emphasis within cognitive psychology on the acquisition of knowledge rather than on the regulation of action. The brain evolved mechanisms to acquire knowledge because knowledge was important in the regulation of successful action.

Reason 2: Many relationships necessary to the successful regulation of action cannot be observed by any individual during his or her lifetime. Asking the question of how a domain-general architecture could acquire all the classes of necessary domain-specific knowledge exposes a fatal weakness in domain-general systems: They are limited to knowing what can be validly derived by general processes from perceptual information. Domain-specific mechanisms are not limited in this way. The world has a statistically recurrent domain-specific structure (e.g., snakes and spiders are often venomous, objects are solid, self-propelled entities are usually animals, the person who nursed you is likely to be your mother, human speech is consistent with Universal Grammar). A domain-general system has to bring the same general procedures to bear on spiders, speech, objects, mothers, and self-propelled entities, and so cannot initially treat any of these categories differently. Its subsequent operation is limited to what can be perceptually derived based on the application of general procedures. In contrast, content-sensitive architectures can come equipped with domain-specific procedures, representations, or representational formats prepared to exploit unobserved – and indeed, individually unobservable – sequelae to membership in various domains. The individual need not observe or experience death from a snake bite to manifest a caution around snakes, or run a long-term epidemiological study of the effects of inbreeding to manifest a distaste for sex with siblings. Chomsky's argument from the poverty of the stimuli is of this kind: Perception alone cannot supply infants with a list of constraints on the hypothesis space of potential human grammars (Chomsky, 1975; Pinker, 1984).

In its most general form, the difficulty of discovering what fitness consequences various actions or choices in knowledge representation have is fatal to any proposed domain-general system. The systematic statistical consequences of many courses of action on fitness are not stably assessable for several generations, and then only by evolutionary biologists, Divine Beings, or – and this is the essential point – natural selection. Because the promotion of fitness means differential representation of genes in subsequent generations, the time at which the consequences of an action can be assessed is remote from the time at which the action must be taken. Adaptive courses of action can be neither deduced nor learned by general criteria alone because they depend on statistical relationships between features of the environment, behavior, and fitness that emerge over many generations and are, therefore, often not observable during a single lifetime.

For example, how would a general-purpose mechanism situated in an ancestral hunter-gatherer ever discover that it should regulate behavior in approximate accordance with Hamilton's kin selection equation – that X should help Y whenever $C_x < r_{xy}B_y$?[2] When an individual sees a relative, there is nothing in the stimulus array that tells her how much she should help that relative. And there is no consequence that she can observe that tells her whether, from a fitness point of view, she helped too much, not enough, or just the right amount. Even worse, there is no one in the situation from whom she could learn, because selection will have created mechanisms in her relatives that cause them to encourage her to behave in ways that violate the above equation. A design feature that causes X to help her brother will spread through the population when it causes her behavior toward her full brother to fall within the bounds dictated by $C_x < \frac{1}{2} B_{brother}$. But selection should also have designed mechanisms that cause her brother to encourage her to help him whenever $\frac{1}{2}C_x < B_{brother}$, as well as mechanisms that cause their mother to encourage her to help her brother whenever $C_x < B_{brother}$. In other words, what counts as adaptively "correct" behavior is individual-specific. Learnability theorists of language have pointed out that a learning theory is inadequate if the information required for induction is absent from the child's environment. In the case of helping kin, the information is not only absent, but other individuals in the situation should be designed to try to socialize the child into behaving in ways that are contrary to the very rule that the child must induce.

In contrast, natural selection *can* detect these statistical relationships. This is because natural selection does not work by inference or simulation. It takes the real problem, runs the experiment, and retains those design features that lead to the best available outcome. Natural selection "counts up" the results of alternative designs operating in the real world, over millions of individuals, over thousands of generations, and weights alternatives by the statistical distribution of their consequences. In this sense it is omniscient – it is not limited to what could be validly deduced by one individual, based on a short period of experience, it is not limited to what is locally perceivable, and it is not confused by spurious local correlations. It uses the statistical foundation of the actual lives of organisms, in the actual range of environments they encounter, under the statistical regularities they experience and, using alternative developmental programs leading to alternative designs, tests for the best solution. Some statistical regularities may be picked up by some kind of inductive learning system, but many can only be detected by the feedback process of natural selection.

Reason 3: Combinatorial explosion paralyzes any system that is truly domain-general. A domain-general evolved architecture is defined by what it lacks: It lacks any content, either in the form of domain-specific knowledge or domain-specific procedures, that can guide it toward the solution of an adaptive problem. As a result, a domain-general system must evaluate all alternatives it can define. Permutations being what they are, alternatives increase exponentially as the problem complexity increases. By the time you analyze any biological problem of routine complexity, a mechanism that contains no domain-specific rules of relevance, procedural knowledge, or privileged hypotheses could not solve the problem in the amount of time the organism has to solve it (e.g., Carey, 1985; Cosmides & Tooby, 1987; Gallistel, Brown, Carey, Gelman, & Keil, 1991; Keil, 1989; Markman, 1989; Tooby & Cosmides, 1992). Indeed, a great deal of research on domain-specific reasoning in children has been motivated by this concern, including many of the chapters in this volume (see also Carey & Gelman, 1991; Keil, 1989; Markman, 1989; and Volume 14 of *Cognitive Science*).

In short, although some mechanisms in the cognitive architecture may be domain-general, these could not have produced fit behavior under Pleistocene conditions (and therefore could not have been selected for) unless they were embedded in a constellation of specialized mechanisms that have domain-specific procedures, or operate over domain-specific representations, or both.

Evolutionary biology, computational theories, and learnability

An evolutionary perspective can aid research on domain specificity in cognitive development in two ways. (1) It allows one to pinpoint the important, long-enduring adaptive problems for which humans are most likely to have cognitive adaptive specializations – that is, it suggests what domains might be fruitful to investigate. (2) Evolutionary biology provides richly contentful theories and relevant data that allow one to construct detailed computational theories or task analyses of these domains. This facilitates both the experimental investigation of the associated cognitive mechanisms and the application of learnability (or, more generally, solvability) criteria.

Why a theory of adaptive function is important

Many psychologists study the mind without asking what it was designed to do. Instead, they hope to uncover its structure by studying things it is *capable* of doing. Playing chess, remembering nonsense syllables or long strings of numbers, programming computers, doing college-level statistics – these are all activities that we *can* do, but they are certainly not activities that our minds were *designed* to do. It is highly unlikely that the cognitive architecture of the human mind includes procedures that are *dedicated* to solving any of these problems: The ability to solve them well would not have enhanced the survival or reproduction of the average Pleistocene hunter-gatherer, and the performance of modern humans on such tasks is generally poor and uneven. In all probability, a wide and somewhat idiosyncratic array of mechanisms and knowledge bases is mobilized when we try to solve this kind of problem, so the study of such problems is unlikely to lead us to carve nature at the joints (Marr & Nishihara, 1978).

There is a big difference between studying what a mechanism *can* do, and what it was *designed* to do. Suppose you have to figure out how an appliance works by studying some of the things it *can* do. I tell you that it can be used as a paperweight, that you can use it to warm your hands on a cold day, and that you can kill someone who is taking a bath by throwing it into the tub with him. By studying each of these uses of the appliance, you will learn a little bit about its structure – it is heavy enough to keep paper from blowing away, it generates heat, it is electrical – but you won't get a very coherent idea of what it is or how it works. It sounds like an electrical, heat-generating paperweight. Where do you go from here? Where is the heuristic value in this research strategy?

Suppose, on the other hand, that I tell you that the appliance is a mechanism that was designed to toast slices of bread – it is a "toaster." Your research strategy for discovering how it works would be completely different. Knowing its function, you would look for mechanisms that were *specially designed* for fulfilling that function; in this case, you would look for mechanisms that were specially designed for toasting bread. For example, you might hypothesize that the appliance has elements that generate heat; that it has two of these heating elements, one for each side of a slice of bread; that these elements are parallel to each other; that the distance between them is a little wider than the width of the average slice of bread; that it has a mechanism for detecting when the bread is toasted and for turning off the heat, a mechanism that allows you to retrieve the toasted bread without burning your fingers, and so on. It also tells you what features of the toaster are functionally arbitrary; the trait, "heavy enough to use as a paperweight," is not relevant to a toaster's function – it is merely a byproduct of the fact that the toaster's functioning parts are heavier than paper.

Knowing what the appliance was designed to do – what its function is – has enormous heuristic value because it suggests what design features it is likely to have. It allows you to pinpoint the kinds of problems a toaster should be very good at solving. Although it does not tell you the exact structure of the mechanisms that solve these problems (will the toast be delivered by a pop-up mechanism or by opening a door?), it suggests sharply focused hypotheses about the structure of these design features. It allows you to develop a task analysis for that problem, or what David Marr would call a "computational theory" for that problem domain: a theory specifying what functional characteristics a mechanism for solving that problem must have (Marr & Nishihara, 1978; Marr, 1982).

Evolvability constraints and computational theories

The most important contribution that evolutionary biology can make in the study of domain-specific mechanisms is in the development of computational theories of adaptive information-processing problems. Natural selection theory is a theory of *function*: It allows one to pinpoint adaptive information-processing problems that the human mind was selected to solve and therefore should be good at solving. Because an adaptive problem and its cognitive solution – a mechanism – need to fit together like a lock and a key, understanding adaptive problems tells one a great deal about the associated cognitive mechanisms. Natural selection shapes domain-specific mechanisms so that their structure meshes with the evolutionarily stable features of their particular problem-domains. Understanding the evolutionarily stable features of problem-domains – and what selection favored as a solution under ancestral conditions – illuminates the design of cognitive specializations. Although a computational theory of an adaptive problem cannot, by itself, tell you the exact structure of the information-processing mechanisms that solve the problem, it does suggest what design features they are likely to have and places important constraints on the family of possible mechanisms.

For example, the evolution of altruism, or helping behavior, was a puzzle for evolutionary theory. How can a new design feature spread through the population until it becomes species-typical if it causes an individual to harm its own reproductive success – the number of offspring it has – in order to increase another individual's reproductive success? The individual who has the new design feature is, by definition, selecting itself out.

In 1964, W. D. Hamilton provided an answer to this question. Using mathematical game theory, he showed that if an organism helps a kin member whenever the cost to itself (in reproductive terms) is less than the benefit to its kin member, discounted by the probability that the kin member shares the same design feature, then that helping design can spread through the population. Any design feature that causes an individual to help more than this – or less than this – would be selected against. This constraint is completely general: It is inherent in the dynamics of natural selection, true of any species on any planet at any time.

This means that the cognitive programs of an organism that confers benefits on kin cannot violate the [Cost to self < (Benefit to kin member) × (coefficient of relatedness to kin member)] constraint of Hamilton's kin selection theory. Cognitive programs that systematically violate this constraint cannot be selected for. Cognitive programs that satisfy this constraint can be selected for. A species may lack the ability to confer benefits on kin, but if it has such an ability, then it has it by virtue of cognitive programs that produce behavior that respects this constraint. One can call theoretical constraints of this kind *evolvability constraints*; they specify the class of mechanisms that can, in principle, evolve (Tooby & Cosmides, 1992).

The specification of constraints imposed by the evolutionary process – the specification of an adaptive function – does not, in itself, constitute a complete computational theory. Evolvability constraints merely define what counts as adaptive behavior. Cognitive programs are the means by which behavior – adaptive or otherwise – is produced. The important question a computational theory must address is: What kind of cognitive programs must an organism have if it is to behave adaptively?

Evolutionary biologists do not usually think of their theories as defining information-processing problems, yet this is exactly what they do. For example, Hamilton's kin selection theory raises – and answers – questions such as: How should the information that X is your brother affect your decision to help him? How should your assessment of the cost to you of helping your brother, versus the benefit to your brother of receiving your help, affect your decision? Will the information that Y is your cousin have a different effect on your decision than if you thought Y were your brother? In general, how should information about your relatedness to X, the costs and benefits to you of what X wants you to do for him, and the costs and benefits to X of your coming to his aid, affect your decision to help X?

As these questions show, an organism's behavior cannot fall within the bounds of the constraints imposed by the evolutionary process unless it is guided by cognitive programs that can solve certain information-processing problems that are very specific. To confer benefits on kin in accordance with the evolvability constraints of kin selection theory, the organism must have cognitive programs that allow it to extract certain specific information from its environment: Who are its relatives? Which kin are close and which distant? What are the costs and benefits of an action to itself? To its kin? The organism's behavior will be random with respect to the constraints of kin selection theory unless (1) it has some means of extracting information relevant to these questions from its environment, and (2) it has well-defined decision rules that use this information in ways that instantiate the theory's constraints. We are one of the species that has evolved the ability to help kin. Consequently, we can be expected to have evolved mechanisms that are dedicated to solving such problems, and can therefore solve them quickly, reliably, efficiently, automatically, effortlessly, and unconsciously. Trying to study domain-specific processes without a detailed computational theory that is either derived from, or at least compatible with, evolutionary biology would be like trying to study language acquisition without knowing the grammar of any human language.

The development of detailed computational theories of adaptive problems not only facilitates the experimental investigation of human cognition, but it also lays the groundwork for conducting a learnability (or, more generally, a solvability) analysis (e.g., Pinker, 1979, 1984; Tooby & Cosmides, 1992; Wexler & Culicover, 1980). The fact that many adaptive problems are of a very specialized kind suggests that many cognitive processes will be far more specific than is usually assumed, even by psychologists sympathetic to a domain-specific viewpoint. For example, evolutionary biology identifies a large number of distinct problems posed by social life that learnability analyses indicate must involve very different procedures for their solution. Rules that will cause one to accurately detect cheaters in a situation of social exchange, for example, do not map onto the rules of inference of the propositional calculus (Cosmides, 1989; Cosmides & Tooby, 1992; Gigerenzer & Hug, 1992). Nor do they map onto rules for detecting violations of aggressive threats. For example, a social contract has a different cost-benefit structure from a threat; a social contract is not in effect unless both parties agree to it, whereas a threat is a unilateral speech act; a social contract does not have a biconditional entailment structure whereas a threat does; from the point of view of a single actor, there is only one way of violating a social contract, whereas there are two ways of violating a threat, and so on. Rules of inference for detecting cheaters on social contracts cannot, in principle, detect bluffs and double-crosses in situations of threat. Different rules are required for these different domains: The "grammar" of social contracts is very different from the grammar of threat. If someone were to propose a learning mechanism that accounts for the acquisition of both social contract algorithms *and* threat algorithms, their theory would have to meet stringent learnability criteria: Given the informational environment to which a child is exposed, this same mechanism would have to induce two entirely separate sets of rules that act on very different mental representations, plus metarules for when to apply each set of rules. Developing computational theories of different social problem domains has led us to believe that it is unlikely that "social cognition" will turn out to be a unitary domain (Cosmides & Tooby, 1989, 1992).

Domain-specific reasoning in children

Long-term, across-generation recurrence of conditions – external, internal, or their interaction – is central to the evolution of adaptations, and it is easy to see why. Transient conditions that disappear after a single or a few generations may lead to some temporary change in the frequency of designs, but the associated selection pressures will disappear or reverse as often as conditions do. Therefore, it is only those conditions that recur, statistically accumulating across large numbers of generations, that lead to the construction of complex adaptations. As a corollary, anything that is recurrently true (as a net statistical or structural matter) across large numbers of generations could potentially come to be exploited by an evolving adaptation to solve a problem, or to improve performance. For this reason, a major part of adaptationist analysis involves sifting for these environmental or organismic regularities or invariances.

For those who study cognitive adaptations, the long-enduring structure of the world provides a deeply illuminating source of knowledge about the evolved architecture of the mind. As Shepard has put it, there has been the evolution of a mesh between the principles of the mind and the regularities of the world, such that our minds reflect many properties of the world (Shepard, 1987a). Many statistical and structural relationships that endured across human evolution were "detected" by natural selection, which designed corresponding computational machinery that is specialized to use these regularities to generate knowledge and decisions that would have been adaptive in the environment in which humans evolved.

Our domain-specific cognitive adaptations can, through exploiting the world's subtle enduring statistical structure, go far beyond the information they are given, and reconstruct from fragmentary cues highly accurate models of local conditions by exploiting these relationships (e.g., a self-propelled entity is usually an animal; sharp discontinuities in reflected light intensity usually indicate the presence of an edge). This evolutionary Kantian position has already been strongly vindicated in the fields of perception and psychophysics (see, e.g., Shepard 1981, 1984, 1987a, 1992; Marr, 1982), where the representations that our evolved computational systems construct go far beyond what is "logically" warranted solely by the sensory information itself, usually settling on single preferred interpretations. Our minds can do this reliably and validly because this fragmentary information is operated on by evolved procedures that were selected precisely because they reflect the subtle relationships enduringly present in the world (e.g., shading cues indicate shape and depth, time-location relationships indicate the most probable kinematic trajectories followed by solid objects). These mechanisms supply a privileged organization to the available sense data so that the interaction of the two generates interpretations that usually correspond to actual conditions in the external world. In the absence of specialized mechanisms that assume certain relationships are characteristic of the world, recovering accurate models of the external world from sense data would be an insoluble computational problem (Marr, 1982; Poggio, Torre, & Koch, 1985).

Parallel ideas form the centerpiece of Chomskyan psycholinguistics: Children must be equipped with specialized mechanisms ("mental organs") organized to exploit certain grammatical universals of human language, because otherwise language learning would be an unsolvable computational problem for the child (Chomsky, 1957, 1959, 1975, 1980; Pinker, 1979, 1982, 1984, 1989; Wexler & Culicover, 1980). The discovery and exploratory description of such universal subtle relationships present in the "world" of human language is a primary activity of modern linguists and psycholinguists. Proposed mechanisms for language learning that do not include specialized procedures that exploit these relationships have been repeatedly shown to be inadequate (Pinker, 1989, 1991; Pinker & Prince, 1988). As in perception, adaptations for grammar acquisition must mesh with the enduring structure of the world. But in this case, the recurrent structure to be meshed with is created by the species-typical design of other (adult) human minds, which produce grammars that manifest certain relationships and not others.

This same logic is what places the recent advances in the study of children's reasoning in the mainstream of evolutionary psychology. Indeed, the field of cognitive development has been revolutionized by the discovery that the principles of inference that infants and children bring to the tasks of learning are organized to reflect the particular recurrent structure of specific problem-domains, such as object construal and motion, the differences between artifacts and living kinds, physical causality, and so on (see, e.g., the articles in Carey & Gelman, 1991 and in this volume). These evolved, domain-specific cognitive specializations have been shown to be specialized according to topic and to develop in the absence of explicit instruction.

For example, contrary to the Piagetian notion that infants must "learn" the object concept, recent research has shown that (at least) as early as 10 weeks – an age at which the visual system has only just matured – infants already have a sensorily integrated concept of objects as entities that are continuous in space and time, solid (two objects cannot occupy the same place at the same time), rigid, bounded, cohesive, and move as a unit (e.g., Spelke, 1988, 1990, 1991). Indeed, when infants of this age are shown trick displays that violate any of these assumptions, they indicate surprise – one could almost say in such cases that the object concept embodied in their evolved mechanisms causes them to "disbelieve" the evidence of their senses (Leslie, 1988). By 27 weeks, infants already analyze the motion of inanimate objects into submovements and use this parsing to distinguish causal from noncausal relationships (Leslie, 1988; Leslie & Keeble, 1987). Needless to say, these are all relationships that accurately reflect the evolutionarily long-enduring structure of the world. A Piagetian architecture that had to laboriously discover them would be a poor and inept design compared to one that spontaneously organized its knowledge in terms of such stably true principles.

Brown (1990) has shown that early causal principles such as "no action at a distance" guide learning about tool use in children as young as 18 months; these children categorize tools for use according to functional properties (e.g., a hooked end for pulling) over nonfunctional properties (e.g., color). In contrast, the same children have great difficulty learning how to use a tool when its mechanism of action appears to violate one of their concepts about physical causality – concepts that mirror certain aspects of Newtonian mechanics.

The living world of plants and animals is structured into species and other more inclusive units that have large sets of properties in common – wolves resemble other wolves, mammals other mammals, and so on. This is another enduring set of relationships in the world that our minds should have evolved special design features to exploit. Ethnobiologists and cognitive anthropologists such as Atran and Berlin have shown that the principles of categorization humans spontaneously bring to this task reflect certain aspects of this enduring structure, and are the same cross-culturally (Atran, 1990; Berlin, Breedlove, & Raven, 1973). .

The enduring relationships created by the existence of such "natural kinds" and of artifacts have apparently selected for additional reasoning specializations as well. To begin with, very young children make sharp distinctions between the animate and inanimate worlds. Throughout our evolutionary history, being an animal has been reliably – if imperfectly – correlated with self-generated motion, whereas inanimate objects rarely move unless acted upon by an outside force. Recent research suggests that young children use this cue to distinguish the animate from the inanimate worlds, and make very different inferences about the two (Gelman, 1990b; Premack, 1990). More generally, experiments by Keil (1989) and others indicate that the kind of inferences children spontaneously make about natural kinds, such as animals, plants, and substances, differ sharply from those they are willing to make about human-made artifacts. Artifacts are defined by how their perceptual attributes subserve their (intended) function. In contrast, natural kinds are viewed as having invisible, defining "essences" that cause their perceptual attributes. (Indeed, the species-typical genetic endowments of species, and the common ancestry of larger taxa do cause an indefinitely large set of similarities to be shared among members of a natural kind, as does a common chemical structure for different instances of a substance.)

In an important series of experiments, Gelman and Markman (1986, 1987; Markman, 1989) found that natural-kind membership is a powerful organizer of inference in young children. In general, being a member of a natural kind carries more inferential weight than being perceptually similar. In addition, children give more weight to natural-kind membership when reasoning about traits that actually are more likely to vary as a function of membership in a natural kind, such as breathing, than when reasoning about traits that are more likely to vary as a function of perceptual similarity, such as weight or visibility at night (for a summary, see Markman, 1989).

Another important set of evolutionarily long-enduring regularities is the recurrent design features of other human minds. Evolved domain-specific cognitive specializations are even more necessary in this area, not only because other minds constitute the single most important selective force facing any individual human, but also because mental states such as beliefs, motives, intentions, and emotions cannot be directly observed. To allow a human to represent at least some of the mental states that generate others' behavior, special inferential systems must be available to bridge the gap from the observable to the unobservable. For example, if there is a reliable correlation over evolutionary time between the movement of human facial muscles and emotional state or behavioral intentions, then specialized mechanisms can evolve that infer a person's mental state from the movement of that person's facial muscles (Ekman, 1973, 1984; Fridlund, 1991). Indeed, evidence drawn from cognitive neuroscience indicates that we do have mechanisms specialized for "reading" facial expressions of emotion (Etcoff, 1983, 1986). If humans organize their understanding of each other through invoking the operation of unobservable entities such as beliefs, desires, and intentions, it cannot be because perception alone drove them to it.

An intensive research effort in the field of cognitive development has recently provided substantial support for the hypothesis that our evolved psychological architecture includes procedures that cause very young children to reliably develop models of other human minds (e.g., Astington, Harris, & Olson, 1988; Leslie, 1987, 1988; Perner, 1991; Wellman, 1990; Wimmer & Perner, 1983). Developmental psychologists have been finding that even 2- and 3-year-olds make different inferences about "mental entities" (dreams, thoughts, desires, beliefs) than about "physical entities." Moreover, children typically "explain" behavior as the interaction of beliefs and desires. Such inferences appear to be generated by a domain-specific cognitive system that is sometimes called a "theory of mind" module (Leslie, 1987). This module consists of specialized computational machinery that allows one to represent the notion that *agents* can have *attitudes* toward *propositions* (thus "Mary" can "believe" that "X," "Mary" can "think" that "X," and so on). Between the ages of 3 and 5 this domain-specific inferential system develops in a characteristic pattern that has been replicated cross-culturally in North America, Europe, China (Flavell, Zhang, Zou, Dong, & Qui, 1983), Japan (Gardner, Harris, Ohmoto, & Hamazaki, 1988), and a hunter-gatherer group in Camaroon (Avis & Harris, 1991). Moreover, there is now evidence suggesting that the neurological basis of this system can be selectively damaged; indeed, autism is suspected to be caused by a selective neurological impairment of the theory of mind module (Baron-Cohen, Leslie, & Frith, 1985; Leslie, 1987, 1988; Leslie & Thaiss, 1990).

This research suggests that a panhuman theory of mind module structures the folk psychology that people develop. People in different cultures may elaborate their folk psychologies in different ways, but the computational machinery that guides the development of their folk notions will be the same, and many of the representations developed will be similar as well. It appears that humans come into the world with the tendency to organize their understanding of the actions of others in terms of beliefs, desires, and other mental entities, just as they organize patterns in their two-dimensional retinal array under the assumption that the world is three-dimensional and that objects are permanent, bounded, and solid.

These principles can be expected to apply far beyond these few presently documented cases. The world is full of long-enduring structure – social, biological, physical, ecological, and psychological – and the mind appears to be full of corresponding mechanisms that use these stable structural features to solve a diverse array of adaptive problems. Like a key in a lock, the functional organization of each cognitive adaptation should match the evolutionarily recurrent structural features of its particular problem-domain (Shepard, 1987a; Tooby & Cosmides, 1990a). Because the enduring structure of ancestral environments *caused* the design of psychological adaptations, the careful empirical investigation of the structure of environments from a perspective that focuses on adaptive problems and outcomes can provide powerful guidance in the exploration of our cognitive mechanisms.

The future of domain-specific research

Domain-specific procedures or domain-specific representations?

One of the satisfying aspects of the recent florescence of research on domain specificity in cognitive development has been its rigor relative to alternative approaches within the field. Despite its relative sophistication, however, it is important to realize that the research program is only in its beginning phases, and we are a long way from having complete models of the phenomena in question. The ultimate goal of cognitive research should be the achievement of a fully specified formal model of some cognitive mechanism, implementable – at least in principle – by automata. This requires the full specification of, for example, (1) the initial set of procedures, (2) the initial set of representations, (3) the representational formats, (4) the environment the architecture operates in, and (5) the way in which procedures create the relationship between representational inputs and outputs.

However, in reading the literature on domain-specific reasoning in children, one could come away with the impression that the study of cognition is nothing more than the study of representations. But representations are, by themselves, inert. Obviously, there must be procedures that operate on representations if the brain is to process information. So the next step for many researchers lies in discovering where the domain specificity lies – in the child's mental representations, in the procedures that operate on these representations, or in both.

The literature on domain-specific reasoning in children is often unclear on this issue. Some researchers appear to favor the notion that certain content-imbued, domain-specific representations are reliably developing aspects of our evolved architecture, but that the procedures that operate on these representations are themselves domain-general. R. Gelman, for example, can be read as arguing that domain-specific skeletal principles (representations or procedures?) provide an initial categorization of the world, thereby determining what data gets processed, but that the processors themselves are statistical inference engines that are reasonably domain-general, able to take a wide variety of contents as inputs (R. Gelman, 1990a, 1990b). In contrast, Spelke often seems to imply that the infant's object concept is embodied in procedures that are domain-specific but amodal in the sense that they can operate on both visual and tactile data (Spelke, 1988, 1990). Both procedures and representations are hypothesized to be domain-specific in Leslie's conception of the child's theory of mind module (Leslie, 1987, 1988). In yet another variation on the theme, Karmiloff-Smith argues that infants have domain-specific procedures, but that some kind of process – presumably a domain-general one – operates on these procedures in such a way that the knowledge embodied therein is transformed into representations that can themselves be acted upon by yet other procedures, whether domain-specific or domain-general (e.g., Karmiloff-Smith, 1991).

Any of these possibilities may be correct. Indeed, all may be correct, although for different domains. Our point is that the study of domain specificity in cognitive development will advance significantly when researchers propose more precise computational models – models that attempt to specify the nature of both the representations *and* the procedures that give rise to domain-specific reasoning in children. Once such models are proposed, learnability analyses can determine whether they can, in fact, give rise to the performance they are credited with, and experimentation can explore the details of the mechanisms involved.

From domain-specific knowledge acquisition to domain-specific behavioral regulation

The work on domain specificity in cognitive development has not been, for the most part, motivated by evolutionary considerations or, indeed, by any larger program intended to discover how the human mind regulates behavior. Instead, it was spurred by philosophical arguments that combinatorial explosion will prevent a blank slate – or its technologically modern equivalent, the general-purpose computer – from learning anything in real time (e.g., Carey, 1985; Keil, 1989; Markman, 1989). Indeed, the problem that combinatorial explosion poses for the acquisition of knowledge is certainly a sufficient justification for looking for domain-specific mechanisms. But this approach is limited in its heuristic power. The invocation of combinatorial explosion cannot, by itself, generate hypotheses about which domains we are likely to have domain-specific mechanisms for reasoning about. In contrast, by considering what adaptive problems our ancestors would have had to be good at solving, as well as what kind of information would have been available for solving such problems under ancestral conditions, one can make many educated guesses about which domains are likely to have associated cognitive competences (for an array of examples, see the chapters in Barkow, Cosmides, & Tooby, 1992).

The origins of cognitive psychologists' interest in knowledge acquisition are well known. Cognitive psychology developed in substantial measure as an outgrowth of epistemology, and so it has inherited a preoccupation with such traditional philosophical concerns as knowledge acquisition, concept formation, language, and perception. Questions of how adaptive behavior is generated or how adaptive problems – such as mate selection – were solved have been largely ignored. Yet, from an evolutionary perspective this relative emphasis appears strangely disproportionate. Cognitive mechanisms capable of acquiring knowledge evolved solely because they subserved a larger cognitive architecture that regulated behavior. Specific knowledge acquisition mechanisms evolved only because they enhanced the system's ability to generate adaptive behavior under ancestral conditions. Surely this larger encompassing architecture with its constituent array of problem-solving specializations is equally worthy of study by cognitive psychologists. We suspect that the heavy emphasis on knowledge acquisition rather than behavioral regulation has caused many researchers to grossly underestimate the number of domain-specific mechanisms that are necessary to account for human thought and behavior. The evolvability considerations discussed earlier suggest that our species-typical architecture can be expected to contain not only a large number of domain-specific mechanisms that generate knowledge, but also a large number of domain-specific mechanisms that otherwise function to regulate and generate behavior (see, e.g., Cosmides, 1989; Cosmides & Tooby, 1989, 1992).

As a scientific matter, mechanisms describable at the cognitive level underlie and organize all of human thought and behavior – not just knowledge acquisition – and so cognitive psychology needs to broaden its scope to include them. This changes cognitive psychology into a wide-ranging discipline in which every kind of behavior or psychological phenomenon must eventually be addressed. Indeed, once cognitive psychologists begin to consider what kind of mechanisms would have been capable of generating adaptive behavior under ancestral conditions, the area of inquiry is explosively expanded. Not only should we expect to find domain-specific mechanisms that give rise to the object concept and an implicit theory of mind, but we should also find domain-specific mechanisms that give rise to incest avoidance, social exchange, aggressive threat, parenting, mate choice, disease avoidance, food aversions, predator avoidance, habitat selection, and so on (see, e.g., Buss, 1992; Cosmides & Tooby, 1992; Fernald, 1992; Mann, 1992; Orians & Heerwagen, 1992; Profet, 1992; Shepher, 1983; Symons, 1979; Wolf & Huang, 1980).

In such cases, the domain specificity may be found not in the form of knowledge structures per se, but in the specialized way in which various procedures and cues interact to produce an adaptively appropriate behavior. Rhesus monkeys, for example, have domain-specific mechanisms specialized for learning to avoid venomous snakes. If a laboratory-reared monkey sees a snake, it exhibits no fear. It does exhibit fear toward snakes, however, if it sees another monkey emiting a fear reaction toward snakes or snake facsimiles. Yet the monkey does not become afraid of *any* stimulus toward which it sees other monkeys reacting with fear. For example, if it sees another monkey emit a fear reaction toward an artificial flower, the lab-reared monkey does not become afraid of artificial flowers (Mineka & Cook, 1988). The rhesus monkey's fear-producing mechanism is highly domain-specific, but its domain specificity lies in the way in which a precise configuration of cues activates procedures that give rise to adaptively appropriate behavior. There is evidence for a similar mechanism in humans (Cook, Hodes, & Lang, 1986).

By asking what kinds of mechanisms would have been capable of giving rise to adaptive behavior under ancestral conditions, cognitive psychologists can also determine what kind of knowledge an individual would need to acquire in order to generate the appropriate behavior. This allows one to pinpoint domains for which we should have domain-specific mechanisms governing knowledge acquisition. Thus, knowing that our ancestors must have evolved mechanisms that would have caused them to avoid incest under ancestral conditions tells one that we must have evolved mechanisms that allow us to categorize the social world into kin versus non-kin. Moreover, it tells one that these evolved mechanisms must use cues, such as coresidence at an early age, that were reliably associated with kinship during our evolutionary history (Wolf & Huang, 1980). Knowing that our ancestors must have evolved mechanisms that, under ancestral conditions, would have caused them to choose habitats that were well-suited for supporting human life tells one a great deal about the kind of habitat knowledge people can be expected to seek out, and what kind of habitats they can be expected to prefer (e.g., Kaplan, 1992; Orians & Heerwagen, 1992). Knowing what would have counted as a good mate under ancestral conditions can tell one what kinds of information about the opposite sex a person will find interesting and what kind of mates they will tend to prefer. And so on. By using evolvability criteria and remembering that our evolved mechanisms were designed not to seek truth as an end in itself, but instead to generate adaptive behavior, one can both expand and focus the search for domain-specific cognitive mechanisms.

Evolution, domain specificity, and culture

The new research on domain-specific reasoning in cognitive development indicates that the human mind is permeated with content and organization that does not originate in the social world. This content was placed in the mind by the process of natural selection, and it is a reliably developing feature of our cognitive architecture. At a minimum, children's cognitive mechanisms were selected over evolutionary time to "assume" that certain things tend to be true of the world and of human life (e.g., objects are solid, other humans have minds, the self-propelled are animate). The specialized procedures, representational formats, cues, and categorization systems of these mechanisms impose – out of an infinite set of potential alternatives – a detailed organization on experience that is shared by all normal members of our species. Such a conclusion radically transforms our view of culture (for an extended analysis, see Tooby & Cosmides, 1992).

Traditionally, the mind has been considered to be a general-purpose computer or blank slate, with all of its content deriving from general-purpose mechanisms operating on environmentally or socially generated content. To speak crudely, the external social world was thought to impose its content on the internal. On this view, "culture" was seen as a unitary phenomenon that can be expressed in three different ways: (1) Culture as the socially learned: It is conceived as being some kind of contingently variable informational substance that is transmitted by one generation to another. (2) Culture as adult mental content: Because the individual mind is considered to be initially content-free and general-purpose, all or nearly all adult mental organization and content is assumed to be "cultural" in origin. (3) Culture as within-group similarities: Humans everywhere show patterns of local within-group similarity in their behavior and thought, accompanied by significant intergroup differences. The existence of separate streams of transmitted information is then assumed to be the exclusive explanation for these group patterns: Cultures are these sets of similarities, and intergroup differences are unreflectively called "cultural" differences. Under the standard view, these three logically separable concepts – the socially learned, mental content, and intragroup similarities – are all seen as one and the same thing – "culture."

But if all humans share a universal highly organized architecture that is endowed with many mechanisms that are rich in content, then the equation of these three breaks down. To begin with, the socially transmitted can no longer be equated with the contentful organization of human mental life and viewed as its sole cause because evolution is another cause of reliably developing mental content. Instead of all mental content being a social product, in many cases the causality is reversed. The evolved structure of the mind itself imposes content on the social world. In this alternative view, each domain-specific cognitive adaptation is a building block in a new theory of culture, because each can be expected to impose its particular organization on its special area of human knowledge and action (Sperber, 1985, 1990; Atran, 1990; Boyer, 1990; Hirschfeld, 1989; Cosmides & Tooby, 1989, 1992; Tooby & Cosmides, 1992; Chomsky, 1980). The design of our evolved domain-specific mechanisms will themselves govern what is or can be socially transmitted (see, e.g., Sperber, 1985, 1990). Certain representations may be viewed as subsisting within individual domain-specific mechanisms, and the programming of these mechanisms will regulate how specific representations move from individual to individual, distributing themselves in the population in response to different social and ecological conditions (Boyer, 1990; Sperber, 1990). At a deeper level, the existence of domain-specific mechanisms also means that there is a level of universal human mental content – that is, for certain things there is a single universal human "culture" (e.g., Universal Grammar, social exchange logic, object permanence, theory of mind).

In short, understanding that the human mind includes a large number of complex, evolved, domain-specific cognitive processes fundamentally changes one's view of transmitted "culture" and of the origins of mental content. At a minimum, as Sperber (1985) has cogently argued, it tells one that the equipotentiality assumption implicit in most cultural transmission theories – the assumption that mental representations with different content are equally easy to transmit – is false. Representations whose content taps into a domain for which we have specialized mechanisms will be transmitted very differently than representations whose content does not tap into such a domain. Second, it casts the strongest doubt on the notion that the individual is the passive recipient of cultural transmission. The Hamiltonian revolution in evolutionary biology has demonstrated that individuals' fitness interests were often in conflict during human evolution. One would expect our domain-specific psychological mechanisms to reflect this fact, causing individuals to resist socialization in certain domains and under certain circumstances, and to accept it in other domains and circumstances. For example, as we discussed earlier, one would expect a child to resist attempts by her parent to socialize her into helping her sibling whenever $C_x < B_{sib}$, and behave in ways that satisfy the $C_x < \frac{1}{2}B_{sib}$ rule (Tooby & Cosmides, 1989; Boyd & Richerson, 1985).

Finally, domain-specific mechanisms provide an alternative explanation for within-group similarities – aside from attributing them to the operation of cultural transmission. Domain-specific adaptations raise the possibility that within-group similarities (and intergroup differences) are "evoked" rather than socially learned (Tooby & Cosmides, 1989, 1992). The possibility of *evoked culture* breaks down the traditionally hypothesized equivalence between shared intragroup similarities and the socially transmitted.

Some (or all) domain-specific cognitive adaptations should be designed to respond in structured ways to inputs from local situations. As a result, humans in groups can be expected to express, in response to local conditions, organized within-group similarities that are caused not by social learning or transmission, but rather by the activation of these content-imposing mechanisms. Of course, these generated within-group similarities will simultaneously lead to systematic differences between groups that face different conditions.

To take a single example, differences in attitudes and social rules involving food sharing may be evoked by ecological variables (Cosmides & Tooby, 1992). One finding from the theoretical literature of evolutionary ecology on optimal foraging is that different kinds of sharing rules benefit individuals in different situations. For example, when the variance in foraging success of an individual is greater than the variance for the band as a whole, bandwide food sharing buffers the variance. In essence, the individual stores food in the form of social obligations. Bandwide sharing is a "from each according to his ability to each according to his need" type of system – food is distributed relatively equally to everyone in the band, no matter who found it. In contrast, when the variance in foraging success for an individual forager is low, that individual is better off sharing just within his or her family, in accordance with kin selection principles. If everyone reliably has access to the same goods, there is no particular benefit to sharing.

Optimal foraging theory is one component of a task analysis, or, in David Marr's terms, a computational theory of the adaptive problem of foraging. It defines the nature of the problem to be solved, and thereby specifies constraints that any mechanism that evolved to solve this problem can be expected to satisfy. In this case, optimal foraging theory suggests (1) that we should have domain-specific information-processing mechanisms governing foraging and sharing, and (2) these mechanisms should be sensitive to information regarding variance in foraging success, causing us to prefer one set of sharing rules for high variance items and another set for low variance items.

Kaplan and Hill's (1985) study of the Ache, a hunter-gatherer group living in eastern Paraguay, provides a particularly elegant test of this hypothesis because it controls for "culture." Meat is a very high variance food item among the Ache: On any given day, there is a 40% chance that a hunter will come back empty-handed. Collected plant foods, in contrast, are very low variance items. Kaplan and Hill found that the Ache engage in bandwide sharing of meat, whereas they share plant food primarily within the nuclear family. Thus the same individuals, in the same "culture," engage in different patterns of sharing for different foods, depending on the variance they experience in obtaining them.

Cashdan (1980) found a very similar situation among different groups of the Kalahari San. The Kalahari San are widely cited in anthropological circles for their strict economic and political egalitarianism. For example, the !Kung San, who experience extreme variability in the availability of food and water, have very strong social sanctions that reinforce sharing, discourage hoarding (calling someone "stingy" is a terrible insult), and discourage displays of arrogance and authority. For example,

The proper behavior of a !Kung hunter who has made a big kill is to speak of it in passing and in a deprecating manner (Lee, 1969; Draper, 1978); if an individual does not minimize or speak lightly of his own accomplishments, his friends and relatives will not hesitate to do it for him. (Cashdan, 1980: 116)

But it turns that some San bands are more egalitarian than others, and their degree of egalitarianism is related to variance in their food supply. The //Gana San of the northeastern Kalahari are able to buffer themselves from variability in the food and water supply in ways that other San cannot, through a small amount of food cultivation (including a kind of melon that stores water in the desert environment) and some goat husbandry. In contrast to the !Kung, the //Gana allow considerable economic inequality, they hoard more, they are more polygynous and, although they have no clear-cut authority structure, wealthy, high-status //Gana men are quick to claim that they speak for others and that they are the "headman" – behavior that would be considered unconscionable among the !Kung. Again, even though the !Kung and the //Gana are culturally similar in many ways – they share the same "meme-pool," so to speak – their social rules regarding sharing and economic equality differ, and these differences track the variance in their food supplies.

These phenomena are quite possibly instances of evoked culture. Rather than being the result of cultural transmission (at least in any traditional sense), they are evoked by the local situation. Because foraging and sharing are complex adaptive problems with a long evolutionary history, it is difficult to see how humans could have escaped evolving highly structured domain-specific psychological mechanisms for solving them. These mechanisms should be sensitive to local informational input, such as information regarding variance in the food supply. This input can act as a "switch," turning on and off different modes of activation of the appropriate domain-specific mechanisms. The experience of high variance in foraging success should activate rules of inference, memory retrieval cues, attentional mechanisms, and motivational mechanisms that allow bandwide sharing to occur and that make it appealing. The experience of low variance in foraging success should activate rules of inference, memory retrieval cues, attentional mechanisms, and motivational mechanisms that make within-family sharing possible and appealing. These alternative modes of activation of the domain-specific mechanisms provide the core knowledge that must be mutually manifest to the various actors for bandwide or within-family sharing to occur. This core knowledge can then organize and provide points of attachment for symbolic activities that arise in these domains.

Such alternative modes of activation can create alternative sets of complexly patterned social rules and activities. These will emerge independently, that is, in the absence of direct cultural transmission, in culture after culture when the individuals therein are exposed to the informational cues that activate these alternative modes.

In summary, cognitive psychology gains an entire new dimension of rigor when its natural relationships to the larger scientific landscape are recognized and exploited. Cognitive mechanisms are adaptations that were produced over evolutionary time by the operation of natural selection, and they acquired their particular forms as solutions to evolutionarily long-enduring adaptive problems. Indeed, the origins of domain specificity can be located in the evolutionary process, in the selective advantages conferred by functional design in adaptive problem solving.

Despite institutional histories to the contrary, anthropology and psychology cannot be seen as truly independent disciplines. The centerpiece of anthropological theory is the centerpiece of psychological theory: a description of the reliably developing architecture of the human mind, a collection of cognitive adaptations. These evolved problem solvers are the engine that link mind, culture, and the world. Domain-specific performance is the signature of these evolved mechanisms, a signature that can lead us to a comprehensive mapping of the human mind.

Notes

1. In certain situations two or more alternative designs can be stably maintained in a population through frequency-dependent selection, as in the case of contagion-retarding protein variation (Tooby, 1982). However, natural selection in interaction with sexual recombination tends to impose a specieswide uniformity in our complex adaptations, providing an explanation for the existence of a universally shared human nature (Tooby & Cosmides, 1990b). Nonfunctional traits can vary freely, but the developmental programs underlying our complex adaptations are constrained to be virtually species-typical.
2. In this equation, C_i and B_i refer to costs and benefits to individual i, measured as decreases and increases in i's reproduction caused by the design feature in question. $r_{i,j}$ – the coefficient of relatedness between individuals i and j – refers to the probability that i and j share the same design feature by virtue of common descent.

References

Astington, J. W., Harris, P. L., & Olson, D. R. (Eds.). (1988). *Developing theories of mind.* New York: Cambridge University Press.

Atran, S. (1990). *The cognitive foundations of natural history.* New York: Cambridge University Press.

Avis, J., & Harris, P. L. (1991). Belief-desire reasoning among Baka children: Evidence for a universal conception of mind. *Child Development, 62,* 460–467.

Barkow, J., Cosmides, L., & Tooby, J. (Eds.). (1992). *The adapted mind: Evolutionary psychology and the generation of culture.* New York: Oxford University Press.

Baron-Cohen, S., Leslie, A., & Frith, U. (1985). Does the autistic child have a "theory of mind"? *Cognition, 21,* 37–46.

Berlin, B., Breedlove, D., & Raven, P. (1973). General principles of classification and nomenclature in folk biology. *American Anthropologist, 75,* 214–242.

Boyd, R., & Richerson, P. J. (1985). *Culture and the evolutionary process.* Chicago: University of Chicago Press.

Boyer, P. (1990). *Tradition as truth and communication: Cognitive description of traditional discourse.* New York: Cambridge University Press.

Brown, A. (1990). Domain-specific principles affect learning and transfer in children. *Cognitive Science, 14,* 107–133.

Buss, D. (1992). Mate preference mechanisms: Consequences for partner choice and intrasexual competition. In J. Barkow, L. Cosmides, & J. Tooby (Eds.), *The adapted mind: Evolutionary psychology and the generation of culture.* New York: Oxford University Press.

Carey, S. (1985). Constraints on semantic development. In J. Mehler & R. Fox (Eds.), *Neonate cognition* (pp. 381–398). Hillsdale, NJ: Erlbaum.

Carey, S., & Gelman, R. (Eds.). (1991). *The epigenesis of mind.* Hillsdale, NJ: Erlbaum.

Cashdan, E. (1980). Egalitarianism among hunter-gatherers. *American Anthropologist, 82,* 116–120.

Cheney, D. L., & Seyfarth, R. (1990). *How monkeys see the world.* Chicago: University of Chicago Press.

Chomsky, N. (1957). *Syntactic structures.* The Hague: Mouton & Co.

Chomsky, N. (1959). Review of Skinner's "Verbal Behavior." *Language, 35,* 26–58.

Chomsky, N. (1975). *Reflections on language.* New York: Random House.

Chomsky, N. (1980). *Rules and representations.* New York: Columbia University Press. *Cognitive Science, 14* (1990). Special issue on structural constraints on cognitive development.

Cook, E. W. III, Hodes, R. L., & Lang, P. J. (1986). Preparedness and phobia: Effects of stimulus content on human visceral conditioning. *Journal of Abnormal Psychology, 95,* 195–207.

Cosmides, L. (1989). The logic of social exchange: Has natural selection shaped how humans reason? Studies with the Wason selection task. *Cognition, 31,* 187–276.

Cosmides, L., & Tooby, J. (1987). From evolution to behavior: Evolutionary psychology as the missing link. In J. Dupre (Ed.), *The latest on the best: Essays on evolution and optimality.* Cambridge, MA: MIT Press.

Cosmides, L., & Tooby, J. (1989). Evolutionary psychology and the generation of culture, Part II. A computational theory of social exchange. *Ethology and Sociobiology, 10,* 51–97.

Cosmides, L., & Tooby, J. (1992). Cognitive adaptations for social exchange. In J. Barkow, L. Cosmides, & J. Tooby (Eds.), *The adapted mind: Evolutionary psychology and the generation of culture.* New York: Oxford University Press.

Daly, M., Wilson, M., & Weghorst, S. J. (1982). Male sexual jealousy. *Ethology and Sociobiology, 3,* 11–27.

Darwin, C. (1859). *On the origin of species.* London: Murray.

Dawkins, R. (1976). *The selfish gene.* New York: Oxford University Press.

Dawkins, R. (1982). *The extended phenotype.* San Francisco: W. H. Freeman.

Dawkins, R. (1986). *The blind watchmaker.* New York: Norton.

Ekman, P. (1973). Cross-cultural studies of facial expression. In P. Ekman (Ed.), *Darwin and facial expression: A century of research in review.* New York: Academic Press.

Ekman, P. (1984). Expression and the nature of emotion. In P. Ekman & K. Scherer (Eds.), *Approaches to emotion.* Hillsdale, NJ: Erlbaum.

Etcoff, N. (1983). Hemispheric differences in the perception of emotion in faces. Doctoral dissertation, Boston University.

Etcoff, N. (1986). The neuropsychology of emotional expression. In G. Goldstein & R. E. Tarter (Eds.), *Advances in clinical neuropsychology, Vol. 3.* New York: Plenum.

Fernald, A. (1992). Human maternal vocalizations to infants as biologically relevant signals: An evolutionary perspective. In J. Barkow, L. Cosmides, & J. Tooby

(Eds.), *The adapted mind: Evolutionary psychology and the generation of culture.* New York: Oxford University Press.

Flavell, J. H., Zhang, X-D, Zou, H., Dong, Q., & Qui, S. (1983). A comparison of the appearance-reality distinction in the People's Republic of China and the United States. *Cognitive Psychology, 15,* 459–466.

Freyd, J. J. (1987). Dynamic mental representations. *Psychological Review, 94,* 427–438.

Fridlund, A. J. (1991). Evolution and facial action in reflex, social motive, and paralanguage. *Biological Psychology, 32,* 3–100.

Gallistel, C. R. (1990). *The organization of learning.* Cambridge, MA: MIT Press.

Gallistel, C. R., Brown, A. L., Carey, S., Gelman, R., & Keil, F. C. (1991). Lessons from animal learning for the study of cognitive development. In S. Carey & R. Gelman (Eds.), *The epigenesis of mind.* Hillsdale, NJ: Erlbaum.

Gardner, D., Harris, P. L., Ohmoto, M., & Hamazaki, T. (1988). Japanese children's understanding of the distinction between real and apparent emotion. *International Journal of Behavioral Development, 11,* 203–218.

Gelman, R. (1990a). Structural constraints on cognitive development: Introduction to a special issue of *Cognitive Science. Cognitive Science, 14,* 3–9.

Gelman, R. (1990b). First principles organize attention to and learning about relevant data: Number and the animate-inanimate distinction as examples. *Cognitive Science, 14,* 79–106.

Gelman, S., & Markman, E. (1986). Categories and induction in young children. *Cognition, 23,* 183–208.

Gelman, S., & Markman, E. (1987). Young children's inductions from natural kinds: The role of categories and appearances. *Child Development, 58,* 1532–1540.

Gigerenzer, G., & Hug, K. (1992). Domain-specific reasoning: Social contracts, cheating and perspective change. *Cognition, 43,* 127–171.

Hamilton, W. D. (1964). The genetical theory of social behavior. *Journal of Theoretical Biology, 7,* 1–52.

Hirschfeld, L. (1989). Rethinking the acquisition of kinship terms. *International Journal of Behavioral Development, 12,* 541–568.

Jackendoff, R. (1992). *Languages of the mind.* Cambridge, MA: MIT Press.

Kaplan, H., & Hill, K. (1985). Food sharing among Ache foragers: Tests of explanatory hypotheses. *Current Anthropology, 26,* 223–239.

Kaplan, S. (1992). Environmental preference in a knowledge-seeking, knowledge-using organism. In J. Barkow, L. Cosmides, & J. Tooby (Eds.), *The adapted mind: Evolutionary psychology and the generation of culture.* New York: Oxford University Press.

Karmiloff-Smith, A. (1991). Beyond modularity: Innate constraints and developmental change. In S. Carey & R. Gelman (Eds.), *The epigenesis of mind.* Hillsdale, NJ: Erlbaum.

Keil, F. C. (1989). *Concepts, kinds, and cognitive development.* Cambridge, MA: MIT Press.

Leslie, A. M. (1987). Pretense and representation: The origins of "theory of mind." *Psychological Review, 94,* 412–426.

Leslie, A. M. (1988). The necessity of illusion: Perception and thought in infancy. In L. Weiskrantz (Ed.), *Thought without language* (pp. 185–210). Oxford: Clarendon Press.

Leslie, A. M., & Keeble, S. (1987). Do six-month-old infants perceive causality? *Cognition, 25*, 265–288.

Leslie, A. M., & Thaiss, L. (1990). Domain specificity in conceptual development: Evidence from autism. Paper presented at conference on "Cultural knowledge and domain specificity," Ann Arbor, Michigan.

Lewontin, R. C. (1967). Spoken remark in P. S. Moorhead & M. Kaplan (Eds.), *Mathematical challenges to the Neo-Darwinian interpretation of evolution. Wistar Institute Symposium Monograph, 5*, 79.

Lewontin, R. C. (1978). Adaptation. *Scientific American, 239*, 156–169.

Mann, J. (1992). Nurturance or negligence: Maternal psychology and behavioral preference among preterm twins. In J. Barkow, L. Cosmides, & J. Tooby (Eds.), *The adapted mind: Evolutionary psychology and the generation of culture*. New York: Oxford University Press.

Markman, E. M. (1989). *Categorization and naming in children: Problems of induction*. Cambridge, MA: MIT Press.

Marr, D. (1982). *Vision: A computational investigation into the human representation and processing of visual information*. San Francisco: Freeman.

Marr, D., & Nishihara, H. K. (1978). Visual information-processing: Artificial intelligence and the sensorium of sight. *Technological Review*, October 28–49.

Mineka, S., & Cook, M. (1988). Social learning and the acquisition of snake fear in monkeys. In T. R. Zentall & B. G. Galef (Eds.), *Social learning: Psychological and biological perspectives* (pp. 51–73). Hillsdale, NJ: Erlbaum.

Orians, G. H., & Heerwagen, J. H. (1992). Evolved responses to landscapes. In J. Barkow, L. Cosmides, & J. Tooby (Eds.), *The adapted mind: Evolutionary psychology and the generation of culture*. New York: Oxford University Press.

Perner, J. (1991). *Understanding the representational mind*. Cambridge, MA: MIT Press.

Pinker, S. (1979). Formal models of language learning. *Cognition, 7*, 217–283.

Pinker, S. (1982). A theory of the acquisition of lexical interpretive grammars. In J. Bresnan (Ed.), *The mental representation of grammatical relations*. Cambridge, MA: MIT Press.

Pinker, S. (1984). *Language learnability and language development*. Cambridge, MA: Harvard University Press.

Pinker, S. (1989). *Learnability and cognition: The acquisition of argument structure*. Cambridge, MA: MIT Press.

Pinker, S. (1991). Rules of language. *Science, 253*, 530–535.

Pinker, S., & Bloom, P. (1990). Natural language and natural selection. *Behavioral and Brain Sciences, 13*, 707–784.

Pinker, S., & Prince, A. (1988). On language and connectionism: Analysis of a parallel distributed processing model of language acquisition. *Cognition, 28*, 73–193.

Poggio, T., Torre, V., & Koch, C. (1985). Computational vision and regularization theory. *Nature, 317*, 314–319.

Premack, D. (1990). The infant's theory of self-propelled objects. *Cognition, 36*, 1–16.

Profet, M. (1992). Pregnancy sickness as adaptation: A deterrent to maternal ingestion of teratogens. In J. Barkow, L. Cosmides, & J. Tooby (Eds.), *The adapted mind: Evolutionary psychology and the generation of culture*. New York: Oxford University Press.

Ramachadran, V. S. (1990). Visual perception in people and machines. In A. Blake & T. Troscianko (Eds.), *AI and the eye*. New York: Wiley.

Rozin, P. (1976). The evolution of intelligence and access to the cognitive unconscious. In J. M. Sprague & A. N. Epstein (Eds.), *Progress in psychobiology and physiological psychology*. New York: Academic Press.

Rozin, P., & Kalat, J. W. (1971). Specific hungers and poison avoidance as adaptive specializations of learning. *Psychological Review, 78*, 459–486.

Shepard, R. N. (1981). Psychophysical complementarity. In M. Kubovy & J. R. Pomerantz (Eds.), *Perceptual organization*. Hillsdale, NJ: Erlbaum.

Shepard, R. N. (1984). Ecological constraints on internal representations: Resonant kinematics of perceiving, imagining, thinking, and dreaming. *Psychological Review, 91*, 417–447.

Shepard, R. N. (1987a). Evolution of a mesh between principles of the mind and regularities of the world. In J. Dupre (Ed.), *The latest on the best: Essays on evolution and optimality*. Cambridge, MA: MIT Press.

Shepard, R. N. (1987b). Towards a universal law of generalization for psychological science. *Science, 237*, 1317–1323.

Shepard, R. N. (1992). The perceptual organization of colors: An adaptation to regularities of the terrestrial world? In J. Barkow, L. Cosmides, & J. Tooby (Eds.), *The adapted mind: Evolutionary psychology and the generation of culture*. New York: Oxford University Press.

Shepher, J. (1983). *Incest: A biosocial approach*. New York: Academic Press.

Sherry, D. F., & Schacter, D. L. (1987). The evolution of multiple memory systems. *Psychological Review, 94*, 439–454.

Shiffrar, M., & Freyd, J. J. (1990). Apparent motion of the human body. *Psychological Science, 1*, 257–264.

Spelke, E. S. (1988). The origins of physical knowledge. In L. Weiskrantz (Ed.), *Thought without language* (pp. 168–184). Oxford: Clarendon Press.

Spelke, E. (1990). Principles of object perception. *Cognitive Science, 14*, 29–56.

Spelke, E. (1991). Physical knowledge in infancy: Reflections on Piaget's theory. In S. Carey & R. Gelman (Eds.), *The epigenesis of mind* (pp. 133–169). Hillsdale, NJ: Erlbaum.

Sperber, D. (1985). Anthropology and psychology: Towards an epidemiology of representations. *Man (N.S.), 20*, 73–89.

Sperber, D. (1990). The epidemiology of beliefs. In C. Fraser and G. Gaskell (Eds.), *The social psychological study of widespread beliefs*. Oxford: Clarendon Press.

Staddon, J. E. R. (1988). Learning as inference. In R. C. Bolles & M. D. Beecher (Eds.), *Evolution and learning*. Hillsdale, NJ: Erlbaum.

Symons, D. (1979). *The evolution of human sexuality*. New York: Oxford University Press.

Symons, D. (1992). On the use and misuse of Darwinism in the study of human behavior. In J. Barkow, L. Cosmides, & J. Tooby (Eds.), *The adapted mind: Evolutionary psychology and the generation of culture*. New York: Oxford University Press.

Tooby, J., & Cosmides, L. (1989). Evolutionary psychology and the generation of culture, Part I. Theoretical considerations. *Ethology and Sociobiology, 10*, 29–49.

Tooby, J., & Cosmides, L. (1990a). The past explains the present: Emotional adaptations and the structure of ancestral environments. *Ethology and Sociobiology, 11*, 375–424.

Tooby, J., & Cosmides, L. (1990b). On the universality of human nature and the uniqueness of the individual: The role of genetics and adaptation. *Journal of Personality, 58,* 17–67.

Tooby, J., & Cosmides, L. (1992). The psychological foundations of culture. In J. Barkow, L. Cosmides, & J. Tooby (Eds.), *The adapted mind: Evolutionary psychology and the generation of culture.* New York: Oxford University Press.

Wellman, H. M. (1990). *The child's theory of mind.* Cambridge, MA: MIT Press.

Wexler, K., & Culicover, P. (1980). *Formal principles of language acquisition.* Cambridge, MA: MIT Press.

Williams, G. C. (1966). *Adaptation and natural selection.* Princeton: Princeton University Press.

Wimmer, H., & Perner, J. (1983). Beliefs about beliefs: Representation and constraining function of wrong beliefs in young children's understanding of deception. *Cognition, 13,* 103–128.

Wolf, A. P., & Huang, C. (1980). *Marriage and adoption in China 1845–1945.* Stanford: Stanford University Press.

Part III

The origins of domain knowledge: Conceptual approaches

5   ToMM, ToBy, and Agency: Core architecture and domain specificity

Alan M. Leslie

Our understanding of Agency is, in part, the result of domain-specific learning. The nature of this domain-specific learning needs to be understood in relation to the organization of information processing in the infant. As a result of adaptive evolution, the infant is a specialized processor of information with an architecture that (in part) reflects properties of the world. On this assumption, it should be possible to establish links between properties of the world, processing subsystems specialized for tracking those properties, and domains of knowledge. It is argued in the case of Agency that three main classes of world properties are reflected in three corresponding processing subsystems producing three distinct levels of knowledge. These three related triples are, respectively, *mechanical* Agency, *actional* Agency, and *attitudinal* Agency. Each of these three linked property classes, processing subsystems, and knowledge levels are discussed in turn but the focus will be mainly on mechanical Agency. In developing these ideas this discussion deals more generally with the nature of early mechanical understanding and its relation to conceptual development. A number of the ideas put forward in Leslie (1988) are revised and extended.

One lesson of cognitive science is that different types of knowledge often have different locations within the global organization of human information processing. In development, different types of commonsense knowledge may originate from different locations in core cognitive architecture. Early mechanical understanding and the notion of Agency can be studied within such a framework.

Parts of this chapter were written while I was visiting the Psychology Department at UCLA. I greatly benefited from discussions and conversations with a number of people there including Randy Gallistel, Nancy Kanwisher, and Liz Spelke who passed through, but most particularly with Rochel Gelman who gets my special thanks. I am also grateful to Geoff Hall, John Morton, and Jean Mandler for helpful comments on an earlier draft.

119

Domain specificity

The trouble with the notion of domain specificity is that there could turn out to be too many domains. For example, we may be tempted to describe knowledge of chess as a domain distinct from car driving, or we may wonder whether chess and checkers form one domain or two. In the study of development, it is customary to stick quite closely to the description of the child's conscious knowledge or lack thereof, often to the exclusion of all else. This one-dimensional approach to cognition encourages the proliferation of "domains." However, to study the cognitive mechanisms that produce development it is necessary to do more than enter the remote lands of childhood and carry back reports of quaint beliefs and astounding ignorance. To the extent that there are mechanisms of domain-specific development, then a deeper notion of domain is possible – one that is less software dependent, less profligate, and more revealing of the design of human cognition. This kind of domain specificity reflects the specialization of mechanisms in core cognitive architecture.

By core cognitive architecture I mean those human information processing systems that form the basis for cognitive development rather than its outcome (Leslie, 1988). Understanding this core is the primary aim of all theories of cognitive development. One view of the core is that it is essentially homogeneous and that any differentiation of its architecture is the product of development. The general all-purpose learning device of classical associationism is an elegant and influential example of this view. An alternative view of the core is that it contains heterogeneous, task-specialized subsystems. Vision is an obvious example of a specialized subsystem with a specialized internal structure. The language faculty is another. I propose and discuss a third specialized system that interfaces input and central processes and that structures the development of conceptual knowledge.

Types of domain-specific mechanisms

Different kinds of specialized core devices can underlie domain specificity. Some mechanisms may perform specialized tasks, not because they are particularly special on the inside – they have no special processes nor a prestructured representational system – but because they occupy a special position within the overall processing organization. The positioning of the device guarantees it will receive input from a particular class of object in the world and that it will end up representing a certain kind of domain-specific information. Mechanisms for face recognition may be an example of this. Faces seem to be processed by a device that employs general, non-specialized pattern processing (Diamond & Carey, 1986; Ellis & Young, 1989; Tanaka & Farah, 1991) but that receives only faces as input. Johnson and Morton (1991) propose that in the first few weeks of life the face recognition device, which they call "CONLERN," receives restricted input because of another device they call "CONSPEC." Unlike CONLERN, CONSPEC *is* internally specialized – it contains a rudimentary template of a face that serves to direct attention to faces. On this story, CONLERN becomes a face recognition device because it receives only face inputs.

A different kind of core domain-specific device is exemplified by a mechanism that acquires the syntactic structure of the natural language to which it is exposed. The study of language acquisition suggests that such a device not only occupies a special position in overall organization and is fed a special class of input, but also processes that input in a relatively specialized way, and, in so doing, employs a specialized representational system (e.g., Chomsky, 1975, 1986; Pinker, 1989).

The language faculty is probably not the only member of a class of core domains concerned with knowledge of formal systems. Formal core domains plausibly include *number* and perhaps *music*, as well as grammar. In formal domains, structural relations are key and there is no organizing role for the notion of cause and effect. By contrast, the notion of cause and effect is the central organizing principle in the core domains of object mechanics and "theory of mind." Like Carey (1985), I believe that these two core domains comprise the major part of our initial capacity for causal conceptual knowledge. These causal domains are my focus here and I shall argue that specialized core devices drive their development.

An overview of the core architecture of Agency

I want to examine a relatively neglected topic in studies of development, namely, the notion of Agency. I capitalize the first letter because, in some uses, an agent is simply a cause. The notion of an Agent, however, is more restricted and, in the first instance, applies to a certain class of object. Before discussing the properties that distinguish this class of object and define the notion of Agent, I want to draw attention to a distinction that is probably important but that I shall not pursue here. This is the distinction between Agent and animate object. Most objects that are Agents are animate and certainly all the objects that ever, in the course of evolution, contributed to the adaptation of our cognitive systems for dealing with Agency were animate. Nevertheless, I assume that the notion of animateness is external to Agency and proprietary to the biological domain. I can leave open the question whether or not biological knowledge constitutes a domain in core architecture (but see Keil, this volume), and if so what type.

I propose that the notion of Agency emerges from domain-specific learning and reflects properties of core architecture. In exploring the relationship between core architecture and our ability to understand the behavior of Agents, I will postulate two processing devices: First I shall discuss **ToBy** (Theory of Body mechanism), the seat of the infant's theory of physical

Table 5.1. *Core architecture for the cognition of Agency*

A Tripartite Theory of Agency		
Real World Properties of Agents	Processing Device	Levels of Understanding or "theories"
mechanical	**ToBy**	"Agents and Objects"
actional	**ToMM** (system$_1$)	"Agents and Action"
cognitive	**ToMM** (system$_2$)	"Agents and Attitudes"

bodies; later I shall discuss **ToMM** (the Theory of Mind Mechanism), the seat of the child's "theory of mind."[1]

I propose that understanding Agency is not achieved by a single conceptual system nor by a single processing system. Instead, it involves three distinct, hierarchically arranged processing components or modules. The three components correspond to or achieve three distinct levels of understanding or "theories" of Agency.

The first component, which I call **ToBy**, embodies the infant's theory of physical objects. **ToBy** is concerned with Agents in a mechanical sense – that is, with the mechanical properties of Agents. Distinguishing Agents from other physical bodies that are not Agents and describing their mechanical interactions are important functions of **ToBy**.

The next two components and their corresponding levels of understanding are concerned with the "intentional" properties of Agents. Although the movements and states of mere objects are simply features *of* the world, the movements and states of Agents, as well as being *of* the world, are also *about* the world (see, e.g., Dennett & Haugeland, 1987, for this notion of "aboutness"). The aboutness or intentionality of action and cognition are dealt with at the next two levels respectively. Together these two components, which deal with the intentionality of Agents, make up the device I call **ToMM**. Unlike **ToBy**, **ToMM** is exclusively Agent-centered. The first subcomponent of **ToMM** ("*system$_1$*") is concerned with Agents and the goal-directed actions they produce. This second level theory of Agency can be called "Agents and Action."

The third and final level of the hierarchy is concerned with the mental states of Agents and their role in producing behavior. At this level, Agents are represented as holding attitudes to the truth of propositions – attitudes such as *wanting*, *believing*, and *pretending* that p, where p is a proposition of some kind. This third level theory of Agency can be called "Agents and Attitudes." Although the first level of Agency is part of the infant's "theory of physical bodies," the latter two levels are part of the infant's theory of mind. This tripartite theory of Agency is summarized in Table 5.1.

This hierarchy is not a series of stages of development in the traditional sense. Instead, each level corresponds to a separate subsystem. Each component or subsystem constitutes a learning device with a specialized agenda for information acquisition, a specific way of organizing or describing the inputs it receives, a specific location within the larger architecture, and therefore with particular relationships to other components. The development of each subsystem can proceed in parallel and unfold according to its own distinct character and inputs. Naturally, each subsystem could *begin* its development in sequence, determined in part by the maturational status of the appropriate neural circuits and in part by the availability and quality of inputs. Thereafter, each subsystem can develop in parallel.

My discussion concentrates upon the first of these levels, mechanical Agency, and deals with the other two levels only to mark off what else I think comprises the core notion of Agency that is not dealt with at the first level. I begin then with the emergence of a processing mechanism (probably somewhere around 3 or 4 months of age) that equips the infant to attend to the mechanical properties of objects and events.

ToBy: A mechanics module

Piaget's (1953, 1955) view of the infant's developing knowledge of the physical world was tied to his view of core architecture and thus to his view of infant learning mechanisms. As in classical associationism, core architecture is assumed to be homogeneous and unstructured. The core, according to Piaget and to classical associationism, consists of two things: an ability to represent microfeatural sensations, and a set of completely general learning procedures. For Piaget, the learning procedures operate iteratively over the microfeatures (and neonatal reflexes) to build schemas. Differentiation or specialization of architecture is purely the result of psychological development and never initially its cause. The homogeneity assumption dictated the gradual and uniform cognitive development that Piaget thought he observed in examining structured action in infancy. Thus, Piaget believed that it was not until the end of infancy, toward the close of the second year, that infants construe the physical world as a rigid three-dimensional space containing stable, enduring objects whose behavior is regulated by causality. Before then, the infant processes the world as a disorganized display, whose chaos gradually gives way to familiarity, but whose meaning depends entirely on the infant's present activity. The world beyond subjective activity is, for the infant, simply a void.

The picture, which we read in Piaget, of the infant's painfully slow construction of an objective world seems now to reflect more on the limitations of the infant's capacity for planned, structured activity, for example, in manual search tasks (Diamond, 1988), and less on the infant's capacity to represent stable bodies with mechanical properties. A different picture of infantile representation emerges when visual attention measures are used to probe infant cognition. Measuring the infant's attention to events apparently taps a different psychological system than that which governs manual search behavior. Piaget's view overlooks even this gross degree of modularity. According to the new measures, infants, a few months after birth, apprehend cohesive, bounded, spatiotemporally continuous objects (see Spelke, 1990, for review), attribute specifically causal properties to collisions between objects (see Leslie, 1988, for review), and model some of the properties of hidden objects (see Baillargeon, 1991b, for review). Apparently infant competence even extends to construing the hidden mechanism in Piaget's classic invisible displacement event (Leslie & DasGupta, 1991). The infant's processing of the physical world appears to organize rapidly around a core structure representing the arrangement of cohesive, solid, three-dimensional objects embedded in a system of mechanical relations, such as pushing, blocking, and support.

These findings, in my view, inform us about a specialized learning mechanism adapted to create conceptual knowledge of the physical world, and to do so at an early period in development when general knowledge and general problem-solving abilities are quite minimal. Leslie and Keeble (1987) suggested that modular organization provides a way to work around the inevitably limited general capacities and knowledge characteristic of the preschool period. Core modularity provides a way to ensure rapid and uniform knowledge acquisition in domains that have adaptive significance to our species. Such acquisition secures, in turn, the early success of informative communication and thus the ability to take part in and benefit from the cultural transmission of knowledge. Although the best evidence for modular or compartmentalized processing comes from the study of perceptual input systems (Fodor, 1983; Marr, 1982), developmental benefits would also accrue from componential organization at more central levels of processing.

Alternatively, one could adopt a view that stresses the similarities and continuities between commonsense theories and theories that are the products of science or other forms of deliberate, reflective thinking. One version of this view places the conscious manipulation of concepts at center stage. Although imagining the child consciously solving a problem gives one a reassuring sense of having understood a piece of development, in fact this assurance is entirely illusory. Conscious thought is no better understood than the mass of unconscious processes upon which it depends.

If one takes a "child-as-scientist" view and pictures the child as an ordinary everyday scientist, working hard to contribute additional phenomena to an existing theoretical framework, then of course one addresses the nature of that original framework. The ideas set forth here can be aligned with such a picture. If instead one recoils from initial structure and starts from an unconstrained, general core architecture, the child-as-scientist metaphor changes in a critical way. Now the metaphor requires one to picture the child as a *great* scientist, begetter of conceptual revolution and radical theory shift.

This child-scientist produces her conceptual revolutions without the benefit of formal instruction, does so regularly, and in several different domains simultaneously. Her astonishingly successful and prolific early career is diminished only by the fact that all other children make essentially this same progress too, in essentially the same way, without effort, and, by and large, independently of IQ.

In view of these facts, it seems likely that some theories bootstrap thanks to specialized devices in core architecture. These processes can establish the core knowledge and ability on which pedagogy itself depends. **ToBy**, I will argue, is responsible for the early and rapid emergence of knowledge of physical bodies. Following Marr (1982), we may ask what is the goal of the information processing task this device carries out. **ToBy**'s goal, in general, is to arrive at a description of the world in terms of the mechanical constitution of physical bodies and the events they enter into. There are two main parts to achieving this goal. The first part, following Spelke, is to find the stable three-dimensional objects in the world. The second part, following Gelman and Talmy, is to find the "sources of energy" that produce their motions (Gelman, 1990) or, more generally, the distribution or dynamics of forces in a scenario (Talmy, 1988).

ToBy and FORCE

ToBy is concerned with the mechanical properties of objects and events. My first assumption is that **ToBy** employs a primitive notion that I shall call FORCE. I reserve the word *energy* for talking about mechanical forces *in the world*. For the cognitive correlate of energy, I use the term FORCE. FORCE is meant to be a "primitive" – a commonsense notion introduced by a modular system that has resulted from evolutionary adaptation. FORCE is not the scientific term developed culturally. I want to mark this distinction in my terminology. The fact that in the world object motions are invariantly the result of energy distribution is what makes it advantageous that the psychological system has a way of attending to and representing sources of energy. This does not mean that **ToBy** possesses a complete or even very deep system for thinking about the physical world, when viewed from the point of view of modern or even of, say, Aristotelian scientific theory. Others have discussed psychological notions similar to FORCE (for example, some aspects of Shultz's [1982] "generative transmission," and Anderson's [1990] force models), the closest being Talmy (1988).

The employment of the notion of FORCE is principally what makes it the case that **ToBy** is concerned with *mechanics*. It also dictates that **ToBy** be interested in three-dimensional bodies. This follows from the fact that, in the world, only three-dimensional bodies have mechanical properties. More terminology: It seems likely that some version of the distinction reflected in language by the distinction between "mass" noun (e.g., *butter*, *water*) and "count" noun (e.g., *dog*, *table*) is available to **ToBy**. For count objects, particular individuals can be identified and counted (three tables, many dogs), whereas masses cannot ("much water" but not "three waters") unless a count object organizes the mass (e.g., "three glasses of water"). I shall try to use the term *object* where a specifically count object is intended and "body" when surfaces, masses, *and* objects are intended.

ToBy is concerned with three-dimensional objects as the principal bearers, transmitters, and recipients of FORCE. Although entities such as letters or moving patches of light on a surface may be treated as objects by perceptual processes that trace their identity (Treisman, 1988), they fail to be bodies with mechanical properties.[2]

A dual route to mechanical analysis

ToBy is not concerned with entities that, like patches of light or letters on a page, lack mechanical properties. In contrast, three-dimensional objects can hardly fail to have mechanical properties. Spelke (1988, 1990, this volume) has argued persuasively that infants share with adults certain core aspects of the notion of physical object as bounded, cohesive, solid, three-dimensional bodies whose existence is spatiotemporally continuous. Infants also apparently regard objects as opposed to masses as countable (S. Carey, personal communication). Such a notion of physical object, which I attribute to **ToBy** and its specialized representational system, requires the availability of mechanical description. Therefore, I argue for the following proposition. The concern with picking out and tracking physical objects – a concern that unites adult and infant – is in one guise a concern with the mechanical structure of the world. The key player in this mechanical world is the three-dimensional object.

I wish that my account could have been as simple as the previous paragraph promises. However, mechanical events typically involve an element of motion. It is a fact about the world that the motion of three-dimensional objects is the result of the distribution of energy. Motion is therefore a source of information about FORCE. It is a fact about the visual system that it processes motion without reference to whether or not the bearer of motion is a three-dimensional object. Vision deals with the complexities of recognizing the form of three-dimensional objects too late in the stream of processing to be of use in the analysis of motion. Motion analysis takes place independently of the processing of luminosity, color, and texture, and earlier than the analysis of shading and the occlusion of surfaces (VanEssen, 1985; Livingstone & Hubel, 1988). These two facts, one about the world, the other about visual processing, suggest there will be a second route to mechanical analysis, a route that is independent of three-dimensional objects. Supporting evidence for this would be the existence of special visual sensitivities to patterns of motion that are highly informative with respect to FORCE dynamics. Some

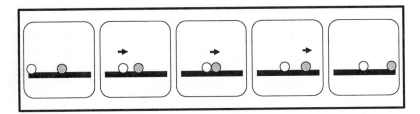

Figure 5.1. The "billiard ball" launching event.

of these patterns were discovered by Michotte (1963), chief among them being the "billiard ball launching" event.

In a launching event, one object moves toward another stationary object, strikes it sending that object off, while the first object now becomes stationary at the point of impact (see Figure 5.1). Michotte discovered that adults had an immediate impression of cause and effect when viewing this configuration. Two things are striking about his discovery. First, events exactly like this almost never occur in the real world. (For example, such a pattern with objects of equal mass occurs only in 180-degree collisions if the objects have perfect elasticity.) Second, the impression of causality occurs despite the fact that the objects involved are only pencil marks on paper or patches of light on a wall. The observers know perfectly well that there is no real mechanical connection between the motions of the insubstantial, two-dimensional entities. Nevertheless, the causal impression is quite incorrigible. This led Michotte to argue, correctly in my opinion, for the radical notion that adults are subject to a perceptual *illusion* of causality.

In a series of studies, I showed that, by $6\frac{1}{2}$ months and possibly earlier, infants too are subject to the launching illusion (Leslie, 1982, 1984b; Leslie & Keeble, 1987; reviewed in Leslie, 1988). I proposed that the perception of cause and effect in infant and in adult were linked through a modular component of motion analysis that serves to kick start development in infants and has the side-effect of creating a causal illusion in adults. I shall call this component the *Michotte module*.[3]

The *dual route* to mechanical analysis suggests that **ToBy** has two principal inputs from vision: one from a three-dimensional object recognition device, and one from motion analysis systems, including the Michotte module. Following Warrington (Warrington & James, 1986; Warrington & Taylor, 1978) and Marr (Marr, 1982; Marr & Nishihara, 1978) and others, I make the following assumption. The representation of the shape of an object involves a process distinct from the representation of other kinds of information about objects such as their use or function. In brain-damaged patients either kind of information may be impaired independently of the other. The visual three-dimensional object recognition device is concerned purely with the "geometry" of objects, recognizing them by matching to a three-dimensional shape model stored in a catalogue.[4] Specifically, visual object recognition is not concerned with the mechanical properties of the object, and therefore is not concerned with whether the object is cohesive, substantial, mechanically bounded, or numerically identical over time. These aspects of the "object concept" are the concern of **ToBy**. I shall refer to the output of the visual object recognition module as the *purely visual object* to underline the distinction between an object-recognized-by-shape and an object-constituted-mechanically.

In summary: Together with information on surface layout, **ToBy** takes, as input, descriptions that make explicit the geometry of the objects contained in a scene, their arrangement and their motions, and onto such descriptions paints the mechanical properties of the scenario. In doing this, **ToBy** interprets the motions, arrangements, and geometry of the objects in terms of the sources and fates – the dynamics – of FORCE.

Purely visual causality versus mechanical causality

The two principal visual inputs to **ToBy** determine a dual route to generating mechanical descriptions. **ToBy** paints mechanical properties onto purely visual objects (and more generally, onto bodies and surfaces). However, as we have seen, certain patterns of motion also attract FORCE descriptions even though no three-dimensional objects are involved.

The Michotte module, although it renders a perception of cause and effect, does not produce a FORCE description. Instead, the cause and effect of the Michotte module is a disembodied or purely visual cause and effect. This assumption is close to what Michotte himself believed. Michotte rejected the notion that his launching effect depended upon the perception of force (Michotte & Thinès, 1963) and instead, related it to what he called "ampliation of the movement." This was a phenomenological notion that seems to be best interpreted as a purely visual – that is, spatiotemporal – extension of the movement of the first object in the second.

The distinction between Marr's purely visual three-dimensional object, on the one hand, and the mechanical object (the cohesive, solid, bearer of FORCE), on the other hand, is echoed in the distinction between Michotte's "purely visual" causality and mechanical causality based on the dynamics of FORCE. These distinctions probably reflect a more general architectural distinction. It seems characteristic of vision that what it makes explicit are the *spatial* properties of surfaces, objects, and motions. Marr called this "the quintessential fact of human vision – that it tells us about shape and space and spatial arrangement" (Marr, 1982: 36). Any information processing system has to represent information. Any system of representation brings particular kinds of entity and particular kinds of information to the fore – makes them "explicit" to use Marr's term – whereas other kinds of information

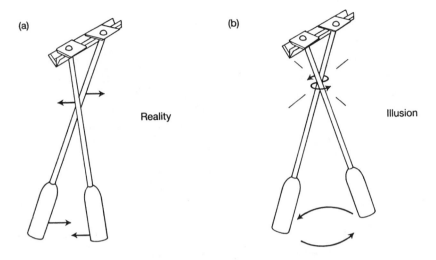

Figure 5.2. Pulfrich double pendulum illusion. Wearing a neutral density filter over one eye but viewing the swinging rods with both eyes creates a stereoscopic depth illusion. The result is that subjects see the solid rods passing through one another (after Leslie, 1988).

are left implicit or are pushed into the background. Approaching vision as an information processing system, it is apparent that what is made explicit by visual processing is spatial information, including, of course, spatial arrangement over time (i.e., motion).

I want to claim that the concern of vision for spatial description excludes the description of mechanical properties. Mechanical properties are left implicit "in the background." For example, in the stereoscopic illusion produced by a Pulfrich double pendulum (see Figure 5.2), the solid rods of the pendulum appear to pass through one another (Leslie, 1988). Vision is not constrained to suppress the illusory trajectories of the rods simply to prevent the mechanical anomaly of the appearance of passing through, though other *spatial* anomalies can have this suppressing effect (Leslie, unpublished). It appears that a mechanical solidity constraint is not employed in visual processing. Furthermore, the ease of forming a visual image of two solid objects passing through one another suggests that neither vision nor visual imagination employs a solidity constraint. Despite this, infants only a few months old are surprised to view a scenario in which a hidden object appears to violate the solidity constraint (Baillargeon, 1986; Baillargeon, Spelke, & Wasserman, 1985). Despite the indifference of vision and visual imagination, the solidity constraint shows up in naive mechanical reasoning. The reason for this intriguing pattern, I suggest, is that mechanical constraints are not the province of vision – neither of visual imagination nor of visual experience – but of **ToBy**.

Space and mechanics are not the same (or may the FORCE be with you)

Although spatiotemporal patterns are highly confounded with *contact* mechanics, the two are not the same. Unfortunately, the correlation can encourage the idea that mechanical notions reduce to mere spatiotemporal patterns and that mechanics is not fundamental to our understanding of the world. This is, of course, the starting point of classical empiricism (e.g., Hume, 1740) and the idea finds many echoes elsewhere. Michotte provides examples: His distinction between "mere displacement" and "movement" (Michotte & Thinès, 1963) cries out for interpretation in terms of whether the moving entity is seen as the dominant bearer of FORCE (= "movement") or not (= "displacement"), as in the case of one object transporting another. Likewise, as I will argue below, "ampliation" of the movement in a launching event is most naturally interpreted as the transmission of FORCE from one object to another through contact.

More recently, Mandler (1992) has put forward an account of infant competence that assumes that mechanical notions can be reduced to spatiotemporal patterns.[5] Mandler argues that conceptual development proceeds out of a perceptual analysis of the spatiotemporal properties of objects and events. This perceptual analysis yields a kind of representation that she calls "image schemas." Image schemas are analogue spatial representations and provide the earliest "concepts." The core architecture for conceptual development, in Mandler's view, employs a purely analogue, "non-propositional" format of representation. Specifically, image schemas are said to underlie the infant's notions of causation (launching), containment, and agency. The image schemas for these events are illustrated in Figure 5.3.

The reader should guard against the temptation to read mechanical meaning into the spatiotemporal patterns depicted by the image schemas in Figure 5.3. It is more natural for us to think about launching, containment, and agency events as mechanical events rather than as purely spatiotemporal patterns. Because of this, we may inadvertently think about the representation (the image schema) in terms of what it *refers to* rather than in terms of how it represents what it refers to. Of course, what the schema for, say, launching refers to is, as a matter of fact about the world, a mechanical event. But that is not how Mandler wants us to interpret her notion. Image schemas are defined by Mandler as representations that make explicit *spatial* (that is, spatiotemporal) information, not mechanical information. Indeed, this is crucial to her claim that analogue, spatial image schemas *alone* provide sufficient grounding for conceptual development.

However, the evidence for infants' grasp of launching (and as we shall see later, also for their grasp of containment and of Agency) shows that they understand the mechanical, and not just the spatiotemporal, properties of such events. Leslie and Keeble (1987) were able to demonstrate a causal

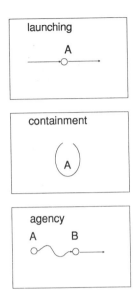

Figure 5.3. Mandler's "image schemas" for launching, containment, and agency (after Mandler, 1992).

illusion of launching in 6-month-olds precisely because they found a way to vary the mechanical properties of the test stimuli *while equating the changes in spatiotemporal properties*. This allowed them the conclusion that infants had reacted to something above and beyond spatiotemporal properties, namely, the causal (mechanical) properties of launching. More generally, we have to ask ourselves why infants analyze out the particular spatiotemporal patterns Mandler identifies. There are myriad other spatiotemporal patterns that could have been latched onto instead. The answer is, I believe, because these are the spatiotemporal patterns upon which the infant's theory of mechanics bestows immediate significance.

   Image schemas, then, make explicit the wrong kind of information, if they are to play the role in conceptual development that Mandler assigns to them. We might enlarge on Mandler's theory and propose that **ToBy** operates over image schemalike representations, enriching them by painting on mechanical information. But this will create a different class of internal representation: The schemas will no longer be simple analogue images, but will become instead *mechanical diagrams*. Diagrams are partly spatial analogue representations, to be sure, but they are also partly symbolic. And mechanical diagrams, whether appearing statically upon the printed page and being interpreted by a reader or unfolding over time in a baby's head and being processed by the baby's cognitive system, depend for their efficacy upon the availability of mechanical notions. Such notions must rest upon at least a rudimentary theory of mechanics.

Mandler interprets work by Choi and Bowerman (1991) on "spatial" verb systems in support of her thesis about the primacy of spatial representation in development. But verb systems too encode mechanical notions; they pick out the spatial relations that have a significant mechanical interpretation. To take but one example from Choi and Bowerman, cited by Mandler, Korean (unlike English) uses a systematic marking for whether two objects or parts of an object fit together tightly or fit together loosely. There are, of course, geometric correlates of fitting tightly and fitting loosely – roughly, the closeness or remoteness of contact. But just as in the hand-as-agent experiments I will discuss below, the spatial relationship is relevant precisely because of the mechanical properties it signals. The significance of this spatial relationship – why it is attended to, why it is informative and worth encoding in a verb system – is clearly mechanical: How much force is required to make or break the contact? Will one object provide support for the other? Will the fitting just drop out if I don't hold it in there? And so on. The significant generalization to make from these cases is not primarily in terms of spatial representation but in terms of *the interpretation the spatial relations receive in a FORCE theory of contact mechanics*. This is the critical information grasped by early learners of verb systems. I believe much the same goes for most of the examples from perception in prelinguistic infants, which Mandler discusses, including launching, Agency, and containment.[6]

Part of the motivation Mandler has for proposing the notion of image schema as the basis for conceptual development and language acquisition is to avoid attributing "propositional" (i.e., predicate-argument) representation to the infant. However, the plausibility of this solution is diminished if mechanically interpreted FORCE diagrams are a minimum requirement for internally representing the notions Mandler targets. For example, this would require enriching analogue spatiotemporal representations by adding on symbol structures. Actually, predicate-argument structures are eminently suited to representing FORCE dynamical notions. Representing mechanical *roles* and mechanical *relations* raises many of the "binding" problems that predicate-argument structures are so good at solving. Indeed, mechanical roles and relations seem to be reflected directly in much of the verb-argument structure of natural language (Talmy, 1988) that appears largely to be specialized for this task, perhaps as a result of the adaptive coevolution of cognitive and linguistic abilities (Pinker, 1989; Pinker & Bloom, 1990).

Motion and motive FORCE

I now need to say something about how **ToBy** equips the infant to understand and learn about the moving world of physical objects. I shall consider this question in connection with three classes of events. I start with one of the simplest of all events.

Nothing terrestrial moves without having a source of energy. As Gelman

(1990) points out, this underwrites a basic or "first principle" of attending to motions, namely: Attend to the source of energy. Following this principle, there are only two possibilities when observing an object that begins to move. The first is that it was made to move by something else (which you may or may not be able to see) in which case its energy came from some other object. Or the object has an internal source of energy, in which case it is an Agent. So, in painting on a FORCE description, **ToBy** attends to sources of energy. The more an object changes motion state by itself and not as a result of external impact, the more evidence it provides, the more likely it is, that it is an Agent.[7] Notice that none of this follows simply from seeing the spatiotemporal characteristics of the motions per se, but from *interpreting* those characteristics in terms of FORCE source. As always, spatiotemporal properties are confounded with mechanical ones. Without access to the mechanical interpretation, however, none of the inferences concerning cause or Agency can be drawn and we are stuck, like David Hume, with the "impressions of our senses," namely, meaningless spatiotemporal patterns. As we shall see in the following third example, having access to this very simple FORCE dynamical interpretation (internal/external source) allows the infant to recognize a more complex class of events, namely, interactions.

My second example is the launching through collision event that has already been mentioned. Hume's celebrated analysis of causation began with this event. He considered one billiard ball colliding with and launching another to be "as perfect an instance of the relation of a cause and effect as any which we know..." (Hume, 1740). But he was quite unable to say *why* it should seem so perfect. Lacking any place for core mechanical understanding in his framework, Hume had to rely on the statistics of association. But launching has special properties for infants as well as for aficionados of the billiard table. From the point of view of **ToBy**'s contact mechanical theory, launching is the simplest and most complete instance of the transmission of FORCE.

Under a FORCE interpretation, the two objects in launching are assigned different and imbalanced mechanical roles, one as pusher (transmitter of FORCE), the other as pushed (recipient of FORCE). As I noted earlier, when Leslie and Keeble (1987) found a way of unconfounding spatiotemporal properties, 6-month-olds showed they were sensitive to these mechanical roles. One group of infants watched a film of a causal looking launching event, while another group was shown a variation on launching. In this variation, the causal impression is destroyed by introducing a short delay (half second) between the impact of the first object and the reaction of the second. Adults do not think this delayed event looks like pushing and being pushed. Leslie and Keeble habituated one group of infants to a causal sequence and another group to a noncausal sequence. They then tested the two groups by showing them exactly the same film they had respectively seen before, except that the film projector now ran in reverse. The spatiotemporal properties of the sequences thus change: The spatial direction of motion changes (e.g., from left to right) and the temporal order of motion changes (e.g., red object moves first, green object second changes to green first, red second). But these spatiotemporal changes occur equally for *both* groups. Moreover, whatever degree of spatiotemporal continuity there was in the pattern of motion the infant was habituated to is still there unchanged in the test presentation. It must be: It is the same piece of film they saw before.

However, specifically in the case of launching, reversal produces a change in *mechanical roles* and this change introduces a difference between the two groups. In the causal event, reversal swaps the roles of pusher and pushed between the objects. The pusher becomes the pushed. In the noncausal event, these roles are absent and so they cannot be reversed. Thus, if infants appreciate the mechanical structure of launching, they will recover attention more to its reversal than to the reversal of a variant that lacks that same mechanical structure. That is what Leslie and Keeble found. Six-month-olds interpret spatiotemporal patterns in terms of mechanical structure.

Recently, Baillargeon (1991a) has found that young infants have expectations regarding the amount of FORCE a moving object imparts to a stationary one on impact, with greater FORCE being delivered by larger objects and resulting in greater distances traveled.

The third and final class of event takes us back to Agency and the interaction between an Agent object and a non-Agent object, as when a hand picks up a doll. Leslie (1982) habituated 5- and 7-month-old infants to such an event. Half the infants were then tested on the same event but with a number of visible changes including a different hand, different direction of movement, different pace, and so on. These infants did not recover interest to these changes. The other group of infants saw an event in which the only change was a small gap introduced between hand and doll so that when the hand again picked up the doll it looked "as if by magic." These infants did recover interest. This was followed up by Leslie (1984a) who showed that 6-month-olds were surprised at the lack of contact only during the pick-up and not when the hand and doll were stationary. Most important, they were surprised only when a hand was involved. If an event with the same spatiotemporal pattern of motion was shown that did not include a hand (the doll was "picked up" by a Styrofoam block), the infants were unconcerned about the spatial contact (see Figure 5.4). These results show that infants were concerned about spatial contact only when they thought a mechanical relationship was involved. And they thought a mechanical relation was involved only when a hand was at work.

Consider: An infant can often observe hands moving "on their own." This gives **ToBy** strong evidence that hands have an internal source of power. Hands are Agents. When the infant then sees a hand moving simultaneously and in contact with another object, *in spite of the precise spatiotemporal reciprocity of the two motions*, **ToBy** interprets the event as having a particular

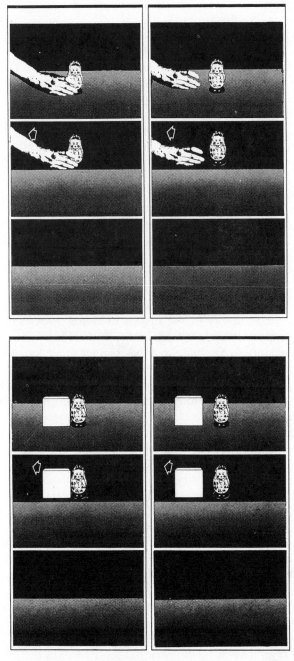

Figure 5.4. Infants perceive hands as Agents. This differentially influences their interpretation of the spatial relation in the top and bottom pairs of events (from Leslie, 1984a).

mechanical direction and involving unequal mechanical roles. The hand, as
the source of FORCE in the event, must pick up and pull the doll rather than
the other way around (where the doll pushes the hand backward). This is (to
us) such an obvious way to interpret this event that it is worth laboring the
point. In the past, the infant has observed hands and dolls individually exhibiting different kinds of spatiotemporal motion. But it does not follow merely
from this fact that, in the future, when the hand and doll move together, the
infant must see the hand as the causally active object, that is, as doing the
picking up. But this *does* follow if the infant interprets the different prior
spatiotemporal patterns as revealing different mechanical properties. Mandler
and I agree that these studies show the infant's grasp of Agency. However,
I sharply disagree with her proposal that this is achieved by a purely
spatiotemporal analysis. The theory of **ToBy** provides, in my view, a fuller
account of the mechanism whereby infants learn to identify and comprehend
the behavior of Agents.[8]

Two questions for *ToBy*

In Piaget's (1955) theory of the origins of causal notions there are
said to be two initial aspects to causality that gradually diverge in development.
One is simply the tendency to associate together regular sequences of events.
The other, which Piaget calls "efficacy," is the infant's supposed awareness of
sensations of effort and desire accompanying action. I draw attention to efficacy
because it might at first sight be confused with the following, in my opinion,
sounder idea. Because of its position in global architecture, **ToBy** can use
evidence provided by senses that are less wholly spatial than vision. In
particular, **ToBy** can take advantage of information from kinesthetic, haptic,
and pressure senses. If, as seems reasonable, one assumes that these senses
can provide (for example, in the course of acting upon objects) input that is
interpretable as information about FORCE, then the infant has a further
valuable source of evidence about the physical world. Notice that this proposal
endows the infant with the perception of mechanical properties of objects
and events – things objectively in the world – rather than merely with a subjective awareness of bodily sensations. This general idea receives support
from the findings of Streri and Spelke (1988) on the haptic perception of
object cohesion.

A second line of investigation suggested by **ToBy** concerns infants'
knowledge about types or *kinds* of objects. According to the theory of **ToBy**,
perceptual categorization of objects is distinct from other forms of knowledge about object-kind. The three-dimensional model catalogue, for example, could provide the basis for perceptual categorization of purely visual
objects. But what about an infant's knowledge of object-kinds as it relates to
the mechanical object? The results on understanding hands as sources of
power suggests that this is one object-kind that infants do known about and

distinguish from other kinds of objects. Little other than this is known at present. The theory of **ToBy** predicts that mechanical properties will provide the central information in the early formation of (conceptual) object-kinds. As we shall see in the following section, information about how Agents typically use an object will come to assume importance too. Acquiring this information demands more than mechanical FORCE descriptions of Agents. A new level in the theory of Agency is required and by assumption a further mechanism beyond **ToBy**.

Beyond ToBy

I come now to the limitations on **ToBy** as a theory of Agency. The mechanical properties of Agents are not the only properties that set them apart from other objects. When Agents behave they act in pursuit of goals and react to their distant environment (perception). Neither of these facts fits in with or is representable by **ToBy**'s contact mechanics. A goal is a state of affairs that an Agent tries to bring about. Typically, this state of affairs does not yet exist – the Agent acts to make it actual; the desired state of affairs is a little in the future, one might say. Sometimes action in pursuit of a goal fails and the strived for state of affairs does not come about – it remains "in the future." Understanding the pursuit of a goal by an Agent, then, is understanding action in relation to circumstances that are at a distance in time. Understanding perception, on the other hand, typically involves understanding a causal relation at a distance in space. Neither of these fits with **ToBy**'s spatiotemporal contact principle of "no action at a distance." **ToBy** is concerned with mechanical relations that obtain locally and contiguously in space and time. The brain mechanisms implementing **ToBy**, then, will presumably operate at this strictly local scale. Understanding Agents and Action,[9] however, requires an analysis over a larger scale to capture relations between Agents and states of affairs at "distant" times and places. I assume, therefore, that actional (as opposed to mechanical) properties of Agents are not processed by **ToBy** but by a different mechanism, operating after **ToBy**. I call this mechanism **ToMM**. **ToMM** is concerned with the *intentional* properties of Agents.

Agency and the "fictional causes" problem

We come now to what seems to me to be the really difficult problem that the existence of Agents puts in the way of an information processing system that wants (blindly of course) to evolve the capacity to understand their behavior. Up to now, we have considered only the mechanical domain. When considering merely physical objects, only *actual* circumstances are relevant in accounting for *actual* behavior; only really present objects can possibly be relevant to prediction; only states of affairs that actually obtain can possibly contain actual causes of actual behavior. This is perhaps the most basic and truistic assumption of all in causal domains: that only real causes real. Without this assumption, there is no notion of cause, there are no constraints on possibility, no causal explanation, no causal prediction, in short, no causal knowledge. To suppose that something unreal caused something real does not even begin to make sense. And yet, here is an example of a kind of reasoning we do everyday: Why did John jump into the doorway? To avoid the rain. Was it really raining? No, he only thought it was raining.

Because Agents have cognitive properties (as well as mechanical and actional properties), they sometimes (often) behave in response to situations that are not actual but are merely fictional. This sounds like we assume that something fictional is causing something actual. Since that is crazy, I am going to assume that that is not what we are doing. The problem that **ToMM** solves is how to describe the relation that holds between the actual behavior of Agents and fictional circumstances while maintaining a causal, that is, rational framework. **ToMM**'s job is to square this circle.

A short digression on actional Agency

In describing the actional properties of Agents above, I touched on a weak version of the fictional causes problem in the notion of goal-directed action. In this case, however, there is no reason to see the goal state of affairs as causing the behavior. Instead, just as in mechanical Agency, where the Agent is seen as having an internal source of causal power or FORCE, so in actional Agency is the Agent seen as a having an internal source of striving or acting (toward the goal). The action or "pressure" to bring about the goal state of affairs arises from *within* the Agent and "flows outward" from the Agent (see Talmy, 1988, for a discussion of how basic verb structures in English express this kind of picture).

The notion of the Agent acting or striving to bring about a goal state is akin to Wellman's (1990) attribution of a "drive theory" of desire to the young child. Wellman is right in postulating an early notion of desire that is not propositional attitude based. However, the way he formulates his drive theory cannot be correct. Wellman says the child simply conceives of another person as having an internal drive toward an object but without the possibility of embedding this object in a proposition, as it were. Wellman depicts the child as imagining a pair of hands in the other person's head stretched out to an apple, "wanting" the apple. In denying the child the ability to represent any propositionlike content as the focus of the desire state, Wellman wishes to avoid attributing a propositional attitude notion of desire to the very young child. However, his formulation has the unfortunate effect of making the child's putative drive notion almost useless for predicting behavior. When Wellman's child thinks of Mary as wanting an apple, he is incapable of representing what Mary wants to do with the apple or what state she wants the apple to be in. Somehow Mary just "wants" an apple. Of course, the reader of Wellman's theory will involuntarily supply an enriched interpretation to Mary's "want": by default, that Mary wants to *eat* the apple. But the young child, according to Wellman, cannot do this. When Wellman's child thinks that Billy wants a swing, he cannot represent whether Billy wants to sit on the swing, swing on the swing, just sidle up and be close to the swing, or anything else specific. To do so would be to represent Billy as desiring a state of affairs rather than just an object. Billy simply "wants" the swing, full stop. Unfortunately, such a notion is pretty useless for predicting behavior.

However, there is another way to formulate Wellman's insight that there may be a notion of desire that is not based on a propositional attitude, but one gets to this not by dropping the state of affairs (described by the proposition in a propositional attitude), but by dropping the attitude. In its simplest form this notion represents the Agent as "ACTING to bring about [a state of affairs]." In a more complex form this notion might represent the Agent as having a disposition or standing readiness to ACT to bring about [a state of affairs]. Further elaborations of this general class of notion include disposition strength, preference, ACTING to avoid [a state of affairs], and so on. The state of affairs in brackets would, of course, be represented by the child however he normally represents states of affairs, and if this is normally represented in a "propositional" format then so be it. Such a notion, however, is not a propositional attitude because "ACTING to bring about..." does not describe an attitude to the truth of a proposition; it describes an attempt to change physical circumstances. It will be necessary for the child to be able to represent possible or future states of affairs, but then this is already assumed by the kind of understanding of the *physical* world that has been demonstrated in babies, as discussed in earlier sections.

Attitudes and fictions

In actional notions of Agency, one sees only a weak form of the fictional causes problem. In the case of propositional attitudes like *believing* (and *pretending*), one sees the full-blown fictional causes problem. Although the theory of Agents and Action allows one to understand behavior in relation to circumstances that are remote in time and space, it does not allow one to construe behavior in relation to (caused by) circumstances that are fictional *in the here and now*. Interpreting behavior in this way is made possible by the third and final layer of the theory of Agency: Agents and Attitudes. The notion of a propositional attitude solves the fictional causes problem. It does so essentially by describing the Agent as actively holding an attitude to the truth of a proposition.

In a successful mental state attribution, the state of affairs described by the proposition that the Agent is related to may be actual, merely possible, or even impossible. But the attitude the Agent takes (to its truth) is always real.

For example, John *believed* it was raining. The rain was not real but John's attitude of believing in the rain certainly was real. And it is John's attitude (to the truth of the proposition in question) that caused his behavior (not the proposition nor the state of affairs described by the proposition).

There is, of course, a price to be paid for solving the problem posed by the fact that the behavior of Agents is determined by cognitive properties.[10] The price to be paid is that special concepts have to be available – that is to say, a specialized representational system is required. I have called this system the "metarepresentation" (Leslie, 1987b) or, more recently, the "M-representation" (Leslie & Thaiss, 1992; Leslie & Roth, 1993). In the closing pages, I briefly sketch how **ToMM** might come to solve these problems.

To summarize: **ToMM** itself has an internal structure with at least two major subcomponents, which I shall call *system₁* and *system₂*. *System₁* deals with the second level of the theory of Agents, namely, Agents and Actions. *System₁* employs the "ACT to bring about state of affairs" system of representation. *System₂* implements the third level of the theory of Agents, namely, Agents and Attitudes. *System₂* employs the M-representation.[11]

System₁: Agents and Action

Whereas **ToBy** appears to begin development at around 3 to 4 months, the **ToMM** *system₁* probably begins to develop later, perhaps around 6 to 8 months.[12] One of the first signs of *system₁* is the following of eye gaze. From about 6 months onward, infants will begin to turn and visually search in the direction of gaze adopted by an *en face* adult (Butterworth, 1991). Butterworth found that the accuracy of the infant in locating the object that the adult is looking at increases rapidly between 6 and 12 months. Also during this time, infants begin to attend to the uses Agents make of objects; by 12 months infants display knowledge of the conventional function of some everyday objects, such as spoons and brushes (Abravanel & Gingold, 1985). This suggests that they are able to appreciate and are storing knowledge about the instrumental roles that objects can play in Agent's goal-directed actions.

If *system₁* underlies the infant's ability to represent the actional properties of Agents, then it really comes into its own when representing situations in which two Agents come together and *interact*. Agent's goals can mesh in different ways. At a general level: One Agent's goal may coincide with another Agent's goal. This produces enhancement or helping. Alternatively, one goal may be opposed to another. This produces blocking or harming (cf. Premack, 1990). More specifically, during the second half of the first year, infants begin to produce "requesting" behaviors, for example, in request reaching or "asking" to be picked up (Bates, Benigni, Bretherton, Camaioni, & Volters, 1979; Bruner, 1976). These requests call upon another person to achieve or help in achieving some current goal of the infant's. Similarly, during this time, infants begin deliberately to acquiesce in or comply with the actions of others, for instance, positioning to be picked up. Also during this time, they begin deliberately to try to block the goals of the other person, such as in "refusing" behaviors (Bates et al., 1979; Bruner, 1976). Again during this time, infants begin to show they appreciate the role structures of some simple goal-directed (inter)actions by being able to reverse the roles, for example, in the "give and take" behaviors that appear around 10 months (Bruner, 1976).

Premack (1990) makes a number of interesting suggestions concerning infants' sensitivity to goal-directedness. One suggestion is that goal-directedness or "intentionality" may be perceived on the basis of a class of motion pattern. If so, this would parallel the case of mechanical causality, for example, launching. In terms of the present framework, Premack suggests a specialized device that renders a "purely visual goal-directedness." This is an interesting idea that, if true, would comport with and extend the examples discussed earlier.

It remains very much an open question whether infants bring some simple theory of the kinds of goals Agents may have or whether all this must be learned. The simple representational system I have proposed for *system₁* will at least allow the infant to learn about some immediate goals Agents may have by watching for outcomes. The outcome state of affairs can then be entered into the action representation as the goal state of affairs. Even in this limited scheme, outcome information can be useful, given some experience, for construing later actions of Agents that are directed to the same kind of goal, even when the intended outcome is not achieved.

System₂: Agents and Attitudes

ToMM *system₂* begins to develop last, during the second year of life. Perhaps the clearest early sign of the employment of the M-representation is the ability to pretend and understand pretense in others (Leslie, 1987). This emerges between 18 and 24 months. During this period, infants become able to construe the behavior of other Agents as relating to fictional states of affairs, specifically, as issuing from the attitude of pretending the truth of a proposition that describes a fictional state of affairs. For example, a mother's actual behavior of talking to a banana can be understood by constructing the M-representation, **mother pretends (of) the banana** (that it is true that) **"it is a telephone."** This links her behavior, via an attitude, to a fiction. For fuller discussion see Leslie (1987), Leslie and Thaiss (1992) and Leslie and Roth (in press).

Shared pretense can be properly regarded as an example of intentional communication (Leslie & Happé, 1989). What is particularly interesting about this communication is that it forces the child to compute *speaker's meaning* in Grice's (1957) sense. Thus, mother continues pretending and says, "The telephone is ringing. It's for you." She hands the child the banana. To comprehend this otherwise bizarre behavior, the child must not construe mother's words simply in terms of their linguistic meaning. She must also compute what mother intends them to mean on this occasion. In this example, "telephone" is intended to refer to the banana whereas "is ringing" is intended as a predicate true not directly of the remarkably silent banana but only of the banana via its pretend identity as a telephone. If the child does not compute speaker's meaning in relation to speaker's mental state (i.e., speaker pretends that . . .), she will fail to comprehend mother's actions, linguistic and otherwise.

Before the emergence of pretense, however, from around 12 months onward, the infant already communicates informatively with other Agents and understands *some* of the informative communications other Agents direct at him or her. These new communications go beyond the "instrumental" request and other earlier instrumental communicative behaviors of the first year that are under the control of $system_1$ (and possibly, in certain cases, of $system_0$ [see Note 11]). For example, the infant begins to understand informative pointing gestures around 14 months (Blake, McConnell, Horton, & Benson, 1992; Butterworth, 1991). Informative *showing* also typically makes its appearance early in the second year along with verbal communication.

There are a number of quite tricky questions that this brisk summary skips over. For example, what is the relation between linguistic abilities and **ToMM**? My assumption is that structural linguistic knowledge and language processing mechanisms are essentially independent of **ToMM**. **ToMM**'s development may impact, however, on communicative language use.

Another set of questions concerns the development of attention to Agents, joint attention with Agents and gestures, such as pointing and informative showing, directed to Agents. In one guise, **ToBy** and **ToMM**'s sub-systems form a hierarchy of control mechanisms governing attention and responsiveness to Agents. The critical point in understanding the development of attention to Agents, joint attention, and social responsiveness over the first two years is how these hierarchical control mechanisms develop. A given response may have different significance depending upon its controlling mechanism. For example, though we begin to smile after the first few weeks of life and continue smiling (on and off) for the rest of our lives, *what* we are smiling *at* changes drastically with development. The 1-week-old smiles only when asleep, the awake 6-week-old smiles at high-contrast stimuli, months later the infant will direct smiles at familiar animated faces but not at other high-contrast stimuli, and still later when sharing pretense, and so on. The development of "the smile response" is really the development of its controlling mechanisms. Similar considerations no doubt hold for other social responses such as pointing, showing, vocalizing, joint attention, and so forth. One way to study these questions is to examine those tragic cases where brain growth proceeds abnormally as in childhood autism. Some of these issues are explored at greater length in Leslie and Roth (1993).

In general, the developments in relation to messages and communication discussed in this section are indicative of the 1-year-old's new approach to Agents as possessors, transmitters, and recipients of *information*. Viewing Agents as transmitters of information, and not just FORCE, heralds the beginnings of the capacity to solve the problems created by the fact that in the real world Agents' behavior is determined by cognitive properties. The solution to this problem hinges on understanding how *meaning* enters into the causation of behavior. The social intelligence that now dominates this planet is the result of the evolution of neural mechanisms that rapidly find this solution.

Summary

I have presented a three-level theory of our understanding of Agency. Each of these levels corresponds to an information processing subsystem specialized for making certain kinds of information explicit. Each subsystem attends to one of the three classes of properties that distinguish Agents from non-Agents. These classes are: The behavior of Agents reflects the mechanical property of having an internal source of energy; the behavior of Agents reflects the actional property of pursuing goals and perceiving the environment; and finally, the behavior of Agents is determined by cognitive properties. It seems likely, given the distinctive computational demands of tracking the world at each of these levels, that correspondingly distinct devices are required in cognitive architecture. Agency as a domain of knowledge, then, has a complex structure. Understanding conceptual development in this domain requires understanding how this structure reflects core architecture – those aspects of the organization of human information processing that form the basis for development rather than its outcome.

Notes

1. I hope the reader will simply sound out these acronyms like a name rather than internally spell out what they stand for every time they are read. This way they will come to sound like old friends.

2. One possibility is that **ToBy**'s initial notion of object is parallel to the notion of an "object file" (Kahneman & Treisman, 1984), that is, a spatiotemporally continuous entity none of whose properties, such as size or shape, are considered critical, or even relevant, for determining its identity. The "file" itself is what allows the object to be referred to. The various properties that might be associated with the object are gathered together and "held" in the file but are regarded as accidental to the identity of the object. The idea is like "rigid designation" (Kripke, 1972): referring to *this* thing whatever it is. Such a parallel would have to be qualified so that **ToBy**'s object files applied only to three-dimensional

objects. However, **ToBy** may employ some initial idea of object type and/or be ready to assign objects to kinds. In this case, **ToBy** might try to decide questions of identity with respect to kind. In the case of object files the question is, Is this the same individual thing (whatever it may be)? versus, in the case of object kinds, Is this the same one of a given kind? I leave this as an open empirical question about which we know very little from studying infants, though I will suggest below that there is at least one object kind infants know about early on (viz., hands).

3. Schlottmann and Shanks (1992) provide further evidence for a Michotte module in adults. They forced their subjects to attend to the predictive relationship between the movements of the objects in collision events. The contingency of the second movement on the first was varied and subjects' predictive judgments showed they were sensitive to the degree of contingency. However, contingency had no effect whatsoever on their "causal perception" of single launching events. The illusion of a mechanical cause was highly sensitive to *contiguity* whereas predictive judgments were much less so. Schlottmann and Shanks take the dissociation between contiguity and contingency as support for "a distinct mechanism of causal perception" (p. 340). In terms of **ToBy**, what determines judgments of mechanical cause in collision events is how well the conditions for the transmission of FORCE have been met, not the statistics of the event set. Use of statistical relations in judgments of cause probably assumes importance to the extent that the analysis of mechanism becomes more difficult, less visible, and less complete.

4. So far as I can see, nothing of what I say hinges on the details of Marr's "three-dimensional model" account of object recognition; other accounts in the same general class, such as Biederman's (1987) theory of "geons," are equally compatible.

5. I use the term *spatiotemporal* in preference to Mandler's use of the term *spatial* since this better expresses the importance of motion in her account.

6. One might gain the impression from reading Mandler (1992) that image schemas abstract over shape and volume such that what is made explicit is a two-dimensional spatial arrangement, so that containment is represented as an x inside a circle. However, Mandler's intention is that the schema be a kind of three-dimensional model of the entity and container. In either case, whatever spatial properties of the INSIDE relation an image schema captures, it is only in the case of three-dimensional objects that INSIDE becomes mechanical containment. That is, when three-dimensional objects are involved, the spatial aspect of containment can take on mechanical significance and be consequential: The contained object cannot escape by passing through the walls of the container; thus when the container is moved it will transport the contained object to whichever location the container is moved; the object can however enter and escape through an aperture in the container, if certain metrical conditions are met, and so forth. These mechanical consequences follow from (1) the spatial relation, INSIDE, *together with* (2) certain assumptions drawn from the theory of object contact mechanics, such as solidity and transmission of FORCE (in this case, entrainment or transport). Infants around 6 months, perhaps earlier, already appreciate such mechanical containment (Leslie & DasGupta, 1991). But in the spatial image schema these mechanical properties are not made explicit, in Marr's

sense. Even if the image schema does depict a three-dimensional relationship over time, it still fails to make the mechanical relationships explicit. To achieve this, mechanical properties, such as solidity and transmission of FORCE, would have to be added on to the image. The image schema is therefore unlikely to be the primary basis for conceptual development.

7. Machines do not pose much of a problem for **ToBy**. However, given that they could not have been taken into account during evolution, they might well have been a problem. For example, a robot will be considered an Agent under this scheme, though we would not consider it animate. My assumption, you will recall, is that **ToBy** knows nothing of animateness. Automobiles might appear to be Agents to the extent that they keep changing motion state (but the first time an infant saw a car simply rush past, she might assume that something external has propelled it, like a giant billiard ball). On the other hand, an indistinct blob rushing about, such as a housefly, will usually (and correctly) appear to be an Agent without necessarily appearing to be animate. Separating Agency from animateness (by evolving a modular organization) has had beneficial side-effects, allowing us to apply without obstacle our commonsense understanding of Agency (1) to inanimates and (2) without having to know whether or not something is animate.

   Picking out an object as an Agent has a cascade of effects. As we shall see later in this chapter, to the extent we think something is an Agent, we are willing to try to attribute goals to its behavior, and to the extent we are able to attribute goals to the Agent, we are willing to attribute propositional attitudes to explain, predict, and interpret that behavior. For example, houseflies try to get out through windows because they don't *know* there's glass in the way.

8. Vaina (1983), working within a similar framework to that adopted here, outlines a theory of the "Functional" representation. This deals with the representation of the functional properties of objects such as their "throwability," "pick-upableness," and so on. Although Vaina is careful in her consideration of the kinds of visual information made explicit prior to and forming the input to the computation of the Functional representation, in my view her theory overlooks or gives insufficient weight to two critical things. The first is the necessity to make explicit the mechanical properties of objects and scenarios. The second is to make explicit the actional properties of Agents (see the discussion in the following sections). The functional properties of objects are determined in part by their mechanical properties and beyond this by the kinds of uses Agents make of them in pursuing goals.

9. This makes a nice phrase but I intend to subsume perception under it too. Actually, only perception in a limited sense is subsumed. For example, the relation of "seeing x" is subsumed but not the relation of "seeing that p." The latter falls under Agent and Attitude.

10. Strictly speaking, not *all* the behavior of an Agent is determined by cognitive properties. Mechanical behavior, like being run down by a bus, is not so determined. The *actions* of Agents are determined by cognitive properties.

11. To avoid misunderstanding I should say that neither **ToMM** alone nor **ToMM** and **ToBy** together exhaust social intelligence. For example, mechanisms of face recognition lie outside the systems discussed here but clearly form part of the capacity for social responsiveness. It seems highly likely that such low-level

mechanisms have inputs into **ToMM**. For this reason one might lump together such mechanisms under the heading of *system₀*. There are many interesting possibilities in this regard but I shall not pursue them here.

12.   Although the particular ages I mention are not critical for the theory, they seem to me as a matter of fact to be approximately right.

References

Abravanel, E., & Gingold, H. (1985). Learning via observation during the second year of life. *Developmental Psychology, 218*, 614–623.

Anderson, J. R. (1990). *The adaptive character of thought*. Hillsdale, NJ: Erlbaum.

Baillargeon, R. (1986). Representing the existence and the location of hidden objects: Object permanence in 6- and 8-month-old infants. *Cognition, 23*, 21–41.

Baillargeon, R. (1991a). Infant's understanding of the physical world. Paper presented to symposium, "Infants' reasoning about spatial relationships," SRCD Biennial Conference, Seattle, April 1991.

Baillargeon, R. (1991b). The object concept revisited: New directions in the investigation of infants' physical knowledge. In H. W. Reese (Ed.), *Advances in Child Development and Behavior, Vol. 23*. New York: Academic Press.

Baillargeon, R., Spelke, E. S., & Wasserman, S. (1985). Object permanence in five-month-old infants. *Cognition, 20*, 191–208.

Bates, E., Benigni, L., Bretherton, I., Camaioni, L., & Volterra, V. (1979). *The emergence of symbols: Cognition and communication in infancy*. New York: Academic Press.

Biederman, I. (1987). Recognition-by-components: A theory of human image understanding. *Psychological Review, 94*, 115–147.

Blake, J., McConnell, S., Horton, G., & Benson, N. (1992). The gestural repertoire and its evolution over the second year. *Early Development and Parenting, 1*, 127–136.

Bruner, J. S. (1976). From communication to language – a psychological perspective. *Cognition, 3*, 255–287.

Butterworth, G. (1991). The ontogeny and phylogeny of joint visual attention. In A. Whitten (Ed.), *Natural theories of mind: Evolution, development, and simulation of everyday mind reading*. Oxford: Basil Blackwell.

Carey, S. (1985). *Conceptual change in childhood*. Cambridge, MA: MIT Press.

Choi, S., & Bowerman, M. (1991). Learning to express motion events in English and Korean: The influence of language-specific lexicalization patterns. *Cognition, 41*, 83–121.

Chomsky, N. A. (1975). *Reflections on language*. New York: Random House.

Chomsky, N. A. (1986). *Knowledge of language: Its nature, origin, and use*. New York: Praeger.

Dennett, D. C., & Haugeland, J. C. (1987). Intentionality. In R. L. Gregory (Ed.), *The Oxford companion to the mind* (pp. 383–386). Oxford: Oxford University Press.

Diamond, A. (1988). Differences between adult and infant cognition: Is the crucial variable presence or absence of language? In L. Weiskrantz (Ed.), *Thought without language* (pp. 335–370). Oxford: Oxford Science Publications.

Diamond, R., & Carey, S. (1986). Why faces are and are not special: An effect of expertise. *Journal of Experimental Psychology: General, 115*, 107–117.

Ellis, H. D., & Young, A. W. (1989). Are faces special? In A. W. Young and H. D. Ellis (Eds.), *Handbook of research on face processing* (pp. 1–26). Amsterdam: Elsevier Science Publishers.

Fodor, J. A. (1983). *Modularity of mind.* Cambridge, MA: MIT Press.

Gelman, R. (1990). First principles organize attention to and learning about relevant data: Number and the animate-inanimate distinction. *Cognitive Science, 14,* 79–106.

Grice, H. P. (1957). Meaning. *Philosophical Review, 66,* 377–388.

Hume, D. (1740). *A treatise of human nature.* London: Clarendon Press.

Johnson, M. H., & Morton, J. (1991). *Biology and cognitive development.* Oxford: Blackwell.

Kahneman, D., & Treisman, A. (1984). Changing views of attention and automaticity. In R. Parasuraman and D. R. Davies (Eds.), *Varieties of attention* (pp. 29–61). New York: Academic Press.

Kripke, S. A. (1972). Naming and necessity. In D. Davidson and G. Harman (Eds.), *Semantics of natural language* (253–355). Dordrecht: Reidel.

Leslie, A. M. (1982). The perception of causality in infants. *Perception, 11,* 173–186.

Leslie, A. M. (1984a). Infant perception of a manual pick-up event. *British Journal of Developmental Psychology, 2,* 19–32.

Leslie, A. M. (1984b). Spatiotemporal continuity and the perception of causality in infants. *Perception, 13,* 287–305.

Leslie, A. M. (1987). Pretense and representation: The origins of "theory of mind." *Psychological Review, 94,* 412–426.

Leslie, A. M. (1988). The necessity of illusion: Perception and thought in infancy. In L. Weiskrantz (Ed.), *Thought without language* (pp. 185–210). Oxford: Oxford Science Publications.

Leslie, A. M. (unpublished). Further observations on the Pulfrich double pendulum illusion. MRC Cognitive Development Unit, University of London.

Leslie, A. M., & DasGupta, P. (1991). Infants' understanding of a hidden mechanism: Invisible displacement. Paper presented at symposium on "Infants' reasoning about spatial relationships," SRCD Biennial Conference, Seattle, April 1991.

Leslie, A. M., & Happé, F. (1989). Autism and ostensive communication: The relevance of metarepresentation. *Development and Psychopathology, 1,* 205–212.

Leslie, A. M., & Keeble, S. (1987). Do six-month-old infants perceive causality? *Cognition, 25,* 265–288.

Leslie, A. M., & Roth, D. (1993). What autism teaches us about metarepresentation. In S. Baron-Cohen, H. Tager-Flusberg, and D. Cohen (Eds.), *Understanding other minds: Perspectives from autism* (pp. 83–111). New York: Oxford University Press.

Leslie, A. M., & Thaiss, L. (1992). Domain specificity in conceptual development: Neuropsychological evidence from autism. *Cognition, 43,* 225–251.

Livingstone, M. S., & Hubel, D. H. (1988). Segregation of form, color, movement, and depth: Anatomy, physiology, and perception. *Science, 240,* 740–749.

Mandler, J. M. (1992). How to build a baby, II: Conceptual primitives. *Psychological Review, 99,* 587–604.

Marr, D. (1982). *Vision.* San Francisco: W. H. Freeman & Co.

Marr, D., & Nishihara, H. K. (1978). Representation and recognition of the spatial organization of three-dimensional shapes. *Proceedings of the Royal Society of London*, B, *200*, 187–217.

Michotte, A. (1963). *The perception of causality*. Andover: Methuen.

Michotte, A., & Thinès, G. (1963). La causalite perceptive. *Journal de Psychologie Normale et Pathologique*, *60*, 9–36. Translated by G. Thines, A. Costall, and G. Butterworth in G. Thines, A. Costall, and G. Butterworth (Eds.), *Michotte's experimental phenomenology of perception* (pp. 66–87). Hillsdale, NJ: Erlbaum. (1991).

Piaget, J. (1953). *The origins of intelligence in the child*. London: Routledge and Kegan Paul.

Piaget, J. (1955). *The child's construction of reality*. London: Routledge and Kegan Paul.

Pinker, S. (1989). *Learnability and cognition: The acquisition of argument structure*. Cambridge, MA: MIT Press.

Pinker, S., & Bloom, P. (1990). Natural language and natural selection. *Behavioral and Brain Sciences*, *13*, 707–784.

Premack, D. (1990). The infant's theory of self-propelled objects. *Cognition*, *36*, 1–16.

Schlottman, A., & Shanks, D. R. (1992). Evidence for a distinction between judged and perceived causality. *Quarterly Journal of Experimental Psychology*, *44*, 321–342.

Shultz, T. R. (1982). Rules of causal attribution. *Monographs of the Society for Research in Child Development*, *47*, No. 1.

Spelke, E. (1988). Where perceiving ends and thinking begins: The apprehension of objects in infancy. In A. Yonas (Ed.), *Perceptual development in infancy. Minnesota Symposium on Child Psychology* (pp. 191–234). Vol. 20. Hillsdale, NJ: Erlbaum.

Spelke, E. S. (1990). Principles of object perception. *Cognitive Science*, *14*, 29–56.

Streri, A., & Spelke, E. (1988). Haptic perception of objects in infancy. *Cognitive Psychology*, *20*, 1–23.

Talmy, L. (1988). Force dynamics in language and cognition. *Cognitive Science*, *12*, 49–100.

Tanaka, J. W., & Farah, M. J. (1991). Second-order relational properties and the inversion effect: Testing a theory of face perception. *Perception & Psychophysics*, *50*, 367–372.

Treisman, A. (1988). Features and objects: The fourteenth Bartlett Memorial Lecture. *Quarterly Journal of Experimental Psychology*, *40*, 201–237.

Vaina, L. (1983). From shapes and movements to objects and actions. *Synthese*, *54*, 3–36.

Van Essen, D. C. (1985). Functional organization of primate visual cortex. In A. Peters and E. G. Jones (Eds.), *Cerebral cortex* (Vol. 3) (pp. 259–329). New York: Plenum.

Warrington, E. K., & Taylor, A. M. (1978). Two categorical stages of object recognition. *Perception*, *7*, 695–705.

Warrington, E. K., & James, M. (1986). Visual object recognition in patients with right-hemisphere lesions: Axes or features? *Perception*, *15*, 355–366.

Wellman, H. M. (1990). *The child's theory of mind*. Cambridge, MA: MIT Press.

6   Moral belief: Form versus content

David Premack and Ann James Premack

This is a two-part chapter, the first part of which attributes a moral domain to the infant and presents a model of the domain; and the second part of which shows how the primitives of the domain provide an invariant form in which to express the diverse moral beliefs of different cultures.

Part I: Infant's model

The subject matter of morality is social behavior, the relation among individuals, ultimately how one individual treats another. Human social competence is highly developed, and the ability to make moral judgments about social behavior is part of the competence. Some concepts of moral judgment are not unique, but are shared. For instance, the attribution of intention, which is central to morality, is a fundamental component of theory of mind (Leslie, 1987; Premack & Woodruff, 1978; Wellman, 1990; Wimmer & Perner, 1983), while aesthetics, which enters into moral judgment, is a hidden yet significant component of pedagogy (Premack, 1984, 1991). However, morality is not simply constructed from pieces of other social competences.

This piece began in Israel in 1978, at the Van Leer Jerusalem Institute, where we spent 4 months with a small group, most of them specialists in moral development. Those of us who were nonspecialists listened to the weekly presentations of the specialists with less than total pleasure. The work, though serious, lacked simplicity, so much so that one of us was led to try his own hand, and wrote a piece called "The sheep dog as a model of morality." It succeeded in its secondary purpose, annoying the specialists, but less in its primary one, finding simple principles from which to derive the complexity of moral behavior. This piece, based on lectures to the Collège de France, Paris, 1991, is an improvement on the first one, though less of one than we would have wished. Several people helped with this chapter. Jonathan Bennett read Part I; his continuing comments are a contribution to one's education. John Smith and Hans Kummer reassured us on an evolutionary point most convincingly (by independently agreeing with one another!). Finally, we are indebted to the editorial group that produced this book, in particular Susan Gelman and Larry Hirschfeld, not only for comments but for their kindness in sending relevant articles from Ann Arbor to Paris.

149

Judgments concerning the "rightness" or "wrongness" of acts, an individual's "rights" and "responsibilities," the concept of "ought," are sui generis, and cannot be derived from concepts belonging to other parts of social competence.

What is the source of these distinctly moral concepts, of "right," "wrong," "ought," "responsibility," and the like? Are they irreducible primitives, or can we find their origin in other sources? In this chapter, we trace their origin to "knowledge" or expectancies of the human infant, and present a model that attributes to the infant capacities that concern what *one individual expects of another* – how the concepts of *power, group,* and *possession* affect those expectancies. While one cannot simply derive traditional moral primitives from the model, the expectancies that the model assigns to the infant place the primitives in a new light.

Criteria for evaluating moral acts

An infant distinguishes objects that move only when acted upon by another object from those that are (or appear to be) self-propelled. When shown an object that starts and stops its own motion, the infant interprets the object as intentional; we have found this with 3-year-old children (Dasser, Ulbaek, & Premack, 1989), and propose that it will also be found with infants (Premack, 1990). This distinction is fundamental for our purposes because morality is a property of intentional objects.

When two intentional objects interact in an appropriate manner, the infant attributes to the initiator of the action an intention to affect the recipient either positively or negatively. What criterion does the infant use to distinguish a positive from a negative act?

Human adults make this distinction on the basis of at least three criteria, two of which are available to the infant. The simplest is based on intensity of motion. Soft or weak motions are coded positive, hard or strong ones negative, so that one object gently rubbing another will be coded a positive act, striking another a negative. There is a correspondence between this criterion of the infant's and that of simple organisms. Invertebrates approach weak and avoid strong stimuli.

The older infant will have, in addition to intensity of motion, the criterion of helping and hurting. These criteria derive from the further concepts of goal, liberty, and aesthetics; of these goal is the most fundamental. Humans are extremely predisposed to "see" goal-directed action; they "see" it on the slightest provocation. In fact, all they require in order to perceive goal-directed action is an object they consider to be intentional, directing all its action at the same item, be the item a location, or another object that is either intentional or not.

For instance, if one places a curved line on a computer screen and then "moves" an abstract object – for example, a filled circle – some distance up the line, back down the line, up again, a human observer will attribute a goal to the object – that of "trying to get up the incline." Not in any way special, this example is one of indeterminately many, all of which illustrate the extreme simplicity of the stimulus conditions leading humans to attribute goal. Here is another example of equal simplicity.

Place a broken vertical line on the screen, and "move" an abstract object up toward the break in the line, down, up again; the human observer will attribute to the object the goal of "trying to pass through the aperture."

Informally, we can say that whenever an object, perceived to be intentional, persistently directs its actions toward a single item, a human observer attributes a goal to the object. From this informal description, we can then extract three features essential to the attribution of goal.

First, all of the object's actions must be directed at the same item – the top of a line, an aperture, another object, and so forth.

Second, the object must repeat its action; success must not be achieved by a single act. In the present examples, one ascent or upward movement did not bring the object to the top of the "hill," or allow it to pass through the aperture. The object "failed" and then "tried" again. Ironically, success contributes little to the impression of goal-directedness; it is failure, or the repeated attempt to overcome failure, that leads to the attribution of goal.

Third, the object's repeated acts must not be repeated perfectly. The series of acts directed at the curved and broken lines were not identical; there was variation in the height to which the objects ascended, the speed at which they moved, and/or in other parameters of the movement. Actually, the need for variability pertains less to the attribution of goal than to that of intentionality. Even though an object starts and stops its own motion – thus leading to the attribution of intentionality – if it starts and stops (or subsequently moves) in an invariant manner, it will lose this attribution. Repetition is a threat to the attribution of intentionality; yet, repetition is essential for the attribution of goal. To retain both the attribution of intentionality and of goal, repetition must be accompanied by variability.

Basically, the attribution of goal depends on a relation between an intentional object and a target item, the curved line in one example, broken line in the other. An impressive demonstration of this point can be made simply by removing the target items. If we eliminate these items, while at the same time retaining the exact prior movement of the objects, we will lose the attribution of goal. When seen on an empty screen, these objects, though duplicating their former motion, will no longer appear goal-directed. For the attribution of goal does not depend on an object's motion alone, but on its motion relative to a target item. This is to say also that if we change the location of the lines, so that the objects, while moving as before, no longer now move relative to the lines, we again lose the attribution of goal. The attribution of goal depends on a distinctive relation between an intentional object and a target item.

Even as we can eliminate the attribution of goal by removing a target item, so can we create the attribution of goal by introducing a target item. For instance, an intentional object that is shown "bouncing" up and down in the same location appears to be "playful" rather than goal directed. If, however, a vertical line is placed next to the bouncing object, the line will immediately become a barrier and the object will be seen as "trying to get over it." Notice that the effect of the relation between intentional object and target item is bidirectional. Adding the "targets" transforms the objects, changing them from playful to goal-directed; but adding the intentional objects transforms the lines, changing them into targets – a curved line into a hill, a broken one into a portal, and a vertical one into a barrier.

In all three of our examples, gravity undoubtedly plays a role in the attribution of goal. Why does the intentional object not immediately ascend the hill, rise to the height of the aperture, or surmount the barrier? Why does it rise part way but then fall back? One could explain this by attributing illness, an enfeebled condition, to the intentional objects, but a more probable inference is gravity. It is so for an adult observer; is it also a probable inference for an infant? Unfortunately, this is one of many questions that remain to be answered.

Attributing a goal to one object sets the stage for attributing helping or hurting to a second object. For the latter can be perceived as either assisting or hindering the former in its attempt to attain its goal. For instance, once an object is perceived as "trying to climb a hill," a second intentional object can be introduced that "pushes" the first one either up or down "the hill." We can arrange for the second object to resemble the first one in all critical respects.

Like the first, it engages in action directed at a specific target. In this case not a location – the top of a hill or a portal – but directed toward the other object; it is not immediately successful. It "tries" repeatedly (either to aid or hinder the first object), varying its actions somewhat, changing from "try" to "try." Now, the second object will be perceived too as having a goal, that of helping or hurting the first object. Humans attribute "helping" and "hurting" – second-order goals – under stimulus conditions as simple as those for which they attribute first-order goals. Here is another example of equal simplicity.

An object perceived as "trying to pass through the aperture" can be helped or hindered by a second object that "pushes" it "through" or "away from" the aperture. In this case, as in all others, it is the prior attribution of goal to one object that sets the stage for attributing the goal of helping or hurting to a second object. From the moment a goal is attributed to an object, helping and hurting loom as major possibilities.

Classically, "failure" attends the attribution of goals – higher order no less than first order – yet it may not be a necessary condition for the attribution of goal. Suppose an intentional object, offered a choice among five alternatives, chooses one consistently. Although each of its choices meets with perfect success (there is no "failure" or "trying" of any kind) goal would nonetheless be attributed. While failure, and the repeated attempt to overcome may undeniably be the most common condition for the attribution of goal, successful, consistent choice among alternatives may also lead to the attribution of goal.

Consider now some problems introduced by higher-order helping or hurting. Suppose that the goal sought by A is that of hurting B. C, in assisting A to achieve such a goal, is acting positively with respect to A, but not with respect to B; in fact C is contributing to the hurt done B.

If an intentional object hurts one party while helping another how do we code the net value of this act? Is it positive? or negative? Were we to distinguish degrees of positive or negative, then some combinations of positive and negative acts would have a net positive value. Others a net negative. At the moment, unfortunately, we have no criteria for distinguishing one magnitude of positive (or negative) from another.

We can adopt a system according to which the net value of an act is decided by the value of the first act in a chain that has value. We make this qualification because, of course, not all acts have value; for instance object A's attempt to climb a hill has no value. Only acts that involve a relation between intentional objects have value. But, suppose object B acts to hinder A's attempt to climb the hill – an uncomplicated negative act – and further, that C acts to help B – by itself a positive act. In this circumstance, however, B and C act negatively, B by hurting A, and C by helping B do so. Thus, though C's act is one of helping, it is nonetheless judged negative, because the act it facilitates is both a negative and the first act in the chain to have a value. In this circumstance, C could act positively if it were to hurt B rather than help it. In hindering B from hurting A, C's act would be judged positive.

Goal is the principal source for the attribution of helping and hurting; liberty and aesthetics, to which we turn now, are lesser sources for this same attribution. Though lesser, each is of interest because of the special twist it gives to the conditions that lead humans to attribute helping or hurting.

An infant's use of liberty can be seen in the following example: When shown two bouncing objects, one of which becomes trapped in a virtual hole, the infant will interpret the action of a second object that restores the motion of the first as helping, and code it positive.

This criterion is more complex than may appear because it assumes that the infant can judge what the object would have done had it not been trapped. Suppose the infant is shown one object stop the motion of another: Will it judge this positive or negative? If the object were left alone, would it have stopped or continued? If stopped, the action was a form of assistance, and would be judged positive; but if not, the action was an interference and would be judged negative. Judging whether the action of a second party helps or hinders the first party can be complex, suggesting that the infant's judgment may be imperfect and/or restricted to simple cases.

Now consider an example of aesthetics. We show an infant two balls; the one which bounces higher and faster than the other is preferred by the infant. The preferred ball now moves into the vicinity of the other ball and demonstrates its superior movement several times, as though offering an example. It even assists directly, placing itself below the lesser ball, lifting it, helping it to bounce higher. The infant will interpret the actions in both of these examples as helping, coding them positive. In this case, a positive action consists, not in helping an object maintain its liberty, but in assisting it to move from an existing to a preferred state.

A third level of value concerns characterological judgment, and while this level does not appear explicitly in the child until the seventh or eighth year (with the emergence of personality theory; see Chaplin, John, & Goldberg, 1988; Rholes & Ruble, 1984; but see Eder, 1989, for earlier precursors), it may have an implicit counterpart in the infant; a counterpart that could be detected by appropriate habituation/dishabituation tests. Value now concerns traits of persons, all of them bimodal variants of good/bad, such as kind/cruel, generous/stingy, friendly/hostile, and the like. These traits are assumed to be transsituational, that is, it is the character or essence of the person that is the source of the trait, not the environment in which he finds himself. Although empirically minded personality theorists vigorously dispute this claim (e.g., Mischel, 1968), the species-specific belief is, in fact, that personality traits are transsituational. Supposing the critics to be correct, and the species-specific belief to be false, what bearing would this have on the content of the belief? None. The content of the belief is not contingent on its truth value (see pp. 157–158 for full discussion of this point).

To return to the aesthetic concept of the older infant, there is an interesting relation between the judgment of character and evaluation of the face. People associate good character with beautiful face. Actually, not only face but also body, bodily movement, the whole physical person may be included in the association. Face has been singled out for research, perhaps justifiably because it is believed to be the most sensitive indicator of character. A great deal of research (much of it summarized in Berscheid & Walster, 1969; Dixon, Berscheid, & Walster, 1972) shows that people believe in "Schiller's thesis" (1882): Physical and spiritual beauty are one and the same. The antiquity of this thesis goes well beyond Schiller, of course, for he is merely a prominent advocate of a position espoused by the Greeks.

A recent finding that infants prefer attractive faces (chosen by adult judges) (Samuels & Ewy, 1985), offers a way of determining whether the belief in Schiller's thesis is learned or innate. If infants prefer not only attractive faces but also "attractive" behavior, can we assume that they will expect the two to go together? That is, if shown individuals with attractive faces who engage in negative behavior (or individuals with unattractive faces who engage in positive behavior), will the infant be surprised? More surprised than if shown cases in which there is agreement between the attractiveness of the face and of the behavior? Naturally, one wants to assure that the reaction is specific to disconfirmation of the expectancy that attractive faces and behavior go together; not simply part of a more general reaction to a discontinuity in preferred items, such as a preferred color occurring with a nonpreferred shape.

The power of possession

Normally, we speak of positive or negative acts only with regard to intentional objects. However, morality can be extended to nonintentional objects through the concept of possession. Intentional objects have the capacity to possess, and are seen "to possess" if they are connected to an object and if the two move together. Work by Kummer and Cords (1991) shows that monkeys define ownership on precisely these grounds. An object is considered to be possessed when it is connected to and moves with a monkey. Only when objects were both connected to and moved with a monkey did other monkeys refrain from attempting to take the object from its "owner." They treated such objects as though they were part of the monkey's body, in much the same way as they treated the monkey's arm or leg.

What Kummer and Cords failed to consider was the status of an *intentional* object that was connected to and moved with a monkey. The concept of possession is not restricted to nonintentional objects, of course. The human concept of slavery, for instance, shows that intentional objects can be possessed. This case is important because it demonstrates that possession is not determined merely by co-movement and connection, for when two intentional objects are connected and move together, which is the possessor?

In the latter case, a third factor, the power relation between the two objects, must be considered. Possession requires not only connection and co-movement, but also that the possessed object be less powerful than the possessor.

Power of an intentional object can be manifested in many ways, through size, strength, attractiveness, and so forth, ultimately, however, in its ability to control the movement of another. A decision as to which object is the more powerful must be made only when the possessed object is intentional, for a nonintentional object is incapable of controlling movement and is inescapably the weaker and always the object possessed.

Although the Kummer–Cords data indicate that monkeys need physical connection for the interpretation of possession, human infants probably do not. A physical connection between two objects, such as the cord that attached the object to a monkey, may make it easier to perceive that one object is controlled by the other, but it is not essential. It is the perception that the objects differ in power and one is controlling the other that leads the infant to interpret the relation between them as that of possession.

Ordinarily, acts upon nonintentional objects have no consequences for the infant – one can pound or "pet" an unintentional object but in neither case will the infant assign value to the action. Possession, however, changes the status of nonintentional objects. The infant will code acts upon such objects as positive or negative. In addition, it will expect acts upon these objects to be reciprocated. The infant expects the owner to reciprocate acts upon its possessions in the same degree that it reciprocates acts upon itself.

With regard to the possession of intentional objects, the most common example is, of course, not a slave but a child. The relation between parent and child offers a perfect example of possession. When a child and parent move together, the parent carries the child, leads it by the hand, directs it verbally, one way or another controlling its movement.

What expectancies does the infant have with respect to intentional objects like a child? For instance, does it expect a "child," that is, a possessed intentional object, to reciprocate acts performed upon it by its "parent"? Interestingly, in most societies children are spared the burden of reciprocating their parents' positive acts, while they are at the same time denied the right of reciprocating their parents' negative acts. Thus, a child is not expected to feed the parent in return for the food the parent provided, nor to caress or even thank the parent. At the same time, however, if the parent spanks the child, the child is not allowed to hit back. This combination – no obligation to reciprocate positive acts and no right to reciprocate negative ones – is sufficiently widespread in human cultures to raise the question of whether the combination is part of the infant's expectancies. Does the infant expect to see this pattern of reciprocation in all possessed intentional objects? To answer this question we must test the infant, and fortunately, it is now clear how this can be done. Possession is an important primitive because it has the power to bring into the moral domain objects that ordinarily lie outside it. Once value is assigned to actions, reciprocation follows, and in many respects it is reciprocation that is the crux of morality.

The group: A relation among intentional objects

The concept of group, like that of possession, concerns the relation among objects, but differs in that all of the objects in a group are intentional. Group is the co-movement of objects of equal power. In group, no object controls the movement of the other. An infant will interpret as a group intentional objects of equal size and strength that move together. Group is a relation among equals as possession is a relation among unequals. There is co-movement in both cases, but power is distributed differently among the co-moving elements; equally in the case of group, unequally in the case of possession.

The predilection to bring physically similar objects together, which is found even in the 10-month-old child (Sugarman, 1983), takes an earlier form in the infant, for the infant expects physically alike intentional objects to form groups, and physically unlike ones, not to. When shown a set of, for instance, white intentional objects, an infant will expect them to cohere and move together; it will have the same expectation for a set of black intentional objects; but not for a mixture of white and black objects. However, if the infant is shown that the mixture of black and white objects coheres and moves together, it will interpret them as a group. Although the infant expects like objects to "flock together," when shown the uncoerced co-movement of unlike objects, the infant accepts them as a group in the same degree that it accepts any other. The criteria of uncoerced co-movement takes precedence over physical similarity.

The concept of group entails some extremely powerful consequences. First, the infant expects group members to share reciprocation, that is, it expects each group member to reciprocate acts perpetrated upon other group members. For instance, when the infant observes object C act positively (negatively) on object B, it expects not only B, but also A, B's co-group member, to act positively (negatively) on C.

Second, the infant expects group members to act alike. This represents an extension on the infant's normal inductive assumptions. Even as the infant expects the same individual to repeat itself in some degree, so the infant expects group members to repeat one another in some degree. For instance, the infant's normal inductive assumptions may take this form: When object A acts positively on B some number of times, the infant expects object A to continue doing so. The infant extends this assumption to members of a group. Having perceived one group member to act positively on B some number of times, it expects other group members to do the same. In effect, the infant treats different group members as though they were the same "individual" acting at different times; it equates multiple tokens of a type (group members) with multiple instances of a token (repeated instances of the individual).

Third, the infant expects group members to act positively toward one another. This positive expectation for group members contrasts with an infant's neutral expectations for interactions between unattached intentional objects. As regards the latter, the infant has no expectations, neither positive nor negative.

Evolution and false beliefs

Is the widespread belief in Schiller's thesis, that physical and spiritual beauty are the same, an embarrassment to evolutionary theory? It is probable that this belief is false. Is evolutionary theory compatible with false beliefs? Only a Panglossian distortion of evolutionary theory could suggest that it is not. Evolution does not require a surviving alternative to be ideal, but only that it be the best of the alternatives available at the time. More generally, evolution does not require a cost/benefit analysis to show that, for surviving traits benefits invariably exceed costs. On the contrary, costs may well exceed benefits in a surviving trait, but less so than for traits that did not survive. Hence, certain of the "innate" beliefs of humans may indeed be false, but better than other beliefs available at the time. Finally, it is the mechanism on which beliefs depend – and not the beliefs themselves – that evolve.

Is "ought" an innate concept?

Philosophical treatments of morality distinguish prescriptive statements, and attribute their special status to the concept of "ought," which is presented as an irreducible primitive embodying the fundamental idea of morality. From a psychological point of view there is no reason to dispute the distinction between prescriptive and ordinary statements; there is, however, reason to question the irreducibility of ought. A psychologist wishing to understand the nature of would-be primitives (ought no less than any other), can pursue the goal by asking the following questions:

What is the evidence for the concept of ought, that is, what distinguishes the behavior of an individual who has this concept? When does such behavior first appear in the infant or child, what is the behavior's developmental course, and on what does development depend? If comparable behavior is found in nonhuman species, how does it differ from that found in the human? A psychologist concerned with the topic of morality can reasonably ask these questions without malice, that is, with no intention of diminishing the claim that the focal concept of morality is ought.

While the present list of primitives does not itself contribute to the explication of ought, it is important to note that most of the infant's primitives take the logical form of an expectancy, and it is the examination of the basic nature of an expectancy that will contribute to the explication of ought. An expectancy takes this form: "If an antecedent is satisfied, the individual expects that a consequent will follow." This can be given the quality of ought or "should" by reading, not that the "consequent *will* follow," but rather that it "*should* or *ought* to follow."

This strong reading is not equally appropriate for all expectancies, however. As an example, the expectancies to which should or ought do *not* apply are those that depend entirely on experience. An individual who expects the written sequence, say, 8, 12, 19 does so simply because he experienced this sequence some number of times. If the sequence is written 8, 12, 11, the individual will show evidence of his original expectancy by dishabituation, that is, by looking longer at the sequence than if it had not been changed.

Expectancies of this kind are not resistant to change. They can be altered by simply varying the individual's experience. The expectancy 8, 12, 19 can be converted into a host of alternatives – 8, 11, 9; 8, 19, 12; and so on – by simply changing the sequence given the individual. Neither "*ought* nor *should* follow" are proper for expectancies of this kind. For expectancies that owe their existence entirely to the experience of an individual and are consummately subject to change, the consequent "*will* follow" is the only appropriate reading.

There is, however, another kind of expectancy that is neither based on individual experience nor is it readily subject to change. Indeed, this kind of expectancy is so resistant to change, it might well be considered incorrigible. According to the model, such an example is the infant's expectancy that reciprocation will preserve valence. Another is the infant's expectancy that one solid object will obstruct the passage of another (Baillargeon, Spelke, & Wasserman, 1985).

This kind of expectancy, unlike the first, cannot be altered by a simple change in an individual's experience. That is, if shown one solid object apparently pass through another, an infant would not abandon the expectancy of the impermeability of solid objects. Though if shown, say, a small red object pass through a large green one, looking time would ultimately decline, the infant would not abandon the belief that solid objects cannot pass through one another. And when shown a new circumstance it would revert to its original expectancy.

Could infants actually learn arbitrary boundary conditions of their general expectancies, for example, learn that small red objects *can* pass through large green ones? Could they learn this while at the same time retaining their original expectancy? An untested question. Whether they could or not, it is certain that their original expectancies would remain intact. While chemical or surgical intervention might change such an expectancy, experience alone could not.

Expectancies of this kind, that are both innate and impervious to change by experience, are those for which ought or should are appropriate substitutes for "will." In such cases one can properly say, "when A acts positively on B, B *should* act positively on A"; or "when two solid objects meet, neither *should* pass through the other."

Will the infant respond differently to the disconfirmation of an expectancy that is based merely on experience rather than to disconfirmation based on an innate factor? Perhaps it will. Although, unfortunately, it is not possible to find actual comparisons of infants' reactions under the two conditions, one expects a stronger reaction in one case than the other; for example, surprise rather than mere dishabituation or increased looking time.

However, despite the infant's (possible) distinctive reaction to disconfirmation of the innate expectancy, problems remain for the illumination of ought. If ought is sui generis, then disconfirmation of an expectancy with a moral content should differ from one with merely a physical content. Yet, such a result is doubtful. The infant's expectancy concerning reciprocation and the preservation of value may be said to have a "moral" content, whereas its expectancy concerning the impermeability of solid objects may be said to have a "physical" content. Nevertheless, we expect the infant's reaction to their disconfirmations to be the same.

Will the infant not react differently to an intentional violation of an expected condition than to one that is not? Intention is the key to ought, so that one object's failure to preserve valence when reciprocating another's act is an intentional violation and therefore an example of ought. In contrast, such is not the case for the failure of one nonintentional solid object to block the passage of another. Will the infant take this factor into account?

Because the infant does not draw the distinction which is the traditional basis of ought, it will not. Briefly, the infant does not distinguish between the intentional and nonintentional acts of *intentional* objects. Such a conception is found only in the adult; there is no provision for such an interpretation in the infant.

As seen by infants, intentional objects are capable of two kinds of movement, those that meet the criteria for the assignment of value and those that do not. A movement that meets the criteria, therefore any movement to which value is assigned, is an intentional act. Positive or negative acts, in the eyes of the infant, are always intentional. Because the infant's criteria are not exhaustive, some movements will occur for which the infant makes no assignment of value. Rather than interpreting them as accidental or unintentional, however, the infant does not interpret them at all.

One example for which value is not assigned is that of one intentional object "following" another, that is, "copying" its path while remaining a fixed distance behind. Following does not meet any of the infant's criteria for the assignment of value, being neither soft nor hard, helpful nor harmful, and so forth. Therefore, an infant observing object A follow object B would assign no value to the act. Neither would it expect reciprocation from object B, for reciprocation is restricted to acts that have been assigned value.

In contrast, an infant observing one object "chase" another, that is, "copying" its path while increasing its speed, advancing on the object as though to overtake it, would assign value to the act and would expect reciprocation. In sum, because an infant does not attribute unintentional acts to intentional objects, it would have no use for ought, a concept that emphasizes the distinction between intentional and unintentional acts.

It seems likely that the infant will not react to the semantic content of an expectancy; the disconfirmation of all innate expectancies, whether moral or physical, will produce the same outcome. Should the infant react differently to innate expectancies, on the one hand, but not to those of moral content, on the other, ought may be a cultural distinction. In cultures that observe the distinction, what is the age at which children acquire the concept of ought? Is there anything that differentiates cultures that draw the distinction?

Incidentally, it is not only infants whose judgments of intentionality fail to conform with those of adults; similar failures are reported in even 4- to 5-year-old children (e.g., Smith, 1978; King, 1971; Berndt & Berndt, 1975). Human actions that adults dismissed as "accidental," involuntary, or failing to achieve an intended effect, 4-year-olds judged to be intentional. Children of this age appeared to rely on a criterion of the kind proposed here, one based exclusively on "self-propelledness," considering as intentional: falls, sneezes, and even acts that achieved nonintended outcomes. Not until the age of 6 did children's judgments of intentionality conform to those of adults.

Part II: Form versus content

Moral beliefs of different cultures can be compared to the languages used in the cultures. They have a great deal in common, despite their evident differences. We are fortunate to have a theory of language which enables us to say what different languages have in common. While there is vigorous dispute concerning virtually every detail, there is nonetheless a theory. We have no comparable theory in the case of morality, and therefore must build one. The moral "knowledge" which we assigned the infant in Part I is a step in such a direction.

Just as there are primitives from which one builds sentences so are there primitives from which one builds moral beliefs. These primitives do not affect the content of either a sentence or a moral belief, but the form. Thus, while the content of moral beliefs will vary widely over cultures, the form will not.

One should be clear from the outset as to what one can hope to obtain from such a set of primitives. How did moral beliefs evolve? How do people acquire them? What role does attachment to the caregiver play? Do special emotions or attitudes – guilt, shame, mercy – attach uniquely to morality? What is the role of empathy? The Oedipus complex? Internalization of parental attitudes? These are not questions to be answered from a list of moral primitives. Nor are language primitives able to answer how language evolved, how the child acquires it; what is the role of pragmatics, truth claims, the interrogative, predication, and the like. What can be learned from primitives is their role in providing a basic form – of sentence or moral belief – that can express indefinitely many contents.

In this section, we will comment on the primitives described in Part I, and show how they cohere to provide the basic form of a moral belief. The primitives are: intention; positive/negative (right/wrong); reciprocation; possession; power; group.

1. Intention: Morality is a property of intentional objects. Although broadened by the implications of possession, in the basic case, the class of objects to which morality applies is co-equal with the class of objects to which intention applies.

2. The action of one intentional object on another is judged positive or negative (right or wrong) on the basis of several criteria. The simplest is intensity of motion. Soft acts are judged positive, hard ones negative (soft and hard being defined relative to an adaptation level). The older infant will have, in addition to intensity of motion, the criterion of helping and hurting, derived from the further concepts of goal, liberty, and aesthetics. Goal is

fundamental, for once a goal is attributed to one object, the stage is set for the attribution of helping or hurting to another object. Liberty and aesthetics are lesser or more specialized sources of helping and hurting. The attribution of goal is the basic precondition for the assignment of value to the social actions of intentional objects.

It is important to see that evaluation in the moral domain has a distinctive character, and is not simply equivalent to preference. It could be the case that every domain, not only that of intentional objects, has a unique evaluative dimension. But that does not appear to be the case; only the moral domain has a special evaluative dimension. In all other domains, evaluation concerns preference, and preference is a highly nondomain-specific process that can apply to all domains including the moral one.

Moral evaluation is principled, based not on preference but on the criteria described above. For example, does the action of a second object help or hurt a first object? If it enables the first one to carry out its goal, it helps; otherwise it hurts. The fact that the judgment is principled does not guarantee that it is correct, however. Nothing grants omniscience to moral judgment. The decision above may be mistaken, based on a misreading of the action of the second object. Moral judgment is not necessarily less subjective or prone to error than judgment in the nonmoral domain; it differs simply in not being based on preference.

For instance, the model's claim that reciprocation will preserve valence is not conditional on an infant's preference.

Some observers may have no preference – being equally disposed to look at the positive moral case as at the negative – and some may even prefer to observe the negative case in which the goal-seeking of the first party is impaired by the second. But that does not bear on the moral judgment of the case. Suppose that object B acted negatively in reciprocating A's positive action – thus failing to preserve valence; this should surprise infants who prefer negative acts no less than it surprises those who prefer positive acts (or have no preference at all).

3. Reciprocation is the expectation that the action of one intentional object on another will lead to a reversal of roles, and that the reversal will preserve the valence of the original action. For instance, if A acted negatively on B, then B will act negatively on A. We can distinguish weak and strong forms: On the strong form, all actions will be reciprocated with preservation of valence; on the weak form, *if* an action is reciprocated it will preserve valence. The weak form seems more tenable: All reciprocated actions will preserve valence but not all actions will be reciprocated.

The main source of the compunctiousness, the "ought–should" character, of moral judgment may be the primitive itself, but reciprocation may be a secondary source. We argued in Part I that noncontingent expectancies,

expectancies not derived merely from experience, have the force of "should." The expectancy that reciprocation *will* preserve valence can be interpreted as *should* preserve valence.

Will empathy contribute to the obligational quality of moral belief? One might suppose that it would. A child who can identify and sense the distress of another will be inclined to help the other (Hoffman, 1977). But that must be qualified. We must distinguish between the ability to identify the emotions of others, and the disposition to do something helpful about them. When an individual senses another's distress does he invariably act to dispel it, or are there occasions on which he will take advantage of what he detects, doing injurious things he would not do otherwise (in natural disasters, victims are assisted by some, looted by others)? Bischof-Kohler (1990) recognizes this possibility, observing that empathy may trigger "malicious gloating," and that in phylogeny empathy set the stage for "intentional cruelty." In any case, before accepting empathy as a source of moral obligation we must know more about the linkage between sensing negative emotion and acting to alleviate it.

4. Possession extends the moral domain to nonintentional objects. While acts directed at ordinary nonintentional objects are not assigned valence, those directed at possessed nonintentional objects are. In addition, since intentional objects are subject to possession, we must accommodate the competing effects of possession and reciprocation. In the model, possession overrides reciprocation. The infant does not expect *possessed recipients* to reciprocate. If an individual acts negatively on an intentional object he owns, the infant does not expect reciprocation from the recipient; nor, does the infant expect the recipient to reciprocate positive acts. This denies a possessed recipient retribution, and exempts it from gratitude. On these assumptions, possession totally overrides reciprocation. Though we suspect that is correct, the model could be adjusted to make the competition between possession and reciprocation less one-sided.

5. The concept of power is presupposed by both possession and group. It is inequality that makes possession possible in the first place; intentional objects of equal power cannot possess one another. When intentional objects of equal power move together, they constitute a group, not a possessed object and its possessor. Power can be indexed in several ways – size, beauty, sagacity, and so forth – but most incontrovertibly by the ability of one object to control another, either forcing the weaker object to act in certain ways or denying it action that it would otherwise take.

6. When intentional objects of equal power move together, the infant perceives them as a group. Physical likeness among such objects promotes the concept of group but is not needed. The formation of a group has internal consequences, as described in Part I. For example, group members are expected to tend to act alike, not to act negatively on one another, and to

reciprocate on behalf of other members. These are internal consequences: They concern how a group member perceives another – what one is expected to give another member, and what one expects to receive in return.

The formation of a group also gives rise to *external* consequences: These concern how group members perceive nonmembers. Such consequences of group formation, not discussed in Part I, will be discussed below.

From the perspective of an observer, the formation of a group does not change the status of group nonmembers. Nonmembers do not acquire the special prerogatives that members extend to one another; nonetheless they do not lose their original status (i.e., remaining intentional objects with respect to all actions judged by standard moral criteria). Thus, an observer of group formation perceives members as gaining prerogatives (relative to one another), but does not regard nonmembers as having lost prerogatives. This is not, however, how a group member perceives a nonmember.

In distinguishing members from nonmembers, a group member both extends prerogatives to members and withdraws them from nonmembers. Thus, becoming a member of a group entails two consequences: the loss of one's neutral predilections toward others, and the acquisition of two new attitudes – positive toward members of the group, negative toward nonmembers.

In Part I, the model assigns knowledge of internal group properties to the infant, but is silent about external group properties. Are external group properties part of the infant's knowledge, and therefore properly part of the model, or are they something a child learns? We propose them as part of the infant's knowledge, with two caveats. First, knowledge of external group properties develops later than knowledge of internal properties of the group. Second, this primitive may give rise to a sex difference. Knowledge of external group properties may be more likely to develop, or to attain a greater strength, in the male infant. If we regard sex as producing overlapping distributions rather than categorical difference, then the mean of the distributions will be greater for the male than for the female infant. Indeed, the distributions may be such that some females (but probably no males) will escape knowledge of external group properties altogether. While *all* infants will expect one group member to act positively on another, and *most* will expect a group member to act negatively on a nonmember, *some* female infants will not expect the latter. If a female infant, lacking negative expectancy, is found to have the expectancy as a child, it will be because of what she has learned.

Intergroup hostility, a staple of human history, may owe more to the "devaluation" by members of nongroup members than to any other factor. From the momentum of the crusades, continuing into the present, intergroup hostility appears to have secured its future in human affairs. Frequently, the hostility between human groups bears an eerie resemblance to that of chimpanzee groups. Chimpanzees patrol territorial boundaries, seek isolated outgroup members, and kill them when they are found (Goodall, 1986). Sex difference is a prominent feature of such intergroup hostility. Only male chimpanzees patrol, seek out, and kill (Goodall, 1986); similarly, mainly human males bomb, pillage, and bayonet; females remain home cooking, cleaning, and caring for children. How might we explain this difference?

We suggested one explanation, that is, the knowledge of external group properties in the male infant. Now we add a second – an explanation that could act in concert with the first. Males appear more prone to form and join groups than females. Male chimpanzees spend much of their time in like sex groups, whereas females, rather than bonding with one another, spend long periods alone with their offspring (Goodall, 1986). But why is the bond that mothers form with their children less dangerous than that of group membership? Why does it not lead to the devaluation of other? Mother and child are *not* co-members of a group, their relation is that of possession, and possession does not entail devaluation of other. Membership in a group, however, involves automatic devaluation of other.

If human males resemble chimpanzee males in having a penchant for groups, spending more time in them, and participating with greater fervor, it will be the male who, as a group member, perceives nonmembers as less than fully qualified intentional objects, and denies them normal moral rights. Is this a characteristic of human males? Regrettably, though the question is relatively straightforward, relevant data seem unavailable.

From this list of primitives we can now construct the general form of a moral belief. (1) The belief concerns a relation between intentional objects, typically people (but sometimes gods); nonintentional objects enter the relation only insofar as they are possessions. (2) The relations are coded right or wrong, those coded right being enjoined, those coded wrong forbidden. (3) The group to which the participants belong is distinguished from all other groups, and only relations among members of this group count.

Within the boundaries of this form, there are then virtually no constraints on the content. The criteria – intensity, goal, liberty, aesthetics – by which moral acts are judged do not themselves constrain the content of moral belief. Liberty, for example, is not defined relative to a particular kind of action, either on the part of the first or second party. Any action by a second party that preserves the action of a first party counts as liberty, and the action of the first party can be of any kind. The same applies to helping and hurting, both of which are defined by their relation to the goal seeking of a second party, but not by the content of that goal. Whatever the goal that is sought by a first party, action by a second party that facilitates or hinders the achievement of that goal counts as helping or hurting.

Moral beliefs can concern the treatment of parents by children, the worship of gods, the dress code of widows, how a fire should be built, whether dogs should be kicked, and the like. Beliefs can concern topics that do not explicitly involve relations between people – dress code, fire preparation, diet – because they implicitly involve such relations. An improperly built fire may imperil another; an improper diet may cause immoral behavior, so may improper dress.

Turiel (1983) has argued that people distinguish moral beliefs from conventional ones, and that there are intrinsically moral events. However, as we can see moral beliefs can have any content. Moreover, it is not events that are intrinsically moral or nonmoral. What is intrinsically moral are the distinctive judgments made on relations among intentional objects, and the criteria used to make these judgments.

Further, moral beliefs are not innate, as Turiel's position implies, while mere conventions are learned. Moral beliefs are as dependent on learning as any other beliefs; they result from a conjunction of innate and learned factors, the innate factors being the infant's primitives. Shweder, Mahapatra, and Miller (1990), on the basis of an extensive comparison of Hindu and American moral beliefs, reject Turiel's thesis; they could find no events that were intransigently moral or nonmoral.

Moral beliefs must be defined with sufficient abstractness to enable a form/content distinction. Rather than provide the content of moral belief, the primitives supply the frame into which content is poured. Although the *form* of moral belief reflects the infant's primitives, content does not. The content of moral beliefs reflects the power struggles of the culture.

Organized religion is only one of several groups engaged in this struggle. That only males can conduct priestly function, or constitute a minion; that widowers can remarry while widows cannot; are reflections of male dominion over the female. The requirement that children respect and obey their parents reflects the struggle between generations. Although the messages of such power struggles differ widely, all have been formulated with the same primitives.

There appear to be many intrusions into the content of moral beliefs from sources outside morality. Nothing, for instance, in the moral primitives concerns the traditional content of Western religion; yet it is commonplace for gods, original sin, eternal life, redemption, and the like to appear in Western moral belief. Why? And why has organized religion historically presented itself as the custodian of morality? On what grounds? This historical anomaly needs explanation.

References

Baillargeon, R., Spelke, E. S., & Wasserman, S. (1985). Object permanence in five-month-old infants. *Cognition, 20,* 191–208.

Berndt, T. J., & Berndt, E. G. (1975). Children's use of motives and intentionality in person perception and moral judgment. *Child Development, 46,* 904–912.

Berscheid, E., & Walster, E. H. (1969). *Interpersonal attraction.* Reading MA: Addison-Wesley.

Bischof-Kohler, D. (1990). The development of empathy in infants. In M. E. Lamb & H. Keller (Eds.), *Infant development: Perspectives from German-speaking countries*. Hillsdale, NJ: Erlbaum.

Chaplin, W. F., John, O. P., & Goldberg, L. R. (1988). Conceptions of states and traits: Dimensional attributes with ideals as prototypes. *Journal of Personality and Social Psychology*, *54*, 541–557.

Dasser, V., Ulbaek, I., & Premack, D. (1989). The perception of intention. *Science*, *293*, 186–188.

Dixon, K. K., Berscheid, E., & Walster, E. (1972). What is beautiful is good. *Journal of Personality and Social Psychology*, *24*, 285–290.

Eder, R. A. (1989). The emergent personologist: The structure and content of $3^1/_2$-, $5^1/_2$-, and $7^1/_2$-year olds' concepts of themselves and other persons. *Child Development*, *60*, 1218–1228.

Goodall, J. (1986). *The chimpanzees of Gombe*. Cambridge, MA: Harvard University Press.

Hoffman, M. L. (1977). Empathy, its development and prosocial implications. In C. B. Keasy (Ed.), *Nebraska Symposium on Motivation*, *25*, 169–217. Lincoln: University of Nebraska Press.

King, M. (1971). The development of some intention concepts in young children. *Child Development*, *42*, 1145–1152.

Kummer, H., & Cords, M. (1991). Cues of ownership in long-tailed macaques, Macaca fascicularis. *Animal Behavior*, *42*, 529–549.

Leslie, A. M. (1987). Pretense and representation: The origins of "theory of mind." *Psychological Review*, *94*, 412–426.

Mischel, W. (1968). *Personality and assessment*. New York: Wiley.

Premack, D. (1984). Pedagogy and aesthetics as sources of culture. In M. S. Gazzaniga (Ed.), *Handbook of cognitive neuroscience*. New York: Plenum Press.

Premack, D. (1990). The infant's theory of self-propelled objects. *Cognition*, *36*, 1–16.

Premack, D. (1991). The aesthetic basis of pedagogy. In R. R. Hoffman & D. S. Palermo (Eds.), *Cognition and the symbolic processes*. Hillsdale, NJ: Erlbaum.

Premack, D., & Woodruff, G. (1978). Does the chimpanzee have a theory of mind? *The Behavioral and Brain Sciences*, *1*, 516–526.

Rohles, W. S., & Ruble, D. N. (1984). Children's understanding of dispositional characteristics of others. *Child Development*, *55*, 550–560.

Samuels, G., & Ewy, T. M. (1985). Aesthetic perfection of faces during infancy. *British Journal of Developmental Psychology*, *3*, 221–228.

Schiller, J. C. F. (1882). *Essays, esthetical and philosophical, including the dissertation on the "Connexions between the animals and the spiritual in man."* London: G. Bell.

Shweder, R. A., Mahapatra, M., & Miller, J. G. (1990). Culture and moral development. In J. Kagan & S. Lamb (Eds.), *The emergence of morality in young children*. Chicago: University of Chicago Press.

Smith, M. C. (1978). Cognizing the behavior stream: The recognition of intentional action. *Child Development*, *49*, 736–743.

Sugarman, S. (1983). *Children's early thought: Developments in classification*. Cambridge: Cambridge University Press.

Turiel, E. (1983). *The development of social knowledge: Morality and convention*. Cambridge: Cambridge University Press.

Wellman, H. (1990). *Children's theories of mind.* Cambridge, MA: MIT Press.

Wimmer, H., & Perner, J. (1983). Beliefs about beliefs: Representation and constraining function of wrong beliefs in young children's understanding of deception. *Cognition, 13,* 103–128.

7 Domain-specific knowledge and conceptual change

Susan Carey and Elizabeth Spelke

Overview

We argue that human reasoning is guided by a collection of innate domain-specific systems of knowledge. Each system is characterized by a set of core principles that define the entities covered by the domain and support reasoning about those entities. Learning, on this view, consists of an enrichment of the core principles, plus their entrenchment, along with the entrenchment of the ontology they determine. In these domains, then, we would expect cross-cultural universality: cognitive universals akin to language universals.

However, there is one crucial disanalogy to language. The history of science and mathematics demonstrates that conceptual change in cognitive domains is both possible and actual. Conceptual change involves overriding core principles, creating new principles, and creating new ontological types. We sketch one potential mechanism underlying conceptual change and motivate a central empirical problem for cognitive anthropology: To what extent is there cross-cultural universality in the domains covered by innate systems of knowledge?

Domain-specific cognition

The notion of domain-specific cognition to be pursued here is articulated most clearly by Chomsky (1980a). Humans are endowed with domain-specific systems of knowledge such as knowledge of language, knowledge of physical objects, and knowledge of number. Each system of knowledge applies to a distinct set of entities and phenomena. For example, knowledge of language applies to sentences and their constituents; knowledge of physical objects applies to macroscopic material bodies and their behavior; knowledge of number applies to sets and to mathematical operations such as addition. More deeply, each system of knowledge is organized around a distinct body of core principles. For language, these are the principles of universal grammar;

169

for physical objects, the principles might include Newton's axioms and the principles of continuity and solidity; for number, they might include the principles of one–one correspondence and succession.

This notion of domain specificity provides a basis for determining, and distinguishing among, the domains of human knowledge: Two systems of knowledge are distinct just in case they center on distinct principles. For example, if knowledge of language and knowledge of number were found to center on the same core principles, psychologists should conclude that they constitute a single system of knowledge, despite the many obvious differences between the abilities that knowledge of language and knowledge of number support. Indeed, Chomsky (1980b) has suggested that language and number are connected in this way. This notion similarly provides a basis for distinguishing the genuine cognitive domains from more trivial collections of beliefs: Only genuine domains are characterized by distinct sets of core principles. In particular, reasoning about material bodies, about persons, and about sets may well depend on distinct systems of knowledge of physics, psychology, and number. In contrast, reasoning about billiard balls, about bricks, and about plates probably depends on a single knowledge system: The core principles underlying reasoning about one of these collections of objects probably apply to the other collections as well (Carey, 1985).

Domain-specific perception

If human reasoning depends on domain-specific knowledge systems, then reasoners face a crucial task: They must single out the entities to which each system of knowledge applies. For example, a well-developed system of knowledge of psychology is useless unless a reasoner can determine when he or she is faced with a person. Similarly, systems of knowledge of physics and number can function only insofar as a reasoner can single out material bodies and sets. The mechanisms that single out such entities need not be (and never are) flawless: It is sufficient for the reasoner to pick out some of the persons, some of the material bodies, and the like. Without some mechanisms for singling out entities within a domain, however, reasoning cannot proceed. A domain-specific reasoner cannot simply ask of some part of the layout, "How does this thing behave?" The reasoner also must ask, "What kind of thing is this?" (see Wiggins, 1980).

We will call the processes that single out material bodies, persons, and sets *domain-specific perception*. These processes may not be perceptual, however, in a narrow sense. Most of the processes studied in psychophysics, sensory physiology, and computational vision do not function to single out the entities about which one reasons but rather they function to construct representations of the continuous surrounding surface layout. Vision, for example, appears to culminate in representations of the distances, orientations, colors, textures, and motions of light-reflecting surfaces (Gibson, 1950; Marr, 1982).

These representations are not sufficient for the operation of domain-specific reasoning. To reason about material bodies, one must carve the surface layout into unitary, bounded, and persisting things (Spelke, 1988). To reason about number, one must represent a collection of bodies, surfaces, or other entities as a set (Gelman & Gallistel, 1978; also see Shipley & Shepperson, 1990; Wynn, 1992). To reason about human action and mental life, one must represent a portion of the surface layout as a sentient, purposive being. The processes that culminate in such representations are our focus here.

There are two general ways in which the task of apprehending the entities in a domain could be accomplished: Domain-specific perception either could depend on principles that are distinct from the principles guiding domain-specific reasoning, or domain-specific perception and reasoning could depend on a single set of principles. Consider, for example, the domain of reasoning about human action and experience. It is possible that perceivers single out human beings by virtue of a face-recognizer, a voice-recognizer, a gait-recognizer, and the like. Whenever the perceiver is confronted by eyes, hair, and other features in the proper configuration, his or her face-recognizer would signal the presence of a person. This signal would then trigger the operation of the processes of psychological reasoning, whereby the actions of the person are understood in terms of the person's goals and feelings. On this view, apprehending persons and reasoning about human actions depends on distinct principles: principles governing the physical arrangement of eyes, noses, and so forth, on one hand, and principles concerning the relation among purposes, perceptions, and the like, on the other. Psychological reasoning would proceed appropriately, because the mechanisms that embody these distinct principles would be suitably linked together.

Alternatively, perceivers may single out persons by analyzing the behavior of entities, asking whether an entity's behavior appears to be directed to some goal, to be guided by perceptions of its environment, to be colored by emotions, and so on. Entities would be perceived as persons insofar as their behavior was consistent with such an analysis. On the second account, processes of perceiving and reasoning about psychological beings are intimately connected: They are guided by the same system of knowledge.

In human infancy, we suggest, perception and reasoning are guided by a single knowledge system in at least three domains: physics, psychology, and number. We begin with the case of physics by reviewing the findings of studies of object perception and physical reasoning in infancy (see Spelke, 1990, or Spelke & Van de Walle, in press, for a more extensive review).

Perceiving and reasoning about physical objects

Research on object perception provides evidence that young infants can perceive the unity, boundaries, complete shapes, and persistence of objects under some conditions. Object perception appears to depend on amodal mechanisms that divide the surface layout into bodies in accordance with a small number of principles, each of which reflects constraints on object motion.

Consider first young infants' perception of the unity of a visible object. Experiments using preferential looking methods, which rely on infants' well-documented tendency to look longer at displays that they perceive to be novel, provide evidence that infants as young as 3 months of age perceive a three-dimensional object presented against a uniform background as a connected body that will maintain its connectedness as it moves. For example, infants who were familiarized with a cohesive object subsequently looked longer at the outcome of an event in which the object broke in two than at the outcome of an event in which the object moved as a whole (Spelke, Breinlinger, & Jacobson, 1992). Infants' preference for the former outcome reliably exceeded that of infants in a baseline condition who viewed the same outcome displays with no preceding events. The experiment provides evidence that infants perceived the original object as a connected body that should maintain its connectedness over motion.

Further experiments focusing on infants' preferential looking or object-directed reaching provide evidence that young infants perceive the distinctness of adjacent objects if the objects undergo different rigid motions (Hofsten & Spelke, 1985; Spelke, Hofsten, & Kestenbaum, 1989). Infants also perceive the distinctness of stationary objects if the objects are spatially separated: Spatially separated objects are perceived as distinct units even if they are separated only in depth such that the gap between them is not directly visible (Hofsten & Spelke, 1985; Kestenbaum, Termine, & Spelke, 1987; Spelke, Hofsten, & Kestenbaum, 1989).

The above findings suggest that infants perceive objects in accord with two constraints on object motion. First, objects are connected bodies that maintain their connectedness as they move: Two spatially separated objects, or two adjacent objects that slide with respect to one another, are therefore perceived as distinct. Second, objects are not connected to other objects and retain their separateness as they move: Two stationary and adjacent objects, lacking any spatially or spatiotemporally specified boundary, are therefore perceived as one connected body. These two constraints can be captured by a single *principle of cohesion*: Surfaces in the layout lie on a single object if and only if they are connected.

Now consider infants' perception of the unity of an object whose ends are visible or tangible but whose center is hidden. Four-month-old infants have been familiarized with such an object and then presented with a fully visible complete object or with two objects separated by a gap where the original object had been hidden. If infants perceived the original object as a connected body, then they should look longer at the two-object test display, relative to infants in a baseline condition who viewed the same test displays with no previous familiarization.

Such experiments provide evidence that 4-month-old infants perceive a visible, center-occluded object as a connected body if the ends of the object undergo a common rigid motion (Kellman & Spelke, 1983; Slater, Morison, Somers, Mattock, Brown, & Taylor, 1990; Craton & Baillargeon, personal communication, 1991). Rigid motion in any direction, including motion in depth, specifies the connectedness of the object (Kellman, Spelke, & Short, 1986); a pattern of common retinal displacement in the absence of true motion does not (Kellman, Gleitman, & Spelke, 1987). Studies in the haptic mode provide evidence that infants perceive the unity of objects whose ends are tangible under the same conditions as they perceive the unity of objects whose ends are visible (Streri & Spelke, 1988; 1989; Streri, Spelke, & Rameix 1992). Infants aged $4^{1}/_{2}$ months held the two ends of a haptic assembly in their two hands, without visual or haptic access to the full assembly. They perceived the assembly as one connected body when the ends moved together and as two spatially separated bodies when the ends moved independently.

The findings of these studies suggest that infants perceive objects in accordance with two further constraints on object motion. First, surfaces move together only if they are in contact: The two rigidly moving ends of a center-occluded visible object or of a haptic assembly are therefore connected. Second, surfaces move independently only if they are spatially separated: Two independently movable seen or felt objects are therefore separated by a gap. These two constraints can be encompassed by a single *principle of contact*: Surfaces move together if and only if they are in contact.

Finally, consider infants' perception of objects that move fully out of view. Experiments using visual preference methods provide evidence that young infants perceive the persisting identity or distinctness of objects over successive encounters in accordance with the principle of contact (discussed earlier) and the principle of continuity: An object moves on exactly one connected path over space and time. First, Van de Walle and Spelke (1993) presented infants with an object that moved back and forth behind an occluder such that its two ends were visible in immediate succession but never simultaneously: The left side of the object moved behind the occluder until the object was fully hidden, and then the right side of the object began to appear from behind the opposite side, moving at the same speed and on the same path. Subsequent looking preferences between nonoccluded complete and broken displays provided evidence that the infants perceived the object as a connected body, in accordance with the contact principle. Second, Spelke and Kestenbaum (1986) and Xu and Carey (1992) presented infants with events in which an object moved out of view behind the first of two spatially separated occluders, and after a pause an object moved into view from behind the second occluder. Subsequent visual preferences between fully visible one- and two-object displays provided evidence that infants perceived two objects in this event in accordance with the continuity principle: Because no object appeared between the two screens, the object moving on the left must have been distinct from that on the right.

In summary, young infants appear to perceive objects in accordance with the principles of cohesion, contact, and continuity. We now consider whether infants respect these principles when they reason about objects that move from view.

A variety of experiments provide evidence that young infants represent the existence of an object that moves from view and make certain inferences about the object's continued motion (e.g., Baillargeon, 1986; Leslie, 1991; Spelke, Breinlinger, Macomber, & Jacobson, 1992). These experiments have used preferential looking methods to assess infants' reactions to an "invisible displacement task" (Piaget, 1954), in which an object moves from view and infants must infer its further motion. The experiments provide evidence that infants make some, but not all, of the inferences about object motion made by older children and adults. A consideration of infants' successes and failures may thus shed light on the principles guiding infants' inferences.

Experiments from three laboratories offer evidence that infants' inferences accord with two constraints on object motion: continuity (objects move only on connected paths), and solidity (objects move only on unobstructed paths, such that two objects never occupy the same place at the same time) (Baillargeon, 1986; Leslie, 1991; Spelke et al., 1992). In one experiment (Spelke et al., 1992, Exp. 1), 4-month-old infants first were familiarized with an event in which a ball fell behind a screen on an open stage and was revealed on the stage floor. Then a second surface was placed above the stage floor and a test sequence was presented in which the ball fell behind the screen, and the screen was raised to reveal the ball at rest either on the upper surface or on the lower surface. The latter position was inconsistent with the continuity and solidity constraints, because the ball could reach the lower surface only by jumping discontinuously over or by passing through the upper surface. Infants looked longer at the inconsistent than at the consistent test outcome. Their preference for the inconsistent outcome reliably exceeded the preferences of infants in a separate control condition, who viewed the same outcome displays preceded by consistent events. The experiment therefore provides evidence that 4-month-old infants infer that a hidden object will move on a connected and unobstructed path, in accordance with the continuity and solidity constraints. Further experiments provide evidence for the same ability at ages ranging from $2^1/_2$ months to 10 months, with a variety of displays and events (e.g., Baillargeon, 1986; Baillargeon, Graber, DeVos, & Black, 1990; Leslie, 1991; Spelke et al., 1992).

The continuity and solidity constraints are closely related: Whereas the continuity constraint dictates that an object must move on at least one connected path (i.e., the path of an object can contain no gaps), the solidity constraint dictates that an object must move on at most one connected path (i.e., the paths of two objects cannot intersect in space and time). Both constraints therefore can be captured by the principle of continuity: An object traces exactly one connected path.

Additional experiments provide evidence that infants infer that a hidden object will move in accordance with the principles of cohesion and contact. Carey, Klatt, and Schlaffer (1992) tested 8-month-old infants with events in which one object was lowered, raised, and lowered again behind a screen, and then the screen was raised to reveal one or two objects on the display floor. Infants looked longer at the two-object event, relative to the length of infants' looks in a baseline control experiment. The experiment provided evidence that infants inferred that the object would move in accordance with the cohesion principle: Unlike nonsolid substances (which were tested in other experiments), moving objects do not leave parts of themselves behind. Ball (1973) familiarized infants with an event in which one object moved out of view behind a screen and then a second object, which was initially half visible and stationary, moved fully into view. Then infants were tested with nonoccluded displays in which the first object either came into contact with the second object or stopped short of the second object. Infants looked longer at the no-contact event, relative to baseline controls. The experiment provides evidence that the infants inferred that the first object contacted the second object, in accordance with the contact principle (for further evidence, see Leslie, 1988).

In summary, infants appear to infer that hidden objects will move in accordance with the principles of cohesion, contact, and continuity. These are the same principles that guide infants' perception of the unity, boundaries, and persistence of the objects they see and feel. A single system of knowledge therefore appears to underlie object perception and physical reasoning in infancy. We now ask briefly whether a single system of knowledge also guides infants' perception and reasoning in the domains of psychology and number.

Perceiving and reasoning about persons

The system of knowledge guiding reasoning about human action and mental life is currently a subject of much study and some debate (see Astington, Harris, & Olson, 1988; Leslie, 1987; Perner, 1991; Wellman, 1990). Central to our understanding of other human beings, however, appears to be the notion that people are sentient beings who choose their actions (see Wellman, 1990, for a discussion). If this notion is central to reasoning about human action, then the system of knowledge of psychology is distinct from that of physics. We must ask, therefore, how reasoners single out a person as an entity in the domain of their psychological reasoning.

Babies appear to have an innate representation of the structure of the human face; this representation allows neonates to direct attention to faces that move across the field of view (see Johnson & Morton, 1991, for a review). Perhaps babies use that representation to identify people as entities expected to be capable of perceptions and purposive action. Evidence from a number of sources suggests this is not the case: Infants, children, and adults identify animate, sentient beings by taking account of their actions, not by analyzing their surface appearance.

Consider first young children's reactions to dolls. Many young children are delighted by dolls, with whom they engage in rich pretend interactions. At no age, however, do children appear to be led by dolls' human features to treat dolls as animate, sentient beings (R. Gelman, 1990; R. Gelman, Spelke, & Meck, 1983). Even infants respond differently to dolls and to living faces: A stationary doll's face is an object of interest or delight, whereas a stationary human face, seen under similar circumstances, can evoke fear or aversion (Tronick, 1982). In addition, young infants appear to respond to objects that lack any clearly animate features (e.g., mobiles) as animate and social beings, if the behavior of those objects approximates the behavior of a responsive social agent. These findings, and other findings with adults (Heider & Simmel, 1944), suggest that children and adults use some principles of their intuitive psychology not only to reason about persons but also to perceive persons as persons (for more detailed expositions of this view, see R. Gelman, 1990; and Premack, 1990).[1]

Perceiving and reasoning about number

The origin and the nature of knowledge of number has been a topic of philosophical debate at least since Hume (e.g., Kitcher, 1983). Psychological research on infants (e.g., Wynn, 1992) and animals (see Gallistel, 1990, for a review) strongly supports the existence of innate knowledge of number that includes core principles of one-to-one correspondence and succession (every number has a unique successor, Gallistel & R. Gelman, 1992). If this view is correct, then number would appear to be a domain of knowledge distinct from physics or psychology. How do reasoners single out the entities in this domain, apprehending sets and their numerosity?

A controversy exists concerning the relations between perceiving and reasoning about small sets. On one view, perception of small sets depends on a special pattern-recognition process, "subitizing," whereas perception of large sets depends on a counting process (Klahr & Wallace, 1973; Davis & Pérusse, 1988). The principles of operation of the subitizing process are unknown, but they are believed to be distinct from the principles governing numerical reasoning. On a different view (Gallistel, 1990; Gallistel & R. Gelman, 1992), sets of all sizes are enumerated by a counting process. Proponents of both views agree that the principles at the core of the counting process include one-to-one correspondence and succession, and that these principles underlie not only counting but also the operations of spontaneous arithmetic.

In our terms, the difference between these two views of the process of enumerating small sets is exactly the difference between the thesis that a single system of knowledge underlies number perception and numerical reasoning, and the thesis that distinct systems underlie these abilities. Note that on both views, a single set of principles is thought to enable humans to perceive and reason about large sets.

In summary, domain-specific reasoning and domain-specific perception appear to depend on a single system of knowledge in the domains of physics, psychology, and number (at least for large sets). We now ask how knowledge grows and changes in these domains.

Cognitive development

It is natural to suppose that humans learn about the world by observing it. We learn that bodies fall by watching them fall; we learn that insults make people angry by watching people react to insults; we learn that $2 + 2 = 4$ by observing two sets of two things combine into one set of four things. Variants of this thesis may be offered. Children may learn through active manipulation (releasing or throwing objects, hitting people, combining sets), or by social interaction (tossing balls around, participating in social exchanges, playing number games).

If any of these proposals is correct, then children and adults will learn only about the things they perceive. A child who cannot perceive any object that falls, any person who is moved to anger, or any sets of two things that combine into a set of four things, will never learn about these entities, however much he or she observes, manipulates, or communicates about the surrounding layout. Perception limits the development of knowledge.

The consequences of this limit depend on the relation between the principles governing perception and those governing reasoning. If perception and reasoning are guided by distinct principles, experience may overturn the original principles governing reasoning. For example, suppose that perception of persons depends on a face-recognizer, whereas initial reasoning about persons depends on notions that action is internally generated in accordance with perceptions and feelings. Encountering a doll, the child would perceive a person. The behavior of this person, however, would not appear to result from choices but from the blind operation of the laws of mechanics. Because the doll must be admitted to the class of persons (we are assuming that the face-recognizer, not the psychological reasoner, makes this decision), the child is now in a position to learn that his or her initial psychology is false: Not all persons are purposive, sentient beings. With increased exposure to dolls, stuffed animals, portraits, and the like, this learning will grow and be extended. Learning will therefore bring changes to the child's initial system of knowledge.

If the same system of knowledge guides perception and reasoning, in contrast, it would seem that children *cannot* learn, by observing the world, that their initial system of knowledge is false. For example, suppose that both perception and reasoning about persons are guided by the notion that people are sentient and purposive. When children encounter an entity that looks like a human being but does not engage in self-generated action, they will not conclude that their notion of person is false but rather that this entity does not fall within the domain of their psychology: It is not a person.

In any domain in which perception and reasoning depend on the same system of knowledge, learning from observation, from action, or from social interchange will tend to preserve the initial system of knowledge. Knowledge will grow by a process of enrichment, whereby core principles become further entrenched. The initial system of knowledge will not be overthrown by any process of induction from experience, because only objects that conform to that system are available to be experienced. Cognitive development will result in the enrichment of knowledge around unchanging core principles.

Some aspects of mature, commonsense reasoning appear to support the view that knowledge of physical objects, persons, and number develops by enrichment. In the domain of physics, principles such as cohesion, contact, and continuity appear to be central to mature intuitions about object persistence (see Hirsch, 1982) and object motion (see Spelke, 1991, for discussion). In the domain of psychology, the notion that people choose their actions appears to be deeply ingrained in mature commonsense reasoning (Wellman, 1990). Finally, in the domain of number, Gallistel and R. Gelman (1992) argue that the most intuitive mature conceptions of number are those that derive from the principles of one-to-one correspondence and succession.

Nevertheless, this reasoning leads to a contradiction. Conceptual change in the domains of physics, psychology, and number is not only possible but actual. In the history of science and mathematics, it has occurred with the development of Newtonian and quantum mechanics, with the attempt to construct a purely behavioristic or mechanistic psychology, and with the discovery of rational, real, and complex numbers. In each of these cases, the development of science has led to the construction of new principles and to the abandonment of principles that formerly were central to knowledge in the domain. In each of these cases, new types of entities were discovered or posited. The existence of conceptual change in science challenges the view that knowledge develops by enrichment around a constant core, and it raises the possibility that there are no cognitive universals: no core principles of reasoning that are immune to cultural variation.

Conceptual change

The nature and existence of conceptual change has been extensively analyzed and debated since Feyerabend (1962) and Kuhn (1962) independently adopted the mathematical term "incommensurability" (no common measure) to refer to mutually untranslatable theoretical languages (see Suppe, 1977, for a comprehensive critique of the early Kuhn/Feyerabend positions). These debates have led to a softening of Kuhn's and Feyerabend's early claims. In particular, current analyses of conceptual change in science deny that the meanings of all terms in a theory change when some do, that theories completely determine evidence and therefore are unfalsifiable, or that theory change is akin to religious conversion. These analyses nevertheless hold that the core insight of the Kuhn/Feyerabend early work stands: The history of science is marked by transitions across which students of the same phenomena speak incommensurable languages.

Carey (1991) summarizes the recent analyses of conceptual change that have been offered by philosophers of science (Kitcher, 1988; Kuhn, 1982; see also Hacking, 1993; Nersessian, 1992) and by cognitive scientists (Thagard, 1988; see also Chi, 1992; Vosniadou & Brewer, 1992). Conceptual change consists of conceptual differentiations, such that the undifferentiated parent concept plays no role in subsequent theories (Carey, 1991; Kuhn, 1977), and of the creation of new ontological categories (Thagard, 1988; Chi, 1992). Conceptual change involves change in the core principles that define the entities in a domain and govern reasoning about those entities. It brings the emergence of new principles, incommensurable with the old, which carve the world at different joints.

Cognitive science and the history of science

Some doubt the relevance of historical analyses of conceptual change to cognitive science and especially to cognitive development. Scientific reasoning and concepts, one might argue, are different from ordinary reasoning and concepts. Only the former undergo changes in core principles.

We consider it a serious empirical question as to whether the core concepts of commonsense reasoning are subject to change. Whatever answer one gives to this question, however, the existence of conceptual change in science challenges the argument for enrichment given above. If the development of domain-specific reasoning is constrained by domain-specific perception, and if the same system of knowledge underlies both reasoning and perception, then no person at any level of expertise is in a position to learn that his or her initial system of knowledge is false. This argument applies to any perceiver and reasoner, whether human or animal, layperson or scientist. The existence of conceptual change in domain-specific core knowledge presents a serious counterexample to the argument for enrichment and needs to be explained (Carey, 1991).

Those who emphasize the differences between intuitive theories and explicit scientific theories often imply that those differences in themselves *explain* conceptual change. In particular, the community of scientists, the self-reflective nature of explicit theory construction, and the instructional institutions that create scientists may be engines of conceptual change (e.g., Spelke, 1991). We grant that developed science differs from intuitive knowledge in these three ways. Nonetheless, communication among scientists, reflection, and instruction do not in themselves provide a mechanism for conceptual change.

First, processes that occur within an interactive community of scientists cannot, in themselves, bring about conceptual change, because the interactions within a scientific community can only be as effective as the conceptions of its individual members permit. Communication between scientists succeeds only insofar as two scientists can single out the same things to talk about (see Kuhn, 1962). The arguments against the possibility of conceptual change therefore apply to the community of scientists as well as to the individual scientist.

Next, consider the possibility that reasoners use "disciplined reflection" to revise conceptions within a domain. Many have argued that metacognitive abilities enable human intelligence to extend itself beyond its initial limits (e.g., Rozin, 1976; Sperber, this volume). By itself, however, reflection can do nothing to extricate developing conceptions from the self-perpetuating cycle described above. We as humans can only reflect on the entities we perceive. If our initial conceptions determine those entities, then we will be able to reflect only on entities whose behavior accords with our initial conceptions. Reflection by itself will not produce conceptual change.

Finally, instructional institutions that create scientists cannot in themselves account for conceptual change, for two reasons. First, instruction cannot account for individual discovery or invention. Second, instruction, like all communication, is limited by the student's ability to apprehend the objects to which it applies. If a student is not able to apprehend the entities in a to-be-learned theory, he or she may mouth the correct words but will assign to them meanings licensed by his or her own concepts (see the science misconceptions literature reviewed in Carey, 1986, and the chapter by Vosniadou, this volume).

In sum, we do not dispute that Western science is a social process, the product of self-reflective, metaconceptually sophisticated adults, and that systematic instruction is required to form these adults. These facts, however, do not provide an account of conceptual change. We require such an account: an explanation of how a reasoner can move beyond the core principles in a system of knowledge. Once such an account is provided, we may ask how it tempers the generalization that knowledge develops by enrichment around a constant core.

Mechanisms of conceptual change

Mappings across domains

The formal reflections of scientists provide one source of evidence concerning the processes of conceptual change. We begin with the reflections of the physicist, historian, and philosopher of science, Pierre Duhem. Duhem (1949) suggested that scientific physics is not built directly upon commonsense understanding of physical phenomena but depends instead on translations between the language of ordinary experience and the language of mathematics. According to Duhem, the objects of science are not concrete material bodies but numbers. To provide explanations for physical phenomena, physicists first translate from a physical to a mathematical description of the world, and then they look for generalizations and regularities in the mathematical description. These generalizations, when translated back into the language of everyday objects, are the physicist's laws.

In our terms, scientists who effect a translation from physics to mathematics are using their innately given system of knowledge of number to shed light on phenomena in the domain of their innately given system of knowledge of physics. Scientists do this by devising and using systems of measurement to create *mappings* between the objects in the first system (numbers) and those in the second (bodies).[2] Once a mapping is created, the scientists can use conceptions of number to reason about physical objects. They therefore may escape the constraints imposed by the core principles of physical reasoning. In effect, the mapping from physics to number creates a new perceptual system for the domain of physics, centering not on the principles of cohesion, contact, and continuity but on the principles of one-to-one correspondence, succession, and the like. The entities picked out by this new perceptual system need not be commensurable with those picked out by the old.

Duhem focuses exclusively on the construction of a translation, or mapping, from physics to mathematics. Conceptual change may occur as well through mappings across other domains. In particular, conceptual changes in science appear to have resulted from the construction and use of mappings from psychology to physics. By viewing animals and people as complex machines, mechanistic biology and mechanistic psychology aim to explain animal and human action in terms of physical principles. We return to these conceptual changes below.

How do scientists construct mappings across domains? Science's informal documents (lab notebooks, journals) provide an excellent source of data concerning this process. Recently, cognitive scientists as well as historians and philosophers of science have begun to mine this source (e.g., Gruber, 1974, on Darwin; Nersessian, 1992, on Maxwell; Tweney, 1991, on Faraday). Nersessian (1992) concentrates on two interconnected pairs of processes that recur in historical cases of conceptual change: (1) the use of physical analogy, and (2) the construction of thought experiments and limiting case analyses. These processes serve both to reveal tensions and inadequacies within a system of knowledge and to restructure that system through the construction of mappings across knowledge domains.

Physical analogies

Nersessian's analysis of Maxwell's use of physical analogies provides a worked example of the productive use of such mappings in the process of conceptual change. According to Nersessian, Maxwell himself used the term "physical analogy" in explaining his method. A physical analogy exploits a set of mathematical relationships as they are embodied in a source domain, so as to analyze a target domain about which there is only partial knowledge. In Maxwell's case, the source domain was fluid mechanics as an embodiment of the mathematics of continuum mechanics, and the target domain was electromagnetism. By constructing the analogy between these two areas of physics, Maxwell was able ultimately to construct an effective mathematical theory of electromagnetism.

Nersessian notes several important lessons from this case study. First, the analogy from fluid mechanics to electromagnetism did real inferential work: Important mistakes in Maxwell's first characterization of the electromagnetic field are traceable to points at which this analogy breaks down. Second, the process of constructing mappings across domains is difficult: Each mapping must be explored and tested in depth to determine its usefulness. Third, "imagistic representations" play an important part in constructing the mapping from physics to number: They express mathematical relationships in a directly comprehensible way and thus serve as a good bridge between domains. Fourth, the process of constructing a mapping across domains is not one of transferring the relations from source domain to target in one fell swoop by plugging in and testing values. Rather, a scientist explores different possible mappings from the source domain onto the target domain, imposing different conceptualizations of the target domain in so doing. Finally, the mapping thus created can produce conceptual change in both domains. By using the Newtonian mathematics of continuum mechanics to understand electromagnetic fields, Maxwell constructed a mathematics of greater generality than that of his source domain (Nersessian, 1992).

Thought experiments and limiting case analyses

Another modeling activity is the construction of thought experiments, including limiting case analyses. Philosophers of science have often discussed how (or whether) thought experiments can be *experimental*: Can they have empirical content even though they involve no data? Kuhn (1977), analyzing a thought experiment that figured in the process by which Galileo differentiated instantaneous velocity from average velocity, argued that one function of thought experiments is to show that current concepts cannot apply to the world without contradiction. Nersessian (1992) extended Kuhn's analysis by arguing that thought experiments involve mental model simulations, which are part of the source of their empirical content.

Nersessian's example is Galileo's famous thought experiment showing that heavier objects do not fall faster than lighter ones. Galileo imagined two objects, a large heavy one and a small light one, in free fall. According to Aristotelian and scholastic physics, the heavier object should fall faster. He then imagined joining the two objects with an extremely thin rod, creating a composite object. This thought experiment suggests two contradictory outcomes: (1) The composite object is heavier still and therefore should fall even faster, and (2) the slower speed of the smaller object should impede the speed of the larger object, so the composite object should fall more slowly! Galileo went on to construct a limiting case analysis concerning the medium in which objects fall to resolve the contradiction. He concluded that in a vacuum, objects of any weight will fall at the same speed. This thought experiment and limiting case analysis played a role in constructing a differentiated, extensive conception of weight. That conception, in turn, depends on the mathematical distinction between a sum and an average.[3]

Conceptual change and cognitive universals

If processes such as those discussed by Nersessian are necessary components of the engine for conceptual change, we can account for the plausibility of the intuition that conceptual change results from the cooperative activity of a scientific community, from reflection, and from instruction. Galileo, Maxwell, Faraday, Einstein, and Darwin left writings, diaries, and notebooks showing that they used the heuristic processes Nersessian describes, and that they were fully conscious of doing so. They used these processes in the context of a self-reflective understanding of the goal of constructing new scientific theories. When one constructs a mapping across domains for the first time, one never knows how useful or deceptive it will prove to be. Thought experiments, physical analogies, and limiting case analyses serve as devices to communicate new conceptualizations to the scientific community, but these new conceptualizations will be adopted only insofar as they provide resolutions to standing puzzles and promote a productive research program. The jury is the social institutions of science.

But do heuristic processes of the kind Nersessian describes, and the mappings that result from them, also occur outside of developed science? Do they bring conceptual change to lay adults and children, creating cultural differences in core knowledge systems? The evidence considered thus far is consistent with three different hypotheses concerning conceptual change outside of science, each with different consequences for the existence of cross-cultural cognitive universals.

According to the *strong universality hypothesis*, only metaconceptually sophisticated scientists can overturn the core principles that innately determine ontology and reasoning. If this hypothesis is true, then the intuitive theories of people in all cultures will be enriched versions of those innate principles. The core principles of commonsense reasoning will be universal.

According to the *weak universality hypothesis*, children and lay adults can overturn innate, core principles of reasoning, but only through experience in a culture with a developed science. The source of conceptual change is the assimilation by children of the conceptions of the adults around them as those conceptions are expressed in adult language, in the measurement devices and technology of the culture, and in systematic instruction in school. And the source of the lay adult's conceptions, in turn, is the cultural assimilation of conceptual changes *originally* made by metaconceptually sophisticated scientists. If the weak universality hypothesis is true, then the intuitive knowledge systems of all cultures will share a common innate core, except in the case of cultures with a developed science.

According to the *no universality hypothesis*, the processes of conceptual change observed in scientists also occur spontaneously in children and lay adults. Although infants the world over share a set of initial systems of knowledge, those systems are spontaneously overturned over the course of development and learning, as children and adults construct, explore, and adopt mappings across knowledge systems. Because of the diversity of the potential mappings across domains, it is unlikely that the knowledge systems of members of different cultures will share a common core.

In the rest of this chapter, we turn to evidence bearing on these hypotheses. Rather than rely on cross-cultural data, we will examine a population that stands outside the cultural institutions of science and that lacks metaconceptual awareness of theory construction and choice: American children. Even though children do not engage in the social process of explicit theory construction and are not self-reflective theorizers, there is ample empirical evidence for conceptual change in childhood. Conceptual change occurs both spontaneously, as the child masters the language and the intuitive knowledge systems of the adult culture, and also as the result of systematic instruction in school. The existence of conceptual change in childhood militates against the strong universality hypothesis.

Conceptual change in childhood

Number

The preschool child's concept of number is the *positive integer* (see R. Gelman, 1991), as defined by the core principles of one-to-one correspondence and succession. This core notion changes early in the child's school years as the child constructs the concept of *0* (Wellman & Miller, 1986), the concept of *infinity* (in the form of a realization that there is no highest number; R. Gelman & Evans, 1981), and the concept of *rational number* (R. Gelman, 1991), and as the child becomes explicitly aware of the core principles defining number and thereby becomes able to reason about conservation of number (see R. Gelman & Gallistel, 1978, for a review).

It could be argued that the construction of *0* and *no highest number* involve change in the concept of number, as both changes begin to separate number from counting. Moreover, the construction of the concept of *rational number* brings an even deeper conceptual change. Coming to see .5 or $^1/_3$ as numbers requires abandoning the identification of number with counting, abandoning the successor principle, and constructing a new understanding of division (as a different operation from repeated subtraction). The new principles that jointly determine what constitutes a number and that govern reasoning with numbers include closure under division, construed in this new way.

R. Gelman (1991) suggested that changing conceptions of number depend in part on the construction of mappings between number and physical objects (as the child learns measurement) and on the construction of mappings between number and geometry (via devices such as the number line). Children's ability to benefit from these mappings suggests that the strong universality thesis is false for the domain of number. It is not clear, however, whether children or adults would spontaneously devise measurement devices or construct number lines in the absence of a developed science and mathematics. The weak universality hypothesis and the no universality hypothesis are both consistent with the above studies.

Biology and psychology

The principles determining the entities of the earliest psychology – capacity for self-generated motion and attention and contingent reaction to surrounding events – actually determine the ontological kind *animal*, not just *person*. For this reason, Carey (1985) speculated that young children's intuitive biology is not differentiated from their intuitive psychology. Her claim that 4-year-olds do not have an autonomous domain of intuitive biology has come under much scrutiny (e.g., Inagaki & Hatano, 1988; Springer & Keil, 1989; Wellman & S. Gelman, 1992). Regardless of whether preschool children should be granted an autonomous biology, however, it is clear that their understanding of biological phenomena differs radically from that of older children. In Hatano and Inagaki's (1987) terms, children progress from a vitalistic biology to a mechanistic biology.

Much of the evidence for this conceptual change was reviewed in Carey (1985, 1988): Evidence for the differentiation of the concepts *dead* and *inanimate*, for a change in the status of *person* as *animal*, and for the coalescence of the concepts *animal* and *plant* into a new concept, *living thing*. To that evidence, Keil and his colleagues have added many new phenomena suggesting conceptual change over these years (Keil, 1989; Springer & Keil, 1989). Keil's data serve two important purposes: They provide information concerning the precise characterization of the preschool child's initial biological concepts, and they provide evidence for conceptual change in the concept of *animal* and perhaps the concept of *person*.

Take Keil's transformation studies. Preschool children believe that a skunk can be turned into a raccoon through surgery; by age 9 (and earlier in some studies), children believe that the animal resulting from such a transformation is still a skunk that just looks like a raccoon (Keil, 1989). Preschool children do not think, however, that anything that looks like a raccoon is a raccoon: A skunk wearing a raccoon costume and pictured to look identical to a raccoon is judged to be a skunk (Keil, 1989). Similarly, a dog with all its insides removed (the blood and bones and stuff like that) is judged not to be a dog any more (S. Gelman & Wellman, 1991). These data suggest that to preschool children, the core of the notion of *animal kind* includes bodily structure: It is not enough to look just like an animal (e.g., a stuffed dog) or a particular kind of animal (e.g., a raccoon-costumed skunk), in order for an entity to be an animal or a particular kind of animal. Rather, the body of the entity must have the right structure, including internal structure. But these data also show that 9-year-olds have constructed a deeper notion of how that bodily structure must come to be: For 4- to 6-year-olds, surgery will do it; for 9-year-olds, bodily structure must result from a natural growth process. We take this developmental difference to reflect changes in the principles that define the entities in the domain of biology: By age 9, aspects of the life cycle have become part of the core principles. Changes of this sort are typical of historical cases of conceptual change (Kitcher, 1988).[4]

That this change actually reflects conceptual change rather than enrichment is further shown by changes in children's understanding of why children resemble their parents. Both Springer and Keil (1989) and S. Gelman and Wellman (1991) claim that preschool children understand that babies (including animal babies) inherit an innate potential from their parents to develop certain traits rather than others. However, their data do not establish that the preschool child has an understanding of the *biological* inheritance of properties.

We take an understanding of inheritance of properties to include, at a minimum, two essential components. First, children resemble their parents: Black parents tend to have black children, blue-eyed parents are more likely to have blue-eyed children than are brown-eyed parents, dogs have baby dogs rather than baby cats, and so on. Second, the *mechanism* underlying this resemblance crucially involves birth. There are many ways children may come to resemble their parents: Curly-haired parents may have curly-haired children because they give them permanents; prejudiced parents may have prejudiced children because they taught them to be so. Such mechanisms are not part of a biological process of inheritance of properties. To be credited with a biological concept of inheritance, children need not understand anything like a genetic mechanism, but they must distinguish the process underlying family resemblance from mechanical or psychological processes. At a minimum, children should realize that the process through which an animal originates – birth – is crucially involved in the process through which animals come to have their specific characteristics.

Without doubt, preschool children understand that offspring resemble their parents. Springer (1992) told 4- to 8-year-olds that a pictured animal had an unusual property (e.g., this horse has hair inside its ears) and then probed for projection of the property to a physically similar horse, described as a friend who is unrelated to the target, and to a physically dissimilar horse, described as the target's baby. At all ages, the property was projected more to the baby than to the friend. This important result confirms the mounting evidence that preschool children are not appearance-bound (S. Gelman, Coley, & Gottfried, this volume) and establishes the family resemblance component of a belief in inheritance of properties. However, because Springer did not probe the mechanism responsible for inheritance, his study does not bear on the second component. Springer distinguished what he considers a biological relationship (parentage) from a social relationship (friendship), but, as Carey (1985, 1988) points out, parentage is also a social relationship. At a minimum, one would like to see biological parentage distinguished from adoptive parentage.

The same issue arises with respect to the data of Springer and Keil (1989). Four- to seven-year-old children, plus adults, were told that both parents have a particular atypical property (e.g., pink rather than the usual red hearts) and were asked whether an offspring would have that property. They manipulated further information about the unusual property (whether the parents were born with the property or acquired it in an accident, whether the property was internal or external to the body, and whether the property had "biological" functional consequences).[5] Two important results emerged. First, only adults based their judgments solely on information about how the parents acquired the property: That is, only adults related birth to inheritance. In one study, 7-year-olds were beginning to take this variable into account. Second, even preschool children made systematic judgments, influenced by whether or not the property was described as having biological consequences. From this result, Springer and Keil concluded that preschoolers have a biological concept of inheritance, but that it is different from the adult's concept. Again, a comparison between natural parentage and adoptive parentage is necessary to determine whether preschoolers' concept of inheritance goes beyond an understanding of family resemblance.

S. Gelman and Wellman (1991) specifically contrasted nature versus nurture. For example, they asked whether a cow, Edith, who had been separated from other cows at birth and raised with pigs, would (1) moo or oink and (2) have a straight or curly tail. Even 4-year-olds judged that Edith would moo and have a straight tail. But the story asserts that Edith is a cow, in spite of having been raised in the company of pigs. There is a wealth of evidence, much of it from Gelman herself (S. Gelman, Coley, & Gottfried, this volume), that preschoolers take category membership as predictive of category-relevant properties, even in the face of conflicting information. Furthermore, the task does not stress that the baby cow is raised in a pig family, a child among other children who are pigs. S. Gelman and Wellman also posed a story about a seed from an apple, planted in a flower pot, and found that by age 5, children judged it would come up an apple rather than a flower. This scenario contrasts environment (in the company of flowers) with parentage (seed from an apple) and confirms Springer's (1992) finding that *family* resemblance is crucial. The experiment does not provide evidence, however, for an understanding of biological inheritance and a differentiation between biological and adoptive parentage.

Solomon, Johnson, Zaitchik, and Carey (1993) have carried out several studies contrasting adoptive with biological parentage. For example, a story is told about a (tall) shepherd whose son is taken at birth to be adopted by a (short) king and raised as the prince. The child is then asked whether the boy, when he grows up, will be tall like the shepherd or short like the king. Adults project physical properties such as height on the basis of biological parentage. This pattern does not begin to emerge until age 7: the age at which Springer and Keil (1989) begin to see the effect of information as to whether the property of the parent was inborn or acquired. As of now, there is no evidence that preschoolers have a conception of biological inheritance that goes beyond expectations of resemblance between parents and their offspring.

These data are consistent with those reviewed in Carey (1985), indicating changes in children's understanding of reproduction during the early school years. Preschool children do not take reproduction as one of the core principles defining animals and governing inferences about them. By age 10, in contrast, knowledge of reproduction begins to organize children's understanding of animals, as reflected both in the beginning understanding of inheritance and as reflected in judgments of what makes a skunk a skunk (Keil, 1989). This change is part of the construction of the new ontological category, *living thing*, which includes plants as well as animals (Carey, 1985). New core principles and new entities in the domain are hallmarks of conceptual change.

How do these fundamental changes in children's concept of *animal* bear on children's innate concept of *person*? Does the notion of a person as a sentient, freely acting being change once children begin to construct a mechanistic biology? If so, how does this change come about, if the principles at the center of the initial concept of person underlie not only psychological reasoning but also perception of persons?

Although answers to these questions are far from clear, we offer the following observations. First, biological concepts appear to exert some influence on mature, commonsense psychology. For example, Western adults are inclined to consider the living descendant of two persons as a person, even if that person lacks all capacity to act (e.g., while sleeping or in a coma). Adults also are inclined to deny personhood to apes, dolphins, and parrots, however impressive their behavioral accomplishments. *Person* is, at least in part, a species concept (see, e.g., Wiggins, 1980). Second, the initial conception of a person as a freely acting, sentient being remains a powerful part of Western adults' commonsense understanding of human action, surviving in uneasy coexistence with the later-developing biological conception. Tensions between these conceptions can be found not only in scientific psychology and philosophy of mind but also in everyday life, as current debates over abortion, criminal responsibility, and other topics demonstrate.

Finally, note that the development of mechanistic biology and mechanistic psychology depend in part on the construction of mappings across the domains of psychology and physics. The research reviewed above provides evidence that the construction of these mappings is a difficult and extended process. Insofar as it succeeds, however, there arises the possibility for conceptual change. A person may be viewed not only as a free agent but also as a complex machine and a member of a living kind (see Gentner & Grudin, 1985, for a historical analysis of changes in metaphors for the mind over 90 years of scientific psychology).

Studies of American children's changing biological and psychological conceptions cast doubt on the strong universality hypothesis, but they do not distinguish between the weak and the no universality hypotheses. To explore the conjecture that conceptual change in biology and psychology requires a developed scientific tradition, we need empirical studies of the intuitive biological and psychological theories held by children and adults in a wide range of cultures. Atran (1990) finds evidence for cross-cultural universality of folk taxonomies in biology but does not review research on folk explanations of biological phenomena: disease, reproduction, inheritance, and the functions of body parts. To our knowledge, the only work exploiting recent methodologies to diagnose intuitive biological conceptions is that of Jeyifous (1986), building on the work of Keil (1989). Jeyifous's results suggest that the developing conceptions of biology sketched in this section occur in cultures isolated from Western biological thought. For example, unschooled rural Yoruba children shift from the judgment that an operated-upon raccoon has become a skunk to the judgment that it is still a raccoon at about the same age as their American counterparts. If this shift reflects conceptual change, then Jeyifous's finding suggests two conclusions. First, conceptual change does not require developed scientific institutions. Even though Yoruba biology differs greatly from intuitive American biology, both involve a notion of animal kind that is deeper than bodily structure, whereas the preschool child's biology (in both cultures) does not. Second, even though conceptual change is seen in both cultures, cross-cultural universality is still observed. Of course, whether intuitive Yoruba biology is commensurable with intuitive American biology is an open empirical question.

Matter and physical objects

We have suggested that objects, for babies, are defined by the principles of cohesion, continuity, and contact: Objects are coherent solids that maintain their boundaries as they move along spatiotemporally continuous paths, and that act upon each other only on contact. There are tensions in the baby's application of these principles, however, and these tensions may provide the seeds for future conceptual change. The principles do not apply equally well to persons (who commonly appear to violate the contact principle, while behaving in accord with the principles of cohesion and continuity). Similarly, nonsolid substances such as liquids, gels, and powders obey the principle of continuity (e.g., sand cannot pass through solid barriers) but not the principle of cohesion (e.g., sand can disperse and coalesce as it moves). Although innate principles determine an ontology for the child, they do not define entirely nonoverlapping sets of entities. How do children conceptualize the entities in the overlapping sections of their ontological universe, and how do their conceptions change with development and experience? We focus here on changing conceptions of nonsolid substances and on emerging conceptions of *matter*.

The distinction between objects and nonsolid substances is very salient to young children. Objects are typically quantified as individuals whereas nonsolid substances are typically not quantified as individuals. This quantificational distinction is marked as the count/mass distinction in the syntax of many of the world's languages, and it conditions 2-year-old children's hypotheses about word meaning (Soja, Carey, & Spelke, 1991). But do young children appreciate that both objects and nonsolid substances are material?

Four-year-old children treat both objects and nonsolid substances as subject to the continuity principle: They judge that it is impossible for water to fill a box if the box is already filled by a steel block of the same dimensions (Carey, 1991). Moreover, 3- and 4-year-olds distinguish objects from ideas, dreams, and images on the basis of two properties that are relevant to the distinction between material and immaterial entities: objective perceptual access and causal interaction with other material entities (Estes, Wellman, & Woolley, 1989). Children's abilities to distinguish some material entities (i.e., objects) from some immaterial entities (i.e., ideas) on the basis of some properties that for adults are part of the core of the distinction between material and immaterial entities does not show, however, that children draw a material/immaterial distinction. Rather, children might draw a distinction between objects and mental entities, or between real and imaginary entities, on the basis of these properties. Two types of further information are required before we attribute a material/immaterial distinction to the child: We need to probe more widely the entities that fall under the distinction, and we need to analyze the explanatory work the distinction does for the child, in relation to the explanatory work that the material/immaterial distinction does for adults.

Carey (1991) presents such an investigation and concludes that preschool and early elementary-aged children *do* draw a material/immaterial distinction. The child's concept of matter, however, is incommensurable with that of the adult. Conceptual change in the years from 4 to 12 involves each of the interrelated concepts of *matter*, *kind of stuff*, *weight*, *density*, and *air*. The analysis includes two examples of initially undifferentiated concepts that are incommensurable with adult concepts: *weight/density* and *air/nothing*.[6] The principles that pick out material entities and guide reasoning about them for preschool children include the principle that a given region of space can be occupied by only one portion of matter at a time (the continuity principle), the principle that material entities are publicly observable, and the principle that material entities interact causally with each other (the contact principle). Unlike adults, the young child does not take weight to be a core property of matter. This is seen by the judgment that heat, light, and electricity are "made of some kind stuff," just like cars, trees, and animals and unlike ideas and dreams. More strikingly, weight is viewed as an accidental property of prototypical material entities. For example, most children up through age 10 judge that a pea-sized piece of styrofoam, although material, weighs nothing at all. Weight therefore is not a necessary property of entities judged material.

Because weight is not a necessary property of material entities, it cannot provide a measure of amount of matter. Like the Greeks (Jammer, 1961), young children have no measure of matter (Piaget & Inhelder, 1941; Carey, 1991). For young children, weight (an extensive magnitude) is not differentiated from density (an intensive magnitude) and therefore cannot be an extensive property of matter (Carey, 1991; Smith, Carey, & Wiser, 1985). Children know that if object A weighs 250 grams and if object B weighs less than A, then object B will weigh less than 250 grams. But the same children are perfectly happy to judge that object A can be broken into 10 pieces, each of which weighs 0 grams!

Finally, preschool children, and roughly half of our sample of 6- to 10-year-olds, have not constructed a model of matter as continuous and homogeneous. Asked to imagine cutting a piece of steel in half repeatedly, they claim one finally will arrive at a piece that is so small that it no longer occupies space, and also that one will arrive at a piece of steel in which one could (in principle) see all the steel: There would be no more steel inside. The other half of the elementary schoolchildren, and all the 12-year-olds, judged that steel is continuous, homogeneous, and infinitely divisible: No matter how small the piece, it would still occupy space and would have more steel inside it. (By age 12, in spite of science education, most children have constructed a continuous model of matter.) The continuous model of matter supports the distinction between weight and density, providing the possibility that weight may become one of the core properties of material entities.

How do children come to reconceptualize matter and material objects? Mappings between the domains of physics and number, constructed through the processes described by Nersessian, appear to play a role in this process. Carol Smith and her collaborators (e.g., Smith, Snir, & Grosslight, 1992; Smith, Grosslight, Macklin, & Davis, 1993) have explored the use of physical analogies to drive 11- to 13-year-olds' reconceptualization of matter, especially the differentiation of weight from density and the construction of weight as an extensive quantity. The ideas are tested in the arena of science education. The curriculum that Smith et al. have developed centers around computer-implemented, interactive visual models that serve to represent the mathematics of intensive and extensive quantities. For example, in one model, weight is represented by the number of dots, volume by the number of boxes of a fixed size, and density by the number of dots per box. Students first work with the models, exploring the mathematical relations between the extensive and intensive quantities internal to the models. Then students work on mapping the models to the material world, by exploring such phenomena as the constant ratios of size to weight within each material and the laws of floating and sinking. This mapping is slow and difficult: Without having differentiated weight from density, students cannot readily succeed in mapping number of dots per box to density, rather than to absolute weight or to some other physical variable.

To facilitate this mapping, Smith et al. use the physical analogy of dissolving sugar in water as a source domain (in which sweetness is the intensive quantity and amounts of sugar and water are the extensive quantities) as well as the visual model of the intensive quantity (dot crowdedness). The visual model embodies the mathematics of extensive and intensive quantities and serves as a bridge between mathematical representations and the target domain. As did Maxwell, students explore the analogy in a piecemeal manner, over time. When they encounter the phenomenon of thermal expansion and attempt to model it, they must change the model (material kinds do not have constant densities). This process consolidates and extends their understanding of the mathematics of intensive and extensive quantities, and it contributes to change in their concept of matter. It results in a mapping between physics and mathematics that gives rise to a new core concept: *quantity of matter*.

Smith et al. also employ thought experiments and limiting case analyses in their curricular intervention. Here we provide one example of a limiting case analysis (concretely exemplified rather than part of a thought experiment). Students who lack an extensive concept of weight maintain that a single grain of rice weighs nothing at all. As a classroom exercise, teams of students discover how many grains of rice placed on one edge of a playing card balanced on a thick fulcrum cause it to topple (around 50). They are asked to explain why the card fell. (Most say, "the rice was heavy.") Then the playing card is balanced on a thinner fulcrum, such that 10 grains of rice suffice, and again students explain that the rice was heavy enough to topple the card. Then the card is balanced on a very very thin fulcrum, and a single grain of rice placed on its edge causes it to fall. Students are asked to reconsider whether a single grain of rice weighs a tiny amount or nothing at all. Seven-year-olds are unmoved by this experience; they insist that the single grain of rice weighs nothing. A classroom of 10- or 11-year-olds presents a completely different picture. First, they are very interested in the experiment, and a lively discussion ensues, pitting those who now think that a grain of rice weighs a tiny amount against those who still maintain it weighs nothing. In every class observed thus far, the proponents of the former view have spontaneously produced two arguments: (1) a sensitivity of the measuring device argument and (2) the argument that a single grain of rice must weigh something, because if it weighed 0 grams, then 50 grains of rice would weigh 0 grams as well.

Note that these two arguments depend on the mapping from physical objects to number: It is only in the realm of mathematics that repeated division of a positive quantity always yields a positive quantity, and that repeated addition of 0 always yields 0. In the realm of physics, in contrast, every physical interaction has a threshold. Repeated division of an object always results, eventually, in objects that are too small to be detected by any given physical device. Moreover, a collection of objects, each of which falls below the threshold of a given device, may well be detectable by the device. Like the Aristotelian physicists discussed by Jammer (1961, see note 3), 7-year-old children who resist Smith's limiting case analysis and continue to insist that a single grain of rice weighs nothing are not necessarily irrational. Rather, they may be reasoning consistently within the domain of perceivable objects and outside the domain of number. Smith's limiting case analysis forms part of the process of constructing a mapping between weight and number and fosters the development of an extensive concept of weight. It does not, however, guarantee that the mapping will be constructed and used.

Smith et al. (1993) recently documented that their model-based curriculum, including thought experiments and limiting case analyses, is more effective in inducing conceptual change than is a control curriculum that does not involve these heuristics. Wiser (1988) has obtained similar results from the use of physical analogy in inducing conceptual change in high school students' thermal concepts, especially the differentiation of heat and temperature.

These results support Duhem's and Nersessian's proposals concerning the mechanisms effecting conceptual change. In addition, they reveal that meta-conceptually unsophisticated individuals, who are not part of the social process of scientific theory building, can use the heuristics that scientists use to effect conceptual change. The success of these curricula suggests that conceptual change in childhood is the same sort of process as is conceptual change in the history of science. Studies of conceptual change in physics provide evidence against the strong universality hypothesis.

As in the case of number and psychology, however, the weak universality hypothesis is left untouched. Smith's students did not spontaneously explore the mapping between number and weight, and they did not invent the physical analogy, the thought experiments, or the limiting case analyses. These were constructed to be instructional aids by adults who understood the students' conceptions of matter and who knew what conceptual change they wanted to effect. This demonstration therefore leaves open the possibility that only metaconceptually aware theory builders invent thought experiments, limiting case analyses, and physical analogies in order to construct and use mappings between different knowledge domains.

In summary, studies of conceptual change in childhood show the strong universality hypothesis to be false. Children and adults, like scientists, can bring about changes in their core, domain-specific systems of knowledge by constructing and using mappings across those systems. These studies weaken the expectation of cross-cultural cognitive universals, even in domains supported by innate principles. The personal qualities of mature scientists and the cultural institutions of science are not necessary for conceptual change. Psychologists and anthropologists therefore cannot expect that intuitive theories held by lay people the world over will be enriched versions of the innate principles in these domains.

Conclusions

Studies of conceptual change, both in the history of science and in childhood, suggest that human reasoners go beyond the principles at the core of their initial systems of knowledge. Reasoners do this, in part, by constructing mappings across different knowledge domains. Because the possibilities for mapping across different domains of knowledge are vast, there is little reason to expect, a priori, that all adults in all cultures will have commensurable conceptions, even in those domains where humans are endowed with systems of knowledge whose principles both determine the entities of the domain and support reasoning about those entities.

Still, we do not know whether children or adults spontaneously construct mappings across domains, by means of such heuristics as those described above, in the process of developing systems of culturally constructed knowledge. In the absence of developed science, does cognitive development in all cultures require conceptual change, such that the conceptual systems of the members of distinct cultures are incommensurable with the innately given systems? And does the cultural construction of knowledge in these domains lead to intuitive theories across different cultures that are incommensurable with each other? We offer these two related questions as *the* central problems for cognitive anthropology. At least they are the questions we would most like to have answered.

Notes

1. Some researchers take the wide-ranging changes, at about age 4, in children's abilities to reason about false beliefs, about the appearance–reality distinction, and about certain perspective-taking tasks as evidence for conceptual change in the child's theory of mind (e.g., Perner, 1991). Others maintain that the mature psychological conception of a person is an enriched version of the 2-year-old's conception (e.g., Wellman, 1990; Fodor, 1992). We do not take sides in this debate

but note that researchers on both sides hold that the child, even the baby, attributes to people the capacity for self-generated action, for contingent reactions to the baby's own reactions, and for attention to entities in the world. The later development of representational theories of mind would appear to preserve this core conception of people as sentient and purposive beings.

2. Competing views of analogical reasoning within cognitive science (e.g., Gentner, 1989; Holyoak & Thagard, 1989; Carbonell, 1986) flesh out the details of how such mappings are constructed and used.

3. Galileo's thought experiment reveals that the Aristotelian concept of *weight* is undifferentiated between an extensive quantity (the weight of the composite object is additive) and an intensive quantity (the weight of the composite object is an average). According to Jammer (1961), Aristotle's concept of weight was in fact undifferentiated in this way. Indeed, Aristotle considered a version of Galileo's thought experiment and drew the conclusion that the composite object would fall faster, because the weight of any given piece of substance was a function of the totality of which it was part: Both the small and the large object would be heavier when they became part of a single object! Galileo's thought experiment therefore leads to no contradiction within Aristotelian physics. Thought experiments, like any experiments, depend upon current conceptualizations and do not guarantee conceptual change.

4. This deepening continues beyond age 10; ten-year-olds judge that a skunk, accidentally given an injection of a chemical shortly after birth, which caused it to grow into an animal that looks just like a raccoon, has indeed become a raccoon; adults judge it will continue to be a skunk (Keil, 1989).

5. Springer and Keil (1989) offer no analysis of what constitutes a "biological" functional consequence and include such examples as "has stretched out eyes which make it easier to see their enemies."

6. For example, all 4-year-olds and roughly half of the 6-to 10-year-olds maintained that the box mentioned here could contain both the steel block and an equal volume of air at the same time, "because air isn't anything." The same children also asserted that we need air to breathe, that the wind is made of air, that there is no air in outer space or on the moon. In a different interview of 6-year-olds, in which air had not been mentioned, about one quarter of the children posited air as the material of which dreams and ideas are made!

References

Astington, J. W., Harris, P. L., & Olson, D. R. (Eds.). (1988). *Developing theories of mind*. New York: Cambridge University Press.

Atran, S. (1990). *Cognitive foundations of natural history*. Cambridge: Cambridge University Press.

Baillargeon, R. (1986). Representing the existence and the location of hidden objects: Object permanence in 6- and 8-month-old infants. *Cognition, 23,* 21–41.

Baillargeon, R., Graber, M., DeVos, J., & Black, J. C. (1990). Why do young infants fail to search for hidden objects? *Cognition, 36,* 255–284.

Ball, W. A. (1973, April). The perception of causality in the infant. Paper presented at the Society for Research in Child Development, Philadelphia, PA.

Carbonell, J. (1986). Derivational analogy: A theory of reconstructive problem solving and expertise acquisition. In R. Michalski, J. Carbonell, & T. Mitchell (Eds.), *Machine learning: An artificial intelligence approach* (pp. 371–392). Los Altos, CA: Morgan Kaufmann.

Carey, S. (1985). *Conceptual change in childhood*. Cambridge, MA: Bradford/MIT Press.

Carey, S. (1986). Cognitive science and science education. *American Psychologist, 41*, 1123–1130.

Carey, S. (1988). Conceptual differences between children and adults. *Mind and Language, 3*, 167–181.

Carey, S. (1991). Knowledge acquisition: Enrichment or conceptual change? In S. Carey & R. Gelman (Eds.), *Epigenesis of mind: Studies in biology and cognition*. Hillsdale, NJ: Erlbaum.

Carey, S., Klatt, L., & Schlaffer, M. (1992). Infants' representations of objects and nonsolid substances. Unpublished manuscript, MIT.

Chi, MTH. (1992). Conceptual change within and across ontological categories: Examples from learning and discovery in science. In R. N. Giere (Ed.), *Cognitive models of science. Minnesota Studies in the Philosophy of Science, 15*, 129–186. Minneapolis: University of Minnesota Press.

Chomsky, N. (1980a). *Rules and representations*. New York: Columbia University Press.

Chomsky, N. (1980b). Rules and representations. *Behavioral and Brain Sciences, 3*, 1–61.

Davis, H., & Pérusse, R. (1988). Numerical competence in animals: Definitional issues, current evidence, and a new research agenda. *Behavioral and Brain Sciences, 11*, 561–615.

Duhem, P. (1949). *The aim and structure of physical theory*. Princeton: Princeton University Press.

Estes, D., Wellman, N. M., & Woolley, J. D. (1989). Children's understanding of mental phenomena. In H. Reese (Ed.), *Advances in child development and behavior* (pp. 41–87). New York: Academic Press.

Feyerabend, P. (1962). Explanation, reduction, empiricism. In H. Feigl & G. Maxwell (Eds.), *Minnesota Studies in the Philosophy of Science, 3*, 41–87. Minneapolis: University of Minnesota Press.

Fodor, J. (1992). A theory of the child's theory of mind. *Cognition, 44*, 283–296.

Gallistel, C. R. (1990). *The organization of learning*. Cambridge, MA: Bradford/MIT Press.

Gallistel, C. R., & Gelman, R. (1992). Preverbal and verbal counting and computation. *Cognition, 44*, 43–74.

Gelman, R. (1990). First principles organize attention to and learning about relevant data: Number and the animate–inanimate distinction as examples. *Cognitive Science, 14*, 79–106.

Gelman, R. (1991). Epigenetic foundations of knowledge structures: Initial and transcendent constructions. In S. Carey & R. Gelman (Eds.), *The epigenesis of mind: Essays on biology and cognition* (pp. 293–322). Hillsdale, NJ: Erlbaum.

Gelman, R., & Evans, R. (1981). Understanding infinity: A beginning inquiry. Paper presented at the Society for Research in Child Development, Boston, MA.

Gelman, R., & Gallistel, C. R. (1978). *The child's understanding of number*. Cambridge, MA: Harvard University Press.

Gelman, R., Spelke, E. S., Meck, E. (1983). What preschoolers know about animate and inanimate objects, In D. Rogers & I. A. Sloboda (Eds.), *The acquisition of symbolic skills*. New York: Plenum.

Gelman, S. A., & Wellman, H. M. (1991). Insides and essences: Early understandings of the nonobvious. *Cognition, 38*, 213–244.

Gentner, D. (1989). The mechanisms of analogical learning. In S. Vosniadou and A. Ortony (Eds.), *Similarity and analogical reasoning* (pp. 200–241). Cambridge: Cambridge University Press.

Gentner, D., & Grudin, J. (1985). The evolution of mental metaphors in psychology: A 90-year retrospective. *American Psychologist, 40*, 181–192.

Gibson, J. J. (1950). *The perception of the visual world*. Boston: Houghton-Mifflin.

Gruber, H. E. (1974). *Darwin on man: A psychological study of scientific creativity*. New York: E. P. Dutton.

Hacking, I. (1993). Working in a new world: The taxonomic solution. In P. Horwich & J. Thomson (Eds.), *World changes*. Cambridge, MA: MIT Press.

Hatano, G., & Inagaki, K. (1987). Everyday biology and school biology: How do they interact? *The Quarterly Newsletter of the Laboratory of Comparative Human Cognition, 9*, 120–128.

Heider, F., & Simmel, M. (1944). An experimental study of apparent behavior. *The American Journal of Psychology, 57*, 243–259.

Hirsch, E. (1982). *The concept of identity*. New York: Oxford University Press.

Hofsten, C. von, & Spelke, E. S. (1985). Object perception and object-directed reaching in infancy. *Journal of Experimental Psychology: General, 114*, 198–212.

Holyoak, K., & Thagard, P. (1989). Analogical mapping by constraint satisfaction: A computational theory. *Cognitive Science, 13*, 295–356.

Inagaki, K., & Hatano, G. (1988). Young children's understanding of the mind–body distinction. Paper presented at the Meeting of the American Educational Research Association, New Orleans.

Jammer, M. (1961). *Concepts of mass*. Cambridge, MA: Harvard University Press.

Jeyifous, S. (1986). *Atimodemo: Semantic conceptual development among the Yoruba*. Doctoral dissertation, Cornell University.

Johnson, M. H., & Morton, J. (1991). *Biology and cognitive development: The case of face recognition*. Oxford: Blackwell.

Keil, F. C. (1989). *Concepts, kinds, and cognitive development*. Cambridge, MA: MIT Press.

Kellman, P. J., Gleitman, H., & Spelke, E. S. (1987). Object and observer motion in the perception of objects by infants. *Journal of Experimental Psychology: Human Perception and Performance, 13*, 586–593.

Kellman, P. J., & Spelke, E. S. (1983). Perception of partly occluded objects in infancy. *Cognitive Psychology, 15*, 483–524.

Kellman, P. J., Spelke, E. S., & Short, K. (1986). Infant perception of object unity from translatory motion in depth and vertical translation. *Child Development, 57*, 72–86.

Kestenbaum, R., Termine, N., & Spelke, E. S. (1987). Perception of objects and object boundaries by three-month-old infants. *British Journal of Developmental Psychology, 5*, 367–383.

Kitcher, P. (1983). *The nature of mathematical knowledge*. Oxford: Oxford University Press.

Kitcher, P. (1988). The child as parent of the scientist. *Mind and Language, 3,* 217–228.

Klahr, D., & Wallace, J. G. (1973). The role of quantification operators in the development of conservation. *Cognitive Psychology, 4,* 301–327.

Kuhn, T. S. (1962). *The structure of scientific revolutions.* Chicago: University of Chicago Press.

Kuhn, T. S. (1977). A function for thought experiments. In T. S. Kuhn, *The essential tension.* Chicago: University of Chicago Press.

Kuhn, T. S. (1982). Commensurability, comparability, communicability. *PSA 1982, 2* (pp. 669–688). East Lansing, MI: Philosophy of Science Association.

Leslie, A. M. (1987). Pretense and representation: The origins of "Theory of mind." *Psychological Review, 94,* 412–426.

Leslie, A. M. (1988). The necessity of illusion: Perception and thought in infancy. In L. Weiskrantz (Ed.), *Thought and language* (pp. 185–210). Oxford: Oxford University Press.

Leslie, A. M. (1991, April). Infants' understanding of invisible displacement. Paper presented at the Society for Research in Child Development, Seattle, WA.

Marr, D. (1982). *Vision.* San Francisco, CA: Freeman.

Nersessian, N. J. (1992). How do scientists think? Capturing the dynamics of conceptual change in science. In R. N. Giere (Ed.), *Cognitive models of science. Minnesota Studies in the Philosophy of Science, 15,* 3–44. Minneapolis: University of Minnesota Press.

Perner, J. (1991). *Understanding the representational mind.* Cambridge, MA: Bradford MIT Press.

Piaget, J. (1954). *The construction of reality in the child.* New York: Basic Books.

Piaget, J., & Inhelder, B. (1941). *Le development des quantites chez l'enfant.* Neufchatel: Delchaux et Niestle.

Premack, D. (1990). The infant's theory of self-propelled objects. *Cognition, 36*(1), 1–16.

Rozin, P. (1976). The evolution of intelligence and access to the cognitive unconscious. *Progress in Psychobiology and Physiological Psychology, 6,* 245–279.

Shipley, E. F., & Shepperson, B. (1990). Countable entities: Developmental changes. *Cognition, 34,* 109–136.

Slater, A., Morison, V., Somers, M., Mattock, A., Brown, E., & Taylor, D. (1990). Newborn and older infants' perception of partly occluded objects. *Infant Behavior and Development, 13,* 33–49.

Smith, C., Carey, S., & Wiser, M. (1985). On differentiation: A case study of the development of the concepts of size, weight, and density. *Cognition, 21,* 177–237.

Smith, C., Grosslight, L., Macklin, D., & Davis, H. (1993). A comparison of IPS and a parallel model-based curriculum in producing conceptual change. Paper presented at the American Educational Research Association.

Smith, C., Snir, Y., & Grosslight, L. (1992). Using conceptual models to facilitate conceptual change: The case of weight and density. *Cognition and Instruction, 9,* 221–283.

Soja, N., Carey, S., Spelke, E. (1991). Ontological constraints on early word meanings. *Cognition, 38,* 179–211.

Solomon, G., Johnson, S., Zaitchik, D., & Carey, S. (1993). The young child's conception of inheritance. Paper presented at the Society for Research in Child Development, New Orleans.

Spelke, E. S. (1988). Where perceiving ends and thinking begins: The apprehension of objects in infancy. In A. Yonas (Ed.), *Perceptual development in infancy. Minnesota Symposium on Child Psychology*, *20*, 191–234. Hillsdale, NJ: Erlbaum.

Spelke, E. S. (1990). Principles of object perception. *Cognitive Science*, *14*, 29–56.

Spelke, E. S. (1991). Physical knowledge in infancy: Reflections on Piaget's theory. In S. Carey & R. Gelman (Eds.), *Epigenesis of mind: Studies in biology and cognition*. Hillsdale, NJ: Erlbaum.

Spelke, E. S., Breinlinger, K., & Jacobson, K. (1992). Gestalt relations and object perception in infancy. Unpublished manuscript, Cornell University.

Spelke, E. S., Breinlinger, K., Macomber, J., & Jacobson, K. (1992). Origins of knowledge. *Psychological Review*, *99*, 605–632.

Spelke, E. S., Hofsten, C. von, & Kestenbaum, R. (1989). Object perception and object-directed reaching in infancy: Interaction of spatial and kinetic information for object boundaries. *Developmental Psychology*, *25*, 185–196.

Spelke, E. S., & Kestenbaum, R. (1986). Les origines du concept d'objet. *Psychologie Francaise*, *31*, 67–72.

Spelke, E. S., & Van de Walle, G. (in press). Perceiving and reasoning about objects: Insights from infants. In N. Eilan, W. Brewer, & R. McCarthy (Eds). *Spatial Representation*. Oxford: Basil Blackwel.

Springer, K. (1992). Children's beliefs about the biological implications of kinship. *Child Development*, *63*, 950–959.

Springer, K., & Keil, F. C. (1989). On the development of biologically specific beliefs: The case of inheritance. *Child Development*, *60*, 637–648.

Streri, A., & Spelke, E. S. (1988). Haptic perception of objects in infancy. *Cognitive Psychology*, *20*, 1–23.

Streri, A., & Spelke, E. S. (1989). Effects of motion and figural goodness on haptic object perception in infancy. *Child Development*, *60*, 1111–1125.

Streri, A., Spelke, E. S., & Rameix, E. (1992). *Modality-specific and amodal aspects of object perception in infancy: The case of active touch*. Unpublished manuscript.

Suppe, F. (1977). *The structure of scientific theories*. Urbana: University of Illinois Press.

Thagard, P. (1988). *Conceptual revolutions*. Princeton, NJ: Princeton University Press.

Tronick, E. (1982). *Social interchange in infancy*. Baltimore, MD: University Park Press.

Tweney, R. D. (1991). Faraday's notebooks: The active organization of creative science. *Physics Education*, *26*, 301.

Van de Walle, G. A., & Spelke, E. S. (1993). Integration of information over time: Infants' perception of partly occluded objects. Poster presented at the Society for Research in Child Development, New Orleans, LA.

Vosniadou, S., & Brewer, W. F. (1992). Mental models of the earth: A study of conceptual change in childhood. *Cognitive Psychology*, *24*, 535–585.

Wellman, H. M., & Miller, K. F. (1986). The development of understanding of the concept of the number zero, 3–7 year-olds. *British Journal of Developmental Psychology*, *4*, 31–42.

Wellman, H. M. (1990). *The child's theory of mind*. Cambridge, MA: Bradford/MIT Press.

Wellman, H. M., & Gelman, S. A. (1992). Cognitive development: Foundational theories of core domains. *Annual Review of Psychology*, *43*, 337–375.

Wiggins, D. (1980). *Sameness and substance*. Cambridge, MA: Harvard University Press.

Wiser (1988). Can models foster conceptual change? The case of heat and temperature. Harvard University: Educational Technology Center Technical Report.

Wynn, K. (1992). Addition and subtraction by human infants. *Nature*, *358*, 749.

Xu, F., & Carey, S. (1992). Infants' concept of numerical identity. Paper presented at the Boston University Language Acquisition Conference.

8 Is the acquisition of social categories based on domain-specific competence or on knowledge transfer?

Lawrence A. Hirschfeld

The understanding of some conceptual domains is clearly helped by a domain-specific competence, as many of the chapters in this volume establish. This is the case for middle-sized objects physics (Carey & Spelke), living kind classification (Atran, Keil), theory of mind (Gopnik & Wellman, Leslie), and numerosity (R. Gelman & Brenneman). Other conceptual domains lack such an underlying domain-specific competence, including, for instance, astronomy, particle physics, computer technology, or (as the chapters by Boyer and Vosniadou suggest) religious representations and cosmology. In yet other domains the question is moot, as for instance in the case of chemistry or artifacts. The issue is quite undecided too in the domain of social categories (Turiel, 1983).

How does knowledge develop in domains for which there is no ad hoc innately specified competence? The mechanism invoked most often is analogy and transfer from better grounded domains. In particular, it has been suggested that acquisition of social categories is based on a transfer from the biological domain rather than on a domain-specific competence (Atran, 1990; Boyer, 1990; Rothbart & Taylor, 1990). In this chapter, I present evidence and arguments suggesting that the acquisition of social category does not depend on such a transfer. This could be so either because there is a domain-specific innately specified competence just for the social domain, or because social categories fall from the start within the extension of wider competences. I discuss these and other possibilities in the conclusion.

There is no well-described psychological mechanism of analogical transfer but there are lots of plausible examples. Many rich examples are found

I am grateful to Scott Atran, Susan Gelman, Doug Medin, and Ann Stoler for helpful comments on previous drafts of this chapter and to Ed Rothman for suggestions on analyses. I owe an especially great debt to Dan Sperber for his careful readings of earlier drafts and valuable suggestions. Research discussed in this chapter was supported by grants from the Fondation Fyssen and the National Science Foundation (INT-8814397 and RCD-8751136), and funds from the Office of Vice President for Research, University of Michigan.

in the social sciences, in particular the history of science and anthropology. Foremost in anthropologists' interest is the rich exploitation of analogies between the natural and the social domain found throughout the world, the best known example of which is totemism. It is common in the ethnographic record to find evidence for the representation of social and cultural issues "through the symbolic medium of animals" (Turner, 1985: 49; Crocker, 1977; Tambiah, 1969; Lévi-Strauss, 1962) and conversely to see human psychological and social traits attributed to animals (Hallowell, 1976) and occasionally inanimate objects (Daniel, 1984). In these analogies between humans and animals, is one and the same domain generally the source and the other the target of a transfer of representations? Could it be that one domain is based on a domain-specific competence and the other built from this one by analogy? Or do they both involve specific competence from the start, as I will suggest?

In fact two domain-specific competences are reasonably well established: naive psychology in the human (but not the social) sphere and naive biology in the animal sphere. Naive psychology has to do with psychological explanation of individual action, with explaining behavior. Naive biology has to do with explaining appearance and character in terms of underlying species-specific essences, explaining beings. Both the transfer of human psychology to other living kinds and the transfer of essentialist classification to social categories have been claimed to occur. This chapter focuses on the transfer from the biological to the social domain and questions its constitutive role. (The relationship between the two types of transfers is discussed in Hirschfeld, in press-a.)

Unlike living kinds classification, not all social categorization is essentialist. It is a common observation of anthropology that there is a contrast between two types of socially recognized social categories: Some are clearly created by humans, resulting from individual or collective choice, decision, conventions, achievements, and so on. Others are natural-like – they cannot be chosen or achieved (or only by means of processes that are seen as natural-like or supernatural-like themselves). In other words, some social properties are contingent to the person's identity, whereas others are essential (Hirschfeld, 1988). Examples of natural-like categories (on the most common folk interpretation) are castes, aristocracies, witches (vs. taught sorcerers), priestly lineages, ethnicity, race, age, kinsmen, gender, and so forth. Examples of human-made categories are professions, elected positions, economic classes, friends, membership of voluntary association, sorcerers, and the like.

It is for the natural-like categories that the possibility of a transfer from naive biology easily comes to mind. This transfer has been claimed on essentially two grounds: the blatant and much observed similarities between the essentialism of living kind categories and that of the relevant social categories on the one hand, and a reluctance to envisage an innately specified domain-specific competence directly underlying social categorization on the other. On the basis of my own experimental investigations, I maintain that social categories fall within the scope of a domain-specific competence, and are not brought into existence by mere analogical transfer (this does not deny that such transfers take place; on the contrary it may help explain them better).

The issue is relevant both to classical concerns of anthropologists and to contemporary concerns of developmentalists working on knowledge transfer. In fact, I believe that the insights of anthropology *and* psychology may be needed if we are to advance our understanding of this shared problem.

Two transfer models

For at least a century, anthropologists have debated how best to interpret the commonly encountered association of two systems of difference, the natural one of species, and the human one of social categories. The most widely discussed instance of such an association is totemism, the use of differences between natural species to symbolize differences between social groups.

Early accounts of totemic beliefs, in which membership in a certain plant or animal species is identified with membership in a particular social category, often interpreted these associations less as transfers than as equivalencies. To cite one of the best-known illustrations, the Bororo of central Brazil claim that they are parrots (or members of other totemized species) (Crocker, 1977; Turner, 1989). Von den Steinen (1894), who made the initial report, insisted that the Bororo could not distinguish between humans and animals, an interpretation that hardly anyone since has taken seriously. Yet, even modern ethnographers confirm that the Bororo, and other similar groups, make such assertions with apparent sincerity and explicitness that require further interpretation (Crocker, 1977; Turner, 1989). Thus, although subsequent scholars have seen the cognitive link as being less direct than the identification of animals and humans, considerable debate surrounds how to characterize such beliefs. Mauss, for example, prefiguring more recent cognitivist interest in essentialist thinking, suggested that such totemic identifications imply a "kinship of substance between humans and the revered species" (1947: 161).

Most researchers in anthropology, however, have taken totemic claims to be evidence of symbolic, figurative associations, based either on unique cultural considerations (Boas, 1916) or affective ones (Radcliffe-Brown, 1922). Lévi-Strauss's (1962, 1966) landmark work suggests that such symbolic links are best understood as a mode of thought pervasively concerned with the relationship between natural and cultural (as opposed to human) orders. A number of scholars have noted that although the affinity between categories of animal and human variation is intuitive, it is less the function of an objective and perceived parallel than it is the result of an obviously created (and frequently far-fetched) one (Tambiah, 1969; Rosaldo, 1972; Leach, 1964;

Douglas, 1966). The relationship between the natural and human orders does not "jump out" for apprehension, but implies a "historic past when man for all time made his passage from nature to culture" (Tambiah, 1969: 454).

The notion that the natural order impinges, through knowledge transfer, onto our organization of the human world continues to be taken up both by anthropologists and psychologists. Researchers working from a domain perspective have recently suggested that the natural and social orders, however, may be linked through a mode of thought that is less than literal but (cognitively) more than symbolic. Atran (1990), Boyer (1990), and Rothbart and Taylor (1990), for example, have independently argued that the natural and human orders converge when social categories are "naturalized." Naturalization, here, involves a process whereby principles derived from the understanding of biological variation come to govern understanding of social difference. What is imported to the target (social) domain, according to all three proposals, is a belief that members of a category share an essence that gives rise to the surface similarities supposedly common to members of the category.

The naturalization of social categories proposal (hereafter, the *naturalization model*) has developmental consequences as well: On this view, children naturalize social differences by using their enriched knowledge of biological variation to structure their emergent understandings of the social world. "Children might initially borrow from their presumptions of the underlying natures of living things in order to better organize their knowledge of HUMANS and merge this knowledge with that of other LIVING THINGS" (Atran, 1990: 74).

This borrowing, Atran (1990) and Boyer (1990) have separately argued, is well motivated and follows from a confluence of conceptual similarity and cognitive need – much the same impetuses to which Radcliffe-Brown (1922) and Boas (1916) appealed in their early speculations on the cultural origin of totemic beliefs. The argument, however, is about individual representations rather than collective ones, and is framed epistemologically: Children readily transfer principles organizing biological concepts to social ones because of the ontological proximity of the two domains, the fact that humans and animals "are adjacent ontological domains, as it were" (Atran, 1990: 74; see also Greeno, 1983; Spiro, Feltovich, Coulson, & Anderson, 1989). At the same time, the projection of biological principles to the social domain meets demands for cognitive economy (Boyer, 1990; see also Spiro et al., 1989; Vosniadou, 1989; cf. Inagaki & Sugiyama, 1988; Inagaki & Hatano, 1987): Such transfers import constraints on social categories that the semantics of these social categories do not themselves afford.

It may seem obvious today to anybody attending to the literature in cognitive science that if there is a transfer between living kinds and social categories, it goes from the biological to the social. But the reverse order was proposed by Durkheim and Mauss (1903/1963) in a very influential essay, the echoes of which are still to be found in today's social sciences (e.g., Douglas, 1986). They argued that

the first logical categories were social categories; the first classes of things were classes of men, into which these things were integrated. It was because men were grouped, and thought of themselves in the form of groups, that in their ideas they grouped other things, and in the beginning the two modes of grouping were merged to the point of being indistinct. Moieties were the first genera; clans, the first species. (Durkheim & Mauss, 1903/1963: 82–83)

The relation Durkheim and Mauss describe (hereafter, the *societal model*) involves a transfer from the human to the animal orders (for a more recent statement, see Dwyer, 1976).[1] Durkheim and Mauss also contend that the relation involves the transfer of principles for reasoning about human variation to animal variation. Hence, their societal model is clearly the reverse of the naturalization model mentioned earlier.

Implicit in any transfer model is the notion that only some aspects of the source domain are imported into the target domain. An analogy's utility depends in significant measure on this *partial* transfer (Spiro et al., 1989). For example, although the hydrogen atom is like the solar system, this

clearly does not convey that *all* of one's knowledge about the solar system should be attributed to the atom. The inheritance of characteristics is only partial.... The analogical models used in science can be characterized as structure-mappings between complex systems. Such an analogy conveys that like relational systems hold within two different domains.... Thus, a structure-mapping analogy asserts that identical operations and relationships hold among nonidentical things. The relational structure is preserved, but not the objects. (Gentner & Gentner, 1983: 101–102)

For the human and biological domains, the issue can be framed in terms of *which* relational structure is being preserved. There is broad agreement that when young children coordinate their knowledge of the human and the biological worlds, they extend an understanding of something they know a good deal about to something with which they are less familiar.[2] But what is it exactly that young children know much about, and what is it they are rank novices at? It may be informative in this regard to compare the precise aspects of biological and social knowledge that end up being genuinely analogous across domains.

According to the naturalization model proposed by Atran, Boyer, and Rothbart and Taylor, what is transferred are two notions: First, biological variation comes to be seen as an apt model for human variation, and second, members of a given social category come to be viewed as naturally resembling one another. Models by Atran, Boyer, and Rothbart and Taylor all appeal to perceptual availability. It is seen as inescapably apparent that plants and animals vary from one another not continuously or randomly, but so as to constitute discrete kinds. Analogously, children seem to be provided with genuine or spurious evidence that humans too vary from one another in a manner that suggests discrete groupings.

By analogy, then, these limited varieties of humans are typified by shared underlying essences, just as the limited variety of other living things is best typified in terms of shared essences (see also, Hirschfeld, 1989a). Just as there are apples and oranges, there are Japanese and Javanese. Just as all apples share an underlying essence that causes apple blossoms (specifically apple ovaries) to become apples (and not oranges), all Japanese (supposedly) share an underlying essence that causes infant Japanese to become adult Japanese (and not Javanese). Research by Gelman and her associates (Gelman & Wellman, 1991; Gelman, Coley, & Gottfried, this volume) suggests that this sort of essentialist thinking emerges quite early for biological kinds.[3] Work both by anthropologists (Mauss, 1947) and social psychologists (Allport, 1954) indicates that it is a recurrent feature of adult thought across many cultures and historical epochs.

However, as I have pointed out, not all social categories are construed in an essentialist manner. Some social categories are based on an understanding of the behavior per se of members of the category. Although regularities in such behavior may be attributable to some underlying *cause* (say, the recurrent patterns of behavior associated with an occupation that are derived from the function the occupation performs), these causes are not essentialized. A similar argument could be made for regularities in behavior resulting from one's personality. In such cases there is an attribution of underlying cause, but not of underlying essence. If categories of this sort resulted at all from a transfer, it would have to be from naive psychology rather than from naive biology. Here again, the evidence I will present speaks against a transfer explanation and for a domain-specific competence available from the start.

The mental representation of racial categories

I want to argue that, as maintained in the naturalization model, there is a domain-specific competence for the biological domain that underlies essentialist thinking in biology, and that, as suggested in the societal model, there is a domain-specific competence for the social domain (which has the relevant aspects of the social domain in its extension) that underlies essentialist thinking about social categories. If this is right, both the naturalization and societal models are wrong in assuming that competence in one domain is constituted by transfer from the other. The well-documented transfers that do occur are merely made particularly easy and fruitful by the similarities between the two fields (see Hirschfeld, in press-a).

In a modern secular society, there are relatively few natural-like social categories. Most social categories are of the human-made type, such as occupational categories or voluntary memberships, for instance. However those natural-like categories that are found in modern society are of major importance. They occur in four areas: age, gender, race or ethnicity, and kinship.

Age and gender are major areas of study in themselves to which I have no original research to contribute. They are areas, however, in which the naturalization model seems the least plausible: It would be strange to propose that essentialist thinking on human ages or genders is derived from antecedent essentialist thinking on animals, in part because gender essentialism may developmentally precede essentialist thinking on animals (see Bem, 1989; cf. Carey's quote later in this chapter). Not only is it plausible that age and gender understanding is based on a domain-specific competence, but it could well be that, in the case of gender, the relevant domain is not the social domain as a whole, but gender by itself.

In the case of kinship, on the other hand, there is not even agreement among anthropologists or psychologists as to what the adult folk understanding of the area consists of – whether it is essentialist, or based on a conventional labeling of reproductive relations, or what. I have argued in a series of papers, however, that a partly essentialist understanding of kinship is in fact at work, and I will recapitulate the argument in this chapter (see, Hirschfeld, 1986, 1989b).

Still, the best test case of essentialism in modern secular society is that of race. Here the fact that adult folk views of race are essentialist need hardly be argued. The open question is whether these are essentialist as a result of transfer from naive biology, or whether they are so because of domain-specific competence from the start. To decide the issue, I have conducted a series of experiments on the development of racial thinking in young children.

For both children and adults, race (and ethnicity) are a universally salient social contrast (van den Berghe, 1981; Katz, 1982; Aboud, 1988). Yet significant changes in racial thinking are claimed to occur during early childhood. For example, although adults believe that race is closely tied to notions of underlying essence (Allport, 1954), young children are not granted the ability to associate such relatively abstract criteria with racial categories (Aboud, 1988). Second, race, according to the commonsense adult view, is a biological phenomenon spanning both the animal and human domains (van den Berghe, 1981). But it is generally thought that young children do not appreciate the biological implications of race (Aboud, 1988). Finally, whereas older children and adults see humans as "one mammal among many" (Carey, 1985: 94), young children appear to hold humans apart from other biological species, treating humans as a taxonomic (Carey, 1985; Johnson, Mervis, & Boster, 1992; Inagaki, 1990) or ontological isolate (Keil, 1979). To the extent that children's thinking about human racial variation develops in coordination with their biological knowledge, we would expect to find evidence that these knowledge structures emerge and change during early childhood in a way that suggests specific patterns of influence. However this is not what we do find.

Racial awareness in young children

Children are not credited with an understanding of all the factors that make race a highly salient social dimension to adults. They are, however, generally assumed to show an early sensitivity to racial variation, which is viewed as unavoidable on *perceptual grounds* for both adults (Taylor, Fiske, Etcoff, & Ruderman, 1978) and young children (Aboud, 1988; Vaughan, 1987; Katz, 1982). If this were true, children might be led to associate human, racial variation with patterns of nonhuman diversity that similarly "cry out to be named" (Berlin, 1978; see Johnson et al., 1992). That is, children might come to naturalize racial differences because they believe that (at least some) differences in human morphology are similar to the morphological differences between nonhuman animal species. A considerable literature is consistent with this argument: First, perceptual information is thought to play a critical role in the way social categories generally, and racial ones in particular, are derived and represented (Aboud, 1987; Alejandro-Wright, 1985; Furth, 1980; Kosslyn & Kagan, 1981; Rosenberg, 1979). Second, the more perceptually marked a social category, the more precociously it is thought to be acquired (Aboud, 1987; Hartley, Rosenbaum, & Schwartz, 1948).

The naturalization model applied to race predicts therefore that children first perceive phenomenal variation in humans, see some of these as discontinuous and generating discrete human types, and in order to understand these observations resort to the essentialist model already developed, on the basis of a domain-specific competence, for the living kinds domain. The two testable empirical predictions here are (1) that perception of racial differences precedes the formation of racial categories, and (2) that racial categories are constructed from the start so as to incorporate and make sense of the observed differences. I will, however, challenge both predictions.

Note first that the view that racial categories are based on perceptual criteria engenders an empirical paradox. This paradox dissolves if racial categories are seen as perceptually less rich. A good deal of evidence has established that preschool children can readily distinguish between racial groups. An equally extensive literature details young children's readiness to maintain prejudices about their members (Clark & Clark, 1940; Katz, 1982; Semaj, 1981; Sorce, 1979; Durrett & Davy, 1979; Madge, 1976). Yet, racial group membership plays almost no role in shaping preschool children's interactions, including the choice of playmates (Doyle, 1983; Finkelstein & Haskins, 1983; Singleton & Asher, 1979; McCandless & Hoyt, 1961; Lambert & Taguchi, 1956; Stevenson & Stevenson, 1960).

These findings are paradoxical on what may seem a trivial and innocuous assumption, namely, that young children's beliefs about a particular racial group cause them systematically to recognize members of that group. This assumption seems to derive support from studies showing that young children (1) sort humans on the basis of racial morphology and (2) express attitudes toward members of various named races. Thus, it has been assumed that young children put these two competencies together so that the extensions of children's and adults' racial categories are the same. But this assumption is warranted only if young children's perceptual sortings and categorical evaluations are actually combined. If young children's attention is drawn more to the *categories* of race than to their physical correlates, this might not be the case. Young children might – in fact I will show they do – focus on race as a way of abstractly categorizing people rather than as a way of labeling perceptual regularities they apprehend in the human world. If this is so, then, on the one hand, they tend to sort humans "appropriately," and, on the other hand, they tend to give expression to familiar racial attitudes, without however combining these two dispositions.

In short, if children are better at thinking about racial differences than instantiating them, then there is little reason to believe that racial categories would have the same behavioral or attitudinal consequences for children and adults. Assessing this possibility involves examining the sorts of perceptual information contained in early racial concepts. If young children's representations of racial categories are not invariably rich with perceptual information (and therefore not directly associated with specific differences in appearance), preschoolers may be unable to translate their precocious dispreferences for members of minority groups into behavior because they would not be sure which individuals are in fact members of minority groups.

In order to evaluate the standard claim that perceptual information is integral to preschoolers' racial concepts, I conducted several studies exploring the sorts of social information young French children extract from everyday experience (Hirschfeld, 1993). In the first study, I looked at preschoolers' sorting skills over racial variation. The primary data supporting the view that racial categories are rich with perceptual information come from studies showing that 3½-year-olds can readily distinguish between people according to skin color (Clark & Clark, 1940; Lemaine, Santoli, Bonnet, & Ben Brika, 1985; Katz, 1982). Common to all of these studies is a task that asks children to match racial labels with stimuli contrasting *on a single* physical dimension. That is, given an array of dolls, half of which have light skin color and half dark, young children will readily pick out the dark-skinned dolls when asked which are the black (or, in older studies, "Negro") dolls. I used a slightly more complex task, one that more closely paralleled everyday social encounters in that it assessed children's understanding of race in a context of multiple (and thus ambiguous) possibilities: French preschoolers were asked to pair four familiar racial labels with their referents.[4] Performance levels suggest that preschoolers find this (more ecologically valid task) challenging: The 4-year-olds were correct in only 40% of the trials, and 3-year-olds were able to pair racial labels correctly with the appropriate pictures in only 17% of the trials.

Why do these performances differ so from those reported by previous researchers? One explanation is that although children understand that there are physical correlates to race and ethnicity, they know very little about which physical correlates go with which racial and ethnic categories. When the task involves matching a single racial category to a single variation in physical feature (as when children are presented with two dolls, one dark-skinned and one not, and asked to chose which of two dolls is the black one), the choice is relatively easy. When the task involves matching several possible physical types with several racial labels, the choice is not so straight-forward.

If this interpretation is correct, it suggests that children learn about race by attending to verbal, discursive cues rather than to visual ones. Accordingly, young children's knowledge of race as a verbal category should outpace their understanding of race as a visual phenomonen. To explore this possibility, I conducted a second series of studies (Hirschfeld, 1993). In these I collected data on the perceptual richness of early racial categories. Using two narrative tasks, I found that children recalled considerably more racial information after *listening* to a complex verbal narrative than after *viewing* a similarly complex visual one. These differences in rates of recall could not be attributed to the modality of the task itself, because rates of recall of other kinds of social information were greater on the visual than the verbal task. Even when the link between the racial label and its referent was pointed out immediately before viewing the visual text, children's use of racial labels was almost non-existent. Moreover, once memory factors were controlled for, I found no evidence of developmental trends in racial recognition and recall during the preschool years. I also found that by using a narrative task (thus embedding judgments about race in a social context simulating everyday experience), the salience of race as a way of categorizing people was significantly *decreased*, relative to other social categories.

These findings strongly suggest that children initially acquire knowledge that there are racial differences, and only later discover what those differences might be (which is not to say that perceptual information is unimportant to racial concepts, of course). In this respect, young children's understanding of human racial categories differs from their understanding of nonhuman animal categories: Although membership in a natural category can override differences in appearance in guiding young children's inductions about hidden properties (Gelman & Markman, 1986, 1987), in the absence of some perceptual cue, natural category membership alone does not afford this inferential potential (Davidson & Gelman, 1990; Boster, 1988). Given this, the notion that social categories are naturalized *because* human variation in morphology is seen as analogous to variations in natural species morphology is hardly persuasive.

In short, natural and social differences come to be recognized in crucially different ways. Thus, the *perceptual* motivation for subsuming them both under a single principle of organization, transferred from one domain to the other, is lost. This of course does not rule out the possibility that social categories are naturalized via analogic transfer, but it does leave us without a mechanism for explaining how this transfer occurs. There are many kinds of social categories, most of which are not naturalized. If the visual analogy between racial and living kind categories is not available to young children, what prompts them toward an essentialist construal of *this* particular kind of social category?

Social identity and the biological implications of race

In the narrative recall studies just discussed, although patterns of responses derived from verbal and visual representations were strikingly different for the *amount* of information recalled, the *type* of information recalled was quite similar. Certain kinds of social information are more salient in preschoolers' recall regardless of whether the stimulus story was verbal or pictorial. Specifically, young children recall an individual's occupation more readily than either the person's race or nonracial physical features. One explanation of these findings is that when parsing a social context, young children are concerned with discovering the types of persons there are in that context. That is, children are not simply concerned with understanding the context as a situational frame of reference (Ross, 1981), but also with exploring ontological possibilities.

Yet young children also recall a person's race more readily than nonracial but anatomical information (e.g., information about a person's physique or stature). This finding is more curious. Preschoolers, it is widely argued, rely almost exclusively on physical appearance in person categorization (Flavell, 1985; Furth, 1980; Aboud, 1988; Rosenberg, 1979). Young children's greater attention to occupation might be explained by the greater salience of behaviorally relevant dimensions or apparel in representing social experience. It was quite interesting, however, to find that young children recall racial features more frequently than other physically relevant features (e.g., references to physique, like *fat* or *tall*). If, as is standardly claimed, children rely so heavily on appearance and do not understand that some kinds of corporeal appearance are fundamentally different from other kinds of physical differences, why do they find racial variation more salient than other sorts of corporeal differences?

The issue is linked to young children's conceptualization of social identity. The standard view in the identity literature is that young children do not conceive of social difference in biological terms: Although young children can readily categorize people by race and ethnicity, a number of studies suggest that prior to 8 years of age children do not understand that a person's race or ethnicity is immutable (Aboud, 1987, 1988; Semaj, 1980). In other words, young children do not understand that a person's racial identity remains intact in the face of changes in appearance. They fail to understand this, Aboud (1988) argues, because they are aware only of obvious features of race and ethnicity. Thus, they would not appreciate that race and ethnicity are derived from one's family background (Alejandro-Wright, 1985). For example, in one study, Aboud and Skerry (1983) found that most Jewish children under 8 years of age, when shown a picture of themselves dressed in Eskimo clothing, identified themselves as Eskimo rather than Jewish. This overreliance on physical appearance in identity judgments may be quite general. Studies by Keil (1989), for example, indicate that 4-year-olds fail to grasp identity constancy, in the face of changes in outward appearance, for nonhuman animals. Similarly, a number of studies suggest the same for human gender (Gelman, Collman, & Maccoby, 1986; Carey, 1985; Emmerich, Goldman, Kirsch, & Sharabany, 1977; Slaby & Frey, 1975; Kohlberg, 1966).

These conclusions, however, contrast strikingly with other recent work on naive biology that challenges the view that young children believe, at least for nonhuman living things, that outer appearances determine other relevant aspects of a creature's intrinsic nature. Preschoolers appear to have a more adultlike grasp of causality (Gelman & Kremer, 1991; Massey & R. Gelman, 1988) and are considerably less reliant on appearances in deciding whether a living kind has a nonobvious property (Gelman & Markman, 1986) or underlying essence (Gelman & Wellman, 1991) than the externalist model implies (see also Brown, 1989; Carey, 1985). In the light of these other results, it is intriguing that identity studies should find that young children have so little appreciation of the biological importance of gender, racial, and other social properties. These categories are biologically relevant to adults. As Atran (1990), Boyer (1990), and Rothbart and Taylor (1990) point out, much of the inferential potential of such social categories derives from their association with biological categories.

If an understanding of social categories in terms of underlying essences were absent in young children, then this would suggest a marked disjunction between early naive understandings of the social and biological worlds. The later emergence of a biological construal of race or gender, accordingly, would suggest that the biological model is being transferred to the social domain. Many believe that this is already established:

It is perfectly clear . . . that for children below age 7, gender is not a basic biological fact about people. Rather, its meaning to children is social: what they wear, how they cut their hair, what they like to play with, and how other people react to these choices. Coming to see gender as a biological given is part of the emergence of biology as a separate domain of intuitive theorizing that occurs during the first decade of life. One source of this change is very likely learning about reproduction, for gender differences play a crucial role in explaining the origin of babies. (Carey, 1985: 54)

As we have seen, if we replace *gender* with *race* in the this quote we would accurately capture the standard view on racial category acquisition (Aboud, 1987; 1988).[5]

However, people – and children in particular – can have an essentialist understanding of gender that is a priori but not biologically well informed. In particular, reproduction is only one aspect of the biology of gender and race, and too much emphasis on it may obscure the extent that preschool children do in fact find biological implications in these concepts. For example, although young children may not appreciate some of the biological significance of gender, this does not mean that they do not comprehend that nonobvious physical properties are central to gender constancy. Bem (1989) found that even young children preserved gender constancy over transformations in appearance once the children had the domain-specific knowledge that genitalia are nonobvious defining attributes of male and female. (Genitalia are nonobvious in the sense that they are typically not available for inspection – in contrast to the sorts of cultural cues that gender constancy tasks [often, misleadingly] test over.)

Sensitivity to gender emerges early, during middle toddlerhood (Katz, 1983; Lewis, 1981). Other social categories, including race and occupation, are mastered somewhat later, midway through the preschool years (for race, see Hirschfeld, 1988; Aboud & Skerry, 1984; for occupation, see Blaske, 1984). Here again the fact that children fail to appreciate the biological significance with which adults invest race does not imply that their understanding of race is not essentialist.

Identity, growth, and inheritance

A test of the difference between an essential and a contingent construal of a feature is whether an individual changes identity when gaining or losing that feature, or the extent that such a change is conceivable at all. Thus according to adult commonsense, change of dress does not signal a change of identity, whereas change of sex does. Change of race, in contrast, is not conceived of as a genuine possibility at all. I conducted a series of studies in order to explore the meaning of different social identities to preschoolers, and in particular to assess the degree to which their understanding of racial features is essentialist. For this, I used a task that probed children's expectations about possible and impossible identity-relevant changes within the context of normal growth and inheritance. Specifically, I wanted to see if young children would use their knowledge of social categories – particularly their understanding of corporeal qualities such as physical size and skin tone, on the one hand, and noncorporeal features such as occupation and clothing, on the other – in making judgments about preserved identity. Earlier work suggests that young children would rely on such cues as a function of the contribution these cues make to outward appearances. This previous work also implies that conceptually enriched contrasts (say, between features that are corporeal vs. noncorporeal or between qualities that are relevant to collectivities vs. those not relevant to collectivities) would not influence young children's judgments of identity.

Most studies of identity constancy ask children to assess the possibility or consequences of changes in characteristic, but nonessential cues (dress) versus changes in characteristic but essential features (skin color). Implicit in such contrasts is the notion that inessential features are noncorporeal, whereas essential ones are literally embodied. Although these tasks all use familiar properties, they do not all involve familiar *transformations*. Children (or adults presumably) typically do not witness abrupt and major changes in a person's physical being or presentation of self. Accordingly, asking children to determine whether someone's identity remains the same under several different *meaningful* but unfamiliar changes in appearance may confuse young subjects because it is not clear whether the pretransformed and posttransformed individuals are supposed to be (as opposed to could be) the same individual (Bem, 1989). Similarly, asking children whether *they* would change gender or race if their outward appearance were altered (e.g., Aboud & Skerry, 1983; Guardo & Bohan, 1971) may be more informative of children's beliefs about *personal* identity than of their understanding of *social* identity.[6]

Children do, however, have considerable experience with – and knowledge of – the major physical and behavioral changes that occur *across the life span* (i.e., growth) and *across generations* (i.e., inheritance). Moreover, young children appear to understand that these natural transformations are both lawful and nonrandom, and this understanding apparently involves domain-specific knowledge (Rosengren, Gelman, Kalish, & McCormick, 1991; Springer & Keil, 1989; Keil, 1989).

With this in mind, I showed 3-, 4-, and 7-year-olds a series of pictures, each portraying an adult of a specific race, body type, and wearing occupationally relevant apparel (e.g., a stout, black police officer). I then showed children another series of pictures, each pair of pictures portraying a child sharing two of the three social features (body build, race, and occupation) with the target picture. Each of the pair contrasted on one social dimension with the target picture (e.g., one pair consisted of a thin, black child wearing a police hat, toy gun, and whistle and a plump, white child wearing the same costume). All possible contrasts were presented. Two conditions were used, an Inheritance condition and a Growth condition. In the Inheritance condition children were asked which of the contrast pair was the child of the target adult; in the Growth condition children were asked which of the contrast pair was a picture of the target adult as a child. See Figure 8.1.

I found no difference in children's judgments about growth and judgments about inheritance, indicating that young children see the social qualities that preserve identity in growth as essentially those that are inherited across generations.[7] Children's performances, however, varied significantly as a function of their age. Performances also varied depending on the type of comparison children were asked to make (i.e., whether the contrast was race

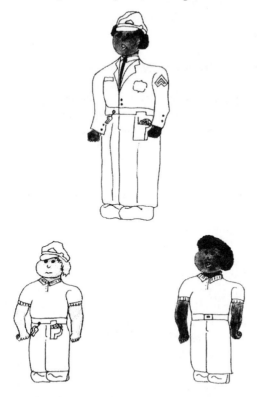

Figure 8.1. Sample items from identity constancy task. Occupation vs. race contrast, male set.

to occupation, occupation to body build, or race to body build). Children chose race over body build significantly more than race over occupation, both of which were choosen significantly more than occupation over body build. However, when each age group is considered separately, only race over body build choices were significantly above chance for the youngest children. For the 4-year-olds, all three contrasts differed from chance. For the oldest subjects, race over body build choices and race over occupation choices were also reliably above chance.[8]

In short, in contrast to earlier studies, I found that children do not consider all physical properties of a person to be equally informative of their identity, and by extension, they do not believe that all such properties are equally resistant to modification (identity, by definition, being that aspect of a person that does not change). If children were focusing only on changes in corporeal appearance when making judgments about identity, children should find modifications in skin color as likely to signal a change in identity as changes in body build. Clearly this is not the case. My findings also do not support the view that a clear appreciation of the biological nature of race emerges only in middle childhood. In contrast to earlier findings, I found that by 4 years of age, children find race to be more essential to identity than either occupation or body build. Moreover, the congruence in performance in the Growth and Inheritence conditions points to a biological understanding of essential traits.

Carey and Spelke (this volume) specifically reject the notion that young children appreciate the biological relevance of physical features: "As of now, there is no evidence that preschoolers have a conception of biological inheritance that goes beyond expectations of resemblance between parents and their offspring." They cite a set of studies (Solomon, Johnson, Zaitchik, & Carey, 1993) showing that preschoolers do not project physical properties, such as height, on the basis of biological parentage. But, as my studies demonstrate, preschoolers do not believe that physical properties such as height are the most identity-relevant features – skin color and even occupation are better predictors. Thus, their findings confirm rather than controvert my claim. Their results do not establish that preschoolers deny the biological (as opposed to social) implications of physical properties; they establish that preschoolers do not view *some* physical properties as biologically caused. Other physical features are conceived by preschoolers as having biological implications.

Carey and Spelke (this volume) also argue that preschoolers do not believe that physical properties are acquired through birth; young children, they contend, believe the children resemble their parents for social rather than biological reasons. In another set of studies (Hirschfeld, 1993) I present evidence showing that preschoolers do in fact expect that a child's skin color is determined by birth, not by environmental factors. In that study preschoolers, second graders, and sixth graders were presented a (picture) story in which infants are switched at birth in hospital. They were then asked to identify pictures of the children these infants would become. Almost 80% of the preschoolers, 80% of the second graders, and all of the sixth graders expected the children to have skin color that matched their birth rather than their adoptive parents.

These findings point up another interesting quality of racial categories that was alluded to earlier. Although the discovery of racial categories by young children cannot be attributed to observation of perceptual differences, perceptual information is not unimportant to racial concepts. Based on the results of the narrative studies, I contended that young children know that some perceptual features are relevant to race (say, skin color), whereas others are not (say, finger length). Young children, however, seem largely unconcerned about *which* (of a range of) relevant physical features go with which racial category in the early representations of racial concepts. The present data lend further support to this claim, in that they suggest that young children associate some physical features (skin color) with preserved identity, but not others (body build). The data do not imply that young children uniquely associate a particular skin color with a specific racial group.

Identity and strategies for social reasoning

One particular result needs explaining: Three-year-olds seem to understand that skin color is more important to identity than body build, but not that skin color is more important than apparel. This is puzzling. Clothing, on the face of it, is much less related to a person's intrinsic nature than, say, body weight. Studies with slightly older preschoolers suggest that children recognize this: Relative to race, age, and gender, young children find dress the least important factor when sorting persons (Davey, 1983).

There are at least two possible explanations for the pattern of results I obtained. One might be tempted to attribute the difference in the performances of the 3-year-olds (who did not find race more important than occupation in judgments of identity) and 4-year-olds (who did) to a developmental shift from a reliance on appearance to a reliance on a deeper understanding of social difference. Older children who rely on the intrinsic physical features might be using a theory-laden strategy (because they favor physical features that are diagnostic of socially relevant groups over those that are not). In contrast, children who employ a strategy privileging shared costume in judgments about both inheritance and growth would be relying on an appearance-oriented rather than a theory-driven approach to categorization. Children using this latter strategy would not yet have shifted from a focus on inessential characteristics and superficial appearances to one targeting defining attributes (Keil, 1989; Keil & Batterman, 1984). This interpretation, however, rests on the assumption that when children rely on occupation in determining social identity, they are actually making judgments about similarity in *dress*. These judgments are appearance- rather than theory-driven to the extent that a reliance on costume does not involve enriched conceptual complexes. But is this really the case?

The difference in importance of apparel for children in my study (in contrast to Davey's earlier work) could also be explained in terms of the different *meaning* apparel had in my and Davey's tasks. Although associated with sartorial cues, occupational categories, which are both enduring and named, may be conceptually more suggestive than clothing by itself. This would account for young children's increased attention to apparel on my task. The results of the identity study, however, do not allow us to assess whether children are distinguishing between clothing as a mark of occupation from clothing itself.

To explore whether children's choices reflect an appreciation that certain kinds of clothing are in fact important cues about group membership, children participating in the inheritance study were given a second task in which they were shown two sets of pictures. Each set consisted of a target picture depicting a child with clothes of a certain color and apparel associated with an occupation, for example, a child wearing a pink dress and a waitress's apron. Children were asked to make an identity judgment from two stimulus pictures in which an adult version of the child in the target picture was portrayed either (1) wearing clothes of the same color, but without the occupational emblems or (2) wearing different colored clothing but with the same occupational emblem as depicted in the target picture. In short, the task contrasted shared clothing with shared occupation. Overall, children showed no preference – clothing predicted identity as frequently as occupation. When the male and female items are considered separately, however, a different pattern emerges. Children's responses indicated that they expect occupation to be preserved for *males* but not for females.[9]

These results indicate that young children find occupational apparel meaningful – at least for males. They do not tell us what that meaning might be. Children who opt for shared costume in determining identity are clearly not attending to superficial similarities in appearance per se. Instead, this strategy could indicate that a notion of common *activities* rather than similarity in apparel underlies their reasoning. One reason to interpret their choices in this way is that occupation is important to older as well as younger children. The proportion of children who rely on costume remains stable during the preschool years, but the overall pattern changes because older preschoolers rely more heavily on race and less on body build than younger preschoolers: Seven-year-olds, although strongly favoring race in determining identity, continue to consider costume to be as good a predictor of identity as body build.[10]

This raises an interesting possibility: Variations in performance on these tasks (some favoring race, others occupation) may reveal *two* conflicting patterns of judgments rather than a lack of patterning. For example, the youngest children on the first identity task displayed no preference for race or occupation when making judgments of preserved identity. Rather than reflecting a confusion about, or indifference to, the roles that occupation and race play in a person's identity, these responses might indicate the existence of two relatively balanced preferences. Some children might consistently favor race, whereas other children might consistently favor occupation in making judgments of identity.

In short, children might be relying on two reasoning strategies to account for regularities in social life – one rooted in the way people enter into habitual interactions and association, the other concerned more with a person's intrinsic and corporeal nature. Furthermore, these reasoning strategies might be unevenly distributed: Different children rely more on the one aspect than the other in representing social variation. Nonetheless, both are implicated in social understanding. It is plausible, and perhaps probable given recent work on intrapopulation variation in apparently shared mental models (see Boster, in press; D'Andrade, 1990), that children could arrive at more or less similar views of a phenomenon, while using distinct strategies (see Shweder & LeVine, 1976, for an analogous pattern of emergent understanding of dreams in Hausa children).

To assess this possibility I looked at individual children's patterns of response to see whether variation in performance was meaningful. I was interested in knowing if children's choices were regular, particularly in determining the nature of any regularity that could be conditioning their judgments. Did children use a transitive reasoning strategy in making their choices? Or could a child, for example, choose race over occupation and occupation over body weight, but nonetheless choose body weight over race? Such a pattern would violate both transitivity and consistency. Presumably the more consistent the child's choices, the more stable is the underlying strategy; conversely, the less clear a child is about the underlying strategy for drawing judgments of identity, the less consistent their choices would be. In fact, I found that most children's choices were transitive. Overall, 57 of 78 children (73%) made all and only regular, transitive choices. Consistency varied largely as a function of age: Seventeen out of 25 (68%) of the 3-year-olds, 18 out of 29 (62%) of the 4-year-olds, and 22 out of 24 (92%) of the 7-year-olds made only regular choices.

The task actually gave children two opportunities for inconsistency. The first is the question just reviewed of transitivity across contrast pairs (race to occupation, occupation to body build, race to body build). The second opportunity for inconsistency involved the possibility of performing differently on different items. Two sets of stimuli pictures were used: one centering on a police officer, the second set involving a nurse. Overall, no item effect was found, and the children tended to treat both sets in the same way. Again, the number of item-consistent responses varies as a function of age: Eight out of 17 (47%) of the 3-year-olds, 13 out of 18 (72%) of the 4-year-olds, and 21 out of 22 (95%) of the 7-year-olds chose consistently (i.e., if they chose race first on the male set, then they chose race first on the female set; if they chose occupation first on the male set, then they chose occupation first on the female set).

Those instances in which the children treated the two sets differently, although infrequent, are nevertheless informative. There were six possible inconsistent choices: Children could select race first on the male set, and occupation or body build on the female set. They could select occupation first on the male set but race or body build first on the female set. Finally, they could select body build first on the male set but race first or occupation first on the female set. The distribution of inconsistent responses is interesting. First, two of the six possible inconsistencies dominated, ones in which race was first on one set but occupation on the other. For example, most (five of nine) of the 3-year-olds' inconsistent responses were occupation first on the male set, but race first on the female set. Similarly, most of the 4-year-olds' inconsistent choices (four out of five) also involved occupation first on one set and race first on the other. This pattern of error (which was significantly different from chance) suggests that younger children are confused about which of two transitive strategies applies.[11]

Taken together these data indicate that young children's emerging understanding of social difference involves two competing reasoning strategies in assigning individuals to social categories: They may focus on natural-like features or they may focus on patterns of habitual behavior. In so doing, they are concerned with determining what kinds of social beings there are either in terms of intrinsic nature (racial kinds) or habitual patterns of goal-oriented activity (occupational kinds). Even when they show a preference for one type of category, they do not ignore the other. Even those children who are more interested in occupational categories than racial ones approach the racial categories with an essentialist bias, as shown by the fact that they attribute greater weight to intrinsic features such as skin color than to more contingent ones such as body build.

The experimental evidence I have presented provides evidence against the standard view of the development of racial categories and more generally on the naturalization model according to which essentialism is imported in the social domain rather than present there from the start. In this light, the study of actual transfers, whether spontaneous or culturally sanctioned, must be reconsidered.

Kinship categories

Are there other instances of this mediation in reasoning strategies in social cognitive development? Are there other kinds of social understanding in which intrinsic natures and patterns of habitual association shape social categorization, instances in which young children opt either for an interactional or an essentialist interpretation of social difference? Kinship, I believe, provides such a case. Elsewhere I have developed this notion in detail, both in terms of children's and adults' representations (1986, 1989b). Here I will present the argument in skeletal form.

Virtually all accounts of kinship term acquisition assume that mature definitions of kinship concepts *necessarily* include knowledge of reproductive histories; a broad consensus has emerged to the effect that genealogical predicates are the essential feature of kinship terms (see Hirschfeld, 1986, 1989b). Because young children lack an understanding of these predicates, this implies that by definition they are not fully representing the adult concept of kinship. Yet, very young children, who clearly do not understand the nature of the reproductive relationships kinship putatively reflects, *do very well when using kinship terms*. In fact, young children make almost no mistakes in everyday conversation. Correctly using kinship terms thus cannot be contingent on understanding the biological template of kinship.

Why? The simplest explanation, as I have argued before (1986, 1989b), is that kinship really is not, even for the adult, about episodic predicates such as paternity and maternity. Rather, kinship relations involve a recognition of "natural commonality."[12] Natural commonality cannot be a function of the objective biological distance between two individuals: Kinship systems across cultures are notoriously willing to embrace as kin one set of relatives of the same biological distance while ignoring similarly (biologically) close, but structurally distant individuals (say, when favoring marriage with a cross-cousin [i.e., cousins related through a brother and a sister in their parents' generation], while forbidding [as incestuous] marriage with a parallel cousin [i.e., cousins related through two brothers or two sisters in the parents' generation]). Nor is natural commonality a simple function of *physical* resemblance – no one (including those who do not understand the genetic cause of the disorder) imagines that all Down Syndrome children are related simply because they resemble each other. Rather, natural commonality seems to embrace a number of qualities, including physical resemblance, and putative paternity and maternity. It is, accordingly, a quality that a person's intrinsic nature gives rise to in subsequent generations.

Still, in young children this is clearly not a fully elaborated construct. Young children appear to rely on two principles to construe the meaning of kinship terms. On the one hand, they use a notion of family, the expectation that there is a collectivity of individuals that is interrelated in some basic, predictable, and enduring way, which share, I propose to interpret, a certain natural commonality. On the other hand, children, like adults, rely on certain patterns of habitual association and interaction in constructing kin term meanings.

From a reanalysis of studies on the acquisition of kinship terms, I (Hirschfeld, 1989b) concluded that the family concept is spontaneously relevant for young children, allowing them to infer nonobvious relations of kinship and natural commonality from patterns of coresidence. Their understanding of the notion of family, or of underlying commonality, however, is flexible enough to extend unproblematically beyond the domain of social relations. Markman (1973, 1981) tested the influence of collection and class terms in class inclusion problems, finding that collection terms facilitate performance on these tasks. Her initial study used *family* as the collection term stimulus. Interestingly, in a subsequent set of studies, using *family* as well as *army* (vs. soldiers), *hockey team* (vs. hockey players), Fuson, Lyons, Pergament, Hall, and Kwon (1988) failed to replicate Markman's findings – that collection terms facilitate conservation judgments – except in those cases in which *family* was the stimulus collection term in question. Apparently the family concept is associated with more efficacious processing of inferential tasks unrelated to kinship per se.

In constructing kin term meanings, children also rely on observed patterns of behavior – specifically, the enduring and habitual associations having to do with the sharing of sleeping, eating, and other sustenance relations typically grouped under the rubric of coresidence. This appears to be true of adults as well as children, though most cognitive accounts of kinship have ignored this aspect of the kinship concept.

Again, we can see how social reasoning, and particularly the creation of social ontologies, involves reliance on two types of understanding – one concerned with the natural, intrinsic quality of the individual, the other with the precipitate of that individual's actions and associations. Each culture's kinship system appears to weight these differently – my father's best friend (nicknamed "Uncle" Bob) is somewhat less a kinsman to me than he might be to a Bororo. Moreover, as our studies indicate, at different points in development distinct weights seems to be given to each type of understanding. This variation also points up what may be a significant contrast between young children's (and adults') intuitions about kinship and other social differences: With kinship young children seem willing *to combine* reasoning strategies – using both an interactional and an essentialist conceptualization of difference – whereas other kinds of social construal appear to drive children *to make a choice* in favor of one of the two reasoning strategies, the essentialist one in the case of racial categories, or the behavioral one in the case of occupational categories. Neither strategy however is borrowed from another domain; their coordination, rather, is characteristic of a competence that is specific to the social domain.

Conclusion

Biologists and anthropologists, arguing from a comparative perspective, have long contended that beliefs about race cannot be derived from observations of human variation alone. Specific cultural, historical, and environmental constraints are also required (Gould, 1980; Van den Berghe, 1981; Alland, 1971). I have argued that young children's expectations about race cannot be derived from observations of physical difference either. Children are prepared to find that humans come in groups, that is, they have societal identities. Children naturalize societal identities not because they identify patterns of human variation with patterns of nonhuman species variation. They adopt from the start an essentialist approach to some social categories.

The form of essentialism that is found in the understanding of kinship involves an underlying essential property, a natural commonality, that differs from the underlying essences of living kind classification in two ways: It is a relational rather than an individual property, and it can be possessed to a greater or lesser degree. That is, kinship depends on a relationship as defined by a specific individual, not in terms of independent collectivities. Second, the amount of natural commonality between two individuals related by kinship by definition depends on the degree of kin relation. Close kin resemble each other more than distant kin resemble each other. Although race may be conceptualized in terms of gradients, so that "mixed-bloods" are thought to share less essence than "full-bloods," all things being equal, members of a racial group share the same amount of underlying essence. These differences between racial and kin-based essentialist thinking render implausible the view that essentialism in the understanding of kinship might be based on a transfer from biological essentialism.

Race is not the only conceptual domain where global, domain under-standings appear to precede more specific ones. Several authors have recently stressed the importance of top-down strategies to young children's ontological understanding. These include strategies that initially pick out and elaborate general classes of events or objects rather than the specific objects being discriminated. Carey (1978) describes a similar process in her work on color term acquisition: Children apparently recognize the fact that color terms pick out relevant chromatic contrasts before they effectively represent what the specific chroma are. Mandler, Bauer, and McDonough (1991) suggest that because children make some distinctions at the basic level, we cannot con-clude that they are making the distinction because of their understanding of the mechanisms underlying basic level contrasts:

> children might be able to discriminate a variety of four-legged animals, perhaps even have different labels for them and be able to say that dogs 'woof' and horses 'neigh'. Nevertheless, if their knowledge base consists only of a few such unorganized and isolated bits of information it might not be sufficient to support a theory that these objects are different kinds of things. (Mandler et al., 1991: 270)

In fact, the child's theory may well support the notion that there are different kinds of things; it simply may not specify how one goes about discovering them. This is plausible for living kinds generally, and, I would argue, likely for societal kinds in particular.

I have argued that the social domain is within the scope of some innately specified competence. This leaves open several possibilities. The simplest is that there is a dedicated domain-specific competence for the social domain (or several such competences for different aspects of the social domain). But this is by no means the only possibility. There might be megadomains that have the social sphere or part of it in their extension. So, for instance, there might be a domain of kinds based on underlying essences that would include both living kinds and natural-like societal kinds (and possibly substances, too). And there might be a domain of intentional and dispositional explana-tion of behavior that would include the psychology not just of humans in general but also that of categories of humans and of animal species (Hirschfeld, in press-a).

Such competences might alternatively be described not in terms of megadomains but in terms of modes of construal (Keil, this volume). A mode of construal may fit more than one conceptual domain. Thus Keil has pro-posed that biological kinds become linked with a specific mode of (teleolo-gical) construal. Still, this particular mode of construal need not be mapped during development onto all and only biological kinds. Although adults, and most children, would probably not ask what purpose a protuberance on a rock serves, and would plausibly ask what the pincers on a bug were for, we, and our children, may well wonder what a particular custom is for (as a large number of anthropologists have done). The retort that customs are a property of people, preeminent biological kinds, will not do; customs are not "of people" but "of peoples."

It could also be that an adequate understanding of a domain requires that we understand something of its specific relations to other domains. If this is the case, it may be that a productive characterization of domain differences will not turn on the contents of a given domain or depend on whether the domain is a product of an innately guided learning program. Rather it may depend on how a domain's knowledge is articulated, extended, and elaborated across domains, what Rozin and Schull (1988) call the issue of accessibility. Accessibility, the domain-specific process of knowledge coordination, has the advantage of rendering such epistemic links in domain-specific terms – something the notion of knowledge transfer affords less well. In turn, it renders constructs like mental economy domain-specific as well: Ultimately, understanding accessibility will mean that we not only recognize that mental economy happens, but we may well also understand how it happens.

From a domain-general perspective the issue of least effort in knowledge transfer is an important question; from a domain-specific view it is a crucial one. According to the domain-specific account, domain knowledge is the product of distinct, specialized devices that "communicate with other cognitive structures in only very limited ways" (Garfield, 1987: 1). "Limited" though they might be, these communications are critical both to conceptual development (Brown, 1989) and evolutionary change (Rozin & Schull, 1988). The empirical focus of this chapter, the relationship between emergent biological and human understandings, is a case in point. But even in this instance, where the cross-domain coordination of knowledge is both empirically and theoretically crucial, the analytic *focus* of previous studies has overwhelmingly been on the conceptual reorganization of only one of these domains (typically, naive biology; see Carey, 1985; Inagaki, 1990). Perhaps because of this, little attention has been paid to *how* (as opposed to *that*) psychological principles are imported into biological reasoning. I have tried to redress this here.

It is somewhat surprising that so little research from the domain perspective has been devoted to exploring how knowledge from different domains comes to be articulated. The domain specificity argument, after all, is compelling in large part because it is counterintuitive: Despite convincing evidence that much human knowledge is represented in distinct and uniquely organized domains, it is also widely accepted that our appreciation of the world is conditioned on the intuition that knowledge is generalizable across instances and coherent across areas of understanding. In other words, regardless of how it is represented, people do not appear to *experience* their knowledge as modular. Much psychological work has focused on mechanisms functioning to meet and overcome *challenges* to this perceived cognitive consistency (in social psychology, Festinger, 1957; in cognitive psychology, Holland, Holyoak, Nisbett, & Thagard, 1989; in developmental psychology, Piaget, 1967). In its turn, much anthropology is equally concerned with cognitive coherence: exploring and identifying the cultural mazeways producing local structures that frame shared interpretation and common potential for action (Quinn & Holland, 1987).

Cases of such articulations aside, previous transfer studies disclose a paradox: Although the *intuition* that problems are solved through analogical reasoning is robust, attempts to demonstrate such abilities experimentally have not been altogether successful (Novick, 1988; Resnick, this volume). Brown (1990, 1989) observes similar "puzzling disparities" in the developmental literature, where within-domain transfers in early childhood are readily found, but parallel, cross-domain transfers among older children have been much more difficult to document. It is plausible to interpret, as Brown (1989) has, the difficulty researchers have experienced in attempting to duplicate experimentally this seemingly "intuitive" transfer of problem-solving procedures across domains as evidence for the robustness of domain-specific devices – thus standing on its head, the logic of the naturalization model (according to which, the ease of transfer evidences the operation of a domain-specific device).

In order to decide between these various alternatives much more empirical work has to be done. It would be interesting to study the acquisition of natural-like categories in societies where they predominate, like caste in India. More experimental work must be done on kinship understanding across cultures. Adult social categories also need to be better analyzed in a cognitively informed manner. One general recommendation will have, I hope, received support from this discussion: The anthropological and the psychological approaches can be fruitfully combined and must be if we are to understand better the mechanisms of social understanding.

Notes

1. "For Rofiafo, species are objectively 'out there,' but the concept, species, is an internalized transformation from human social relations," specifically those of kinship (p. 434).
2. This, incidentally, is taken to be the case not only in the transfer from the biological to the social assumed in the naturalization model, but also in the suggestion of Carey (1985) and Inagaki and her colleagues (1990; Inagaki & Hatano, 1987) that naive psychology of human behavior is transfered to other living kinds.
3. I have recently completed work indicating that parallel notions about social kinds develop at about the same time (Hirschfeld, in press-a).
4. The labels were (in their English translation) *Arab*, *Chinese*, *white*, and *black*.
5. Carey (1982: 96) makes a similar claim about the relationship between kinship terms and knowledge of reproduction: "until the child has learned something of the biological context of parenting, he cannot have the concept of *brother* according to which adults and animals have brothers." Yet this is not quite the

same as arguing that young children do not have some biologically relevant understanding of terms like *brother*. Elsewhere (Hirschfeld, 1989b), I have argued that the notion of family relations, and family background, are central to young children's earliest representations of kinship terms. Young children clearly use perceptual cues, like coresidence, in construing the meaning of kinship terms, yet they do not *reduce* kinship terms to such perceptual features, as many accounts have suggested. This is clear from the fact that young children invariably understand that noncoresiding kinsmen, such as grandparents and cousins, are indeed relatives (see Hirschfeld, 1989b).

6. Work on children's social identity suggests a parallel between children's and adults' social reasoning: A number of researchers have recently argued that for young children, as for adults, personal identity and reference group orientation are largely independent of each other (Cross, 1991; Jackson, McCullough, & Gurin, 1988; Spencer, 1985). This distinction has important implications for interpreting young children's performances on identity constancy tasks. First, it is not always evident whether personal identity or reference group identity is implicated in performances on tasks commonly used to assess identity constancy. Second, children might consider membership in certain groups to contribute more to group identity than other kinds of membership – thus being more stably associated with group identity. Adults typically consider race to contribute more profoundly than occupation to an individual's group identity. Some children, nonetheless, might believe that groups based on common activities and associations (signaled by common costume) are more salient for group identity than are shared physical features. Such children would underestimate the role of race on the sorts of identity constancy tasks described above, not because they do not understand racial constancy, but because they have certain beliefs about group identity. Third, some children may focus on activities and associations when reasoning about categories to which adults attribute deep and distinct essences (e.g., gender) – and thus believe that if one's activities and associations change then one's category identity changes, not because they do not understand constancy, but because their reasoning strategy selectively attends to patterns of habitual associations and activities over presumptions of underlying essence.

7. One interpretation of these results is that children conceptualize social qualities preserving identity in both circumstances as resulting from the person's intrinsic nature in that it is this intrinsic quality that is constant over both growth and inheritance. This suggests one parallel between naturalized social categories and biological categories, since biological properties are conceptualized by young children as part of a living thing's intrinsic nature (Atran, 1990; Gelman & Coley, 1990).

8. Specifically, a 3 (age group) × 2 (Inheritance vs. Growth condition) analysis of variance (ANOVA) with types of comparison as repeated measure revealed significant effects for age, $F(2, 72) = 4.89$, $p < .02$, and type of comparison, $F(2, 72) = 9.54$, $p < .0001$. Post-hoc comparisons indicated that race over body build choices ($M = 1.62$) were significantly higher than race over occupation choices ($M = 1.39$), which in turn were significantly higher than occupation over body type choices ($M = 1.15$). There was no effect for condition. For the youngest group, only race over body build choices were significantly above chance, $t(24) = 3.17$, $p < .05$. For the 4-year-olds, all three were above chance; race over

body build, $t(28) = 3.78, p < .001$, race over occupation, $t(28) = 2.20, p < .04$, and occupation over body build, $t(28) = 2.29, p < .03$. For the oldest subjects, race over body build choices were significantly above chance, $t(23) = 23.00, p < .0001$, as were race over occupation choices, $t(23) = 4.65, p < .0001$.

9. The number of times children selected shared occupation was summed across items for each age group and the data entered into a 3 (age) × 2 (gender of person portrayed) ANOVA. The analysis revealed a significant main effect for gender item, such that occupation was more salient in identity judgments about the male items ($M = 1.20$ [out of 2]) than in judgments about the female item's identity ($M = .81$), $F(1, 35) = 7.07, p < .02$. Considering all three age groups together, the mean number of times that occupation was chosen over clothing tended to be above chance for the male items ($M = 1.18$), $t(37) = 1.74, p < .09$. Three-year olds, however, were significantly above chance ($M = 1.36$), $t(10) = 2.39, p < .04$. The mean number of times occupation was chosen over clothing for female items, in contrast, was significantly *below* chance, $t(37) = -2.09, p < .05$.

10. The mean number of choices (out of two) by type of comparison for three age groups are:

	3-year-olds	4-year-olds	7-year-olds
Race over body build	1.37*	1.52*	1.96*
Race over occupation	1.20	1.31*	1.67*
Occupation over body build	1.09	1.27*	1.08

*above chance, $p < .05$

11. Note that the youngest children's inconsistencies are even more restricted: All involved occupation first for the male items when race was first on the female items. The role that different social categories play in shaping children's expectations is evident here: In justifying their responses, several subjects made statements suggesting that they believe that a male's occupation is more important to individual identity than a female's.

12. In earlier papers I called this "natural resemblance." This expression does capture the idea of a natural property that, unlike the essences underlying natural kinds, is a comparative, that is, a more-or-less property. However unlike "commonality," "resemblance" as ordinarily understood is both observer and context relative. For instance, there is more natural commonality between two brothers than between two distant cousins in the English kinship system, whatever the context or the point of view.

References

Aboud, F. E. (1987). The development of ethnic self-identification and attitudes. In J. S. Phinney & M. J. Rotheram (Eds.), *Children's ethnic socialization* (pp. 32–55). Newbury Park: Sage Publications.

Aboud, F. E. (1988). *Children and prejudice.* New York: Basil Blackwell.

Aboud, F. E., & Skerry, A. (1983). Self and ethnic concepts in relation to ethnic constancy. *Canadian Journal of Behavioural Science, 15*(1), 14–26.

Aboud, F., & Skerry, A. (1984). The development of ethnic attitudes: A critical review. *Journal of Cross-Cultural Psychology, 15*, 3–34.

Alejandro-Wright, M. N. (1985). The child's conception of racial classification: A socio-cognitive developmental model. In M. B. Spencer, G. K. Brookins, & W. R. Allen (Eds.), *Beginnings: The social and affective development of black children* (pp. 185–201). Hillsdale, NJ: Erlbaum.

Alland, A. (1971). *Human diversity.* New York: Columbia University Press.

Allport, G. (1954). *The nature of prejudice.* Cambridge: Addison-Wesley.

Atran, S. (1990). *Cognitive foundations of natural history.* New York: Cambridge University Press.

Bem, S. (1989). Genital knowledge and gender constancy in preschool children. *Child Development, 60,* 649–662.

Berlin, B. (1978). Ethnobiological classification. In E. Rosch & B. Lloyd (Eds.), *Cognition and categorization.* Hillsdale, NJ: Erlbaum.

Blaske, D. (1984). Occupational sex-typing by kindergarten and fourth-grade children. *Psychological Reports, 54*(3), 795–801.

Boas, F. (1916). The origin of totemism. *American Anthropologist, 18,* 319–326.

Boster, J. (1988). Natural sources of internal category structure: Typicality, familiarity, and similarity of birds. *Memory & Cognition, 16*(3), 258–270.

Boster, J. (in press). The information economy model applied to biological similarity judgments. In J. Levine, L. Resnick, & S. Behrend (Eds.), *Socially shared cognition.* American Psychological Association.

Boyer, P. (1990). *Tradition as truth and communication.* New York: Cambridge University Press.

Brown, A. (1989). Analogical learning and transfer: What develops? In S. Vosniadou & A. Ortony (Eds.), *Similarity and analogical reasoning* (pp. 369–412). New York: Cambridge University Press.

Brown, A. (1990). Domain-specific principles affect learning and transfer in children. *Cognitive Science, 14*(1), 107–134.

Carey, S. (1978). The child as language learner. In M. Halle, J. Bresnan, & G. A. Miller (Eds.), *Linguistic theory and psychological reality* (pp. 264–293). Cambridge, MA: MIT Press.

Carey, S. (1982). Semantic development: The state of the art. In E. Wanner & L. Gleitman (Eds.), *Language acquisition: The state of the art.* New York: Cambridge University Press.

Carey, S. (1985). *Conceptual development in childhood.* Cambridge, MA: MIT Press.

Clark, K., & Clark, M. (1940). Skin color as a factor in racial identification of Negro preschool children. *Journal of Social Psychology, 11,* 159–169.

Crocker, J. (1977). My brother the parrot. In J. Sapir & J. Crocker (Eds.), *The social use of metaphor: Essays on the anthropology of rhetoric* (pp. 164–192). Philadelphia: University of Pennsylvania Press.

Cross, W. E. (1991). *Shades of black: Diversity in African-American identity.* Philadelphia: Temple University Press.

D'Andrade, R. (1990). Some propositions about the relations between culture and human cognition. In J. Stigler, R. Shweder, & G. Herdt (Eds.), *Cultural psychology: Essays on comparative human development.* New York: Cambridge University Press.

Daniel, E. Valentine. (1984). *Fluid signs: Being a person the Tamil way.* Los Angeles: University of California Press.

Davey, A. (1983). *Learning to be prejudiced: Growing up in multi-ethnic Britain.* London: Edward Arnold.

Davidson, N., & Gelman, S. (1990). Inductions from novel categories: The role of language and conceptual structure. *Cognitive Development, 5*, 151–176.

Douglas, M. (1966). *Purity and danger: An analysis of concepts of pollution and taboo.* London: Routledge & Kegan Paul.

Douglas, M. (1986). *How institutions think.* Syracuse: Syracuse University Press.

Doyle, A. (1983). Friends, acquaintances, and strangers: The influence of familiarity and ethnolinguistic background on social interaction. In K. Rubin & H. Ross (Eds.), *Peer relationships and social skills in childhood.* New York: Springer-Verlag.

Durkheim, E., & Mauss, M. (1963). *Primitive classification.* Chicago: University of Chicago Press. (Original work published 1903)

Durrett, M. E., & Davy, A. (1979). Racial awareness in young Mexican-American, Negro and Anglo children. *Young Children, 26*, 16–24.

Dwyer, P. (1976). An analysis of Rogaifo mammal taxonomy. *American Ethnologist, 3*(3), 425–445.

Emmerich, W., Goldman, K., Kirsch, B., & Sharabany, R. (1977). Evidence for a transitional phase in the development of gender constancy. *Child Development, 48*, 930–936.

Festinger, L. (1957). *A theory of cognitive dissonance.* Palo Alto: Stanford University Press.

Finkelstein, N., & Haskins, R. (1983). Kindergarten children prefer same-color peers. *Child Development, 54*, 502–508.

Flavell, J. (1985). *Cognitive development.* Englewood Cliffs, NJ: Prentice-Hall.

Furth, H. (1980). *The world of grown-ups: Children's conceptions of society.* New York: Elsevier-North Holland.

Fuson, K., Lyons, B., Pergament, G., Hall, J., & Kwon, Y. (1988). Effects of collection terms on class-inclusion and on number tasks. *Cognitive Psychology, 20*, 96–120.

Garfield, J. (1987). Introduction: Carving the mind at its joints. In J. Garfield (Ed.), *Modularity in knowledge representation and natural-language understanding* (pp. 1–13). Cambridge, MA: MIT Press.

Gelman, S., & Coley, J. (1990). The importance of knowing a dodo is a bird: Categories and inferences in 2-year-old children. *Developmental Psychology, 26*, 796–804.

Gelman, S., Collman, P., & Maccoby, E. (1986). Inferring properties from categories versus inferring categories from properties: The case of gender. *Child Development, 57*, 396–404.

Gelman, S., & Kremer, K. (1991). Understanding natural cause: Children's explanations of how objects and their properties originate. *Child Development, 62*, 396–414.

Gelman, S., & Markman, E. (1986). Categories and induction in young children. *Cognition, 23*, 183–209.

Gelman, S., & Markman, E. (1987). Young children's inductions from natural kinds: The role of categories and appearances. *Child Development, 58*, 1532–1541.

Gelman, S., & Wellman, H. (1991). Insides and essences: Early understandings of the non-obvious. *Cognition, 38*, 213–244.

Gentner, D., & Gentner, D. (1983). Flowing waters or teeming crowds: Mental models of electricity. In D. Gentner & A. Stevens (Eds.), *Mental models.* Hillsdale, NJ: Erlbaum.

Gould, S. (1980). *The panda's thumb: More reflections in natural history*. New York: W.W. Norton & Co.

Greeno, J. (1983). Conceptual entities. In D. Gentner & A. Stevens (Eds.), *Mental models*. Hillsdale, NJ: Erlbaum.

Guardo, C., & Bohan, J. (1971). Development of a sense of self-identity in children. *Child Development, 42*, 1909–1921.

Hallowell, A. (1976). *Contributions to anthropology: Selected papers of A. Irving Hallowell*. Chicago: University of Chicago Press.

Hartley, E., Rosenbaum, M., & Schwartz, S. (1948). Children's perceptions of ethnic group membership. *Journal of Psychology, 26*, 387–398.

Hirschfeld, L. (1986). Kinship and cognition: Genealogy and the meaning of kinship terms. *Current Anthropology, 27*(3), 217–242.

Hirschfeld, L. (1988). On acquiring social categories: Cognitive development and anthropological wisdom. *Man, 23*, 611–638.

Hirschfeld, L. (1989a). Discovering linguistic differences: Domain specificity and the young child's awareness of multiple languages. *Human Development, 32*, 223–236.

Hirschfeld, L. (1989b). Rethinking the acquisition of kinship terms. *International Journal of Behavioral Development, 12*(4), 541–568.

Hirschfeld, L. (1993). Discovering social difference: The role of appearance in the development of racial awareness. *Cognitive Psychology, 25*, 317–350.

Hirschfeld, L. (in press-a). Anthropology, psychology and the meanings of social causality. In A. Premack (Ed.), *Causal understandings in cognition and culture*. New York: Oxford University Press.

Hirschfeld, L. (in press-b). The child's representation of human groups. In D. Medin (Ed.), *The psychology of learning and motivation: Advances in research and theory. Vol. 30*. San Diego: Academic Press.

Holland, J., Holyoak, K., Nisbett, R., & Thagard, P. (1989). *Induction: Processes of inference, learning, and discovery*. Cambridge, MA: MIT Press.

Inagaki, K. (1990). Young children's everyday biology as the basis for learning school biology. *The Bulletin of the Faculty of Education, Chiba University, 38*, 177–184.

Inagaki, K., & Hatano, G. (1987). Young children's spontaneous personification and analogy. *Child Development, 58*, 1013–1020.

Inagaki, K., & Sugiyama, K. (1988). Attributing human characteristics: Developmental changes in over- and underattribution. *Cognitive Development, 3*(1), 55–70.

Jackson, J., McCullough, W., & Gurin, G. (1988). Family, socialization environment, and identity development in Black Americans. In H. P. McAdoo (Ed.), *Black families* (pp. 242–256). Newbury Park, CA: Sage Publications.

Johnson, K., Mervis, C., & Boster, J. (1992). Developmental changes within the structure of the mammal domain. *Developmental Psychology, 28*, 74–83.

Katz, P. (1982). Development of children's racial awareness and intergroup attitudes. In L. G. Katz (Ed.), *Current Topics in Early Childhood Education* (Vol. 4, pp. 16–54). Norwood, NJ: Ablex.

Katz, P. (1983). Developmental foundations of gender and racial attitudes. In R. L. Leahy (Ed.), *The child's construction of social inequality*. New York: Academic Press.

Keil, F. (1979). *Semantic and conceptual development: An ontological perspective.* Cambridge, MA: Harvard University Press.

Keil, F. (1989). *Concepts, kinds, and cognitive development.* Cambridge, MA: Bradford Books/MIT Press.

Keil, F., & Batterman, N. (1984). A characteristic-to-defining shift in the development of word meaning. *Journal of Verbal Learning & Verbal Behavior, 23,* 221–236.

Kohlberg, L. (1966). A cognitive-developmental analysis of children's sex-role concepts and attitudes. In E. Maccoby (Ed.), *The development of sex differences.* Stanford: Stanford University Press.

Kosslyn, S., & Kagan, J. (1981). "Concrete thinking" and the development of social cognition. In J. Flavell & L. Ross (Eds.), *Social cognitive development: Frontiers and possible futures* (pp. 82–96). New York: Cambridge University Press.

Lambert, W., & Tachuchi, Y. (1956). Ethnic cleavage among young children. *Journal of Abnormal & Social Psychology, 53,* 380–382.

Leach, E. (1964). Anthropological aspects of language: Animal categories and verbal abuse. In E. Lennenberg (Ed.), *New directions in the study of language* (pp. 23–63). Cambridge, MA: MIT Press.

Lemaine, G., Santolini, A., Bonnet, P., & Ben Brika, J. (1985). Préferences raciales, identité et soi idéal chez les enfants de 5 à 11 ans. *Bulletin de Psychologie, 39,* 129–157.

Lévi-Strauss, C. (1962). *Totemism.* Boston: Beacon Press.

Lévi-Strauss, C. (1966). *The savage mind.* Chicago: University of Chicago Press.

Lewis, M. (1981). Self-knowledge: A social cognitive perspective on gender identity and sex role development. In M. Lamb & L. Sherrod (Eds.), *Infant social cognition: Empirical and theoretical considerations.* Hillsdale, NJ: Erlbaum.

McCandless, B., & Hoyt, J. (1961). Sex, ethnicity and play preferences of preschool children. *Journal of Abnormal & Social Psychology, 62,* 683–685.

Madge, N. (1976). Context and the expressed ethnic preference of infant school children. *Journal of Child Psycholology and Psychiatry, 17,* 337–344.

Mandler, J., Bauer, P., & McDonough, L. (1991). Separating the sheep from the goats: Differentiating global categories. *Cognitive Psychology, 23*(2), 263–298.

Markman, E. (1973). The facilitation of part-whole comparisons by use of the collective noun "Family." *Child Development, 44,* 837–840.

Markman, E. (1981). Two different principles of conceptual organization. In M. Lamb & A. Brown (Eds.), *Advances in developmental psychology. Volume 1.* Hillsdale, NJ: Erlbaum.

Massey, C., & Gelman, R. (1988). Preschooler's ability to decide whether a photographed unfamiliar object can move itself. *Developmental Psychology, 24*(3), 307–317.

Mauss, M. (1947). *Manuel d'ethnographie.* Paris: Payot.

Novick, L. (1988). Analogical transfer, problem similarity, and expertise. *Journal of Experimental Psychology: Learning, Memory, & Cognition, 14,* 510–520.

Piaget, J. (1967). *Etudes sur la logique de l'enfant. Tome II: Le jugement et le raisonnement chez l'enfant.* Neuchatel: Delachaux et Niestlé.

Quinn, N., & Holland, D. (1987). Culture and cognition. In D. Holland & N. Quinn (Eds.), *Cultural models in language and thought* (pp. 3–40) New York: Cambridge University Press.

Radcliffe-Brown, A. (1922). *The Andaman Islanders*. Cambridge: Cambridge University Press.

Rosaldo, M. (1972). Metaphor and folk classification. *Southwestern Journal of Anthropology, 28*, 83–99.

Rosenberg, M. (1979). *Conceiving the self*. New York: Basic Books.

Rosengren, K., Gelman, S., Kalish, C., & McCormick, M. (1991). As time goes by: Children's early understanding of growth in animals. *Child Development, 62*, 1302–1320.

Ross, L. (1981). The "intuitive scientist" formulation and its developmental implications. In J. Flavell & L. Ross (Eds.), *Social cognitive development: Frontiers and possible futures* (pp. 1–42). New York: Cambridge University Press.

Rothbart, M., & Taylor, M. (1990). Category labels and social reality: Do we view social categories as natural kinds? In G. Semin & K. Fiedler (Eds.), *Language and social cognition*. London: Sage.

Rozin, P., & Schull, J. (1988). The adaptive-evolutionary point of view in experimental psychology. In R. Atkinson, R. Herrnstein, G. Lindzey, & R. Luce (Eds.), *Steven's handbook of experimental psychology*. New York: John Wiley & Sons.

Semaj, L. T. (1980). The development of racial evaluation and preference: A cognitive approach. *The Journal of Black Psychology, 6*(2), 59–79.

Semaj, L. T. (1981). The development of racial classification abilities. *Journal of Negro Education, 50*, 41–47.

Shweder, R., & LeVine, R. (1976). Dream concepts of Hausa children: A critique of the 'doctrine of invariant sequence in cognitive development'. In T. Schwartz (Ed.), *Socialization as cultural communication: Development of a theme in the work of Margaret Mead* (pp. 117–138). Berkeley: University of California Press.

Singleton, L., & Asher, S. (1979). Racial integration and children's peer preferences: An investigation of developmental and cohort differences. *Child Development, 50*(4), 936–941.

Slaby, R., & Frey, K. (1975). Development of gender constancy and selective attention to same-sex models. *Child Development, 46*, 849–856.

Solomon, G., Johnson, S., Zaitchik, D., & Carey, S. (1993, April). *The young child's conception of inheritance*. Paper presented at Society for Research in Child Development, New Orleans.

Sorce, J. (1979). The role of physiognomy in the development of racial awareness. *The Journal of Genetic Psychology, 134*, 33–41.

Spencer, M. (1985). Cultural cognition and social cognition as identity factors in black children's personal-social growth. In M. B. Spencer, G. K. Brookins, & W. R. Allen (Eds.), *Beginnings: The social and affective development of black children* (pp. 215–230). Hillsdale, NJ: Erlbaum.

Spiro, R., Feltovich, P., Coulson, R., & Anderson, D. (1989). Multiple analogies for complex concepts: Antidotes for analogy-induced misconception on advanced knowledge acquisition. In S. Vosniadou & A. Ortony (Eds.), *Similarity and analogical reasoning*. New York: Cambridge University Press.

Springer, K., & Keil, F. (1989). On the development of biologically specific beliefs: The case of inheritance. *Child Development, 60*, 637–648.

Stevenson, H., & Sevenson, N. (1960). Social interaction in an interracial nursery school. *Genetic Psychology Monographs, 61*, 37–75.

Tambiah, S. (1969). Animals are good to think and good to prohibit. *Ethnology, 8*(4), 422–459.

Taylor, S., Fiske, S., Etcoff, N., & Ruderman, A. (1978). The categorical and contextual bases of person memory and stereotyping. *Journal of Personality & Social Psychology, 36*, 778–793.

Turiel, E. (1983). *The development of social knowledge: Morality and convention.* New York: Cambridge University Press.

Turner, T. (1985). Animal symbolism, totemism, and the structure of myth. In G. Urton (Ed.), *Animal myths and metaphors in South America.* Salt Lake City: University of Utah Press.

Turner, T. (1989). "We are parrots," "Twins are bird": Play of tropes as operational structure. In J. Fernadez (Ed.), *Beyond metaphor: The theory of tropes in anthropology* (pp. 121–158). Stanford: Stanford University Press.

van den Berghe, P. (1981). *The ethnic phenomenon.* New York: Elsevier.

Vaughan, G. (1987). A social psychological model of ethnic identity. In J. Phinney & M. Rotheram (Eds.), *Children's ethnic socialization* (pp. 73–91). Beverly Hills, CA: Sage.

Von den Steinen, K. (1984). *Unter den Naturvolkern Zentral-Brasiliens.* Berlin: Verlagsbucklandlub Dietrich Reimer.

Vosniadou, S. (1989). Analogical reasoning as a mechanism in knowledge acquisition: A developmental perspective. In S. Vosniadou & A. Ortony (Eds.), *Similarity and analogical reasoning* (pp. 413–437). New York: Cambridge University Press.

9   The birth and nurturance of concepts by domains: The origins of concepts of living things

Frank C. Keil

The revival of interest in domains of cognition, especially in the contexts of cross-cultural and developmental studies, is a welcome new awareness of how different sorts of concepts and belief systems might become tailored to particular kinds of lawful regularities in our physical and social worlds. To make much progress, however, this new emphasis requires more precise distinctions between types of domains and better descriptions of the ways in which each type might vary across development and cultures. We can talk about domains as rarefied as a cardiologist's knowledge of arrhythmia to those as commonplace as everyday folk psychology. Domains can vary from the highly concrete causally rich relations in a naive mechanics of physical objects to the highly abstract noncausal relations of mathematics or natural language syntax. Lumping together all of these different sorts of domains so as to have similar effects on cognitive development is likely to be misleading and uninformative. In this chapter, I consider some distinctions and their implications for questions concerning the origins of concepts.

The focus of this chapter is on the emergence of biological thought. Concepts of living things may offer an especially clear illustration of how domains might be involved in the origins of more specific concepts, and conversely of how specific concepts become intertwined within larger belief systems. In addition, views of concept structure and use have increasingly invoked the special importance of those belief systems known as theories. Several converging lines of work on both the development (Carey, 1985; Keil, 1989) and the use of concepts (Murphy & Medin, 1985) have argued that most concept structures are inextricably intermixed with causal, explanatory beliefs of a systematic nature. Mere tabulations of feature frequencies and correlations grossly undetermine concept structure. For example, curvedness is equally typical of a banana and a boomerang but is considered much more

Preparation of this paper and much of the research described herein was supported by NIH grant R01HD23922

234

explanatorily central to the boomerang (Medin & Shoben, 1988). A key part of concept acquisition, representation, and use involves structures and relations that transcend models in which typicality governs all aspects of structure.

The increasing consensus on embedding concepts in theorylike structures has not led to a parallel consensus on how this intermixing comes about; and it is through this disagreement that the role of domains in cognitive development becomes especially salient. Two views have come to dominate much of the current discussion. One strongly empiricist account argues that early concepts are devoid of theory, which then gradually gets overlaid. The other view, which will be called the primal theories account, argues that concepts are embedded within theorylike relations from the start. But the embeddings are often incorrect, because only two sets of theories are available at first, a kind of naive physical mechanics and a naive psychology, and all else is forced to fit in one of those two relations.

It is a strong claim to assert that the two domains of physics and psychology have a privileged status as the original theories that spawn all others; but this claim rests on several different and striking pieces of evidence. A large body of recent work with infants and special populations, such as autistic children , suggests innate sensitivities to these two different patterns of regularities. This work is extensively discussed in other chapters in this volume (e.g., Carey & Spelke, Leslie, Hirschfeld, Cosmides & Tooby, Premack, and Gopnik & Wellman) and need not be directly addressed here.

Biological phenomena are among the most pervasive aspects of our daily lives; yet, surprisingly, both of these views suggest a distinct domain of biological thought does not emerge until quite late in the course of cognitive development, often not until 6 or 7 years of age. In the empiricist view, concepts in biology, as in every other domain, emerge via general associative or inductive mechanisms. Patterns of explanation and discovery that eventually become uniquely associated with biology are said to have their origins in completely domain-general mechanisms of learning that work in the same way for all content. Early concepts are structurally indistinguishable across domains, because they are mere tabulations of frequencies and correlations and because restructurings caused by theory do not manifest themselves for several years.

The alternative view holds that biological thought does not spring out unguided tabulations of environmental regularities. Instead, it springs out of a specific mode of construal, a mode that nicely governs its own domain but wrongly engulfs biology until biology is able to stand on its own legs and emerge free and clear. Carey (1985) has summarized this view most explicitly and suggested that many of children's early beliefs concerning biological kinds are couched in a naive psychology, leading to gross misconstruals and distortions of biological things to make them fit the psychological, and to an inability to make important distinctions between biological phenomena and psychological ones. A child would understand eating only in terms of the beliefs and desires related to eating, not in terms of its physiological/nutritional role; similarly, the property of "has babies" would only be understood in terms of the social roles of parenting and not in the reproductive sense.

It does appear that, in some tasks, kindergartners and preschoolers will say that animals eat to the extent that they are sufficiently psychologically similar to the prototypical intentional being, humans. Thus, dogs eat and have babies, but worms don't. Carey quotes one child who said, "worms don't have babies, they just have little worms," to illustrate how they construe having babies solely in psychological terms (namely, those of parenting; Carey, 1989). A lingering question, however, asks why the comment about having little worms was offered at all; if the child had only a social understanding in which worms could not fit, such a comment should be irrelevant and not come to mind.

These examples illustrate why biological concepts provide such a critical assessment of the two broader views of concept structure and acquisition. Both can be assessed for their common contention that initially living things are not appreciated as such; and they can be contrasted as to whether biological concepts are distorted from the start by being forcibly embedded in a different primal conceptual domain or whether they gradually emerge and become distinctive through more general mechanisms of learning. More broadly, they bear on the question of how the earliest sorting of the world into meaningful kinds and regularities is related to later, more sophisticated construals.

Some distinctive properties of living things

For biological thought to be of interest as a distinct domain of cognition, adults should see biological things as having their own special sets of properties and relations. Some distinctions are clearly known only to sophisticated scientists but others may be much more universal. To illustrate, consider these seven distinctions, none of which are strictly true of all biological things and untrue of all else, but which do seem especially to capture the biological world (see also Keil, 1992):

1. Biological things reproduce, preserving the important properties of their kind both at the level of the species and the individual. Linked to reproduction are notions concerning inheritance of properties, including what sorts of properties are inherited and how inheritance works.

2. Biological kinds have a complex, heterogeneous internal structure. Except for broad axes of symmetry, if you chop them up into pieces, the pieces tend to be different from each other as well as not being simply smaller versions of the original. Gold and water clearly don't behave that way. Moreover these heterogeneous units are often arranged in functional hierarchies.

3. Biological kinds grow and undergo canonical and usually irreversible patterns of change, patterns that strongly individuate biological kinds. Crystals

may grow as well, but the change does not usually go through a distinctive patterned sequence (it usually goes through the same cycle over and over again). Finally, the patterns of change move toward an ideal target state for that kind, a state that is not usually the endstate (as elderly members of species illustrate).

4. Something intrinsic to biological kinds produces most of their stable phenomenal properties, which are not usually either external natural forces or human intentional ones.

5. Typical phenomenal properties are usually diagnostic of underlying nonphenomenal ones. We assume not only a kind of essence, but also a rich set of causal links between that essence and the merely phenomenal, at the same time recognizing the potential of the phenomenal to mislead (fishlike mammals, lizardlike snakes, and so on).

6. Properties have purposes for biological kinds. There is a compelling, albeit sometimes mistaken sense (see Gould & Lewontin, 1978) that the properties of biological kinds are there for reasons, that they solve design problems for the kinds that possess them. This sense of teleological justification is much weaker for such nonbiological natural kinds such as gold, water, and icicles. Properties of artifacts also have purposes of course, but the purposes for biological kinds tend to be more self-serving (e.g., rabbits have fluffy fur to keep themselves warm) whereas those for artifacts tend to be other serving (coats have fluffy polyester to keep people warm).

7. Biological kinds have parts that work together to support each other in a complementary manner, a lay version of homeostasis.

These seven distinctions are not independent of each other and can be collapsed and expanded in various ways, but they do illustrate the feasibility of having a different set of beliefs and different patterns of explanation for biological kinds.

These distinctions therefore now provide a context for evaluating the empiricist view that biological thought coalesces out of atheoretical associations and inductions unencumbered by belief.

The empiricist case

In some ways, biological knowledge does seem to rise out of raw induction over regularities in the world. For almost a century it has been claimed that immature concepts are unprincipled tabulations of all salient information that correlates with instances (salience being only perceptually driven). These early concepts then shift to more principled, tightly organized ones, or theory-driven ones, usually at around 6 years of age. This change has been referred to as: holistic to analytic, concrete to abstract, accidental to essential, among others, and has been mentioned by almost all the major developmental theorists of the century, including Vygotsky, Werner, Piaget, and Bruner (e.g., Bruner, Oliver, Greenfield, et al., 1966; Inhelder & Piaget,

1964; Vygotsky, 1934/1986; Werner, 1948). In addition it maintains a lively presence in current proposals concerning shifts from concepts organized on the basis of attribute similarity to those organized on the basis of higher-order relational similarity (Gentner & Toupin, 1988). There is also a long philosophical tradition of similar claims, with views ranging from Locke and Bacon to Quine (1977). This particular brand of empiricism tends to have a stagelike flavor in that concepts throughout the first years of life are said to be fully devoid of theory, which only comes to have influence in middle childhood. Thus, any early domains of cognition would be organized exclusively by principles of phenomenal similarity, not by appeal to any deeper explanatory principles. A different sort of empiricism might argue that theoretical domains emerge little by little such that, even in infancy, some very crude theoretical biases start to be abstracted away from the regularities implicit in the social and physical worlds. This second view is discussed later in this chapter.

My first studies on concepts for biological kinds also seemed to support the notion of a shift from a preschool atheoretical child to one empowered with new, domain-specific theoretical insights. For example, if all the salient characteristic features of one kind are changed into those of another contrasting kind, such as permanently changing surface parts to make a horse look and act like a zebra, younger children say the kind has been changed. Apparently a phenomenal zebra is a zebra, pure and simple.

The concepts appeared to be organized solely in terms of tabulations of typical features with no appeal to deeper principles or biases. Resistance to biological kind change by older children appeared to be caused by the emergence of biological beliefs that override the typical feature cluster, so that even though the thing looks and acts like a zebra, they know that feature clusters alone are not enough.

These apparent shifts from a preschool phenomenal similarity to a later, theory-driven restructuring would seem to support soundly the empiricist model, especially the stagelike version. There are, however, serious drawbacks both of a conceptual and a more practical nature. First, empiricist accounts have great difficulty demonstrating how an interconnected set of explanatory beliefs, or an intuitive theory, could ever emerge. There is no known route from association to domain-specific theories or belief clusters that does not build in preexisting biases to construct certain classes of theories over others; and those biases cannot simply be perceptually driven. For centuries, empiricists have claimed that all knowledge could be bootstrapped up out of constraints laid down by a set of sensory and perceptual primitives, but we have yet to see any such model actually work even for a notion as apparently simple as causation. Any attempt to design a working model invariably builds either domain-specific constraints into the learning procedure itself, or supplies data that is carefully filtered so as to embody such constraints. Perhaps a better general learning procedure will someday succeed with unbiased data, or perhaps the true data of experience embodies far more patterns conducive to the formation of domain-specific thought than are currently understood; but, for now, the lack of any positive models decreases the plausibility of such claims.

The second danger with the empiricist approach is that the last decade of developmental psychology has been full of demonstrations that prior researchers have underestimated young children's abilities to transcend the merely phenomenal. Again and again, preschoolers, and now even infants, have been shown not to be seduced by surface similarity and instead rely on deeper relations and principles (Baillargeon, 1987; Spelke, 1988). No matter how young children are, they always seem to make appeals to coherent sets of underlying principles that can override surface similarity.

However, even if the empiricist program is problematic, one still has to explain the "empiricist look." An account is needed to explain why more than half a century of research claimed there was a shift from organizing concepts in terms of raw, holistic similarity to seeing the world in terms of deeper, explanatory principles. One such account arises from viewing concepts themselves as intrinsic blends of association and belief.

Even the expert's most sophisticated theories eventually dwindle in explanatory power as increasingly subtle distinctions and relations are explored. As the theory loses its explanatory power, a back-up mechanism is needed for clustering entities and storing information, and it usually involves some associative means of storing feature frequencies and correlations. Thus adults cannot get by with theory-driven similarity alone; and perhaps in a complementary manner, the youngest child cannot get by with just phenomenal similarity based on association. There may never be at any age purely associative concepts, except for artificial and meaningless categories such as "blik," meaning small blue squares with stripes. Given that these sorts of artificial concepts were the most common stimuli used in concept learning studies for much of the 1960s and 70s, it is not surprising that young children's concepts might therefore be described in purely associative terms. The apparent developmental shift to understanding an arbitrary rule for organizing such categories may have therefore been misleading. Rather than tacking explanatory belief systems onto concepts as a kind of developmental afterthought, even the youngest children may always be trying to shoehorn new entities into their presently available systems. Only in desperation would they have a representation of a category, or what we might call a pseudoconcept, be purely associative without the nurturance and support of beliefs and principles, for those are what add the flesh and muscle to induction.

Biological concepts might appear to undergo a qualitative shift from no theory to theory, but instead we may be witnessing the emergence of ever more powerful theories that are increasingly able to explain what formerly was representable only by association. The illusion of a qualitative shift occurs because observers tend to presuppose parts of the child's theory so automatically that they may notice only the associative residual that becomes incorporated into the expanding theory or belief set. Some parts of theories may be so basic that they are rarely considered explicitly. It is more natural to notice those parts that change, and thus see an illusory shift from concepts and domains organized by associative similarity to those organized by theory and explanatory belief.

This alternative view of early concept development predicts that even the youngest children should be able to go beyond the phenomenal if the experimenter finds a way to tap into the core beliefs that organize those children's domains.

In my own research I have come to realize that young children will indeed override the phenomenal similarity spaces that we take to be the hallmarks of simple associative representations; and they will do so in their judgments not only as to whether something is an animal or a plant, but also as to what kind of animal or plant it is. Thus, almost no kind of change can really turn an animal into a plant and even the horse/zebra transformation will be rejected as a true change if the transformation doesn't tap into anything preschoolers see as biologically relevant, such as using a skintight costume to effect the phenomenal change as opposed to using permanent changes of surface parts (Keil, 1989).

These and other studies, such as several performed by S. Gelman and her colleagues (e.g., Gelman & Coley, 1991; Wellman & Gelman, 1988), strongly argue against young children blindly following tabulations of feature frequencies and correlations in their construals of biological kinds. They do not prove that domain-general tabulation procedures cannot work; but given the absence of positive demonstrations of such procedures, they have shifted the burden of proof. One doesn't have to run newborns to cast doubt on the empiricist program; instead it suffices to show that relevant developmental trends do not extrapolate backward in a way that supports such a view. Rather than being the more parsimonious view, the empiricist account has to explain how a set of properties and relations becomes differentially salient for picking out and thinking about living things, especially when many of those properties are not obvious in immediate experience. I therefore move on to the primal theories view, under the assumption that there is no positive evidence that even very young children structure their concepts in terms of raw similarity spaces constrained only by perceptual principles and associativelike laws. As mentioned previously, a more subtle empiricist view is considered later in this chapter.

Evaluating the primal theories view

Given that the stagelike class of empiricist models runs into both conceptual and pragmatic problems, the primal theories view suggests itself as a possible alternative. The primal theory model predicts that early biological thought is not a separate domain but is instead absorbed largely into an intuitive theory of mind and behavior. To test this prediction, thought about many facets of biology should be examined to see if there are any systematic distortions in the modes of construal yielded by primal theories. If not, one wants to ask whether some other coherent set of beliefs seems to be organizing biological thought as a whole or whether it is splintered into many subdomains of biology, with no unified models of explanation and understanding. These alternatives can be assessed only by detailed studies of several different sub-domains of biology, such as beliefs about species and other taxonomic concepts, growth, reproduction, inheritance, disease, and physiology, among others.

It is only through such comparisons that we gain insight into the difference between highly local expertise domains and the possibility of much broader modes of explanation and construal. My colleagues and I are in the midst of an extensive series of studies covering many different biological phenomena. Whenever possible in these studies we contrast physical and psychological relations with biological ones suggested by the seven principles described earlier in this chapter. This chapter illustrates the approach with examples from beliefs about inheritance and disease.

The biological transmission of properties

All people across history and culture have assumed that living things transmit some of their properties to their offspring (Jacob, 1982). At the same time all adults realized that only some properties have this special status of being transmittable; and indeed they almost certainly have a range of intuitive probabilities attached to different properties. Differences between the adult intuitive probabilities and those of children might shed light on the emergence of biological thought. Ken Springer and I (Springer & Keil, 1989, 1991) have conducted an extensive series of studies exploring how developmental changes in beliefs about properties might shed light on broader questions about the emergence of biological thought. It has become increasingly clear that, although younger children may well have different beliefs about what properties are likely to be inherited and what mechanisms are plausible, their beliefs are never guided by either absorption into a naive psychology nor by reference to phenomenal similarity to the most frequent and/or salient examples. Instead, there are consistent appeals to properties that have functional/physiological roles and to mechanisms that are internal to the organisms involved (Keil, 1992).

In his doctoral thesis, Springer examined links between beliefs about inher-itance and those about kinship (Springer, 1990). Kinship relations involve both the biological and social modes of construal while at the same time keeping those modes distinct. Preschoolers were shown displays of three animals in which animal A was visually similar to animal B but unrelated, and visually less similar to animal C, but related.

Children were asked whether animals B and C had either nonperceivable biological properties (e.g., "has tiny bones inside it") or nonperceivable, non-biological properties (e.g., "is very dirty from playing in the mud") possessed by A. A series of studies showed that preschoolers (roughly $4^{1}/_{2}$ years) were more likely to attribute biological properties to dissimilar related animals than to similar unrelated ones. When the property was nonbiological, it was attributed more often to the similar animal than to the dissimilar but related one. There was, therefore, a strong reversal in the pattern of attribution as a function of the type of property presented, with biological properties inductively projecting along bloodlines and social/behavioral properties along phenomenal similarity.

In sum, judgments of inheritance do not show a collapse of the behavioral into the biological, and they suggest a particular sensitivity to the functional nature of the properties of living things (see also Hirschfeld, this volume). A key question concerns the presence of similar patterns in the realm of disease.

Biological contagion

Social/psychological conditions, such as laughter and depression, can be seen as contagious; but for adults, this psychological contagion is completely distinct from the biological. One way to explore whether young children appreciate the special nature of biological contagion is to ask what sorts of symptoms can be caught. Any set of beliefs about biological contagion must regard only some unusual conditions as communicable; otherwise contact with all other living things would be seen as hazardous.

We have conducted several studies examining what sorts of unusual conditions can be "caught." In one study, the conditions varied on three dimensions: sudden onset versus congenital (i.e., one just got the condition or has always had it); good versus bad (the condition is detrimental vs. beneficial); and behavioral versus physiological (an unusual mental state vs. an unusual functional biological state). Adults put strong emphases on both the behavioral/physiological and sudden onset/congenital contrasts and have weaker intuitions whether good versus bad symptoms are relevant. If children are absorbing all biology into psychology however, we might expect no differentiation of the behavioral versus physical and congenital versus sudden onset. The empiricist view might predict more attention to the good/bad dimension early on because all familiar contagious diseases have salient negative effects.

The symptoms were all intended to be sufficiently dissimilar from familiar diseases so that simple analogies to them would not be helpful. In addition, some of the behavioral afflictions were deliberately constructed to have clear physiological side effects, to assess if younger children would differentiate similar endstates on the basis of different underlying mechanisms. Consider, for example, the case of a little girl who suddenly developed the false belief that her hands were dirty and kept washing them all the time, such that her hands became red and "oozy." There is a clear physiological outcome here much like that of known diseases, but the cause is clearly a set of behavioral symptoms. Once these afflicted people have been described, the child is asked if, after being in close contact for a weekend or so, one would "catch" the affliction.

Children as young as 4 years of age judged the abnormal behaviors not to be contagious regardless of how much close contact one had to the afflicted person. The behavioral/physiological contrast influenced judgments far more strongly than the other two contrasts. The good/bad distinction, which might afford the simplest comparison to known diseases by brute similarity, not only had a smaller overall effect, but also showed a trend in which the younger children were actually less influenced. Apparently, experience with increasing numbers of diseases increased the salience of the good/bad dimension rather than reducing it. The congenital/sudden onset dimension had no influence on judgments in the younger children. Beginning in the second grade, however, it came to have a major influence, a finding in accordance with the rise in importance of congenital factors in judgment of inheritance (see also Keil, 1992).

The rejection of behavioral afflictions is especially impressive considering how often we speak colloquially about the contagiousness of behaviors, such as laughter. The major developmental change of an increasing understanding that congenital things are less likely to be contagious again illustrates that the younger children can and do differ quite dramatically in some ways from adults. Sharing certain biases with adults therefore in no way ensures that younger children will possess the same theories and concepts of disease. It only ensures that common modes of construal at broader levels will prevail.

These children assumed that psychological and biological causes could not mix. They were wholly separate. A clearer understanding of the basis for their judgments would inform questions about how the two domains are organized. To that end we are currently conducting a series of studies asking about more subtle types of behavioral and physiological aberrations in children ranging in age from 3 to 10 years. For example, there is a continuum of sorts from the most mental of aberrations, false and illusory beliefs, to cases of correct beliefs but aberrant mental processes (such as general memory and attentional disturbances), to cases of correct beliefs and mental processes but aberrant behaviors (such as facial tics) to more purely physiological aberrations (such as joints that ache). Although they are still in progress, the early results from these studies suggest that, early on, most behaviors are seen as equally noncontagious. Later, with increasing age, an awareness seems to emerge that the more belieflike an aberration is, the less contagious it is likely to be. It will only be through such detailed analyses that we will gain a clearer idea of why the behavioral/biological distinction is so clear to these children and how such an understanding is related to developing notions of living things.

Disease causes and symptoms

In addition to contagion, beliefs about possible disease agents are a useful way of asking about children's understanding of fundamentally different kinds of causes in a domain where direct experience of the mechanisms responsible for disease is not possible. There are for adults at least, two different causes of diseases: biological agents such as germs and viruses, and nonbiological ones such as poisons and toxins. This contrast allows one to ask if simply knowing that something is biological leads to different patterns of inferences about how it would produce a set of surface outcomes also generated by a nonbiological agent. This was shown to be the case in a preliminary study in which preschoolers judged that an ingested powder that caused, say, purple blotches all over, did so in a very different way from germs that caused the same blotches.

In a second study, the disease agent was simply called a "thing" to block associations to known agents such as germs. Consider three different accompanying descriptions about the thing: a functional or teleological description stating that the thing needed to get inside and use parts of the body to make one sick, a simple mechanical description in which the thing rubbed around inside the body causing sickness through mechanical damage such as abrasion, and an intentional description that directly attributes goals and desires to the thing to make you sick (this is an important contrast case with the teleological description).

For most adults, the teleological description implies that a biological thing is involved. The goals and desires description implies not only a biological thing, but also a psychological one, and the mechanism description suggests a nonliving thing. Children at grades K, 2, and 4 each received these descriptions and were asked to make inferences about other likely properties in a version of a commonly used induction paradigm.

The results are straightforward: (1) describing a thing as using parts of the body resulted in its being seen at all ages as just as alive, just as able to move on its own, just as able to reproduce as an intentional thing described as "wanting to get inside you and make you sick" and just as likely to have heterogeneous internal structure (inside parts that were "different from each other, not all the same") all in strong contrast to the abrasion case. Thus, the functional and intention/desire entities were, on the average, more than twice as likely to have the traits of reproduction, motion, heterogeneous structure, and being alive. This is summarized in Figure 9.1, which shows average results for all these properties because they were not significantly different from each other (see also Keil, 1992).

On the other hand, as seen in Figure 9.2, children at all ages thought that the functional/teleological thing did not know what it was doing any more than a simple mechanical one and in strong contrast to the intentional one, attributing knowledge roughly three times as much to the intention/desire entity.

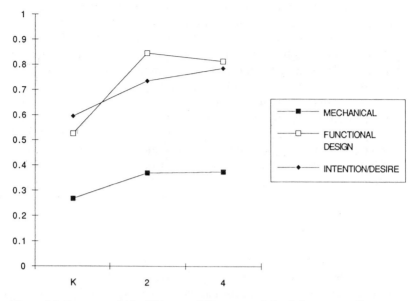

Figure 9.1. Extent to which children at different ages judged that unseen disease agents of each of the three types could reproduce, move, be alive, or have heterogeneous internal structure. Overall means are shown here because differences among the questions were nonsignificant.

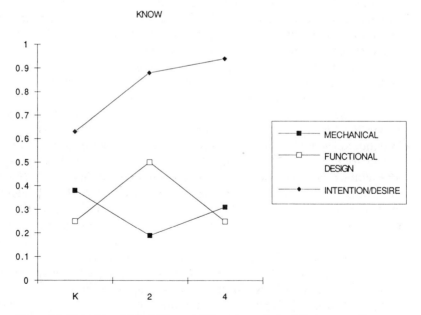

Figure 9.2. Extent to which children at different ages judged that unseen disease agents of each of the three types had knowledge guiding their actions.

This pattern demonstrates that even the youngest children are not simply equating these disease agents to prototypical animals or human exemplars, which do know what they are doing. They are apparently not taking the teleological description as simply making the thing an intentional agent with mental goals. A thing for these children can apparently be biological without being sentient, which is a critical distinction.

These studies on intuitions about invisible disease agents illustrate that young children do not reason about biological things simply by making analogies to the most familiar biological beings with intentions. An independent set of principles appears to be guiding their inferences, a set that relies heavily on notions of function and organized structure in an overall system.

A Teleological Stance

Young children appear to understand the advantages of teleological/functional modes of construal for all biological kinds and may associate them more strongly with these kinds than with other sorts of things. They may also construe biological things as having richer or more causally potent essences. These modes of construal may be the most important constant constraints on emerging biological thought and may be what give coherence to that thought across other developmental changes in beliefs about living things.

Perhaps the domain of biological thought has origins as distinct for humans as those domains of thought about objects and persons. In addition to the intentional and physical stances, there might also be a "design" stance (Dennett, 1987). Such a stance looks at things as if they had functions, or as if their properties were designed for purposes. This stance allows one to understand relations that might well be hopelessly complex or even invisible to a simple mechanical/physical stance. Thinking of systems as solutions to design problems can often provide new insights. Many explanations at the design level cannot be reduced to the mechanical level nor elevated to the intentional level without serious loss of specificity and/or explanatory power.

The argument from design repeatedly occurs throughout history in culture after culture as a motivation for a god or gods (Dawkins, 1986). Even after Darwin and Wallace, some maintain that we overzealously use teleological explanations in evolutionary biology (Gould & Lewontin, 1978). It is therefore of interest to explore the origins of the adult intuition that some kinds of questions just don't fit with nonbiological natural kinds. One can ask why water is transparent, but not in the why sense that asks, "What does being transparent do for water? What good is it? Why wouldn't water be just as good if it was opaque?" All of these sorts of questions, however, are perfectly appropriate for a jellyfish. For adults these kinds of teleological questions and answers are fine for most biological kinds and not for most other natural kinds. They are also appropriate for many artifacts, but in a different sense having to do with natures of the purposes of properties.

Some informal observations of my own children at early ages convinced me that some version of this mode of construal was organizing their concepts. For example, one of our children at $2^1/_2$ years came across a silverfish for the first time, pointed at the pincers, and asked, "What are those things for?" One doesn't find this sort of question nearly so often concerning the properties of nonliving naturally occurring things. In an attempt to ask experimentally whether young children appreciate that preferred explanations for even the same property may vary considerably as a function of the kind of thing involved, several studies have been conducted that ask children to choose between explanation types. The explanations do not really add any new useful information but they do model more abstract types of structural explanations. Thus, in one study 5- to 7-year-old children were told that "Two people are talking about why plants are green. This person says it is because it is better for the plants to be green and it helps there be more plants. This person says it is because there are little tiny parts in plants that when mixed together give them a green color. Which reason is a better one for x (plants/ emeralds)?" The same choice was given for why emeralds were green. Note that both explanations are adequate for plants but only the trivial reductionist one works for the emeralds.

Overall, teleological explanations were favored for biological kinds roughly $2^1/_2$ times more often than were reductionist explanations. Reductionist explanations were preferred for nonbiological natural kinds like emeralds roughly five times as often as the teleological. In a different study, children were presented with two pictures, one of a prickly plant and one of a prickly kind of mineral; indeed, in some cases, the drawings are nearly identical except for the labels. They are told that both are prickly but only one is prickly because being prickly is good for it and they are asked to pick which one (show pointy plant/rocks). Children as young as 5 will show a stronger linkage of the teleological with both plants and animals.

Although this particular technique does not work well with younger children, the children may not be lacking a design stance. Perhaps as early as the first year of life, children are able to adopt clear functional stances toward a variety of artifacts, where they clearly understand that various properties have purposes, and can invent new tools as well (Kolstad & Baillargeon, 1992). But using the design stance is not the same as explicitly being aware of how certain phrasings are compatible with that stance. In addition, a young child might have the stance, and even some sensitivity to the propositional structure of its typical explanations, but not yet know that it has a special affinity with living things. Some of the studies on disease have suggested, in more implicit terms, an early linking of functional relations to biological kinds, but explicit recognition of the role of these sorts of explanations may take considerably more time to develop.

Departures from randomness

Perhaps a less verbal component of the teleological mode of construal involves expectations about the functional architecture of internal parts of different kinds of entities. Certainly one of the hallmarks of living things is that their internal parts are nonrandomly structured. These departures from randomness can range from bilateral symmetry of like elements to spatial clustering of similar parts. Minerals, crystals, and rocks can also have nonrandom structures, but some patterns may be more distinct for living things, and certain kinds of nonrandomness may be less likely for rocks. Suppose that one is shown via "a super x-ray machine" two possible views of the insides of parts of plants, animals, and rocks, where one view is a random array of elements whereas the other has symmetry, or clustering, or repetitive complementary relations, as shown in the Figure 9.3.

Note that, although perhaps visually less compelling, the complementary configurations may be among those most strongly and uniquely associated with living things, as they most strongly imply internal functional architecture. We are now asking whether children as young as three are sensitive to nonrandomness as being associated with living things and whether some types of nonrandomness, such as complementarity, are more strongly linked. Young children may treat discernible parts on living things quite differently than similar parts on nonliving things, such as assuming that they are functional and related in consistent ways to other parts. Preliminary signs are encouraging, but the study is still in the early stages. In conjunction with R. Gelman's work on young preschoolers' expectations about the presence of internal parts for moving things (Gelman, 1990), a theme starts to emerge that even children who are barely talking may still have strong expectations about how different sorts of functional configurations are associated with different kinds of things. From these hunches about functional architectures may arise more explicit and abstract notions of design.

Contrasting artifacts with living things

Because general design explanations also work well for artifacts, the question arises as to how they are to be distinguished from living things. One possibility is in the nature of the functional explanation, for although properties may have purposes for both groups, the purposes are usually more self-serving for the living kind. Roses have thorns to keep animals from getting at them whereas barbed wire has barbs so as to keep animals from getting at something of value to humans. Complex artifacts can have some self-preserving properties and domesticated species can have properties enhanced to serve human needs, but the broader contrast is a good one.

We now have preliminary indications that children as young as 3 years of age see living things as much more prone to having self-serving properties

 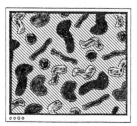

Figure 9.3. Examples of stimuli used in a current study. The child is asked to choose which internal structure (as shown by the super x-ray machine) seems to fit better with the depicted object. In this instance a rock and a flower are shown with choices offered between a random array and one with complementary parts.

that are linked to enhancing the presence of others. Thus, if preschoolers are presented with drawings following roses and barbed wire, will they judge that the rose has barbs for its own good and the barbed wire for the good of others? Very different views about clustering and hierarchical organization of properties may spring from this contrast, the one for living things being relatively bounded, tightly clustered, and self-contained whereas the one for artifacts flows more continuously into considerations of broader social contexts and human needs and intentions.

A second way to cleave artifactual and living things is that living ones have clearer essences and causally more potent ones. There are hints of this in several of the studies described so far, but there are few studies that directly explore this issue. The best indications so far come from developmental studies conducted by S. Gelman and her colleagues and by Atran's cross-cultural analysis of biological belief systems (Gelman & Coley, 1991 and this volume; Atran, 1990 and this volume).

Conclusions: Domains and concepts

There are several implications of this work for issues concerning the relations between concepts and domains. First, two highlights from the empirical findings:

1. Although many developmental phenomena might suggest a shift from preschoolers' being domain-general associative learners to later being domain-specific theorists, a closer look reveals that many apparently associative concepts have cores of explanatory beliefs, which are usually less powerful cores that give way sooner to associative nets, but they are beliefs nonetheless. Children might still be domain-general tabulators at even earlier ages, but several studies have shown how many such apparent cases are illusory. Moreover, there are no clear positive demonstrations of completely unbiased natural concepts in even the youngest of children; thus, the burden has shifted. It might not be even possible to model the emergence of explanatory beliefs out of associative nets. There is no obvious mapping from the kinds of environmental regularities most salient to a simple associative system operating on perceptual primitives to sets of explanatory beliefs.

2. There is no pattern in all the studies reported here that supports a gradual emergence of biological theory out of the folk psychological. As we look at younger and younger children, we do not see their judgments becoming more and more psychologically driven. Although the precise source of biological knowledge is still open to exploration, it does not seem to come from a psychology. At the same time, young children have few explicit beliefs about living things. They clearly have never thought about many of the things we ask and yet they still have strong biases for some classes of mechanisms over others, biases that don't seem to spring out of a naive physics or psychology. Such biases suggest a set of abstract principles that can generatively account for intuitions about an indefinitely large set of novel biological phenomena. What might these principles be in more detail? Returning to the seven contrasts outlined at the beginning of this chapter, they may be largely distilled to ramifications of the teleological and essentialist biases and their interactions.

A great deal of conceptual change does occur with respect to biological thought in the first 10 years of life and many of the studies described here illustrate dramatic changes. A critical question concerns how well most known patterns of conceptual change can be accommodated within a system in which some common principles, such as those implicit in essentialist and teleological biases, are always present. It appears that the modes of construal do not embody specific beliefs about biological things and instead embody biases for certain kinds of explanations and functional architectures over others. If this is so then conceptual change may occur within a larger and highly stable framework that helps orient one cognitively toward biological sorts of things.

We may therefore want to distinguish between broad modes of construal and detailed sets of beliefs in our accounts of how knowledge becomes organized into domains and changes over time. We may be endowed with relatively few modes of construal (or stances if you prefer), such as the mechanical, the intentional, and the teleological (and perhaps a half dozen more); but we may be able to use these as footholds into acquiring much more elaborated belief systems in an extraordinary number of specialized domains.

Even if the mechanical, intentional, and teleological stances precede and guide the differentiation of more local belief systems, those three stances themselves might be initially learned through more general learning procedures. I have suggested that recent infancy research makes such a model unlikely for the mechanical and the intentional; but there is less evidence concerning the earliest origins of a functional mode of construal. However, the extraordinary ease with which all of us do learn about functional objects, such as tools, relative to other species that exhibit sophisticated learning in so many other areas also argues against reduction to general learning procedures. If there is indeed a strong species specificity for a functional/design stance, it can serve as evidence for its domain specificity as well.

If it does turn out to be the case that any or all of these stances are learned through general learning procedures, that finding would be of extraordinary interest in its own right. It would mean that, throughout the world, humans are exposed to patterns of regularities that are so coherent and bounded that general learning procedures invariably extract similar overarching principles for interpreting information in those domains. Those principles would vary dramatically across domains but would be shared across all individuals within each domain. They would be uniquely accessible to humans as opposed to other animals either because of a major difference in human experience or because of the additional power of their general learning procedures. Finally, the general models of learning would have to be able to show not only how those universal stances were so quickly developed in the earliest stages of learning but also how they endured as constraining framework guiding later conceptual change. This particular empiricist alternative has no supporting evidence at present; but it remains a theoretical option, although certainly not a more parsimonious or basic one.

Returning at last to the broader theme of how different domains are involved in the origins of concepts, the emergence of biological thought can be seen as supporting a view in which there are very early skeletal constraints on concepts at the most belief-laden aspects of cognition, constraints moreover that are not equally felicitous with all classes of phenomena. I have called these sets of constraints modes of construal, so as to indicate that they yield different forms of explanation that resonate with specific sets of phenomena; and to indicate that they themselves probably are not either real theories or real concepts, but rather predispositions to interpret patterns of relations at all levels of analysis from the perceptual to the most abstract and conceptual.

These modes of construal could be viewed as opportunistic, exploratory entities that are constantly trying to find resonances with aspects of real world structure. They may well be limited in scope of successful application, but not exclusively tailored for a domain such as biology. Although some of those modes may have evolved in direct response to the pressing needs of being able to learn quickly about particular patterns of causation, it may also be part of their nature to be constantly seeking out new resonances with other sets of phenomena, hence our tendencies (often through metaphor) to anthropomorphize computers, to see personality in fluid dynamic terms, or see design in randomness. This account gains much of its potential interest from the possibility that there may be only a small number of these basic modes of construal that emerge in early life, say, half a dozen or so. Such a modest array of stances would mean that concept structure was neither reducible to one set of laws arising out of a single model of learning, nor splintered into a thousand different areas of expertise and skill. There may be enough diversity of these basic biases to help us understand the major different kinds of patternings in the natural and social worlds, but not so much as to turn the study of concepts into an endless catalogue of different structures in different tiny domains.

Those tiny domains exist in a different sense, but we should see them as having a very different role in the growth of concepts. Expertise and explanation may not be the same. In the extreme, it may be that these fundamental modes of construal are the only explanatory systems ever available to us and that we learn about new patterns by discovering which of these modes, or even what combinations of them, best provide insight into a set of phenomena (and sometimes nothing much works). Some forms of expertise might involve making just such discoveries, such as in learning how to use an intricate combination of the intentional and design stances in understanding computers. Other forms of expertise may rely more heavily on our fallback mechanisms of association, and automatization of highly repetitive routines. These might include the chicken sexing experts discussed by Gibson (1969) and many others since. These experts were able to discern sex in the anatomies of newborn chicks while novices could see no meaningful differences whatsoever. In addition, the original experts were unable to articulate the basis for their judgments. Domains of this last sort have nothing of the flavor of explanation left in them. Indeed, one of the most intriguing aspects of those forms of expertise is that the experts frequently cannot access the beliefs themselves nor directly teach them to others.

My most general point is that we collapse together these different senses of domains at great peril. The fundamental modes of construal give us immediate intuitive feelings not only for how and why things are the way they are, but equally important, of what sorts of things there are; they yield our ontologies. Through metaphor, mixtures of domains, and some incorporations of more general learning mechanisms we can use these modes to understand more circumscribed and local phenomena; but the sense of immediate explanation starts to fade, and is gone altogether, along with any ontological sense, as we move into the cognitively "blind" expertise of the chicken sexer.

References

Atran, S. (1990). *Cognitive foundations of natural history: Towards an anthropology of science*. Cambridge: Cambridge University Press.

Baillargeon, R. (1987). Young infants' reasoning about the physical and spatial characteristics of a hidden object. *Cognitive Development, 2*, 179–200.

Bruner, J. S., Oliver, R. R., Greenfield, P. M., et al. (1966). *Studies in cognitive growth*. New York: John Wiley.

Carey, S. (1985). *Conceptual change in childhood*. Cambridge, MA: MIT Press.

Carey, S. (1989). Conceptual differences between children and adults. *Mind and Language, 3*, 167–181.

Dawkins, R. (1986). *The blind watchmaker*. New York: Norton.

Dennett, D. C. (1987). *The Intentional Stance*. Cambridge, MA: MIT Press.

Gelman, R. (1990). First principles organize attention to and learning about relevant data: Number and the animate–inanimate distinction as examples. *Cognitive Science, 14*, 79–106.

Gelman, S. A., & Coley, J. D. (1991). Language and categorization: The acquisition of natural kind terms. In S. A. Gelman & J. P. Byrnes (Eds.), *Perspectives on language and thought; Interrelations in development* (pp. 146–196). Cambridge: Cambridge University Press.

Gentner, D., & Toupin, C. (1988). Systematicity and surface similarity in the development of analogy. *Cognitive Science, 10*, 277–300.

Gibson, E. J. (1969). *Principles of perceptual and cognitive development*. New York: Appleton-Century-Crofts.

Gould, S. J., & Lewontin, R. C. (1978). The spandrels of San Marco and the Panglossian paradigm. *Proceedings of the Royal Society, London, 205*, 581–598.

Inhelder, B., & Piaget, J. (1964). *The early growth of logic in the child*. New York: Norton.

Jacob, F. (1982). *The logic of life: A history of heredity*. New York: Pantheon Books.

Keil, F. C. (1989). *Concepts, kinds and cognitive development*. Cambridge, Bradford Books for MIT Press.

Keil, F. C. (1992). The origins of an autonomous biology. In M. A. Gunnar & M. Maratsos (Eds.), *Minnesota Symposium on Child Psychology, Volume 25* (pp. 103–138). Hillsdale, NJ: Erlbaum.

Kolstad, V., & Baillargeon, R. (1992). Appearance and knowledge-based responses of 10.5-month-old infants to containers. Manuscript submitted for publication.

Medin, D. L., & Shobin, E. J. (1988). Context and structure in conceptual combination. *Cognitive Psychology, 20*, 158–190.

Murphy, G. L., & Medin, D. (1985). The role of theories in conceptual coherence. *Psychological Review, 92*, 289–316.

Quine, W. V. O. (1977). Natural kinds. In S. P. Schwartz (Ed.), *Naming, necessity, and natural kinds* (pp. 155–175). Ithaca, NY: Cornell University Press.

Spelke, E. S. (1988). The origins of physical knowledge. In L. Weiskrantz (Ed.), *Thought without language* (pp. 168–184). Oxford: Oxford University Press.

Springer, K. (1990). *Children's awareness of the biological implications of kinship.* Unpublished doctoral dissertation, Cornell University.

Springer, K., & Keil, F. C. (1989). On the development of biologically specific beliefs: The case of inheritance. *Child Development, 60,* 637–648.

Springer, K., & Keil, F. C. (1991). Early differentiation of causal mechanisms appropriate to biological and nonbiological kinds. *Child Development, 62,* 767–781.

Vygotsky, L. S. (1934/1986). *Thought and language.* Cambridge, MA: MIT Press.

Wellman, H., & Gelman, S. (1988). Children's understanding of the nonobvious. In R. J. Sternberg (Ed.), *Advances in the psychology of human intelligence* (pp. 99–135). Hillsdale, NJ: Erlbaum.

Werner, H. (1948). *Comparative psychology of mental development* (2nd ed.). New York: International Universities Press.

Part IV

Are domains theories?

10   The theory theory

Alison Gopnik and Henry M. Wellman

This is a book about domain-specific cognition – the proposal that at least some human conceptual abilities are specialized for some types of contents and not for others. In this chapter we address the development of a single domain: everyday understanding of the mind. We suggest that this development is best understood as the formulation of a succession of naive theories. Moreover, this "theory theory" can help to characterize cognitive domains more generally and to explain domain-specific development. Our chapter, therefore, joins company with a number of recent discussions drawing parallels between theory change in science and cognitive development (Carey, 1985, 1988; Gopnik, 1984, 1988; Karmiloff-Smith & Inhelder, 1974; Keil, 1987; Wellman, 1985, 1990).

Theory of mind

In the past five years there has been an explosion of interest in children's early understanding of the mind (Butterworth, Harris, Leslie & Wellman, 1991; Astington, Harris, & Olson, 1988; Frye & Moore, 1991; Whiten, 1991). The research tackling this question has come to be called "children's theory of mind." This title reflects a leading explanatory position among investigators in this area. According to this position, our everyday conception of the mind is an implicit naive theory; children's early conceptions of the mind are also implicit theories, and changes in those conceptions are theory changes. We refer to this explanatory position as the "theory theory."

A. G. was supported by NSF Grant No. DBS 9213959 during the preparation of this manuscript. H. W. was supported by NICHD grant HD-22149 and by a fellowship from the Center for Advanced Study in the Behavioral Sciences. An earlier version of this paper was presented at the 1991 Society for Research in Child Development Meeting. We are grateful to Andrew Meltzoff, Clark Glymour, Doug Medin, Lou Moses, and Chuck Kalish for their helpful suggestions and comments on an earlier draft.

257

If the theory theory has any content, it should be falsifiable. It should lead to empirical predictions about the course of development, and these predictions should be different from those of alternative accounts. We will describe both the nature and predictions of the theory theory in some detail and contrast them with two alternative accounts, a "simulation theory" and an "innate module theory." Some of the predictions of the theory theory are similar to the predictions of one or the other of these alternatives. However, the overall pattern of predictions is distinctive. In the end we suggest that the current data, by and large, support the theory theory.

What is a theory?

When we say that children's understanding of the mind is a theory, we do not necessarily mean that it is an explicitly formulated theory, or that the cognitive enterprises children engage in are identical to those of adult scientists. The question of when and how children come to do science is an interesting one (Kuhn, 1989), but it is not the one we consider here.[1] There are obvious differences between scientists and children. For example, scientific change, as it's usually conceived, takes place over a period of many years and involves the entire scientific community, whereas cognitive change takes place in individual children in a much shorter time period.

Nevertheless, scientific theory change and conceptual change in childhood are both the product of human minds trying to understand the world around them. Scientific change must centrally involve some human cognitive capacity. But although this claim seems nearly self-evident to psychologists, it has not been the prevailing view in philosophy of science itself. Instead, philosophers of science have typically been concerned with logical questions about the nature of scientific knowledge, or, more recently, with sociological and historical questions about the nature of change in the scientific community. To oversimplify, we might say that the original project of classical philosophy of science was to try to show some logical way in which true theories could be constructed from evidence, in the way, for example, that complex logical systems could be constructed from simple axioms. The failure of this project led to a view that emphasized the largely arbitrary, socially determined nature of actual scientific change.

A cognitive interpretation of science might hold some middle ground between these views. On this view scientific theory change may be neither logically necessary nor sociologically arbitrary. Instead, it reflects cognitive processes that genuinely lead to a veridical conception of the world, though not necessarily in a way that is logically guaranteed. Curiously, this view has really only begun to be elaborated in the philosophy of science itself. The cognitive science of science is still in its infancy. Nevertheless, the large body of phenomena described in literature on the history and philosophy of science will inform any such cognitivist view, and any such view will have to provide an account of those phenomena.

From this cognitive point of view, both cognitive developmentalists and philosophers of science face a similar question – how to characterize mechanisms for learning about the nature of the world. Two of the clearest and most impressive instances we have of such learning are the acquisitions of children and the achievements of science. How do children and scientists develop basic knowledge about the world? The hypothesis of the theory theory is that there are deep similarities between the underlying cognitive mechanisms involved in the epistemological endeavors of childhood and of science. Philosophers of science are developing a characterization of cognitive structures – scientific theories, paradigms, research programs – that organize, produce, and store scientific knowledge. Developmental psychologists are developing a parallel notion of everyday theories and research programs that organize, produce, and store everyday knowledge.

Insights from philosophy of science, then, can help to illuminate the epistemological achievements of childhood. But the similarities are better captured by thinking of scientists as big children, rather than thinking of children as little scientists. The progress of science, we believe, reflects certain fundamental processes of conceptual change that are first seen in very young children.

Within philosophy of science there is much argument over what theories are and how they change. In spite of these controversies, there are some very general features that, on almost all conceptions, are characteristic of theories and distinguish them from other types of knowledge. Our reference list will include strange bedfellows to a philosopher of science, including such classic accounts as those of Nagel and Popper as well as revisionist views such as those of Laudan and Kuhn. This reflects the tension between logical and sociological views of science.

Nevertheless both schools have provided us with rich descriptions of the actual course of theory formation and change in science. In what follows we highlight the features of theories and theory change in science that seem to us common across these very different accounts and that seem most relevant and helpful in understanding cognitive development. We do not aim for a definitive account of scientific theories. On the contrary, the point of the theory theory is not to demonstrate that what scientists do is identical with what children do, but to use the scientific notions as a touchstone for characterizing an important sort of cognitive development.

Empirical typologies versus theories: Abstractness and coherence

Theories are always constructed with reference to evidence, some layer of experience different from the theories themselves (Nagel, 1961; Lakatos, 1970; Laudan, 1977; Popper, 1965). The relation between theory and evidence is distinctive. It is not like the relation between experience and other cognitive structures. To capture this, we distinguish between two ways of organizing experience. The first kind we will call "empirical typologies and generalizations," the second "theories." Empirical typologies and generalizations are orderings, partitionings, and glosses of evidence and experience, but they share the same basic vocabulary as the evidence itself. For example, I may look at a collection of plants and divide them into ones with no stems, ones with green stems, and ones with woody stems. Similarly, I may make generalizations about the behavior of objects. If the evening star appears at the same place in the heavens every evening we may make the empirical generalization that it will continue to appear at that place this evening (without any theoretical notions of why this may be the case). If on many occasions moldy bread relieves infected wounds, we might make the generalization that mold relieves infection (Nagel, 1961; Hempel, 1965). In developmental psychology the idea that children have "scripts" or "schemas" (e.g., Nelson, 1985) implies that much early cognition consists of empirical typologies and generalizations. And this may well be true for certain sorts of knowledge.

Empirical typologies and generalizations contrast with theoretical structures. Theories propose theoretical constructs: Abstract entities, events, or forces. These theoretical entities do explanatory work – they provide causal explanations that account for evidential phenomena. These theoretical explanations are typically phrased in a vocabulary that is quite different from the evidential vocabulary.

For example, suppose we postulate Darwinian species as a theoretical construct in evolutionary biology (rather than describing birds, mammals, etc., as empirical types). We will define species in terms that are quite removed from their apparent features; a green stemmed plant and a woody stemmed one may both be ferns because of their reproductive lineage. Similarly, Kepler's theory of the planets postulates elliptical movements that are notoriously not visible when we look at the stars' perceived motions in the sky. In theoretical medicine, we postulate unseen entities, like viruses and bacteria, with distinctive properties. Theoretical constructs are often called unobservable but they need not be definitively unobservable; rather they are appeals to a set of entities removed from, and underlying, the evidential phenomena themselves. Theoretical constructs are designed to explain (not merely type and generalize) those empirical phenomena. So, one characteristic of theories is their abstractness.[2] Theories postulate abstract entities and laws that explain the data but are phrased in a different vocabulary than the data themselves.

Moreover, theoretical constructs do not work independently – they work together in systems characterized by lawlike structures. A second characteristic of theories, therefore, which distinguishes them from empirical generalizations, is their coherence (Hempel, 1965; Quine & Ullian, 1970). The theoretical entities and terms postulated by a theory are closely, "lawfully," interrelated with one another. As a result, changes in one part of a theory have consequences for other parts of the theory.

Explanation. The coherence and abstractness of theories together give them an explanatory force that empirical typologies and generalizations lack. Although empirical typologies and generalizations may be useful, they lack deep explanatory power. To "explain" that this plant is stemless because it belongs in the category of plants without stems, or that the star appeared there by saying that it always appeared there before, is legitimate but shallow. In contrast, explaining the position of the evening star in terms of Kepler's theory, or the properties of plants in terms of their evolutionary history, is, at least, cognitively satisfying in a way that empirical generalizations and typologies are not. Moreover, there are reasons to believe that such explanations are also more accurate. They get us closer to the truth.

Prediction. Similarly, empirical generalizations allow predictions, but the predictions are not far removed from the evidence itself. Moreover, they are phrased (roughly) in the same terms as the evidence itself. If the evening star was the first to appear in the heavens in the past, then it will be the first to appear there tonight (Nagel, 1961). In contrast, the abstractness and coherence of theories give them a very characteristic sort of predictiveness. A theory, in contrast to an empirical generalization, a script, or a schema, makes predictions about a wide variety of evidence, including evidence that played no role in the theory's initial construction. In evolutionary biology, knowing a plant's species enables us to predict what its offspring will look like. Kepler's account allows one to predict the behavior of new celestial objects, moons, for example, which were quite unknown at the time the theory was formulated. Theories in medicine allow us to predict that antibiotics will inhibit many bacterial infections, including some, like scarlet fever, that present none of the symptoms of an infected wound, or some, like Legionnaire's disease, that were unknown when the theory was formulated. They also allow us to predict that such drugs will be useless against viral infections, even when the symptoms of the viral infection are identical to those of a bacterial one.

Some of these predictions will be correct. The theory will accurately predict future events described at the evidential level, and will do so in ways that no single empirical generalization could capture. Others will be incorrect. Because theories go beyond the evidence, and because theories are never completely right, some of their predictions will be falsified. In still other cases the theory will make no prediction at all.

In fact, the theory may in some circumstances have less predictive power than a very large set of empirical generalizations would. This is because explanatory depth and force do not simply equate with predictive accuracy. We can make predictions about events without explaining them: Kepler's theory still leaves many of Tycho Brahe's observations unexplained; there are no theoretical explanations for the efficacy of aspirin, and yet empirical generalizations about its effects are the basis for an industry. Theoretical predictions are different in two ways. First, a few theoretical entities and laws can lead to a wide variety of unexpected predictions. Second, in the case of a theory, prediction is intimately tied to explanation.

Interpretation. As we've seen empirical typologies and generalizations are closely related to the evidence itself. A taxonomy or generalization may call our attention to certain features of the evidence rather than others, but it will rarely lead us to actively misconstrue the evidence. In contrast, theories produce interpretations of evidence, not simply descriptions and typologies of evidence and generalizations about it. It is notoriously true that theoretical preconceptions may lead a scientist to dismiss some kinds of evidence as simply noise, or to reinterpret others as suspect or the result of methodological failures (Lakatos, 1970; Scheffler, 1967). Nevertheless, these influences of the theory on evidential interpretation are not merely arbitrary. There are characteristic ways in which theory and evidence interact (Glymour, 1980).

All of these characteristics of theories ought also to apply to children's understanding of mind, if such understandings are theories of mind. That is, children's theories should involve appeal to abstract unobservable entities, with coherent relations among them. Theories should invoke characteristic explanations phrased in terms of these abstract entities and laws. They should also lead to characteristic patterns of predictions, including predictions about new types of evidence and false predictions. Finally, theories should lead to distinctive interpretations of evidence; a child with one theory should interpret even fundamental facts and experiences differently than a child with a different theory. This distinctive pattern of explanation, prediction, and interpretation is among the best indicators of a theoretical structure, and it provides a way of distinguishing the theory theory from some of its competitors.

Dynamic features of theories. So far we have been talking mostly about the static features of theories, the features that can distinguish them from other cognitive structures such as typologies or schemas. We turn now to theory changes. A most important thing about theories is what philosophers call their defeasibility. Theories are open to defeat or revision via evidence and because of this theories change. In fact, a tenet of modern epistemology is that any aspect of a theory, even the most central ones, may change (Quine, 1961; Laudan, 1977).

Theories change as a result of a number of different epistemological processes. One particularly critical factor is the accumulation of counterevidence to the theory (Popper, 1965). The mere fact of counterevidence, however, may not lead to the theory's rejection; instead the interpretive mechanisms of the theory may simply reinterpret the counterevidence (Lakatos, 1970). This fact has sometimes led to a kind of epistemological nihilism, as if theory change was just a matter of caprice, or sociology (Feyerabend, 1975). But even though a precise logical specification of theory change may elude us, there are certainly substantive things to be said about how it typically takes place. There are characteristic intermediate processes involved in the transition from one theory to another (Kuhn, 1962; Lakatos, 1970; Laudan, 1977).

The initial reaction, as it were, of a theory to counterevidence may be a kind of denial. The interpretive mechanisms of the theory may treat the counterevidence as noise, as something not worth attending to. However, at a slightly later stage the theory may call on ad hoc auxiliary hypotheses designed to account specifically for such counterevidence. Typically, these hypotheses are only invoked to explain particular cases of counterevidence and are not applied more generally. Auxiliary hypotheses may also be helpful because they phrase the counterevidence in the accepted vocabulary of the earlier theory. Such auxiliary hypotheses, however, often appear, over time, to undermine the coherence that is one of a theory's strengths. The theory gets ugly and gerrymandered instead of being elegant and tight.

A third step requires the availability or formulation of some alternative model to the original theory. A theory may limp along for some time under the weight of its auxiliary hypotheses if no alternative way of making progress is available. Even when a viable alternative emerges, its fertility is typically not recognized immediately. The first inklings of the new conceptual structure may appear in the form of relatively small modifications of the conceptual apparatus of the earlier theory. Only later may it become clear that the new idea also provides an alternative explanation for the evidence that was central to the earlier theory.

The development of the heliocentric theory of planetary movement provides some good examples of these intermediate processes. Auxiliary hypotheses involving more and more complex arrangements of epicycles were invoked to deal with specific pieces of counterevidence. At the same time, a new conception of planetary movement, heliocentrism, was beginning to emerge. It is worth noting though that Copernicus's theory itself failed to apply the heliocentric idea very widely. In many respects Copernicus's account is more like the Ptolemaic one, than, say, Tycho Brahe's account. It includes epicycles, for example. Brahe's account acknowledges many of the flaws of the Ptolemaic ones, and uses the idea of heliocentrism to deal with them (other planets revolve around the sun, which revolves around the earth). But even Brahe fails to accept the central idea that the earth itself goes around the sun. Only with Kepler is there a really coherent heliocentric account that deals both with the anomalies and with the earlier data itself.

We propose that these same dynamic features should be apparent in children's transition from one theory to a later one, and specifically from one view of the mind to another. Children should ignore certain kinds of counterevidence initially. Later, they might account for them by auxiliary hypotheses, only invoked to deal with particular kinds of counterevidence. Furthermore, children might first use the new theoretical idea in limited contexts, contexts closely related to the conceptual structure of the earlier theory. Only after the theory change is complete will they finally reorganize their knowledge so that new theoretical entities play a central role.

The child's theories of mind

In this section we briefly outline an emerging picture of children's early understanding of the mind. The description we provide is of a succession of theories, the child's developing theories of mind. The description helps to clarify the theory theory, by outlining one sensible version of the theory for further discussion. The data also fit such a characterization, we believe; one of the strengths of the theory theory is that it usefully organizes a welter of emerging findings.

A number of misconceptions about children's theories of mind are beginning to appear. One is that there is a single "child's theory of mind" that emerges at some point in development. A second is that possessing this theory of mind should be identified with solving the Wimmer and Perner (1983) false-belief task. A third is that before developing this theory of mind the child is a behaviorist. We share none of these assumptions. In fact, we believe that they are inconsistent with the theory theory and the data. As we have seen an essential feature of theories is that they change. In theory change one can identify a succession of different, progressively more accurate theories. Moreover, on the theory theory, no single piece of knowledge, or performance on a single task, should be critical. The important thing about a theory is that it allows inferences about a wide variety of problems. Nor is there any reason to suppose that children are ever behaviorists – the theories we will discuss are all mentalistic ones.

We propose that there is a change from one mentalistic psychological theory to another somewhere between $2^1/_2$ and to 4 years of age.[3] The change is not a simple all or none one, but rather involves a more gradual transition from one view of the mind to another. Indeed this change manifests the telltale intermediate processes that are characteristic of theory change. Two-year-olds have an early theory including a conception of mental states such as desires and perceptions, but this theory is incorrect from an adult perspective, in that it does not posit the existence of representational mental states, prototypically beliefs. In 3-year-olds we see an intermediate phase. Children develop a nonrepresentational account of belief. They also begin to understand representational aspects of their well-developed notions of perception and desire. And they begin to countenance mental representations as a kind of auxiliary hypothesis, invoked to explain salient counterevidence. In a third phase, beginning around the age of 4, children reorganize their central explanatory theory. They begin to realize that what actors think – their representation of the world rather than the world itself – inevitably determines their actions.

The 2-year-old theory

The 2-year-old is clearly a mentalist and not a behaviorist (e.g., Wellman & Woolley, 1990). Indeed, it seems unlikely to us that there is ever a time when normal children are behaviorists. Even in infancy, children seem to have some notions, however vague, of internal psychological states. This is evidenced in very early "conversational" interaction and in facial imitation; almost from birth infants coordinate their actions with those of others in a sensitive and fine-grained way (Meltzoff & Gopnik, 1993; Gopnik, 1993). Later, more clearly, infant mentalism is demonstrated in social referencing and joint attention behaviors; 9-month-olds seek information about other's psychological relations to objects (Wellman, 1993). It seems plausible, therefore, that mentalism is the starting state of psychological knowledge. However, this early mentalistic theory does not include all the sorts of mental states that adults understand.

More specifically, even at 2 years, psychological knowledge seems to be structured largely in terms of two types of internal states, desires, on the one hand, and perceptions, on the other. Desire and perception alone provide examples of the two basic categories of explanatory entities in folk psychology – the two types of theoretical constructs that Searle (1983) calls "world-to-mind" and "mind-to-world" states. An understanding of desire encompasses an early knowledge that what is in the mind can change what is in the world. An understanding of perception, on the other hand, encompasses an early knowledge that what is in the mind depends on what is in the world. Moreover, both desire and perception, as theoretical constructs, work to explain action but may also be divorced from any particular actions that an agent may perform.

More important, however, desire and perception can be, and at first are, understood in non-representational terms. Desires at first are conceived simply as something like drives toward objects (Wellman & Woolley, 1990). Perceptions are at first understood simply as awareness of or visual contact with objects (Flavell, 1988). In neither case need the child conceive of a complex propositional or representational relationship between these mental states and the world. Instead, these very young children seem to treat desire and perception as simple causal links between the mind and the world. Given that an agent desires an object, the agent will act to obtain it. Given that an object is within a viewer's line of sight, the viewer will see it.

These causal constructs are simple, but they have considerable predictive power. In particular, together they allow the first form of "the practical syllogism": "If an agent desires x, and sees that x exists, he will do things to get x." Even that form of the practical syllogism is a powerful inferential folk psychological law. It allows children to infer, for example, that if John wants a cookie and sees one in the cookie jar, he will go there for it. If he doesn't want it, or doesn't see it, he won't. And there is evidence that $2^1/_2$-year-olds make just such inferences (Wellman, 1990, chap. 8).

The 3-year-old theory

By age 3, children begin to show signs of a more elaborate mental ontology. Natural language can provide us with one avenue for exploring these abilities. Before 3, children make extensive and appropriate use of terms for desire and perception (Bretherton & Beeghly, 1982). More cognitive mental terms (think, know, remember, make-believe, dream) only begin to emerge around the third birthday (Shatz, Wellman, & Silber, 1983). There is further evidence that at age 3 children begin to develop a more general notion of belief (Moses, 1993; Wellman & Bartsch, 1988), and also representational but fictional mental states such as pretenses, dreams, and images (Wellman & Estes, 1986; Woolley & Wellman, 1992, 1993).

When these concepts first appear, however, they have an interesting character, framed by the child's larger theory that is still a desire-perception theory. Initially the understanding of belief is largely nonrepresentational, and is modeled on an earlier understanding of desire and especially perception. On this view, belief, like perception and desire, involves rather direct causal links between objects and believers. This view has variously been called a "copy theory" (Wellman, 1990), a "Gibsonian theory" (Astington & Gopnik, 1991b), a "situation theory" (Perner, 1991), or a "cognitive connection" (Flavell, 1988) theory of belief. The similar idea in all these accounts is that belief contents directly reflect the world. In these respects the child's first conception of belief seems to be a relatively simple extension of earlier nonrepresentational theoretical constructs.

The most well-known evidence that children have this nonrepresentational view of belief is their misunderstanding of situations that involve misrepresentation. In the classic false-belief task, for example, children may see a candy box that has pencils instead of candy inside. They are asked what someone else will think is inside the box. Three-year-olds typically say "pencils." They behave as if there is a simple and reliable causal link between the real state of affairs in the world, and our mental states about it. As we will see 3-year-olds also behave as if they hold this view in a variety of superficially quite different tasks. So the first understanding of belief is arguably nonrepresentational in a crucial fashion. The 3-year-old's conception of fictional mental states such as imaginings and dreams suffers from a similar restriction. Three-year-olds (but not 4-year-olds) tend to expect even fictional imagings to reflect the real world truthfully (Woolley & Wellman, 1993).

Conversely, as the third year progresses, children begin to understand representational aspects of desire and perception. Desire and perception may be construed either nonrepresentationally, or representationally. In fact, in the adult theory, desire and perception are as representational as belief. What we want and see (by and large) is not the thing itself but the thing as represented. Understanding some aspects of desire and perception seems to require this sort of representational understanding. For example when we are satiated with something we no longer desire it, but the object itself has not changed; when different types of people have different tastes or values, their desires differ but the objects of desire remain the same; when people see the same object right-side up or upside-down, or through different colored filters, their perceptions of the object may differ. As we will see there is evidence that these representational aspects of desire and perception may be understood earlier than equivalently representational aspects of belief.

The 5-year-old-view

By age 4 or 5, children, at least in our culture, have developed a quite different view of the mind, one that we and others have called a "representational model of mind" (Flavell, 1988; Forguson & Gopnik, 1988; Perner, 1991). On this view almost all psychological functioning is mediated by representations. Desires, perceptions, beliefs, pretences, and images all involve a fundamentally similar structure, a structure sometimes described in terms of propositional attitudes and propositional contents. These mental states all involve representations of reality, rather than realities themselves. In philosophical terms, the child's view of the mind becomes fully "intentional." To use Dretske's (1969) terminology, perceiving becomes perceiving that, desiring becomes desiring that, and we would add, believing becomes believing that. This new view provides a kind of Copernican, or better Keplerian, revolution in the child's view of the mind. In addition to distinguishing different types of mental states with different relations to a real world of objects (desires vs. perceptions), the child sees that all mental life has the same representational character. Many characteristics of all mental states can be explained by the properties of representations. For example, representations change over time, and differ among people with different experiences. This newly unified view not only provides new predictions, explanations, and interpretations, but it also eventually provides a revised view of the very phenomena that were accounted for earlier by the desire-perception theory.

The child's theory as theory

What evidence do we have for these claims about the child's conception of the mind? In particular what evidence do we have for thinking that these understandings are theoretical in the sense that we have been outlining so far? We will argue that (1) the child's understanding involves general constructs about the mind that go beyond any direct evidence. (2) These constructs feature prominently in explanation. (3) The constructs allow children to make predictions about behavior in a wide variety of circumstances, including predictions about behavior they have never actually experienced and incorrect predictions. (4) Finally, these constructs lead to distinctive interpretations of evidence.

Explanations

Children's explanations of action show a characteristic theorylike pattern. In open-ended explanation tasks (Bartsch & Wellman, 1989; Wellman & Banerjee, 1991) children are simply presented an action or reaction ("Jane is looking for her kitty under the piano") and asked to explain it ("Why is she doing that?"). There are many mental states that might be associated with such situations. Yet 3- and 4-year-old children's answers to such open-ended questions are organized around beliefs and desires just as adults' are ("she wants the kitty"; "she thinks its under the piano"). Moreover, there is a shift in explanatory type between 2 and 5. Two-year-old's explanations frequently mention desires, never beliefs. Asked why the girl looks for her doll under the bed, they will talk about the fact that she wants the doll, but not about the fact that she believes the doll is there. Three-year-olds invoke beliefs and desires, and some 3- and 4- and 5-year-olds consistently refer to the representational character of these states, explaining failure in terms of falsity. These same trends can be seen in the explanations children give in their spontaneous speech (Bartsch & Wellman, 1990, and in press).

Predictions

Consider the desire-perception theory. Even that early theory allows children to make a variety of predictions about actions and perceptions, both their own and others'. For example, they should be able to predict that desires may differ, and that, given a desire, an actor will try to fulfill that desire. They should understand that desires may exist without being acted on, and that they may be unfulfilled. They should predict that fulfilled desires will lead to happiness, whereas unfulfilled desires will lead to sadness. And there is evidence that, in fact, all these kinds of predictions are made by very young children (e.g., Astington & Gopnik, 1991a; Wellman & Woolley, 1990; Yuill, 1984). Similarly, a child with the desire-perception theory should be able to predict the perceptions of others in a wide variety of circumstances, including those in which the perceptions are different from their own. Such very early activities as shared attention (e.g., Bakeman & Adamson, 1984) and social referencing (e.g., Hornik, Risenhoover, & Gunnar, 1987) may already indicate some capacity to predict the perceptions of others. Other aspects of this understanding quickly develop. By $2^1/_2$ these Level-1 predictions, as Flavell calls them, are firmly and reliably in place (Flavell, 1988). At this age children can reliably predict when an agent will or will not see (and hear and touch) an object. They can also predict how seeing an object will lead to later actions.

These predictions may seem so transparent to adults that we think of them not as predictions at all but simply as empirical facts. A little reflection, however, should make us realize that the notion of desire or perception used by these very young children is theoretically broad and powerful. Children can use the notion of desire appropriately and make the correct predictions when the desired targets are objects, or events, or states of affairs; they can attribute desires to themselves and others, even when they do not act to fulfill the desires and when the desires are not in fact fulfilled (Astington & Gopnik, 1991a; Wellman & Woolley, 1990). Similarly, children seem to make accurate predictions about perception across a wide range of events, and involving factors as different as screens, blindfolds, and visual angles, and do so across different perceptual modalities (Flavell, 1988). Again, they may do so even when the perceptions do not lead to any immediate observable actions. Moreover, given novel and unfamiliar information about an agent's desires and perceptions, children will make quite accurate predictions about the agent's actions (Astington & Gopnik, 1991a; Wellman & Bartsch, 1988; Wellman & Woolley, 1990).

More significantly, however, these children also make incorrect predictions in cases where the desire-perception theory and its successor, the nonrepresentational theory of belief, breaks down. The most well-known instance of such an incorrect prediction is the false-belief error in 3-year-olds, such as on the candy-pencils task. The focus on false-belief tasks, however, may be unfortunate because it has promoted a mind-set in which any ability to perform "correctly" on a false-belief task is taken as evidence that the child has a representational theory of the mind. As we will see, there are cases in which 3-year-olds indicate some understanding of false belief without having yet formulated a representational theory of the more general sort that we earlier attributed to 4- and 5-year-olds. To begin with, however, it is worth pointing out the much greater ubiquity and generality of incorrect false-belief predictions. Three-year-olds make erroneous predictions, not only in the "classic" tasks, such as the candy-pencils task, but also in many other cases involving beliefs about location, identity, number, and properties. They make incorrect predictions for other children, for adults, for puppets, and for hypothetical story characters. Incorrect predictions are made when the question is phrased in terms of what the other thinks, what the other will say, and what the other will do, and across a wide range of syntactic frames. They are made by American, British, and Austrian children, and by Baka children of the Cameroons (Avis & Harris, 1991; Gopnik & Astington, 1988; Moses & Flavell, 1990; Perner, Leekam, & Wimmer, 1987).

Moreover, and more significantly from the point of view of the theory theory, these incorrect belief predictions are mirrored by similar incorrect predictions on a wide range of other tasks. A brief inventory would begin with appearance-reality tasks. If children are shown a misleading object, say a "hollywood rock" that is really made of sponge, they typically say both that the object really is a sponge and that it looks like a sponge; they fail to distinguish appearance, as represented, from reality. These tasks have themselves proved robust across many variations of culture, question, and material (Flavell, Green, & Flavell, 1986; Flavell, Zhang, Zou, & Qi, 1983).

Also included are judgments about the sources of beliefs. For example, 3-year-old children fail to predict that someone with limited information about an object will have limited knowledge of the object. O'Neill, Astington, and Flavell (1992) showed children two objects that felt identical but looked different; 3-year-olds had difficulty predicting that someone who saw the objects would be able to differentiate between them, but not someone who only felt them. Young children have similar difficulty understanding subjective probability (Moore, Pure, & Furrow, 1990). Three-year-olds understand that some people may know things that others do not but they fail to appreciate that there may be different degrees of belief. That is, they do not predict any difference in accuracy between someone who is certain of something and someone who merely thinks it may be true. Finally, young children evidence related errors in the understanding of pictorial representation systems. Just as 3-year-olds typically predict that all beliefs must be accurate, they also predict that pictures and photographs must be accurate (Zaitchek, 1990).

Arguably all these tasks require a representational model of the mind. The early nonrepresentational theory of belief leads to incorrect predictions in cases of misrepresentation such as false beliefs, and also false photographs or misleading appearances (consider the similar difficulties for Gibsonian accounts in psychology). But the early theory also, in a quite different way, makes it difficult to understand that beliefs may come from many different sources, that they may come in degrees, and that there are intermediate steps between the mind and the world.

We might phrase this by saying that young 3-year-olds believe that cognitive states like belief come in only two varieties, total knowledge, when the world is causally related to the mind, and absolute ignorance, when it is not. In cases of misrepresentation, there is one object in the world and two people are both related to that object, but differences in the causal relations between the minds and the world lead to different representations of that object. In the sources and subjective probability cases there is one object in the world, and two people arrive at the same representation of that object, but the causal relations between each person and the world are different. To distinguish between degrees of belief or sources of belief we need to understand that people's cognitive relations to the world may differ in significant ways even when both their ultimate beliefs and the objects in the world are the same. Moreover, the notion of complex intermediate representational processes relating world and mind provides a causal framework for understanding many cases of misrepresentation. (See Astington & Gopnik, 1991b; Gopnik, 1993; Wellman, 1990, for further discussion).

In some of these tasks the nonrepresentational theory of belief makes no predictions and children answer at random. Significantly, however, in many cases the theory makes consistent incorrect predictions, and young children consistently give the same wrong answer, with correct answers emerging at about 4 years. The tasks involve very different types of situations and questions and their information-processing demands are quite varied. Moreover, the standard methodology of these studies has included control tasks, involving similar or identical situations, questions, and information-processing demands, which children seem entirely capable of answering. It seems then that children's difficulties are not due to some memory, attention, or language comprehension abilities that are unavailable to younger but available to older subjects. Nor do any dimensions of familiarity, at least in any simple terms, seem to underlie the difference between tasks at which children succeed and tasks at which they fail. Instead all these tasks seem to call on the same theoretical conception of the mind. Insofar as that theoretical conception fails, so do the children.

Interpretations

In the tasks we have described so far children are clearly using mental states to explain and predict, both correctly and incorrectly – two of the central functions of theoretical constructs. Children's responses also show strong interpretive effects. Suppose we present the young child with situations or events that amount to counterevidence for the desire-perception theory? If the child is simply reporting her empirical experience or observations, we might expect that she will report that evidence correctly. In fact, however, children consistently misreport and misinterpret evidence when it conflicts with their theoretical preconceptions. Flavell and his colleagues have some provocative but simple demonstrations of evidential misinterpretation (Flavell, Flavell, Green, & Moses, 1990). A child sees a blue cup, agrees that it is blue and not white, and sees the cup hidden behind a screen. At this point another adult comes into the room, and she says, "I cannot see the cup. Hmm, I think it is white." Then the child is asked what color he thinks the cup is and what color the adult thinks it is. To be correct the child need only report the adult's actual words, but 3-year-olds err by attributing to the adult a true belief. Even if corrected, "well actually she really thinks it's white," they continue to insist the adult has a factually correct belief: "She thinks its blue."

Moreover, in several studies, 3-year-olds make standard false-belief errors in reporting their own false beliefs, errors equivalent to their assessment of others' beliefs. In these cases children need not predict a person's belief or actions, they need only report their own past experienced beliefs. In fact, they misreport, that is misinterpret, their own beliefs. Gopnik and Astington (1988), for example, showed children a variety of deceptive objects, such as a candy box full of pencils. The traditional false-belief question was "What will Nicky (an ignorant other) think is inside the box?" The self-report false-belief question was "When you first saw the box, before we opened it, what did you think was inside?" Three-year-olds erred when reporting their own past false belief just as they did in assessing the other's false belief, and in each case they made the same error, reporting the true belief instead. Similarly,

3-year-olds are inaccurate in reporting the sources of their own beliefs, just as they fail to predict accurately the effects of sources on the beliefs of others (Gopnik & Graf, 1988; O'Neill & Gopnik, 1991). However, 3-year-olds are very accurate in reporting simple past perceptions (Gopnik & Slaughter, 1991). In short, many 3-year-olds interpret beliefs in terms of a restricted non-representational theory. When their experiences fit the theory, they report them accurately. When their experiences do not fit the theory, they misconstrue and misreport them to make them fit (Gopnik, 1993).

Transitional phenomena

Three-year-olds, however, unlike 2-year-olds, are no longer completely ignorant about representation and belief. Instead, recent evidence suggests that during the period from 3 to 4 many children are in a state of transition between two theories, similar, say, to the 50 years between the publication of *De Revolutionibus* and Kepler's discovery of elliptical orbits.

In our discussion of interpretation we described how children with the earlier theory begin by simply denying the existence of counterevidence: Johnny and I really did think and act as if there were pencils in the candy box when we first saw it. We have also described children's initial nonrepresentational account of belief. This nonrepresentational account of belief extends their original desire-perception psychology and leads to their errors in false-belief tasks. But when and how, we now ask, do the first signs of an understanding of misrepresentation, the centerpiece of the 5-year-old theory, begin to appear? Recall that in the scientific case the crucial idea of the new theory may first be used in order to deal with only particularly salient types of counterevidence, or be used in ways that involve only slight extensions of the earlier theory. There is evidence for these sorts of transitional phenomena in children's understanding of mind in the period from 3 to 4.

For example, it is possible that 3-year-old children achieve a partial notion of mental representations in the case of "non-real" mental states, such as pretences, dreams, and images. Certainly there is evidence that children actually have such fictional mental states as young as 18 months (Leslie, 1987). Evidence that they understand such states, however, becomes clear only later. But, by the third birthday children have some conceptual knowledge of these aspects of mental life, and moreover, they may distinguish such imaginary or hypothetical states from the states of desire and perception (Flavell, Flavell, & Green, 1987; Wellman & Estes, 1986). However, these states appear to play little role in 3-year-olds' (and for that matter adults') explanation of ordinary behavior. Significantly, these states have little causal connection to objects (that, in fact, is what is distinctive about them). Although 3-year-old children see desires as states that modify the world, and perceptions as states that are modified by the world, pretenses, images, and dreams, on their view, bear no causal relation to the world at all. So, advances in understanding representational mental states may first appear for mental states that play only a peripheral role in children's causal theory of mind and behavior. Furthermore, there is recent evidence that 3-year-olds' conception of fictional mental states is at first marked by a nonrepresentational conception similar to their first nonrepresentational conception of beliefs. As mentioned earlier, 3-year-olds (but not 4-year-olds) tend to expect even fictional imagings to reflect the real world truthfully (Woolley & Wellman, 1993).

Similarly, it seems that first understandings of genuine misrepresentation are developed as only mild extensions of the concepts of desire and perception central to the earlier theory. Desire and perception may be construed either nonrepresentationally, or representationally. In fact, in the adult theory, desire and perception are as representational as belief. What we want and see (by and large) is not the thing itself but the thing as represented. Understanding some aspects of desire and perception seems to require this sort of representational understanding. For example, when we are satiated with something we no longer desire it, but the object itself has not changed; when different types of people have different tastes or values, their desires differ but the objects of desire remain the same. There is evidence that representational aspects of desire may be understood earlier than equivalently representational aspects of belief. Three-year-olds are significantly better at recognizing and reporting changed desires for the very same object than changed beliefs about the same state of affairs (Gopnik & Slaughter, 1991). Similarly, young children are better at recognizing that two people might have similar desires or preferences for the same object than that they have two different beliefs about the same object (Flavell et al., 1990). However, 3-year-old children still do not perform as well on these tasks as they do on simple nonrepresentational desire tasks (Wellman & Woolley, 1990). Similarly, although nonrepresentational aspects of perception are understood by $2^1/_2$ years, representational ones, such as understanding that an object may look right-side up to one observer and upside-down to another, are only understood later (Flavell, 1988; Gopnik & Slaughter, 1991). However, there is evidence that these aspects of perception are understood before corresponding aspects of belief. Both in Flavell's earlier studies and in our recent studies (Gopnik & Slaughter, 1991; Slaughter & Gopnik, 1992), children were better at misrepresentation tasks involving perception than they were at similar false-belief tasks and appearance/reality tasks.

We have suggested that for the 2-year-old the central theoretical constructs are nonrepresentational desires and perceptions whereas for the 4-year-old they are representational beliefs. Three-year-old transitional understandings seem to include both nonrepresentational accounts of belief and representational accounts of imagination, desire and perception. This is reminiscent of the way that Copernicus and Tycho Brahe mix epicycles and heliocentrism.

There is also evidence that early signs of an understanding of misrepresentation may come only when children are forced to consider salient counterevidence to their theory. At times, for example, at least as the fourth year progresses, 3-year-olds are able to recognize the existence of beliefs that clearly misrepresent (e.g., Moses, 1993; Robinson & Mitchell, 1992; Siegal & Beattie, 1991; Wellman & Banerjee, 1991). In particular, Bartsch and Wellman (1989) found, as others had, that 3-year-old children continued to make incorrect false-belief predictions about a person's future actions, predicting persons would act as if they had correct knowledge instead. However, if 3-year-olds were confronted with a person who had already committed an incorrect mistaken action, and were asked to explain this anomalous behavior, at least some of them began to talk about misrepresentation. Mistaken actions constitute anomalies, or counterevidence, to nonrepresentational desire-perception explanations of action. Making this sort of counterevidence particularly salient seemed to help to induce initial representational notions, in this transitional age group. Similarly, in a recent study of children's conception of their own past beliefs, Mitchell and Lacohee (1991) required children to select an explicit physical token of their original belief (e.g., a picture of candy in the candy box) and then were shown the real contents of the box (pencils). When asked about their earlier belief in this experiment, children were confronted with their earlier choice of the physical token, and many were then able to avoid the typical misinterpretation of their earlier belief. That is, these children were able to assemble a beginning sense of misrepresentation if confronted with strong, clear counterevidence to their usually incorrect theoretical interpretation of their past belief.

However, to reiterate, these same 3-year-olds do not often think in terms of misrepresentation or false beliefs. When predicting action they typically, consistently, resistantly act as if the actor's desire along with the objective facts determine action, ignoring the role of false belief. Similarly, when asked the contents of a person's belief, they consistently, resistantly cite the objective facts rather than the subjective representations. The more advanced representational notion of belief initially functions like an auxiliary hypothesis rather than a central theoretical construct. It serves to explain strong counterevidence, under pressure, but is not used generatively to provide new predictions. (Compare the way epicycles function in Ptolemaic and early Copernican theory.) It serves to characterize peripheral phenomena, such as fictional imaginings, before it centrally characterizes beliefs.

Do 3-year-olds really understand false belief then? Did Copernicus really understand planetary movement? The answer in both cases is that the question is a bad one. One of the strengths of the theory theory is that it makes such questions otiose. "Understanding" false belief, or developing an idea of representation, involves the development of a coherent, widely applicable theory. It may be possible to have some elements of that theory, or to apply them in some cases, without operating with the full predictive power of the theory, particularly in a transitional state.

We argue therefore, that the transition from $2^{1}/_{2}$ to 5 shows all the signs of being a theory change. Although initially the theory protects itself from counterevidence, the force of such counterevidence eventually begins to push the theory in the direction of change. The first signs of the theory shift may emerge when counterevidence is made particularly salient. Moreover, the central concepts of the new theory, representation and belief, may first appear as small modifications of concepts that are already well entrenched in the earlier theory, such as desire and perception. Finally, by age 4 or 5 the new theory has more completely taken over from the old. The predictions are widely and readily applicable to a range of cases.

Alternative accounts

So far we have tried to present a picture of how a theory theory would handle the evidence about children's developing theories of mind. We wish to contend not only that the theory theory can account for the developmental data but also that it does so more adequately than other accounts. In this section we consider specifically two alternative accounts of children's understanding of mind: simulation theory and an innate module account. For each of these alternatives we provide a brief description, concentrating on the sorts of evidence that might distinguish that account from the theory theory. No single type of evidence speaks against these accounts; there is no critical experiment that confirms one theory and disconfirms the others. Still, the accounts do have different empirical implications and there is evidence that helps decide between each alternative and the theory theory.

Empirical understanding of the mind: The simulation theory

One alternative to the theory theory is that the child's understanding of the mind is much more closely linked to evidence than to theory. On this view much of the child's understanding of the mind is more like empirical typologies and generalizations than like theories. How might this look? Consider a commonsense account of a person's report of his or her own states of mind. In this account, the person directly experiences his on-going mental states and simply describes them accordingly – I'm wanting this, believing that, imagining the other, and feeling sad about something else altogether. These descriptions type the mental states as one sort or another. Such reports, it could be argued, serve to describe mental states in an appropriate evidential vocabulary – in this case the language of introspective mental experience – just as describing a fern as green, or woody, or big describes it in an appropriate evidential vocabulary – in that case the language of external perceptual experience. In this sort of description, it could be argued, we do not interpret our own mental states in terms of some theory; we merely experience them and are able to type together certain states as experientially similar.

All this has a certain plausibility for knowledge of one's own states, but what about our knowledge of others? On this view knowledge of one's own mind is direct and evidential, but knowledge of other minds is indirect and predictive. Still, the sort of prediction required is only that provided by any empirical generalization. According to this view we straightforwardly generalize mental states from our own experience to others. I know what I experience when "I want an apple" and I generalize that state to others, inferring that she also "wants an apple" in analogous circumstances or when she displays analogous behavior.

This empirical account of knowledge of the mind is congenial with a classic philosophical view of the understanding of the mind. This view, originally identified with Descartes but widely accepted since, is that we have some form of privileged "perceptual" or introspective access to our own mental states. Something like this view is also implicit in the extensive "perspective-taking" literature in the Piagetian tradition – the developing child must generalize his or her own experiences to other minds.

Recently, several philosophers (Gordon, 1986; Goldman, 1989) and psychologists (Harris, 1991; Johnson, 1988) have proposed more specific versions of this general position – a proposal they term simulation theory. According to simulation accounts, we use our empirical generalizations and typologies to attribute to others the states we would have ourselves if we were in the other's situation, or were producing their behavior. We simulate their mental states from our own, hence the name of this account. In a bit more detail, the simulation process works as follows. We feed perceptual inputs appropriate to the other's situation (e.g., what he can see or touch or hear) to our own mind. By running our mind through this contrived, imaginary situation we simply experience the mental state that would result in that situation. Then we attribute that state to the other person. We simulate the other person's mental state by running a working model of a mind – our own mind – in a simulated situation and seeing what the model yields.

The general empirical generalization account and the more specific simulation accounts have a number of telling empirical consequences; we will focus on only two here (see Gopnik, 1993; Gopnik & Wellman, 1992, for further discussion). The first concerns the experience of your own mind. On this view, in a very important sense, access to your own mental states is supposed to be direct and empirical, requiring no inference or interpretation, no conceptual intermediaries, no theorizing; you simply experience your state and describe it. A consequence of this view is that one cannot erroneously misinterpret, or misconceive, one's own mental state. One simply reports the experience as being of one evidential type or another.

On the theory theory, in contrast, erroneous self-interpretations are not only possible, they are to be expected. One typical characteristic of theories, after all, is that they allow and even force interpretation of the evidence. If the theoretical prediction and evidence are in conflict it is often the evidence rather than the theory that is reinterpreted, as we noted earlier.

A second empirical consequence, related to this first one, concerns the course of development. For both theory theory and simulation theory we can predict that there will be development: Initial "easy" problems will be solved correctly before later "hard" ones. But the notions of what will be easy and hard differ dramatically between these two accounts. For simulation theory the critical difference is between states that are directly reported versus those that must be simulated – states of the self versus states of others. A child's errors, again in the tradition of perspective-taking views in development, should occur when they must infer others' states, and can be expected to be essentially "egocentric" errors. That is, the child's early errors consist of not correctly adjusting the child's simulation to the other person's condition, an adjustment that is especially necessary, for example, when self and other are in such different situations that they should be experiencing conflicting mental states.

Note that on a simulation account there is no reason to expect that different mental states should be easier or harder to attribute to others. Take beliefs and desires. Both beliefs and desires are equally available to the child as states of her own mind. At a young age, from a simulation perspective, reading off one's own beliefs and one's own desires should be equally easy; attributing beliefs and attributing desires to someone else should be equally problematic, and equally subject to egocentric error when the other person's beliefs and desires conflict with one's own.

In contrast, for the theory theory the critical difference concerns states that are easy or difficult to conceive of. Earlier we described what we take to be a succession in the child's conceptions of mental states, as the child develops and replaces a succession of theories. Especially important is a difference between an early nonrepresentational understanding of mental states and a later more representational understanding. Early on children have a relatively adequate understanding of nonrepresentational desire-perception states. Later they develop an understanding of the representational state of belief, specifically, and a representational understanding of mind more generally (including a representational understanding of certain aspects of perception and desire). Theoretical conceptions of the sort we have described are equally applicable to the self and others. If a theory has formulated a particular theoretical construct, such as the concept of false representations, it should in principle be able to apply this concept equally well to the child's own behavior and the behavior of others. If the theory does not include this construct, it will not be applicable to either the self or others.

We want to describe several empirical findings that are relevant to the different developmental predictions of the two theories. The first set of findings concern children's ability to understand and report their own mental states. For example, as we noted before, children not only fail to understand that others' beliefs can misrepresent; they also fail to understand that their own beliefs can misrepresent. Children who say that the other person will think there are pencils in the candy box, also say that they themselves thought there were pencils in the candy box when they first saw it. Children who are unable to understand the sources of others' beliefs are also unable to report the sources of their own beliefs. Children seem to misinterpret even their own experience when it conflicts with their theories.

One crucial comparison concerns children's understanding of desires and perceptions versus belief. In three different tasks Gopnik and Slaughter (1991) presented children with situations in which their desires were satiated and so changed. For example, initially the child desired one of two short books. That one was read to him and the child said he now desired the other book. The test question for the past desires was just like the one for past beliefs: "When you first saw the books, before we read one, which one did you want?" In these tasks 3-year-old children were considerably better at reporting past now-changed desires than past now-changed beliefs. Similarly, Gopnik and Slaughter presented children with situations in which their perception was changed. Children saw an object on one side of a screen and they were then moved to the other side of the screen where they saw a different object. They asked, "When you first sat on the chair, before we moved over here, what did you see on the table?" The children were completely able to report their past perception. Again these same children misreported their own past beliefs.

These experiments concern children's reports of their own mental states, beliefs, desires, and perceptions. From a simulation point of view, why do the children make errors when they are, supposedly, simply reading off their own mental states? And why do they make errors for one state but not for the others?

Perhaps the trouble is that the questions require not a report of current mental states, but a (faulty) memory of past states. Harris (1991) has suggested this. However, the crucial data here concern the comparison between children's reports of belief and reports of other states such as desire and perception. These data suggest that young children can report mental states that are just past but now different, for example, they do so for changed desires and perceptions. The poor performance for beliefs that are just past but now different, therefore, cannot just be a memory problem. This finding presents a paradox for simulation accounts. Either reporting immediately past mental states involves directly reporting one's own states or it involves simulating immediately past experiences. If reporting these immediately past states requires simulation, and simulation is hard for 3-year-olds, then why are 3-year-olds so good at simulating their past desires and perceptions? If reporting past states does not require simulation, because these states are just read off, then why are the 3-year-olds so bad at reading off past beliefs?

More generally, the simulation account suggests that children are at first generally egocentric about the mind and then overcome this by learning that they must adjust their simulations for others. The developmental data do not fit this general mold; there is evidence for nonegocentric understanding quite early for some states. We have already described one such set of tasks, the early "Level-1" perspective-taking tasks, in which children can predict that the other child will not see what they see themselves. Similarly, quite young children can predict that someone else will have a desire different from their own (Wellman & Woolley, 1990). One issue for simulation theory, then, must be to explain why children, who can obviously "adjust their simulations" for some states, do not do so for beliefs. Indeed, even for belief itself, the data do not suggest that children's main difficulty involves misattributing their own beliefs to others. Instead, it involves a failure to understand that beliefs can misrepresent.

In this regard a task that makes a particularly interesting contrast to the false-belief task is a "discrepant belief" task (Wellman & Bartsch, 1988). Imagine a task in which the child sees objects at two different locations: There are pencils in the drawer and there are also pencils in the cupboard. The child is told about another person who has seen only the target objects at one location (or alternately that the other person believes there are pencils in only one location). Where will that person look if he wants to find the object? Compare that task to an equivalent false-belief task. In this case the target objects are only in one location, A. The child is told or shown that the other person believes (falsely) that the targets are in location B instead. Where will the other look if he wants to find the target objects? Three-year-olds typically answer correctly on discrepant belief tasks while failing false-belief tasks. On discrepant belief tasks they do not predict that the other would do what they actually do on the basis of their own knowledge (look in both places or in either place indifferently). Instead they predict, correctly, that the other will act on his own belief, one that is discrepant from the child's own belief. At the same time these same children fail the false-belief tasks, asserting that the other will look where the object really is.

In the discrepant belief task the other person possesses a belief that is different from the subject's, but that belief does not misrepresent. There are, in fact, pencils in the location as the other person believes. In this case 3-year-olds pass. In the comparable false-belief task the other's belief is not only different from the child's own belief, it misrepresents; it falsely claims there are candies in the box when there are none. Children's performance on these matched tasks strongly suggests that the problem is not that the child fails to adjust to the other's situation, but it is that the child fails to realize that beliefs can misrepresent.

This is only one example of results that suggest that young children's errors in understanding the mind are not really "egocentric." Even very young children are quite able to attribute to others mental states different from their own. Instead, they err by sometimes misunderstanding what certain mental states are really like.

A related empirical problem is that the simulation theory has difficulty explaining the structure of the explanations that children offer. In children's natural language and particularly their explanations for aberrant actions, they initially explain actions only in terms of desires and perceptions. As they grow older belief explanations also begin to emerge, occasionally including false-belief explanations (Bartsch & Wellman, 1989; in press). From a simulation point of view, the child's own mind, even at the very youngest ages, is a device that itself contains states like beliefs as well as desires. The child's model outputs both beliefs and desires. Why should children's explanations and predictions first privilege desires over beliefs? There is no reason to expect this if the child is simply running simulations and reporting outcomes. On the theory theory, in contrast, there is a good reason why children's explanations and predictions at first ignore beliefs and especially false beliefs or misrepresentations. Young children have yet to come to a theoretical conception of belief as an explanatory psychological construct.

To be clear, our preference for the theory theory over simulation accounts does not mean that we completely reject a role for first-person knowledge in the formation and application of a theory of mind. Our own first-person psychological experience provides a body of data that strongly informs and shapes our concepts of mind. Our claim is that these first-person experiences are also theory-laden. First-person knowledge of our own mental states is not merely experiential, it is a product of conceptual interpretation intertwined with self-experience.

Similarly, we do not wish to deny an important role for the simulation of others' states of mind. A theory of mind must confront the problem of inferring the mental states of others in particular cases. Several devices can be used to aid in this process, but imagining what your own mental states would be rates high among them. We contend, however, that such simulations are theory-driven. To understand another's actions we simulate his or her beliefs and desires. Why those mental states among the myriad possibilities? Why not simulate his or her daydreams, night dreams, aches, and sensations? Our simulations, we argue, are information acquisition attempts framed by a theory. Theories direct their holders to look for some sorts of data and not others; our theory of mind directs us to look for or construct some sorts of information about others. Simulations in this view are a consequence of our theory of the mind.

The innate module theory

A second serious alternative to the theory theory is that an understanding of mind is the result of an innate module. In this theory, basic mental concepts such as belief and desire are not constructed from evidence in the course of childhood development. Instead, an innate structure dedicated to interpreting behavior in terms of beliefs and desires has been forged phylogenetically, in evolution. Ontogenetically, that structure may need to be triggered by certain sorts of inputs, but once triggered it creates mandatory interpretations of human behavior in mentalistic terms. Something like this alternative can be derived from Fodor's writings about modules (1983) and his position that belief-desire conceptions of the mind are innate to humans (1987, 1992). Moreover, Leslie (1987, 1991) proposes that there is a distinct theory of mind module that makes its first developmental appearance with the onset of pretence in 18-month-olds.

There are two separable aspects of this alternative, as we see it. The first is the claim that there is innate knowledge about the mind. The second is the claim that this knowledge is modular. We believe that there is innate knowledge about the mind but we do not believe there is a theory of mind module (see also Astington & Gopnik, 1991; Gopnik, 1993; Meltzoff & Gopnik, 1993).

A naive theory may begin from an innate starting state, an initial mapping of inputs onto representations that is innately specified. However, from the theory theory point of view any starting conceptions would themselves be revised and reorganized as a result of countervailing evidence. What is innate is an initial state, a first theory. We are born with certain kinds of psychological knowledge that begin a process of theory development and revision. Moreover, if children do not have these initial representations, this first theory (in the case of autism, for example) we might expect them to develop a further theory of the mind in radically different ways, if they develop such a theory at all. Such a view seems implicit in the claims of some investigators of theory of mind in autism, such as Baron-Cohen (1990) and Hobson (1989). On this view, however, such initial structures, although innate, would be defeasible; any part of them could be modified or altered with new evidence. It makes sense to us to talk about innate theories, and to see the process of theory change and replacement as one that begins at birth.

When Leslie and Fodor argue for a theory of mind module, however, they are making a much stronger claim. In Fodor's (1983) analysis, for example, modules are not only initially innately specified, but their processing is mandatory, encapsulated, perceptual, and very fast. In addition, modular representations, unlike central knowledge and belief processes, are insensitive to revision via evidence. Along these lines, Leslie, for example (1991), argues that there is an innately specified privileged system of representations of psychological knowledge, analogous to the proposed specialized representational systems of the visual (Marr, 1982) or syntactic (Chomsky, 1975, 1980) systems. This theory of mind module automatically maps given perceptual inputs (say a person's behavior) onto a more abstract set of representations (representations of the actor's mental states). It automatically mandates certain "inferences" or outputs and not others.

It is the mandatory, nonrevisable character of modular processing that we wish to focus on for now. These features mean that the basic representations of the module are, in philosophical terminology, indefeasible. Given a normal brain, once the module has matured and has been triggered, certain representations of the mind will result. Conversely, other representations simply could not be formulated, no matter how much evidence supported them.

The crucial differences between this account and the theory theory, therefore, concern the interplay of experience and conceptual structure. In theories, experience can radically alter the nature of the theoretical concepts. Evidence about planetary movements can lead to the transformation of a geocentric conception into a heliocentric one. In modules the relation between experience and conceptual representation is different – experience is simply represented in this fashion. Relevant experience can trigger our use of a privileged representational system (or not), but the evidential nature of the experience does not reshape and reconstruct such privileged representations themselves.[4]

We would resist calling indefeasible, modular, cognitive structures theories. However, the representations these structures produce may mimic theoretical inferences or representations in various ways. In particular, like theories, modules invoke abstract entities and rules that are only related to perceptual experience in indirect ways. Also like theories, modules allow predictions that go beyond experience, and allow, indeed mandate, the subject to represent evidence in a particular way, a process that may look like interpretation. In modularity accounts, however, the inputs to the representations and the representations themselves, are not related to one another because of their logical or inferential or evidential properties, but simply as a matter of brute biological fact. Modular representations do not lead to predictions because of some set of inductive or deductive generalizations, but because they are designed by evolution to do so.

What kinds of evidence could differentiate between the modularity account and the theory theory? It is worth pointing out that many kinds of evidence that are commonly adduced to support one position or another, in fact, cannot discriminate between these two. The mere fact that there is some psychological knowledge in very early infancy is compatible with either view – that is, with either an innate starting-state theory or an early innate module. In particular, the theory of mind deficits in a biological disorder like autism might stem either from the absence of a theory of mind module, or from the absence of an initial starting-state theory of persons. The fact that the representations in question are abstract, and removed from the evidence of actual experience, is compatible with either view. So is the fact that such structures may develop universally. Children the world over may develop the same understandings because they are specified innately, or they may converge on the same conceptions because the crucial evidence is universally the same, and so are theory-formation capacities. All people do, in fact, have minds, and so it is not too surprising that all normal children reach this conclusion about them. Scientists similarly converge on a common account of the world, not because evolutionary theory or Newtonian physics are innately given, but because they are presented with similar patterns of evidence.

On the other hand, the fact that there is some logic in the relations between input and representations is not itself enough to rule out modularity. Evolution could seize on these relations also, precisely because they were, at least roughly, the correct ones. Arguments from function are equally undiscriminating. If a particular structure is functionally important from the perspective of the mental life of the individual child, or the cultural life of a community, then it is also likely to be important from an evolutionary perspective and vice-versa. Evolutionary just-so stories and ontogenetic ones are largely interchangeable. This is particularly true when there is a long history of cultural transmission of information.

In short, by considering only a given representational system it may be difficult, if not impossible, to distinguish between these views. The static features of theories, their abstractness, coherence, and explanatory and interpretive force, can also be found in modules. The crucial evidence in this case will be developmental. It is the dynamic features of theories, particularly their defeasibility, that allow us to discriminate them from modules.

In fact, modular accounts of the acquisition of representational systems, are, in an important sense, antidevelopmental (see, for example, Pinker's discussion of "the continuity assumption": Pinker, 1984). Apparent changes in representation occurring over time, on these views, can be accounted for only by processes outside the representational system itself. For example, they may reflect the maturation of another representational system, a later model coming on line. Thus, in his latest position Leslie (1991) acknowledges two transitions in children's representations of the mind. First, there is activation of an initial "metarepresentational" mental module at about 18 months. It is the triggering of this module that stimulates engagement in pretense and an understanding of desires and perceptions at about this age. Then there is the activation of a second, additional theory of mind module at about 3 or 4, which Leslie now postulates to account for children's understanding of belief and reality-appearance at this later age. Similarly, in modular linguistic theories it is sometimes proposed that early language, up until about 3 or 4 when complex syntax appears, is not really language at all (Chomsky, 1980). It instead reflects the operation of a quite different representational system that is supplanted by the maturation of a "real" language aquisition device at about 3.

Alternatively, modularity accounts may invoke external "information-processing limitations" or "performance constraints" to explain development. Fodor (1992) and Leslie (this volume) take this tack. On this view early conceptual structures are just like later ones, but various superficial performance problems prevent children from demonstrating this competence. This is also a common move in linguistic accounts (Chomsky, 1980; Pinker, 1983).

The essence of our preference for a theory theory over an innate module account concerns the developmental data. As described earlier, we believe that the developmental data chart a succession of conceptions of mind, each logically related to earlier conceptions and revealing several intermediate transitional and partial conceptions. On the theory theory the principal mechanism for development comes from within the representational system itself; the theory changes as a result of the accumulation of new evidence and also as a result of internal reworkings of the theory itself. According to the theory theory therefore, we would expect to see, not a single privileged representation of the input, but rather a series of developmentally related representations. Erroneous representations that are later restructured should be the rule rather than the exception, under this account. Moreover, as each set of representations is replaced by the next we would expect to see intermediate theory-formation stages and processes. For example, we might first see resistance to and reinterpretation of counterevidence, the invocation of auxiliary hypotheses, and the limited application of ideas in the new theory, before the new theory became completely dominant. We have suggested that just such a sequence is detectable in the child's developing theory of mind.

Such a sequence of several dependent, successor theories, each erroneous in its own way, with characteristic transitions between them, is difficult to explain, in any principled way, by an innate modular maturational account. A postulated succession of two modules, one coming on-line later than and replacing the first seems decidedly ad hoc, in comparison to the theory theory account. Similarly, there is no motivated and general performance limitation account that can describe the pattern of developmental change across the many tasks described above (see Wellman, 1990; Gopnik, 1993). Again the Bartsch and Wellman "discrepant belief" task (see above) is a particularly good indicator of this. The information-processing demands of this task are identical to those of the "false-belief" task, and the task uses precisely the same question. Yet 3-year-olds are consistently quite competent at solving this task. Moreover, erroneous (as opposed to incomplete) representations, which are later modified and restructured, are also difficult to explain on a purely modular account. Evolution might, of course, select for an erroneous representation: The representation just has to be good enough to allow the organism to survive and reproduce. But, if the representational system is good enough, why, on a modularity account, would it be replaced later in development?

It is, of course, logically possible that a maturational sequence of successive modules might just by accident parallel a theory-formation process, and that the triggering inputs just happen to bear the same relation to the privileged representations that evidence bears to theory. Such a view, however, seems unmotivated. It is easy to see how evolution might have selected for an (approximately) correct innately determined representation of the world. It is much more difficult to see how evolution would have selected for a series of representational systems, each maturing separately only to be replaced by another.

What seems more plausible is that evolution selected for a cognitive capacity to revise concepts on the basis of evidence, that is, a theory-making ability. It is also true, as we have said earlier, that an initial state theory, one that influences the later course of development, could be available. Finally, general maturational changes in information-processing capacities could enable children to develop some theories rather than others (in much the same way that computers or telescopes enable scientists to develop some types of new theories). Innate capacities could play a role in the development of a theory of mind in all of these ways, but they would not constitute a theory of mind module.

In sum, the role of evidence in theory change, the actively erroneous character of early theories, and the progressive character of theory formation distinguish theory change from the maturation of an innate module. They are also characteristic of children's developing conceptions of mind.

One important sort of evidence that would help differentiate between the theory theory and an indefeasible module is not yet available: intervention studies that would test whether children arrive at different theories if given different patterns of evidence. Experimental studies of this sort are very difficult to conduct. However, examination of the effects of natural variations in evidence are possible, for example, in cross-cultural investigations or investigations of individual and family differences. In the few studies conducted to date young children's performance on appearance-reality (Gardner, Harris, Ohomoto, & Hamazaki, 1988; Flavell et al., 1983) and false-belief tasks (Avis & Harris, 1991) seems quite constant across cultures. However, we do not know the extent of cross-cultural variation in adult theories of mind. If adults converge on the same theory in different cultures, then we might not expect cross-cultural differences in development. Anthropological reports of cross-cultural variation typically concern rather abstract and sophisticated notions of emotional or moral states (Lutz, 1988) or conceptions of self and personhood (Markus & Kitayama, 1991). It is not clear whether cultures do or do not differ much in the sort of very basic psychological knowledge investigated in theory of mind tasks with 3- and 4-year-olds.

Conversely, several suggestive, but still preliminary, studies point to a significant influence of different patterns of evidential input and variation in the timing of the development of mental concepts. Dunn, Brown, Slomkowski, Tesla, & Youngblade (1991) found that children whose parents talked a great deal about mental states developed false-belief explanations earlier than those whose parents did not. Perner, Ruffman, and Leekam (1992) found that children from large families, and particularly younger siblings, did better on false-belief tasks than children with fewer siblings. This is in spite of the fact that older siblings and children from small families do better on general measures of cognitive ability. Perner and his colleagues suggest that siblings may be a particularly relevant source of evidence for the existence of conflicting states of mind.

Theories and domains

Considerable debate in developmental psychology has centered on the extent to which the mind develops in a general versus specific fashion.

The theory theory provides some important resources for tackling this issue. Again, certain considerations about the nature of theories, articulated by philosophers of science, provide a fruitful starting point for considering naive theories. Of special import here, it seems to us, is a consideration of framework theories in contrast to specific theories (Wellman, 1990). Framework theories, called paradigms, research programs, and research traditions, by philosophers of science, define domains of inquiry. They do so in part by providing an ontology of the fundamental phenomena to be explained: for example, behavior, external stimuli, and overt responses for Behaviorism versus mental states, processes, and intentional action for Mentalism. Specific theories (say the Rescorla–Wagner theory of classical conditioning within Behaviorism) account for specific phenomena by "reducing" them to the ontology and explanatory structures of the framework theory. Notably, framework theories provide a characteristically developmental analysis of theoretical endeavors. A framework theory outlines a domain for discovery – a research program for the development of more detailed explanations and proposals.

This sort of analysis represents an attempt by philosophers of science to characterize an intriguing epistemological structure: framework understandings that predate and inspire, but at the same time are themselves further articulated and developed in more specific understandings of a domain of phenomena. Such structures are both general – encompassing a large domain of phenomena – and specific – specifically different from framework theories for other complementary domains. They are both open-ended and constraining, initiating the development of more specific theories but restricting them by defining the domain of inquiry in the first place.

The theory theory, therefore, predicts a particular combination of specificity and generality. It provides a middle ground between domain-general "stage theories" such as Piaget's on the one hand and accounts of development in terms of skills, or scripts, or "contextual activities" on the other. These latter accounts propose that children develop only an array of different competencies in areas that are highly practiced or repeatedly experienced, an analogy to skill at chess, or understanding restaurants, or sociocultural tasks like weaving. Similarly, some modularity theories propose that there are a great many task- and domain-specific representational systems with relatively little interaction between them (see Cosmides & Tooby, this volume).

A theory, in contrast, and especially a framework theory, should be able to make predictions and explanations across a wide variety of evidence, including evidence that played no role in the theory's initial construction. This predictive and explanatory power is what gives theories their epistemological potency and differentiates theories from skills, rough empirical generalizations, and scripts. Theories typically apply not only to highly familiar or practiced pieces of knowledge but also to brand new ones, sometimes pieces of knowledge that could not have been conceived of or discovered outside of the theory. Equally, we would expect, and indeed have seen, that a theory change may affect knowledge of many different sorts in similar ways and at similar times, provided that the theory gives those events a unifying characterization.

Yet theories are limited in their explanatory and predictive scope; even framework theories explain only some kinds of things and not others. Regardless of the extent of the domain, a theory of mind explains only "mental things"; it does not explain physical events and entities – those are left to a theory of physics. Thus there will be several domains in the child's cognition and experience, domains defined by the framework theory that covers them. Wellman and Gelman (1992) suggest, for example, that in the period between 2 and 5 the child's naive psychology is complemented by a naive mechanics and perhaps also a naive biology. These domains are also defined by framework theories; each theory explains only some things and not others and the "things" to be explained are defined by the theory. The entities and laws of these naive theories (objects and physical movements, for example) are very different from those of a theory of mind. The theory theory predicts, therefore, contra stage theories, that individual children's progress in one domain will be quite independent from their progress in the others. Domains outside the scope of some target theory will remain unaffected by changes to that theory, just as we would not expect a new theory of atomic structure to change our theory of evolution or vice versa.

In this way theories not only reflect domains but also actually constitute them. The much-troubled question of how to specify domains is easily solved on this view: A domain is what your framework theory tells you it is. The question is an empirical one and can be addressed by empirically investigating the scope of a person's fundamental theories, such as the individual's theory of mind.

An important consequence of this view is that domains themselves may change as theories change. Once again this differentiates theories from modules. For example, the Berkeley biologists recently reorganized themselves, at great expense, into a different set of departments. Zoology, botany, physiology, and paleontology were replaced by cell biology, biochemistry, immunology, and genetics. Scientific advances in biology meant that apparently natural domains (plants vs. animals, for instance) had been subsumed by others defined by different theoretical considerations. The new departments reflect a change in the framework theories within biology as a whole. Similarly, some of the changes we have sketched in this chapter seem to us to involve changes in children's very idea of the scope and nature of psychological explanation. The domain at issue is changing with development.

A theory approach to domain specificity provides a cognitive analysis of domains rather than a neurological-biological one. Ultimately, of course, cognition is a product of neurology. And there is evidence to suggest the existence of certain neurologically specifiable domains of thought (see other chapters in this volume). However, it remains to be seen how various psychological domains relate to neurologically specified domains, and it seems unlikely to us that all interesting cognitive domains will be the result of distinct neurological structures. For example, connectionist models demonstrate the possibility of single neural structures that can perform several separate psychological tasks. In general, we do not think that cognitive domains will neatly reduce to neurological domains, just as psychology will not neatly reduce to neurology. We need cognitive analyses to identify cognitive domains. The theory theory offers tools for this task.

Conclusion

In spite of Piaget's arguments for a "genetic" epistemology, many recent approaches to cognitive development, including those information-processing approaches misleadingly called neo-Piagetian, are antiepistemological in a deep sense. That is, they explain behavioral changes not by describing the endogenous development of knowledge itself but by invoking exogenous mechanisms, including maturation, triggered changes in information-processing skills, socially provided knowledge, or tools. Such mechanisms must indeed be responsible for various developmental changes. But the changes we are interested in cannot be accounted for in these ways alone, because they involve changes in the structure of knowledge itself and not simply in its instantiation or application. The philosopher of science's notion of a theory and characterization of theory change provide crucial conceptual tools for talking about such deep cognitive changes, and, as we have tried to show here, such notions provide illuminating insights into children's actual behavior. It is of course true that within philosophy and history of science, theory formation and theory change are far from well understood. In important ways the scientist's ability to learn about the world is still almost as mysterious as the child's. Nevertheless, it seems to us that reducing two mysteries to one is an important advance, and a great deal more than we usually achieve.

Notes

1. Having a theory also need not mean awareness that what you have is a theory. Neither children nor scientists may have much conscious access to the epistemological processes in which they engage. In fact, philosophers of science often dismiss scientists' accounts of their own theory constructing activities as incorrect. By and large, scientists' theories are more explicitly held than children's but even this may be more a matter of degree than kind. In explanation studies, and in natural conversation, 3- and 4-year-olds are quite explicit about their convictions about beliefs and desires and the relations between them. Conversely, it is often true that historians and philosophers of science "reconstruct" theories from the actual writings and practice of science. Abstracting Kepler's heliocentric theory, for example, from the welter of mysticism, superstition, and just plain confusion in his writing may not be all that different than abstracting the 3-year-old's theory of belief from her language and behavior. What children or scientists say about

what they know and do is a useful source of information but in neither case is it definitive.

2. It is important to be as clear as possible about the way in which theoretical constructs are abstract, unobservable, and postulated. We mean abstract in the sense of "thought of apart from" observable particularities – we do not mean abstruse or merely ideal. Theoretical entities are unobservable in the sense of not being obviously a part of the evidential phenomena to-be-explained, not that they are necessarily incapable of being observed in any fashion whatsoever. Thus, we could postulate that genes control inherited features such as eye color and height, in order to provide a theoretical account, and still fully expect that genes are observable in some fashion. It is simply that genes are not directly evident in, observable in, the phenomena of eye color and height themselves. Similarly, postulated does not mean conjured out of thin air; it means recruited for explanatory purposes from outside the evidential phenomena themselves. Thus (natural) selection can be postulated to account for the origin of species but at the same time selection can be fully concrete and observable, in the realm of animal breeding, for example. It is the recruitment of selection to account for natural speciation that is postulational; selection itself is not a mere postulated entity.

3. On the theory theory, the ages of development are not crucial. In fact we would expect to find, as indeed we do, wide variation in the ages at which successive theories develop. We would expect to find similar sequences of development, however. We will use ages as a rough way of referring to successive theories.

4. In some modular systems, there are several alternative branching routes, so to speak, that determine the eventual form the module may take. These are generally described as "parameters" set by the input. The relation between input and the setting of the parameter is still, however, a relation of triggering. In contrast, in a theory theory, by analogy with scientific theories, there should be very wide scope for novel theories, not simply a choice of several options.

References

Astington, J. W., & Gopnik, A. (1991a). Developing understanding of desire and intention. In A. Whiten (Eds.), *Natural theories of mind* (pp. 39–50). Oxford: Basil Blackwell.

Astington, J. W., & Gopnik, A. (1991b). Theoretical explanations of children's understanding of the mind. *British Journal of Developmental Psychology, 9*, 7–31.

Astington, J. W., Harris, P. L., & Olson, D. R. (1988). *Developing theories of mind.* New York: Cambridge University Press.

Avis, J., & Harris, P. L. (1991). Belief-desire reasoning among Baka children. *Child Development, 62*, 460–467.

Bakeman, R., & Adamson, L. B. (1984). Coordinating attention to people and objects in mother–infant and peer–infant interaction. *Child Development, 55*, 1278–1289.

Baron-Cohen, S. (1990). Autism: A specific cognitive disorder of mind-blindness. *International Review of Psychiatry, 2*, 81–90.

Bartsch, K., & Wellman, H. M. (1989). Young children's attribution of action to beliefs and desires. *Child Development, 60*, 946–964.

Bartsch, K., & Wellman, H. M. (1990). Talking about beliefs and desires: Children's theory of mind manifest in their everyday language. Paper presented at the Piaget Society meetings, Philadelphia.

Bartsch, K., & Wellman, H. M. (in press). *Children talk about the mind.* New York: Oxford University Press.

Bretherton, I., & Beeghly, M. (1982). Talking about internal states: The acquisition of an explicit theory of mind. *Developmental Psychology, 18,* 906–921.

Butterworth, G., Harris, P. L., Leslie, A. M., & Wellman, H. M. (Eds.). (1991). *Perspectives on the child's theory of mind.* Oxford: Oxford University Press.

Butterworth, G. E. (1991). The ontogeny and phylogeny of joint visual attention. In A. Whiten (Ed.), *Natural theories of mind* (pp. 223–232). Oxford: Basil Blackwell.

Carey, S. (1985). *Conceptual Change in Childhood.* Cambridge, MA: MIT Press.

Carey, S. (1988). Conceptual differences between children and adults. *Mind and Language, 3,* 167–183.

Chomsky, N. (1975). *Reflections on language.* New York: Random House.

Chomsky, N. (1980). *Rules and representations.* New York: Columbia University Press.

Dretske, F. (1969). *Seeing and knowing.* Chicago: University of Chicago Press.

Dunn, J., Brown, J., Slomkowski, C., Tesla, C., & Youngblade, L. (1991). Young children's understanding of other people's feelings and beliefs: Individual differences and their antecedents. *Child Development, 62,* 1352–1366.

Feyerabend, P. K. (1975). *Against method.* London: New Left Books.

Flavell, J. H. (1988). The development of children's knowledge about the mind: From cognitive connections to mental representations. In J. Astington, P. Harris, & D. Olson (Eds.), *Developing theories of mind* (pp. 244–267). New York: Cambridge University Press.

Flavell, J. H., Flavell, E. R., & Green, F. L. (1987). Young children's knowledge of the apparent-real and pretend-real distinctions. *Developmental Psychology, 23,* 816–822.

Flavell, J. H., Flavell, E. R., Green, F. L., & Moses, L. J. (1990). Young children's understanding of fact beliefs versus value beliefs. *Child Development, 61,* 915–928.

Flavell, J. H., Green, F. L., & Flavell, E. R. (1986). Development of knowledge about the appearance–reality distinction. *Monographs of the Society for Research in Child Development, 51* (Serial No. 212).

Flavell, J. H., Zhang, X-D., Zou, H., Dong, Q., & Qi, S. (1983). A comparison between the development of the appearance–reality distinction in the Peoples Republic of China and the U.S. *Cognitive Psychology, 15,* 459–466.

Fodor, J. A. (1983). *Modularity of mind.* Cambridge, MA: MIT Press.

Fodor, J. A. (1987). *Psychosemantics: The problem of meaning in the philosophy of mind.* Cambridge, MA: Bradford Books/MIT Press.

Fodor, J. A. (1992). The theory of the child's theory of mind. *Cognition, 44,* 283–296.

Forguson, L., & Gopnik, A. (1988). The ontogeny of common sense. In J. Astington, P. Harris, & D. Olson (Eds.), *Developing theories of mind* (pp. 226–243). New York: Cambridge University Press.

Frye, D., & Moore, C. (1991). *Children's theories of mind: Mental states and social understanding.* Hillsdale, NJ: Erlbaum.

Gardner, D., Harris, P. L., Ohomoto, M., & Hamazaki, T. (1988). Japanese children's understanding of the distinction between real and apparent emotion. *International Journal of Behavioral Development*, *11*, 203–218.

Glymour, C. (1980). *Theory and evidence.* Princeton, NJ: Princeton University Press.

Goldman, A. I. (1989). Interpretation psychologized. *Mind and Language*, *4*, 161–185.

Gopnik, A. (1984). Conceptual and semantic change in scientists and children: Why there are no semantic universals. *Linguistics*, *20*, 163–179.

Gopnik, A. (1988). Conceptual and semantic development as theory change. *Mind and Language*, *3*, 197–217.

Gopnik, A. (1993). How we know our minds: The illusion of first-person knowledge of intentionality. *Behavioral and Brain Sciences*, *16*, 1–15, 90–101.

Gopnik, A., & Astington, J. W. (1988). Children's understanding of representational change and its relation to the understanding of false belief and the appearance–reality distinction. *Child Development*, *59*, 26–37.

Gopnik, A., & Graf, P. (1988). Knowing how you know: Young children's ability to identify and remember the sources of their beliefs. *Child Development*, *59*, 1366–1371.

Gopnik, A., & Slaughter, V. (1991). Young children's understanding of changes in their mental states. *Child Development*, *62*, 98–110.

Gopnik, A., & Wellman, H. M. (1992). Why the child's theory of mind really is a theory. *Mind and Language*, *7*, 145–171.

Gordon, R. M. (1986). Folk psychology as simulation. *Mind and Language*, *1*, 158–171.

Harris, P. L. (1991). The work of the imagination. In A. Whiten (Ed.), *Natural theories of mind* (pp. 283–304). Oxford: Basil Blackwell.

Hempel, C. (1965). *Apects of scientific explanation.*

Hobson, R. P. (1989). Beyond cognition: A theory of autism. In G. Dawson (Ed.), *Autism: New perspectives on diagnosis, nature and treatment* (pp. 22–48). New York: Guilford.

Hornick, R., Risenhoover, N., & Gunnar, M. (1987). The effects of maternal positive, neutral, and negative affective communications and infant responses to new toys. *Child Development*, *58*, 937–944.

Johnson, C. N. (1988). Theory of mind and the structure of conscious experience. In J. Astington, P. Harris, & D. Olson (Eds.), *Developing theories of mind* (pp. 47–63). New York: Cambridge University Press.

Karmiloff-Smith, A., & Inhelder, B. (1974). If you want to get ahead, get a theory. *Cognition*, *3*, 195–212.

Keil, F. (1987). Conceptual development and category structure. In U. Neisser (Ed.), *Concepts and conceptual development* (pp. 175–201). New York: Cambridge University Press.

Kuhn, D. (1989). Children and adults as intuitive scientists. *Psychological Review*, *96*, 674–689.

Kuhn, T. S. (1962). *The structure of scientific revolutions.* Chicago: University of Chicago Press.

Lakatos, I. (1970). Falsification and the methodology of scientific research programmes. In I. Lakatos & A. Musgrave (Eds.), *Criticism and the growth of knowledge* (pp. 91–196). Cambridge: Cambridge University Press.

Laudan, L. (1977). *Progress and its problems: Towards a theory of scientific growth.* Berkeley: University of California Press.

Leslie, A. M. (1987). Pretense and representation: The origins of "theory of mind." *Psychological Review, 94,* 412–426.

Leslie, A. M. (1991). Information processing and conceptual knowledge: The theory of TOMM. Paper presented at the meetings of the Society for Research in Child Development, Seattle, WA.

Lutz, C. (1988). *Unnatural emotions.* Chicago: University of Chicago Press.

Markus, H. R., & Kitayama, S. (1991). Culture and the self: Implications for cognition, emotion, and motivation. *Psychological Review, 98,* 224–253.

Marr, D. (1982). *Vision.* New York: W. H. Freeman.

Meltzoff, A. N., & Gopnik, A. (1993). The role of imitation in understanding persons and developing theories of mind. In S. Baron-Cohen & H. Tager-Flusberg (Eds.), *The theory of mind deficit in autism.* New York: Cambridge University Press.

Mitchell, P., & Lacohee, H. (1991). Children's early understanding of false belief. *Cognition, 39,* 107–127.

Moore, C., Pure, K., & Furrow, P. (1990). Children's understanding of the modal expression of certainty and uncertainty and its relation to the development of a representational theory of mind. *Child Development, 61,* 722–730.

Moses, L. J. (1993). Young children's understanding of belief constraints on intention. *Cognitive Development, 8,* 1–25.

Moses, L. J., & Flavell, J. H. (1990). Inferring false beliefs from actions and reactions. *Child Development, 61,* 929–945.

Nagel, E. (1961). *The structure of science.* New York: Harcourt, Brace and World.

Nelson, K. (1985). *Making sense: The acquisition of shared meaning.* Orlando, FL: Academic Press.

O'Neill, D. K., Astington, J. W., & Flavell, J. H. (1992). Young children's understanding of the role that sensory experiences play in knowledge acquisition. *Child Development, 63,* 474–490.

O'Neill, D. K., & Gopnik, A. (1991). Young children's ability to identify the sources of their beliefs. *Developmental Psychology, 27,* 390–399.

Perner, J. (1991). *Understanding the representational mind.* Cambridge, MA: MIT Press.

Perner, J., Leekam, S. R., & Wimmer, H. (1987). Three-year-olds' difficulty with false belief. *British Journal of Developmental Psychology, 5,* 125–137.

Perner, J., Ruffman, T., & Leekam, S. R. (1992). *Theory of mind is contagious: You catch it from your sibs.* Unpublished manuscript.

Pinker, S. (1984). *Language learnability and language development.* Cambridge, MA: MIT Press.

Pinker, S. (1989). *Learnability and cognition.* Cambridge, MA: MIT Press.

Popper, K. R. (1965). *Conjectures and refutations: The growth of scientific knowledge,* 2nd ed. New York: Harper & Row.

Quine, W. V. O. (1961). Two dogmas of empiricism. In W. V. O. Quine (Ed.), *From a logical point of view* (pp. 20–46). New York: Harper & Row.

Quine, W. V. O., & Ullian, J. S. (1970). *The web of belief.* New York: Random House.

Robinson, E. J., & Mitchell, P. (1992) Children's interpretation of messages from a speaker with a false belief. *Child Development, 62,* 639–652.

Scheffler, I. (1967). *Science and subjectivity.* Indianapolis: Bobbs Merril.

Searle, J. R. (1983). *Intentionality.* Cambridge: Cambridge University Press.

Shatz, M., Wellman, H. M., & Silber, S. (1983). The acquisition of mental verbs: A systematic investigation of first references to mental state. *Cognition, 14*, 301–321.

Siegal, M., & Beattie, K. (1991). Where to look first for children's understanding of false beliefs. *Cognition, 38*, 1–12.

Slaughter, V., & Gopnik, A. (1992). *Children's early understanding of perception.* Unpublished manuscript.

Wellman, H. M. (1985). A child's theory of mind: The development of conceptions of cognition. In S. R. Yussen (Ed.), *The growth of reflection.* New York: Academic Press.

Wellman, H. M. (1990). *The child's theory of mind.* Cambridge: Bradford Books/MIT Press.

Wellman, H. M. (1993). Early understanding of mind: The normal case. In S. Baron-Cohen, H. Tager-Flusberg, Cohen, & Volkman (Eds.), *Understanding other minds: Perspectives from autism.* Oxford: Oxford University Press.

Wellman, H. M., & Bannerjee, M. (1991). Mind and emotion: Children's understanding of the emotional consequences of beliefs and desires. *British Journal of Developmental Psychology, 9*, 119–124.

Wellman, H. M., & Bartsch, K. (1988). Young children's reasoning about beliefs. *Cognition, 30*, 239–277.

Wellman, H. M., & Estes, D. (1986). Early understanding of mental entities: A reexamination of childhood realism. *Child Development, 57*, 910–923.

Wellman, H. M., & Gelman, S. A. (1992). Cognitive development: Foundational theories of core domains. *Annual Review of Psychology, 43*, 337–375.

Wellman, H. M., & Woolley, J. D. (1990). From simple desires to ordinary beliefs: The early development of everyday psychology. *Cognition, 35*, 245–275.

Whiten, A. (1991). *Natural theories of mind.* Oxford: Basil Blackwell.

Wimmer, H., & Perner, J. (1983). Beliefs about beliefs: Representation and constraining function of wrong beliefs in young children's understanding of deception. *Cognition, 13*, 103–128.

Woolley, J. D., & Wellman, H. M. (1992). Children's conceptions of dreams. *Cognitive Development, 1*, 365–380.

Woolley, J. D., & Wellman, H. M. (1993). Origin and truth: Young children's understanding of imaginary mental representations. *Child Development, 64*, 1–17.

Yuill, N. (1984). Young children's coordination of motive and outcome in judgments of satisfaction and morality. *British Journal of Developmental Psychology, 2*, 73–81.

Zaitchek, D. (1990). When representations conflict with reality: The preschooler's problem with false beliefs and "false" photographs. *Cognition, 35*, 41–68.

11 Thinking by children and scientists: False analogies and neglected similarities

Paul L. Harris

In this chapter, I distinguish among three types of cognitive activity: the cognitive processes of children; the cognitive processes of individual scientists; and the collective, public enterprise that constitutes the history of science. I propose that when we focus on individual scientists rather than the organized discipline within which they work, there are some neglected similarities between the way that they think and the way that young children think. On the other hand, I argue against the proposal that there are important and interesting analogies between the cognitive processes of children and the collective history of science. In particular, I argue against the claim that individual children show patterns of cognitive development in early childhood that resemble the shifts in theoretical stance that are found in scientific disciplines viewed across several decades or centuries.

On general grounds, this analogy is implausible. First, science as a progressive enterprise is a highly specialized activity involving few individuals even in this century and virtually none throughout most of human history. By contrast, many facets of cognitive development in children are universal, and probably have been throughout most of our history. Second, theory change in science is a collective activity that depends on competitive, interindividual and intergroup communication. Yet, cognitive development in individual children is not in any obvious sense a collective or competitive enterprise.

The standard basis for the alleged analogy is that science exhibits four important cognitive traits: theoretical economy, corrigibility, domain specificity, and an absence of magical thinking. First, a large set of observations is explained – economically – in terms of a small set of theoretical postulates or principles. Second, such principles dominate the scientific outlook especially during periods of so-called normal science, yet they are corrigible; elaboration and revision of the principles bring new phenomena into focus. Third,

This research was partially supported by the E.S.R.C. (United Kingdom) Grant no. R000 23 3543.

science is geared to the construction of domain-appropriate, causal explanations. Finally, scientific thinking is skeptical toward the special or extraordinary causal chains that are accepted as plausible in magical thinking.

The proposal that children think like scientists implies that these same traits are present in the course of cognitive development. For example, it has been claimed that children exhibit explanatory economy in their understanding of physics and of psychology. They adopt a small set of physical principles and use them to explain and predict a wide range of physical movements (Carey & Spelke, this volume). Similarly, they espouse a belief-desire psychology that allows them to predict and explain a wide range of human actions and emotions (Astington, Harris, & Olson, 1988; Gopnik & Wellman, this volume). These explanatory frameworks are radically revised in the course of cognitive development, allowing children to incorporate an increasingly large set of phenomena. Third, although children may adopt limited or false theories, their explanatory focus can be construed as domain-specific: They do not offer mechanistic explanations of human behavior nor Intentional explanations of mechanical phenomena. Finally, their approach to causal explanation appears to be rational and scientific rather than magical.

I shall argue that these four traits do characterize certain public aspects of science but they are a poor description of cognitive development in children. There is little evidence that children adopt theories, invent new theories, recognize domain specificity, or avoid magical thinking. Yet I shall also argue that children are like individual scientists in these respects. A great deal of scientific thinking, as practiced by working scientists, is not guided by theory, is not directed at the invention of new theory, shows no principled signs of domain specificity, and has important links with magical thinking. Scientists do, of course, construct, publish, and refine theories but that is a collective enterprise that is not necessarily reproduced in the cognitive processes of individual scientists and certainly has no obvious parallel in children's cognitive development. In this chapter, I explore these claims in more detail. My plan is to consider each trait in turn, first with respect to thinking by children or lay adults and then with respect to scientists.

Theoretical thinking

Theoretical thinking among children and lay adults

Well-structured theories include a set of explicit postulates or principles, which when appropriately coordinated, yield predictions that may or may not be validated by appropriate observation. Theories are most readily found in science textbooks. Psychologists have claimed that they are also to be found inside the heads of lay adults and children: They have a mental representation of the theoretical principles, which they use to make predictions and explanations. Faced with a problem of explanation or prediction, they presumably determine the relevant theory, such as folk physics or folk psychology, search through the appropriate postulates in that theory, and then make a prediction from those postulates or offer an explanation couched in its terms. Detailed studies of these presumed mental processes have not been carried out, but these steps would seem minimally necessary.

Recently, an alternative account of lay explanation and prediction, which abandons the analogy with scientific theorizing, has been advanced. The basic idea is that children, and indeed adults, do not truly subscribe to wide-ranging theoretical principles but engage in a process of imaginative enactment or simulation. I first discuss this proposal briefly in terms of folk physics before turning to a fuller discussion of folk psychology.

Folk physics. Faced with a prediction problem in physics, subjects engage in a scene-setting phase. They recall an analogous situation, or they retrieve a prototype that contains supposedly relevant features of the problem situation. For example, in the case of a problem concerning movement, it may be critical to construct a prototype with the relevant starting conditions of trajectory, speed, or both. Second, in a transformation phase, subjects initiate an imaginative enactment in which the starting conditions for the intital scene are transformed or extended in some fashion consistent with the specification of the problem. For example, in the scene-setting phase, subjects might imagine the projectile moving along a given trajectory at a given speed; in the transformation phase, they imagine it launched – from a hand or sling. Third, in an outcome phase, they read off the imagined denouement of the transformation. For example, they see in their mind's eye the path along which the projectile continues.

Evidence for the role of this type of enactment is that when adults are interviewed about their solution of simple trajectory problems in physics they (almost without exception) refer to their imaginative processes when asked how they reached a solution (Yates, Bessman, Dunne, Jertson, Sly, & Wendelboe, 1988). Although these self-reports may be inaccurate or they may describe an ancillary process that plays no causal role in helping subjects to make predictions, they undermine the theory view. On that view, one would expect subjects to refer to the principles that guided their predictions, yet there is no evidence that they do so.

A reasonable defense of the theory view, especially when it pertains to young children, is that subjects do use explanatory principles but do not know what principles they use. The principles are not explicit but tacit and inaccessible. Nevertheless, because they are few in number and broad in their application, they can be seen as theoretical. In that case, however, subjects should, at least, be consistent in the kinds of predictions and explanations that they make. Yet in the case of folk physics such consistency is difficult to demonstrate.

Adults make different predictions when invited to focus on features of the situation that might affect their selection of a prototype but should be irrelevant to a principle-based prediction (Yates et al., 1988). For example, when asked to think about a projectile launched from a sling versus a curved tube, they are more likely to predict an outward trajectory for the sling. Subjects presumably imagine different situations for a sling versus a tube (e.g., swinging a heavy object vs. observing a pinball) and are misled by the centrifugal force that is more salient in the former.

If imaginative enactment were a major intellectual strategy, then we would expect to see evidence for its operation early in life. In fact, when children produce or understand a pretend episode, they manifest the basic building blocks of this strategy: They can imagine a set of starting conditions, imagine a transformation of those starting conditions, and identify the likely consequences. For example, we have presented children with episodes in which an initial pretend situation (a receptacle containing a pretend substance or liquid) is transformed (e.g., inverted or squeezed). The children's task is to watch the episode, and identify the outcome that the transformation has produced. The task calls for causal predictions in that the outcome (e.g., a surface below the receptacle that ends up wet or dirty) does not visibly occur – it has to be imagined by the children as they watch. We find that 2-year-olds are adroit at such predictions. They join in with the pretense appropriately (e.g., pretend to dry the "wet" surface) and they can verbally identify the hypothetical outcome (e.g., "wet," "soggy," "mucky," and so forth) (Harris & Kavanaugh, 1993).

Folk psychology. The experiments just described require subjects to imagine physical transformations and predict their outcome. Is it reasonable to extend this type of explanation to psychological causation as well as physical causation? Again, there is convincing evidence from children's pretend play. Toddlers are not only capable of attributing physical properties during their pretense, but they are also capable of attributing psychological states. Two-year-olds can attribute pretend desires, sensations, and emotions to their dolls. For example, a doll is said to "want a bath" and is made to complain about the temperature when it is placed in some (pretend) water: "Oh no, sooo hot!" Moreover, the child can enact an appropriate satisfaction of this need by adding some pretend cold water (Wolf, Rygh, & Altshuler, 1984).

Recent work on the acquisition of folk psychology suggests that despite the facility with which children make attributions of perception, sensation, and desire they have difficulty in appropriately attributing beliefs. In particular, there appears to be a marked improvement between 3 and 5 years of age in their ability to recognize that someone might hold and act on a false belief. In explaining this age change, Gopnik and Wellman (this volume) argue for the so-called theory theory. They propose that the change reflects an underlying shift in children's theory of mind. Whereas children of around 2 years recognize the existence of mental states, they do not understand that mental states can represent (accurately or inaccurately) the state of the world. Sporadically at 3 years and consistently by 5 years, children postulate a representational theory of mind that enables them to grasp that a false believer can entertain an inaccurate representation.

I have proposed a different account, based on the concept of simulation. The full developmental range of this account has been presented elsewhere (Harris, 1991, 1992). Here, I highlight the contrast between simulation theory and the theory theory as formulated by Gopnik and Wellman. According to the simulation account, children have privileged access to their current mental states. They can give relatively accurate reports of what they currently see, want, think, or imagine. Privileged access is not available in the case of other people's mental states or noncurrent states of the self. In order to identify or make predictions about such states, therefore, a simulation strategy is needed. Children must reconstruct in their imagination the causal sequences in which such mental states are embedded.

This can be illustrated by considering one of the standard tests for children's understanding of false belief (Wimmer & Perner, 1983). Children watch while a doll puts some chocolate in a cupboard and leaves the room. The chocolate is then moved in the doll's absence, and the doll returns. Children are told that the doll now wants the chocolate and they are asked to say where the doll will search for it. There is a robust improvement between 3 and 5 years in children's ability to predict that the doll will search in the old rather than the new location. Simulation theory postulates a shift in simulation strategy to explain this age change (Harris, 1991). One strategy is for children to take as a pretend premise the doll's desire for the chocolate, to feed that pretend desire into their own planning system, and to imagine where they themselves would search. So long as their planning system incorporates their own knowledge base as a resource (including knowledge about object permanence, about how to open cupboards, and about where the chocolate actually is) this strategy will lead children to predict that the doll will approach the new location and search there rather than the old. This is the standard false-belief error that 3-year-olds often exhibit.

A more sophisticated simulation strategy is to feed in not just the doll's desire, but in addition, the now contrary-to-fact situation (i.e., the chocolate in its original location), which the doll witnessed before its departure. If these twin inputs are fed into their own planning system (and allowed temporarily to overwrite facts within the knowledge base), children will pass the false-belief task because on this simulation the desired chocolate is to be found (contrary to fact) where it was in the first place.

This type of simulation requires, however, that children overwrite what they currently take to be the case. Thus, according to the simulation analysis, children improve between 3 and 5 years on such tasks not because they have adopted a new theory of mind but because they improve in the accuracy of their simulation, particularly when it calls for such temporary overwriting.

I have focused on the false-belief task for illustrative purposes. However, the age change on this task is part of a more general improvement in simulation accuracy (Harris, 1991; 1992). At 3 years, children typically make allowances for differences in intentional stance. For example, they acknowledge that a doll might currently see, or want something different from themselves. They can also acknowledge that they themselves, at some earlier point in time, might have seen or wanted something different from what they currently see or want. What they do not acknowledge is that such variations in intentional stance can arise concerning realities that are not simply different but are also in obvious conflict with one another. For example, a bar of chocolate cannot be both where it is now and where it was before; an object cannot be both a rock and a sponge; a candy box cannot have only candy, but also some pencils inside it. These realities are mutually exclusive.

The tasks that show an improvement between 3 and 5 years are precisely ones in which children must imagine not just an intentional stance that is not their own current stance, but a situation that they know to conflict with what they currently take to be the case. They must imagine someone (a doll, or themselves at some earlier point in time) apprehending a reality that conflicts with what they now take to be reality. For example, they must imagine someone believing that chocolate is in place A whereas they know it is in place B (the standard false-belief task); or they must imagine someone believing that a box contains candy whereas they now know it contains pencils (the "own" false belief task); they must imagine someone perceiving an object to be a rock whereas they know it to be a sponge (the reality-appearance task); they must imagine someone perceiving an object to be upside down whereas they perceive it to be right way up (the Level 2 perspective-taking task), and so forth. In all these cases, an accurate simulation can only be achieved by feeding in as input a counterfactual reality and allowing it temporarily to overwrite what is known to be the case. Thus, simulation theory can readily explain the improvement that is observed on these several tasks between 3 and 5 years.

However, the simulation account also predicts that such tasks will be easier to solve under either of two conditions: Inputs concerning current reality are attenuated or inputs concerning the counterfactual reality are strengthened. In either case, the likelihood of successful overwriting is increased. Current evidence provides support for both of these predictions.

For example, Mitchell and Lacohee (1991) strengthened the counterfactual input by having children not only say what they thought was in a candy box (i.e., "smarties") but also select and post a picture depicting smarties. After discovering the actual contents of the box (i.e., pencils), children were better at acknowledging their previous claim that it contained smarties.

Wimmer and Perner (1983) and Zaitchik (1991) created false-belief tasks where information about the current whereabouts of the to-be-found object was attenuated. In the case of Wimmer and Perner (1983), the object was not visibly moved to a new location, rather it was removed from the old one and then made to disappear. In the case of Zaitchik (1991), children never saw for themselves the transfer from old to new location; instead they were merely told about it. In both experiments, children were much better at diagnosing the protagonist's false belief than they were in a standard control task.

Notice that all these findings fit readily into the simulation account. The theory theory can be stretched to cover the picture-posting because such behavior would be problematic and potentially instructive for a child who discounts false beliefs. However, it cannot explain the other findings. Neither the object's disappearance nor a verbal report of its transfer should be problematic for a child who discounts false beliefs.

We may now consider two other points of controversy between the theory theory and the simulation theory: the relation between self and other, and the explanation as opposed to the prediction of action.

Self and other. Simulation theory holds that young children, even at 3 years, should be relatively accurate in reporting their own current mental states as compared with their past states or with those of other people. The theory theory makes no claim to such privileged access, arguing instead that mental states, whether belonging to self or other, must all be filtered through the same theoretical lens. Studies in which children have been asked to report on mental states confirm that children do indeed exhibit a similar pattern when asked to report either on their past mental states or those of others (Baron-Cohen, 1991; Gopnik & Slaughter, 1991). For example, in each case, they are more accurate in reporting on past perceptual states than past belief states. This is the type of evidence that theory-theorists have emphasized (c.f., Gopnik & Wellman, this volume). It is quite consistent with the theory theory, but it is no less consistent with simulation theory.[1]

More critical in choosing between the theory theory and simulation theory are children's reports of their own current mental states. The evidence suggests that 3-year-olds are quite accurate in reporting on a variety of mental states: what they currently think, want, perceive, pretend, and so forth (Baron-Cohen, 1991; Gopnik & Slaughter, 1991). To the extent that theory-theorists argue that children's accuracy varies only with the nature of the mental state, ignoring their privileged access, they cannot explain children's relative accuracy in reporting their current mental states.

Explanations of behavior. We may ask children to offer psychological predictions or explanations. A theory usually permits both so that the theory theory is not embarrassed by the fact that children seem to show a similar pattern of development on each type of task. Simulation, by contrast, appears better suited for prediction than explanation. As noted earlier, by feeding in another person's desire into the planning system, it is possible to derive an "as if" output – a hypothetical plan of action, which can be used as a prediction of the person's likely behavior.

Consider, however, the findings reported by Bartsch and Wellman (1989). Children were presented with a description of an action (e.g., "Jane is looking for her kitty under the piano"), and asked to explain it. In line with the theory theory, children referred to Jane's desire ("She wants the kitty") or belief ("She thinks it's under the piano"). If the process of simulation moves in a forward direction – by taking an antecedent state as a premise (e.g., a desire) and simulating the consequent (an action) – how can it explain an apparent reversal of the process when the child is supplied with a consequent such as an action and offers a belief or desire as an antecedent?

A plausible answer to this question is that the notion of antecedents and consequences is altogether too mechanistic to capture our accounts of human action. When we say that Jane is looking under the piano because she wants the kitty or because she thinks it is hiding there, we are referring to mental states that are not simply antecedent to but also concurrent with the action in question. The desire is not a discrete occurrence that triggers the action and then expires; it steers the action. The same is true of the belief: It gives a direction to Jane's action and not just an initial impulse. Thus, a thorough simulation of another's purposeful action would involve a simulation of the mental states that accompany it. If I imagine you looking for something, I do not simulate a bare physical movement but an action plus concurrent gubernatorial states of desire and/or belief.

However, the theory-theorist might produce a further objection (c.f., Gopnik & Wellman, this volume). How is it that young children produce causally appropriate as opposed to inappropriate explanations? In particular, why do they refer predominantly to beliefs and desires rather than to some sensation or emotion that might accompany an action such as searching under the piano? The answer to this objection is that Gopnik and Wellman exaggerate the extent to which children offer belief-desire explanations. It is true that these are quite frequent if children are given prompts (e.g., "What does Jane want?" or "What does Jane think?"). However, these prompts are obviously leading questions; children's replies to such questions cannot be taken as evidence for their preferred explanatory strategy. In fact, when 3-year-olds were asked an initial open-ended question (e.g., "Why is Jane doing that?"), approximately one-third of their explanations focused on relevant beliefs and desires; another third involved other types of psychological explanation (e.g., perceptions, emotions, physiological states, traits, and so forth) and another third involved no psychological state or category at all (e.g., they referred to the location of the kitty). The pattern among 4-year-olds was very similar with only a marginal and nonsignificant increase in belief-desire explanations (Bartsch & Wellman, 1989, Figure 2).

Harris, Johnson, Hutton, Andrews, and Cooke (1989) observed a related phenomenon. Children first watched the standard contents of a container being surreptitiously replaced. For example, Coke might be taken out of a Coke can and replaced with milk. When asked how a character would feel about being offered the can as a drink, 3- and 4-year-olds often referred to what they knew about the situation. They said that the character would feel sad, " 'Cos there's no Coke" even though the character had not yet taken a sip and discovered the surreptitious replacement.

The overall pattern of results reported by Bartsch and Wellman (1989) and by Harris et al. (1989) fits the simulation theory well. It suggests that children imagine themselves in the situation facing the protagonist and when called on to explain his or her action or emotion, they refer to various features of that simulation: Their explanations do refer to beliefs and desires but they also refer to other psychological states. Moreover, in line with the claim that children fail to engage in appropriate temporary overwriting, explanations also refer to features of the situation that are known to the subject but which the protagonist cannot possibly know about.

In sum, the pattern of children's explanations poses serious problems for the theory-theorist rather than the simulation theorist. Consistent with simulation theory, young children are catholic in their spontaneous explanatory strategy. They do not confine themselves to the central concepts of the theory that they are alleged to possess – unless they are prompted to do so by leading questions. Moreover, they often step outside of the psychological domain altogether by referring to the situation in which a protagonist is acting.

Theoretical thinking among scientists. Scientists construct and publish explicit theories and these constitute the written history of science. That does not show, however, that scientists always think by means of such theories. So, although my description of the young children's thinking has implied that it is atheoretical, that does not necessarily mean that children do not think like scientists. It all depends how scientists think.

My remarks in this section are simply intended as a gesture toward a larger body of writing. One of Kuhn's best-known concepts is that of a paradigm (Kuhn, 1970). Despite its familiarity and influence, Kuhn acknowledges that he used the concept in several different senses, and that has led to confusion among his commentators. Sometimes, Kuhn focuses on the sociological impact of a paradigm as a revolutionary but eventually dominant theory. For example, discussing the impact of Franklin on electrical theory, Kuhn (1970: 17) notes that: "to be accepted as a paradigm, a theory must seem better than its competitors." Yet, he also uses paradigm in a much more concrete fashion that ties it to the day-to-day thinking and practice of individual scientists and this is the usage that I wish to emphasize. He describes a paradigm as a particularly clear and illustrative procedure. Acknowledging the central importance of this second definition, Kuhn (1970: 175) formulates it in the following way: "the concrete puzzle-solutions which, employed as models or examples, can replace explicit rules as a basis for the solution of the remaining puzzles of normal science."

When the notion of paradigm is cast in this more concrete and psychological fashion, it is clear that it comes quite close to what I described earlier as operative in children's thinking. The child assimilates a new situation to a previously encountered instance or to a prototypical model of those instances, and then uses the instance or prototype to extrapolate forward to likely outcomes in the new situation. Similarly, the scientist assimilates the outstanding puzzles of normal science back to the paradigmatic exemplar.

Kuhn is at pains to point out that the paradigm is not a set of explicit rules. It operates in a much more concrete or tacit fashion. The main task for the novice scientist is not to understand the explicitly stated laws but to learn to see how new problems can be assimilated to paradigmatic and previously encountered problems. Once that has happened, the student can "interrelate symbols and attach them to nature in the ways that have proved effective before" (Kuhn, 1970: 189).

Earlier, I suggested that a great deal of scientific thinking is not guided by theory. This was obviously a provocative way of stating the claim but if Kuhn is right I think it can be defended. The most immediate guide for the scientist's thinking is the concrete procedure or puzzle solution that is paradigmatic for the scientist's field. There may be an explicit theoretical statement that describes what happens in that procedure. Yet it is the procedure itself that is the inspiration and guide rather than the explicit statement.

The conclusion to this first section then is that children and scientists think alike because in neither case does theory guide their thinking.

Theory change

Theory change in children?

So far, I have argued that children do not think in theoretical terms, but on the basis of working models or concrete paradigms that serve as a basis for prediction and explanation. It obviously follows from this premise that cognitive development in children is not precipitated by theoretical crises nor does it consist in the invention of new theories.

At first glance, this claim appears to be an attack on any analogy between cognitive development in children and intellectual advancement in science. However, that does not necessarily follow. The history of science suggests that a great deal of day-to-day thinking in the laboratory is guided not by an explicitly stated theory but by concrete procedures, specific puzzle solutions, that embody potential solutions to outstanding problems.

If that analysis is correct, we can legitimately pursue the analogy between child and working scientist. Indeed, Kuhn himself has done just that. In an intriguing essay on the role of thought experiments in science, he points to the analogies between children and scientists (Kuhn, 1977). In particular, he discusses Piaget's demonstration of the way in which children, like scientists, may respond inconsistently. Quoting Piaget's description of young children's conception of speed (Piaget, 1970), he describes how children at an intermediate stage are prone to think of "faster" in terms of the leading object of a pair, yet also acknowledge that the trailing car is the faster if it moves so quickly that its speed is highly salient perceptually.

Children can, therefore, be confronted by a paradox: Two cars set off at different times from a starting line. The car that leaves first moves off quite slowly. The car that moves off second goes very fast, but its handicap is such that it still trails behind the slower car at the finishing line. Children who are capable of using both criteria are now confronted by a paradox. As they watch the first car leave the second behind at the start, they should be able to imagine it going on to arrive first at the finishing line, and so it does. So far, so good. Yet in the course of the race they also spot the second car rushing to catch up with the first, tempting them to describe it as the faster of the two and leading them to expect it to arrive first at the finishing line, which it does not. At the end of the race, they have seen one car arrive ahead of the other but they have also seen the loser move more quickly. Faced with this paradox, they vacillate in the car that they choose as the faster.

Recasting this in the terms that I used earlier, I would say that children at this intermediate stage have two distinct internal models for relative speed. One model sets the scene by identifying the car that leaves ahead of the other as the faster of the two; in the transformation phase these relative positions are preserved and the leading car is expected to arrive first at the finish. The other model sets the scene by comparing relative velocities – the faster car is the one that is seen to be moving more quickly; in the transformation phase the faster car is expected to gain on the goal more quickly and to win at the end of the race. The clash between these two working models produces intellectual dislocation in the child. Eventually, the child needs to sort out the appropriate conditions for applying each working model.

Earlier, I reviewed evidence showing that children's predictions on theory of mind tasks exhibit a similar inconsistency. For example, 3-year-olds fluctuate in their acknowledgement of false beliefs. Gopnik and Wellman (this volume) argue that such inconsistency speaks in favor of the child as theoretician: Children's inconsistencies across tasks reflect their struggle to invoke and apply a theoretical principle. At first, they do so inconsistently when faced with counterevidence and later in a more unified and consistent fashion. Thus, they argue that 2-year-olds ignore false beliefs altogether; 3-year-olds occasionally recognize their existence but by 4 or 5 years, children conceive of the mind as a representational device across a broad range of propositional attitudes, including belief.

However, this argument has two weaknesses. First, the evidence does not fit the claim that children achieve theoretical consistency. It is not just 3-year-olds who are inconsistent. The same applies to 4- and 5-year-olds as Wimmer and Perner (1983) found when they made the hidden object disappear rather than move to a new location. Indeed, we need only to complicate the false-belief task a little further – to tell children about a character who has a false belief about another's belief, rather than a physical fact – to find that children well beyond the age of 5 years have difficulties. Here, too, there are marked fluctuations in performance. Under optimal conditions, almost all 9-year-olds answer correctly, but if fewer prompts are given, only about half succeed (Perner & Wimmer, 1985, Table 8). In sum, Gopnik and Wellman propose that children initially invoke a new theory in a piecemeal fashion to deal with counterevidence and then move toward theoretical consistency. For the central problem of belief, that description appears to be simply wrong. Children's prolonged vacillation in acknowledging that a belief may be false appears to reflect a persistent processing difficulty, as implied by the simulation account, rather than a theoretical revolution.

The second weakness of Gopnik and Wellman's account is that it is silent about the source of new theoretical ideas. Confrontation with counterevidence to a given theory (e.g., the nonrepresentational theory that Gopnik and Wellman impute to 2-year-olds) cannot, ipso facto, generate a theoretical alternative (i.e., a representational theory of mind). Gopnik and Wellman are silent about how children arrive at the idea of the mind as a representational device. In this respect, they pay less attention than they might to the history of science: The rise of a new theory is poorly correlated with the range of counterevidence against the old theory. Counterevidence simply signals the need for a new theory but rarely specifies what form it should take.

Theory change in science. Kuhn's point in quoting Piaget at length is to show that there are analogies between children and scientists. In each case, a particular setting may elicit two inconsistent predictions. Important scientific advances may be triggered by the attempt to resolve such inconsistencies. Indeed, in the case of science the inconsistency may occur at the level of thought only. That is to say, there may be little need to carry out the experiment in order to discover that a paradoxical inconsistency has been reached, and a new conceptualization is called for. Thus, Kuhn quotes Galileo's dialogue on speed in which a thought experiment is used to drive home the distinction between "faster" as applied to two bodies at a given instant of time, and "faster" as applied to the comparative time taken to complete a journey of a given length: The runner whose speed is faster when the bell sounds for the last lap may not be the winner of the race.

Notwithstanding the fact that children and scientists may be inconsistent in their predictions, it is important to underline two differences between them. Although one difference operates at the psychological level and the other at the sociological level, I suspect that they are two sides of the same coin.

First, at the psychological level, there is little evidence – throughout a considerable body of research on cognitive development – of children openly acknowledging intellectual puzzlement. It is true, of course, that children bombard adults with questions, especially "why" questions, but these questions are designed to gather information about the world, not to resolve a question about how best to conceptualize it. Thus, children ask questions like: "When will we get there?" or "Why are we going so slowly?" They do not formulate questions designed to sort out how they should conceptualize the world. They do not ask: "How could I say that this car is both faster and slower than the other one?" To the extent that children are not interested in straightening out their concepts, they are not interested in science.

Scientists, in contrast, are forced to have an interest in their concepts, even if their main interest is the mind, or the brain cell, or the atom. There is a twofold stimulus to that interest. First, to borrow from Kuhn once more, the scientist's day-to-day activity is directed toward the solution of some more-or-less explicitly recognized puzzle. The puzzle is not resolved by simply observing nature. It is, in part, a conceptual puzzle. It is resolved when the puzzling observations and the paradigm into which they ought to be assimilated can be reconciled. The resolution will require some additional specification or enlargement of the paradigm, which in turn will call for a written account referring the new observations to the theoretical statements, for which the paradigm serves as a procedural shorthand. Thus, scientists confront themselves by their labors with their theoretical modifications, in ways that children never do. Indeed, I suspect that paradigmatic strain is amplified for scientists (as compared with children) precisely because they work at two levels: the tacit and relatively private level of the paradigm, and the more explicit and relatively public level of theoretical statement. The scientist cannot simultaneously describe the same car as both "faster" and "slower" and ignore the contradiction as a child might. The inconsistency will be picked up either by the scientist or by colleagues.

The upshot of this is that scientists change their theories and know that they do. This brings me to the second point of difference between children and scientists. Knowing that theory change is part of the enterprise, scientists work collectively to bring it about. Their efforts rarely start with a direct attack on a theory. Metatheoretical debate has never cut much ice in science. Scientists concentrate instead on observations that do not readily fit the paradigm. Depending on their intellectual allegiances, their skills, and their temperament, they will adopt a variety of different maneuvers with respect to such puzzles. Renegades may seek to strain the paradigm by creating or adding to the stock of puzzling observations. Connoisseurs will try to show that these puzzling observations are a special case, which from a paradigmatic viewpoint, occur only in suboptimal conditions. Statesmen will reveal how a modification of the paradigm can cope with the puzzle. This triad of opposing strategies has the collective outcome of extending, preserving, and reasserting the paradigm.

Needless to say, nothing like this triad exists in children's cognitive development. They rarely challenge each other's conceptualization though they may scorn each other's factual assertions. Children are mostly left to get on with their own cognitive development. Even though they ask questions and are supplied with answers, such exchanges are often ineffective engines of cognitive development for two reasons. First, the questions and the answers do not always marry up. Second, and more important, these partially successful exchanges are intended to give children a picture of what the world is like rather than to get them to scrutinize their intellectual apparatus.

In summary, when we compare children's everyday thinking and the day-to-day thinking of a working scientist, we do find some similarities. Each of them engage in paradigm-based thinking, and each may encounter anomalous situations that provoke vacillation and inconsistency. Nonetheless, there are important differences. The anomaly for the child is a tacit, inarticulate uncertainty, a tendency toward contradiction. The anomaly for the scientist is engineered and amplified by the institutional machinery of the scientific establishment. Hence, we should beware of likening children's cognitive development to theoretical change in science. That is misleading because it likens a psychological change to one that is ultimately sociological.

Domain specificity

Domain specificity in children's thinking

I turn now to a key but nettlesome issue: Do children adopt domain-specific theories? As I argued in the first section, I do not think they do. Nevertheless, the concept of domain specificity is useful and important. Domain specificity is useful in thinking about perception. It seems clear that infants and young children have a variety of discrete perceptual mechanisms. These mechanisms impose psychological order on perceptual inputs by subdividing or reconfiguring the information that is supplied. For example, in the case of speech perception, discrete categories are imposed on physical continua (Kuhl, 1987). In the case of biomechanical motion perception, a unified but elastic configuration is imposed on discretely moving dots (Bertenthal, Proffitt, Spetner, & Thomas, 1985; Johansson, van Hofsten, & Jansson, 1980).

These processes of subdivision or reconfiguration appear to proceed automatically. They operate from infancy, and they are difficult to override. For example, in the case of speech perception there is some evidence for learning effects, but there is no evidence that the human perceiver can eventually hear the physical continuum that gives rise to the discrete perceptual categories of perceptual awareness (Kuhl, 1987). Those psychological categories constantly filter the original sound source.

To move beyond the claim that children are sensitive to particular perceptual domains to the more radical claim that they construct domain-specific theories, we need to establish a link between perception and explanatory mode.

I shall try to formulate that potential link as sympathetically as possible. It goes as follows. Children are equipped with a set of special-purpose perceptual mechanisms such as those just described. They are also in the business of seeking explanations and making predictions. That dual task is facilitated if a particular mode of explanation is appropriate for a particular perceptual domain. For example, suppose that the perceptual device for detecting biological motion serves as a screening device as well: It classifies perceptual events in terms of whether or not they include biological motion. (There might be subdivisions within this general category: things that move by slithering vs. walking vs. flying. The number and nature of the categories do not matter at this point.) Suppose further that children have different explanatory modes at their disposal. They can search for an immediately prior mechanical event or they can search for relevant Intentional states, particularly beliefs and desires. Suppose further that any event that is classified as including biological motion triggers the Intentional mode of explanation. A child so equipped looks, at first glance, to have got off to a good intellectual start in life. He or she will not waste time trying to offer psychological explanations for perceptual events that do not include biological motion. The nonbiological displacement of rivers, cars, and balloons, and all manner of events that include no motion – changes of light, and sudden claps of thunder – these will all be excluded from psychological explanation. Conversely, faced with the movement of a snake, or a skunk or a sparrow, the child will be predisposed to ask what it wants.

Helpful though such restrictions might be, there is little evidence that children do actually hold to them. A long tradition of work on animism shows that children extend psychological explanations to the nonbiological movements of rivers, clouds, and so forth (Berzonsky, 1971). Indeed, they extend their use of psychological explanations to completely immobile objects. Recall, once more, children's pretend play. Two-year-olds endow lifeless dolls with desires and sensations. Indeed, children of 3 or 4 years of age happily endow totally nonexistent creatures, such as imaginary companions or imaginary monsters, with desires and dispositions (Jersild, 1943; Manesovitz, Prentice, & Wilson, 1973).

In summary, even if we assume that in early infancy a particular type of perceptual input triggers a certain mode of causal explanation, older children can certainly dispense with such triggering. The psychological mode of explanation becomes self-starting, independent of perceptual input, and overextended. Moreover, although I have concentrated on one particular link between perceptual processing and explanatory mode, I suspect that the conclusion is likely to be a fairly general one. Putting it in more general terms, although there may be domain-specific perceptual mechanisms, there are few if any immediate perceptual constraints on explanatory mode. To the extent that explanatory modes can be identified, they appear to be imposed on a variety of perceptual and even hypothetical inputs.

Children's pretend play draws attention to further difficulties facing a mind that thinks in domain-specific terms. It might be argued that children's pretend play does not make naive theories redundant, but underlines the degree to which their thinking is theory-driven. According to this account, pretend play nicely illustrates how children use their naive theories of, say physics and psychology, to predict or enact what will happen in the course of a make-believe incident. Thus, their naive theory of physics allows them to realize that when a cup containing make-believe tea is tipped upside-down, the liquid will spill onto the surface below. Similarly, their naive theory of psychology allows them to realize that a doll who is too hot will want to get colder.

The difficulty with this approach is that it leads to the unlikely claim that children seamlessly integrate several minitheories in the course of a single short pretend episode. Consider once more the brief pretend episode I described earlier. Presumably, a naive psychology would be involved in attributing to the doll a desire for a bath; a naive engineering in turning on the faucets above the bath; a naive physics in knowing that the water will fall into the pretend bath below; a naive psychology would be recruited again to anticipate the doll's complaint about the heat; and engineering and physics must be coordinated to produce the solution: turning on the cold tap in order to mix it with the hot water already in the bath. On this analysis, 2-year-olds have powers of interdisciplinary synthesis that any adult scientist might envy. My point is not, of course, that children do not integrate. I want to argue that children's thinking does have this synthetic aspect: They can indeed integrate information from what might be construed as different domains. However, by not carving up nature into disciplinary domains, they avoid the problem of coordination that would ensue.

How then does the child parse the stream of events? Until now, for the purposes of exegesis, I have tacitly accepted the notion of domain specificity. For example, I have discussed examples first in relation to "folk physics" and then in relation to "folk psychology." Strictly speaking, however, the simulation account suggests a radically different approach. Children's pretend play, and their capacity for simulation in general, appears to be based on causal prototypes or sequences that cross-cut rather than respect disciplinary boundaries. In particular, if a child is to understand the transformations that are brought about (or intended) by human action, it is vital that the child not construct separate mental disciplines, one devoted to psychological events, another to biological or animate motion, and yet a third to the physics of inanimate objects. This is already apparent in the pretend episode discussed earlier.

Consider, in addition, just a handful of the action words that are produced by a majority of $2^1/_2$-year-olds: *bring, build, catch, chase,* and *clean* (Fenson, Dale, Reznick, Thal, Bates, Reilly, & Hartung, 1991). To produce these words appropriately, the child needs to recognize that actors engage in animate motion whose goal is a specific planned transformation of the physical world.

Children's facility in acquiring words for these interdomain events makes it unlikely that they initially parse the event structure of the world by dividing it into mental events, animate movements, and inanimate displacements.

A more plausible parsing system is one that reflects the kind of transformations that they themselves can execute. Such a parsing system for observed outcomes would be compatible with the parsing system that they deploy in planning an action. This type of compatibility between planning and observation will have two advantages: It will permit children to engage in an on-line monitoring of their own goal-directed actions, and it will enable them to attribute action plans to other people. The child seeking to execute some plan can check whether the planned transformation has actually been brought about. For example, if the child plans to *clean* a surface or to *build* a tower, the child can monitor his or her progress to establish when the planned transformation has been achieved. The representational system for planning an action will be compatible with the system for encoding its products so that match and mismatch judgments can be made. Conversely, when monitoring another person making progress toward such a transformation, the child can attribute to that agent the pertinent plan, recognizing for example that the other person wants to clean a surface or build a tower. In this latter case, an observed outcome is mapped back into an attributed plan.

To sum up, I see little evidence of disciplinary specialization in the child's mind. Rather, when engaged in pretending, in planning, or in the interpretation of another person's actions, the child looks out for transformations effected by animate agents. Such planned outcomes cannot be easily assigned to the psychological, the biological, or the physical domain – rather they straddle all three.

Domain specificity in scientific thinking

Let us now turn to see whether there is any warrant for the notion of domain-specific modes of explanation within science itself. Adopting the same general stance, we would expect there to be links between particular types of events and the mode of explanation that is proposed. The history of science suggests, however, that these linkages do not exist, particularly if we survey several centuries. For example, Kuhn (1977) points out that Aristotelian physics typically offered explanations in terms of so-called formal and final causes: Stones fell because their nature or form could only be entirely realized in that position. During the 17th century and 18th century, mechanical explanations couched in terms of the physical impact of one group of particles on another came to predominate, although there were important exceptions (such as Newton). Yet in the 19th century explanations couched in terms of forms, notably mathematical forms, rather than efficient causes were again ascendant.

I suspect that a similar story can be told for other sciences. In the case of biology, for example, Darwinian evolutionary theory overthrew the traditional Aristotelian emphasis on a set of eternal and unchanging forms. Nevertheless, the modern-day conception of a genetic program that guides the transformation from fertilized egg to adult form is not too distant from the Aristotelian conception of a form-giving principle (eidos) (Mayr, 1982).

The implication is that nature does not present itself to us with helpful labels suggesting a particular mode of causal explanation. There is no obvious link between the domain under which an event is classified, and the type of causal explanation that is appropriate for that event. The history of science might have been shorter if such links existed. This does not mean that the notion of domain specificity is unhelpful. It means simply that it will prove most useful in the analysis of perceptual processing – particularly those modes of processing that are not easily overridden by experience.

Magical thinking

Magical thinking in children

Given that nature has no handy labels suggesting how it should be explained, it is not surprising that children go astray in their explanation of unfamiliar phenomena. For example, Carey (1985) reviews a variety of explanations advanced by children for death. Not surprisingly, they try to assimilate it to more familiar phenomena such as sleeping or temporary departure rather than seeing it in biological terms.

It is feasible, however, that children also go astray when they confront much more familiar phenomena. In the previous section, I argued that children cannot rely on any straightforward link between the perceptual appearance of an object or event and the type of explanation that is appropriate to it. To the extent that they learn that the way that something looks may not be a clue to its capacities, they may come to adopt a cautious attitude toward perceptual evidence. As a result, they end up being uncertain whether to be credulous or skeptical toward even the most unlikely causal sequence. In effect, children have an open-minded attitude to what we would dismiss as magic.

Provoked by some findings of Subbotsky (1985), we have begun to examine this possibility in the context of object permanence (Harris, Brown, Marriott, Whittall, & Harmer, 1991). It is generally accepted that infants have a firm understanding of object permanence, certainly by the age of 18 months and possibly a good deal earlier. Are children willing to lend any credence to a violation of object permanence? To investigate, we showed children two large black boxes and invited them to check that the boxes were empty. We asked them to imagine that there was a creature (e.g., a puppy or a monster) inside one of the two boxes. On a pretext of getting some candy, the experimenter then left the children alone with the two boxes. The results were unequivocal. The children often went to investigate the box in which they had imagined the creature. They were likely to approach the box more quickly, for a longer period, and more often than the other control box.

After an absence of 2 minutes, the experimenter returned and interviewed the children about what they had done. They acknowledged looking in the pretend box and frequently acknowledged that they had wondered what was inside it. In a follow-up study (Johnson & Harris, in press), in which we asked children to explain how something might appear in a box that was empty a few moments earlier, children often mention the possibility of magic ("A wizard might have magicked it in" "A fairy flew in when we opened the lid before and made it get in there").

In summary, our results bear out the earlier findings of Subbotsky (1985). Children frequently show an interest in and a credulity toward magical phenomena. They entertain the possibility that objects can be created out of thin air, that one object can turn into another, and that a representation such as a model or picture can turn into what it represents. This is not to suggest that children do not understand ordinary physical principles such as object permanence but rather that they do not always use such principles to cast firm doubt on the possibility of intriguing magical transformations. Recall that children in our study were explicitly invited to imagine that there was a creature inside the box. Hence, the possibility that there was such a creature in the box would have readily come to mind – it would have been easily "available" (Tversky & Kahneman, 1973) – during the experimenter's absence.

Thus, although children acknowledge that the world typically obeys certain physical principles, they are not entirely skeptical about the possible violation of those principles, even those that emerge in early infancy. Although this stance can be labeled in a dismissive fashion as credulous, I think it is appropriate to be more charitable. The child cultivates to some degree an open-mindedness toward the causal outcomes that he or she routinely anticipates. This does not, of course, amount to any systematic attempt to scrutinize or test those expectations, but it does imply an acceptance, and even a hope, that things might be other than they seem.

Magical thinking in science

The standard account of intellectual advancement in the 16th and 17th centuries is that there were two important and concurrent developments. On the one hand, the Scientific Revolution led to a mechanization of the world picture. During the same period, there was a decline in a variety of magical beliefs and practices in the fields of medicine and law (Thomas, 1971). The amateur historian (and occasionally the professional) might be tempted to conclude from these concurrent developments that there is some intellectual opposition between scientific thinking and magical thinking.

Recent work in the history of science suggests that such an opposition is too simplistic. Indeed, far from regarding magical practices and investigations as inimical to the development of science, there is evidence of important continuities and even overlap in technique, preoccupation, and intellectual stance (Henry, 1990). To quote but one example, Ashmole, member of the Royal Society and founder of Oxford's Ashmolean Museum, aimed to revive for scientific use a collection of medieval alchemical texts (Ashmole, 1652). He wrote that the goal of science was the attainment of that "true and pure Knowledge of Nature (which is no other than what we call Natural Magic) in the highest degree of Perfection." Nor were his commendations ignored. Newton himself owned a copy of his book and it is one of the few books in his library that he is known to have annotated heavily (Webster, 1982).

Why exactly should scientists, particularly those of Newton's stature, have interested themselves in magic? Historical scholarship does not yet provide an agreed answer to this question but one fascinating suggestion is worth quoting at some length (Henry, 1990: 594):

Studies of alchemical and other magical texts known to Newton and also of his own alchemical manuscripts, suggest that alchemy provided him with a body of evidence and a set of concepts and arguments which he used to infer the existence of attractive and repulsive forces between particles of matter. In arguing for interparticulate forces capable of acting at a distance Newton was flouting the canons of both Aristotelian and Cartesian mechanics, but he was actually advocating ideas that had been commonplace in natural magic and which had recently been absorbed into the new natural philosophy.

The important implication of this argument is that an interest in magic, far from being an obstacle to the scientific imagination, may have inspired it.

Conclusions

The recorded history of science is predominantly the history of theories that are publicly formulated, and subjected to systematic competition and eventual eclipse by other equally public alternatives. That explicit record is a poor guide to the day-to-day thinking of scientists, let alone children.

I have tried to show that children's thinking is not based on theories but on concrete mental models. Because children do not adopt theories, their thinking does not exhibit theoretical change. Moreover, alert to the possibility that reality is not what it seems, they speculate about magic. In these respects, their thinking is similar to that of scientists.

Working scientists also use concrete mental models that can be mapped into but are distinct from their publicly stated theories. The extension of those theories is a deliberate and collective enterprise however, and no obvious parallel is to be found in children's cognitive development. Making the same point differently, the theoretical consistency, parsimony, and progress that we take to be the hallmark of a mature scientific discipline is achieved despite and not because of any similarities between the cognitive processes of children and scientists.

Finally, it is worth reiterating one notable contrast between children and scientists. Even as they begin to talk, children show a striking disregard for disciplinary boundaries. Their conceptual vocabulary picks out events that cut across the boundaries of physics, biology, and psychology. Scientists need to hold a workshop before they can begin to compete.

Note

1. Gopnik and Wellman appear to have misunderstood the suggestion that children might have difficulty in reporting on beliefs that they do not currently hold. This was not meant to imply that such difficulties are simply memory-related nor that children will have equivalent difficulties in reporting all past mental states. Children's difficulties with false beliefs arise because they must grasp that such beliefs are typically directed at situations that are now deemed counterfactual. This possibility arises in the case of past rather than current beliefs because when we discover that a belief that we currently hold is false, we cease to hold it.

References

Ashmole, E. (1652). *Theatrum Chemicum Britannicum*.
Astington, J. W., Harris, P. L., & Olson, D. R. (1988). *Developing theories of mind*. New York: Cambridge University Press.
Baron-Cohen, S. (1991). The development of a theory of mind in autism: Deviance or delay? *Psychiatric Clinics of North America, 14*, 33–51.
Bartsch, K., & Wellman, H. (1989). Young children's attribution of action to beliefs and desires. *Child Development, 60*, 946–964.
Bertenthal, B. I., Proffitt, D. R., Spetner, N. B., & Thomas, M. A. (1985). The development of infant sensitivity to biomechanical motions. *Child Development, 56*, 531–543.
Berzonsky, M. D. (1971). The role of familiarity in children's explanations of physical causality. *Child Development, 43*, 705–715.
Carey, S. (1985). *Conceptual change in childhood*. Cambridge, MA: MIT Press.
Fenson, L., Dale, P. S., Reznick, J. S., Thal, D., Bates, E., Reilly, J. S., & Hartung, J. P. (1991, March). Technical manual for the MacArthur Communicative Development Inventories. Preliminary version, San Diego State University.
Gopnik, A., & Slaughter, V. (1991). Young children's understanding of changes in their mental states. *Child Development, 62*, 98–110.
Harris, P. L. (1991). The work of the imagination. In A. Whiten (Ed.), *Natural theories of mind* (pp. 283–304). Oxford: Blackwell.
Harris, P. L. (1992). From simulation to folk psychology: The case for development. *Mind and Language, 7*, 120–144.
Harris, P. L., Brown, E., Marriott, C., Whittall, S., & Harmer, S. (1991). Monsters, ghosts and witches: Testing the limits of the fantasy – reality distinction in young children. *British Journal of Developmental Psychology, 9*, 105–123.
Harris, P. L., Johnson, C. N., Hutton, D., Andrews, G., and Cooke, T. (1989). Young children's theory of mind and emotion. *Cognition and Emotion, 3*, 379–400.

Harris, P. L., & Kavanaugh, R. D. (1993). Young children's understanding of pretense. *Society for Research in Child Development Monographs, 58,* Serial No. 231.

Henry, J. (1990). Magic and science in the sixteenth and seventeenth centuries. In R. C. Olby, G. N. Cantor, J. R. R. Christie, & M. J. S. Hodge (Eds.), *Companion to the history of modern science.* London: Routledge.

Jersild, A. T. (1943). Studies of children's fears. In R. G. Barker, J. S. Kounin, & H. F. Wright (Eds.), *Child behavior and development.* New York: McGraw Hill.

Johansson, G., von Hofsten, C., & Jansson, G. (1980). Event perception. In M. R. Rosenzweig and L. R. Porter (Eds.), *Annual Review of Psychology* (pp. 27–63). Palo Alto, CA: Annual Reviews Inc.

Johnson, C. N., & Harris, P. L. (in press). Magic: Special but not excluded. *British Journal of Developmental Psychology.*

Kuhl, P. K. (1987). The special-mechanisms debate in speech research: Categorization tests on animals and infants. In S. Harnad (Ed.), *Categorical perception.* Cambridge: Cambridge University Press.

Kuhn, T. S. (1970). *The structure of scientific revolutions* (2nd edition). Chicago: The University of Chicago Press.

Kuhn, T. S. (1977). *The essential tension.* Chicago: The University of Chicago Press.

Manesovitz, M., Prentice, N. M., & Wilson, F. (1973). Individual and family correlates of imaginary companions in preschool children. *Developmental Psychology, 8,* 72–79.

Mayr, E. (1982). *The growth of biological thought.* Cambridge, MA: Belknap Press.

Mitchell, P., & Lacohee, H. (1991). Children's early understanding of false belief. *Cognition, 39,* 107–127.

Perner, J., & Wimmer, H. (1985). "John thinks that Mary thinks that . . .": Attribution of second-order beliefs by 5- to 10-year-old children. *Journal of Experimental Child Psychology, 39,* 437–471.

Piaget, J. (1970). *The child's conception of movement and speed.* London: Routledge & Kegan Paul (original work published in 1946).

Subbotsky, E. V. (1985). Preschool children's perception of unusual phenomena. *Soviet Psychology, 23,* 91–114.

Thomas, K. (1971). *Religion and the decline of magic.* London: Weidenfeld and Nicholson.

Tversky, A., & Kahneman, D. (1973). Availability: A heuristic for judging frequency and probability. *Cognitive Psychology, 5,* 207–232.

Webster, C. (1982). *From Paracelsus to Newton.* Cambridge: Cambridge University Press.

Wimmer, H., & Perner, J. (1983). Beliefs about beliefs: Representations and constraining function of wrong beliefs in young children's understanding of deception. *Cognition, 13,* 103–128.

Wolf, D. P., Rygh, J., & Altshuler, J. (1984). Agency and experience: Actions and states in play narratives. In I. Bretherton (Ed.), *Symbolic play.* Orlando, FL: Academic Press.

Yates, J., Bessman, M., Dunne, M., Jertson, D., Sly, K., & Wendelboe, W. (1988). Are conceptions of motion based on a naive theory or on prototypes? *Cognition, 29,* 251–275.

Zaitchik, D. (1991). Is only seeing really believing? Sources of the true belief in the false belief task. *Cognitive Development, 6,* 91–103.

12 Core domains versus scientific theories: Evidence from systematics and Itza-Maya folkbiology

Scott Atran

Introduction

This chapter is intended to be an anthropological contribution to two areas of central interest to this volume: (1) the nature of specific cognitive domains common to ordinary folk, and (2) the relationship between the structure of the most basic of these commonsense domains to the structure of corresponding scientific theories. The claim is that for one such domain – folkbiology – conceptual categories exhibit high internal cultural consensus, and significant cross-cultural correlation with scientific taxonomies. Still, this apparently panhuman and domain-specific taxonomic structure may be embedded in different belief systems and may be distinctly interpreted at various levels of expertise.

Because this categorical structure provides such strong constraints on theories, there should be at least some stability and cross-cultural consistency to theory-related inferences. For example, different cultures may have very different beliefs about reproduction; but if their judgments about whether or not two species could interbreed is based on taxonomic relatedness, then these judgments should show the same decreasing function of taxonomic relatedness. Moreover, if the structure of taxonomy is enough to generate "default" probabilities for inferences about any of its categories given any

Fieldwork among the Itza-Maya of San José, Petén (Guatemala) was made possible by grants from the French Ministry of Research, the University of Michigan, and the Spencer Foundation. A number of people are involved in the Itza-Maya project, and their advice and assistance have been invaluable to various aspects of this contribution. I am especially grateful to Ximena Lois (CREA-Ecole Polytechnique) for grammatical and propositional analyses, Valentina Vapnarsky (Université de Paris X) for running sorting tasks and transcribing informant protocols, Richard Frisch (Austrian Academy of Sciences) and Brian Smith (University of Texas, Arlington) for species identifications; and John Coley and Alejandro López (University of Michigan) for help with statistical analyses.

316

other of its categories, then an indefinitely large number of category-based inductions can be made within folkbiology without having to resort to any prior system of causal explanation (cf. Osherson, Smith, Wilkie, Lopéz & Shafir, 1990; Osherson et al., 1991). Thus, we might expect both New Yorkers and Itza-Maya to find it more likely that wolves have sharp canines and eat "gravy train" than do mustangs, given that dogs have sharp canines and eat "gravy train." This, despite the fact that most New Yorkers and Itza-Maya have never seen wolves and mustangs close up.

The general idea is that people may have implicit presumptions about biological relations that underlie morphobehavioral features in the absence of explicit causal theories. Such "proto-theoretical" presumptions would permit token morphological variation within a patterned taxonomic type, and underscore the "default" conditions set by taxonomic structure on any subsequent causal theory. If so, then the emergence of biological theories might be initially attributed to attempts to elaborate a causal account of these antecedent probabilities. The upshot: Rather than theories making categories, it is the domain-specific structure of categories that severely constrains, and thereby renders possible, any theoretical (or culturally peculiar "cosmological") elaboration of them.

The argument turns on a comparative analysis of Itza-Maya folkbiology and corresponding aspects of systematics (the branch of biology that deals with the classification of animals and plants). Statistical measures are used to assess relative agreement on judgments of taxonomic relatedness across: (a) a sample of Itza informants, (b) Itza men and Itza women, and (c) the Itza and (Western) science. The measures are also used to relate taxonomic similarity judgments to levels of: (d) agreement among Itza informants on inferences concerning reproduction, and (e) expertise among Itza men and women.

Aside from notable exceptions,[1] anthropology has been marginal to the relevant debates in psychology and philosophy, usually serving as an indiscriminate background of anecdotes for virtually any imaginable position. Too often, importation of philosophy of science into cognitive psychology seems almost as indiscriminate and anecdotal as the importation of anthropology. Isolated examples are often drawn helter-skelter from scientific disciplines far afield. To be sure, philosophy's impact on cognitive psychology is of more consequence than anthropology's. But along with the intellectual rigor analytic philosophy has brought to bear, it has also been a source of dubious cognitive claims – in particular, the anthropologically curious claim that ordinary notions of the natural world develop like, or toward, scientific theories.

Underlying (1), the argument about domain specificity, is the suggestion that folkbiology is among the most inferentially rich, accessible, culturally stable, and universally distributed knowledge. Arguably, this is because humankind is endowed with domain-specific means for biological sortings (Cosmides & Tooby, this volume). This endowment need not manifest itself as a cognitively isolated "module," with exclusive access to a range of stimuli (cf. Fodor, 1983). Rather, there appears to be a spontaneous and highly selective, but nonexclusive, filtering of input (Keil, this volume), and a well-structured output to which other domains may have differential access (Sperber, this volume). Specifically, folkbiological taxonomy appears to derive from cognitive processes that operate more or less independently of cultural context. More generally, such "core" domains of human knowledge seem to operate under severe cognitive constraints. These both ensure widespread cultural transmission and drastically limit the effects of transmission – whether aleatory or institutionally patterned (e.g., science, cosmology) – on the structure of the domain itself (Atran & Sperber, 1991; Boyer, this volume).

It is logically implausible that humans generalize from limited experience without preexisting cognitive structures that project finite and fragmentary instances to complexly organized and indefinitely extendable classes. It is an empirical question whether or not these principles cross domains, and, if they do, which domains they cross. But there are currently a number of assumptions in the work on category structure whose empirical motivation is questionable. Take, for example, "the working assumption . . . that in the domain of both man-made and biological objects, there occur information rich bundles of attributes that form natural discontinuities [and] these bundles are both perceptual and functional" (Rosch & Mervis, 1975: 586; Hunn, 1987). In assuming folkbiological categories to be, in significant part, functionally determined like artifacts, findings about both domains may be undermined. Certainly (a child's) initial discrimination of "wings" and "trees" does not depend on the observer's functional viewpoint in the way that discrimination of "table tops" or "crates" does; and just as surely one cannot presume that beds and chairs are naturally four-legged, as (even three-legged) tigers are, just because they usually have four legs (Atran, 1987a).

Issue (2), of how lay concepts are created and integrated to form theories, is crucial both to general questions about human conceptual structures and to specific issues in science education. Although there is marked disagreement over the extent to which such "naive theories" change over time (Carey & Spelke, this volume), a number of contributors to this volume hold that children's basic knowledge, and folk knowledge generally, is structured into "naive theories" of mind, biology, and physics. The idea is that "theories not only reflect domains but actually constitute them"; consequently, "there will be several domains in the child's cognition and experience, domains defined by what theory covers them" (Gopnik & Wellman, this volume). From this vantage, theories determine the ontological commitments that "make" the categories of a given domain, such as the categories of folkbiology (Gelman & Coley, 1991).

Apparent lack of consistency between biological beliefs, and lack of criteria for globally assessing correspondence between such beliefs and the available evidence, may be attributed to "cosmological" theories wherein "the causal structure underlying natural kinds" is supposedly different for different cultures (Keil, 1986: 146; Jeyifous-Walker, 1985). Hence, "clearly, people in different cultures have different theories about the world, which should cause them to have different concepts" (Murphy & Medin, 1985: 305). The implication is straightforward: If different cultures have different belief systems about biological kinds, and these belief systems determine categories, then different cultures should have different categories for biological things.

Folkbiological classifications should thus prove to be neither universal nor to mirror the Linnaean system in any interesting way (cf. Rosch, 1975: 198). Carey's (1985) developmental studies are related to this theme. For Carey, naive biology is initially naive psychology extended to nonhuman animals. Only later does this become a naive biology of living kinds, including plants. The child supposedly comes to this understanding through contact with scientific knowledge in school, books, nature programs on television, and so forth. Accordingly, only to the extent that such mediated forms of scientific knowledge are culturally pervasive should there be strong consensus in the way individuals in the society make biological partitionings that include plants, and a significant correlation between the cultural consensus and science.

To disconfirm such views is not to deny that culturally peculiar beliefs or theoretical competence can affect folkbiological structure and inferencing from that structure. It is only to deny that basic concepts of plants and animals must be exhausted by cultural beliefs about them or theoretical knowledge of them. To change the cultural or theoretical context of any given folkbiological system, therefore, is *not* to fundamentally change the object.

It is likely, then, that the collapse of even the most sophisticated system of cultural cosmology would barely affect the products of such basic domain-specific cognitions. Consider the Maya, who are often cited as that non-Western culture with the most developed of cosmological traditions akin to that which produced Western science. An independent Maya tradition, which had a highly ritualized "written" element, endured until the conquest of the Itza-Maya by the Spanish at the end of the 17th century (Villagutierre, 1701/1933). Today, that system has all but disappeared, and the Itza culture of the Petén rainforest in Guatemala is itself on the verge of extinction. In fact, the only aspects of Itza culture that have preserved their integrity since the conquest are the language (Hofling, 1991) and knowledge of plants and animals, including practical knowledge (Atran et al., 1992).

Now, if it is true that the core of Itza knowledge of the biological world is largely independent of institutionally related historical developments such as science or cosmology, then one would expect basic Itza knowledge of living kinds not only to remain structurally stable but also fundamentally similar in conception to the folkbiology of ordinary Americans, French, or Ancient Greeks. By contrast, one might expect noncore elements of Itza cosmology or animal and plant ritual to be less coherent and more fragmentary than basic knowledge of living kinds. Remnants of Maya cosmology may thus be fundamentally different in conception from, say, sophisticated Western religious or scientific elaborations of knowledge about nature. Yet, there should still be a significant correlation between the Itza and science. This is because the inspection and structural evaluation of readily apprehended features of morphology, behavior, and ecology is largely independent of cultural transmission, and because systematics continues to rely on such features to infer phylogenetic relationships.

The domain of folkbiology

The folkbiology of all cultures seems to be hierarchically organized into a shallow taxonomy (Berlin, Breedlove, & Raven, 1973; Bulmer, 1974; Atran, 1990). This is clearly the case for those Maya cultures that have been studied in depth (Berlin, Breedlove, & Raven, 1974; Hunn, 1977; Brown, 1979). Each level of folktaxonomy is in approximate accordance with the corresponding ranks of modern biological systematics. Thus, the two *folk kingdoms*, in any folkbiological taxonomy roughly coincide with the animal and plant realms. Folkzoological *life-form classes* typically include all local species of the same biological class (e.g., bird, fish). By contrast, different folkbotanical life-forms (e.g., tree, grass) often contain species of the same biological family, but nevertheless include all those species whose morphology and ecological proclivity appear to confine them to a broadly similar role in the "economy of nature."

Intermediate family fragments generally contain a few or several species that belong exclusively to the same scientific family (or, in the case of less salient organisms, to scientific orders). *Folk species* habitually include only species of the same scientific genus (dog, maple). Often, however, the locally represented scientific genus is monospecific. This is particularly true of the most salient organisms, that is, the larger vertebrates and phylogenetically isolated phanerogams. *Folk sub-species* and *varietals* most characteristically represent strains of domesticated species (collie, retriever; sugar maple, red maple) or of species that are otherwise particularly significant for the culture (noxious, medicinal, etc.). Folk kingdoms and family fragments often go unnamed, folk sub-species are generally polynomial, whereas life-form classes and folk species are usually labeled by a single lexical item.[2]

In Western science, basic folktaxa eventually split into species (Cesalpino, 1583) and genera (Tournefort, 1694). As in any folk inventory, Ancient Greeks and Renaissance herbalists had to contend with only 500 or 600 local species (Raven, Berlin, & Breedlove, 1971). During the initial stages of Europe's worldwide "Age of Exploration," the number of species increased by an order of magnitude. Foreign species became habitually attached to the most obviously similar European species, that is, to the generic type, in a "natural system" (Atran, 1987b). A similar "fissioning" of intermediate folk groupings occurred when the number of species encountered increased yet another order of magnitude, and a "natural method" for organizing plants and animals into families (Adanson, 1763) and orders (Lamarck, 1809) emerged as the foundation of modern systematics (Atran, 1983). Higher-order folkzoological life-forms provided the initial framework for biological classes, while plant life-forms were abandoned as being intuitively and ecologically "natural," but "philosophically lubricious" (Linnaeus, 1751).

Each taxonomic level is mutually exclusive. Organization of the *locally perceived* flora and fauna is, in a sense, virtually exhaustive in that folk are inclined to attach hitherto unknown or unfamiliar species as varieties or "companions" of better-known species. The primary level of folktaxonomy is that of the folk species, because knowledge of all further biological divisions and connections derives from comparison and inspection of biological groups at this rank. Accordingly, people in any given culture normally and effortlessly conceptualize plants and animals in terms of a few hundred such taxa. Folk are naturally inclined to assign most, if not all, conspicuous organisms to primary taxa at a glance, with no evident reflection or discussion. It seems to matter little whether or not a culture especially values such knowledge, institutionalizes it or promotes its schooling through formal or informal instruction. These taxa are usually labeled in everyday speech by a single, easily remembered lexical item like "fox" and "oak."

Invariably, it appears, humans presume each primary taxon to possess an inherent physical nature, or underlying "essence." This nature is held responsible for the kind's teleological growth, and its characteristic behavior, morphology, and ecological proclivity. It is this presumption that allows people to unambiguously attach morphological variants (e.g., a dog born voiceless and three-legged) to a taxonomic type (by nature a barking quadruped) and to guide creatively inductions about the likely distribution and normal development of biological properties that are not immediately obvious ("mighty oaks from acorns grow"). Thus, from an instance of an organism or attribute, one can "automatically" predict its taxonomic extension to a complex set of indeterminately many living forms and related properties.

Primary folkbiological taxa generally denote the most readily identifiable biological discontinuities in a locale. The spontaneous criteria used to identify the primary taxon of a given organism pertain to overall morphology and characteristic behavior, including growth stages and ecological proclivity. Each primary taxon is associated with a typically homogeneous cluster of readily perceptible attributes that is manifestly different from all other such primary clusters. Relative to one another, these clusters reflect low morphological and biological diversity within the group and wide ecological and evolutionary divergence between groups (Hunn, 1976). The visibly obvious phenotypic "gaps" between primary taxa mark clearly distinct roles in the local economy of nature, which generally correlate with specifiable degrees of adaptive specialization and phylogenetic distance. Roughly:

1. For larger vertebrates and higher vascular plants, primary taxa tend to

coincide with scientific species when those species belong to biological families locally represented by few genera (e.g., falcon and agave families) or by species with no evident local congeners (most mammals and the more phylogenetically isolated flowering plants). This is also for taxa with a high cultural profile (e.g., species of the pheasant and herring families, the genera *Citrus* and *Allium*) or for those that are ecologically remarkable (e.g., the tall canopy trees of the rainforest, each of which may be a veritable microniche).

2. For more polytypic families, primary taxa are likely to correspond to scientific genera (many birds, fish, trees, and herbaceous phanerogams). This is because the perceptible "biological gaps" between genera of a highly polytypic family converge with the perceived distance separating species of a minimally polytypic family.

3. For highly polytypic families of less phenomenally salient organisms (e.g., small rodents, reptiles, and amphibians, many shrubs and grasses), culturally unimportant primary taxa will tend to group genera inasmuch as biological gaps between the genera are less striking to the eye.

4. In the case of invertebrates (worms, flies, bugs) and cryptogams (ferns, mosses, algae), which are harder still to perceive and which operate on an altogether different ecological register, folktaxa often include several genera, families, orders, and occasionally phyla. But even these phenomenally less conspicuous taxa are morphologically consistent, behaviorally or ecologically consequent, and often in broad accord with evolution.

To be sure, cultural factors can increase the psychological salience of secondary biological properties, as with many of the cultivars and cultigens in agricultural societies (Boster, 1980). Yet, by cultivating or otherwise focusing on particular morphological properties for some special purpose, cultures may actually provide organisms exhibiting those properties a wider or more concentrated ecological distribution (cf. Geoghean, 1976). Cultural factors can also reduce the psychological significance of primary taxa, including many kinds of birds, fish, shrubs, and grasses little recognized in modern urban societies (Rosch, Mervis, Gray, Johnson, & Boyes-Braem, 1976; Dougherty, 1978; Brown, 1984). But this need not affect appreciation of robins, sharks, holly, and rye as *(folk)biologically* primary, that is, as absolutely *ranked* folk species like deer and pines. By and large, cultural interest appears secondary to phenomenally salient biological considerations in the composition of primary ethnobiological taxa.

Itza folkbiology provides evidence for these generalizations about the specific taxonomic structure that delimits the domain of folkbiology. There is no common lexical entry for the plant kingdom in Itza, but the numeral classifier *tek* is used with all and only plants. Plants generally fall under one of four mutually exclusive life-forms: *che'* (trees), *pokche'* (undergrowth = herbs, shrubs, bushes), *ak'* (vines), and *su'uk* (grasses). Each life-form is distinguished by a particular stem habit, which is believed to be the natural outgrowth of every primary kind of *pu(k)sik'al* (species-essence) included in that life-form. A number of introduced and cultivated plants, however, are not affiliated with any of these life-forms, and are simply denoted *jun-tek* (lit. "one plant"), as are many of the phylogenetically isolated plants, such as the palms and cacti. All informants agree that mushrooms (*xikin~che'*, lit. "tree-ear") have no *pu(k)sik'al* and are not plants, but take life away from the trees that host them. Lichens and bryophytes (mosses and liverworts) are not considered to be plants, to have an essence, or to live.

As in ordinary English, the Itza term for animals (*b'a'al~che'*, lit. "forest-thing") polysemously indicates both the animal kingdom as a whole (including invertebrates, birds, and fish), and also the more restrictive grouping of quadrupeds (amphibians, reptiles and, most typically, mammals). Birds (*ch'ich'*) and fish (*käy*) exhibit patterns of internal structure that parallel those found with the quadrupeds. But for the unlabeled life-form of invertebrates, whose morphology and ecological proclivity is appreciably different from that of humans and other vertebrates, correspondence of folk to modern systematics blurs as one descends the ranks of the scientific ladder, and violations of the local scientific scheme tend to be more pronounced.

Still, in this respect as in others, the categorical structure of Itza folkbiology differs little from that of any other folkbiological system, including that which initially gave rise to scientific systematics. Thus, for Linnaeus, the Natural System was rooted in "a natural instinct [that] teaches us to know first those objects closest to us, and at length the smallest ones: for example, Man, Quadrupeds, Birds, Fish, Insects, Mites, or firstly the large Plants, lastly the smallest mosses" (1751, sect. 153). For Buffon, Linnaeus's greatest theoretical adversary, the Natural Method also began with:

Quadrupeds, Birds, Fish. It is the same in the realm of plants; he [man] will distinguish trees from plants [i.e., from herbs, grasses, vines, and bushes] very well, by their height, by their substance, by their figure. Here is what simple inspection must necessarily give him, and which with the slightest attention he will not fail to recognize. (1751, I: 32)

A method of measuring interinformant and cross-cultural agreement

Some domains of knowledge are more widely distributed across cultures than others, and information pertaining to these domains is more likely to be shared within a culture than other kinds of information. The extent to which the folkbiological knowledge of different cultures, and of different groups within a culture, is affected by different belief systems and patterns of information transmission may be examined by analyzing patterns of agreement (or disagreement) in judgments of taxonomic similarity. A mathematical tool particularly well-suited to this task is the "cultural-consensus model" (CCM) of Romney, Weller, and Batchelder (1986).

The model assumes that widely shared information is reflected by a high concordance, or "cultural consensus," among individuals. To the extent some individuals agree more often with the consensus on a set of related questions, they are considered more "culturally competent" than others with respect to that set. But the model requires that informants answer independently of one another, and measures competence and consensus without regard to social ties between informants. Thus, although the CCM was designed to evaluate intracultural stability of shared social knowledge, it may be best fitted to ascertain the validity of aggregated responses that are least affected by social networks or institutions (Boster, 1987).

Mathematical estimation of individual knowledge levels, or competencies, can be derived from the pattern of interinformant agreement on the first factor of a principal component factor analysis provided that: (1) there is indeed a single factor solution such that the first latent root (the largest eigenvalue) is large enough in comparison to all other latent roots so that it alone accounts for a significant amount of the variance, and (2) most individual scores on the first factor are strongly positive, whereas no first-factor scores are strongly negative. The mean taken from all first-factor scores then constitutes the overall measure of consensus.

One function of the CCM is to help determine how many informants are needed to establish what the consensus is within a group or culture. Given the model's assumptions, a relatively small informant sample may suffice to indicate a correct appreciation of cultural competence with a fairly high degree of confidence (Romney et al., 1986: 326). For example, if average cultural competence is 0.7, then 5 informants suffice to classify 80% of informant answers with a 95% confidence level in the context of true–false or multiple-choice format (Romney et al., 1986: 326). With 10 informants, the proportion rises to 99% of the answers with a 95% confidence level. Because similarity judgments in our data set have no fixed-response format, the statistical measure developed to assess sample size requirements for the original fixed-format consensus model serves only as an approximate, but reasonably correct, indicator (Romney, personal communication).

Applying the CCM to Itza folkbiology requires setting up a similarity matrix, with each cell reflecting the taxonomic distance that Itza perceive between any given pair of folktaxa. We have identified most local species of local trees, nearly all palms, and most mammals, reptiles, and amphibians subsumed under the Itza life-form, "quadruped" (as in ordinary English, the Itza term for "animal" – *b'a'alche'* – polysemously indicates the animal kingdom, and mammals together with herpetofauna save snakes).[3] Ten Itza informants – five men and five women – were involved in sorting tasks, representing about a fifth of the adult Itza-speaking population. An initial pilot study used pictures and line drawings for animals, and dried specimens presented as herbaria vouchers for plants. But these stimuli (especially pictures) often led to misidentifications of closely related species. To minimize the effects of the particular stimuli chosen on the task, name cards were then used. Itza were familiarized with them, as part of a joint initiative between their community and our team to introduce a standardized transcription of their oral language. Initial results show that literate and illiterate informants respond no differently to the learned name-card tasks. Illiterate informants consistently use the name cards as mnemonic icons.

Informants were first asked to generate as many names for animals and plants as they knew. Cards were made for all of the names elicited, then presented in random sequence to each informant. Informants were asked to discard cards not recognized and to join together cards they thought referred to exactly the same organisms. The (joined) cards were re-presented in random sequence and informants were asked to describe what the corresponding organisms look like, where they live, how they grow and change, and (for animals) how they behave. Answers were tape-recorded for later transcription. Informants were then told: "We would like you to put together those things [that] you think have the same names because they have the same essence" (*ki-k'a-ti ka a-tz'a ket a' b'a'al-o intech tan-a-tukl-ik yan je-b'ix u-k'ab'a-jo men yan je-b'ix u-pusik'al-o*). At this stage, informants would usually join folk sub-species, such as *juj-i kaj* ("village iguana" = *Ctenosaura similis*) and *juj-i ja'* ("river iguana" = *Iguana iguana*), or *u-ch'upal ix-xiat* ("female xate" = *Chamaedoraea elegans*), and *u-xib'al ix-xiat* ("male xate" = *Chamaedoraea oblongota*). Informants were asked why they put cards together.

Next, informants were asked to sort freely all specimens into as many groups of "companions" (*et'ok*) as they wished.[4] Informants were then encouraged to merge successive piles until they felt that that there was no longer any justification for doing so. At each successive stage, informants were asked why they had kept apart the groups of the preceding stage. Each informant's judgment of taxonomic similarity for every pair of cards (representing pairs of folktaxa) was assessed by counting the rank order in which pairs were joined. A pair of folktaxa was given a rank of 0 if the informant believed that the two folktaxa are coextensive. An aggregate similarity matrix was then computed.

The sorting task used with taxonomic judgments is inherently biased to yield tree structures. Because of this, we used an independent triad method for similarity-judgment within selected intermediate taxa, and a method of pairwise similarity-judgment for inferences about reproduction. These tasks do not force subjects to make trees; accordingly, any convergence between performances on the sorting, triad, and pairwise-judgment tasks cannot be attributed to task bias.

Men and women were compared in order to find out how levels of expertise might affect competence. Informant protocols concerning descriptions and justifications of sortings were subject to propositional analysis in order to determine levels of expertise. The expectation was that men should prove more expert because they are usually familiar with a wider range of the biological stimuli included within Itza forest culture. Men often roam extensively over the forest, sometimes leaving the village for weeks at a time. They go in search of game, plant materials for construction, or to clear and monitor a swidden plot (shifting agriculture). Women stay closer to home, and may be more expert with the wild herbs and grasses that go into the day-to-day menus and remedies that they provide their families; but because our present study chiefly involves quadrupeds, trees, and palms, this cannot be addressed here.

Previous research suggests that qualitative differences exist between experts and nonexperts with regard to folk conceptions of animals. For example, using a combination of sorting tasks and propositional analyses, Boster and Johnson (1989), and Chi, Hutchinson, and Robin (1989), both found that experts not only show more domain-related knowledge, but also organize this knowledge by means of a deeper, more causally connected relationship between concepts. Both studies concur that expert concepts "are both more interrelated and more differentiated than those of novices" (Chi et al., 1989: 39), and that "these interrelations of attributes (or rules) are used by experts in forming their groupings" (Boster & Johnson, 1989: 877). Surprisingly, however, the results of these two series of studies lead to seemingly contrary assessments of how expertise affects consensus and approximation to scientific taxonomy.

Thus, Boster and Johnson report that expert fishermen use both morphological and functional criteria to judge similarities among fish, "while novices judge on morphological criteria alone and thereby approach the scientific classification of fish more closely than experts" (p. 866). Moreover, "experts not only show more variation in their sorts of the fish, they also offer more varied justifications for their sorts" (p. 881). This is because experts use a more diverse range of heuristics in sorting fish. The heuristics are apparently based on causal reasoning unavailable to novices, which derives from a wider appreciation of how to catch and prepare fish.

By contrast, Chi and her colleagues report that children who are experts on dinosaurs structure their knowledge into more globally coherent hierarchies than do novices. At each level of the hierarchy, the relations between well-defined families and family groups are also more locally cohesive in terms of the patterns of causal interlinkages and attribute sharing among concepts. As "novices are more likely to categorize only on the basis of explicit physical features" (p. 43), their inferences are less accurate "with respect to an absolute scientific standard," and so they are unable to conceptualize a "higher level of classification that coalesces family structures, in the same way that zoologists classify animals" (p. 55). The accuracy analysis also indicates that experts have less variable and more "stable body of domain knowledge that allows them to generate correct inferences" (p. 53).

To address the arguments raised in both sets of studies, a propositional analysis of informant protocols was designed to take into account the relative importance of: morphology, behavior, habitat, diet, functional relationship to humans, causal connection, reasoning based on taxonomic comparison, and amount and interlinkage of information. We expected men and women not to differ significantly in their adherence to the cultural consensus on folk-biological taxonomy, despite significant differences in interpretation of that structure in terms of the factors mentioned.

To test further the relation between categorization and constraints on theory formation, a second task involving the cultural-consensus model was performed. Following a complete run of the successive sorting task, informants were asked which animals could mate. If they could not, why not? Matings were almost never allowed between folk species, and often disallowed even between folk species (e.g., between river and village iguanas). One of three kinds of reasons was nearly always given for why mating is not possible: The members of the different taxa differ too greatly in size, the members of the different taxa live in different places and never meet, and the members of one or the other taxa have a particularly repellant property vis-à-vis the other taxa in the pile. For example, the jaguar's even-headed temperament, the cougar's aggressiveness, and the margay's small size generally disallow mating between these three members of the Itza spotted-cat taxon, *b'alum*.

Thus, every time informants disallowed mating between biological groups they were asked if mating could occur under one or a combination of the following conditions: (1) If size is an obstacle, then what if a member of the larger group were born a dwarf? (2) If habitat is relevant, what if members of the different groups were forced to live in the same habitat, say, in the same cage? (3) If some noxious property is an obstacle, what if an herbal potion were given to neutralize that property? From the answers, a reproduction-response matrix was created for each informant. For each cell, which represents a biological pair, a reproduction ranking was given: 1 if mating could occur spontaneously, 2 if any one of the three conditions listed above were invoked, 3 if any two conditions were invoked, 4 if all three conditions were invoked, 5 if a more extreme set of conditions were invoked (e.g., supernatural intervention), and 6 if mating could not occur under any circumstances. A score of 0 was given when an informant considered the pair coextensive.

A mean reproduction-response matrix of informants' responses to mating questions was created, then subjected to a factor analysis. The prediction was for a strong correlation between aggregate taxonomic-similarity ranking and aggregate reproduction ranking. We further predicated a significant correlation between informants' assessments of the rank order of similarlity between folktaxa and the scientific distance between pairs of folktaxa (calculated as the number of nodes in the scientific tree required to include all species in the joint extension of any given folktaxonomic pair).[5]

Sorting data combined with reproduction judgments was intended to provide critical evidence on the extent to which biological reasoning is constrained.

The success of the CCM in describing the categorization data addresses the question of the contribution of theories to category formation. The model applied to mating judgments provides a metric for the degree to which these categories constrain inferences associated with them. A robust, and nonobvious, finding would show a highly structured taxonomy that enjoys a strong cultural consensus and is significantly correlated with inferences as diverse as evolutionary theory and Itza-Maya notions about the likelihood of mating between animals that do not normally interbreed.

Results: Consensus, competence, and correlation with science

No significant disagreement appears among informants over what the folkspecies are and to which biological species they typically refer. For quadrupeds, 75% of all folk species correspond to biological species, 14% to scientific genera, and 78% of the folk species are monotypic. For trees, our inventory is not quite complete, but well over half of tree folk species are monotypic and over two-thirds correspond to biological species or genera.

Following an initial run of pile sortings, we found that informants made a number of relatively stable, unlabeled groupings that roughly correspond to scientific taxa: Felidae + Canidae (felines/canines), cow + Perissodactyla (equids and tapirs), Cebidae (monkeys), Dasypractidae (pacas and agoutis), Suiformes (pigs and peccaries), Ruminanta part (deer, goats, sheep), Testudinata (turtles), Anura (frogs, toads), Lacertilia (lizards). The boundaries of other groupings were less clear-cut, both scientifically and across informants. These variously involved: shrews (Insectivora), rodents (other than the dasypractids), mustelids, and opossums (Marsupalia). At a higher level, informants also invariably separated the mammals from the herpetofauna (reptiles and amphibians).

The discussion of results that follow is limited to three representative, unlabeled, or "covert," intermediate Itza folktaxa: felines/canines, lizards and palms. The reasons for this limitation are both practical and theoretical. One aim of our research was to demonstrate the existence of unlabeled categories that fall roughly between the levels of the scientific family and order.[6] Propositional analysis was restricted to informant protocols derived from the first free pile sortings above the folk species level. These initial sortings exhibited all features deemed pertinent to assessing differences in expertise between men and women. To minimize the effects of sorting tasks on notions of reproduction, pairwise mating judgments were elicited. The results presented below are merely meant to be indicative of certain tendencies in taxonomically related judgments. It is not implausible that the results will be modified when the full complement of animals and plants is tested.

For mammal reproduction, pairwise judgments were elicited in random order for all carnivore folk species and their folkzoological allies, including procyonids (raccoons, coatimundis, kinkajous, ringtails) and mustelids (otters, tayras, weasels, skunks) as well as a rodent (porcupine) and a marsupial (oppossum). Except for rare cases of supernatural or forced intervention (e.g., miraculous metamorphosis, sewing sex organs together), there were no imaginable matings of felines or canines with other carnivores. Similarly for reptile reproduction, pairwise judgments were elicited in random order for all folk species of quadrupedal reptiles, including turtles and crocodiles, as well as a toad and a nonpoisonous rat snake. Virtually no matings were thought possible between lizards and other herpetofauna.

Felines/canines form the largest intermediate group (9 folk species recognized) of mammals, and lizards the largest intermediate group of herpetofauna (9–13 folk species). Itza readily distinguish between each carnivore species, roughly grouping them further into canines, small felines, and spotted and large felines. By contrast, most reptile folk species lump biological species, often violating scientific genera and even families. Still, they are broadly split further into iguanalike and gekkolike groups. Overall, carnivore and reptile groupings may correlate similarly with science, although scientific resolution of their primary taxa differ.

Unlike animal family fragments, which usually fall under a single life-form, family-level plant groupings may cut across life-forms. Where they exist, palms constitute one such grouping that is likely to occur in any folkbotanical system. Palms (Arecaceae) and their allies, the Zingiberales (Marantaceae, Heliconiaceae, Musaceae), include trees (*che'*), herbs and shrubs (*pokche'*), vines (*ak'*), or unaffiliated plants. Among the plants they are like the mammals in their discriminability: Most folk species are monotypic and most correspond to scientific species. But for the most tended, there can be a number of folk sub-species. For example, the small, ornamental herb *xiat* (*Chamaedoraea* sp.) has three binomially labeled folk sub-species; the coconut (*Cocus nucifera*) has three folk sub-species, one being further divided into three folk varietals; the bananas (*ja'as* = *Musa* sp.) include two folk sub-species, seven folk varietals and six sub-varietals.

In order to explore the extent and internal structure of the palms we first excluded all tall canopy trees from the plant sorting task, leaving small- and medium-sized trees. Also included in the task were spiney vines (the only local palm vines being spiney), broad-leafed shrubs or herbs and their allies, and a heterogeneous collection of other herbs and vines. We asked informants to join plants that they thought might be "companions," even though they may belong to different life-forms, such as *ak'*, *che'*, and *pokche'*.

Table 12.1 shows results that fit the assumptions of the cultural-consensus model. The folktaxonomic distance scores derived from successive pile-sorting tasks indicate a single dimension of "cultural knowledge" underlying the data for all three subtaxonomies: felines/canines, lizards, and palms. In each case, the first factor eigenvalue accounted for significantly more of the variance than subsequent factors. The results in Table 12.1 also point to a single, underlying body of implicit inferential knowledge about reproduction.

Table 12.1. Consensus: *Eigenvalues as % variance explained*

	1st root	2nd root	3rd root
Cat/dog tax	64.5	12.7	8.4
Cat/dog rep	57.4	11.8	10.5
Lizard tax	42.6	16.4	11.6
Lizard rep	53.5	12.8	9.8
Palm tax	53.9	14.1	9.1

Table 12.2. Competence: *First factor scores*

	Mean	Men	Women
Cat/dog tax	.783	.719	.874
Cat/dog rep	.735	.626	.844
Lizard tax	.637	.699	.575
Lizard rep	.718	.778	.655
Palm tax	.725	.701	.745

Table 12.3. Correlations: *Science, folktaxonomy, & reproduction*

	Science	Tax/rep
Cat/dog tax	$r = .495\ p < .002$	$r = .924$
Cat/dog rep	$r = .453\ p < .006$	$p < .000$
Lizard tax	$r = .537\ p < .003$	$r = .904$
Lizard rep	$r = .450\ p < .016$	$p < .000$
Palm tax	$r = .454\ p < .000$	

Table 12.2 indicates comparable scores of "cultural competence" regarding the three subtaxonomies. A one-way analysis of variance showed no significant differences between men and women on the first two factors of each sorting task. Judging from the samples, then, Itza folkbiological taxonomy evinces a high level of consensus for the culture as a whole, with men and women being equally competent in making "culturally correct" judgments that fit the consensus (but note the suggestion of a relationship between gender and taxonomic group that merits further study).

Table 12.3 suggests a uniformly significant correlation between higher-order Itza folktaxonomy and scientific systematics (the correlation of all Itza groupings to science rises to $r \approx 0.8$ when folk species are also taken into account). High correlations between taxonomic relatedness and likelihood of mating further signal that inferences about potential interbreeding are virtual projections of taxonomic judgments. The indication is that a psychologically robust domain, which is constituted by folkbiological taxonomy, links notions as apparently far flung as evolutionary systematics and Itza speculations about

Table 12.4. *Propositional attributes: One-way analysis of variance*

Rounded means	Cat/dog (Men)	Cat/dog (Women)	Lizard (Men)	Lizard (Women)	*t*-test (men vs. women)
Total # propositions	37.0	31.6	45.8	39.8	
Total # features	40.4	33.4	62.2	44.6	
% comparative statements	44.5	36.7	27.0	23.8	
% causal statements	14.4	3.1	2.3	.9	$p = .02$
% morphological features	49.5	76.9	67.9	78.0	$p = .00$
% behavior/ habitat features	29.7	21.1	19.4	14.5	$p = .02$
% function/ diet features	20.7	1.0	7.3	7.5	$p = .01$
# propositions per sort	6.1	3.7	6.0	5.1	$P = .02$

mating between animals that normally do not interbreed. Similarly, for Aristotle, the likelihood of "monstrous" matings was an inverse function of taxonomic distance (Atran, 1985), however different from Itza his idea of genesis.

Table 12.4 shows two tendencies: Men and women exhibit comparable appreciation of the global coherence of folktaxonomy and a comparable amount of knowledge regarding that taxonomy; but they manifest significantly different levels of expertise. Thus, both groups use comparative taxonomic statements to a high degree (91% of all comparisons made by women, and 83% of those made by men, were to taxonomically related animals). Moreover, there appear to be no statistically significant differences between men and women concerning the total number of features and propositions mobilized to justify their sorts. These results, together with their comparable competence scores, imply more or less equal knowledge of taxonomic structure.

By contrast, men provide more linkages between propositions and features. They also tend to rely less on static morphological features to characterize sorts, and more on complexly related features of behavior, habitat, diet, and functional relationship to people. This appears to make men more "expert" folkbiologists than women, in the sense of being more "rule-bound," or theoretically inclined, to making their sorts locally cohesive.

A comparison of within-group correlations for men and women shows significantly more variation for men in regard to felines/canines ($t = -2.268$, $p = .036$), more variation for women in regard to lizards ($t = 2.999$, $p = .034$), but no significant difference for palms. In Table 12.4, note that difference in expertise between men and women is more apparent for felines/canines than for lizards. One factor may be that only men hunt the canines and felines. Both men and women have little functional relationship with lizards, apart from the occasional eating and tanning of the village iguana. Still, men have more knowledge of more lizards. Although both groups readily recognize the nine folk species mentioned, the men tend to recall up to four more folk species and an equal number of folk sub-species. When faced with one of the lesser-known lizards, women are more inclined to consider it a variant of a familiar kind. Perhaps women's less complete knowledge of lizards, contrasted with a more complete male knowledge unencumbered by functional concerns, accounts for greater internal consistency among men.

In sum, statistical findings tend to support claims that: (1) Folkbiology comprises a core domain of human cognition; (2) the conceptual structure of this domain is pretheoretical; (3) it is constituted by highly structured, natural taxonomy; (4) this categorical structure severely constrains, so as to correlate and even render possible, speculations as seemingly diverse as evolutionary theory and Itza-Maya notions about the likelihood of mating between caged, drugged, and dwarfed animals that do not normally interbreed. Additional studies underway also suggest that inferences about the distribution of unknown biologically related properties (e.g., diseases) among biological categories also closely follow taxonomic structure, whether for Maya, Western folk or scientists.

Taxonomy and essence without cause

Using the cultural consensus model, Johnson, Mervis, and Boster (1992) have recently explored developmental changes in the organization of information within the mammal domain of native American English speakers. Results on triad tests of similarity judgments for 7-year-olds, 10-year-olds, and adults indicate no significant differences in mean competence values (first factor = .59, .63, and .61) or in correlations with scientific taxonomy (r = .36, .39, and .47). There was, however, a positive relationship between competence value and approximation to scientific taxonomy as a function of age (r = .66).

In particular, adults were far more likely than either group of children to pair humans with primates when presented with a human–primate–nonhuman primate triad, and to consider nonhuman primates to be most like the same kind of thing. Because adults were more apt to conceive of humans as just one animal among many, and as more similar to the primates, the authors argue that the main effect of cultural instruction on the folkbiology of mammals is that: "children probably have to be taught that humans are similar to other primate and nonprimate mammals in that all possess lungs, are warm blooded, bear live young, nurse their young, etc." (p. 81). Once children accept these facts, there presumably is a qualitative shift in knowledge about animals, the emergence of a primate category and the "deep" taxonomic restructuring of information relevant to humans and other primates.

The authors surmise that "children and adults clearly share the same cultural consensus model about mammals." This implies that folkbiological taxonomy primarily involves a spontaneous appreciation of morphology that is largely independent of cultural transmission or differences in underlying theory. But far from questioning whether folkbiological taxonomy is theory-based, the authors claim results that "fit with Carey's [1985] conclusion that there are two models of the animal domain: psychological and biological."

What, then, of Carey's contention that 7-year-olds rely on "psychological theory," whereas 10-year-olds and adults use "biological theory"? Johnson et al. claim that 10-year-olds fail to use biological theory in classifying humans and other primates because they rely on such theory only "when they are placed in situations relatively similar to those in which the facts relevant to the biological model were taught them" (p. 82). Situations of the sort occur when visible morphology is a good predictor of taxonomic similarity; but insofar as humans *are* prima facie distinct from other animals, "visible morphology is a poor predictor when humans are involved" (p. 81).

There are problems with this account. First, it is not evident that visible morphology is a poor predictor of the similarity of humans to primates as opposed to nonprimates. In many cultures, including Maya culture, humans entertain a host of privileged nontaxonomic relations with primates that are obviously based on morphological and behavioral attributes. Nevertheless, before Aristotle introduced humankind as a *genos* of natural history alongside animals and plants (*de Generatione Animalium* 731b25-732a2), perhaps no culture ever conceived of people as part of folkbiological taxonomy. This may owe to the fact that humans and animals belong to different basic conceptual domains.

The relevant biological lesson about humans for the theoretical development of systematics may be not so much that they are primates, but that they are animals. Indeed Linnaeus, who introduced the order of primates to natural history, was able to do so partly on the basis of a comparison with another species he introduced into systematics, *Homo Sapiens*, placed as a separate (mono-specific) class alongside Quadrupeds, Birds, Fish, and Insects (1735). For Linnaeus, as for people schooled in America today, the introduction of humans and primates into biological thought initially had only marginal effect on the structure and content of a patently folk-based scientific taxonomy.

Second, the authors present no direct evidence that children of any age require a "psychological model" for their folkbiological taxonomies. Suppose, as Carey suggests, notions of biological essence and categorical structure arise only after the living-kind domain is first conceived in psychological terms. Suppose also that plants are not initially assimilated into the living-kind domain because they are not readily construed in psychological terms. Then, how comes it that plants and animals are structured in virtually identical fashion by American children at an early age (Dougherty, 1979)?

Given that non-Western children are even less likely to be exposed to relevant biological theory, it would seem odd that 4-year-old Tzeltal Maya consistently taxonomize over a hundred plant taxa, excluding "pseudo" – folk-taxonomic flowers: "He still depends somewhat on location or context [i.e., ecological proclivity] for naming many plants, and he is not able to take into account accurately the full variety of forms and growth stages exhibited by a single kind of plant, although he is distinctly aware of such possibilities" (Stross, 1973: 137). Of course, this finding would seem less odd if the categorical structure of living kinds, including plants and animals, were the product of domain-specific processes that are largely theory- and culture-independent.

The fact that young children mistakenly assent to the possibility of a biological transformation between morphologically distinct species, far from indicating a lack of theory to distinguish biological species, may simply indicate the child's continuing search for essentially allowable expressions of non-obvious morphological variation. Children who incorrectly allow, for example, that beetles can become frogs (Keil, 1989: 211), thus may also be able to adduce correctly that, for example, tadpoles can become frogs. And children who incorrectly allow, for example, that "a young *karanto* vine, growing under the spreading branches of an *'iw* tree which it in no way resembles, [be] called *yal 'iw* ('baby 'iw')" (Stross, 1973: 132), may thereby conjecture that, for example, herblike saplings become trees and wormlike caterpillars become butterflies.

The idea of underlying essence, which seems to be universally and spontaneously available to people for hierarchically classifying and understanding living kinds according to species and ranked groups of species, might be variously extended to other domains. Because humans must cognitively adapt knowledge to the world in which they actually live, they are compelled to integrate their various core domains. Human cognition, it appears, is eclectic. People tend to make use of whatever cognitive means they readily have at their disposal in order to make further sense of the world. Suppose "humans" and "animals" are adjacent ontological domains, as it were (cf. Keil, 1979), then one might expect children to borrow initially from their knowledge of "humans" to begin organizing and merging their knowledge of "animals" and "plants." So, although children may initially entertain only presumptions, rather than knowledge, of the underlying natures of animals and plants, they could use their knowledge of human biology (cum psychology) to begin the process of organizing and merging their knowledge of animal and plant natures.

Conversely, children might initially borrow from their presumptions of the underlying natures of living kinds to better organize their knowledge of "humans" and merge this knowledge with that of other "living things." For instance, apparent morphological distinctions between human groups are readily (but not necessarily) conceived as apparent morphological distinctions between animal species – that is, in accordance with presumptions about underlying physical natures. These presumptions may help to underscore notions of social hierarchy and the tenacity of racism (Hirschfeld, this volume). But whereas the presumed "natural" linkage between the underlying essence and typical morphology of living kinds yields remarkably stable taxa within and across cultures, the largely conventional linkage between "species" of human groups and salient aspects of morphology or behavior shows much wider variation extending even to such traits as speech or apparel.

This suggests that basic cognitive aptitudes, such as those governed by core domains, may have an ineluctable role to play in the formation of culture. By contrast, cognitive proclivities that are less rigidly determined, but still closely adapted to the specific structure of core cognitions, may play a role that is not inescapable. Yet, being so closely linked to core knowledge, these domain-integrating cognitions may readily become central historical subjects in cultural evolution. Once unleashed in a community's cognitive environment, they may prove so psychologically "contagious" that they appear to be inevitable features of human nature, like racism . . . or science.

Conclusion: Science, a doubtful model for basic concepts

In the philosophy of science, which informs much theorizing in cognitive science, there is a widespread belief that ordinary conceptions of the natural world develop like, or toward, scientific theories (Russell, 1948; Quine, 1969; Popper, 1972; Kripke, 1972; Putnam, 1986). But from an anthropological vantage, this may seem a curious belief. For science constitutes a rather specialized activity of thought, one that is hardly required for an apprehension of humankind's immensely rich and varied everyday world. Most people become perfectly competent cultural performers without ever knowing about, or thinking in line with, science. This is not to deny the cultural importance of science or its power to expand the frontiers of human knowledge. It is only to doubt that scientific thinking and theory are so relevant to understanding general conceptual development. By contrast, the cognitive structures of ordinary conceptual domains may strongly constrain, and thereby render possible, the initial elaboration of corresponding scientific fields.

Of course, there is considerable educational restructuring to do in learning science. Inter alia, this involves using analogies from other fields (e.g., biology as essentially chemistry and physics) and signaling "anomalies" that confront unwarranted extensions of intuition (e.g., species as eternal) with counterintuitive facts (species as imperceptibly graded). But rather than wholesale abandonment of common sense as an outworn "theory" (McCloskey, 1983), there may be cause for selective use and refinement of preexisting knowledge in instruction (diSessa, 1988). Awareness of the distinct structural natures and maturational schedules of specific cognitive domains may be significant to this learning process. Thus, it may turn out that early comprehension of biological species and taxonomy facilitates assimilation of new species and properties as well as comprehension of the underlying nature and organization of physical substances and chemical compounds. But if so, the very same facility to conceive of things according to essentially based standards may hinder learning about evolutionary theory (Hull, 1991).

Still, knowing when to use or overcome basic commonsense conceptions first requires an understanding of how they are structured. Even more important, addressing the right domain at the right time might dramatically improve learning, whereas failing to do so could result in a regrettable loss of opportunity for a mind to reach its ordinarily rich capacity.

Notes

1. Much of the exceptional work is by Brent Berlin, his associates, and former students, such as Eugene Anderson, James Boster, Eugene Hunn, Janet Keller, and Terence Hays.

2. Berlin (1992) refers to folk species as "generics," whereas Bulmer (1974) denotes most folk species as "speciemes." But a principled distinction between species and genus is generally not pertinent to a folk context (e.g., local genera are frequently monospecific and often interact as ecological isolates).

3. The Itza readily identify about half of the 200 or so species of quadrupeds and 400 or so species of trees in Petén (cf. Standley & Steyermark, 1946–1977; Cambell & Vannini, 1989): nearly all of the 50 or so species of mammals (excluding bats), except for the 5 species of small cricetid mice, which they do not readily distinguish; nearly all turtles (6 species), crocodiles (2 species), toads (2 species), deadly vipers and coral snakes (7 species), and the taxonomically isolated *Boa constrictor*; between one-quarter and one-third of the 40 or so species of lizards; one-fifth to one-quarter of the 20 or so species of frogs; one-fifth to one-quarter of the 50 or so species of colubrid snakes. Most species of canopy trees are easily recognized; trees that are simultaneously smaller, infrequently encountered, and of no apparent use tend to have no name and are variously labeled a "companion" of this or that better known tree.

4. The reasons for asking the Itza to sort on the basis of "companionship" were as follows: In the original sequential generation of animal names, the order elicited from informants provided broad linkages based on being: (1) wild (*b'a'al~che'-i k'ax*) or domestic (*b'a'al~che'-i kaj*), (2) eaten (*k-u-jan-b'il*) or not (*ma' tan-u-jan-b'il*), and (3) of the land (*i lu'um*), water (*i ja'*), or air (*i ik'*). The history of ethnobiology shows that such readily elicited functional groupings do not adequately capture the deeper taxonomic relations, which are seldom institutionally represented or even consciously formulated. Yet, prior questioning of informants about the semantic relations between "companionship" and "essence" revealed an unarticulated conception of "essential companionship" underlying their unarticulated folkbiological taxonomy. For example, Itza never consider the domestic, inedible, and terrestrial dog (*pek'*) to be an essential companion of the domestic, inedible, and terrestrial horse (*tzimin*). By contrast, they usually do consider the carnivorous dog a distant companion of the carnivorous otter (*pek'-i ja'*), although the latter is wild and aquatic. Similarly, they generally take the perissodactylous horse to be a distant companion of the perissodactylous tapir, although the latter is wild, edible, and semiaquatic. When the Spanish introduced

the horse, the Itza initialy marked it "Castillian tapir" (*tzimin kastil*). Today, it is the tapir that is marked as "forest horse" (*tzimin che'*).

5. A taxonomic code was created to supply the information necessary to compute the scientific distance among folktaxa used in the sorting tasks. The nine code fields provided unique identifiers for primary group (Tetrapoda), crown division (Amphibia, Amniota), cladistic division or class (Chelonia, Diapsida, Mammalia), suborder or corresponding clade (e.g., Lacertilia = Sauria = lizards), superfamily or corresponding clade, family, genus, and species. The codes represent a working compromise between cladistics and classical systematics. *Scientific distance* between folktaxa is calculated by counting the nodes one has to ascend in the scientific taxonomic tree to arrive at a node that includes *all* the species covered by both folktaxa in any given cell of the $1/2 [N \times (N - 1)]$ pairwise similarity matrix of folktaxa. The measure of scientific distance is modified from Hunn (1977) and Boster, Berlin, and O'Neill (1986).

6. Cesalpino referred to intermediate groups, such as the legumes and malvales, as *genera innominata*; just as Aristotle had used the idea of *eide anonyma* to denote unlabeled groups like the felines and equids. To a significant extent, the history of systematics involves the attempt to fix the taxonomic boundaries of these initially covert groupings in order to form a mutually exclusive series of families and orders that exhaustively cover the planet. Indeed, a key motivation of theoretical systematics, including evolutionary theory, was to provide an ontological account of such groups in terms of the causal processes that generate them. For example, the family relationship between the land birds of the Galapagos Islands and the American continent "admit of no sort of explanation on the ordinary view of creation" (Darwin, 1883: 353–354). Although the existence of such groups may be intuitively obvious, it is not at all obvious what in the world would lead to their coming into being.

References

Adanson, M. (1763). *Familles des plantes*, 2 vols. Paris: Vincent.

Atran, S. (1983). Covert fragmenta and the origins of the botanical family. *Man, 18*, 51–71.

Atran, S. (1985). Pre-theoretical aspects of Aristotelian definition and classification of animals: The case for common sense. *Studies in History and Philosophy of Science, 16*, 113–163.

Atran, S. (1987a). Constraints on the ordinary semantics of living kinds: An alternative to recent treatments of natural-object terms. *Mind and Language, 2*, 27–63.

Atran, S. (1987b). Origins of the species and genus concepts. *Journal of the History of Biology, 20*, 175–279.

Atran, S. (1990). *Cognitive foundations of natural history: Towards an anthropology of science*. Cambridge: Cambridge University Press.

Atran, S., & Sperber, D. (1991). Learning without teaching: Its place in culture. In L. Landsmann (Ed.), *Culture, schooling and psychological development*. Norwood, NJ: Ablex.

Atran, S., Frisch, R., Lois, X., & Vapnarsky, V. (1992). Aspects of Itza–Maya subsistence and systematics, present and past: A contribution to the natural history of the Petén tropical forest, Guatemala. Paper presented to The Third International Conference of Ethnobiology, November 1992, Mexico City.

Berlin, B. (1992). *Ethnobiological classification: Principles of categorization of plants and animals in traditional societies.* Princeton, NJ: Princeton University Press.

Berlin, B., Breedlove, D., & Raven, P. (1973). General principles of classification and nomenclature in folk biology. *American Anthropologist, 74,* 214–242.

Berlin, B., Breedlove, D., & Raven, P. (1974). *Principles of Tzeltal plant classification: An introduction to the botanical ethnography of a Mayan-speaking people of Highland Chiapas.* New York: Academic.

Boster, J. (1980). *How the exceptions prove the rule: An analysis of informant disagreement in Aguaruna manioc classification.* Unpublished dissertation, University of California, Berkeley.

Boster, J. (1987). Introduction to: Intracultural variation (special issue). *American Behavioral Scientists, 31,* 150–162.

Boster, J., Berlin, B., & O'Neill, J. (1986). The correspondence of Jivaroan to scientific ornithology. *American Anthropologist, 88,* 569–583.

Boster, J., & Johnson, J. (1989). Form or function: A comparison of expert and novice judgments of similarity among fish. *American Anthropologist, 91,* 866–889.

Brown, C. (1979). Growth and development of folk botanical life-forms in the Mayan language family. *American Ethnologist, 6,* 366–385.

Brown, C. (1984). *Language and living things: Uniformities in folk classification and naming.* New Brunswick: Rutgers University Press.

Bulmer, R. (1974). Folk biology in the New Guinea Highlands. *Social Science Information, 13,* 9–28.

Cambell, J., & Vannini, J. (1989). Distribution of amphibians and reptiles in Guatemala and Belize. *Proceedings of the Western Foundation of Vertebrate Zoology, 4,* 1–21.

Carey, S. (1985). *Conceptual change in childhood.* Cambridge, MA: MIT Press.

Cesalpino, A. (1583). *De plantis libri XVI.* Florence: Marescot.

Chi, M., Hutchinson, J., & Robin, A. (1989). How inferences about novel domain-related concepts can be constrained by structured knowledge. *Merrill-Palmer Quarterly, 35,* 27–62.

Darwin, C. (1883). *On the origin of species by natural selection,* 6th ed. New York: Macmillan. (Originally published in 1872)

diSessa, A. (1988). Knowledge in pieces. In G. Forman & P. Pufall (Eds.), *Constructivism in the computer age.* Hillsdale, NJ: Erlbaum.

Dougherty, J. (1978). Salience and relativity in classification. *American Ethnologist, 5,* 66–80.

Dougherty, J. (1979). Learning names for plants and plants for names. *Anthropological Linguistics, 21,* 298–315.

Fodor, J. (1983). *Modularity of mind.* Cambridge, MA: MIT Press.

Gelman, S., & Coley, J. (1991). Language and categorization: The acquisition of natural kind terms. In S. Gelman & J. Byrnes (Eds.), *Perspectives on language and thought: Interrelations in development.* Cambridge: Cambridge University Press.

Geoghegan, W. (1976). Polytypy in folk biological taxonomies. *American Ethnologist, 3,* 469–480.

Hofling, C. (1991). *Itza Maya texts with a grammatical overview.* Salt Lake City: University of Utah Press.

Hull, D. (1991). Common sense and science. *Biology and Philosophy, 6,* 467–479.

Hunn, E. (1976). Toward a perceptual model of folk biological classification. *American Ethnologist, 3,* 508–524.

Hunn, E. (1977). *Tzeltal folk zoology: The classification of discontinuities in nature.* New York: Academic.

Hunn, E. (1987). Science and common sense: A reply to Atran. *American Anthropologist, 89,* 146–149.

Jeyifous-Walker, S. (1985). *Atimodemo: Semantic conceptual development among the Yoruba.* Unpublished dissertation, Cornell University.

Johnson, K., Mervis, C., & Boster, J. (1992). Developmental changes within the structure of the mammal domain. *Developmental Psychology, 28,* 74–83.

Keil, F. (1979). *Semantic and conceptual development: An ontological perspective.* Cambridge, MA: Harvard University Press.

Keil, F. (1986). The acquisition of natural kind and artifact terms. In A. Marrar & W. Demopoulos (Eds.), *Conceptual Change.* Norwood, NJ: Ablex.

Keil, F. (1989). *Concepts, kinds, and cognitive development.* Cambridge, MA: MIT Press.

Kripke, S. (1972). Naming and necessity. In D. Davidson & G. Harman (Eds.), *Semantics of natural language,* Dordrecht: Reidel.

Lamarck, J. (1809). *Philosophie zoologique.* Paris: Dentu.

Linnaeus, C. (1735). *Systema naturae.* Leiden: Haak.

Linnaeus, C. (1751). *Philosophia botanica.* Stockholm: G. Kiesewetter.

McCloskey, M. (1983). Naive theories of motion. In D. Gentner & A. Stevens (Eds.), *Mental models.* Hillsdale, NJ: Erlbaum.

Murphy, G., & Medin, D. (1985). The role of theories in conceptual coherence. *Psychological Review, 92,* 289–316.

Osherson, D., Smith, E., Wilkie, O., López, A., & Shafir, E. (1990). Category-based induction. *Psychological Review, 97,* 185–200.

Osherson, D., Stern, J., Wilkie, O., Stob, M., & Smith, E. (1991). Default probability. *Cognitive Science, 15,* 251–269.

Popper, K. (1972). *Objective knowledge: An evolutionary approach.* Oxford: Clarendon Press.

Putnam, H. (1986). Meaning holism. In L. Hahn & P. Schlipp (Eds.), *The philosophy of W. V. Quine.* La Salle, IL: Open Court.

Quine, W. (1969). Natural kinds. In *Ontological relativity and other essays.* New York: Columbia University Press.

Raven, P., Berlin, B., & Breedlove, D. (1971). The origins of taxonomy. *Science, 174,* 1210–1213.

Romney, A. K., Weller, S., & Batchelder, W. (1986). Culture as consensus: A theory of culture and informant accuracy. *American Anthropologist, 88,* 313–338.

Rosch, E. (1975). Universals and cultural specifics in categorization. In R. Brislin, S. Bochner, & W. Lonner (Eds.), *Cross-cultural perspectives on learning.* New York: Halstead.

Rosch, E., & Mervis, C. (1975). Family resemblances: Studies in the internal structure of natural categories. *Cognitive Psychology, 7,* 573–605.

Rosch, E., Mervis, C., Gray, W., Johnson, D., & Boyes-Braem, P. (1976). Basic objects in natural categories. *Cognitive Psychology, 8,* 382–439.

Russell, B. (1948). *Human knowledge: Its scope and limits.* New York: Simon & Schuster.

Standley, P., & Steyermark, J. (1946–1977). *Flora of Guatemala*, vol. 24, pts. 1–13. Chicago: Field Museum of Natural History.

Stross, B. (1973). Acquisition of botanical terminology by Tzeltal children. In M. Edmonson (Ed.), *Meaning in Mayan languages*. The Hague: Mouton.

Tournefort, J. (1694). *Elémens de botanique*. Paris: Imprimerie Royale.

Villagutierre Soto-Mayor, J. (1933). *Historia de la conquista de la provincia de el Itzá*, 2nd ed. Guatemala City: Sociedad de Geografía e Historia. (Orginally published in Madrid in 1701)

13 Essentialist beliefs in children: The acquisition of concepts and theories

Susan A. Gelman, John D. Coley, and Gail M. Gottfried

In their first few years of life, children are making sense of the world at two levels at once: at the fine-grained level of everyday object categories (deciding which things are trees and which are dogs and which are cookies), and at a broader level that some have called commonsense "theories." Both are remarkable achievements. First, consider categorization. If children's vocabulary is any indication, by the age of 6 they have carved up the world into thousands of distinct categories (Carey, 1978). Many children undergo a vocabulary "explosion" at roughly 18 months of age (Halliday, 1975; McShane, 1980; Nelson, 1973), when the rate of acquisition suddenly rises exponentially. One child studied in detail by Dromi (1987) produced as many as 44 new words in one week, and roughly 340 new words in her first 7 months of speech. No other species acquires symbolic communication at this rate. Even studies that successfully teach apes to acquire sizeable vocabularies in sign language are incomparable, with no noticeable vocabulary explosion (e.g., after more than 4 years of exposure to sign language, Washoe acquired only about 132 signs; Gardner & Gardner, 1989).

At around the same time that children learn to classify individual entities and undergo rapid vocabulary growth, they are developing broad systems of belief about the world. Not only do children learn to identify certain objects as "dogs," but they also learn that dogs belong to the class of animals, and that animals engage in characteristic biological processes such as growth, inheritance, and self-generated movement. Children are learning about physical laws such as gravity, mental states such as dreams, and social relationships within units such as families. They are learning where things come from, how things change over time, what causes an event to occur, and why. These belief systems include understanding causal relations, and they allow children to make predictions and provide explanations.

The writing of this paper was supported by NSF grant 91-00348 to S. Gelman. We thank Larry Hirschfeld for his helpful comments on an earlier draft.

We believe that these two developments are not independent – that in fact, they go hand-in-hand. Children's concepts are embedded in larger structures that resemble theories (see also Carey, 1985). In this chapter we illustrate the point with the domain of living things. There are two motivations for examining this domain. First, young children are fascinated by living things (especially animals) and devote considerable attention to them. Even infants pay special attention to things that move on their own (Poulin-Dubois & Shultz, 1990), and animal terms typically constitute a sizeable portion of children's early vocabulary (Nelson, 1973). If we assume that children are most likely to build theories about objects of great interest, then the domain of living things is a likely place to look for theorylike beliefs. Second, living things figure prominently in debates concerning the domain specificity of children's thought (see Keil, this volume; Carey & Spelke, this volume; Atran, this volume). It is unclear whether biology constitutes a separate domain for young children, and if so what form it takes. Thus, a close examination of children's theories of living things may provide additional information on this issue.

The structure of the chapter is as follows. First we outline some properties of commonsense theories. Then we present a variety of studies suggesting that children appeal to something like theories when reasoning about living things. We advance the notion of "psychological essentialism" (Medin, 1989) to characterize the results of these studies, which examine children's beliefs about causal mechanisms, innate potential, and maintenance of identity over transformations. Finally we consider alternative accounts of these data, and conclude that children appeal to theorylike entities that may derive from domain-general expectations.

What is a theory?

Everyday thought is theorylike, in the sense that people make use of unobservable, causal-explanatory constructs (see also Carey, 1985; Gopnik & Wellman, in press, for discussion). We distinguish between a commonsense or folk theory and a scientific theory (see also Brewer & Samarapungavan, 1991; Carey, 1985; Gopnik & Wellman, this volume; Kaiser, McCloskey, & Proffitt, 1986; Karmiloff-Smith & Inhelder, 1975; Keil, 1989; McCloskey, 1983; Murphy & Medin, 1985). A commonsense theory does not entail the detailed, explicit, formal understanding that Ph.D. biologists or physicists have.[1] People's beliefs seem to lack the coherence and systematicity typically associated with scientific theories (diSessa, 1988). Even when people have implicit understanding of a theoretical principle, they may be poor at stating that principle explicitly. And even when a hypothesis is strongly held, people seldom conduct rigorous or adequate experiments to test their hypotheses (Wason, 1960). In ordinary circumstances, people rarely engage in hypothetico-deductive reasoning (Shaklee, 1979).

Nonetheless, adult thought is theorylike in its appeal to domain-specific causal laws. For example, we believe that if one marble collides with another, it will cause the second marble to move; or that releasing a pebble from a height will cause it to fall. These mechanical cause/effect relations operate on physical objects only; mental states cannot be described in the same terms. Conversely, the laws of reinforcement apply only to entities capable of psychological processes (e.g., people, dogs), not to objects in the domain of physics. Biology, too, has its own laws relating to eating, breathing, inheritance, growth, and so on.

In order to account for these causal relations, people invent powerful, unobservable constructs. In the preceding physical examples, we appeal to force and energy to explain why one object causes another to move; we appeal to gravitational forces to explain why an object falls from a height. In psychology we refer to beliefs and desires. For living things we refer to genetic dispositions and innate potential. Force, gravity, beliefs, desires, and genes are not visible or easily measured. They are constructions designed to explain events that we *can* see.

People's tendency to create explanatory constructs can lead us to classify together entities that have salient differences but share *theory-relevant properties*. For example, adults generally classify plants and animals together into a category of living things, largely because we believe that both plants and animals grow, need water, reproduce, and have the ability to heal themselves (Backscheider, Shatz, & Gelman, in press; Hickling & Gelman, 1992). Furthermore, adults sometimes refrain from classifying together things that seem superficially the same but differ in theory-relevant properties. In one such theory-based decision, adults exclude whales from the category of fish; although the two animals have similar appearances and habitats, there are important differences in underlying features such as breathing ability and blood temperature. Thus, theory-based classification is available to adults in our culture.

It is important to raise two additional issues that bear on theory-based categories. First, not all categories have this form – a point to which we return in the section, "How domain-specific are essences?" (cf. discussion in Markman, 1989). Second, classifications that appear theory-based are not always a direct consequence of theories. Specifically, people (especially children) may sometimes learn the "theory-based" classification before they learn the theory. For example, they may learn that whales are not fish before they learn that whales can't breathe underwater, have warm blood, and bear live young. Learning that whales are not fish may even encourage a child to search for underlying differences between the two.

In this chapter we examine theorylike beliefs by discussing the unobservable constructs children invoke to account for biological properties and events. In particular, we focus on what Medin (1989; Medin & Ortony, 1989) calls "psychological essentialism."

Essentialism

Psychological essentialism is the idea that people have an implicit assumption about the structure of the world and how it is represented in our categories. Specifically, people seem to assume that categories of things in the world have a true, underlying nature that imparts category identity.[2] People's assumption has two parts: (1) that the world has a natural order that is independent of the observer (a realist assumption), and (2) that categories – and words referring to categories, such as common nouns – map onto that structure. On this view, categories are discovered rather than arbitrary or invented; they carve up nature at its joints. The underlying nature, or category *essence*, is thought to be the causal mechanism that results in those properties that we can see. For example, the essence of tigers causes them to grow as they do – to have stripes, large size, capacity to roar, and so forth. It is important to keep in mind that in discussing essentialism, we are endorsing a psychological claim about people's beliefs, not a metaphysical claim about the world (see also Medin & Ortony, 1989).

Essences are predictive of, but distinct from, more obvious or observable features (Gelman & Medin, 1993; but see Jones & Smith, 1993, for an alternative view). Surface features are correlated with and provide good clues about category membership (e.g., wings, feathers, and flight of a bird). Yet this information is fallible (not all birds have these features; some nonbirds do). In contrast, the essence may not be immediately observable, yet it is important because it determines category identity. It can be thought of as an unseen quality that is responsible for the observable features that hold together a category. Medin (1989) describes the essence as follows:

People act as if things (e.g., objects) have essences or underlying natures that make them the thing that they are. Furthermore, the essence constrains or generates properties that may vary in their centrality. One of the things that theories do is to embody or provide causal linkages from deeper properties to more superficial or surface properties. (p. 1476)

Recently, several theorists have argued, independently, that an essentialist assumption is extremely common among adults. Atran (1990; this volume) reports that essentialist beliefs can be found across widely varying cultures. Mayr (1988) traced essentialist arguments back hundreds of years and proposed that a belief that an unchanging essence determines category membership was one of the biggest obstacles to grasping evolutionary theory. Although indirect evidence suggests that an essentialist stance is prevalent among adults in our culture, the idea has received surprisingly little direct confirmation.

Where does essentialism come from? Is it a basic human assumption, or simply a by-product of our culture and modern-day science? One way to investigate the issue is to study young children, who have not yet been exposed to formal scientific training. They are not taught about DNA or molecules in nursery school, and parents rarely talk about the molecular and genetic distinctions between different species of plants or animals. Furthermore, years of experimentation have documented that children are especially attentive to surface appearances (Flavell, 1977). On many tasks children have difficulty looking beyond the most superficial cues (cf. Piaget's conservation task, in which children below age 6 or 7 fail to appreciate that the quantity of a liquid is unchanged as a result of pouring the liquid into a differently shaped container). If children assume the existence of nonobvious entities, and furthermore assume that such hidden entities can be critical to an object's identity, then we can infer that an essentialist assumption is powerful and basic.

There is already reason to suspect that children may be essentialists. To begin with, evidence is growing that children assume that events are caused (*causal determinism*; A. Brown, 1990; Bullock, Gelman, & Baillargeon, 1982; Gelman & Kalish, 1993). Studies with infants indicate that they seem surprised when viewing events with no apparent cause (Baillargeon, 1993). By preschool age, when children view an event that appears to violate known causal laws (e.g., a screen passing through a box), they attempt to dismantle the apparatus, apparently in search of a hidden causal mechanism (Chandler & Lalonde, in press). Furthermore, children have surprising difficulty grasping random phenomena. Piaget and Inhelder (1975) showed children random devices such as spinners, and found that the youngest children often insisted that they could predict where the pointer would fall. The same kind of pattern is found when children are asked to explain adverse events, such as someone falling ill. Children tend to blame the illness on the victim himself or herself, rather than allow that it happened randomly, an explanation known as "immanent justice" (Karniol, 1980; Kister & Patterson, 1980; Piaget, 1948; White, Elsom, & Prawat, 1978). In all these examples, causal determinism refers to events, but it could as easily refer to properties of objects. That is, children may reason causally not only about events such as falling ill, but also about object features, such as the spots on a giraffe or the ability of a rabbit to hop.

If children do assume causal determinism, then essentialism could be just one step away. That is, upon viewing events or features with no observable cause, children may impute internal, nonobvious, or invisible cause. This would be a way of resolving the apparent contradiction between no visible cause and the need for all events to be caused. Bringing in a hidden cause need not be a conscious or explicit strategy; rather, it may naturally follow from the assumption of causal determinism in such situations. Thus, it is at least plausible that essentialist reasoning is present even from earliest childhood.

What counts as evidence of essentialism?

People may believe that a category has an underlying essence even if they believe they will never know what it is. Using Medin's terminology, they have an essence placeholder. We reason about categories *as if* they have an essence, even while the specifics of the essence are unknown or unknowable. One practical consequence is that it is difficult to find direct evidence of essentialism.

Simply forming a category is insufficient evidence for belief in an essence. At least in principle, one can form complex biological concepts without assuming essences. Pigeons appear able to classify *trees* or *fish* quite accurately on experimental tasks (Herrnstein, Loveland, & Cable, 1976), yet presumably pigeons don't assume essences. In a sense, then, the question is whether biological concepts (e.g., "tree," "dog") take a different form in young children versus pigeons.

We describe various kinds of evidence that are consistent with, and may provide some support for, psychological essentialism: (1) *Explicit articulation of an essentialist philosophy*. This type of evidence is the most direct, but least likely to be found – especially in young children, who are notoriously inarticulate when it comes to explaining their own reasoning processes. (2) *Appeal to invisible causal mechanisms*. An essentialist assumption may emerge as a reference to an unseen entity or quality that is intrinsic to an object, and causes surface features. For example, among educated adults in the United States, DNA is believed to be unseen (by the naked eye), intrinsic to an organism, and possessing the power to determine changes that occur via growth. (3) *Assumption of innate dispositions or potential*. People may refer to inborn capacities, presumably determined by the object's essential nature, that emerge later in life. For example, the human child is believed to have innate potential that is causally responsible for the development of crawling, walking, and language. (4) *Unalterability, or maintenance of identity over superficial transformations*. A belief in essences leads to a belief in unchanging category membership, even in the face of certain dramatic changes in observable properties (i.e., an assumption of unalterability; see Rothbart & Taylor, in press). For example, essentialism would support the belief that an animal should retain membership in a category despite growth, metamorphosis, or plastic surgery that greatly alters its appearance. (5) *Inductive potential*. If we assume that category members share an essence, then we can also assume that this essence leads to deep or unlimited commonalities among category members. For example, given an essentialist bias, giraffes would be assumed to be alike with respect to internal organs, skeletal structure, body temperature, means of nurturing their young, life expectancy, speed of locomotion, and so on. (6) *Taxonomies*. Atran (1990) proposes that evidence for essences can be found in consensus about the taxonomy within which categories fall, "despite obvious variation" among category members (pp. 6, 62). This may be the least direct of the various kinds of evidence, because of the assumptions it makes about taxonomies (which are debatable; see Collins & Loftus, 1975; Hampton, 1982) and their origins.

Combining any of the above pieces of evidence should provide even stronger evidence. For example, if one appeals to an invisible causal mechanism that is unalterable, produces unlimited commonalities (not just one effect), and commonalities that hold among all category members despite superficial differences, then we would have more compelling evidence for psychological essentialism.

In the following sections we review evidence for three of the more direct kinds of evidence for essentialism: appeal to invisible causal mechanisms, assumption of innate potential, and maintenance of identity over superficial transformations.

Causal explanations

A critical aspect of essences is their causal force. Locke (1894/1959) talks about the essence as the causal mechanism that gives rise to those properties that we can see. If children are essentialists, they should search for underlying causes that result in observable features (e.g., assuming some underlying nature that causes category members to be alike). "Features" include not only perceptual appearances, but also behaviors and/or events that are shared by category members. For example, the essence of a tiger causes it to have stripes, large size, capacity to roar, and the like. As mentioned earlier, there is some hint in the literature that children may assume that events are caused. There is also evidence that, when explaining events with no observable cause, children appeal to underlying causes (Shultz, 1982). For example, upon viewing a radiometer (a device that spins when light is beamed on it), children as young as 4 years of age typically said "yes" when asked if there was "some invisible thing that goes from the light to the propeller." How powerful is this assumption of underlying cause, and does it apply more for some domains than others?

We have conducted a study of children's causal explanations to examine whether children view underlying nature as causing natural events to occur (Gelman & Gottfried, 1993). Four-year-old children viewed brief videotapes in which actual animals and objects moved across a surface. All the items were unfamiliar, to ensure that responses did not simply reflect specific experiences with these particular objects, either direct observations or statements made by more knowledgeable others. After viewing each event, subjects were asked to make two judgments about causal mechanisms, an External Cause judgment ("Did a person make this move?") and an Internal Cause judgment ("Did something inside this make it move?"). In addition, children were asked to make an Immanent Cause judgment ("Did this move by itself?"). We also encouraged children to justify their responses after every question.

To determine whether children's judgments vary as a result of the ontological status of an object, the moving objects were chosen from three distinct categories: animals (e.g., chinchilla), wind-up toys (e.g., wind-up toy sushi), and transparent artifacts (e.g., plastic pepper mill). Children were randomly assigned to one of two conditions that differed in the kinds of events presented. In the Baseline condition (also known as the Carried condition), all objects were pushed or carried by a person, whose hand was always visible on the videotape. Here, children should appeal to external cause, reporting that a person made all the objects move. In the second condition (referred to as the Alone condition), the objects started at a standstill and moved without any apparent human intervention.[3] In this condition, we predicted that children should resist external explanations and more consistently appeal to inherent, internal causes. That is, because no person was visible and the object's motion appeared to be self-generated, children were expected to impute an internal cause (Gelman & Kremer, 1991). This finding would provide evidence for a belief that an underlying essence caused the object to move.

Of interest is whether inferences about internal cause would be equally strong for the three kinds of objects. Past research has suggested that an assumption of internal cause should be powerful for animals (Massey & Gelman, 1988); it is unclear whether the same applies for artifacts, which typically move as the result of human agents. The transparent artifacts provide the strongest test of children's belief that events without obvious external cause are internally or inherently caused. Because the children viewed transparent objects moving by themselves and could see that nothing was inside the objects, there was a potential conflict between the assumption of internal cause and the evidence provided by the children's own eyes. Only if the internal cause assumption is very strong would it override the visual evidence.

Children's responses to the causal mechanism questions ("Did a person make this move?" "Did something inside this make it move?") were clearly different for the animals and artifacts. For the wind-up toys and transparent artifacts in the Baseline (Carried) condition, children were much more likely to attribute the cause of motion to a person than to anything inside. With animals, however, the pattern is reversed. Children regularly denied that a person made the animals move. This result is striking, given that the animals were carried and that the person's hand was visible throughout the event.

When the object appeared to be moving alone (Alone condition), children were less likely to claim that a person caused the movement. Rather, they claimed that something inside the item made it move. Interestingly, children displayed this pattern not only for the animals but also for the artifacts, including the transparent ones. That many children attributed internal mechanisms to transparent objects with no apparent insides shows the strength of their belief that internal mechanisms cause objects to move on their own.

Children's responses to the immanent cause question showed the same pattern as the internal cause question, only more dramatically. Over 90% of the children in each condition claimed that the animals moved by themselves. Even when a person bodily carried the animal from one end of the screen to the other, children insisted that the animal itself was responsible (e.g., one child responded for each of the animals, "It wasn't [intended] *for* moving with a person"). For toys and transparent artifacts, only children in the Alone condition said the objects moved by themselves. The absence of an external agent led them to endorse immanent cause.

It is somewhat misleading to look only at children's yes–no responses to the question, "Did it move by itself?" When children responded that an object moved by itself, they could simply have been reporting their observations, rather than implying any particular cause. In other words, "It moved by itself" could be equivalent to claiming that a person did not make it move. However, an analysis of children's explanations for how the objects moved by themselves shows that children provided causal mechanisms that were distinct to the domain of the object.

The children seemed to have particular difficulty explaining the artifact events. On average, children said that they just didn't know how it moved or that some supernatural agent was involved, about 5 times more often for artifacts (toy or transparent) than for animals. Of the more interpretable responses, children primarily used two kinds of justifications not found with animals. First, they often mentioned a person as an agent. Even though they saw on the videotape that the item started from a standstill and moved on its own, they mentioned some person winding up, pushing, or moving the object. The second response was to refer to other natural causes that were not inherent to the object per se, such as electricity, batteries, or magnets. Children even occasionally tried to reconcile their judgments with what they saw on the video: One child suggested there were "invisible batteries" making a transparent artifact move, and one suggested that an "invisible person" made a wind-up toy move.

For the animals, children's justifications were nearly always coherent. The children never referred to an external agent, as they did with the artifacts. Rather, 93% of the codable justifications referred to properties intrinsic to the animal, such as its bones or other parts. The children also occasionally claimed that the animal caused itself to move, with justifications such as, "Because he makes it move himself" or "Only itself can do it." Although children claim that all the objects move by themselves, how they resolve the question of causal mechanism differs sharply by ontological category.

The results of this study show that when children cannot find an external cause, they invoke one that is internal or immanent. Interestingly, children invoke *internal* cause for animals and equally for both opaque and transparent artifacts, but they consistently deny any *external* cause to explain the biological events, even when a human bodily carries the animal. Rather, biological events are viewed as resulting from immanent cause. Children regularly appeal to intrinsic factors even without knowing the internal mechanism (e.g., responding "it just did it itself"). Thus, children seem to be displaying a belief in some underlying causal mechanism, without knowing exactly what that mechanism entails.

Innate potential

A second possible indication of essentialism is belief in innate potential, that a set of characteristics will unfold with maturation, even though they show no sign at birth. For example, a lion cub has the potential to grow into something large and fierce, even though when it is born it is small and helpless. The fact that such characteristic attributes emerge so predictably suggests that the individual possesses nonobvious, intrinsic qualities. To explain developmental changes like this, we as adults might say that lions have an essential nature that is responsible for how they grow.

To test whether preschool children have an idea of innate potential, Gelman and Wellman (1991) conducted a study that can be thought of as pitting nature against nurture. On each of a series of items, 4-year-old children learned about a baby animal that was raised among members of a different species, in an environment more suited to the adoptive species. We attempted to describe the environment as an interactive, nurturing one, in order to increase the plausibility that the environment could exert important effects. Thus, in each scenario, the adopting species were said to "take care of" the adopted animal. Also, every picture of the adopting species contained a mixed-age, familylike grouping. The main issue was what children predicted about the animal's appearance and behavior, after it reached maturity. Would it show the potentialities inherent in its category membership, or would it display the properties one would expect from its environment?

For example, children first saw a picture of a baby kangaroo that looked like a nondescript little blob of an animal. They learned that the baby kangaroo was taken to a goat farm when she was a baby, and raised by goats. Then they saw a picture of the goat farm (4 adult goats and 2 kids). We stressed that the baby grew up without ever seeing another kangaroo.

Both pictures – of the baby and of the contrasting environment – remained in view while children were asked two questions about how the animal would be after it grew up. In this case they heard, (1) Was she good at hopping or good at climbing? (2) Did she have a pouch or was she without a pouch? We pretested all the properties, to make sure that children of this age could answer them correctly when there was no conflict – for example, they said that goats are good at climbing and don't have a pouch.

The results are as follows. Children nearly always answered on the basis of category membership or innate potential. For example, they said that a baby kangaroo raised among goats will grow up to hop and have a pouch. Children were not just reporting associations to the category label (for example, saying "pouch" as an unthinking response to "kangaroo"), because they were sensitive to question type. Children relied more on innate potential when the question concerned a behavior (for example, what noise a cow will make) than when it concerned a static property (for example, whether a cow will have a straight tail). If children were simply reporting associations with the category label, there should have been no difference between behaviors and properties.

However, we wanted to obtain more direct evidence that children were not simply reporting category associations. We conducted two additional studies on the issue. In one study, we asked children about the properties of baby animals.[4] For example, we asked the children whether or not the kangaroo, when it was a baby, had a pouch or could hop. If children were simply reporting category associates, they should report that the baby kangaroo has all the properties of the adult kangaroo. However, if children were considering the particulars of the individual animal, then they should say that the baby kangaroo does not yet possess its full adult properties. In addition, we included inherent properties (e.g., did it have eyes?) and impossible properties (e.g., did it have wings?) as baseline control questions.

Results showed that the children attributed the behavioral properties to the babies as often as the intrinsic properties, suggesting a possible tendency to report category associates for questions about behavior. However, children generally reported that the babies did not have the physical features of the adult animal (e.g., the pouch). Thus, children do not simply report category-associated properties upon hearing questions about category members. Furthermore, the data converge to suggest a stronger understanding of innate potential: Animals will develop properties that they don't yet possess as infants, despite being raised in an unusual environment with no same-species cohort.

Gelman and Wellman (1991) also conducted a "nature-nurture" study with seeds. For example, children saw a seed that came from an apple and was planted in a flowerpot. The test question was, "When that seed grew, what popped up out of the ground? Was it an apple tree or a flower?" Children saw pictures of the seed and of the environment (e.g., apple seed, flowerpot). Seeds provide a strong control for children's tendency to report category associates, because specifying the origin of a seed does not entail stating its category identity (e.g., "comes from an apple" differs from its original identity of "apple seed" and its future identity of "apple tree"). In addition, a seed looks nothing like its eventual endstate (plant or tree). Finally, the use of seeds allows us to examine a very different kind of parent–offspring relationship, in which characteristics cannot be transmitted by means of modeling, reinforcement, or training. Results of this study showed that 58% of the younger 4-year-olds and 92% of the older 4-year-olds answered primarily on the basis of innate potential. The mixed performance of the young 4-year-olds appears to be due to a less-developed understanding of the relation between seeds and plants at that age (Hickling & Gelman, 1992). Nonetheless, it is striking that most of the children consistently reported that a seed has the innate potential to develop in accordance with the parent species. Four-year-old children act like essentialists. They assume that members of a category share an innate potential, and that innate potential can overcome a powerful environment.

Maintenance of identity

An underlying essence would allow individuals to undergo marked change yet retain their identity. We know that adults in our culture believe that radical changes, such as metamorphosis, are possible (Rips, 1989). Furthermore, Keil (1989) has shown that second graders (though not preschoolers) realize that animals but not artifacts can maintain identity over such transformations. Children were shown pictures of animals, then told about transformations performed by doctors that changed the characteristic features of the animal into those of another animal. For example, a tiger had its fur bleached and a mane sewed on, so that it now resembled a lion. Children were then asked whether the posttransformation animal was a lion or a tiger. Second and fourth graders maintained that the identity would not change. This finding implies an early-developing belief that animals, but not artifacts, possess essences that are responsible for maintenance of identity.

Work with younger children demonstrates a similar kind of understanding. Gelman and Wellman (1991) used a paradigm very similar to that of Keil (1989), but with simpler transformations: Each item had either its "insides" or its "outsides" removed. Test items were selected to be clear-cut examples (for adults) of objects for which insides, but not outsides, are essential. For example, blood is more important than fur to a dog; the engine of a car is more important than the paint. As a control, we also selected a set of items for which the insides are not integral parts (e.g., a jar, a refrigerator).

Gelman and Wellman asked 4- and 5-year-old children to consider three transformations: (1) removal of insides (e.g., "What if you take out the stuff inside of the dog, you know, the blood and bones and things like that, and got rid of it and all you have left are the outsides?"); (2) removal of outsides (e.g., "What if you take off the stuff outside of the dog, you know, the fur, and got rid of it and all you have left are the insides?"); (3) movement (e.g., "What if the dog stands up?") as a control. For each transformation, children heard two questions: (1) identity ("Is it still a dog?"), and (2) function ("Can it still bark and eat dog food?").

The results from every test item indicate that children say that if you remove the *insides*, the identity and function of an object will change. Not so for the outsides, even when removing them would sharply change the object's appearance. As predicted, the children correctly reported that the identity of the containers (e.g., refrigerator) would not change if the insides were removed.

An additional series of studies by Rosengren, Gelman, Kalish, and McCormick (1991) examines children's understanding of maintenance of identity, using the natural biological transformation of growth. Rosengren et al. reasoned that an important piece that may be missing from past research is what *mechanism* is underlying the change. In other words, children may be sensitive to whether the mechanism is a natural biological transformation or one that defies biological laws. The implication is that, even though children report that some transformations lead to identity change, they may realize that natural transformations (such as growth) do not.

Rosengren et al. conducted a series of experiments demonstrating that children as young as 3 years of age expect animals to undergo changes over time (via growth) without affecting identity, that children believe that such changes are strongly constrained (e.g., one can only get bigger not smaller over time), and that these changes are specific to the domain of living things. For example, 3-year-olds, 5-year-olds, and adults were shown a picture of an animal and told, "Here is a picture of Sally when Sally was a baby. Now Sally is an adult." They were then shown two pictures: one identical to the original and one the same but larger, and were asked which was a picture of Sally "as an adult." At all age groups, subjects tended to choose the larger picture, showing that they expected the object to undergo change in size with growth.

By 5 years of age, children realize that growth is inevitable. For example, in another condition children saw a picture of a juvenile of a species that undergoes radical metamorphosis (such as a caterpillar). They then saw a picture of the same creature, only smaller (e.g., a smaller caterpillar), and a picture of a larger animal differing in shape (e.g., a moth). Again, subjects were asked to choose which picture represented the animal after it became an adult. Three-year-olds were at chance, but 5-year-olds chose the metamorphosized animal significantly above chance levels. By the age of 5 years, then, children believe that an individual can naturally undergo even substantial shape changes over time.

These data are demonstrational. The studies conducted by Gelman and Wellman (1991) and by Keil (1989) show that children realize that sometimes, the features most critical to an object's identity may be internal and nonobvious. The experiments of Rosengren et al. (1991) demonstrate maintenance of identity over changes wrought by growth. In both cases, children endorse the possibility that objects have important underlying properties.

Other evidence

A variety of additional studies also provide evidence consistent with an essentialist bias. On these tasks, subjects reveal that they look beyond surface similarity when reasoning about categories. Two and one-half-year-old children appreciate that animal categories support inductive inferences regarding familiar properties (Gelman & Coley, 1990), and 3- and 4-year-olds use categories (animals, plants, substances, and artifacts) to guide inferences about novel properties (Gelman, 1988; Gelman & Markman, 1986, 1987). Four-year-old children also appreciate the importance of internal, intrinsic causal mechanisms for living things and artifacts. For example, children report that a bird flies because of its heart and muscles, that a car moves uphill because of its motor, and that a flower blooms on its own (Gelman & Kremer, 1991; see also Gelman, 1990). Children also realize that human intervention has limited effects in the natural world (Gelman & Kremer, 1991). By age 5 years, children recognize that some underlying properties of animals, such as insides, can be predictive of an animal's surface appearance (Backscheider, Coley, & Gutheil, 1991). The common thread running through all these findings is that children attribute unseen constructs to account for observable phenomena. See Gelman and Coley (1991) for a more detailed review of these lines of evidence.

Alternative explanations

The studies reviewed in this chapter do not provide direct evidence for psychological essentialism. They do, however, strongly suggest that children appeal to invisible causal mechanisms, assume innate potential, maintain identity over superficial transformations, and assume unlimited commonalities among category members when they reason about objects. Although not constituting unambiguous evidence for essentialism, these studies do allow us to rule out several competing explanations.

The first, most obvious point is that children's judgments do not simply reflect reliance on perceptual similarity. For example, maintenance of identity over superficial transformations requires overlooking appearances (e.g., perceptual similarity alone would not predict that a caterpillar can become a butterfly). Although appearances are important, preschoolers can go beyond them.

Second, children are not simply reporting observations from past experience. It is unlikely that children can *perceive* essences, because many biologists and philosophers insist that animal species do not have essences (Mayr, 1988). Furthermore, experience alone does not present inheritance mechanisms or immanent causation as observable entities. Experience also would not be sufficient to account for the systematic errors that children make (cf. Taylor & Gelman, 1991, in which children reported that gender-role properties are innately determined).

Finally, children are not explicitly taught an essentialist philosophy. In fact, considering the input, it is remarkable that children hold any consistent set of beliefs. Children hear stories in which princes turn into frogs, people become statues, and elephants hatch out of bird eggs. Even in ordinary language, biological concepts – concerning disease, growth, or genetic relationships – leak over into other domains (computer viruses, sick jokes, dying cars, grandfather clocks, fabrics that breathe, a growing national debt). Still, it may be that these uses are marked in some way as figurative or fictional. To provide a fair look at the issue, we need to see how parents discuss biological concepts in ordinary speech.

We recently gathered data on parental input to 20- and 36-month-olds (Gelman, Coley, Rosengren, Hartman, & Pappas, 1993). Thirty-two mothers and their children came into our laboratory and looked through two books together, one with scenes of animals and the other with scenes of artifacts. We created the books so that they would be as similar as possible in every way except for the objects shown on each page. Every page included objects in which appearances were potentially misleading, as we thought it might prompt parents to talk about nonobvious ways that categories are constructed. For example, on one page parents saw a scene with two bats, a blackbird, and a cave.

We videotaped the sessions and then analyzed the verbal transcripts and both parent and child gestures for any mention or reference to categories. We were especially interested in talk about anything that might be construed as an essence.

We found that, although parents placed great emphasis on categories, frequently pointing out category relations and similarity among category members, they rarely mentioned nonobvious features such as insides, innate potential, origins, or essences. For example, only one mother of the 20-month-olds (out of 16) discussed insides at all, and she made only one mention; origins were never discussed in this age group. Among mothers of the 36-month-olds, insides were mentioned a total of 9 times, with 8 of the 9 mentions referring to the insides of artifacts. In other words, on average only 10 out of 4,372 codable utterances (0.2%) concerned insides. Origins were mentioned a total of 3 times, meaning that on average only about 0.07% of codable utterances yielded discussion of origins. Thus, overt discussion of biological essences was vanishingly rare, even in a sample that was highly educated and motivated.

It seems, then, that children's belief in the importance of nonobvious properties cannot be attributed to what they are directly taught by parents. Neither can it be "read off" their experiences of the physical world, nor reduced to a general similarity bias. Essentialism is not directly available in either the physical environment or the parental input.

How domain-specific are essences?

An essentialist stance appears to describe a variety of concepts, not only within the biological realm (as illustrated earlier; see also Mayr, 1991; Atran, 1990), but also including the following domains (although the authors cited do not always interpret their findings as evidence of essentialism): beliefs about ethnicity (Rothbart & Taylor, in press; Stoler, 1992, in press), personality traits (Yuill, 1992); race and occupation (Hirschfeld, this volume); gender (Gelman, Collman, & Maccoby, 1986; Taylor & Gelman, 1991); the workings of the mind (Wellman, 1990); social attributions (Hilton, 1992); and perhaps physical causality (Shultz, 1982). We illustrate this point with traits.

Yuill (1992) proposes that a trait such as generosity does not merely describe a cluster of related behaviors (sharing, helping, etc.), but rather is an inner quality that *causes* one to demonstrate these behaviors. The link between an overt behavior and the trait that explains it is analogous to the link between a biological structure or process and the essence that causes it (Gelman, 1992). Just as the trait of shyness can cause a person to avoid large parties, so does the essence of a panda cause it to have black-and-white fur and to eat bamboo. The person and the panda are each hypothesized to have an underlying quality (shyness or panda genes, respectively) that gives rise to certain observable properties as well as other, less obvious ones (beliefs and desires in one case; biological structures and processes in the other).

Confronted with this variety of essentialist thinking, some scholars have proposed that an essentialist assumption is domain-general (Medin, 1989). Mayr (1991: 41) implies a similar position:

Essentialism's influence was great in part because its principle is anchored in our language, in our use of a single noun in the singular to designate highly variable phenomena of our environment, such as mountain, home, water, horse, or honesty. Even though there is great variety in kinds of mountain and kinds of home, and even though the kinds do not stand in direct relation to one another (as do the members of a species), the simple noun defines the class of objects.

Yet proposing an entirely domain-general essentialist assumption is on the face of it somewhat problematic: What is the evidence for adherence to underlying causal properties for wastebaskets? Indeed, Keil (1989) provides ample evidence that natural kinds are more likely than artifacts to be treated as having essences, even by the second grade. Similarly, Gelman (1988; Gelman & O'Reilly, 1988) finds that the inductive potential of animal categories is greater than that of artifact categories, suggesting that animal kinds are assumed to have a more tightly knit causal structure. The results from the Gelman and Gottfried study (1993) also revealed distinct differences in children's explanations of animate versus inanimate motion, even when the source of visible movement was equated. Thus, a wholly domain-general essentialist assumption seems problematic.

Specifying the exact nature of the proposed essentialist bias requires explaining this pattern of broad but not boundless applicability. There are at least four potential classes of explanation: (1) borrowing from a base domain, (2) domain specificity in a broad, undifferentiated domain, (3) multiple domain-specific notions, and (4) domain generality with different, domain-specific instantiations. We favor the last possibility, although all four are worthy of serious consideration.

Borrowing from a base domain

First, it may be that essentialism begins as a domain-specific assumption, which is then analogized to other domains. This possibility requires that there is a base domain to which essentialism applies most readily or naturally. Biology is one candidate for such a basic essentialist domain (Atran, 1990), from which the essentialist stance may be extended, by analogy, to other domains. This model is what Hirschfeld (this volume) refers to as the "naturalization" model (see also Atran, Boyer, this volume, for supporting arguments).

Whether biology is the most plausible base domain is an open question. The evidence we have detailed here suggests that biological kinds appear to have essences for very young children. Additionally, biological essences appear to be universally assumed (Atran, 1990), whereas other sorts of essences, such as traits, may not be (Yuill, 1992). However, the domain of social interactions may also form the base. Dwyer (1976: 433) suggests that, for the Rofaifo (a group of people living in the Papua New Guinea Highlands), "species ... in my interpretation, share an essence which is abstracted from human social structure.... This essence approximates symbolically, though it is not standardly labeled as such, a lineage (or kin descent group)."

One advantage to the naturalization model is that, because analogies are imperfect, it predicts some variation in how essentialism is instantiated. Indeed, some important differences do emerge between different views of essences. For example, psychological traits can be altered; biological essences are immutable. Essences always have some outward manifestation (no matter how subtle); traits apparently need not. Essences hold true for all members of a category and so concern *category* identity, whereas traits distinguish people from one another and so concern *individual* identity. The naturalization model handles this variation by positing that traits only resemble essences – they are not equivalent.

A problem we have with this view is that it would require the analogizing to take place extremely early in development. Even preschool children have many kinds of categories that appear to have essences, including biological, psychological, and social categories. For example, Taylor and Gelman (1991) found that children are *more* likely than adults to apply an essentialist model to categories of gender (e.g., boy, girl). If essentialism is generalized so rapidly and widely with so little instruction, it calls into question what a domain is, and how useful or appropriate a domain-specific approach is.

Domain specificity within a broad domain

A second possible approach is to posit that essentialism is domain-specific, but that early in development children's domains are relatively undifferentiated and broader than those of adults. For example, children may have an undifferentiated domain of social things, in which are lumped together things that for the adult will be differentiated into biology, psychology, and social interaction (Carey, 1985). Or, children may have an undifferentiated domain of biological things, in which sex, occupation, race, caste, and ethnicity are lumped.[5] That is, distinctions that for the adult are eventually viewed as social constructions could be believed to be biological categories by children. The plausibility of this position rests in part on how broadly children assume essences. If the assumption extends to physical causality as well as psychological and social causality, then the "broad domain" position is less compelling. The plausibility also rests on the contention that children fail to differentiate among biology, psychology, and social convention, a matter of current debate (Carey, 1985; Inagaki & Hatano, 1988).

Multiple domain-specific essences

Another way to resolve the issue of broad but not unbounded essentialism is to posit multiple domain-specific notions of essentialism. On this view, different kinds of categories (living kinds, social kinds) are independently imbued with their own kind of essence. This explanation receives some compelling support (see Hirschfeld, this volume), although its plausibility would be limited if too many distinct kinds of essences were discovered. That is, it would be unparsimonious to propose one kind of essence to explain children's appeal to invisible causal forces such as wishes, thoughts, and desires as demonstrated in theory of mind research, another kind of essence to explain children's appeal to invisible causal forces in physics, a third to explain children's appeal to invisible causal forces in biology, and a fourth to explain children's appeal to invisible causal forces in the social realm. The plausibility of this approach may rest in its ability to incorporate these varied findings.

Domain generality with domain-specific instantiations

A final possibility is that essentialism is a domain-general assumption, but one that gets invoked differently in different domains, responding to the causal structure of each domain. On this view, the assumption of essences is a general one and so readily applies to new domains that have never before been encountered (e.g., viruses, computers). However, it does not sensibly apply to all domains. The analogy we have in mind is that an essentialist assumption is like a hammer. A hammer is not specifically restricted for use with nails, and can be used with a variety of other objects as well (e.g., screws, staples). Nonetheless, the hammer is designed to fit best with nails or naillike objects, and cannot be used to drive all objects (including books and hats) into walls or boards. Similarly, an essentialist assumption may be "designed" in such a way that it functions only when it meets domains with the appropriate features.

On this fourth view, essentialism would have to begin at a level of generality sufficient to encompass beliefs about traits, biological essences, beliefs and desires, race and gender, and any other categories that children treat as having essences. Children's assumptions may be something like causal determinism coupled with a willingness to consider causes inherent to the object. These assumptions would yield different implications in different domains, given the information provided in the environment. In the case of an animal, the child would notice the animal moving on its own, would see no apparent external cause (either human or mechanical), and so would conclude that some inner, inherent nature is responsible for its movement. R. Gelman (1987, 1990) proposed a similar principle, an "innards principle," to account for her data regarding movement judgments and descriptions of insides that children report for animals versus inanimate objects (Massey & Gelman, 1988). In contrast, in the case of a wastebasket, any behaviors or functions of the object could be readily traced to the people who made and use the wastebasket; hence, there would be no need to appeal to properties inherent in the object or a wastebasket essence.

We favor this last account regarding the domain generality of essentialism for several reasons: It predicts a broad yet not promiscuous application of essentialism, it allows essentialism to emerge in even novel domains, it is consistent with the developmental evidence that essentialism emerges early, and it provides a parsimonious account of why essentialism emerges in multiple domains. However, at present it remains speculative.

The discussion of domain generality raises questions concerning the relation between essentialism and commonsense theories, to which we turn now.

Are essences components of theories?

Essences look like they could be a component of a theory: They are unobserved, imputed entities that are assumed to have causal force. On the surface, then, it would seem that evidence for essentialism could constitute evidence for a theory. In other words, if children have essentialist beliefs about categories of living things, this could imply that children have a theory of living things.

On the other hand, theories are by their very nature domain-specific, and we have just argued in the previous section that essentialism may be a domain-general bias. Moreover, regardless of the stand one takes on the domain specificity of essences, essentialism does not in principle require a theory. It could be an isolated assumption about category structure that is independent of larger belief systems (Atran, this volume). Theories may follow after the fact, and indeed there is some evidence that larger belief systems show much more variability and malleability than essentialism. Furthermore, there is evidence that at least part of the time, it is the adults who form theories, encode them in language, and then pass them down to children. Children assume that there is much more in common to members of a category than meets the eye, but do not put forth detailed hypotheses about the biological processes involved.

We believe that an essentialist assumption fosters theory building and eventually becomes part of a number of distinct theories, even if it is not part of a theory from the start. Developmentally, there may not be a qualitative break between where an essentialist assumption ends and a theory begins. It is again useful to invoke the distinction between scientific beliefs and commonsense beliefs. The question is not whether children have scientifically accurate classifications, nor whether they hold logically consistent belief systems. Rather, the question is whether children reason about causality, make ontological commitments, and hold interrelated beliefs. An essentialist assumption fosters looking for causes, expecting inductions within categories, nonobvious similarities, and so on. Even if these beliefs are not (at first) tightly structured into a coherent, domain-specific system, they are the building blocks or components of later theory building.

Conclusions

We have suggested in this chapter that young children seem to carry with them an essentialist bias, a bias that is then extended into adulthood. Even if we don't carve up the world at its joints, an essentialist assumption makes it seem as if we do. This belief about the structure of the world is both adaptive and pernicious. Psychological essentialism is adaptive in that it leads us to search for new knowledge and to revise categories on the basis of that knowledge. But this kind of belief is potentially dangerous as well: It may promote stereotyping and inflexible thinking. As Gould (1990: 73) notes: "Some classifications channel our thinking into fruitful directions because they properly capture the causes of order; others lead us to tragic and vicious errors (the older taxonomies of human races, for example) because they sink their roots in prejudice and mayhem."

But how pervasive (i.e., domain-general) is an essentialist assumption? Experimental evidence for an essentialist world-view is at present most abundant in the biological domain. That is, when reasoning about animals, preschool children expect category members to maintain their identity over superficial transformations, to have innate potential, to have rich inductive potential, to be driven by immanent causes. Nonetheless, children appear to have something like an essentialist stance in a variety of other domains as well. Accordingly, we have proposed that essentialism in children stems from a domain-general assumption. To state it rather crudely, children assume that events and features are caused, and appear biased to search for internal or inherent causes. These general strategies combine to encourage people to construct essentialist accounts when encountering events or features with no external causal mechanism. This would include a wide variety of seemingly natural behaviors or feature clusters, ranging from the flight of a bird to the customs of an ethnic group.

Beyond what it tells us about essentialism, this work suggests that early understanding of living things appears to be theorylike. An essentialist assumption, like a theory, can foster a search for invisible causal mechanisms responsible for an object's actions, development, and maintenance of identity. An essentialist assumption, like a theory, leads to the expectation of nonobvious similarities among category members, and unlimited inductive potential. An essentialist assumption does not constitute a theory per se, but it does contain several key elements of a folk theory.

To conclude, concept acquisition and theory building seem to go hand-in-hand from the earliest points in development. Cognitive development is not a process of building up from simple units (such as concepts) to larger structures (such as theories). Both are developing simultaneously. We are unlikely ever to find a point when children have concepts without theorylike beliefs.

Notes

1. Note, however, that it is unclear that individual scientists' theories are as objective, consistent, etc., as is often assumed (Brewer & Samarapungavan, 1991).
2. Historically, there are many different essentialist beliefs, entailing distinct kinds of claims (Schwartz, 1977). Here we attempt to characterize some components of everyday, lay essentialist assumptions. We realize that these will not necessarily overlap with essentialist beliefs of any one philosopher or scientist.
3. We moved the transparent artifacts by means of an attached clear thread that was not visible on the videotape.
4. We thank Grant Gutheil for suggesting this experiment.
5. It may also imply that certain things that adults treat as biological are omitted, because for adults a complete domain of biological things might include viruses, bacteria, and plants.

References

Atran, S. (1990). *Cognitive foundations of natural history: Towards an anthropology of science.* Cambridge: Cambridge University Press.

Backscheider, A. G., Coley, J. D., & Gutheil, D. G. (1991, April). *Children's use of information about insides and behavior in predicting animals' appearances.* Paper presented at the biennial meeting of the Society for Research in Child Development, Seattle, WA.

Backscheider, A. G., Shatz, M., & Gelman, S. A. (in press). Preschoolers' ability to distinguish living kinds as a function of regrowth. *Child Development.*

Baillargeon, R. (1993). The object concept revisited. In C. Granrud (Ed.), *Visual perception and cognition in infancy* (pp. 265–315). Hillsdale, NJ: Erlbaum.

Brewer, W. F., & Samarapungavan, A. (1991). Children's theories versus scientific theories: Differences in reasoning or differences in knowledge? In R. Hoffman & D. Palermo (Eds.), *Cognition and the symbolic processes: Applied and ecological perspectives.* Hillsdale, NJ: Erlbaum.

Brown, A. L. (1990). Domain-specific principles affect learning and transfer in children. *Cognitive Science, 14,* 107–133.

Bullock, M., Gelman, R., & Baillargeon, R. (1982). The development of causal reasoning. In W. J. Friedman (Ed.), *The developmental psychology of time* (pp. 209–254). New York: Academic Press.

Carey, S. (1978). The child as word learner. In M. Halle, J. Bresnan, & G. A. Miller (Eds.), *Linguistic theory and psychological reality* (pp. 264–293). Cambridge, MA: MIT Press.

Carey, S. (1985). *Conceptual change in childhood*. Cambridge, MA: MIT Press.

Chandler, M. J., & Lalonde, C. (in press). Surprising, magical, and miraculous turns of events: Children's reactions to violations of their theories of mind and matter. *British Journal of Developmental Psychology*.

Collins, A. M., & Loftus, E. F. (1975). A spreading-activation theory of semantic processing. *Psychological Review, 82,* 407–428.

diSessa, A. A. (1988). Knowledge in pieces. In G. Forman & P. B. Pufall (Eds.), *Constructivism in the computer age* (pp. 49–70). Hillsdale, NJ: Erlbaum.

Dromi, E. (1987). *Early lexical development*. Cambridge: Cambridge University Press.

Dwyer, P. (1976). An analysis of Rofaifo mammal taxonomy. *American Ethnologist, 3,* 425–445.

Flavell, J. (1977). *Cognitive development*. Englewood Cliffs, NJ: Prentice-Hall.

Gardner, R. A., & Gardner, B. T. (1989). A cross-fostering laboratory. In R. A. Gardner, B. T. Gardner, & T. E. Van Cantfort (Eds.), *Teaching sign language to chimpanzees* (pp. 1–28). Albany, NY: State University of New York Press.

Gelman, R. (1987, August). *Cognitive development: Principles guide learning and contribute to conceptual coherence*. Paper presented at the Meetings of the American Psychological Association, Division I, New York.

Gelman, R. (1990). First principles organize attention to and learning about relevant data: Number and the animate–inanimate distinction as examples. *Cognitive Science, 14,* 79–106.

Gelman, S. A. (1988). The development of induction within natural kind and artifact categories. *Cognitive Psychology, 20,* 65–95.

Gelman, S. A. (1992). Children's conception of personality traits – Commentary. *Human Development, 35,* 280–285.

Gelman, S. A., & Coley, J. D. (1990). The importance of knowing a dodo is a bird: Categories and inferences in 2-year-old children. *Developmental Psychology, 26,* 796–804.

Gelman, S. A., & Coley, J. D. (1991). Language and categorization: The acquisition of natural kind terms. In S. A. Gelman & J. P. Byrnes (Eds.), *Perspectives on language and thought: Interrelations in development* (pp. 146–196). Cambridge: Cambridge University Press.

Gelman, S. A., Coley, J. D., Rosengren, K., Hartman, E., & Pappas, T. (1993). *Parental input about category structure*. Manuscript in preparation.

Gelman, S. A., Collman, P., & Maccoby, E. E. (1986). Inferring properties from categories versus inferring categories from properties: The case of gender. *Child Development, 57,* 396–404.

Gelman, S. A., & Gottfried, G. M. (1993). *Causal explanations of animate and inanimate motion*. Manuscript in preparation.

Gelman, S. A., & Kalish, C. W. (1993). Categories and causality. In R. Pasnak & M. L. Howe (Eds.), *Emerging themes in cognitive development, Vol. 2* (pp. 3–32). Springer-Verlag.

Gelman, S. A., & Kremer, K. E. (1991). Understanding natural cause: Children's explanations of how objects and their properties originate. *Child Development, 62,* 396–414.

Gelman, S. A., & Markman, E. M. (1986). Categories and induction in young children. *Cognition, 23,* 183–209.

Gelman, S. A., & Markman, E. M. (1987). Young children's inductions from natural kinds: The role of categories and appearances. *Child Development, 58,* 1532–1541.

Gelman, S. A., & Medin, D. L. (1993). What's so essential about essentialism? A different perspective on the interaction of perception, language, and conceptual knowledge. *Cognitive Development, 8,* 157–167.

Gelman, S. A., & O'Reilly, A. W. (1988). Children's inductive inferences within superordinate categories. *Child Development, 59,* 876–887.

Gelman, S. A., & Wellman, H. M. (1991). Insides and essences: Early understandings of the non-obvious. *Cognition, 38,* 213–244.

Gopnik, A., & Wellman, H. M. (in press). Why the child's theory of mind really is a theory. *Mind and Language.*

Gould, S. J. (1990). Taxonomy as politics. *Dissent,* 73–78.

Halliday, M. A. K. (1975). *Learning how to mean: Explorations in the development of language.* London: Edward Arnold.

Hampton, J. A. (1982). A demonstration of intransitivity in natural categories. *Cognition, 12,* 151–164.

Herrnstein, R. J., Loveland, D. H., & Cable, C. (1976). Natural concepts in pigeons. *Journal of Experimental Psychology: Animal Behavior Processes, 2,* 285–302.

Hickling, A. K., & Gelman, S. A. (1992). *Young children's understanding of seed and plant growth.* Paper presented at the Conference on Human Development, Atlanta, GA.

Hilton, J. (1992, November). *When categorization fails: Stereotyping and the dilemma of consistency.* Colloquium presented at Princeton University.

Inagaki, K., & Hatano, G. (1988). *Young children's understanding of the mind–body distinction.* Paper presented at the meeting of the American Educational Research Association, New Orleans, LA.

Jones, S. S., & Smith, L. B. (1993). The place of perception in children's concepts. *Cognitive Development, 8,* 113–139.

Kaiser, M. K., McCloskey, M., & Proffitt, D. R. (1986). Development of intuitive theories of motion: Curvilinear motion in the absence of external forces. *Developmental Psychology, 22,* 1–5.

Karmiloff-Smith, A., & Inhelder, B. (1975). If you want to get ahead, get a theory. *Cognition, 3,* 195–212.

Karniol, R. (1980). A conceptual analysis of immanent justice responses in children. *Child Development, 51,* 118–130.

Keil, F. C. (1989). *Concepts, kinds, and cognitive development.* Cambridge, MA: MIT Press.

Kister, M. C., & Patterson, C. J. (1980). Children's conceptions of the causes of illness: Understanding of contagion and use of immanent justice. *Child Development, 51,* 839–846.

Locke, J. (1894/1959). *An essay concerning human understanding, Vol. 2.* New York: Dover.

McCloskey, M. (1983). Intuitive physics. *Scientific American, 248,* 122–130.

McShane, J. (1980). *Learning to talk*. Cambridge: Cambridge University Press.

Markman, E. M. (1989). *Categorization and naming in children: Problems of induction*. Cambridge, MA: MIT Press.

Massey, C., & Gelman, R. (1988). Preschoolers' ability to decide whether a photographed unfamiliar object can move itself. *Developmental Psychology, 24*, 307–317.

Mayr, E. (1988). *Toward a new philosophy of biology*. Cambridge, MA: Belknap Press of Harvard University Press.

Mayr, E. (1991). *One long argument: Charles Darwin and the genesis of modern evolutionary thought*. Cambridge, MA: Harvard University Press.

Medin, D. (1989). Concepts and conceptual structure. *American Psychologist, 44*, 1469–1481.

Medin, D., & Ortony, A. (1989). Psychological essentialism. In S. Vosniadou & A. Ortony (Eds.), *Similarity and analogical reasoning* (pp. 179–195). Cambridge: Cambridge University Press.

Murphy, G. L., & Medin, D. L. (1985). The role of theories in conceptual coherence. *Psychological Review, 92*, 289–316.

Nelson, K. (1973). Structure and strategy in learning to talk. *Monographs of the Society for Research in Child Development, 38* (1–2, serial no. 149).

Piaget, J. (1948). *The moral judgment of the child*. London: Routledge & Kegan Paul.

Piaget, J., & Inhelder, B. (1975). The origin of the idea of chance in children (L. Leake, Jr., P. Burrell, & H. Fischbein, Trans.). New York: Norton. (Original work published in 1951)

Poulin-Dubois, D., & Shultz, T. F. (1990). The infant's concept of agency: The distinction between social and non-social objects. *Journal of Genetic Psychology, 151*, 77–90.

Rips, L. J. (1989). Similarity, typicality, and categorization. In S. Vosniadou & A. Ortony (Eds.), *Similarity and analogical reasoning* (pp. 23–59). Cambridge: Cambridge University Press.

Rosengren, K. S., Gelman, S. A., Kalish, C. W., & McCormick, M. (1991). As time goes by: Children's early understanding of growth in animals. *Child Development, 62*, 1302–1320.

Rothbart, M., & Taylor, M. (in press). Category labels and social reality: Do we view social categories as natural kinds? In G. Semin & K. Fiedler (Eds.), *Language, interaction, and social cognition*. Sage Publications.

Schwartz, S. P. (Ed.). (1977). *Naming, necessity, and natural kinds*. Ithaca, NY: Cornell University Press.

Shaklee, H. (1979). Bounded rationality and cognitive development: Upper limits on growth? *Cognitive Psychology, 11*, 327–345.

Shultz, T. R. (1982). *Rules of causal attribution*. Monographs of the Society for Research in Child Development, *47*, No. 1.

Stoler, A. (1992). *The power of essentializing: Tensions between cognitive and political representations of race*. Unpublished manuscript, University of Michigan, Department of Anthropology.

Stoler, A. (in press). Children on the colonial divide: Sentiment and citizenship in colonial Southeast Asia. In G. Eley (Ed.), *Power: Thinking through the disciplines*. Ann Arbor: University of Michigan Press.

Taylor, M. G., & Gelman, S. A. (1991, April). *Children's beliefs about sex differences: The role of nature vs. nurture*. Paper presented at the Biennial Meetings of the Society for Research in Child Development. Seattle, WA.

Wason, P. C. (1960). On the failure to eliminate hypotheses in a conceptual task. *Quarterly Journal of Experimental Psychology, 12*, 129–140.

Wellman, H. M. (1990). *The child's theory of mind*. Cambridge, MA: MIT Press.

White, E., Elsom, B., & Prawat, R. (1978). Children's conceptions of death. *Child Development, 49*, 307–310.

Yuill, N. (1992). Children's conception of personality traits. *Human Development, 35*, 265–279.

Part V

Domains across cultures and languages

14 First principles can support both universal and culture-specific learning about number and music

Rochel Gelman and Kimberly Brenneman

There is a growing body of evidence that infants attend selectively to some fundamental aspects of number and music. Such findings suggest that attention to and learning about number and music are perhaps due to the presence of innate, skeletal principles in each domain. In our chapter, we develop this position while showing how it is consistent with the different ways that cultures support learning and development in specific knowledge areas. Pairing considerations of number and music enables us to show that domain specificity and cultural variation need not be treated as antithetical.

Whereas it is still common for scholars in some fields to assume that "primitive" peoples lack a concept of number (see the following discussion), there is wide acceptance of the idea that all peoples develop musical competence, mainly because the latter can happen without benefit of formal instruction, use of special symbol systems, or the need to represent abstract, relevant dimensions like pitch, key, harmony, rhythm, and so forth. Indeed, accounts of the evolutionary function of the human music capacity often include the idea that, in preliterate societies, music serves to efficiently organize information that cannot be written down. For example, Gardner (1983) describes a possible role for music in organizing religious rites and work groups in the Stone Age, and Sloboda (1985) hypothesizes that music provides a mnemonic framework within which the structure of cultural knowledge and societal relations is stored and communicated. Whatever the role of music in preliterate groups, Donald (1991) points out that these societies always have complex rituals based on some form of music.

In contrast to music, discussions of number are almost always paired with one version or another of the idea that, to become truly competent with

Preparation of this chapter was supported in part by grants from NSF and UCLA to R. Gelman and an NSF Fellowship and UCLA grant to K. Brenneman.

369

numbers, one must learn a symbol system for counting, master the meaning of cardinal terms, and/or develop the abstract and logical abilities that underlie the capacity to think about and use numerical concepts. These contrasting beliefs about the underlying learning paths to musical and numerical skill could be paralleled by the claim that infants' ability to respond initially to music-relevant relationships in a sound sequence is based on the kinds of simple perceptual processes that support "primitive" cultures' development of complex, but nonabstract, music skills. The argument would continue that infants' and "primitives'" numerically relevant responses to number are likewise based on simple perceptual processes and therefore cannot be truly numerical. According to this view, real learning about number is different because it clearly must be based on more abstract processes, the use of logic, the ability to use language, and/or instruction (e.g., Saxe, 1989).

The claim that "primitive" people and young children are restricted to perceptual processes and therefore lack abstract numerical abilities, is less prevalent than it once was, especially in anthropology (e.g., Crump, 1990). Nevertheless, the claim is still made, especially in treatments of the history of numbers (e.g., Andrews, 1977; Beckmann, 1924; Dantzig, 1954; Ifrah, 1981/1985; Kline, 1972; Menninger, 1969) or when developmental theory is applied (e.g., Hallpike, 1979; McLeish, 1992). The widespread view is that very young children lack simple, nonverbal numerical concepts. Theorists much prefer to attribute data on early, preverbal, or "primitive" number use to some variant of a perceptual pattern detector or "perceptual intuition" (e.g., Cooper, 1984; Fuson, 1988; Klahr & Wallace, 1973; McLeish, 1992; Mandler, 1992). For example:

Anthropological studies on primitive peoples ... reveal that those savages who have not reached the stage of finger counting are completely deprived of all perception of number. Such is the case among numerous tribes in Australia, the South Sea Islands, South America and Africa. Curr, who has made an extensive study of primitive Australia, holds that but few of the natives are able to discern four, and that no Australian in his wild state can perceive seven. The Bushmen of South Africa have no number words beyond one, two, and many, and these words are so inarticulate that it may be doubted whether the natives attach a clear meaning to them. (Dantzig, 1954: 2)

In our own time, a few "primitive" peoples of Oceania, Africa and America are still at the "zero" degree of experience with numbers. Guided solely by their natural ability to recognize concrete quantities at a glance, they can conceive, discern, and designate only a single object or a pair, and so their numerical notions are limited to "one," "two," and "many." (Ifrah, 1981/1985: xii)

It is now well-known that infants within the first year of life can discriminate between sets of different small numerosities: ... This kind of behavior ... has played an important role in nativist theories of number development. However, from a Piagetian perspective a concept is far more than discrimination: It implies the representation of some commonality that has been abstracted from a set of exemplars. (Sophian, 1991/1992: 28–29)

Even human beings, for whom the abstract activity of counting seems the most natural thing in the world, find it incredibly difficult to learn. One of the discoveries of 20th-century scientists (made independently by Montessori, Piaget, and Vygotsky) was that adults forget how gradual and time-consuming the process of learning to think in the abstract is. (McLeish, 1992: 8)

It is the very presumption that responding to and creating music neither requires abstract representational abilities nor formal instruction, whereas learning to use the number system does, which leads us to pair these domains. Accounts of initial learnings about number and music differ dramatically in the extent to which education is granted a causal role. Although it is generally assumed that learning about the music of a culture can proceed without formal instruction, the same is not true for learning about number. This difference provides us with a way to decouple the contributions of general learning and school-based, instructional processes from the contribution of innate, domain-specific principles to knowledge acquisition in a domain. For there is evidence that just as musical knowledge develops without benefit of formal instruction, so does knowledge about number. This parallel is one reason we propose that the acquisition of knowledge in both domains grows on a skeleton of innate, domain-specific knowledge.

In the following discussion we start with a crucial matter: a definition of a domain and a description of the innate principles that guide knowledge acquisition within certain domains. We briefly review why an assumption of *some* innate knowledge in a domain does not rule out the need for learning in this domain. These sections provide the foundation on which we build the thesis that learning about both number and music is facilitated, but not guaranteed, by the presence of skeletal, domain-specific principles. We next discuss why our account of principle-first learning is stronger than the learning account offered by Associationism. Finally, we return to the idea that innateness and cultural creativity are not opposites and indeed work together to guide the acquisition of human knowledge.

Defining domain specificity

We follow Gelman and Greeno (1989) and Gallistel (1990) by defining a domain of knowledge in much the same way that formalists do, by appeal to the notion of principles. A given set of principles, the rules of their application, and the entities to which they apply together constitute a domain. Because each set of principles constitutes a different structure, we can characterize a domain in terms of a set of interrelated principles that define entities and operations on them. In contrast, general processes such as discrimination or general-purpose processing mechanisms like short term memory do not constitute domains, any more than the process of long division or the American subtraction algorithm constitutes a domain of mathematics. Similarly, the process of musical transcription and the circle of fifths are not domains. Scripts, at least in the form in which they are often given, do not constitute domains; they are analogous to the heuristic prescriptions for solving problems in mathematics or creating a coherent musical composition. As such, these heuristics should not be confused with the mathematical domains themselves (algebra, geometry, theory of functions, and so on) or the specific genres of music to which they might apply (e.g., classical or jazz). In sum, the test for a conceptual domain is whether it can be characterized in terms of a coherent set of operating principles and their related entities.

We turn now to evidence that both number and music form conceptual domains. Our discussion of the number domain draws heavily on data indicating that infants respond to numerically relevant displays in a way that suggests the operation of certain arithmetic principles. We also answer standard criticisms of our approach as well as offer evidence against alternative interpretations of the data we use to support our position. Our approach to the music domain differs somewhat in that we rely on animal and neuropsychological data to support our claim that the acquisition of musical knowledge is in large part guided by domain-specific, rather than domain-general, skills. As in our discussion of number, we present an alternative account of musical development and the skills of infants. We then explain why our approach is more consistent with the acquisition data of the neurologically normal, human population.

About number

Counting is part of a number-specific domain because the representatives of numerosity (what Gelman & Gallistel, 1978, dubbed *numerons*) generated by counting are operated on by mechanisms informed by, or obedient to, arithmetic principles. For counting to provide the input for arithmetic reasoning, the principles governing counting must complement the principles governing arithmetic reasoning. For example, the counting principles must be such that sets assigned the same numeron are in fact numerically equal and the set assigned a greater numeron is more numerous than a set assigned a lesser numeron. Or, principles of multiplication must be applied consistently both to whole numbers and fractions. It will not do to say that in both cases the product is always more than the two entities being multiplied because this is not true when two fractions are multiplied.

For a variety of converging reasons, Gallistel and Gelman (1992) conclude that infants' numerically relevant responses to sets of inputs are supported by a skeleton of nonverbal counting and related numerical reasoning principles. First, infants discriminate between the Ns in a display whether they are alike or not, stationary or not, and visual or auditory (Starkey, Spelke, & Gelman, 1983; van Loosbroek & Smitsman, 1990). They also prefer one of a pair of slides that depicts the number of household objects matching the number of drumbeats they hear – whether or not the interval between the beats varies

(Starkey, Spelke, & Gelman, 1990). Second, although these numerical abilities appear to be restricted to displays with small set sizes (N ≤ 3 or 4), this limitation does not license the conclusion that infants' responses reflect their reliance on nonnumerical, perceptual processes. If this alternative were true, then it would be hard to explain how infants also respond correctly to the effects of addition and subtraction (Baillargeon, Miller, & Constantino, 1992; Starkey, 1992; Wynn, 1992).

Third, one need not appeal to the rich abstraction abilities that Piaget (1952) and others do to grant that the domain-specific principles we have just outlined underlie infants' abilities to respond to number. Counting mechanisms exist that pay no attention to surface characteristics of objects; in these cases there is no need for high-level classification abilities to render something akin to Russell's class of all classes. In fact, the Gelman and Gallistel counting principles are indifferent to item kind (Gelman & Gallistel, 1978; Gallistel & Gelman, 1990). All that is required is the ability to keep together a collection of separable things; one need not even notice the characteristics of these things. (See Shipley & Shepperson, 1990, for further discussion of this point.) Similarly, one does not have to use linguistic tags to honor the requirements of the counting principles of one-one, stable-ordering, and cardinality. One does have to assign one and only one tag to each item in the display, assign the tags in a stable order across trials, and have a way of letting the last tag represent the value of the set. These requirements are all met by Gallistel and Gelman's (1992) nonverbal counting model, one they use to account for both infant and animal data.

Additionally, the Gallistel and Gelman model offers a straightforward account of the findings that infants' ability to discriminate accurately between set sizes is restricted to small Ns, for it distinguishes between the tendency to tag exactly as many times as there are items to tag and the tendency to do this variably. Following Meck and Church's (1983) model of the animal data (which show some animals dealing with Ns > 50), Gallistel and Gelman assume that both the mean number of tags and variance associated with a given value of N increases as set size does. The variance associated with each N is due to two factors, one from counting errors and the other from the inherent variance in the representations rendered by the count-ordered quantities. Because the animal data show overlap in the distribution of variances for Ns as small as 4, the same could be true for another nonverbal species, the human infant. Unfortunately, the pertinent infant data regarding the degree of variability as a function of set size are not available. Therefore, it is premature to favor some nonspecified "perceptual apprehension" mechanism over a nonverbal counting model to account for the number data from infants.

Finally, when Gallistel and Gelman conclude that infants have innate knowledge of number, they definitely do not mean that the infants have access to this knowledge. Nor do they mean that it is represented in a symbolic form. Instead, the idea is that the principles that define a domain are represented within the structure of the information processing mechanisms that assimilate and direct action. Infants' tendencies to use their information processing systems lead them to attend to data that are related to the structures inherent in these processing systems. Doing so leads to the very conditions necessary for learning to progress in the domains outlined by these structures.

About music

In the domain of music, we can say sequences of sounds are perceived as music when processing is governed by mechanisms that attend to and code pitch sequences as being tonally (or harmonically) and rhythmically related. Our arguments about innate, principled attentional mechanisms in the music domain are more speculative than those we offer for the human number capacities, however, the kind of processing mechanism that could be involved here has been worked out for some songbirds. Marler (1991) discusses the innate learning preferences of songbirds and the mechanisms that underlie these preferences. He indicates that species vary in the complexity of their songs, the degree to which learning requires simple or complex inputs, how much they have to practice as juveniles, and so on. Similarly, songs vary with respect to the number of different musical notes they include, the number and length of note sequences, internal phase structure, and tempo.[1] Despite this variation there is a general specification across species for input that adheres to the tonality characterizing the songs of most songbird species (Marler, 1991; Nowicki & Marler, 1988).

Work on bird song learning has led to the specification of inputs that are relevant to learning about song. For example, the male white-crowned sparrow is born with a template for his adult song. But he will not grow up to sing that song unless: (1) during a critical period early in development, he is exposed to a sample of it; and (2) during his juvenile period he has an opportunity to practice singing and, therefore, to go through a lengthy trial-and-error period before settling on the song that matches the template. Although practice is required here, the bird does not have to hear any further inputs during the juvenile period. What was heard early in life, before the bird could sing, suffices to tune the template that provides feedback, much like auditory memories of a correct way to play the piano do as a student practices and improves a lesson.

That the musical development of human beings may also be guided by this type of domain-specific mechanism, rather than pure perceptual processes, is suggested by the case of an autistic man, NP. NP was able to reproduce a sequence of sounds on a piano after minimal exposure. His skill, however, was specific to tonal sequences (Sloboda, Hermelin, & O'Connor, 1985). He had difficulty reproducing an atonal sequence ("Whole tone scale" from Bartok's *Mikrokosmos*). Therefore, NP was not simply a human tape recorder, capable of playing back any sound sequence. It is highly unlikely that his skill resulted from a domain-general memory capacity. Otherwise he should have been equally able to reproduce tonal and atonal pieces. His advanced development in a specific area was most likely based on domain-specific principles that privileged inputs based, in part, on certain tonality relevant features. The case of NP strongly suggests that nature provides human beings with learning mechanisms that are attuned to certain features of environmental input. We are not as far along in specifying what these features might be as are those who study avian species, which is why our comments on this issue cannot help but be speculative in nature (but see Takeuchi & Hulse, 1993).

Perhaps some would argue that our universal skills for music grow out of our ability to use language; the two share characteristics, such as rhythm, prosody, and pitch contours. This is unlikely given evidence from comparative animal work, neuropsychology, and evolutionary theory and given the structural differences between the two types of input. First, we know that the relevant input for birds acquiring song is composed of both phonetic and tonal features (Marler, 1991) and that, at the neuronal level, cells that respond preferentially to the harmonic aspects of song have been located in the HVc (forebrain nucleus hyperstriatum ventrale, pars caudale) of the zebra finch (Margoliash & Fortune, 1992). And although tonality is not a necessary feature of the relevant speech input needed for a child to learn language, the case of NP suggests that there is reason to suspect that tonality serves an important role in the definition of relevant musical input for human learners. The idea that music and language are not part of the same system and that one is not dependent on the other is reinforced by cases, including that of NP, in which music and language functions are dissociated. For example, a patient may retain musical functioning in the context of a severe aphasia and an autist may possess musical skill in the context of a subnormal IQ and poor language functioning (Gardner, 1983; Sloboda, Hermelin, & O'Connor, 1985; Winner, 1982).

Those who theorize about the evolutionary origins of musical and linguistic skill offer further reasons to treat these as separate capacities. Donald (1991) reviews Darwin's ideas on this matter and adds his own insights. How the human capacity for song arose from primate ancestors is a matter of more debate (see Sloboda, 1985), so we concern ourselves here with how music and language evolved once they were established in some form in the human being. According to Darwin, rudimentary song was a precursor to language. Control of the voice for communication of certain emotional content was first shown in the prosody of rudimentary song. This early prosody served as the basis for the capacity to produce melodic and harmonic song as well as the prosodic features of speech. Donald notes that improvements in voluntary control of prosody by the vocal apparatus would have formed a basis for phonetic control as language developed. However, he continues, although music and language might have a similar origin in rudimentary song it does not follow that they are part of the same system. Donald draws attention to the fact that musical skill is separable from verbal skill (Gardner, 1983). Given that aphasias result (nearly always) from damage to the left hemisphere whereas aprosodias and amusias result from damage to the right, he concludes that "language and rudimentary song are not aspects of a single system" (p. 40).

Finally, we know that the rules about the relationships between and among entities in music are quite different from those that govern the production of language. True, "parentese" (the speech adults address to young language learners) and music are similar on certain levels. Both have wide pitch ranges, dynamic contours, and rhythmic qualities. However, the structural differences between the two cannot be ignored. Music is based on contours provided by the relationship between discrete notes, whereas infant-directed parentese is characterized more by pitch glissandi within and between discrete words (see Fernald & Mazzie, 1991, for examples). Also, the varied rhythmic aspects of musical input are structured by a steady, underlying beat whereas the rhythms of speech are not. Additionally, we know that the physical characteristics of phonemes vary as a function of their context (Liberman, Cooper, Shankweiler, & Studdert-Kennedy, 1967). For example, the actual "b" sound depends on which phonemes come before and after. In music, tones are defined by their frequency so that context does not affect how middle C (or any other note) is formed and produced. These differences are reflected in the fact that it is easy to specify the note that sounds like middle C on the piano but not at all easy to specify the phoneme that sounds like *ba* across the different words that share this same speech sound.

Because both speech and music are temporally arranged sequences of sound characterized by prosody, rhythm, and contour, it makes sense that some processing similarities would occur. For example, infant attention to phrase structure occurs both for music (Krumhansl & Jusczyk, 1990; Jusczyk & Krumhansl, in prep) and speech (Hirsh-Pasek, Kemler Nelson, Jusczyk, Cassidy, Druss, & Kennedy, 1987; Kemler Nelson, Hirsh-Pasek, Jusczyk, & Cassidy, 1989). Despite certain processing similarities, we expect that the infant system treats the two types of input as different. A direct test of this hypothesis seems not to have been done, however (P. Jusczyk, personal communication). Even without the result from such a study, the theoretical and empirical evidence from animal work, neuropsychology, and evolutionary theory suggests that speech and music are neither subsets of each other nor parts of the same system.

First principles support domain-specific learning

The structure of a domain

When we postulate that young children's cognitive development is directed by domain-specific principles, we find it helpful to use the metaphor of a skeleton. Were there no skeletons to dictate the shape and contents of the bodies of pertinent knowledge, then the acquired representations would not cohere. Just as the skeletons of different creatures are assembled according to different principles, so are separate, coherent bodies of knowledge. Skeletons need not be evident on the surface of a body; similarly, the underlying axiomlike principles that enable the acquisition of coherent knowledge need never be accessible to conscious description. Most of us could not formally describe the tonal system of our culture, yet we use the principles of the system to guide judgments of, for example, how well a given note "fits" in a musical context (Krumhansl & Keil, 1982).

The skeleton metaphor is less than perfect because it gives the impression that all principles are in place before the body of knowledge defined by them is acquired. This need not be; it is possible, even likely in many cases, that only some subset of a domain's principles serve this function. It is also conceivable that the initial ones are replaced or expanded over the course of learning. Such replacement or revision of principles is especially likely if the learner acquires new or enriched theories, such as those Carey (1985) has described for biology, or if the learner receives domain-relevant instruction. An example of the latter might be the restructuring of knowledge that comes as young musicians expand their representation of rhythm to include both the principles of meter and the principles of rhythmic figure (see Bamberger, 1990). A developing capacity for mapping language onto principles that are not at first stateable or even symbolically represented may also lead to replacement or expansion (Gelman, M. Cohen, & Hartnett, 1989; Karmiloff-Smith, 1986; 1992).

Relevance

In much the same way that the innate learning mechanism in avian species attends to stimuli that are tonally, phonemically, and/or rhythmically relevant to acquiring the species' song, so do the initial principles of a human, cognitive domain mark out the stimuli that are candidates for assimilation to that domain, stimuli that will feed coherent development within that domain. Our ideas for relevance in a domain are quite like those outlined by Sperber and Wilson (1986) for relevance in communication. They write that a phenomenon is relevant to the extent that it possesses features that make it recognizable and easily processed in a cognitive context and to the extent that it adds new knowledge to that already in the context. We might replace the term "cognitive context" with "domain structure" to show the parallel between their ideas and ours. Initial domain structure defines the constraints on the class of relevant inputs and then serves to store, in a coherent fashion, the data that are assimilated. Structural constraints do not force learners to attend to the data; they simply provide guidance as to what are and, hence, what are not the pertinent data. That is, these initial principles are implicit in the processes that govern early behavior and early information processing. Because they lead infants to process data in ways that are consistent with the implicit principles, they account for infants' attention to seemingly surprising things. For example, in the case of number, principles implicit in preverbal counting mechanisms (Gallistel, 1993) can account for infants' attention to stimuli in a number-relevant way (Cooper, 1984; Moore, Benenson, Reznick, Peterson, & Kagan, 1987; Sophian & Adams, 1987; Starkey, Spelke, & Gelman, 1983; Strauss & Curtis, 1984).

Or, we suggest that, in the case of music, perceptual mechanisms sensitive to certain interval relationships between discrete pitches may provide early support for the acquisition of a given tonal system. For example, most of the world's musical systems include an interval that corresponds to the Western perfect fifth (Sloboda, 1985), which is a musically and psychologically important interval in various systems, including those of North India and the West (see Castellano, Bharucha, & Krumhansl, 1984). Its universality suggests that the perfect fifth might be a structure to which the human system is innately sensitive, a conjecture that is supported by the neurophysiological result that the auditory perceptual apparatus of the squirrel monkey is especially sensitive to this relationship (Rose, Brugge, Anderson, & Hind, 1967). Along similar lines, because the Western musical system expresses tonality through harmony rather than through melody (Castellano, Bharucha, & Krumhansl, 1984), certain chords (rather than just intervals) are particularly important and frequently used structures in music. The major triad (in solfège, *do mi sol*) is one such chord and is viewed as something of a prototype of tonal structure (A. Cohen, Thorpe, & Trehub, 1987).

If certain intervals (and perhaps triads) are universally or widely important to music, innate sensitivity to just these sorts of arrangements might be expected. In fact, Western infants are better able to process the perfect fifth interval than an augmented fifth (Trainor, 1993a, b). Similarly, some work has addressed whether Western infants treat the major triad differently from other chords that are nondiatonic or based on an augmented triad. Not all studies have found a statistically significant difference in infants' treatment of sequences based on the major triad versus other triads, but some work provides an indication that the infant system might find the major triad to be an especially coherent structure (e.g., A. Cohen, Thorpe, & Trehub, 1987; Trainor, 1993b; see Trehub, 1987, for a review). For example, one report indicates that infants better remember melodies based on the major triad than they remember those that are not (A. Cohen et al., 1987, Exp. 2). This result suggests that the major triad forms a more stable and coherent context for melodic memorization for infants than do augmented triads (which include accidentals).

The coherence of the major triad could be related to either the simplicity of the ratio (4:5:6) relations among the three frequencies involved in the major triad or to enculturation in the West. The first hypothesis is based on the idea that the frequency relations among the notes in the major triad are simpler than those formed by an augmented triad (12:15:19) and that processing differences are based in the structure of the auditory system (see Trainor & Trehub, 1992). The second hypothesis is that exposure to more tunes based on the major triad than on the augmented triad underlies the processing and memorial differences between the two. As Cohen and her colleagues point out, cross-cultural research is necessary to determine the relative validity of the "simple ratio" and "enculturation" accounts. One such study might involve testing the coherence of the Western major triad for infants (such as those in North India) born into cultures that do not make regular use of tonal triads. If it is the simple ratio formed by the three tones of the major triad that renders it coherent to the infant system, then we would expect it to do so across cultures.

Our point is that cultures whose musical system does not depend on harmony for the expression of tonality may not take advantage of the way the human system reacts to the simple ratios formed by the tones in the major triad, but it does not follow that the system, especially the less-tutored one, does not find such a structure particularly salient and coherent. In sum, we propose that perceptual attention to certain simple frequency ratio relations between tones that form the fifth or the major triad could support the learning of culture-specific tonal hierarchies, simply because (practically) all of the world's tonal systems privilege certain of the uneven intervals in the scale. The perfect fifth is of universal musical importance, and because both infants and nonhuman primates are especially sensitive to this interval, the argument that the human system attends to the fifth, from early on, seems particularly compelling and ripe for cross-cultural, empirical study. Our position relative to the coherence of the major triad is necessarily more speculative but we believe its consonance with our general theoretical viewpoint and its susceptibility to further empirical test make it an attractive one, nonetheless.

Principles need not be in symbolic form

What is the nature of the principles that define a domain and guide attention to relevant information? One characteristic is that principles need not be represented within the system in some symbolic form and, a fortiori, not in a linguistic form. They can be, and most likely are, represented initially within the structure of the information processing mechanisms that assimilate experience and direct action (cf. Karmiloff-Smith, 1992). Marr (1982) covers many cases in which he believes that the algorithms by which the visual system processes visual input incorporate implicitly various principles about the structure of the world. Gallistel (1990; Cheng & Gallistel, 1984) argues that the principles of Euclidean geometry are implicit in the mechanisms by which the rat constructs and uses a map of its environment. The case of the "missing fundamental" indicates that the human auditory system imposes harmonic structure on certain arrangements of frequencies; when the higher harmonics of a certain frequency, say 300 Hz, are presented simultaneously, the listener perceives a tone at 300 Hz even though it has not been sounded. From the firing pattern of neurons responding to the harmonics, the auditory system infers the fundamental frequency (e.g., 300 Hz). As far as we know, no one has studied whether this response occurs in infant systems, but its presence early in life would have obvious implications for the argument that certain principles are represented within the structure of processing mechanisms. Along similar lines, the human infant system does not treat the discrete tones of music as single tones that happen to occur at similar times; rather, it seems to infer a structural relationship. Both pitch relationships (such as contour) and relational aspects of temporal structure are encoded rather than individual frequencies of tones and their specific durations (Trehub, 1987).

For the domains in question, assimilation of the environment benefits from available learning processes that are constrained by implicit commitments to deep principles about the world. That is, perceptions and conceptions of entities in the domain are facilitated because the processing systems that are involved are such that they will be especially prone to respond to those kinds of data that are relevant. Again, we are reminded of Sperber and Wilson's (1986) discussion of relevance and their statement that both perceptual mechanisms and perceptual salience are relevance-oriented (p. 152). That is, certain aspects of perceptual mechanisms create a situation in which a specific type of phenomenon can be processed with minimal cognitive effort while allowing for some gain in information about a domain.

Our account of knowledge acquisition within domains, and other accounts in its class, are clearly learning accounts. They differ from more traditional ones in that they postulate innate mechanisms that contribute to the learning of domain-relevant information. The idea is that domain-specific principles guide attention to, and mediate the interpretation of relevant environmental input. True, we posit innate, skeletal principles in some domains, but our definition of a domain is not tied to an assumption of innateness. Whether knowledge represented within a domain can be said to be innate depends on the nature of the evidence. As an illustration, consider tonal and atonal music.

Because there are universal characteristics among the world's various tonal systems, we argue that acquisition of *some* tonal system that shares these features is guided by innate principles. We do not make the same argument for the learning of serial, 12-tone music. Knowledge about this system is certainly acquired (often with some difficulty) by those who receive instruction. In contrast, implicit knowledge of a culture's tonal system is acquired without specific tutoring. Interestingly, nonhierarchical, atonal music systems are not the primary way of organizing musical knowledge in any of the world's cultures (Sloboda, 1985), a fact that adds weight to the argument that certain tonal systems are more "natural" for human systems that are structuring and learning about the aural environment.

More about learning

First principles can impede later learning

The difficulty that most have understanding and learning about 12-tone music is also illustrative of the fact that innate principles do not always facilitate learning. They may provide us with a model of a domain that does not map onto the model needed to learn a certain aspect of the domain. Anyone who remembers struggling with fractions can tell us that some inputs for learning require hard work on the part of both the learner and the teacher. Given that children (or novices) do not always possess the adult (or expert) model for a given domain of understanding, inputs that seem relevant from the adult's perspective need not overlap with those that are relevant from the novice's point of view. This is an unsettling conclusion in that it undermines our faith that we, as possessors of the adult model, can readily create the environments that will best foster its acquisition. As an illustration of the problem, consider how young musicians acquire knowledge of the formal aspects of rhythm (Bamberger, 1990) and how elementary schoolchildren interpret their lessons about fractions (Gelman, 1991).

Bamberger (1990) devotes herself to a discussion of how "minds behind musical ears" might attend to rhythmic features and construct rhythmic entities that are quite different from those attended to and constructed by those who have internalized standard music notation. A child and a teacher may listen to the same short tune but hear very different things. The child, attending to figural aspects of the tune's phrases, hears the first and final phrases as different based on where the phrases occur in the tune, in what context they occur, and with what structural function. The teacher, attending to the pitches and durations of notes in the phrases, hears the first and final phrases as identical. According to Bamberger, educators must look at (rather than through) their own ways of organizing a domain of knowledge in order to make sense of how another person might be organizing the same information.

A related point applies to lessons about fractions. For we now know that young children have a robust tendency to apply their idea that numbers are "what one gets when counting things" to their interpretation of inputs that are meant to foster learning about fractions (Gelman, M. Cohen, & Hartnett, 1989; Gelman, 1991). For example, when 5- to 8-year-old children are asked to order $1/_{56}$ and $1/_{75}$, they choose $1/_{75}$ as the larger number because "75 is more than 56." That is, they answer as if they were asked to compare representations of natural (count) numbers.

These two examples are instances of a more general point. Although principles can foster learning, they can also serve as barriers to learning. If what is to be learned does not share the same structure as available knowledge, then the risk is high that data meant to foster new learning will be assimilated to what is known and, therefore, will be misinterpreted. At this point the learning can become difficult and variable.

But new learning can and does occur. How can this be if the learner's model does not match that of the teacher? We propose that if a law of structural redundancy applies to an account of learning, it provides a potential solution to the fact that, at a given point in time, learners might not share their teacher's interpretations of lessons. If conditions are such that multiple examples of the same equivalence class occur over time, the probability increases that the learner's inclinations and interpretations overlap with at least some of the ubiquitous, relevant inputs. As a result the learner could begin to build local commensurates between what is known and what is to be learned (Gelman, 1991). We turn now to a deeper discussion of this issue.

Characterizing learning in and about environments

Equivalence classes and the law of redundancy. Given that we commit ourselves to the idea that learning is the construction of a model of the world and that it is guided by model-building principles, certain characteristics of the learning process follow. First, the requisite inputs that foster development of the model-building principles and the related model must be described in relational or structured ways. For example, inductions about number depend on opportunities to encounter structured, mathematically relevant inputs, a condition that is not met by low-level sensory bits that are temporally and/ or spatially paired. Based on this characterization of relevant inputs for learning, it is no longer obvious that frequent repetitions of the exact same to-be-learned material are either sufficient or necessary for induction. For if learners construct interpretations of what they experience, there is no guarantee that a given stimulus is interpreted the same way at different times. This is because the mental structures that an individual brings to the learning task can change as a function of the given input, the effect of which could be a different future interpretation of the same physical stimulus.

Also, in the constructivist view, environments conducive to knowledge acquisition must share structural relations with the model-building system. This fact mitigates the previous discussion about the possible effects of repeated presentations of the exact same stimulus over time. For the law of frequency can be replaced by a law of redundancy. Now the argument is that learning is facilitated by the presentation of multiple exemplars of inputs that share the same structural description, some of which will overlap with the model-building system. In this case, learning about structure should be fostered by opportunities to encounter different exemplars from the same equivalence class, which is what happens with mathematics lessons in Japanese classrooms (Stigler & Baranes, 1988). Children are encouraged to think of given number facts, for example, $10 + 4$, in terms of their mathematical equivalents, such as $5 + 5 + 4$, $4 + 10$, $2 + 2 + 2 + 2 + 2 + 2 + 2$, and so on.

Similarly, learning about tonality may be simplified by the kinds of musical inputs we provide for children, as these inputs are often different nursery songs that strictly adhere to tonal principles, without sharp or flatted (accidental) notes (A. Cohen, et al., 1987; Dowling, 1988). By providing varied instances of inputs that share the same tonal structure, we may aid acquisition of an internal representation of the Western tonal system. Of empirical interest is whether the children's songs of all cultures are structured so as to adhere strictly to the particular tonal system of the culture. Another case that suggests the importance of varied input is that of Anang children learning music. These Nigerian children receive many and varied musical experiences, including singing, dancing, playing instruments, and listening (Gardner, 1983). Perhaps this variability in part accounts for the anthropological finding that all members of Anang society are musically proficient. Just as the physical body requires nutrients from a number of sources in order to develop optimally, so it may be that a variety of exemplars of relevant input may be better for the developing skeleton and body of knowledge.

The foregoing highlights a general reason for our choosing a principle-first account of knowledge acquisition in certain domains. Because first principles guide attention to inputs with a certain structural description, varied opportunities for learning can be attended to. Different cultures can vary in the sample of relevant inputs offered to the young. As long as the samples come from the equivalence class defined by the principles of the domain, cultural variation as to how skeletons are developed can even be the norm. Without the guidance of principles, it is difficult to imagine how structured knowledge could develop from spatially and/or temporally contiguous bits of perceptual information in any culture, let alone in the varied ones of the world. In the absence of such a structure, why should the learner ever relate, for example, one numerically relevant incident with the next, and the next, and so on. In sum, we favor our account over an Associationist one, in part because it explains how the young mind determines what constitutes relevant input and how it binds one relevant encounter with other relevant encounters in a coherent way.

Can cultural differences exist if knowledge structures are innate?

Given the above, cultural differences in count lists or tonal systems do not weaken our argument for innate principles and domain-specific knowledge. Innate knowledge structures do not preclude learning; rather, they encourage it. Our version of nativism in no way precludes learning about the specific ways in which knowledge is organized and used within particular cultures. Quite the contrary, it fits well with the facts.

Cultural inventiveness within biological boundaries. Nature provides learners with a "leg up" in certain cognitive domains; first principles guide attention to the domain-relevant inputs provided by the environment in a culture-specific way. Certainly, the music systems of the world vary widely in structure. Likewise the attitude toward music and its function in the society varies across cultures. Nevertheless, certain universal features, such as an underlying beat structure, the importance of the octave, and a hierarchical tonal system, occur (see Sloboda, 1985). These universals provide us with clues about the contribution of nature to development in the domain of music whereas cultural differences suggest the various ways that human learning can be flexible regardless of innate knowledge. Marler (1991) makes the point for bird song, and we make it for human beings; song development (whether of bird species or human cultures) is a creative process, but inventiveness is governed by certain rules and learning preferences, which are given by nature.

As an illustration of cultural creativity at work within biological guidelines, consider bird song. Despite nature's prescription for relevant input, learning does not lead to the same product even *within* an avian species. For example, dialects among chiffchaffs can be so different that a bird from Germany does not recognize the song of a chiffchaff from Spain (Gallistel, Brown, Carey, Gelman, & Keil, 1991). Dialects of the white-crowned sparrow differ markedly even within the small area surrounding the San Francisco Bay (Marler, 1991). If something as innate as "animal instinct" is not immutable, then it comes as no surprise that human behavior varies as a function of culture and location. Cultural variation is not a death knell for innateness because creativity is guided by innate influences. As Marler (p. 38) puts it, "We cannot begin to understand how a young bird learning to sing interacts with its social and physical environments, and assimilates information from these interactions, without taking full account of innate contributions to the assimilation process." We propose that the story is the same for human infants and children interacting with and assimilating information from social environments that include number-relevant and music-relevant input.

Like the innate learning preferences common to individuals in an avian species, universal principles of counting (e.g., no double counting) or aspects of tonal systems (e.g., uneven intervals between notes in a scale) indicate knowledge that is shared among members of the human species. For both avian and human species, culture influences the form that this knowledge takes, by adding varied amounts and kinds of relevant information to the skeleton provided by the innate organizing principles. The point is that nature does not require that we count with one and only one list or that we use one and only one type of musical scale, just that we do use a list or a scale. Recall Sperber and Wilson's (1986) ideas about relevance; an input is relevant: (1) if it overlaps a bit with "old" information so that it can be recognized and anchored to it; and (2) if it adds some "new" knowledge to the cognitive context. We propose that innate domain-specific principles are just the "old" information that make recognition of relevant inputs possible for the infant system, regardless of cultural specifics. The "new" knowledge to be gained from relevant input is both confirmation of the innate principles and information about the specific way a culture has adapted to the universal features of, for instance, number or music. There are many exemplars in the equivalence class of relevant inputs to a developing domain, and cultures are in part *defined* by the unique inputs they provide to learners.

Symbol systems as evidence. Cross-cultural differences in number and music systems have received a lot of attention, perhaps in part because the symbol systems used differ among cultures. Although we do not take the fact that different languages exist as evidence that certain features of language are not universal, the fact that numbers and music are written differently across cultures leads some to conclude that underlying principles must vary with culture. This interpretation may be particularly seductive in the case of music. What we find is that, although the system that, for example, North Indians use to notate music differs from that used in Western cultures, the two systems have certain underlying commonalities. For example, the mechanics used to indicate pitches differ greatly between the two systems. In North Indian notation, note names that correspond to Western solfège terms are written out whereas Western notation indicates exact frequencies. The North Indian singer may start in the key and octave that is most comfortable, but, for the Western performer, key and octave are given by the notation (Batish & Batish, 1989). Subsequent changes in the pitch height or octave of a tone are indicated to the North Indian performer with a dot above the tone-name if the tone is to be raised or with a dot below the name if the tone should be lowered. Despite these differences in mechanics, however, both notational systems include information about the proper intervals between notes so that this aspect of the piece remains constant even if the key or octave of the piece varies from performer to performer. Obviously, it is the succession of intervals between notes, rather than a specific key or octave, that gives a tune its musical identity. (Transpositions or performances by a tenor vs. a soprano are the same song.) It is this crucial aspect of a piece that both North Indian and Western notational systems specify.

Both North Indian and Western cultures have solved the notational problem in distinct ways, but these solutions are similar in critical ways because the surface features of each system are determined by certain universal aspects of musical structure. The equivalence class of notational schemes that incorporate these underlying structural principles is large and allows for wide cultural variation. Cultural variation may result from the different function or role of music in various societies. In the West, orchestral music is popular. Instruments must be pretuned and exact musical frequencies must be notated in the score if "intonational nightmares" are to be avoided. In traditional North Indian music, music is individualistic and orchestras rare so that it is not necessary to standardize the notation of exact frequencies (Batish & Batish,

1989). Batish and Batish point out that the North Indian notational scheme will have to adapt to changing times, perhaps becoming more Westernized, as the use of ensembles and orchestras to perform film music becomes more popular. The notational system of a culture reflects the role that music plays in that society much like language can reflect the experience of a culture, but because certain aspects of music are universal, so must certain aspects of notational systems, such as attention to pitch intervals, be universal.

Those who learn or develop a symbol system do so within the context of certain specific domains of knowledge, each characterized by its own principles. Any general re-representation ability that develops must honor the constraints of the domain-specific knowledge being re-represented. The meaning of notational symbols is defined by the domain of knowledge that is being re-represented. As an illustration, consider the symbol created when one writes two numbers with one over the other and a line between them. In the numerical domain this symbol refers to a specific numerical entity, for example, 4 over 4, which is mathematically equivalent to other symbol combinations, such as 2 over 2, 1234 over 1234, and 1. In music, the notational configuration of a number over a number with a line between them is created when a time signature is placed on a musical staff. In this case, the notation refers not to a single numerical entity but to the number of beats per measure and to the type of note (e.g., quarter, half, eighth) that defines the beat. As a time signature, 4 over 4 does not share an identity relation with 2 over 2, and, indeed, in the musical domain, time signatures of 1234 over 1234 and 1 do not exist. Not only is 4 over 4 not musically equal to either of them but neither notates a relationship that is meaningful in the domain of music. Of course, in the number domain, the line between numbers is necessary to indicate that they are to be divided. For time signatures, the line is part of the staff, not part of the time signature symbol itself. The point is that to know why the line matters in fractions but not in time signatures, one would need to understand the domain of knowledge to which the symbol refers. Clearly, the meaning of any given notational symbol is domain-specific even when the same physical form (e.g., 4 over 4) of the symbol is used to represent knowledge in various domains. Although the re-representational ability is general, the meaning of any given notational system or symbol can be defined only with respect to the principles of the domain of knowledge that it re-represents.

Innate and universal constraints within a domain will necessarily yield culturally varied notational systems that, nevertheless, pay attention to the same sorts of things. With notation we have a parallel to the situation with counting and musical systems themselves; musical systems or counting behavior must be informed by and adhere to underlying principles, but there are many ways to do this. Variations across cultures simply reveal some of these ways. Our point is that cultural differences need not indicate that some aspects of human knowledge are not universal, for structures that vary on the surface are often built on the same type of foundation.[2]

Notes

1. Marler refers to these features as "syntactic" even though they have more in common with features of music than with features of linguistic syntax.
2. Trehub and Trainor's (1993) chapter on infants' processing of musical patterns appeared after this chapter went to press. Readers will find data and discussion that are relevant to the position we have developed for music.

References

Andrews, F. E. (1977). *Numbers, please.* Columbia, OH: Teacher's College Press.
Baillargeon, R., Miller, K. F., & Constantino, J. (1992). *Ten-month-old infants' intuitions about addition.* Unpublished manuscript. University of Illinois, Champaign-Urbana.
Bamberger, J. (1990). *The mind behind the musical ear: How children develop musical intelligence.* Cambridge, MA: Harvard University Press.
Batish, S. D., & Batish, A. (1989). *Ragopedia* (Vol. 1). Santa Cruz, CA: Batish Publications.
Beckmann, H. (1924). Die Entwichlung der Zahleistung bei 2–6 jährigen Kindern. *Zietschrift für Angewandte Psychologie, 22,* 1–72.
Carey, S. (1985). *Conceptual change in childhood.* Cambridge, MA: MIT Press/Bradford Books.
Castellano, M. A., Bharucha, J. J., & Krumhansl, C. L. (1984). Tonal hierarchies in the music of North India. *Journal of Experimental Psychology: General, 113,* 394–412.
Cheng, K., & Gallistel, C. R. (1984). Testing the geometric power of an animal's spatial representation. In H. Roitblat, T. G. Bever, & H. Terrace (Eds.), *Animal cognition* (pp. 409–423). Hillsdale, NJ: Erlbaum.
Cohen, A. J., Thorpe, L. A., & Trehub, S. E. (1987). Infants' perception of musical relations in short transposed tone sequences. *Canadian Journal of Psychology, 41,* 33–47.
Cooper, R. G., Jr. (1984). Early number development: Discovering number space with addition and subtraction. In C. Sophian (Ed.), *The origins of cognitive skills* (pp. 157–192). Hillsdale, NJ: Erlbaum.
Crump, T. (1990). *The anthropology of numbers.* Cambridge: Cambridge University Press.
Dantzig, T. (1954). *Number: The language of science* (4th ed.). New York: The Free Press.
Donald, M. (1991). *Origins of the modern mind.* Cambridge, MA: Harvard University Press.
Dowling, W. J. (1988). Tonal structure and children's early learning of music. In J. A. Sloboda (Ed.), *Generative processes in music: The psychology of performance, improvisation, and composition* (pp. 113–128). Oxford: Clarendon Press.
Fernald, A., & Mazzie, C. (1991). Prosody and focus in speech to infants and adults. *Developmental Psychology, 27,* 209–221.
Fuson, K. C. (1988). *Children's counting and concepts of number.* New York: Springer-Verlag.
Gallistel, C. R. (1990). *The organization of learning.* Cambridge, MA: MIT Press.

Gallistel, C. R. (1993). A conceptual framework for the study of numerical estimation and arithmetic reasoning in animals. In S. Boysen & J. Capaldi (Eds.), *The development of numerical abilities: Animal and human models* (pp. 211–224). Hillsdale, NJ: Erlbaum.

Gallistel, C. R., Brown, A. L., Carey, S., Gelman, R., & Keil, F. C. (1991). Lessons from animal learning for the study of cognitive development. In S. Carey & R. Gelman (Eds.), *The epigenesis of mind: Essays on biology and cognition* (pp. 3–36). Hillsdale, NJ: Erlbaum.

Gallistel, C. R., & Gelman, R. (1990). The what and how of counting. *Cognition, 34,* 197–200.

Gallistel, C. R., & Gelman, R. (1992). Preverbal and verbal counting and computation. *Cognition, 44,* 43–74.

Gardner, H. (1983). *Frames of mind: The theory of multiple intelligences.* New York: Basic Books.

Gelman, R. (1991). Epigenetic foundations of knowledge structures: Initial and transcendent constructions. In S. Carey & R. Gelman (Eds.), *The epigenesis of mind: Essays on biology and cognition* (pp. 293–322). Hillsdale, NJ: Erlbaum.

Gelman, R., Cohen, M., & Hartnett, P. (1989). To know mathematics is to go beyond thinking that "fractions aren't numbers." *Proceedings of the Eleventh Annual Meeting of the North American Chapter, International Group for Psychology of Mathematics Education.* New Brunswick, NJ.

Gelman, R., & Gallistel, C. R. (1978). *The child's understanding of number.* Cambridge, MA: Harvard University Press.

Gelman, R., & Greeno, J. G. (1989). On the nature of competence: Principles for understanding in a domain. In L. B. Resnick (Ed.), *Knowing and learning: Essays in honor of Robert Glaser* (pp. 125–186). Hillsdale, NJ: Erlbaum.

Hallpike, C. R. (1979). *The foundations of primitive thought.* Oxford: Clarendon Press.

Hirsh-Pasek, K., Kemler Nelson, D. G., Jusczyk, P. W., Cassidy, K. W., Druss, B., & Kennedy, L. (1987). Clauses are perceptual units for young infants. *Cognition, 26,* 269–286.

Ifrah, G. (1981/1985). *From one to zero: A universal history of numbers.* New York: Viking.

Jusczyk, P., & Krumhansl, C. L. (in prep.). Pitch and rhythmic patterns affecting infants' sensitivity to musical phrase structure.

Karmiloff-Smith, A. (1986). From meta-processes to conscious access: Evidence from children's metalinguistic and repair data. *Cognition, 23,* 95–147.

Karmiloff-Smith, A. (1992). *Beyond modularity: A developmental perspective on cognitive science.* Cambridge, MA: MIT Press/Bradford Books.

Kemler Nelson, D. G., Hirsh-Pasek, K., Jusczyk, P. W., & Cassidy, K. W. (1989). How the prosodic cues in motherese might assist language learning. *Journal of Child Language, 16,* 55–68.

Klahr, D., & Wallace, J. G. (1973). The role of quantification operators in the development of conservation of quantity. *Cognitive Psychology, 4,* 301–327.

Kline, M. (1972). *Mathematical thought from ancient to modern times.* New York: Oxford University Press.

Krumhansl, C. L., & Jusczyk, P. W. (1990). Infants' perception of phrase structure in music. *Psychological Science, 1,* 1–4.

Krumhansl, C. L., & Keil, F. C. (1982). Acquisition of the hierarchy of tonal functions in music. *Memory & Cognition, 10,* 243–251.

Liberman, A. M., Cooper, F. S., Shankweiler, D. P., & Studdert-Kennedy, M. (1967). Perception of speech. *Psychological Review, 74,* 431–461.

McLeish, J. (1992). *Number: The history of numbers and how they shape our lives.* New York: Fawcett Columbine.

Mandler, J. M. (1992). How to build a baby: II. Conceptual primitives. *Psychological Review, 99,* 587–604.

Margoliash, D., & Fortune, E. S. (1992). Temporal and harmonic combination-sensitive neurons in the zebra finch's HVc. *Journal of Neuroscience, 12,* 4309–4326.

Marler, P. (1991). The instinct to learn. In S. Carey & R. Gelman (Eds.), *The epigenesis of mind: Essays on biology and cognition* (pp. 37–66). Hillsdale, NJ: Erlbaum.

Marr, D. (1982). *Vision.* San Francisco: Freeman.

Meck, W. H., & Church, R. M. (1983). A mode control model of counting and timing processes. *Journal of Experimental Psychology: Animal Behavior Processes, 9,* 320–334.

Menninger, K. (1969). *Number words and number symbols.* Cambridge, MA: MIT Press.

Moore, D., Benenson, J., Reznick, S., Peterson, M., & Kagan, J. (1987). Effects of auditory numerical information on infants' looking behavior: Contradictory evidence. *Developmental Psychology, 23,* 665–670.

Nowicki, S., & Marler, P. (1988). How do birds sing? *Music Perception, 5,* 391–426.

Piaget, J. (1952). *The child's conception of number.* London: Routledge and Paul.

Rose, J. E., Brugge, J. F., Anderson, D. J., & Hind, J. E. (1967). Phase-locked response to low frequency tones in single auditory nerve fibers of the squirrel monkey. *Journal of Neurophysiology, 30,* 769–793.

Saxe, G. B. (1989). Transfer of learning across cultural practices. *Cognition and Instruction, 6,* 325–330.

Shipley, E., & Shepperson, B. (1990). Countable entities: Developmental changes. *Cognition, 34,* 109–136.

Sloboda, J. A. (1985). *The musical mind: The cognitive psychology of music.* Oxford: Clarendon Press.

Sloboda, J. A., Hermelin, B., & O'Connor, N. (1985). An exceptional musical memory. *Music Perception, 3,* 155–170.

Sophian, C. (1991/1992). Learning about numbers: Lessons for mathematics education from preschool number development. In J. Bideaud, C. Meljac, & J-P. Fischer (Eds.), *Pathways to number* (pp. 19–40). Hillsdale, NJ: Erlbaum.

Sophian, C., & Adams, N. (1987). Infants' understanding of numerical transformations. *British Journal of Developmental Psychology, 5,* 257–264.

Sperber, D., & Wilson, D. (1986). *Relevance.* Oxford: Blackwell.

Starkey, P. (1992). The early development of numerical reasoning. *Cognition, 43,* 93–126.

Starkey, P., Spelke, E. S., & Gelman, R. (1983). Detection of intermodal correspondences by human infants. *Science, 222,* 179–181.

Starkey, P., Spelke, E. S., & Gelman, R. (1990). Numerical abstraction by human infants. *Cognition, 36,* 97–127.

Stigler, J. W., & Baranes, R. (1988). Culture and mathematics learning. In E. Rothkopf (Ed.), *Review of research in education, 15,* 253–306.

Strauss, M. S., & Curtis, L. E. (1984). Development of numerical concepts in infancy. In C. Sophian (Ed.), *Origins of cognitive skills* (pp. 131–155). Hillsdale, NJ: Erlbaum.

Takeuchi, A. H., & Hulse, S. H. (1993). Absolute pitch. *Psychological Bulletin, 113*, 345–361.

Trainor, L. (1993a, March). *The development of sensitivity to Western melodic structure*. Presented at the biennial meeting of the Society for Research in Child Development, New Orleans.

Trainor, L. (1993b, March). *What makes a melody intrinsically easy to process: Comparing infant and adult listeners*. Presented at the biennial meeting of the Society for Research in Child Development, New Orleans.

Trainor, L. J., & Trehub, S. E. (1992). A comparison of infants' and adults' sensitivity to Western musical structure. *Journal of Experimental Psychology: Human Perception and Performance, 18*, 394–402.

Trehub, S. E. (1987). Infants' perception of musical patterns. *Perception and Psychophysics, 41*, 635–641.

Trehub, S. E., & Trainor, L. J. (1993) Listening strategies in infancy: The roots of music and language development. In S. McAdams & E. Bigand (Eds.), *Thinking in sound: The cognitive psychology of human audition* (pp. 278–327). Oxford: Clarendon Press.

van Loosbroek, E., & Smitsman, A. W. (1990). Visual perception of numerosity in infancy. *Developmental Psychology, 26*, 916–922.

Winner, E. (1982). *Invented worlds: The psychology of the arts*. Cambridge, MA: Harvard University Press.

Wynn, K. (1992). Addition and subtraction by human infants. *Nature, 358*, 749–750.

15 Cognitive constraints on cultural representations: Natural ontologies and religious ideas

Pascal Boyer

The point of a cognitive approach to cultural representations is to put forward a series of causal hypotheses in order to account for certain features of cultural phenomena. Central to such an inquiry is the notion of *cognitive constraints*; given the general properties of human minds, certain types of representations are more likely than others to be acquired and transmitted, thereby constituting those stable sets of representations that anthropologists call "cultures." To many anthropologists, cultural phenomena seem to lie outside the scope of cognitive constraints, due to three types of reasons: their ontological status, their variability, and their transmission. Cultural anthropology generally focuses on abstract systems of "symbols," "codes," or "meanings," the properties of which are supposed to be independent of the way they are represented in human minds. Second, cultural representations are considered as intrinsically variable; as a consequence, it seems difficult to appeal to universal properties of human minds in their description or explanation. Finally, the content and organization of cultural representations, in competent members of a culture, seem to be entirely constrained by what subjects were taught through social interaction. Against these assumptions, I will take as a starting point the following principles:

1. Cultural systems can and must be studied as sets of mental representations acquired and stored by human minds, because acquisition and memorization processes impose strong constraints on the contents and organization of cultural representations.

2. Their undeniable variability should not lead us to ignore important recurrent features, which deserve an explanation.

3. Finally, the argument that all cultural material is acquired through social interaction is much too vague. It may well be the case that some important aspects of cultural representations are precisely not acquired through socialization.

391

In the space of these pages I will not attempt a general defense of this framework.[1] What I will do is show to what extent it can help us reformulate classical anthropological problems. Religious ideas seem the "most cultural" part of culture, and consequently the least likely to be explained in cognitive terms. My argument here is that, if cognitive hypotheses are relevant in the explanation of religious ideas, then other aspects of cultural representations will be a fortiori amenable to such a description.

The implicit assumption behind the notion of cognitive constraint is that cultural transmission is an inherently *selective* process. Given certain circumstances and a variety of mental representations entertained by a population of subjects, some of those representations are more likely than others to be stored in the subjects' memories and transmitted to other subjects. The transmission process itself, by virtue of its structural properties, and by virtue of the cognitive processes it requires, favors the survival of particular cultural representations. An important consequence of this principle is that we need not assume that there is any compelling reason why cultural material is the way it is. On the other hand, there may be compelling reasons why, once a certain cultural material has appeared, it is particularly likely to be transmitted from generation to generation.[2]

Recurrence and cultural underdetermination

The search for universal cognitive constraints does not entail the postulation of cultural *universals*. In all human groups one can find a set of ideas concerning nonobservable, extranatural agencies and processes. Beyond this minimal point, however, we find a family resemblance rather than universal features. For instance, it is assumed in many (but not all) human groups that a nonphysical component of persons can survive after death. Also, such intangible entities are generally construed as intentional beings, that is, beings who entertain beliefs and desires. In the same way, it is very often (though not always) assumed that certain people are especially likely to receive direct inspiration or messages from extranatural agencies, such as gods and spirits. It is also often assumed that such capacities are relatively stable, in the sense that the persons in question are fundamentally, sometimes naturally, different from the others. In most (not all) human groups it is assumed that certain salient events (e.g., illness or misfortune) are symptoms of underlying causal connections between supernatural beings and the world of the living. It is also often admitted that performing certain ritual recipes in the exact way and order prescribed can bring about changes in physical states of affairs. In most human groups, one can find a set of divination recipes, which supposedly guarantee the truth of the statements produced by the technique.

These recurrent features of religious representations are of course not a discovery of the cognitive framework presented here. They have constituted a starting point of most anthropological theories of religion, ever since Tylor,

Frazer, or Durkheim. In such frameworks, however, certain recurrent features were often singled out as hypothetical religious universals. It was then necessary to explain why they were not clearly present in all societies observed. Against this fruitless, and in fact futile search for universals, the theory offered here starts from the more realistic assumption that certain features of cultural representations are recurrent in many different cultural environments, and this recurrence is clearly above chance. The central assumption in this framework is that cognitive constraints on acquisition and representation may provide an explanation for this phenomenon of recurrence.

In order to provide a satisfactory, and psychologically plausible account of religious representations, we must first dispel certain conceptual ambiguities that are pervasive in the anthropological literature, notably as concerns (1) the subjective "unnaturalness" of religious assumptions, (2) their cognitive diversity, and (3) the extent to which they depend on cultural transmission.

Unnaturalness as an intuitive property

Religious representations typically center on claims that violate commonsense expectations concerning ordinary things, beings, and processes. For instance, religious entities are described as invisible beings, yet located in space, intangible yet capable of mechanical action on physical objects. Some of those beings are construed as unaffected by the ordinary process of growth, aging, and death that characterizes all living beings. Also, certain artifacts are described as having causal properties that extend beyond the characteristics of ordinary objects. One could multiply examples of such claims. One task of a cognitive framework is to explain why and how human minds are led to entertain such notions and to find them particularly plausible. Central to this investigation is the question of the relation between religious claims on the one hand, and representations of the everyday, ordinary world on the other. We must give a precise description of the connections between ordinary cognition and the extraordinary claims of religious ontologies.

In anthropological theories, however, this problem has been more often avoided than approached. One recurrent argument is that the unnaturalness of religious ideas is only the consequence of an ethnocentric perspective. The claims that seem unnatural to Western observers are in fact taken as perfectly natural by the people concerned; and they *are* natural, once we take into account a certain background of beliefs, theories, worldviews, and so forth. If such is the case, then the question of a connection between representations of the everyday and representations of the supernatural is eliminated.

This argument, however, just flies in the face of the facts. Let me illustrate this with a simple example, taken from my own ethnographic work among the Fang of Cameroon. Many Fang people consider that witches are persons with an additional organ, which leaves their bodies at night and has all sorts of bizarre skills. The *evur* can fly on banana leaves, it can make another person's blood turn black and thick, it can kill fetuses in the womb, and so on. Such notions seem odd because they violate general principles of everyday cognition. Members of the same species are usually assumed to have the same organs; flying on banana leaves is known to be rather difficult, and so forth. Now these are the very reasons that make such ideas worthy of attention, for Fang people. They find stories of flying organs and mysterious witchcraft killings fascinating as well as terrifying, precisely because they violate their expectations about biological and physical phenomena. Such stories are certainly taken by most subjects as accounts of *real* events, a fact that poses many problems of psychological description. But they are not taken as accounts of *ordinary* real events. Their "attention-demanding" quality depends on the counterintuitive claims they comprise.

Many anthropologists would be reluctant to admit this, because they think it implies that people like the Fang have the same "conception of nature" (and "supernature") as the observer; but, they would argue, we know that our own, Western conception of "the natural" is a philosophical elaboration, constructed in particular historical circumstances. The objection, however, is irrelevant to the present discussion. The "unnatural" character of religious claims does not stem from any explicit, accessible conception of nature; it is an *intuitive property*. Representing as nonordinary, counterintuitive, the events or states evoked in religious claims do not require an explicit, accessible conception of nature or supernature. They require only intuitive expectations about the behavior of physical objects in space, the biological processes that lead to death and decay, and so on. In some cultural contexts, some people develop explicit notions or even theories about what is natural and what is not. These ideas, however, do not govern their intuitions. On the contrary, it is very likely that such explicit notions are constructed by generalizing over a range of stable intuitions about the naturalness of actual or imagined events and states. In other words, saying that there is a set of representations about unnatural objects only commits us to the following assumption: The people in question have some cognitive means (of which they are not necessarily aware) to sort out events and states that violate intuitive expectations, from events and states that do not.

Cognitive diversity as domain specificity

In anthropological discussions, religious representations are often presented as consisting of shared, integrated, explicit, context-free general statements, for example, "the spirits dwell in the rivers," "the ancestors are invisible," and so on. This is rather misleading; very few people ever represent religious assumptions in this way. As all anthropologists know, describing them in this "theoretical" style is an oversimplification. Not all ideas in a religious system are shared by all participants; not all of them are integrated in a single overarching system; certainly many of them are not explicit. More important perhaps, many religious representations are about particular, contextual realities rather than the abstract types to which they belong, for instance, a certain action performed by a certain person, rather than about "the ritual X." This is why anthropological monographs generally complement such abstract descriptions with a wealth of detailed anecdotal material, the point of which is to give the readers some idea of the actual complexities of religious thinking.

I will not dwell here on this aspect of ethnographic descriptions. I want to focus on another, more damaging type of oversimplification. In our approach to religious representations, we tend to think that certain general cognitive principles, notably as regards the acquisition and representation of concepts, apply to all domains of religious representations in the same way. This is congruent with a classical Piagetian picture of cognitive development, following which the child gradually acquires and complexifies a series of structural principles. These principles, when they are acquired, are applied to all conceptual domains in the same way. Against this oversimplified picture, I will mention in the following pages a variety of recent studies suggesting that different conceptual domains are acquired by activating significantly different structural principles.[3]

Before examining this question in detail, we can already divide the putative "domain" of religious representations into a series of "repertoires" of representations that are likely to display significant differences in terms of acquisition and fixation of beliefs. Here I will distinguish between four such repertoires, namely, the *ontological*, the *causal*, the *action*, and the *social categories* repertoires respectively. The *ontological* repertoire is the set of ideas people entertain about the existence of nonobservable entities. This catalogue will include ideas about there being, for example, a distant impersonal Creator somewhere in the skies, water-spirits near ponds and rivers, or invisible ancestors lurking in the darkness of the forest. The *causal* repertoire is a catalogue of ideas and assumptions about causal links between the entities described in the ontological repertoire, on the one hand, and observable events and states of affairs on the other. Thus a causal repertoire may include assumptions such as "gods get angry if no sacrifice is performed" or "reciting a formula will guarantee good crops." The *episode* repertoire consists of descriptions of a certain range of actions and interactions, which are connected to the ideas contained in the ontological and causal repertoire. Describing a religion involves describing a certain set of particular actions or states that are deemed to be of particular types. Obviously, ritual performances are among the most salient types of religious episodes. The *social categories* repertoire is a catalogue of representations concerning differences between people. In this catalogue we include people's ideas concerning their priests, shamans, or other religious specialists, but also any ideas concerning other differences that are relevant in religious action. The rationale for the division between those four categories is that the elements from different repertoires are likely to behave in functionally different ways, in the acquisition and fixation of belief. In this chapter, however, I examine only the recurrent *ontological* assumptions that underlie most religious systems (for a consideration of all four repertoires, see Boyer, 1993).

Cultural transmission

Cultural anthropology generally assumes a commonsense, pre-theoretical view of cultural acquisition, which I will call the theory of *exhaustive cultural transmission*. The main assumption is that the representations entertained by adult, competent members of a group are entirely determined by what was given to them through social interaction. This conception of cultural acquisition, which constitutes what Bloch called the "anthropological theory of cognition" (Bloch, 1985), is often taken for granted in anthropological theories. The main point of this theory is that people brought up in a "culture" are given a ready-made conceptual scheme, which is absorbed, as it were, in a mysterious way that is never described. This "theory of cognition" implies that cultural transmission is, by and large, a *passive* process. Minds are conceived as containers of ideas, which are more-or-less empty at the onset of cultural acquisition, and are gradually filled with whatever ready-made products are given by "the culture." What is studied by anthropologists is supposed to consist of representations created by human groups, in the absence of any relevant cognitive constraints.

This notion of cultural transmission is supported by our intuitive, commonsense notion of cognitive development, which generally has a strong empiricist bias. That is to say, we tend to think that the way children gradually acquire adult competence, in most cognitive domains, is mainly driven by experience. Subjects memorize observational data, and use recurrent features of those data as the starting point in the elaboration of abstract hypotheses. These hypotheses themselves are sometimes refuted, and generally modified on the basis of further experiential data. Cognitive growth is therefore construed as the accumulation of data, combined with the resulting accumulation of gradually more refined hypotheses. Obviously, the commonsense conception leaves some space for direct tuition, which is not experience-driven, in more complex domains.

Against the anthropological conception of cultural acquisition, I argue here that cultural representations are *underdetermined* by cultural transmission. The range of representations people entertain about religious matters is underdetermined by tuition in at least three different ways. First, in most cultural environments, there is very little explicit tuition, abstract instruction, or commentary about what is denoted by religious terms. People are seldom taught the local "theory" of ancestors or spirits in abstract terms. Local exegeses and rationalizations are, by and large, comments on the use of local categories rather than instructions as to their putative denotation.[4] Second, even in situations in which some religious tuition is given, it is generally given in a way that is too incomplete or inconsistent to constitute the basis for certain inferences. Third, and most important, the input is also essentially incomplete. Most religious notions could not be acquired and transmitted in the absence of certain unstated assumptions. For instance, in certain rituals people acquire general notions concerning ancestors from singular occasions of mystical "encounters" with them. This implies that instance-based generalizations are legitimate, as concerns certain aspects (and not others) of the ancestors' behavior. It is impossible to learn anything about the ancestors without underlying principles that guide inductive generalizations.

My main contention here is twofold: (1) that some implicit assumptions and principles of intuitive knowledge are carried over in religious representations; (2) that these principles and assumptions play a crucial role in the acquisition and transmission of the representations concerned. In the following pages I will substantiate these claims, on the basis of an ethnographic example, and then examine the implications of these connections for a general account of religious ideas.

Explicit assumptions and their background

In this section, I make use of a particular aspect of Fang religious ideas, namely, the various assumptions concerning the "ghosts" or "ancestors." I first present a very concise account of the assumptions on which this notion is based, and the way they are acquired by Fang subjects. I then try to show that this apparently simple acquisition process in fact requires the operation of background assumptions, the acquisition of which is far more difficult to describe in the ordinary anthropological framework of "exhaustive cultural transmission." Although I describe the example in some detail, the conclusions I draw from this case apply to religious ontologies in general.

An example: "Ghosts" among the Fang

The Fang consider that the forest is peopled with wandering shadows, among which are the spirits of the dead, called *bekong*. They dwell in invisible villages (some people see them as underground villages, others as camps in the darkest recesses of the forest) and breed wild animals. Many people report strange situations, which are interpreted as signs of the ghosts' presence. A fleeting shadow is seen in a clearing, or a chased animal suddenly disappears in a bush. Such encounters typically occur in liminal spaces (a clearing, which is neither forest nor village) and at liminal times (dawn and dusk). There is considerable ambiguity concerning the exact process through which death transforms people into *bekong*. For most people, however, it is the person's *nsisim* ("shadow") that leaves the body and becomes a *kong*. This makes sense, as the term *nsisim* is often used as a conventional metaphor for individual identity, for what makes a person different from others.

A number of general principles are used to describe the ghosts. They center on the physical properties of the ghosts, and the type of observable phenomena that can be brought about by their action. To start with their properties, everyone characterizes the ghosts as invisible and intangible beings. The "encounters" mentioned above are interpreted as situations in which a ghost wants to send a signal to the living, or wants to be noticed for some reason. More serious encounters, and conversations with the ghosts, occur only in dreams or in a trance. Ghosts are also described as intangible, in the vague sense that they can go through physical obstacles. Moreover, they are described as able to move extremely fast, although no one ever supposes that they could be in two places at once. The *implications* of such principles, and even their entailments, are often surrounded with uncertainty. Although everyone is quite definite that ghosts usually cannot be seen, and that they are never hindered by physical obstacles, no one ever speculates on the possible implications of such capacities. The way these seemingly nonphysical entities eat and drink and the way they domesticate and use wild animals is mysterious, though it constitutes a mystery in which no one seems to show any interest.

On the other hand, the effects of the ghosts' actions are of considerable interest, and the subject matter of frequent statements. It is assumed, and explicitly stated on many occasions, that ghosts can send illnesses at people when they are angry with them. The ghosts are likely to interfere in the affairs of the living, whenever the latter violate ritual prohibitions, or deviate from the traditional ways. In the Fang nosology, such situations constitute an explicitly recognized etiological category. There are ritual specialists, and prescribed ritual remedies for such diseases, which of course include many types of misfortune, beyond somatic illnesses.

This constitutes a very concise summary of what most Fang people accept as valid statements concerning the *bekong* and their actions. We have here the main elements that would be examined in an anthropological description of this notion. Such a description, however, is essentially fragmentary. This is not just a question of ethnographic detail. Obviously, the account presented here should be completed with a number of precise indications, as regards the ideas, images, and actions that are connected with this notion of *bekong*. I would claim, however, that anthropological descriptions in general are incomplete in a more fundamental sense, because they leave aside certain aspects of conceptual structure without which we cannot understand the phenomenon of cultural transmission. I will try and spell out these aspects that are systematically omitted in anthropological descriptions and theories.

Before proceeding any further, I must insist on two general characteristics of the principles mentioned earlier. First, the explicit assumptions express *counterintuitive* claims, which are clearly treated as such by everyone. The fact that some beings can go through obstacles, become invisible, or keep wild animals the way humans breed domesticated species, are explicitly treated as out of the ordinary. Second, the transmission of such principles does not seem mysterious at all. Many of them are explicitly stated as valid generalizations, for instance, "the *bekong* live in the forest," "dead people become *bekong*," and so on. Others can be acquired by generalizing over repeated instances. For instance, one seldom hears the general statement "the *bekong* can provoke misfortune"; its application to a singular case, however, is frequent enough to suggest the generalization even to very lazy inductivists.

The background: Tacit assumptions

In the previous section, I gave a summary of the counterintuitive claims that constitute the focus of Fang discourse about the ghosts. There is no shortage of material, in terms of stated principles, particular anecdotes, and more-or-less mythical stories concerning the ghosts. From such cultural material, people naturally derive their general notions about the strange physical and causal properties of the ghosts. In order, however, to extract such principles from such material, it is necessary to accept a number of implicit premises. Any inductive generalization requires a background of assumptions concerning the type of features that can be generalized. This very general point has important consequences for the precise question of cultural acquisition, as we will see in the following discussion.

Without providing a detailed explanation of Fang notions about ghost-behavior, I must specify those principles that are necessary in order to produce generalizations in this domain. First and foremost, people can take singular episodes, and ritual statements, as the basis for hypotheses about ghosts in general, because they can understand ghost-behavior in *psychological* terms. This requires a set of principles, which are both tacit and indispensable. No one states them, no one is even aware of them, yet if they were not activated the anecdotes for instance would make no sense. For instance, it is necessary to assume that the ghosts have psychological mechanisms such that they can perceive what people do, form some beliefs on the basis of those perceptions, and keep those beliefs in memory. It is also assumed that the ghosts have mental capacities such that, if they find a certain state of affairs E to be desirable, and know that another state of affairs, C, is necessary to achieve E, then they will desire to achieve C. The ghosts are described as *wishing* that certain rituals were performed. They are described as *knowing* that people, if afflicted by misfortune, will eventually oblige. They are said to *decide*, in consequence, that some illness should be "sent" to the living. When people are making inferences from the partly explicit cultural material that is given, they necessarily rely on such tacit principles, describing the ghosts' putative psychological mechanisms. These principles are not given in the utterances and other types of explicit information on the ghosts. They are not implicitly transmitted, in the sense that they could be readily deduced from that explicit information. On the contrary, it is because they are assumed to be valid that inferences about the ghosts' behavior can be drawn at all.

These implicit assumptions concerning the ghosts' psychology are themselves based on a further set of assumptions concerning the stability of their properties as a kind. Obviously, the fact that one can infer general principles from a limited series of examples presupposes that at least some properties of the ghosts are stable. This is especially the case as regards the causal propensities of the ghosts. Subjects spontaneously assume that all or most ghosts have the powers that are exemplified in particular anecdotes or stories. This would not be possible, without the prior assumption, that ghosts are, precisely, a kind, that one can safely produce instance-based general principles.

Such tacit assumptions are never mentioned in anthropological descriptions. This is mainly because it seems unnecessary, perhaps even slightly absurd, to insist on such self-evident principles. After all, one would be really surprised if ghosts were described as desiring an effect E, knowing that its condition is C, and *not* desiring C. Obviously, spelling out the default values in a conceptual system is an unrewarding exercise, in that it requires that we dwell on the banal, if not the platitudinous. This, however, is indispensable in order to have a psychologically realistic description of acquisition. In the following sections, I show how the intuitive empiricist picture of cultural acquisition must be abandoned, if we take into account the necessary presence of such tacit assumptions.

Intuitive ontologies

In the Fang example, we have distinguished between two types of assumptions that combine in the conceptual structure of a category like *bekong*. They are different in terms of attention-demanding potential (counterintuitive vs. self-evident assumptions), as well as representational status (explicit vs. tacit assumptions). The most important difference for our problems, however, is the mode of acquisition. As I pointed out, the processes whereby people acquire the counterintuitive aspects of the conceptual structure do not seem particularly mysterious. Against the background of prior hypotheses concerning the stability of the ghosts as a kind and the fact that their mental processes are similar to that of human beings, the cultural material seems sufficient to support the type of generalizations that constitute adult competence in this domain. On the other hand, such simple processes of inductive generalization are insufficient, if we want to describe the way the background principles themselves are acquired. Their acquisition process must therefore be described if we want to have a complete account of the acquisition of religious ontologies. To do this, we must leave aside strictly anthropological matters for a while, and turn to developmental evidence.

Ontological categories

Research into the representation of ontological distinctions was initiated by F. Keil (1979). Keil assumed that ordinary concepts and predicates carry implicit ontological categories, for example, EVENT, OBJECT, LIVING THING, ANIMATE, HUMAN, and so forth, which are (1) organized in a hierarchy and (2) made manifest by predicate selection. Not all predicates can be applied to a given term, and the applicability of a given predicate allows one to predict the applicability of others. If it is possible to say that a given X "is breathing," then Xs might also, in certain cases, be "furious," but could certainly not be described as "difficult to make" or "happening tomorrow." Keil's experimental research (1979, 1986) showed that even young children make surprisingly fine-grained ontological distinctions, between, for instance, living things and artifacts, and they have precise intuitions on the applicability of predicates. Children, whose vocabulary does not include abstract terms like "event," "property," and "living kind," nevertheless make clear distinctions between those ontological categories. The ontological "tree" is of course gradually developed, mainly by subdividing categories that originally merge two or more adult categories. The most important aspect of these studies, and a highly relevant point to anthropological models, is that it is possible for the subjects to make spontaneous ontological assumptions about terms for which they have virtually no conceptual structure.[5]

Intuitive domain-specific principles

A number of recent developmental studies have emphasized the fact that domain-specific principles correspond to these broad ontological categories. Developmental research on such specific principles has focused on many different domains (for a general survey, see Atran, 1989). The presumptions apply to ontological domains such as physical objects, artifacts, living kinds, and persons. Each of these domains seems to be structured by principles or presumptions that develop early, and seem relatively independent from the structuring principles of other domains. These principles constitute what is often called "intuitive" or "naive" theories (as opposed to scientific theories). They are generally implicit, and seem to play a crucial role in the development of later, partly explicit representations of the domains concerned. Early cognitive development relies on the construction of a naive theory of physical objects (Spelke, 1990), a naive biology (Keil, 1986, 1989) and a naive theory of mental processes (Astington, Harris, & Olson, 1988; Wellman, 1990), to mention a few domains explored so far.

A crucial point is that intuitive "theoretical" principles seem to develop *spontaneously*, in the sense that they are underdetermined by direct or implicit tuition or by objective changes in the available information. The development of "essentialist" assumptions in the representation of living kinds, for instance, occurs in children who have very rudimentary notions of biological processes, and therefore make a clear-cut distinction between, for example, members of a living species and members of a class of artifacts, without the conceptual means to explain the distinction. This principle may be interpreted as an enrichment of a deeper principle, which establishes a fundamental difference in expectations concerning animate as opposed to inanimate objects. There is considerable evidence that this distinction is present even in infants (R. Gelman, Spelke, & Meck, 1983; Bullock, 1985; Richards & Siegler, 1986) and may be grounded in an early sensitivity to the difference between self- and non-self-generated movement in physical objects (Massey & R. Gelman, 1988). In other words, even if essentialist principles develop over time, and are enriched by various "microtheoretical" assumptions, they require presumptions of differences in causal structure that appear extremely early. Obviously, such presumptions are not taught, and they are certainly underdetermined by experience. Far from being inferred from experience, "the initial principles of a domain establish the boundary conditions for the stimuli that are candidates for feeding coherent development in that domain" (R. Gelman, 1990: 83).

This point is of course crucial for cultural anthropology. If intuitive principles are not inferred from experience, then they cannot vary as a function of the cultural environment. Indeed, there is a range of evidence to show that important variations in cultural settings do not affect the content of intuitive presumptions or their developmental schedule in a significant way. As regards biological knowledge, the universality of its basic principles is a familiar point (see Berlin, Breedlove, & Raven, 1973; Brown, 1984; Atran, 1985, 1987, 1990). Furthermore, other aspects of conceptual development appear to be similar, even in domains that could give rise to strong cultural influences. For instance, Walker [Jeyifous] observed that the defining-to-characteristic shift, as described by Keil in American children, occurs in the same form at the same age in Yoruba subjects. Moreover, the shifts display the same domain-specific characteristics. If anything, more variation can be found within Yoruba subjects, between rural and urban subjects, than between the Yoruba average and the American results (Walker [Jeyifous], 1985, 1992a, 1992b). Given the enormous differences in sociocultural settings, it would require some quasi-miraculous coincidence for such shifts to occur at the same age in the same way in the cultures compared.[6]

The Fang case: Ghost-physics and ghost-psychology

To return to the example of the Fang *bekong* mentioned earlier, the common understanding of the notion can be paraphrased, roughly, as follows: *Bekong* are invisible, intangible sentient beings. This of course constitutes an obvious violation of a commonsense principle, following which intentional beings are physical objects. There is a direct link between intentionality, and other characteristics of sentient beings on the one hand, and "corporeality" on the other. Given such premises, the special characteristics of *bekong* make them a conceptual oddity, a puzzling invention. This is very much the way they are construed by the Fang, and most statements about what *bekong* are, or what they can do, are typically accompanied by remarks concerning the uncertainty that results from this oddity. *Bekong*, however, are also assumed to have many other properties, among them psychological processes. Those processes, in striking contrast to the assumptions concerning physicality, are intuitive in the sense that they are a straightforward projection of the assumptions made about people's mental processes.

Ordinary folkpsychology is based on a number of intuitive presumptions, which are both "transparent" and theoretically complex. People's common-sense interpretation of other people's behavior is consistently directed by implicit principles concerning motivation, intentions, memory, reasoning, and so on. Some of these principles are specific, in that they depend on assumptions that concern only other people's behavior, as opposed to any other kinds of data. Moreover, these assumptions appear early enough to be construed as orienting principles, which structure experience, rather than as generalizations inferred from experience by some cross-domain inductive mechanism.

One must distinguish here between implicit assumptions concerning mental contents (the intuitive "theory of mind" or "psychology" proper), and a host of explicit assumptions concerning more complex aspects of mentation (what is often called a "folk psychology"). To give a simple example, it seems obvious to any human subject, from a very early age, that other people's minds perform practical syllogisms. In other words, a default value in the intuitive explanation of behavior is that "all else being equal, if people want a state X and know that 'no X without Y', then they are led to want Y." In all cultural environments, however, intuitive psychology is complemented with a host of specific principles concerning more complex aspects of human behavior. They focus on such domains as motivation, personality types, and the likely psychological effect of certain situations. Many people in the United States, for instance, produce inferences based on the following principle: "Weak-willed people, if they want X and know that 'no X unless Y' but find Y hard to achieve, will give up on X unless they really have a strong desire that X." This type of dynamic explanation is part of a series of hypotheses that are often explicitly represented and used in argument. Here I consider only assumptions of the first type, which are particularly relevant to our problems of religious assumptions.[7]

Intuitive principles comprise a number of assumptions about mental objects and their dynamic interaction. Because they are intuitive, self-evident, and make it possible to complexify one's knowledge of other minds, such assumptions are best elucidated by developmental research. Their effect is clearer in subjects who have no explicit vocabulary to express them, and no awareness of their implicit use in particular explanations. To take the most fundamental facts, even small children seem to conceive mental entities (thoughts, feelings, dreams) as nonphysical objects; this goes against the classical Piagetian notion of childhood realism, following which children do not distinguish between objects and their representation (Wellman & Estes, 1986). Moreover, children have rudimentary, yet precise notions concerning causality in mental events. They know that perception causes beliefs, which can cause intentions, and that these causal links are not reversible. This causal schema is a fundamental feature of what D'Andrade called the "folk-model" of the mind (D'Andrade, 1987).[8] Cultural variations do not seem to have any significant effect on these phenomena. For example, Avis and Harris (1991) made a series of studies on the representation of false belief in Pygmy children. These tests replicate the substance of familiar American experiments, and offer substantially the same results. From an early age (about 4 to 5) children develop an awareness of false belief, an awareness of the fact that other people may store representations of the world that do not correspond to an actual state of affairs, and that they may act on the basis of such a misrepresentation.

To recapitulate: In the analysis of a paradigmatic example of religious notion (the Fang *bekong*), we find that some principles of intuitive, domain-specific conceptual structures can play an important role in shaping and constraining people's beliefs about apparently fantastic religious entities. In this case, the principles in question are notably principles dealing with the explanation of behavior in terms of intentions and beliefs. The existence, and importance of such principles cast doubt on the anthropological notion of exhaustive cultural transmission. The principles of intuitive mentalistic psychology must be included in our description of the Fang notion *bekong*, if we want to have a plausible psychological description of the way people acquire the notion, build a relatively coherent representation of these entities, and make inferences about their behavior. Now these principles are part of a set of cognitive systems that are not culturally transmitted, and in fact are not transmitted at all.

Recurrent violations and a cognitive optimum

Let me now try to show how this type of explanation could be extended further. A natural extension of the Fang example would be to assume that principles of intuitive knowledge may well play a similar part in the construction of religious concepts in general. At this point, obviously, I will have to rely on vastly simplified generalizations to support the speculative claims. I hope this way of proceeding can at least generate a picture of religious ontologies that is at least as plausible as the notion of unbounded cultural construction.

The simplest way to describe these recurrent themes is perhaps to try and construct a list of these ontological assumptions that are the basis of religious systems and violate intuitive expectations. I do not claim that my list is exhaustive, or even precise enough to be of great explanatory power. It should, however, give some indication of the type of explanation the research program is about.

Let me begin with the most obvious, and probably the most common way in which religious ideas can be counterintuitive. This is the postulation of a class (or classes) of beings whose specific properties make them either very strange physical objects, or apparently nonphysical ones. The Fang ancestor-ghosts are, of course, among such entities. Religious systems are almost invariably based on such assumptions, so much so that the idea of nonphysical beings has often been taken, from Tylor onward, as the very definition of religion. The claims concerning the physical properties of such entities typically focus on their intangibility, invisibility, instantaneous changes of location or ubiquity, and so forth.

Another typical violation concerns the fact that many religious entities are construed as having a particular biological destiny. The entities either do not die, or were not born, or do not grow. Typically, ancestors are biologically "blocked" at the age of death, and gods are either ageless or have a characteristic "age" that does not change with time. In other words, they are explicitly characterized as beings whose existence violates expectations about living beings, as regards the normal cycles of birth, maturation, reproduction, death, and decay.

A third type of violation concerns the strange mental and communicational characteristics of the supernatural personnel. This is obvious in popular Western Christian conceptions, for instance, which assume that God can detect, not only people's actions, but also their thoughts and intentions. As is well known, this explicit assumption can generate many cognitive paradoxes. For example, it is difficult to assume the capacity of intention-reading, and to understand what goes on in a prayer (because God knows one's intentions). However, the assumption is necessary to the type of intention-based morality that is admitted in such groups. Paradoxes can also be generated by other common explicit assumptions, such as the idea that the gods can foresee future events.

A conjectural interpretation

How should a cognitive theory of religious ideas approach such seemingly odd principles and assumptions? Anthropologists, being trained both to detect cultural differences and to focus on the counterintuitive nature of religious claims, tend to provide a distorted view of the cognitive processes involved. Against the grain of received anthropological wisdom, I would therefore argue that (1) violations of intuitive ontologies are far more limited than we usually assume, and (2) the amount of intuitive understanding that is required to acquire religious notions is far greater than the anthropological descriptions lead one to think.

Let me offer a brief illustration of this idea, as concerns the three main types of violations already mentioned above. As I said, many creatures such as spirits or ghosts are explicitly described as having counterintuitive physical properties. I tried to show, on the Fang example, that in order to acquire ideas about ancestor-ghosts, one must admit implicit intuitive assumptions about belief-desire psychology. In other cases, the distribution of intuitive and counterintuitive assumptions may be different. The general point, however, is that it would be difficult to acquire and represent ideas about such nonphysical beings except against a background of intuitive theories.

The same arguments can be put forward in the description of odd biological properties, or odd mental-communicational capacities. The beings that are explicitly construed as eternal actually have many properties that are directly transferred from intuitive presumptions. Greek gods are eternal and feed on the smell of sacrifices; their common representation, however, included many aspects transferred directly from commonsense understandings, having to do, for example, with their reasonings or feelings. Such beings typically display, again, a form of belief-desire psychology that seems self-evident because it is directly transferred from commonsense intuitive "theories." An omniscient God is nevertheless submitted to intuitive principles of psychology, and produces *modus ponens* inferences or practical syllogisms in much the same self-evident way as ordinary people.

Cognitive optimum

In slightly metaphorical terms, one could describe the interaction of violations and confirmations as a kind of division of labor. As I tried to show throughout this chapter, religious concepts could not be acquired, and more radically could simply not be represented, if their ontological assumptions did not confirm an important background of intuitive principles. At the same time, they would not be the object of any attention, if they did not contain some principles that are simply ruled out by intuitive expectations. In a speculative way, one could assume that certain combinations of intuitive and counterintuitive claims constitute a cognitive optimum. Obviously, most religious assumptions focus on objects that seemingly violate commonsense assumptions. It can be shown, however, that in order to acquire these notions, subjects have to rely, implicitly, on the intuitive principles I have described. In this framework, a religious category would be described as cognitively optimal if (1) it contains some explicit violation of commonsense thinking and (2) it makes implicit use of the intuitive principles of commonsense knowledge. The hypothesis is that religious representations that are cognitively optimal will be the most recurrent ones. Being easier to learn and memorize, they will have a greater "survival value," in terms of cultural transmission, than other representations.

For the sake of intuitive clarity, this speculative model could be expressed in metaphorically teleological terms, as follows. In order to create religious representations that have some chance of cultural survival, that is, of being acquired, memorized, and transmitted, one must strike a balance between the requirements of imagination (attention-demanding potential) and learnability (inferential potential). If a religious concept comprises only counterintuitive claims, it will fail on the second criterion. Take the imaginary example of a god that would be construed as omnipotent but having no mind, so that one cannot have any description of his/her/its mental processes. This would make it practically impossible to make sense of the relationship between the god and human action. Conversely, a concept that confirms only intuitive ontologies is ipso facto nonreligious and has little attention-demanding power. One of the optimal ways of striking the balance is to take all intuitive ontologies as confirmed, except a few assumptions that are then explicitly described as violated in the case of the religious entity.

Of course, all this is teleological fiction. To put things in a less crudely intentional way: In any cultural environment, indefinitely many religious representations are constantly created and communicated. Only some of them, however, have the potential to support both imaginative scenarios and intuitive inferences. These are the ones that combine a rich intuitive base, with all its inferential potential, and a limited series of violations of intuitive theories, which are attention-demanding. Because of these characteristics, such assumptions are more likely than other assumptions to be easily acquired, memorized, and transmitted. It should not be surprising, therefore, that they constitute the most recurrent aspects of religious systems. Again, they are certainly not universal; but they are more frequent than other types of religious ideas, and my analysis, based on the notion of intuitive assumptions combined with explicit circumscribed violations, accounts for this statistical phenomenon in an economical way.

What makes these hypotheses speculative is of course the quasi-absence of reliable cognitive data on religious ideas. Anthropologists, who are themselves supposedly driven by a sense of relevance, generally focus on the explicit violations, and ignore the self-evident, transparent assumptions necessary to the acquisition and representation of religious ideas. So we are left with detailed descriptions of assumptions of the first type, which provide at best only indirect evidence of the way commonsense assumptions are projected. I hope it is now obvious that my account, however speculative, is at least as plausible as the anthropological notion of exhaustive cultural transmission. It is plausible in the sense that (1) it is certainly consistent with, though not entailed by, the anthropological and psychological data available, and (2) it does not generate the difficult problems created by ordinary anthropological accounts. So it should at least be considered as a plausible alternative to those accounts.

Conclusions: Naturalness of religious claims

To sum up, the argument of this chapter proceeded in four steps, each of them taking us further from the classical anthropological account of religious ontologies:

1. Developmental studies show that ontological categorization can be spontaneously produced by nondemonstrative inferences, on the basis of a fragmented input. In other words, ontological assumptions need not be transmitted in order to be represented.

2. Ontological assumptions carry important quasi-theoretical information. Ontological categories in part correspond to domain-specific principles, which structure intuitive expectations concerning the behavior of the objects concerned, as well as the inferences that can be made about them.

3. Assumptions that violate intuitive theories are systematically coupled with assumptions that confirm them. It is of course possible for human minds to speculate about entities that are entirely freed from the constraints of intuitive ontologies. Such notions, however, are not usually found in religious ontologies.

4. Even assumptions violating intuitive principles are themselves constrained by those principles, in the sense that not all combinations of violated and confirmed assumptions are equally easy to conceptualize.

These remarks make it possible to reformulate, in a psychologically realistic way, two fundamental anthropological problems: that of the resemblance of people's ideas within a certain group, and that of recurrent ideas between different groups.

Let me first consider the question of within-group resemblance. We do little more than label problems instead of solving them, when we describe the acquisition of religious ideas as the transmission of some culturally specific "conceptual scheme" or "worldview" through "socialization." Furthermore, we make a crucial error when we take those convenient labels for real objects. In any human group, different people's religious ideas are similar in a number of important ways. In order to account for this *limited* convergence, it is not necessary to assume that those people share some "collective representations," whose existence and transmission are deep mysteries. More economically, the resemblance between people's representations can be explained by the fact that, confronted with the same input, they tend to make similar inferences. They tend to complement the counterintuitive religious claims with the same tacit assumptions because they are equipped with the same intuitive principles and have the same inferential capacities. In other words, what is provided by cultural transmission is a series of explicit *cues*, which are likely to trigger in most subjects roughly similar spontaneous inferences.

As regards the recurrence of certain types of religious notions in very different cultural environments, we can view it as a consequence of optimal combinations of violation and confirmation of intuitive knowledge. This conclusion may seem somewhat counterintuitive. The feature that makes religious ideas particularly interesting, and that in fact constitutes the category of "religious ideas" is a striking divergence from everyday understandings. I am claiming here, however, that this feature is not the most relevant one in a causal explanation of the recurrence of religious ideas. Religious ideas constitute a fascinating domain, for anthropologists as well as practitioners, because they put forth extraordinary claims. They are learnable and communicable because their mental representation includes, and is constrained by, domain-specific assumptions that are part of a universal intuitive understanding of basic ontological categories.

Notes

1. The hypotheses put forward in this chapter are presented in more detail in Boyer (1992, 1993). The critique of ontological assumptions concerning cultural systems can be found in Boyer (1987), and the points about transmission of cultural systems are examined in more detail in Boyer (1990, chap. 1). See also Hirschfeld, Atran, and Yengoyan (1982) on the conceptual ambiguities in the anthropological notion of culture. More generally, the possibility of a cognitive framework in anthropological descriptions has been defended by Sperber (1985) and Atran (Atran & Sperber, 1991).
2. This notion of a selective model is explained in more detail in Boyer (1992). See Cavalli-Sforza and Feldman (1981), Cavalli-Sforza (1986), Lumsden and Wilson (1981), Boyd and Richerson (1985), and Durham (1991) for examples of theories of cultural transmission based on the notion of variation and selective retention. This assumption is also the starting point of Sperber's notion of an "epidemiological" approach to cultural representations (Sperber, 1991).
3. On this point, to which I return later, see the other contributions in this volume.
4. For a more detailed exposition and discussion of these properties of religious interaction, see Boyer (1987, 1990, chap. 1).
5. For instance, Keil used stories that make a passing mention of objects called "hyraxes" and "throstles." The only thing that is said about them is that the hyraxes "are sometimes sleepy" and that the throstles "need to be fixed." Kindergarten children, who have never heard of those things, nevertheless infer, on the basis of such sentences, that it is possible that a hyrax might be "hungry," and that a throstle might be "made of metal"; on the other hand, they consistently deny that a hyrax could be "made of metal" (Keil, 1986). The subjects do not need any explicit instruction, e.g., to the effect that "hyraxes are animals."
6. Obviously, one may retort that there seems to be ample anthropological evidence, to the effect that basic ontologies are in fact culturally relative. Beyond their invariably anecdotal, non-controlled nature, which after all is the hallmark of ethnography, such arguments are often based on a mistaken inference from "collective representations" (that is, ritualized statements, mythologies, cosmologies, etc.) to individual cognitive processes. Anthropologists who make such claims should remember that they bear the burden of the proof, to show how, for instance, people could make sense of each other's behaviour without a belief-desire psychology, or develop notions of living kinds as kinds, without essentialist assumptions. Anthropological accounts, however, never provide either reliable evidence of genuinely strange ontologies, or a plausible theoretical account of conceptual development based on these strange principles.

7. On such theories of the mind, see the various studies in Heelas and Lock (1981). There is no space here to discuss this important work, which focuses on explicit, and culturally variable notions of thought, self, memory, and so forth.
8. This causal model is a folk-model only in the sense that it is not a *scientific* one. The term *folk*, here, does not entail that it is a cultural creation.

References

Astington, J. W., Harris, P., & Olson, D. R. (Eds.). (1988). *Developing theories of mind*. New York: Cambridge University Press.

Atran, S. (1985). The nature of folk-botanical life-forms. *American Anthropologist, 87*, 298–315.

Atran, S. (1987). Ordinary contraints on the semantics of living kinds. A commonsense alternative to recent treatments of natural-object terms. *Mind and Language, 2*, 27–63.

Atran, S. (1989). Basic conceptual domains. *Mind and Language, 4*, 5–16.

Atran, S. (1990). *Cognitive foundations of natural history: Towards an anthropology of science*. Cambridge: Cambridge University Press.

Atran, S., & Sperber, D. (1991). Learning without teaching: Its place in culture. In L. Landsman (Ed.), *Culture, schooling, and psychological development* (pp. 39–55). Norwood, NJ: Ablex.

Avis, J., & Harris, P. L. (1991). Belief-desire reasoning among Baka children: Evidence for a universal conception of mind. *Child Development, 62*, 460–467.

Berlin, B., Breedlove, D., & Raven, P. (1973). General principles of classification and nomenclature in folk-biology. *American Anthropologist, 75*, 214–242.

Bloch, M. (1985). From cognition to ideology. In R. Fardon (Ed.), *Power and knowledge. Anthropological and sociological approaches*. Edinburgh: Scottish Academic Press.

Boyd, R., & Richerson, P. J. (1985). *Culture and the evolutionary process*. Chicago: University of Chicago Press.

Boyer, P. (1987). The stuff "traditions" are made of: On the implicit ontology of an ethnographic category. *Philosophy of the Social Sciences, 17*, 49–65.

Boyer, P. (1990). *Tradition as truth and communication: A cognitive description of traditional discourse*. Cambridge: Cambridge University Press.

Boyer, P. (1992). Explaining religious ideas: Outline of a cognitive approach. *Numen, 39*, 27–57.

Boyer, P. (1993). *The naturalness of religious ideas: Outline of a cognitive theory of religion*. Los Angeles/Berkeley: University of California Press.

Brown, C. H. (1984). *Language and living things: Uniformities in folk-classification and naming*. New Brunswick, NJ: Rutgers University Press.

Bullock, M. (1985). Animism in childhood thinking: A new look at an old question. *Developmental Psychology, 21*, 217–225.

Cavalli-Sforza, L. L. (1986). Cultural evolution. *American Zoologist, 26*, 845–855.

Cavalli-Sforza, L. L., & Feldman, M. W. (1981). *Cultural transmission and evolution: A quantitative approach*. Princeton, NJ: Princeton University Press.

D'Andrade, R. (1987). A folk-model of the mind. In D. Holland & N. Quinn (Eds.), *Cultural models in language and thought*. Cambridge: Cambridge University Press.

Durham, W. (1991). *Coevolution: Genes, culture and human diversity*. Stanford: Stanford University Press.

Gelman, R. (1990). First principles organize attention to and learning about relevant data: Number and the animate–inanimate distinction as examples. *Cognitive Science, 14*, 79–106.

Gelman, R., Spelke, E., & Meck, E. (1983). What preschoolers know about animate and inanimate objects. In D. Rogers & J. A. Sloboda (Eds.), *The acquisition of symbolic skills*. London: Plenum.

Heelas, P., & Lock, A. (1981). *Indigenous psychologies: The anthropology of the self*. New York: Academic Press.

Hirschfeld, L. A., Atran, S., & Yengoyan, A. (1982). Theories of knowledge and culture. *Social Science Information, 21*, 161–198.

Keil, F. C. (1979). *Semantic and conceptual development*. Cambridge, MA: Harvard University Press.

Keil, F. C. (1986). The acquisition of natural kind and artifact terms. In A. Marrar & W. Demopoulos (Eds.), *Conceptual change*. Norwood, NJ: Ablex.

Keil, F. C. (1989). *Concepts, kinds and conceptual development*. Cambridge, MA: MIT Press.

Lumsden, C. J., & Wilson, E. O. (1981). *Genes, minds and culture*. Cambridge, MA: Harvard University Press.

Massey, C., & Gelman, R. (1988). Preschoolers' ability to decide whether pictured unfamiliar objects can move themselves. *Developmental Psychology, 24*, 307–317.

Richards, D. D., & Siegler, R. S. (1986). Children's understanding of the attributes of life. *Journal of Experimental Child Psychology, 42*, 1–22.

Spelke, E. S. (1990). Principles of object perception. *Cognitive Science, 14*, 29–56.

Spelke, E. S. (in press). Physical knowledge in infancy: Reflections on Piaget's theory. In S. Carey & S. Gelman (Eds.), *Biology and cognition*.

Sperber, D. (1985). Anthropology and psychology: Towards an epidemiology of representations. *Man, 20*, 73–89.

Walker [Jeyifous], S. (1986). *Atimodemo: Semantic conceptual development among the Yoruba*. PhD thesis, Cornell University.

Walker [Jeyifous], S. (1992a). Supernatural beliefs, natural kinds and conceptual structure. *Memory and Cognition, 20*, 655–662.

Walker [Jeyifous], S. (1992b). Developmental changes in the representation of word-meaning: Cross-cultural findings. *British Journal of Developmental Psychology, 10*, 285–299.

Wellman, H. M. (1990). *The child's theory of mind*. Cambridge, MA: MIT Press.

Wellman, H., & Estes, D. (1986). Early understanding of mental entities: A re-examination of childhood realism. *Child Development, 57*, 910–923.

16   Universal and culture-specific properties of children's mental models of the earth

Stella Vosniadou

This chapter develops some ideas about domain specificity and cultural knowledge based on a series of studies of children's concept of the earth (see Vosniadou, 1989, 1991; Vosniadou & Brewer, 1992, in press). More specifically, I argue that the concept of the earth is originally embedded within a naive theory of physics and is constrained by certain entrenched presuppositions that apply to physical objects in general. Although the process of conceptual change appears to be fundamentally the same in children growing up in culturally diverse backgrounds, there is considerable cultural mediation in the construction of the specific mental models of the earth that children in different cultures form. Finally, it is also argued that the acquisition of the culturally accepted model of a spherical earth as an astronomical object surrounded by space cannot be accounted for as a product of enrichment, but involves a major conceptual reorganization proceeding through the suspension or revision of some of the presuppositions that belong to a naive theory of physics.

Domain-specific constraints

A number of chapters in this volume present persuasive evidence to support the view that the human mind operates on the basis of different

The research reported in this chapter was supported in part from a grant from the National Science Foundation, BNS-85-10254, and in part by a grant from the Office of Educational Research and Improvement under Cooperative Agreement No. G0087-CI001-90 with the Reading Research and Education Center. This publication does not necessarily reflect the views of the agencies supporting the research.

I would like to thank Anthi Archodidou for her help in analyzing the cross-cultural data. I would also like to thank Bill Brewer and Ala Samarapungavan for their help in conducting the cross-cultural studies, and, particularly, David Herdrich for allowing me to use the photographs from the study conducted in Samoa.

412

domain-specific constraints, reflecting the structure of the specific adaptive problems humans needed to solve over the course of evolution (e.g., Cosmides & Tooby, this volume; Wierzbicka, this volume; Atran, this volume).

One important domain of knowledge for which it is very likely that domain-specific constraints have been developed is the domain of knowledge about the physical world. Recent work with infants (e.g., Spelke, 1991; Baillargeon, 1990) has succeeded in describing some of the basic principles that seem to guide the process of acquiring knowledge about the physical world. Spelke (1991), for example, has described five constraints about the behavior of physical objects that infants appear to appreciate from early on, namely, *continuity, solidity, no action at a distance, gravity*, and *inertia*.

In an earlier paper (Vosniadou, 1989) I have argued that such constraints, or entrenched presuppositions,[1] as I call them, are organized in a "global theory" of naive physics, which is not available to conscious awareness and hypothesis testing. This naive theory of physics constrains the process of acquiring knowledge about the physical world in ways analogous to those that research programs and paradigms have been thought to constrain the development of scientific theories (e.g., Kuhn, 1977; Lakatos, 1970).

In this chapter I argue that the concept of the earth emerges within such a naive theory of physics and is constrained by the same kinds of presuppositions that constrain physical objects in general. Unlike many other concepts that remain embedded in the same conceptual domain throughout development, the concept of the earth undergoes a major reorganization. This reorganization involves the reconceptualization of the earth as an astronomical body, and proceeds through the suspension and revision[2] of some of the presuppositions that belong to a naive theory of physics.

The results of the cross-cultural studies of the concept of the earth that my colleagues and I have undertaken support the aforementioned argument regarding this concept. It is not clear, however, whether such a conceptual reorganization applies only to the concept of the earth or to the domain of astronomy in general. In other words, it could be argued that the domain of astronomy is not a "core" conceptual domain (see Atran & Sperber, 1987; Boyer, this volume), but a "peripheral" domain that emerges out of a core theory of naive physics. Alternatively, it may be the case that the domain of astronomy is a "core" conceptual domain but the concept of the earth is not seen to belong to it. More research on the development of the concepts of the "sun," "moon," "stars," and "planets" is needed in order to answer this question.

In the pages that follow I will describe some of the research providing the empirical evidence for this argument, starting with a general discussion of the theoretical framework guiding our choice of methodology, and proceeding with a description of some of the results of the specific studies that have been undertaken.

Mental models and underlying conceptual structures

How do we go about determining the range of an individual's knowledge about a given concept and the larger theoretical structures in which this concept is embedded (e.g., Murphy & Medin, 1985)? In our studies of the concept of the earth (Vosniadou & Brewer, 1992) we ask children a series of questions regarding the shape of the earth and the region on the earth where people live. Some of these questions require a verbal response whereas others elicit drawings or the construction of physical models. We assume that children use whatever relevant conceptual knowledge they have to create a mental representation of the earth that allows them to answer our questions. We try to understand and describe these mental representations and to use them to understand the underlying conceptual structures that generate them.

We have adopted the construct of the mental model to characterize children's representations in observational astronomy. The construct of the mental model has been used in a number of different ways (e.g., Johnson-Laird, 1983; Gentner & Stevens, 1983). It is used here to refer to a particular kind of mental representation that differs from other kinds of representations in that it is an analog to the state of affairs (perceived or conceived) that it represents (see Johnson-Laird, 1983).

We assume that a mental model is a dynamic structure created on the spot for the purpose of answering questions, solving problems, or dealing with other situations. Mental models are generated from and constrained by underlying conceptual structures.[3] For example, if one is told that "George dropped the hammer," one's mental model of the location of the hammer will be constrained by an underlying structure related to the assumed properties of gravity.

A given mental model provides only partial information about conceptual knowledge. Consider, for example, the situation in which George was an astronaut who dropped the hammer while he was in a spaceship orbiting the earth. Two individuals who constructed the same mental model of the location of the hammer in the first example may differ in their conceptualization of the location of the hammer in the second example, depending on their exact understanding of gravity. Thus, although a single mental model may be undetermined with respect to the underlying conceptual structure generating it, understanding the kinds of mental models individuals use to answer a variety of questions related to a given concept can provide important information about the content and structure of the knowledge base.

Finally, it is important to note that certain kinds of questions have a far greater potential for providing information about conceptual structures than others. Compare, for example, the (factual) questions, "What is the shape of the earth?" and "Does the earth move?" with the (generative) questions, "If you were to walk for many days in a straight line, where would you end up?" "Would you ever reach the end or the edge of the earth?" and "Does the earth have an end or an edge?"

Children who have been exposed to the culturally accepted information that the earth is a sphere that rotates around its axis may say that the earth "is round" and that "it moves" in response to the first, factual, questions. However, the culturally accepted responses to these questions do not necessarily imply that the children have fully understood what it means for the earth to be round or to rotate around its axis. We know that information acquired through instruction is often stored in a separate microstructure (see Chi, 1988), or becomes assimilated to existing knowledge structures to form a misconception (e.g., Vosniadou & Brewer, 1992).

In contrast to the factual questions, the second, generative questions cannot be answered by simply repeating information received through instruction. We hypothesize that in these situations individuals search their knowledge base for relevant information and use this information to create the mental model of the earth that includes information about its end or edge. Different mental models of the earth will provide different responses to these questions and will lead to different hypotheses about underlying conceptual structures. For example, children who conceptualize the earth as a flat disc with people living on the top of the disc, will say that the earth has an end/edge. Children who form the mental model of a spherical earth with people living all around it, on the outside, will however know that there is no end/edge to the earth and that if one walked for many days one would eventually come back to where one started.

To conclude, generative questions, the kinds of questions that require the explanation of phenomena not directly observed and not likely to have been answered through direct instruction, have a greater potential for revealing information about underlying conceptual structures than factual questions, which elicit information that may have been superficially memorized through instruction.

Mental models of the earth: The first U.S. sample

The first study we conducted (Vosniadou & Brewer, 1992) involved 60 boys and girls from middle-class backgrounds, who attended elementary school in Urbana, Illinois. There were 20 first graders (mean age 6 years and 9 months), 20 third graders (mean age 9 years and 3 months), and 20 fifth graders (mean age 11 years). The children were asked 48 questions concerning the earth, the sun, the moon, and the stars, in an individual interview. Fifteen of these questions, which concerned the earth and the region of the earth where people live, were used to derive children's mental models of the earth.

The results revealed considerable surface inconsistency in children's responses to the individual questions. For example, many children said that the earth "is round" and drew a circle to depict its shape, but then went on to claim that there is an end/edge to the earth from where one can potentially fall off. The following is an excerpt from the interview with a third-grade child, Jamie, which illustrates this point.

Jamie (third grade)
E: What is the shape of the earth?
C: Round.
E: Can you draw a picture of the earth?
C: (Child draws a circle to depict the earth.)
E: If you walked for many days in a straight line, where would you end up?
C: Probably in another planet.
E: Could you ever reach the end or the edge of the earth?
C: Yes, if you walked long enough.
E: Could you fall off that end?
C: Yes, probably.

A number of other responses clearly suggested the presence of alternative conceptions about the shape of the earth. The excerpts from the interviews with Terina and Mathew below illustrate some of these alternative conceptions.

Terina (fifth grade)
C: The earth is round but when you look at it it is flat.
E: Why is that?
C: Because if you were looking around it would be round.
E: What then is the real shape of the earth?
C: Round, like a thick pancake.

Mathew (first grade)
E: If you walked and walked for many days where would you end up?
C: If we walked for a very long time we might end up at the end of the earth.
E: Would you ever reach the edge of the earth?
C: I don't think so.
E: Say we kept on walking and walking and we had plenty of food with us?
C: Probably.
E: Could you fall off the edge of the earth?
C: No, because if we were outside of the earth we could probably fall off, but if we were inside the earth we couldn't fall off.

As we can see from these examples, Terina seems to think that the earth is round and flat like a thick pancake, and Mathew believes that the earth is a hollow sphere with people living deep inside it.

In order to examine whether children's seemingly inconsistent responses were internally consistent with respect to certain alternative mental models of the earth, such as the disc earth or the view that the earth is a hollow sphere, we devised the following methodology. First, a number of possible earth shape models were derived from our data as well as from previous research in this area (e.g., Nussbaum & Novak, 1976; Nussbaum, 1979; Sneider

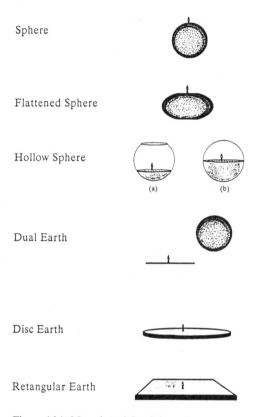

Sphere

Flattened Sphere

Hollow Sphere

(a)   (b)

Dual Earth

Disc Earth

Retangular Earth

Figure 16.1. Mental models of the earth.

& Pulos, 1983). Then, we generated the responses we expected children to give had they formed and used that mental model in a consistent way. Once generated, the pattern of expected responses was compared to the pattern of obtained responses. Children were assigned to a given mental model of the earth if their responses showed no more than one deviation from the expected response pattern (see Vosniadou & Brewer, 1992, for a detailed description of this procedure).

Following this methodology, we were able to account for 82% of our data. In other words, 49 out of 60 children in our sample were found to use in a consistent fashion one of a small number of well-defined mental models of the earth. These mental models are shown in Figure 16.1 and their frequency of occurrence is described in Table 16.1.

As shown in Table 16.1, the majority of the children in our sample formed a mental model of the earth that was different from the culturally expected model of the earth as a sphere. The following five alternative models of the earth were identified: The *rectangular earth* model, according to which the

Table 16.1. *Frequency of earth shape models as a function of grade*

	Grade			
Earth shape concepts	1	3	5	Total
1. Sphere	3	8	12	23
2. Flattened sphere	1	3	0	4
3. Hollow sphere	2	4	6	12
4. Dual Earth	6	2	0	8
5. Disc	0	1	0	1
6. Rectangle	1	0	0	1
7. Mixed	7	2	2	11
Total 20	20	20	20	60

earth is a flat, solid, supported object shaped like a rectangle. The *disc earth*, according to which the earth is also a flat, solid, and supported object, shaped like a disc. The *dual earth* model, according to which there are two earths: a flat, solid, and supported earth on which people live, and a spherical earth that is suspended in the sky, like a planet. The *hollow sphere* model, according to which the earth is a hollow sphere with people living on flat ground deep inside it. Finally, there is the *flattened sphere* model, according to which the earth is shaped like a thick pancake, round on the sides but flat on the top and bottom, where the people live.

Children's mental models of the earth are embedded within a naive theory of physics

Given the massive exposure to information regarding the spherical shape of the earth provided to children in our culture, why do children find it so difficult to form the culturally accepted model of a spherical earth? In Vosniadou and Brewer (1992), we have argued that children find it difficult to believe that the earth is a sphere surrounded by space because they see the earth as a physical object, rather than as an astronomical object, and apply to it the presuppositions that apply to physical objects in general (e.g., solidity, continuity, gravity, etc.). Two of these presuppositions are particularly important, because they are contrary to the culturally accepted information that the earth is a sphere, and as such, have the potential of explaining the alternative models of the earth that children construct. These are the presupposition of an up/down gravity and the presupposition that the ground on which people live is flat.

The up/down gravity presupposition is the presupposition that objects require support and that unsupported objects fall in a downward direction. This makes sense in the context of a conception of space, according to which the ground is flat and the locations of "up" and "down" are defined in terms of this flat ground (and not in terms of the center of the earth). The beginnings of these presuppositions can already be identified in the conceptions of the 6- to 9-month-old infant (see Spelke, 1991; Baillargeon, 1990).

All of the alternative mental models of the earth we have identified are constrained by the belief that the ground on which people live is flat and that unsupported objects fall downward. This is obvious in the case of the rectangular earth and the disc earth models. In the dual earth model, the earth on which people live is also thought to be flat. In the hollow sphere model, the earth is seen as a sphere but the people are supposed to live on flat ground inside the sphere. Finally, in the flattened sphere model, the earth is also thought to be flat in the areas where the people live. There would be no reason for children to form these systematic misrepresentations of the earth if they did not believe that the earth is flat and that objects require support.

It should be made clear here that what we mean by "flat" does not refer to the simple product of a phenomenal perception of flatness but represents (as all entrenched presuppositions do) the complex interpretation of everyday experience by a constructivist mind. In other words, a "flat" earth is not an earth without mountains or oceans, but, rather, an earth where the ground extends along the same horizontal plane, as opposed to something that forms a sphere, and where "up" and "down" are clearly defined with respect to this horizontal plane.

Initial, synthetic, and scientific mental models

If we are correct in our analysis that children's mental models of the earth are embedded within a naive theory of physics, then we should expect that the first, initial models children form, before they are exposed to the information that the earth is a sphere, should be models according to which the earth is conceptualized as consisting of a flat, "supported" ground, with people living on top of it. An additional set of inferences, regarding the existence of an end/edge and the particular shape of this end can produce a class of mental models according to which the flat, supported earth is shaped like a rectangle, square, disc, and so on. These criteria are all met by the rectangular and supported disc models.

The remaining mental models of the earth we have identified can be explained as attempts on the part of the children to reconcile the presuppositions that objects require support and that the ground is flat with the culturally accepted notion of a spherical earth surrounded by space. For this reason, we call these models synthetic.

An examination of the models we have obtained shows that there is a progression of more and more advanced synthetic models, depending on how many of the above-mentioned presuppositions children have suspended or revised. For example, the dual earth model is less advanced than the hollow sphere and flattened sphere models. The children who form the dual earth model have retained both of the entrenched presuppositions that gave rise to their initial model in the first place. These children answer our questions in a way that shows that they still believe that the ground is flat, that the earth is supported, and that the people and objects on the earth live on flat ground. Children who form the dual earth model reconcile the information that the earth is a sphere with their presuppositions by assuming that adults refer to a different object when talking about the round earth.

Children who believe in the hollow sphere model seem to have suspended the up/down gravity presupposition as far as the earth as a physical object is concerned. We call this process "presupposition suspension" because it does not necessarily require a revision of the explanatory framework within which the concept of gravity is embedded. These children accept the notion that the earth is a sphere surrounded by space but have not yet understood how it is possible for the people and objects on the earth to stand on the outside of this sphere (particularly the "sides" and "bottom" of the sphere) without falling. By assuming that the earth is hollow and that people live on flat ground deep inside the earth, these children find a way to reconcile their up/down gravity presupposition with the culturally accepted model of a spherical and "unsupported" earth.

Finally, the children who have formed the flattened sphere model seem to have revised their presupposition that unsupported objects fall. We call this process "presupposition revision" because it requires changing the concept of an up/down gravity to one according to which gravity operates by pulling objects toward the center of the earth. These children have not yet solved the flat/sphere paradox, however. As a result, they think that the areas of the earth on which people live are flat.

The data on the frequency of the earth shape models by grade, presented in Table 16.1, are in general agreement with the theoretical analysis in terms of entrenched presuppositions. The synthetic models that require the fewer changes (e.g., the dual earth model) are more frequently found in the youngest children, whereas the models that require the largest number of changes, (e.g., the sphere) are more frequent in the older children.

In conclusion, children start by conceptualizing the earth as a physical body rather than as an astronomical body and apply to it the presuppositions that constrain physical objects in general. Two of these presuppositions – that the ground is flat and that physical objects require support, are particularly important because they are inconsistent with the culturally accepted information that the earth is a sphere. The process of changing from the initial model of a flat, supported earth to the culturally accepted model of a spherical earth proceeds through the construction of intermediate, synthetic models. Synthetic models are formed when children try to reconcile the information regarding the spherical shape of the earth with the aforementioned presuppositions. This type of conceptual change cannot be accounted for through the mechanism of enrichment. It requires the suspension or revision of the relevant presuppositions.

Cross-cultural studies

The aim of the cross-cultural studies that we have undertaken was to investigate the similarities and differences in the mental models of the earth and of the solar system that children growing up in different cultures construct. We also wished to examine whether the synthetic models children form, before they arrive at the dominant scientific model of the spherical earth are influenced by the nature of the alternate cosmological accounts available to children in different cultures.

Two specific hypotheses were formulated regarding cultural influences on the formation of children's mental models of the earth: (1) the universality of entrenched presuppositions hypothesis, and (2) the cultural mediation hypothesis. These hypotheses will now be discussed in detail.

The universality of entrenched presuppositions

I have argued that the entrenched presuppositions we have identified represent children's interpretations of their experience of the physical world, which are organized within a naive theory of physics. To the extent that children's experiences of the physical world are the same, their presuppositions should also be the same. Children who grow up in the flat midwestern United States, the mountainous regions of Greece, or in the coastal areas of India or Samoa, should all notice that unsupported things fall and infer that the ground extends along the same plane. These children should form similar presuppositions about the nature of the physical world regardless of the particular region of the earth in which they grow up.

Second, if children in the United States start by conceptualizing the earth as a physical object and not as an astronomical object, there is no reason to believe that children growing up in different cultures would do otherwise. We therefore predicted that the children in our cross-cultural studies would all start by forming mental models of the earth consistent with the presuppositions that constrain physical objects in general.

The cultural mediation hypothesis

If entrenched presuppositions are universal, then the specific synthetic models of the earth that children in different cultures would construct should all belong to a class of mental models having the common characteristic of being constrained by the two presuppositions earlier discussed. There is no reason why we should expect these synthetic models of the earth to be identical because entrenched presuppositions constrain individuals' mental models only to a certain extent. For example, the presupposition that unsupported things fall does not specify the exact nature of the substance that should support the earth. It is possible to imagine that the earth floats on water rather than that it is rooted in dirt, or that it is supported by an enormous elephant or a giant turtle, as in some ancient cosmologies. These models are very different, yet they are all constrained by an underlying presupposition that something must support the earth.

Furthermore, although the notion that the earth is a sphere is well accepted in all cultures studied, there are nevertheless important differences in the indigenous cosmologies to which children in these cultures are exposed. The situation is often complicated in cultures such as in India, Greece, or Samoa, where the indigenous cosmologies can be quite different from the current scientific model, and where the indigenous cultural models, often embodied in mythology, are often more accessible to children than equivalent pre-Copernican alternatives are in the American culture.

It is therefore quite possible that the indigenous cosmologies, to which children in different cultures are exposed, will influence their generation of models in the domain of astronomy. Furthermore, where the native cosmology of the culture is closer to the child's direct phenomenal experience, it is likely that the reorganization of the initial models through contact with aspects of the scientific model presented in tradition will be culturally mediated as well. For example, one well-articulated cosmology in the Indian tradition proposes that the earth is shaped like a large disc or a shallow dish floating on water. Thus, it is possible that young children who are told that the earth is round and must reconcile this information with their experience of the earth's flatness are more likely to generate a disc or a pancake model of earth than a spherical model in the absence of other information (see Samarapungavan & Vosniadou, 1988, for a discussion of this issue).

To sum up, the hypothesis that entrenched presuppositions are universal predicts that the class of possible initial models of the earth constructed by children in different cultures would be constrained by the same entrenched presuppositions. The cultural mediation hypothesis predicts that children in different cultures will construct different alternative models of the earth, from the class of possible models, reflecting their cultural experiences.

The cross-cultural data

Cross-cultural studies provide a strong test of the hypothesis regarding the universality of entrenched presuppositions and of the cultural mediation hypothesis. In this chapter we present data from four studies that attempted to test these hypotheses. All of these studies investigated children's cosmologies using the same 207-item questionnaire, developed as part of a larger project on knowledge acquisition in astronomy. We will examine only the responses of the children that pertain to their ideas about the shape of the earth. The four studies were conducted in the United States (Vosniadou & Brewer, in preparation), in Samoa (Brewer, Herdrich, & Vosniadou, 1987), in Greece (Vosniadou, Archodidou, & Kalogiannidou, submitted), and in India (Samara-pungavan & Vosniadou, 1988).

The subjects in the American study were 60 children (20 each from grades 1, 3, and 5), attending elementary school in Urbana, Illinois. The subjects in the Samoan study were 26 children (approximate ages 6, 8, and 12), who attended an elementary school in the village of Aoa, on the northeast coast of the island Tutuila. The Greek sample consisted of 109 children (19 kindergartners, 35 first graders, 30 third graders and 26 sixth graders), who attended elementary school in the town of Thessaloniki in the northern part of Greece. The Indian sample consisted of 36 children (19 6-year-olds and 19 8-year-olds), who were students in a private school in the city of Hyderabad, in the southern part of India. In order to have comparable data, only the results from the 6/7- and 8/9-year-old children will be presented.

All the children were interviewed individually using translations of the same questionnaire by native speakers, except in India where English was used as the medium of communication. The questions about the shape of the earth were similar to the ones described in the first U.S. study. In addition, the children were asked to make a physical model of the earth using clay. The mental models of the earth were derived in the same way as in the first U.S. study, except in the case of the Samoan children, whose mental models were derived only on the basis of their clay models.

The results of these studies showed that it was possible to identify a small number of mental models of the earth that were used by the majority of the children in a consistent way. The percentage of mental models of the earth for the combined 6/7- and 8/9-year-old cross-cultural sample is shown in Figure 16.2. As can be seen, it is possible to group these models into initial, synthetic, and scientific. The initial models are the models of a rectangular, supported disc, and ring earth. They are considered to be initial because they do not show any influence from the culturally accepted model of a spherical earth. The remaining mental models of the earth (with the exception of the spherical model itself) are synthetic models. The specific characteristics of these models will be discussed in greater detail later.

Initial models. The models of a rectangular earth and a supported disc were similar in all the children, except the children from India. The Indian children conceptualized the earth to be supported by water, and not by ground or dirt as the other children. Approximately 67% of the Indian 6-year-olds with disc or rectangle models believed that the earth was supported by an ocean of water. The following is an example of a disc earth model from the protocol of a child from India.

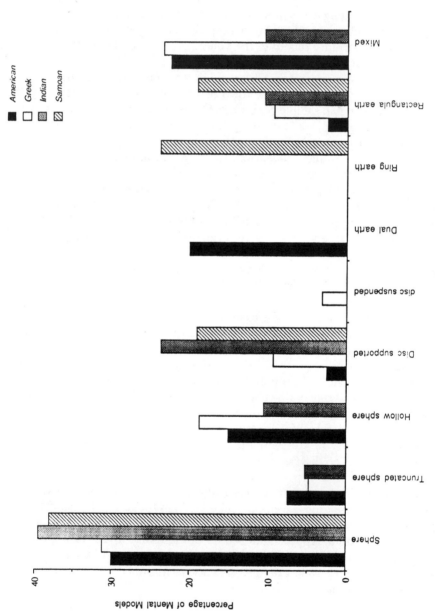

Figure 16.2. Percentage of mental models of the earth in children from the United States, Greece, India, and Samoa.

Figure 16.3. "Ring earth" mental model.

Rakesh (6 years old)
E: What is the shape of the earth?
C: Round like a circle.
E: Where do people live on the earth?
C: In the middle on top.
E: Is there an end or an edge to the earth?
C: Yes.
E: Can a person fall off there?
C: Yes.
E: Where would they fall?
C: Into the ocean.
E: What is below the earth?
C: Ocean.

The Samoan children produced a model of the earth that did not exist in the other samples. This was the model of a ring earth. The children who formed this model rolled the clay into a long rope, which they then wrapped around to form a ring. An example of this model appears in Figure 16.3.

From the descriptions of the children who constructed this model, it appears that the ring earth is not hollow in the middle but represents something like a disc-shaped earth. The ring form appears to have been chosen to emphasize the outer edges of the disc, and probably indicated the areas on the earth where people live. We have interpreted this model to reflect the fact that the predominant way physical and social space is organized in a Samoan

Figure 16.4. Organization of physical space in a Samoan market.

village is in the form of a ring. This applies not only to the village plan, with huts arranged on a circle along the sides of the village, but also to the interior of a Samoan house and a Samoan market, as shown in Figure 16.4.

Despite their differences, all of the obtained models of the earth in the cross-cultural studies we conducted are consistent with the hypothesis that the entrenched presuppositions identified in the first study with American children are universal. The models identified were either constrained by both presuppositions earlier discussed or were attempts to reconcile these presuppositions with the culturally accepted model of a spherical earth.

Synthetic models. The synthetic models obtained in the cross-cultural studies were similar to the synthetic models obtained in the first American study, with two exceptions. The new synthetic models were (1) the model of a truncated sphere, and (2) the model of a suspended disc. Only two flattened sphere models were obtained in the entire sample, and for this reason they were placed in the same category as the suspended disc models. The only difference between the flattened sphere and the suspended disc models is in the area where the people are supposed to live on the earth. In a suspended disc the people are supposed to live only on the top part of the disc. In a flattened sphere, the people are supposed to live both on the flat "top" and the flat "bottom" of the sphere.

The synthetic models obtained in the cross-cultural studies, including the two new models, were consistent with the hypothesis that they represented attempts to reconcile the culturally accepted information of a spherical earth with the two entrenched presuppositions already discussed. This finding is consistent with the universality of entrenched presuppositions hypothesis. In addition, the cultural mediation hypothesis was also supported. An examination of the various mental models obtained shows that the different cultural groups had different preferred initial or synthetic models of the earth, a finding consistent with the cultural mediation hypothesis. As shown in Figure 16.2, the American children favored the dual earth model, which was not obtained in the other cultures investigated. The Greek children preferred the hollow sphere model, whereas the Indian children thought of the earth as a flat disc supported by an ocean of water. The ring earth was the favorite model of the Samoan children.

A χ^2 applied to these data in order to test the hypothesis that the cultures investigated would produce different mental models of the earth was significant at the $p < .001$ level ($\chi^2 = 87.642$, 24df). Therefore, the results clearly support both the hypothesis in the universality of the entrenched presuppositions as well as the cultural mediation hypothesis.

To sum up, it has been argued that children in different cultures all start by conceptualizing the earth as a physical body and apply to it the constraints that usually apply to physical objects within a fundamentally similar theory of naive physics. Despite the universality of this process, there is considerable room for cultural variation to develop, because the children eventually change their concept of the earth from that of a flat and supported physical object to the culturally accepted model of a spherical earth surrounded by space.

Before closing, I would like to draw attention to some of the important similarities that exist in the development of the concept of the earth in elementary schoolchildren cross-culturally, and in the history of science. Original conceptions of the earth were that it is flat and supported, suggesting that the concept of the earth emerged within a theory of naive physics and was constrained by similar presuppositions. Although the earth was conceptualized as spherical already at the time of Aristotle, it was not thought to be similar to the other celestial bodies. Unlike the planets, it was considered to be stationary and to occupy a space in the middle of the universe. It was not until the time of Copernicus that the earth was conceptualized as a planet. These changes in the historical development of the concept of the earth are characteristic of some of the major conceptual reorganizations in the history of science and they require similar kinds of presupposition revision as the ones described in this chapter with elementary schoolchildren.

Conclusions

I have argued that children's concept of the earth is originally embedded within a "core" theory of naive physics and is constrained by the same kinds of presuppositions that apply to physical objects in general. Two of these presuppositions – that the ground is flat and that objects require support – are particularly important because they are contrary to the culturally accepted model of a spherical earth and can explain the formation of synthetic models or misconceptions.

The results of the studies presented here support this argument and are generally consistent with the view that the human mind operates on the basis of relatively few domain-specific constraints that guide the process of knowledge acquisition in a way that allows for considerable cultural diversity to occur.

Finally, the results reported here provide interesting information about the nature of conceptual change with development. Although the kind of conceptual change we have described to take place in the mind of the elementary schoolchild does not involve changes from one domain-specific theory to another, as described by Carey (1991), it cannot be accounted for through the mechanism of enrichment as argued by Spelke (1991). It requires the suspension and revision of some of the entrenched presuppositions that are part of a naive theory of physics and their replacement with a different explanatory framework. This process appears to be not only an intricate part of conceptual development within a cultural context,[4] but also a part of the process of conceptual change in the history of science.

Notes

1. Entrenched presuppositions can be thought of either as innate domain-specific constraints or as empirically acquired domain-specific constraints, products of an inferential process based on everyday experience (see Keil, 1991 for an interesting discussion of different kinds of constraints possible).
2. The suspension of a presupposition refers to the process whereby the range of a presupposition's applicability becomes restricted. For example, children may decide that the presupposition that objects require support does not need to be applied to the earth itself. Revision of a presupposition requires change in the explanatory framework within which a given concept is embedded.
3. There is considerable interest in the question of whether mental models are constructed on the spot or stored as separate structures in long-term memory and retrieved when needed. My position on this issue is that mental models represent dynamic structures that are created on the spot to meet the demands of specific problem-solving situations. This does not exclude the possibility, however, that some specific mental models, or parts of them, which have been proven useful in the past, are stored as separate structures and retrieved from memory.
4. Spelke (1991) makes a distinction between "spontaneous" development and "development as a result of instruction." Whereas some kinds of conceptual changes are clearly the product of explicit instruction and others are not, the notion of spontaneous development is problematic. All conceptual development takes place within a cultural context and is influenced by the cultural systems of beliefs existing within the culture. If conceptual reorganizations have occurred in the cultural context, as in the case of the earth, they will influence conceptual development as well, even without explicit instruction.

5. The Samoan data were collected by David Herdrich and the Indian data by Ala Samarapungavan.

References

Atran, S., & Sperber, D. (1987, June). *Learning without teaching: Its place in culture.* Paper presented at the workshop on "Culture, Schooling and Psychological Development," Tel Aviv University.

Baillargeon, R. (1990). *The development of young infants' intuition about support.* Paper presented at the 7th International Conference on Infant Studies, Montreal, Canada.

Brewer, W. F., Hendrich, D. J., & Vosniadou, S. (1987, January). *A cross-cultural study of children's development of cosmological models: Samoan and American data.* Paper presented at the Third International Conference on Thinking, Honolulu, HI.

Carey, S. (1991). Knowledge acquisition-enactment or conceptual change? In S. Carey & R. Gelman (Eds.), *The epigenesis of mind: Essays on biology and cognition.* Hillsdale, NJ: Erlbaum.

Chi, M. T. H. (1988). Children's lack of access and knowledge reorganization: An example from the concept of animism. In F. Weinert & M. Perlmutter (Eds.), *Memory development: Universal changes and individual differences* (pp. 169–194). Hillsdale, NJ: Erlbaum.

Gentner, D., & Stevens, A. L. (Eds.). (1983). *Mental models.* Hillsdale, NJ: Erlbaum.

Johnson-Laird, P. N. (1983). *Mental models.* Cambridge, MA: Harvard University Press.

Keil, F. (1991). The emergence of theoretical beliefs as constraints on concepts. In S. Carey & R. Gelman (Eds.), *The epigenesis of mind: Essays on biology and cognition.* Hillsdale, NJ: Erlbaum.

Kuhn, T. S. (1977). *The essential tension.* Chicago: University of Chicago Press.

Lakatos, I. (1970). Falsification and the methodology of scientific research programmes. In I. Lakatos & A. Musgrave (Eds.), *Criticism and the growth of knowledge* (pp. 91–195). Cambridge: Cambridge University Press.

Murphy, L. G., & Medin, D. L. (1985). The role of theories in conceptual coherence. *Psychological Review, 92,* 289–316.

Nussbaum, J. (1979). Children's conception of the earth as a cosmic body: A cross-stage study. *Science Education, 63,* 83–89.

Nussbaum, J., & Novac, J. D. (1976). An assessment of children's concepts of the earth utilizing structured interviews. *Science Education, 60,* 535–550.

Samarapungavan, A., & Vosniadou, S. (1988, April). *What children from India know about observational astronomy: A cross-cultural study.* Paper presented at the annual meeting of the American Educational Research Association, San Francisco, California.

Sneider, C., & Pulos, S. (1983). Children's cosmologies: Understanding the earth's shape and gravity. *Science Education, 67,* 205–221.

Spelke, S. E. (1991). Physical knowledge in infancy: Reflections on Piaget's theory. In S. Carey & R. Gelman (Eds.), *The epigenesis of mind: Essays on biology and cognition.* Hillsdale, NJ: Erlbaum.

Vosniadou, S. (1989). On the nature of children's naive knowledge. *Proceedings of the 11th Annual Conference of the Cognitive Science Society* (pp. 404–411). Hillsdale, NJ: Erlbaum.

Vosniadou, S. (1991). Designing curricula for conceptual restructuring: Lessons from the study of knowledge acquisition in astronomy. *Journal of Curriculum Studies*, *23*, 219–237.

Vosniadou, S., & Brewer, W. F. (1992). Mental models of the earth: A study of conceptual change in childhood. *Cognitive Psychology*, *24*, 535–585.

Vosniadou, S., & Brewer, W. F. (in press). Mental models of the day/night cycle. *Cognitive Science*.

Vosniadou, S., Archodidou, A., & Kalogiannidou, A. (in press). Cultural mediation in the formation of mental models about the shape of the earth. *Psychological Issues*. (In Greek).

17 Cognitive domains and the structure of the lexicon: The case of emotions

Anna Wierzbicka

... I necessarily arrived at this remarkable thought, namely, that a kind of alphabet of human thoughts can be worked out and that everything can be discovered and judged by a comparison of the letters of this alphabet and an analysis of the words made from them.

(Leibniz, 1956: 342)

Introduction

How is knowledge stored and organized in the human mind? By knowledge I do not mean school knowledge or book knowledge, but the basic everyday knowledge that provides us with a frame of orientation in daily life, in interaction with other people, in our natural modus operandi.

In my view, there can hardly be a better way of approaching this question than by analyzing language (and languages). "Languages are the best mirror of human mind ... and precise analysis of the meanings of words would allow us – better than anything else – to know the operations of the mind" (Leibniz, 1949: 368).

In language, grammar provides a basic framework for the interpretation of the world and of human existence in the world, with its fundamental semantic categories such as person, number, gender, tense, aspect, mood, "evidentiality," degree, and so on (cf. Jespersen, 1924), whereas the lexicon divides and organizes the "contents of the world" into more or less coherent and self-contained domains. By studying the structure of the lexicon, we can discover what these domains are and how they are organized, and thus reveal fundamental aspects of human interpretation of the world and the organization of knowledge and experience.

I realize of course that this position is controversial and that it is not shared by mainstream modern psychology, which at times seems to behave as if language was largely irrelevant to the study of mind.

Noam Chomsky's claims about the study of generative grammar as a source

of insight into human cognition were received by many psychologists with
great interest, and brought about something of a rapprochement between
psychology and the study of language. But this rapprochement was short-
lived. In any case, neither Chomsky nor Chomskyans have ever taken any
serious interest in the meaning of words. Their approach could not therefore
have tested Leibniz's claim that precise analysis of the meanings of words is
the best possible guide to the operations of the mind.

Most contemporary psychologists do not see language as a reflection of
thought. In their studies of human cognition they tend to rely, instead, on measures such as reaction time, rate of learning, developmental sequences, "semantic memory" experiments, ranking of various items, sorting tasks, and so on.

But when human beings try to study human beings there is no escape from
language, and even supposedly nonlinguistic methods themselves are also
based on unconscious (and often unjustified) linguistic assumptions. For example, recent studies of human categorization have blurred the differences
between the cognitive organization of the domain of living things and that of
artifacts, suggesting some dubious generalizations. In particular, many people, for a while, accepted generalizations that failed to recognize the crucial
fact that whereas "naive" categorization of living kinds reflected in language
involves hierarchical ranking (e.g., creature–bird–sparrow; thing growing out
of the ground–tree–oak), artifactual supercategories (such as, e.g., furniture,
clothing, or kitchenware) do not (cf. Wierzbicka, 1984, 1985; Atran, 1990;
D'Andrade, 1985). The very fact that the names of supercategories such as
bird or *tree* are count nouns (three birds, three trees) whereas the names of
artifactual categories are not (*three furnitures, *three clothings, *three kitchen-
wares) should have alerted the researchers to the conceptual confusion
inherent in their analytical framework – but the necessary attention to language was lacking.

To take another example, one closer to the main theme of the present
chapter, the psychological investigation of human emotion and of the expression of emotion in the human face is often marred by unconscious linguistic
assumptions. Lexical categories of the English language tend to be treated as
neutral analytical tools; and distinctions made overtly by the English lexicon
(but lacking in other languages) are treated as if they were drawn by nature
itself. For example, English concepts such as *sadness, happiness,* or *disgust*
are absolutized and are regarded as innate and universal – despite their origin
in the English language. "Nonlinguistic" experiments are set up and their
results are said to confirm the "universal" role of such concepts without
proper attention being given to the bias built into the experimental procedure
itself. What is often overlooked is that most experimental procedures involve
the use of language – and if language itself is not made an object of attention,
then the folk model reflected in language stands between the investigators
and the object of their investigation, and obscures the view (cf. Wierzbicka,
1986a, 1992d).

In my view, then, modern psychology's lack of interest in the meanings of words has had detrimental consequences both for its own development and for its impact on neighboring disciplines. But linguistics itself, until recently, paid little attention to methodical, large-scale semantic inquiries of a kind that might throw light on the organization of knowledge in the human mind. The main reason for this was the absence of a suitable methodology and also the widespread lack of faith in the very possibility of developing such a methodology. Particularly harmful in this respect was the attractive but not very constructive doctrine of "family resemblances," which was put forward by Wittgenstein in his *Philosophical investigations* (1953), and which has gained extraordinary popularity in contemporary philosophy, psychology, anthropology, and also linguistics (cf. Wierzbicka, 1990a).

If it is assumed that meanings have no clear boundaries and that they are mutually related by vague and elusive family resemblances, then it is natural to conclude that no precise definitions of word meanings can be given. But without such definitions meanings can be neither stated nor compared. As a result, all serious investigation of the lexicon comes to a halt; and in particular, the lexicon cannot be used as a way of accessing the organization of cognitive domains.

The doctrine of family resemblances never had any basis in serious study of the lexicon. It was the speculative idea of a philosopher – to be sure, a philosopher of almost unparalleled genius and charisma, but nonetheless one who was not immune to error.

I believe that lexicographic research of recent years has proved Wittgenstein wrong (on this particular point). As I will try to illustrate, meanings do have boundaries, words can be rigorously defined, lexical fields with analogous semantic structures can be uncovered, and on this basis more or less reliable and accurate cognitive maps can be drawn.

The views expressed and illustrated in this chapter, although controversial, are supported by a large and constantly growing body of empirical investigations. Limitations of space preclude the presentation of any detailed report of these investigations here, and for justification of the claims made I must refer the reader to other, more empirically and descriptively oriented studies, such as, in particular, Wierzbicka (1985, 1987, 1988a, 1989a & b, 1990b, 1991c & d, 1992b, c, & d) or the studies in Ameka (1992), Wierzbicka (1986b, 1990c), and Goddard and Wierzbicka (in press).

My basic assumptions can be stated as follows:

1. The lexicon of any language can be divided into two parts: a small, enumerable, set of words (or morphemes) that can be regarded as indefinable, and a large set of words that can be defined in terms of the indefinables. The meaning of any definable word can be seen as a configuration of the semantic primitives encoded in the indefinables.

2. Although the set of indefinables is in each case language-specific, one can hypothesize that each such set realizes, in its own way, the same universal

and innate "alphabet of human thoughts" (Leibniz, 1956: 342). For example, *this* is an English word, and *hic* a Latin one, but both can realize the same "atom" of human thought. We could say, therefore, that the set of indefinables is universal, although every language has its own, language-specific "names" for them. Consequently, the number of indefinables is probably the same in all languages, and the individual indefinables can be matched cross-linguistically. Of course the indefinables of different languages cannot be expected to be equivalent in all respects; they can, nonetheless, be regarded as SEMANTI-CALLY equivalent. (For discussion and justification of this point see, in particular, Wierzbicka, 1980, 1989a, b.) In this sense (and only in this sense) semantic primitives can be identified with lexical universals.

3. Meanings are very complex structures, built not directly from simple elements such as "someone," "want" or "this," but from structured components such as "I want something," "this is good" or "you did something bad." Components of this kind are ordered, and as they often contain the temporal element "after," or the causal component "because," sequences of such components can be often regarded as "scripts" or "scenarios" (cf. Schank & Abelson, 1977, and Abelson, 1981).

The list of postulated indefinables with which I began has expanded in the course of two decades from 14 (cf. Wierzbicka, 1972) to something like 35. The current list includes the following elements (cf. Wierzbicka, 1989a, b, 1992e; Goddard, 1989a, b): "I," "you," "someone" ("who"), "something" ("what"), "people," "this," "the same," "other," "two," "many," "all," "think," "say," "know," "want," "feel," "do," "happen," "good," "bad," "big," "small," "can," "place" ("where"), "time" ("when"), "after," "under," "kind of," "part of," "like" ("how"), "because," "if," "very," and "no" ("I don't want").

These elements have their own, language-independent syntax. For example, the verblike elements: "think," "know," "say," "feel," and "want" combine with "nominal" personal elements "I," "you," and "someone," and take complex, propositionlike complements (such as "I think: you did something bad"). The "nominal" element "someone" combines with the determinerlike elements "this," "the same," "two," and "all" (whereas "I" does not combine with them). And so on. (For fuller discussion, see Wierzbicka, 1991c.)

Generally speaking, the minilexicon of universal semantic primitives can be thought of as a minilanguage. It is a model not just of the innate "alphabet of human thoughts" but of the innate "language" of human thoughts; or rather, of the "language" of subconscious mental operations and of subconscious cognitive processes ("lingua mentalis"). Being derived from natural language, and being a tool for the description of meaning, this minilanguage has come to be called the "Natural Semantic Metalanguage," or NSM (cf. Goddard, 1989a, b).

Because the meaning of a word is, so to speak, a configuration of components built out of universal semantic primitives, it doesn't depend on the meaning of other words in the lexicon (as semantic field theorists have claimed). But to establish what the meaning of a word is one has to compare it with the meanings of other, intuitively related words. By comparing a word with other words that intuitively are felt to be related to it we can establish what each of these words really means; having done this, we can compare them again, this time more precisely, identifying the elements that are different. Proceeding in this way, we can often discover remarkable symmetries and regularities in the semantic structure of words – as well as unexpected asymmetries and irregularities. We can discover self-contained fields of semantically related words with analogous semantic patterning. We can also discover irregular and open-ended networks of overlapping families of words.

The idea that words form more or less natural nonarbitrary groupings is intuitively appealing, even irresistible. But if we couldn't decompose meanings into components, then we couldn't really investigate this possibility in a systematic and methodical way. If we have a list of hypothetical indefinables, however, and if we learn how to discover configurations of indefinables encapsulated in individual words, then we can reveal the hidden structure of these words and ipso facto we can reveal the structural relations linking together different words. Thus semantic primitives offer us a tool for investigating the structure of semantic groupings or fields, and consequently they provide a guide to the organization of language-based cognitive domains.

These general assumptions will now be illustrated by reference to a specific semantic domain: that of emotion terms. For reasons of space, the present discussion must be brief, sketchy, and selective. (For further discussion of this domain, see Wierzbicka, 1986a, 1988b, 1990d, 1992c & d; Goddard, 1991.)

Emotion concepts

Scenarios and cognitive structures

Emotion concepts encoded in the English lexicon constitute a coherent and reasonably self-contained (though not sharply delimited) cognitive domain, with a characteristic and specifiable type of semantic structure. All the words belonging to this domain can be defined in terms of cognitive structures that are typically (though not necessarily) associated with the emotions in question. Because the whole domain of emotions is too large to be analyzed here, I will limit myself to discussing one section of this domain. Before doing this, however, I will first illustrate my method of analysis with three other examples belonging to three different sections of the field of emotions – *sadness* (*sad*), *joy* (*joyful*), and *anger* (*angry*) – accompanied by brief explanatory comments. (For a more detailed study and discussion of these and many other emotion concepts, see Wierzbicka, 1992a, c, & d.)

Sad   X feels something
    sometimes a person thinks something like this:
       something bad happened
       I would want: it didn't happen (i.e., I wish: it hadn't happened)
       because of this, I would want to do something if I could
       I can't do anything
    because of this, this person feels something bad
    X feels like this

In a prototypical scenario, the "bad event" is in the past ("something bad happened," for example, somebody died). The component "I would want: it didn't happen" signals something like regret. The imaginary – but only imaginary – wish to do something ("I would want to do something if I could"), combined with a feeling of helplessness ("I can't do anything"), implies something like resignation.

Joyful   X feels something
    sometimes a person thinks something like this:
       something very good is happening
       I want this
    because of this, this person feels something very good
    X feels like this

Joy is a fairly simple concept, with just two cognitive components (embedded under "think"), and one without a counterpart among the negative emotion terms. In particular, it does not parallel *sadness*, insofar as *sadness* refers, prototypically, to past events (losses, deaths, separations, and so on), whereas *joy* implies that something very good is happening "now" (although this "now" can be interpreted very broadly). In addition, *sadness* includes further components, which endow it with a rather passive, resigned aura ("I can't do anything [about it]"), whereas *joy* does not include comparable components and is compatible with active manifestations.

Angry   X feels something
    sometimes a person thinks something like this:
       this person (Y) did something bad
       I don't want this
       because of this, I want to do something
       I want this person (Y) to feel something bad
    because of this, this person feels something bad
    X feels like this

In a prototypical *anger* situation, the emotion is triggered by a negative judgment about something that someone did ("this person did something bad"). This judgment triggers a volitional response: a refusal to accept what has happened ("I don't want this") and a desire to act ("I want to do something"). More specifically, the desire to act takes the form of an impulse to do something that would make the culprit feel something bad; but, unlike the case of *hatred*, this last impulse is controlled and doesn't have to be given full rein. (There is a difference between "I want this person to feel something bad" and "I want to do something bad to this person.") Thus, the attitude of the *angry* person is active (they do not accept the situation and they want to do something about it) and it is in principle directed toward somebody; however the active impulses of the angry person can be inhibited and don't have to be acted out. But if the inner activity is totally extinguished then there is no more *anger*, at least in the ordinary sense of the word (as opposed to the professional jargon of psychologists, counselors, and so on).

As these three preliminary examples show, the definition of an emotion concept takes the form of a prototypical scenario describing not so much an external situation as a highly abstract cognitive structure: roughly, to feel a certain emotion means to feel like a person does who has certain (specifiable) thoughts, characteristic of that particular situation (and to undergo some internal process because of this). Typically, though not necessarily, these thoughts involve references to "doing" or "happening," to something "good" or "bad," and to "wanting" or "not wanting."[1]

For example, the English words *joy*, *sadness*, and *anger* can be linked with the following hypothetical thoughts: "Something very good is happening," "I want this" (*joy*); "something bad happened," "I would want: it didn't happen" (*sadness*); "this person did something bad," "I don't want this" (*anger*). This does not mean that the feelings described by these words HAVE to be caused by these thoughts, because, as Johnson-Laird and Oatley insist, "a basic emotion such as sadness can be felt for no known reason" (1989: 92; see, however, Ortony & Clore, 1989). But an analysis based on a prototypical script solves this difficulty: It is one thing to feel something BECAUSE of a particular thought, and another to feel LIKE a person would who is thinking that particular thought.

As I tried to show in my earlier discussions of this topic (cf. Wierzbicka, 1972, 1973), emotions are often overtly described in terms of a prototypical situation ("I felt as one does when ...," or "I felt as one would if ..."). I hypothesize that ready-made emotion terms such as *sadness* or *joy* provide handy abbreviations for scenarios that members of a given culture see as particularly common and salient.

It should be noted that prototypical scenarios of emotion concepts proposed here differ considerably from those proposed in recent psychological literature, where usually no attempt is made to capture the invariant of a given emotion concept, or to express it in simpler and more universal concepts than those that are being analyzed. As an illustration of these differences in approach, I reproduce below (in a slightly abbreviated form) the "prototype of sadness" proposed by Shaver, Schwartz, Kirson, and O'Connor (1987: 1077). For reasons of space, no further comments will be offered, but the differences between this "script" and the explication proposed here will be evident. (For details of this "script," see Shaver et al., 1987):

The prototype of sadness
An undesirable outcome; getting what was not wanted . . .
Discovering that one is powerless, helpless, impotent
Empathy with someone who is sad, hurt, etc.
Sitting or lying around; being inactive, lethargic, listless
Tired, rundown, low in energy; Slow, shuffling movements; Slumped, drooping
    posture
Withdrawing from social contact; Talking little or not at all
Low, quiet, slow, monotonous voice; Saying sad things
Frowning, not smiling; Crying, tears, whimpering
Irritable, touchy, grouchy; Moping, brooding, being moody
Negative outlook; thinking only about the negative side of things
Giving up; no longer trying to improve or control the situation
Blaming, criticizing oneself
Talking to someone about the sad feelings or events
Taking action, becoming active . . . Suppressing the negative feelings

A "script" of this kind includes lots of ideas that may come to mind in connection with the concept of "sadness," but it does not separate essential features from more or less accidental ones. For example, something like "an undesirable outcome" may indeed be a necessary part of the "sadness scenario"; but "withdrawing from social contact" or "slumped, drooping posture" is not. (Listing various possible ways of behaving that may be associated with sadness is no substitute for defining *sadness*: On the contrary, to be able to say that a sad person is likely to cry or to assume a "slumped, drooping posture" we have to know how to define *sad* independently.) Furthermore, describing *sadness* via a tendency "to say sad things" is circular, and analyzing it via other emotion concepts (such as *surprise, empathy,* or *irritation*) makes any comparison between these concepts impossible.

It might be suggested that whereas the "sadness scenario" proposed by Shaver et al. is redundant and includes a good deal of material that is unnecessary (because it may or may not be associated with sadness), the scenarios proposed here are incomplete, because they mention thoughts and feelings but don't refer to the bodily aspect of the emotions in question at all. I agree that the concept of 'emotion' implies more than thoughts and feelings, and I explicate the concept as follows (cf. Wierzbicka, in press):

  a. X thought something
  b. because of this, X felt something
  c. because of this, something happened to X

Component c of this explication can be taken as referring to physiological reactions, facial expression, posture, and so on.

It would be easy, of course, to add such a component to the explication of individual emotion terms, such as *sad* (*sadness*), *joyful* (*joy*), or *angry* (*anger*). I have refrained, however, from doing so, because I don't have the space here to discuss distinctions such as those between, for example, "being sad" and "feeling sad." As they stand, all the explications proposed in this chapter apply equally well to "being" (in a certain emotional state), for example, "being sad," and to "feeling" (a certain feeling), such as "feeling sad." (For a fuller discussion of the relationship between "emotions" and "feelings," see Wierzbicka, in press; for an earlier, and different, discussion, see Wierzbicka, 1980: 142–149; see also Ortony & Clore, 1989.)

Is there an "emotional keyboard"?

In a section entitled "Semantics and emotions: A developmental puzzle," Shweder writes:

What is the role of cultural meaning systems in the growth of an emotional life? Consider this question in terms of an emotional keyboard, with each key being a discrete emotion: disgust, interest, distress, anger, fear, contempt, shame, shyness, guilt, and so on. A key is struck when a situation or object is interpreted in a certain way – as loss, frustration, novelty, or "a little thing that squirms in the night." . . . While a differentiated emotional keyboard may be available to most four-year-olds around the world, the tunes that get played and the emotional scores that are available diverge considerably for adults. (1991: 258–259)

If there was indeed such an "emotional keyboard" this would mean that there was at least one domain-specific set of innate elements underlying the development of human cognition. But is there such a keyboard?

I think there are reasons to doubt it.

To begin with, it is now known that none of the categories corresponding to the so-called basic emotions – that is, fear, anger, disgust, surprise, happiness, and sadness (cf. e.g., Ekman, 1989; Izard, 1977; Johnson-Laird & Oatley, 1989) – is universal; and if these are not universal, then there can be no question of the universality of the less "basic" emotion categories, such as shame, shyness, guilt, or contempt. For example, the English word *anger* differs in meaning from its closest counterpart in Ilongot, *liget* (cf. Rosaldo, 1980; Wierzbicka, 1988c, 1992c), or Ifaluk, *song* (cf. Lutz, 1988; Wierzbicka, 1988b, 1992c), or Yankunytjatjara, *pika* (cf. Goddard, 1991); and the English word *sadness* differs in meaning from its closest counterpart in the Australian language Pitjantjatjara, *tjituru-tjituru* (cf. Goddard, 1987; Wierzbicka, 1992d). "Anger" is, then, no more a universal category of human experience than is "liget" or "song"; and "sadness," no more than "tjituru-tjituru."

If there was a universal emotional keyboard, then the keys of this keyboard could not be identified in terms of culture-specific categories such as "anger" or "sadness." Unfortunately, it is precisely such terms, taken from the set of English folk categories, that have been used as basic conceptual tools in the bulk of research on universals in human emotions; partly as a consequence of this, the results arrived at have an Anglo bias built into them and are far from conclusive.

This is not to deny, of course, that this research led to some important discoveries, or that it demonstrated that there are some universals of human emotion and emotional expression. But we still do not know WHAT these universals are.

Even the most carefully selected photographs of human faces (coming as close as possible to the researchers' idea of a "happy" face, a "sad" face, an "angry" face, and so on) fail to be consistently matched by informants with assorted labels such as "happy," "sad," or "angry." The caption under one of Ekman's tables showing the results of such matching says that "Everyone agrees on what the faces say" (1975: 36), but in fact the table shows a considerable amount of disagreement among informants (although the consensus is high above chance). Characteristically, the highest measure of consensus (about 90%) is associated with smiling faces, described by researchers (in English) as "happy." For "fear," "anger," or "disgust" the level of consensus is usually much lower.

Results of this kind suggest, to my mind, that human beings may be able to read in some (smiling) faces the message: "I feel something good now" (not the message "I feel happy now," because the concept of "happy" is no more than an artifact of the English language), and in some other faces, the message "I feel something bad now."

It is also possible that among "feel-bad" messages, human beings anywhere in the world may be able to distinguish (at least in some cases) between messages referring to the past and those referring to the future (along the lines of "I think something bad happened" vs. "I think something bad will happen"); or that they may be able to read some facial messages referring to human action (e.g., "I want to do something bad to someone," as in an "aggro" face with a squarish mouth and clenched teeth). But possible correlations of this kind do not imply any innate emotional keyboard. (For a different interpretation, see Ortony & Turner, 1990; Wierzbicka, 1993.)

Evidence available to date suggests that the "tunes" may indeed differ from culture to culture (for example, the *liget* tune may be different from the *anger* tune or from the *song* tune), and that there may indeed be more uniformity among children than among adults, but what exactly this uniformity consists in is far from clear at this stage. Ekman, Izard, and their associates are no doubt right in assuming that one path to the understanding of human emotions is to study the human face. I would add that another important path is to study the semantics of emotion concepts encoded in the lexicon of human languages (cf. Harré, 1986); and also, that to be able to investigate the semantics of human faces, we need a suitable methodology, and such a methodology emerges from the study of emotion concepts encoded in language. (For further discussion, cf. Wierzbicka, 1993.)

The research into the semantics of emotion concepts encoded in language suggests that, as mentioned earlier, these concepts indeed constitute a coherent cognitive domain, with a specific type of semantic structure. So far, I have illustrated this type of structure with the explications of three concepts: *sadness*, *joy*, and *anger*. In what follows, I will illustrate it further with a series of explications pertaining to one subdomain of the field of English emotion concepts.

Toward a typology of emotion concepts

Like any other set of complex entities, emotion concepts can be classified in many different ways. As this discussion suggests, one illuminating way to do so would be to distinguish concepts involving the component "I feel something good" from those involving the component "I feel something bad." Because some emotion concepts – for example, "surprise" or "amazement" – are neutral (neither necessarily good nor necessarily bad), this would lead us to a three-way division ("positive," "negative," and "neutral" emotion categories).

Among "bad feelings," it is useful to distinguish those that are oriented to the future from those focusing on the past or on the present. This can be done in terms of the following semantic components:

> I think something bad happened (e.g., sadness)
> I think something bad is happening (e.g., horror)
> I think something bad will happen (e.g., fear)

Another useful distinction is that between bad things happening "in general" (as in the examples above) and bad things happening specifically "to me":

> I think something bad happened to me (e.g., despair, grief)
> I think something bad is happening to me (e.g., pain, distress)
> I think something bad will happen to me (e.g., dread, terror, panic)

Distinctions of this kind enable us to see qualitative contrasts behind what may appear to be merely "stylistic" differences or differences of degree. For example, in the literature on "basic emotions" and the expression of emotion, concepts such as 'sadness' and 'distress' are often used interchangeably; and if informants cannot reliably distinguish a "sad" face from a "distressed" one, this is not regarded as evidence against the claim that "sadness" (or "distress") is one of the "discrete," "basic" human emotions. In fact, however, the two concepts are different, though of course related, as one can see by comparing the explication of *sadness* given earlier to that of *distress* given later (for further discussion and justification, see Wierzbicka, 1992a, d):

Distress X feels something
> sometimes a person thinks something like this:
>> something bad is happening to me now
>> I don't want this
>> because of this, I would want to do something
>> I don't know what I can do
>> I want someone to do something

because of this, this person feels something bad
X feels like this.

As just one little piece of evidence for the reality of these distinctions I will
note the common phrase "distress signals," which is used with reference to
ships. This ship's crew may well wish to signal a message along the following
lines: "Something bad is happening to us," "we don't want this," "because of
this, we would want to do something," "we don't know what we can do," "we
want someone (else) to do something." But there would be no point in any
ship sending out "signals of sadness" (or, for that matter, signals of unhap-
piness, sorrow, depression, or grief).

Because most emotion concepts include several different components, there
are many different dimensions of contrast between them ("good" vs. "bad,"
"happen" vs. "do," "now" vs. "before now" or "after now," "someone" vs.
"me," "I can't do anything" vs. "I don't know what I could do," and so on),
and, consequently, many different (overlapping) classes of emotion concepts
can be singled out. The most useful and illuminating classifactory schemes
are not necessarily those that would recommend themselves most from an
abstract, a priori point of view, because the conceptualization of emotions
reflected in natural language is usually much less symmetrical and "logical"
than a priori abstract schemes would lead one to expect. In particular, it is
well known that languages tend to differentiate "bad feelings" far more than
"good feelings" (cf. Averill, 1980). (Partly for this reason, no doubt, it is
much easier to identify a so-called happy face than to identify a so-called sad
or distressed one.) In particular, the idea that "something bad will/can happen"
is usually given much more attention than the corresponding idea that
"something good will/can happen"; and the idea that "someone did (or is
doing) something bad" is usually lexically elaborated far beyond the corresponding idea that "someone did (or is doing) something good."

The subdomain of emotion concepts referring to "things going against our
wishes" is no exception in this respect, with, for example, *irritation, annoyance,* or *resentment* (unlike [being] *displeased* or *discontent*) having no positive counterparts at all.

Things happening that one doesn't want

"Bad things" that happen to us are not always easy to distinguish
from things that are not necessarily "bad" but that go against our wishes.
Similarly, people's "bad actions" are not always easy to distinguish from
actions that are simply contrary to our wishes. From a semantic point of view,
however, "undesirable" or "unwanted" is not the same thing as "bad" (just
as "desirable" or "wanted" is not the same thing as "good"). In this section,
I will discuss a number of English words referring to actions and events that
we don't want without necessarily regarding them as "bad." These words
include *mad, annoyed, displeased, irritated,* and *resent.*

Mad   X feels something
sometimes a person thinks something like this:
    something happened now
    I don't want this
    because of this, I want to do something now
    I want to do something bad to someone
    I can't not do it
    because of this, this person feels something very bad
    X feels like this

In various discussions of English emotion concepts it is usually assumed that *mad* (in the relevant sense) designates a kind of *anger*, being simply more specific, and more colloquial, than *angry*.

In fact, however, there are important semantic differences between the two concepts, which largely explain why *mad* sounds more colloquial, and also why children acquire this concept much earlier than they acquire the concept of *anger* (cf. Smiley & Huttenlocher, 1989: 36).

To begin with, *mad*, unlike *angry*, does not imply a judgment about somebody else's action ("this person did something bad"); it implies only that "something happened that I don't want." (Cf. the following utterance, reported in Gordon, 1989: 341: "I get mad when I fall down and hurt myself.")

Second, *mad* implies an immediate and short-term reaction ("something happened NOW"), whereas *angry* may refer to longer stretches of time. (This feature of *mad*, too, is illustrated by the example of the child falling and hurting herself.)

The volitive reaction implied by *mad* implies a similar immediacy: "I want to do something NOW," whereas *angry* is compatible with a long-term reaction ("I want to do something" – but not necessarily NOW).

A person who is *mad* is more "dangerous" to other people than a person who is simply *angry* (hence the link with the other sense of *mad*, close to *insane*). Being *mad* implies an impulse to do something bad to someone ("I want to do something bad to someone"), whereas *anger* implies a more general impulse to "do something" (as well as a desire for the culprit to "feel something bad"). In *mad*, the impulse to do something is also less rational, and it may be quite irrational: If there is no assumption that "SOMEONE did something bad" then why should one "want to do something bad to SOMEONE"? (This is another link between the *mad* of "bad and violent emotion" and the *mad* of "insanity.") In addition, the impulse to "do something bad" is perceived as uncontrollable: "I can't not do it" (another link with insanity).

Finally, *mad* implies a greater intensity of feeling ("this person feels something VERY bad"). One could say, for example, that someone was "rather angry," but not that someone was "rather mad."

Annoyed   X feels something
sometimes a person thinks something like this:

     this person (Y) did something
     I didn't want this
     I would want: this person (Y) didn't do it
    because of this, this person feels something bad
    X feels like this.

Annoyance – unlike *anger* or *indignation* – does not imply any judgment ("this person did something bad"); rather, it implies only that what the other person did was against the experiencer's wishes. For example, we can be annoyed with a visitor coming to see us at a time when we are very busy or when we are talking to somebody special and would rather be left alone with that special person. The person who is *annoyed* does not have an urge to hit, to smash something, or even to shout. There is no active opposition, no "I don't want this" in their attitude. Rather, there is a realization that what happened is contrary to their prior wishes ("I didn't want this"), and a resulting "bad feeling."

Normally, one gets *annoyed* with people (or animals), not with inanimate objects; and it is people's actions that *annoy* us, rather than agentless events. For example, one may be *annoyed* when woken up by an early telephone call (or perhaps even by the bark of a dog); but not if one is woken up by a sudden gust of wind.

Displeased   X feels something
    sometimes a person thinks something like this:
     this person (Y) did something
     it is not good
     I didn't want this
     I wanted something not like this
     I thought: because of this, this person (Y) will do it (i.e.
       what I want)
    because of this, this person feels something bad
    X feels like this

People who are *displeased*, like people who are *annoyed*, have no impulse to hit, smash, or shout. On the other hand, they may frown; and if they speak, they may reprove, rebuke, or reprimand the person who has caused their displeasure. This suggests the absence of the components "I don't want this," and "because of this, I want to do something." Here, as in the case of *annoyance*, the wanting is in the past: At the present moment, one registers that what happened was contrary to (or inconsistent with) one's wishes ("I didn't want this," "I wanted something not like this"). But *annoyed* does not imply an expectation that one is in control, whereas *displeased* does. One can be *annoyed* by a fly flying and buzzing near us, but one can hardly be *displeased* with it. Normally, we are *displeased* with a person who we thought was partly under our control and for whom we had certain plans, designs, and expectations; this person has done something, but we see what they have done as not good and as different from what we had in mind. A boss can be *displeased* with a secretary, and a parent with a teenage son or daughter, but (normally) not vice versa. In some respects, then, being *displeased* is like being *disappointed*, but in the latter case the experiencer is not in control, and it is events, not necessarily people's actions, that disappoint us. In the case of *displeased*, we do feel in control, and it has to be other people who have not measured up to our expectations and our plans for them. Furthermore, in the case of a disappointment, we were expecting something GOOD, which – we thought – was going to happen TO US; in the case of *displeased*, both these dimensions are lacking.

Another instructive comparison is that between *displeased* and *discontent*. Here, too, our wishes and expectations fail to be met. But – unlike the case of *displeased* – it can be events and situations rather than people that make us *discontent*; furthermore, the cause of our discontent is in the present, not in the past ("something is happening," not "someone did something," as in the case of *displeased*); the experiencer is directly affected ("something is happening TO ME"); and he or she still wants something ("I want something other than this"), whereas *displeased* does not imply this.

Thus, the thought structures of *disappointed* and *discontent* can be represented as follows (I do not include here the full explications of these concepts):

Disappointed	I thought: something good will happen to me
	I wanted it
	I know now: it will not happen
Discontent	something is happening to me
	this is not good
	I wanted something not like this
	I want something not like this

In contrast to these two explications, that of *displeased* contains the component "this person did something" (which links it with *anger*), and also "I wanted something not like this," "I thought: because of this, this person will do it," which jointly convey an assumption of partial control.

Irritated X feels something
        sometimes a person thinks something like this:
           something is happening
           it has been happening for some time
           I don't want this
           I can't not think about it
           because of this, I would want to do something
        because of this, this person feels something bad
        X feels like this

A fly buzzing around someone's head may either *irritate* them or *annoy* them. What is the difference? The nonemotional sense of the word *irritate* provides a helpful clue. If someone's skin is irritated by rough wool, or a synthetic watchband, the skin seems to be saying, metaphorically speaking, "this thing has been in contact with me for some time," "I don't want this," "in fact, I can't stand it," "because of this, I would want to do something" (and it reddens as if to express the message). Interestingly, a patch of skin can also be "angry," which also appears to imply an "active" (even more "active") message: "I don't want this," "because of this, I want to do something." But, needless to add, skin cannot be "annoyed," as it cannot be "displeased," "disappointed," or "frustrated."

When I discover that I have accidentally burnt my toast I could be *annoyed* but probably not *irritated* – presumably, because the event is completed, short-term, and already in the past. But if a member of my family constantly burns his or her toast and then throws it out, wasting bread and blocking access to the toaster, this pattern of behavior may well come to *irritate* me; and sooner or later, I am likely to betray (if not to show intentionally) that it is getting on my nerves and that I wish he or she would stop it.

These are, then, the crucial elements of *irritation*: Something is seen as part of an on-going process, the experiencer doesn't want it, cannot stop thinking about it, and has an impulse to oppose it. This impulse is not as strong and as conscious as in the case of *anger* ("I WOULD want to do something" vs. "I WANT to do something"). The *irritated* person is also less likely to be feeling in control of the situation than an *angry* one – a difference that can be explained partly in terms of the contrast between "I WOULD want to do something" and "I WANT to do something," and partly in terms of the component "I can't not think about it," which presents the experiencer as a sufferer rather than an agent. Moreover, in *irritation* the impulse to act is not directed against a specific person; on the contrary, *irritation* is likely to spill over in any direction. Finally, the event that *irritates* us does not have to be seen as bad, and consequently can be quite trivial. For example, one can be irritated by somebody's slow eating even if one can't see anything objectively "bad" in this. But normally one would not get *angry* with someone for eating slowly, unless this was seen as deliberate and for some reason reprehensible.

Resent   X feels something (when X thinks of Y)
        sometimes a person thinks something like this of someone:
           this person is doing something
           because of this, something is happening to me
           I don't want this
           because of this, I would want to do something
           I am not doing it now
        because of this, this person feels something bad
        X feels like this

One cannot *resent* rain, heat, or the barking of dogs. One can only *resent* human actions. These actions do not have to be seen as "bad," but they have to be contrary to our wishes ("I don't want this") and they have to affect us personally ("because of this, something is happening to me"). The inner opposition to the action is strong and unequivocal ("I don't want this"), but the urge to act upon it is inhibited ("I WOULD want to do something" rather than "I WANT to do something"). Furthermore, this impulse is not acted out – at least not immediately – not because it is suppressed but because it is, so to speak, consciously bottled up ("I am not doing it now").

Given that it does not imply a negative judgment ("this person did/is doing something bad") *resent* seems to be a surprisingly strong emotion, and this conscious bottling up of the inner opposition may well be largely responsible for this.

Conclusion

In trying to discover how knowledge (or at least basic, "foundational" knowledge) is stored and organized in the human mind we can rely, in a considerable measure, on language. There may be concepts that are not lexicalized in natural language, but these are probably less common, less basic, and less salient in a given speech community than those that have achieved lexicalization; they are also less accessible to study. Words provide evidence for the existence of concepts. Lexical sets, sharing a similar semantic structure, provide evidence for the existence of cohesive conceptual wholes (or fields). If it is hypothesized that knowledge is organized in the mind in the form of "cognitive domains," then conceptual fields detectable through semantic analysis of the lexicon can be regarded as a guide to those domains.

All conceptual structures detectable through language can be seen as different configurations of innate and universal concepts such as "someone" and "something," "do" and "happen," "know," "think" and "want," or "good," and "bad." These elements have no "domain specificity": They constitute a universal set not only in the sense that they appear to be the same in all languages but also in the sense that they provide the basic conceptual building blocks for all cognitive domains. Complex configurations of these building blocks, however, often do form coherent conceptual fields, whose structures can be studied by analyzing individual words and uncovering recurring structural patterns. For example, emotion terms, speech act verbs (cf. Wierzbicka, 1987), and names of animals (cf. Wierzbicka, 1985) can all be regarded as such coherent conceptual fields.

Different fields differ considerably in terms of their complexity. Generally speaking, abstract concepts are much simpler in their structure than concrete concepts. In particular, names of "natural kinds" such as *mouse* or of "cultural kinds" such as *bottle* are much more complex than names of speech acts (such as *threat*) or of emotions (such as *fear*). This means that some fields comprise concepts that can be represented directly as certain configurations of conceptual primitives, whereas others can only be reduced gradually to the level of primitives. For example, an explication of *mouse* that only included hypothesized conceptual primitives would be so complex that it would be virtually unreadable. Ultimately, however, all explications have to rely – directly or indirectly – on the primitives. Progress and understanding can be achieved only by reducing what is complex to what is simpler, and the notion of "simpler" would have no sense if there was no absolute and nonarbitrary measure of conceptual simplicity. Such a measure is provided by the set of innate conceptual primitives. If these primitives can be identified in all languages of the world, they can provide an "absolute" and nonarbitrary "measure" in terms of which concepts can be compared across language and culture boundaries. This ensures that different "language and culture systems" (cf. Grace, 1987) are not incommensurable and can be studied from a neutral, culture-independent perspective.

Concepts encoded in the lexicon of a natural language are often vague, imprecise, fuzzy, and referentially indeterminate. They are often centered around a prototypical scene or a prototypical scenario. They are also often "naive," impressionistic, subjective, and anthropocentric. But none of this means that they cannot be portrayed in a precise, rigorous, and fully "objective" manner. Universal semantic primitives offer a set of tools with which conceptual structures, and the cultural knowledge encoded in them, can be purposefully and systematically explored.

In particular, semantic analysis carried out in terms of universal semantic primitives offers some evidence for the issue of domain specificity. For example, it suggests that the names of emotions constitute a domain with a sui generis conceptual structure, involving a prototypical thought and a prototypical feeling linked with it. The specificity of this domain does not consist in the presence of some innate and universal "emotional keyboard," comprising unanalyzable "basic emotions." All the emotion concepts reflected in either verbal or nonverbal communication (for example, in the lexicon of human language or in the human face) are analyzable and can be seen as configurations of the same conceptual elements that underlie all the other cognitive domains. Nonetheless, the type of configuration is domain-specific. The basic conceptual model that underlies this domain is based on the idea that sometimes people FEEL something BECAUSE they THINK something, and that what a person feels can be described as being LIKE what someone feels when they think something (the crucial concepts involved being FEEL, THINK, BECAUSE, and LIKE).

An example of a cognitive domain with a very different – and also sui generis – type of semantic configuration is provided by the domain of living kind concepts. First of all, living kind concepts are immensely complex, and cannot be analyzed directly in terms of conceptual primitives. This feature distinguishes them from, for example, emotion concepts, but not from the domain of artifacts, which have a comparable level of complexity and which also involve many levels of structure (cf. Wierzbicka, 1984, 1985, and 1991b). This link between natural kinds and cultural kinds is based primarily on the notion of KIND, which is crucially involved in these two domains, but not, for example, in the domain of emotions (the importance of the difference between KIND and LIKE, categorization and resemblance, being one of the most significant insights emerging from recent work in cognitive science, cf., e.g., Gelman & Coley, 1991; Keil, 1989; Atran, 1990).

But despite these links between the domain of artifacts and that of living kinds it is also clear that the two differ in a number of significant ways. To begin with, the "naive" categorization of living kinds reflected in language involves hierarchical ranking (e.g., creature – bird – sparrow; thing growing out of the ground – tree – oak), whereas the artifactual supercategories (such as, for example, furniture, clothing, or kitchenware; or weapon, tool, or vehicle) are not based on a "hierarchy of kinds" (cf. Wierzbicka, 1984, 1985, 1992f; Atran, 1990).

Furthermore, the domain of living kinds appears to be conceptualized partly in terms of "hidden essences," which are linked with species names (and perhaps with the idea of reproduction), whereas with artifactual concepts this is not the case (cf. Schwartz, 1978; Atran, 1990).

Finally, living kind concepts are subject to interspeaker variability and can expand with the speaker's experience with denotata (a process that should not be confused with any increase in scientific knowledge); a similar variability does not seem to occur in the domain of artifacts (although names of technical inventions such as *television*, *radio*, or *computer* raise interesting problems in this connection, too, as they do with respect to "hidden natures"; cf. Keil, 1989).

The organization of cognitive domains is reflected in language, and above all in the structure of the lexicon. There is a danger that in this area of the study of cognition, as in many others, if no special effort is made to adopt a cross-cultural and cross-linguistic approach, the analytical tools employed may prove to be more or less culture-bound (cf. Lutz, 1985). The use of universal semantic primitives can offer a safeguard against this danger.

Note

1. "Wanting" and "not wanting" is such an important ingredient of most emotion concepts that it might be suggested that its role is as crucial as that of thoughts and feelings. But in fact, there are emotion concepts that do not include any volitional components. "Surprise" is one such concept (cf. Wierzbicka, 1992a). "Guilt" is another:

   X feels guilty
   > X feels something
   > sometimes a person thinks something like this:
   >> I did something
   >> something bad happened because of this
   > because of this, this person feels something bad
   > X feels like this

References

Abelson, Robert. (1981). Psychological status of the script concept. *American Psychologist, 36*(7), 715–729.

Ameka, Felix. (Ed). (1992). *Journal of Pragmatics, 18*(1). Special issue on interjections.

Atran, S. (1990). *Cognitive foundations of natural history.* Cambridge: Cambridge University Press.

Averill, James R. (1980). On the paucity of positive emotions. In K. R. Blankstein, P. Pliner, & J. Polivy (Eds.), *Advances in the study of communication and affect, vol. 6: Assessment and modification of emotional behavior.* (pp. 7–45). New York: Plenum Press.

D'Andrade, Roy G. (1985). Character terms and cultural models. In Janet Dougherty (Ed.), *Directions in cognitive anthropology* (pp. 321–343). Urbana: University of Illinois Press.

Ekman, Paul. (1975). The universal smile: Face muscles talk every language. *Psychology Today, September,* 35–39.

Ekman, Paul. (1989). The argument and evidence about universals in facial expressions of emotion. In H. Wagner & A. Manstead (Eds.), *Handbook of social psychophysiology* (pp. 143–164). New York: John Wiley.

Gelman, Susan, & John Coley. (1991). Language and categorization: The acquisition of natural kind terms. In S. A. Gelman, & J. P. Byrnes (Eds.), *Perspectives on language and thought: Interrelations in development.* Cambridge: Cambridge University Press.

Goddard, Cliff. (1987). *A basic Pitjantjatjara/Yankunytjatjara to English dictionary.* Alice Springs: Institute for Aboriginal Development.

Goddard, Cliff. (1989a). Issues in natural semantic metalanguage. *Quaderni di Semantica, 10*(1), 51–64 (Round Table on Semantic Primitives, 1).

Goddard, Cliff. (1989b). The goals and limits of semantic representation. *Quaderni di Semantica, 10*(2), 297–308 (Round Table on Semantic Primitives, 2).

Goddard, Cliff. (1991). Anger in the Western Desert: Semantics, culture and emotion. *Man* (n.s.), *26,* 602–619.

Goddard, Cliff, & Anna Wierzbicka (Eds.). (in press). *Semantic and lexical universals.* Amsterdam: John Benjamins.

Gordon, Steven L. (1989). The socialization of children's emotions: Emotional culture, competence, and exposure. In Carolyn Saarni & Paul L. Harris (Eds.), *Children's understanding of emotion* (pp. 319–349). Cambridge: Cambridge University Press.

Grace, George W. (1987). *The linguistic construction of reality.* London: Croom Helm.

Harré, Rom. (1986). An outline of the social constructivist viewpoint. In Rom Harré (Ed.), *The social construction of emotions* (pp. 2–14). Oxford: Blackwell.

Izard, Carroll. (1977). *Human emotions.* New York: Plenum Press.

Jespersen, Otto. (1924). *The philosophy of grammar.* London: George Allen & Unwin.

Johnson-Laird, P. N., & Keith Oatley. (1989). The language of emotions: An analysis of a semantic field. *Cognition and Emotion, 3,* 81–123.

Keil, Frank. (1989). *Concepts, kinds and cognitive development.* Cambridge, MA: MIT Press.

Leibniz, Gottfried Wilhelm. (1704/1949). *New essays concerning human understanding.* La Salle, Ill.: Open Court.

Leibniz, Gottfried Wilhelm. (1956). *Philosophical papers and letters.* Chicago: University of Chicago Press.

Lutz, Catherine. (1985). Ethnopsychology compared to what? Explaining behavior and consciousness among the Ifaluk. In Geoffrey M. White & John Kirkpatrick (Eds.), *Person, self, and experience: Exploring Pacific ethnopsychologies* (pp. 35–79). Berkeley: University of California Press.

Lutz, Catherine. (1988). *Unnatural emotions.* Chicago: University of Chicago Press.

Ortony, Andrew, & Gerald L. Clore. (1989). Emotions, moods and conscious awareness. *Cognition and Emotion, 3*(2), 125–137.

Ortony, Andrew, & Terence J. Turner. (1990). What's basic about basic emotions? *Psychological Review, 97,* 315–331.

Rosaldo, Michelle. (1980). *Knowledge and passion: Ilongot notions of self and social life.* Cambridge: Cambridge University Press.

Schank, Roger, & Robert Abelson. (1977). *Scripts, plans, goals and understanding: An inquiry into human knowledge structures.* Hillsdale, NJ: Erlbaum.

Schwartz, S. P. (1978). Putnam on artifacts. *Philosophical Review, 87,* 566–574.

Shaver, Phillip, Judith Schwartz, Donald Kirson, & Cary O'Connor. (1987). Emotion knowledge: Further exploration of a prototype approach. *Journal of Personality and Social Psychology, 52,* 1061–1086.

Shweder, Richard A. (1991). *Thinking through cultures: Expeditions in cultural psychology.* Cambridge, MA: Harvard University Press.

Smiley, Patricia, & Janellen Huttenlocher. (1989). Young children's acquisition of emotion concepts. In Carolyn Saarni & Paul L. Harris (Eds.), *Children's understanding of emotion* (pp. 27–49). Cambridge: Cambridge University Press.

Wierzbicka, Anna. (1972). *Semantic primitives.* Frankfurt: Athenäum.

Wierzbicka, Anna. (1973). The semantic structure of words for emotions. In Roman Jakobson, C. H. van Schooneveld, & D. S. Worth (Eds.), *Slavic poetics: Essays in honour of Kiril Taranovsky* (pp. 499–505). The Hague: Mouton.

Wierzbicka, Anna. (1980). *Lingua mentalis: The semantics of natural language.* Sydney: Academic Press.

Wierzbicka, Anna. (1984). Apples are not a 'kind of fruit': The semantics of human categorization. *American Ethnologist, 11*(2), 313–328.

Wierzbicka, Anna. (1985). *Lexicography and conceptual analysis.* Ann Arbor: Karoma.

Wierzbicka, Anna. (1986a). Human emotions: Universal or culture-specific? *American Anthropologist, 88*(3), 584–594.

Wierzbicka, Anna (Ed.). (1986b). *Journal of Pragmatics.* Special issue on particles.

Wierzbicka, Anna. (1987). *English speech act verbs: A semantic dictionary.* Sydney/New York: Academic Press.

Wierzbicka, Anna. (1988a). *The semantics of grammar.* Amsterdam: John Benjamins.

Wierzbicka, Anna. (1988b). L'amour, la colère, la joie, l'ennui: La sémantique des émotions dans une perspective transculturelle. *Langages, 89,* 97–107.

Wierzbicka, Anna. (1988c). Emotions across culture: Similarities and differences. (Reply to Kolenda). *American Anthropologist, 90*(4), 982–983.

Wierzbicka, Anna. (1989a). Semantic primitives and lexical universals. *Quaderni di Semantica, 10*(1), 103–121 (Round Table on Semantic Primitives, 1).

Wierzbicka, Anna. (1989b). Semantic primitives: The expanding set. *Quaderni di Semantica, 10*(2), 133–157 (Round Table on Semantic Primitives, 2).

Wierzbicka, Anna. (1990a). "Prototypes save": On the uses and abuses of the notion of "prototype" in linguistics and related fields. In S. L. Tzohatzidis (Ed.), *Meanings and prototypes: Studies in linguistic categorization.* London: Routledge & Kegan Paul.

Wierzbicka, Anna. (1990b). The meaning of colour terms: Semantics, culture and cognition. *Cognitive Linguistics, 1*(1), 99–150.

Wierzbicka, Anna (Ed.). (1990c). *Australian Journal of Linguistics, 10*(2.) Special issue on the semantics of emotions.

Wierzbicka, Anna. (1990d). The semantics of emotions: *Fear* and its relatives in English. *Australian Journal of Linguistics* (Special issue on the semantics of emotions), *10*(2), 359–375.

Wierzbicka, Anna. (1991a). *Cross-cultural pragmatics: The semantics of human interaction.* Berlin: Mouton de Gruyter.

Wierzbicka, Anna. (1991b). Semantic complexity: Conceptual primitives and the principle of substitutability. *Theoretical Linguistics, 17,* 75–97.

Wierzbicka, Anna. (1991c). Lexical universals and universals of grammar. In Michel Kefer & Johann van der Auwera (Eds.), *Meaning and grammar: Cross-linguistic perspectives* (pp. 383–415). Berlin: Mouton de Gruyter.

Wierzbicka, Anna. (1991d). Ostensive definitions and verbal definitions: Innate conceptual primitives and the acquisition of concepts. In Maciej Grochowski & Daniel Weiss (Eds.), *Words are physicians for an ailing mind* (pp. 467–480). Munich: Otto Sagner.

Wierzbicka, Anna. (1992a). Defining emotion concepts. *Cognitive Science, 16,* 539–581.

Wierzbicka, Anna. (1992b). Semantic primitives and semantic fields. In Adrienne Lehrer & Eva Feder Kittay (Eds.), *Frames, fields, and contrasts: New essays in semantic and lexical organization* (pp. 209–227). Hillsdale, NJ: Erlbaum.

Wierzbicka, Anna. (1992c). *Semantics, culture, and cognition: Universal human concepts in culture-specific configurations.* New York: Oxford University Press.

Wierzbicka, Anna. (1992d). Talking about emotions: Semantics, culture, and cognition. *Cognition and Emotion* (Special issue on basic emotions), *6*(3/4), 285–319.

Wierzbicka, Anna. (1992e). The search for universal semantic primitives. In Martin Pütz (Ed.), *Thirty years of linguistic evolution* (pp. 215–242). Amsterdam: John Benjamins.

Wierzbicka, Anna. (1992f). What is a *life form*? Conceptual issues in ethnobiology. *Journal of Linguistic Anthropology, 2*(1), 3–29.

Wierzbicka, Anna. (1993). Reading human faces: Emotion components and universal semantics. *Pragmatics and Cognition, 1*(1).

Wierzbicka, Anna. (in press). Emotion, language, and "cultural scripts." In Shinobu Kitayama & Hazel Rose Markus (Eds.), *Emotion and culture.*

Wittgenstein, Ludwig. (1953). *Philosophical investigations.* New York: Macmillan.

Part VI

Implications for education

18   Teachers' models of children's minds and learning

Sidney Strauss and Tamar Shilony

Laypersons, teachers, and psychologists believe that learning takes place in people's minds. They all believe that learning takes place as a consequence of instruction, if we interpret instruction in its widest sense (Atran & Sperber, 1991).

Western laypersons have folk psychology notions of the mind and its functioning. But their notions are not all that naive because Western adults have considerable practice at learning and, even more important, thinking about learning. Entry into school, the culturally designated place for learning to take place, generally begins at age 6. Thus students who have finished their high school education have been in formal learning situations for 12 years. Over a considerable period of time, then, they have practiced what they and others think it takes to learn. In the sense that they have not studied formally about the mind and learning in, say, psychology courses, they can be considered laypersons. But it is a big stretch to call them laypersons and holders of a naive psychology after they have been in places where learning is the main goal and where they have been reflective about what that learning is.

Teachers are professionals who have been educated to teach in such a way as to cause change in others' minds. That change is learning. The cause of that change is thought to be teaching. The differentiation between teaching and learning is often unclear, even in the educational literature. Some of our best friends refer to it as the teaching/learning process. The mind is understood as something that cannot be accessed directly, and it is only through our students' behaviors (questions they ask, answers they give to our questions, etc.) that we can infer if our teaching has caused the desired learning

The research reported in this chapter is based on an MA thesis submitted by Tamar Shilony to Tel Aviv University in partial requirement for the MA degree. The study was guided by Sidney Strauss. The research was supported by the Chief Scientist's Office of the Israeli Ministry of Education. Thanks are extended to Nachshon Meiran for statistical assistance and to David H. Feldman, Gaea Leinhardt, and Ference Marton for helpful discussions.

455

in their minds. In other words, we teachers do something (employ teaching strategies) outside of our students' minds, in order to cause changes (learning) to take place in their minds.

Psychologists of the stripe who do work in the area of learning have come up with a number of ways to describe what learning is; however, there is little consensus about which models best describe it. There is no agreed-upon set of principles, rules, or laws of learning, and there does not seem to be one in the offing. So, as much as theoreticians and experimentalists have made progress in understanding learning, their work is still controversial. And, unlike the work on teachers' conceptions about domains, such as physics where there is agreement about its laws, we cannot speak of misconceptions when investigating teachers' understandings of children's minds.

One theme of this book is to tackle issues pertaining to domain specificity. We have chosen to address one of its aspects: We asked ourselves if teachers have mental models of the structure of others' minds, of how the mind works when learning takes place, and of the roles of teaching in fostering that learning.

There are two principal reasons we chose to examine the nature of teachers' mental models of the mind. First, we are interested in teacher education. We hold the position that, by analogy to the education of children, before teaching children concepts, notions, and the like, from some domain of knowledge, we must first understand the structure of children's intuitive knowledge of that domain. The reason for this is that those intuitive knowledge structures, which are quite resistant to change through instruction, are the systems that interpret instruction (diSessa, 1982, in press; McCloskey, 1983; McCloskey & Kargon, 1988).

We believe that, in principle, similar considerations hold for teacher education. That is, before we teach teachers psychological models of children's minds, we should first understand what their intuitive models of children's minds are because their models interpret our instruction.

Second, and more pertinent to the theme of this book, we reasoned that studying teachers' understanding of the mind might be a window into what happens to what has been claimed to be children's models of the mind. In other words, young children have notions as to what the mind is. We are interested to know the fate of those notions in adulthood. In order to examine this, we must first know what children's models of the mind are. Then we will be in a position to show how we can claim lineage between children's and adults' models.

We now briefly present others' findings about children's early notions about the mind, so that we will have something against which we can compare adults' models. For our purposes here, the most relevant findings of children's models of the mind are those reported by Wellman (1988, 1990, this volume).

In a number of research studies, Wellman and his co-workers attempt to describe children's theories of mind: how children understand how reality external to the mind comes to be known. Their research findings suggest that 3-year-old children hold a direct copy theory of mind, whereas many children ages 5 and 6 have a homunculus theory of mind. We slightly elaborate on these theories.

The direct copy theory of mind is that there is a reality that comes to be known and that what is known is the result of a direct copy of reality in the mind. Very young children think that things outside the mind come to be understood by our minds because those things transmit themselves unto the mind, which then copies them as faint traces. Those traces are the substance of our mental beliefs about the world that is external to our minds. Wellman points out that although these very young children seem to hold a theory that explains how we come to know reality, they do not seem to have firm notions about the processes that enable the direct copy to be made. This theory has, as a root metaphor, the idea that the mind is a container that holds ideas and thoughts, which are passively acquired.

The homunculus theory is held by many children at age 6. At its core is the conception of the mind as an active constructor and interpreter of the world. This theory of the mind is seen against the backdrop of children's more general view of themselves as active agents. At age 6, they apply that conception to the mind itself. Children begin to speak about the mind's "behavior," the way it "works," how one's mind gets "tricked," and so forth. Wellman interprets these expressions as being emblematic of the homunculus theory of the mind.

These two theories of the mind are probably additive in the sense that children may hold them, or aspects of them, simultaneously. In other words, it may be the case that the homunculus theory of mind does not replace the direct copy theory of mind; instead, they may exist side-by-side.

So now, having presented these two theories, we have something general against which we can compare adults' models of the mind. So far, so good. But even were we to find that adults' models are similar to either or both of the children's models, then what could that tell us? Why would we claim that adults' models may be descendants of the children's models? This, of course, is a question that haunts every developmental theory and all empirical research in developmental psychology, and we will leave answers to that question to people far wiser than we.

However, so as not to dodge these questions completely, we make a claim that bears on the issue of descendancy. We argue that one way to determine if there is lineage in what we are studying is to see if the original, ancestral model is resistant to instruction. The claim is that if children have a tacit, nonreflective model of the mind and if that tacit model is not explicitly addressed in teaching, then it will remain quite unchanged after teaching. We chose to study teachers' models of the mind because they have been taught to influence minds through instruction, and they have taken educational psychology courses that cover topics on learning and development. Were we to find that teachers hold a common intuitive model of children's minds that is different than the models they were taught at universities, we might have some evidence that their models were resistant to university instruction. And if their models resemble those intuitively held by children, we could make a *very* tentative claim that there might be an ancestor–descendant link between them.

Before we present our work, we feel compelled to add a caveat. We have deliberately stayed away from using terms such as "naive *theories* of the mind" because we do not want to enter the minefield of debate surrounding what constitutes a theory, when one can plausibly argue that children's or adults' understandings of their world have theorylike characteristics, and so forth. We chose to use the somewhat weaker term "mental model" because it implies less of a commitment to the nature of the organizing structure that interprets the world and guides behavior. Choosing the weaker terminology does not mean we have extracted ourselves completely from the minefield, of course, but it gives a different feel to what we are looking for.

Our research also falls within the purview of teachers' cognition, an area of study that has burgeoned recently. We now briefly present that area so as to frame our work.

Conceptual framework

Clark and Peterson (1986) classified research on teachers' thinking into three categories: preactive and postactive planning, interactive thinking, and teachers' theories and beliefs. Space considerations do not allow a full treatment of these categories, but suffice it to say that our research is located within the third area of teachers' thinking: teachers' theories and beliefs.

We argue that teachers' implicit beliefs about children's minds, learning, and instruction have a bearing on how they practice their profession as teachers. The nature of professional knowledge has occupied the concerns of Schon (1983, 1987) and his co-workers (Argyris & Schon, 1974) and they, too, worked out a classification system of kinds of knowledge professionals have. Among them are the following: theories of practice, theories in use, and espoused theories. Espoused theories, which we examined in the present study, are those theories professionals espouse when asked how they would act in a certain professional situation. In the case of teachers, espoused theories about learning and instruction could be those theories teachers espouse when asked how they would teach in a certain situation. Because teachers instruct for learning to take place in others, we can infer their mental models of learning through the ways they speak about instruction. We have more to say about this later.

One of the most significant aspects of teachers' professional knowledge is to make subject matter understandable to the children being taught. This has been called pedagogical content knowledge by Shulman and his co-workers

(Shulman, 1986; Wilson, Shulman, & Richert, 1987). Pedagogical content knowledge includes knowing students' preconceptions about subject matter, which concepts or skills are particularly difficult for children to learn, what makes them difficult, ways to make those difficult concepts and skills easier, and how they are different at different ages.

There has been surprisingly little research done in this area (Ammon & Hutcheson, 1989; Black, 1989; Elbaz, 1983; Munby, 1983; Peterson, Fennema, Carpenter, & Loef, 1989; Wilson et al., 1987; Yaakobi & Sharan, 1985). As interesting as these studies were in their own right, they did not help us in designing our study. The challenge facing us, then, was to conduct a study that attempted to describe teachers' espoused pedagogical knowledge and to infer their models of the mind and its functioning in learning from our discussions with them about instruction.

Common models and contrasting groups

Our goal was to find a mental model that was common to teachers even though the teachers were quite different on a number of important dimensions. The common mental model allows us to identify parameters that may vary among different teachers. Without having this common mental model, it is difficult to know what to look for when attempting to determine how contrasting groups of teachers conceptualize children's minds because there is no framework to indicate what categories exist to be tested. Once this common mental model has been determined, research into how contrasting groups differ within that framework could yield important information for teacher education and for the ancestral–descendant lineage between children's and adults' models of the world of the mind.

Having said that, let us turn to the two contrasting groups of high school teachers we chose to study: (1) experienced versus novice teachers and (2) teachers of different subject matter – the sciences and the humanities. We sought to study both what unites them (the common mental model) and what makes them different.

Experienced versus novice teachers

We chose this terminology over the more accepted terminology (expert, novice) because the term "expert" implies much more than the term "experienced" (Berliner, 1987). Teachers with considerable experience in teaching may not necessarily be expert. Teachers with relatively little experience are novices, though.

With this caveat in mind, we briefly discuss research in the area of the expert–novice distinction with an eye toward what it might tell us about differences we may expect between experienced and novice teachers' espoused pedagogical knowledge. Those who have done expert–novice research have attempted to capture the ways individuals develop and differ from each other. Research in this area has often been on subject matter from the sciences, chess, and other areas that have some precision (Chi, Feltovich, & Glaser, 1981; Dreyfus & Dreyfus, 1986). Findings from research of this sort have revealed four areas in which experts and novices differ: The *knowledge base* of experts is larger than that of novices; *knowledge representation and organization* is deeper among experts than novices; and *strategies* chosen in problem solving are different for the two groups.

Experiments to determine if the above holds for expert and novice teachers obtained results similar to those in the four aforementioned areas (Benjamin, 1989; Berliner, 1986, 1987; Carter, 1990; Carter, Cushing, Sabers, Stein, & Berliner, 1988; Feiman-Nemser & Buchmann, 1985; Lampert & Clark, 1990; Leinhardt, 1989; Leinhardt & Fienberg, 1988; Livingston & Borko, 1989; Pintrich, 1990; Wilson et al., 1987). Unfortunately for the purposes of the present study, these investigators studied topics (e.g., the flow of a class as understood by expert and novice teachers), which, although of interest, do not help us predict what we would find in our study of teachers' espoused pedagogical knowledge, that is, their models about the nature of children's minds and how learning takes place.

Because there is no theory that could guide us, and because there were no empirical precedents for research of the kind we set for ourselves, we had no basis for predicting how teachers' mental models might look nor could we predict what differences might be found between experienced and novice teachers within this model. We included this contrasting group to see if we could detect differences between them were we to find a common mental model.

Teaching different subject matter

We chose to include in our study teachers who taught different subject matter (the sciences and the humanities) to see if that variable would make a difference in the mental models they have about children's minds. We chose these disciplines because we thought there may be relations between teachers' understanding of the epistemologies of their discipline and their epistemologies of children's minds.

Yaakobi and Sharan (1985) showed that teachers of different disciplines have different understandings of the nature of knowledge in the subject matter they teach. Teachers of the sciences think that the knowledge and concepts in their field are "out there," accepted, true, and verifiable. In contrast, teachers of the humanities think that knowledge in their discipline emerges from subjective personal invention, reflecting the creativity of individuals.

We argue that teachers of the sciences might believe that the role of instruction is to get the disciplinary knowledge that is "out there" into the minds of children, and learning might be the "taking in" and remembering of what was taken in. This view is similar to the direct copy theory of mind held by younger children. In contrast, teachers of the humanities might view the role of instruction as one in which conditions are created for personal interpretation and invention. Learning in this view, then, might be the making of these personal inventions. This view is similar to the homunculus theory of mind held by older children.

Once again, because there were no theories that could guide hypotheses about the role of subject matter taught, nor have there been empirical precedents to serve as guidelines for predicting how these proposed differences may be played out in teachers' mental models of pedagogy and learning, we have no hypotheses to make, and can pose only general research questions.

The main research question that guided our research study was: Do teachers have a common mental model of children's minds and of learning? We also asked if there was a difference among teachers with varying teaching experience and teachers of different subject matter in the strength with which they held their positions about the model. This was done to determine if there is some similarity between children's models of the mind (which we did not test) and adults' models of the mind, these adults having been taught about the mind and its workings. Our findings could inform issues of the fate of children's models of the mind.

The subjects were 20 high school teachers who were divided into two groups of equal numbers of science and humanities teachers. As a result, there were five teachers in the four groups created by the two independent variables: experience and subject matter taught.

Experienced teachers were those who had at least seven years teaching experience, and the novices were those who had no more than two years teaching experience. The sciences included physics, chemistry, biology, and mathematics, and the humanities included history, literature, and the Bible, which is taught as literature in Israeli public schools.

Each teacher was interviewed in one session on an individual basis in a semistructured clinical interview technique. The interviewer asked the same initial question to each teacher and, based on the teacher's answers, the interviewer followed up with further questions. The interview lasted approximately one hour.

The question asked was as follows:

When you arrive at school, your principal approaches you with a problem. Two teachers called in sick and will be out for at least a month. You have been asked to take over their classes for that period of time. The teachers teach the same subject matter as you, and you can teach anything you'd like, even if it doesn't appear in the curriculum. The school you work at is a comprehensive school that goes from first to twelfth grade, and the teachers who are sick teach second and sixth grades. Choose whatever content you'd like to teach, and let's talk about how you'd teach that content to children who are aged 7, 12, and 17.

For reasons of clarity of presentation, we now present the mental model we thought to be common to the teachers in our study. In building this model, we analyzed teachers' protocols when they spoke about learning and instruction. This analysis yielded a model that included 11 general categories of knowledge teachers held about children's minds, learning and instruction, and components that comprised these categories. The model is found in Figure 18.1.

The child's mind is the box and, through instruction, teachers attempt to get material that exists outside the mind of children into the mind in such a way that it remains there for a long time, which is another way of saying that it gets learned. Teachers have an engineering vision of how to accomplish that, a point we pick up on at the end of this chapter.

On the left side of Figure 18.1 are categories that are not part of learning as such, but they do influence it. There are five categories here: (1) Characteristics of the Material to be taught (e.g., it is concrete); (2) the Teacher as Intermediary between the material and the learner (e.g., the teacher breaks a problem into parts for the children); (3) aspects of Instruction (e.g., asking questions); (4) aspects of the Child's Environment (e.g., mass communication); and (5) Characteristics of the Learner (e.g., abilities, intelligence).

We now move from the categories that are not learning as such to the sixth (6) category that involves how the material enters the child's mind. We have labeled that category "Means" because this category's components are the means by which material external to the mind enters it. This category gets at the seam between the external world and the mind. Notice that this seam has openings that allow the material to enter, and the openings have flaps that can be up, thus allowing material to enter, or flaps that can be down, thus preventing the material from entering the mind. In the discussion we see that the emotional state of the child controls these flaps.

The mind itself has five categories: (7) Already-Learned Knowledge that exists in the mind. These are the concepts, skills, and so forth that have already been learned; (8) characteristics of the Already-Learned Knowledge, such as the amount of knowledge; (9) mental Processes that allow the new material that just entered the mind to become part of the already-learned knowledge or, in other words, to become learned. An example would be analogies between the new and old knowledge. The next category, Products (10), deals with what happens to the old knowledge when the new knowledge gets learned. For example, the old knowledge gets expanded. We labeled this Products because they are the products of learning. And there is a category of the mind (11) that involves ways the learner Demonstrates Uses of the New Knowledge. For example, the learner can solve problems that are similar to those just learned.

These are the 11 categories we hypothesize to comprise teachers' mental models of children's minds, how learning takes place, and the role of instruction in fostering learning. There are a total of 152 components for the 11

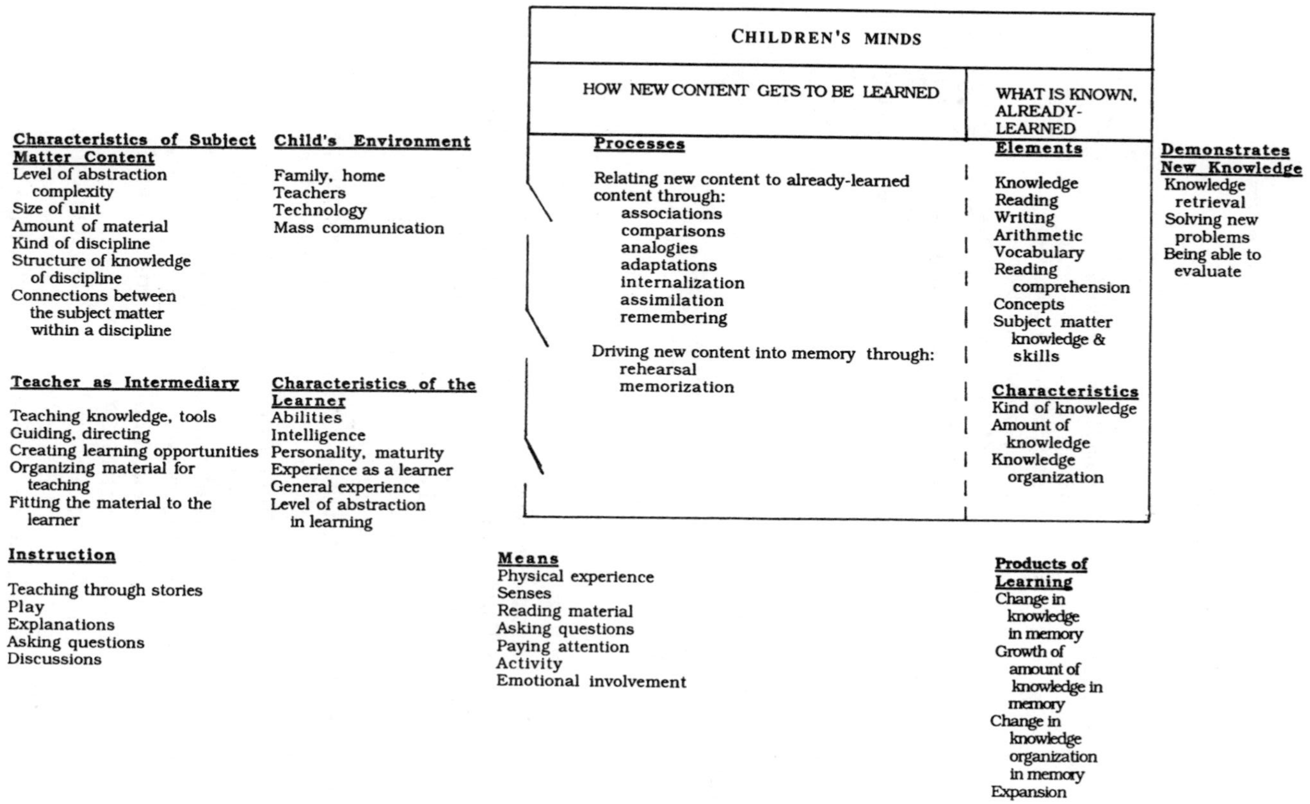

CHILDREN'S MINDS

HOW NEW CONTENT GETS TO BE LEARNED

Processes

Relating new content to already-learned content through:
- associations
- comparisons
- analogies
- adaptations
- internalization
- assimilation
- remembering

Driving new content into memory through:
- rehearsal
- memorization

WHAT IS KNOWN, ALREADY-LEARNED

Elements
- Knowledge
- Reading
- Writing
- Arithmetic
- Vocabulary
- Reading comprehension
- Concepts
- Subject matter knowledge & skills

Characteristics
- Kind of knowledge
- Amount of knowledge
- Knowledge organization

Demonstrates New Knowledge
- Knowledge retrieval
- Solving new problems
- Being able to evaluate

Products of Learning
Change in knowledge in memory
Growth of amount of knowledge in memory
Change in knowledge organization in memory
Expansion

Characteristics of Subject Matter Content
- Level of abstraction
- complexity
- Size of unit
- Amount of material
- Kind of discipline
- Structure of knowledge of discipline
- Connections between the subject matter within a discipline

Child's Environment
- Family, home
- Teachers
- Technology
- Mass communication

Teacher as Intermediary
- Teaching knowledge, tools
- Guiding, directing
- Creating learning opportunities
- Organizing material for teaching
- Fitting the material to the learner

Characteristics of the Learner
- Abilities
- Intelligence
- Personality, maturity
- Experience as a learner
- General experience
- Level of abstraction in learning

Instruction
- Teaching through stories
- Play
- Explanations
- Asking questions
- Discussions

Means
- Physical experience
- Senses
- Reading material
- Asking questions
- Paying attention
- Activity
- Emotional involvement

Figure 18.1. Teachers' mental model of children's minds.

Table 18.1. *Components with more than 50% of the teachers mentioning them for categories with high intercorrelations within categories and low intercorrelations between categories*

Categories	Components	%
Characteristics of subject matter	Level of abstraction	75
	Complexity	65
	Kind of discipline	65
Teacher as intermediary	Teaching knowledge, tools	80
	Guiding, directing	85
	Creating learning opportunities	60
	Developing children's thinking	55
	Organizing material for teaching	55
	Connecting new material to the old	75
	Pacing the presentation of content	50
	Fitting the material to the learner	75
	Teaching the right amount of/variety of material	55
	Teaching material at the right level of abstraction	80
	Creating interest in the subject	65
	Creating a learning atmosphere	65
Characteristics of already-learned knowledge	Amount of knowledge	65
	Knowledge organization	55
	Kind of knowledge	55
Ways the learner demonstrates new knowledge	Application of knowledge and tools	80
	Translation of feelings, thoughts into words, writing, or paintings	75

categories. Due to space considerations, we present a selection of them in Tables 18.1 and 18.2 and in the Appendix. The Appendix includes an example of a description, explanation, judgment, or justification that was classified as an instance of a component. For a full treatment of criteria for classifying teachers' statements into components and for a complete presentation of our data, see Strauss and Shilony (1992).

Now that we have presented the model under test, we must provide operational definitions of what we put to test. The main research question posed was: Do teachers have a common mental model of children's minds and of learning? Operationally, components of a common mental model were claimed to have psychological reality if they met two criteria: (1) correlations within the components of each category were higher than the correlations of the same components with components of other categories, and (2) at least 50% of the teachers mentioned a certain component.

As for the first criterion, the results indicate that four categories met it: (1) characteristics of the subject matter, (2) characteristics of the learner, (3) characteristics of the knowledge already learned, and (4) ways the learner demonstrates the knowledge already learned. The results of the second

Table 18.2. *Components with more than 50% of the teachers mentioning them where there are no separate categories*

Categories	Components	%
Characteristics of the learner	Abilities	50
	Intelligence	65
	Personality, maturity	55
	Curiosity, interest	65
	Mental development	85
	General experience	65
	Experience as a learner	50
	Experience with content being studied, with use of skills	50
	Cumulative life's experiences	55
	Dependence/independence in studies	60
	Level of abstraction in learning	90
Instruction	Teacher's image of the learner	90
	Teaching through stories	75
	Play	50
	Getting them to do something	90
	Explanations	55
	Asking questions	70
	Discussions	60
	Giving examples	50
	Concretization	80
	Evaluating knowledge during instruction	50
	Using means to get information/evaluate the child	50
	Teacher's role as a pedagogue, educator	50
Child's environment	Family, home	55
Means used by the learner to learn material that entered the mind	Physical, sensorial experience	80
	Reading, using the material	75
	Activity	80
Mental processes that take place in the learner's mind	Connections	55
	Comparisons	50
	Processes of	
	analyzing the material	80
	organizing the material	55
	classifying the material	85
	translating the material	80
	reaching conclusions	50
	thinking	95
	learning, knowledge change	75
	Information input and processing	
	Speed of information input and processing	55
	Efficiency of information input and processing	55
Knowledge that already exists in the child's mind	Vocabulary	50
	Concepts	55
	Knowledge and tools about subjects from a discipline	70

Table 18.2. (*Cont.*)

Categories	Components	%
Products of learning	Increase in amount of knowledge	70
	Knowledge organization	55
	Broadening, generalization of knowledge	60
	Storage of knowledge	55
	Learning	85
	Development	70
	Experience	60
	Level of abstraction	60
	Responses, behavior	50

operational criterion (at least 50% of the teachers mentioned a certain component) were that a quite large number of components met this criterion. Data showing the components that met this criterion for the four categories that met the first criterion are found in Table 18.1.

There were also quite a large number of components that met the second criterion (i.e., at least 50% of the teachers mentioned them), but not the first. This means that their categories were not significantly separated from one another in the teachers' minds. These components are found in Table 18.2. For ease of reading, the components are organized in terms of categories, but we reiterate that these components are *not* organized into categories that are separate and distinct in teachers' minds.

We have now determined that the teachers interviewed in this study have a common mental model of children's minds and of learning. It is not as elaborate and full as the model we put to test; nevertheless, it has some of its characteristics. In addition, although some categories were not separate and distinct in the teachers' mental models, their components were mentioned by at least 50% of the teachers. This suggests that these components have psychological reality for the teachers, but they do not coalesce around categories that are distinct in teachers' minds.

The main purpose of this study was to determine the nature of a mental model teachers hold about children's minds and learning. One reason we did this was to see if it bears a resemblance to intuitive, commonsense models of the mind held by children. The model we found resembles some information processing models of memory and learning (Atkinson & Shiffrin, 1968). What is remarkable about this is that these teachers were never taught about information processing approaches in their educational psychology courses; they were generally taught about Piaget and sometimes about Vygotsky. So what we discovered is a mental model that teachers have constructed from something other than courses taken in their teacher preparation. Or, to put it more strongly, the mental model we discovered in teachers may have resisted formal instruction. Let us describe this model further.

The mental model of the child's mind and learning belies an engineering vision on the part of teachers. In their view, the object of pedagogy is to get external subject matter into the place in the mind where knowledge is stored. That is one engineering problem. To solve it, one first serves up knowledge that is initially external to children's minds in such a way that it can enter it. A second engineering problem is to get that new knowledge to a place where it will be stored. After the knowledge enters it, the teacher does things external to children's minds (teaches), believing that if children were to do what the teacher requests, then the new knowledge would be passed in the child's mind from the place where it entered to the place where it will be stored. We elaborate on this a bit.

When teachers spoke about how they would teach children certain content, they typically began speaking about learning in terms of the subject matter they wanted to teach. They believed that knowledge in various disciplines differs in kind, abstraction, and complexity. One of their chief concerns about these differences was about how to package content knowledge for their pupils so that it can be learned.

In order for that to occur, the content has to enter children's minds, and teachers conceive of the mind as having openings of a certain size that allow information to enter. Their notion of "opening size" recalls the notion of working memory capacity. Teachers believe that good pedagogy involves serving up knowledge in chunks that can "get through" the openings. For example, teachers said that if ideas in the subject matter were too complex, they won't even be able to get "in."

Even if the material is the right complexity, it may never enter the mind if children's affective states are not motivated to receive the content. Conceived of metaphorically, the entrances to children's minds have "flaps" that are open when children are attentive. If children are uninterested or unmotivated, the flaps go down, and material cannot enter the mind.

Teachers believe that once content "gets through," it must somehow connect up with already-existing knowledge by means of analogies, associations, familiar examples, and so on. This corresponds to an "elaborative processing" model. Accordingly, teachers believe they should facilitate connection making between new and old knowledge. If there is no already-existing knowledge to get connected to, the new knowledge can be driven into memory through repetition, rehearsal, and practice.

How does new knowledge affect the structure of prior knowledge? Teachers have beliefs concerning what happens to old knowledge when new knowledge finally gets to the place in the mind where it is remembered. Among the changes teachers mention are those in the amount and organization of previous knowledge; broadening and generalizing previous knowledge; higher levels of abstraction than what was in previous knowledge; and more.

Our second research question was about how different amounts of experience in teaching and how different subject matter taught could affect teachers' mental models. In particular, we looked at the strength of the positions teachers held within their mental models. The findings indicated that these two variables, as tested, did not have many significant effects. However, now that we know what the teachers' common mental model looks like, we have a basis for testing in the future how these individual differences and others get expressed within it.

What is the status of this model? First, it is an idealization in two senses: (1) it is *our* model of the teachers' model of children's minds and (2) no teacher holds this model in its entirety. As for the latter, we found that at the more general level of description of the model, the level of categories, all teachers are included in it. However, at the more specific level of the model's description, the level of components, many but not all teachers are included in it. For example, all teachers spoke about the category that refers to characteristics of the subject matter, but not all the teachers mentioned the following component of that category: the structure of the knowledge of a discipline.

This model is also implicit. Teachers are not aware they hold it. In other studies we conducted, when we asked them what they think learning is, we were told what they were taught in their educational psychology courses. But in the present study, we asked teachers to tell us about what and how they would teach subject matter of their choice and, in telling us that, they revealed their implicit models of what children's minds look like and how learning takes place because the purpose of their teaching was to foster learning in children.

If this model was never taught to these teachers but nevertheless they seem to hold it, then where could it have come from? There may be several sources. One may be as mundane and powerful as classroom size, and the ways one teaches many children. Teachers have repertoires of teaching strategies that accommodate this reality. Had they been teachers who taught only tutorials in an apprenticeship relationship with their pupils, then they may have constructed a different model of children's minds and learning.

Yet another source of the teachers' model may be a larger and more encompassing model of communication, where teaching others may be seen as a place where communication takes place. Reddy (1979) offers an intriguing and helpful understanding of two models of communication. The first is what he calls the conduit metaphor of communication, which he believes is the dominant metaphor in our society. It suggests that messages and ideas are objectlike, and are transmitted across space from one person and are received by another. Reflect for a moment on the meaning of these metaphors: "I finally managed to get my ideas across to my students today." "Play around with your thoughts so that they'll come out different." "He didn't quite catch on to it." These metaphors convey a sense of ideas as being tangible and external to individuals, and communicating them means passing them along channels to receptive others who take them in and understand them as they were intended. Bertrand Russell called this the bucket theory of the mind. And Wellman called this the direct copy theory of mind.

It might be the case that, in our study, we were not only tapping teachers' models of the mind and its functioning, but we may also have touched on teachers' models of communication, where teaching others is a place where communication gets played out. And because the central metaphor of communication is one that encourages a conception of knowledge, ideas, thoughts, and so forth as being passed on to others who receive them as is, our teachers' model of the mind and instruction may have been influenced by it.

In contrast to this dominant metaphor, Reddy suggests that a metaphor of the tool-maker may be more appropriate for describing communication. This metaphor suggests that individuals are always in the process of sense making, and that our messages, thoughts, and so on are being constructed by others, and invented anew as we attempt to grapple with their meanings. This view is akin to the one teachers were taught when they learned Piaget's theory. What happened between what they were taught and what they believe implicitly about the mind and learning is a question that those of us involved in teacher education ought to try to answer.

Still another source of the teachers' model of the mind could be that it is grounded in the models of the mind we may all have as youngsters. We have now arrived at the point where we can examine if an ancestor–descendant link exists between children's and adults' models. We have been claiming that two conditions must be met even to begin to argue that a link exists between them. First, we must demonstrate similarities between the models. Second, we should find that the teachers' model is resistant to instruction. We have already shown that the teachers' common mental models of the mind are different than anything they were taught, so the resistance condition seems to have been met. Now we must show that children's and adults' models have some resemblance.

This is particularly difficult to demonstrate for several reasons. First, we did not test children's models of the mind. Second, because we did not know what to expect in the way of how teachers understand chidren's minds, we could not conduct a study that could parallel Wellman's work. And even were these two reasons taken care of, there is the extremely problematic issue of how one can find similarities between models that have been constructed by youngsters and elaborated by adults.

Adults' models of the mind are clearly different than those of children. Adult models are more articulated than children's. Adults have metaconceptual abilities that allow them to think with their minds about their minds. Very young children do not have this ability. Adults' models can be made explicit, whereas young children's probably cannot. Adults have the ability to extend their models through formal instruction (even though our study shows that they don't seem to do that). Young children may not be so affected.

Despite these differences, we are claiming that there might be some similarity between the models. Clearly, whatever similarity that might be found will be at a very general level. We have seen that Wellman suggests that children develop two different models of the mind: a direct copy and a homunculus model. Notice that both models are based on the notion that there is a world external to the mind. Once that is posited, one is obligated to ask how that external world comes to be known by the mind. In other words, if the world is external and becomes represented in the mind, the question becomes: How does what is external become internal?

One area of similarity is that both the children's and adults' models are based on the separation between the mind and the external world. This distinction is vital, as we argued previously, because what follows from it is the need to address how the external world comes to be known in our minds.

Another similarity is that both older children and adults entertain the view that the world comes to be known by a mind that is an active interpreter of the world. Wellman shows us how younger children who hold the direct copy model of the mind have an understanding that the mind is a recipient container that holds images from the world. We believe the teachers' model is not of that order. Older children hold the view that the mind is an active interpreter of the world, that it does not simply reflect what is out there.

The teachers' model that we uncovered bears a family resemblance to this second view. Teachers see the mind as having openings that allow the world to penetrate it, but what gets through has much to do with what is already known. A child who knows more (has more information in memory store) takes in more than the child who knows less. Once the information from the world gets into the mind, it gets moved along to the place where it gets stored (remembered). That moving along is done by the mind, in broad-stroke terms, either by connections being made between the new and the already-known, or by drill and practice that drives the new information into memory. In both cases, the mind actively moves knowledge to the place where what is already learned is stored. This moving along is not done passively, but requires the activity of the mind.

In the most general of comparisons, we have attempted to show that there is some resemblance in the overall view children and adults have about the mind. As tentative as this claim is, we would like to take it one step further and ask about how the hypothesized lineage came into being. Why should there be any resemblance between children's and adults' models of the mind?

Here we borrow from R. Gelman, who claimed that skeletallike principles in very young children's mathematical principles constrain adults' conceptualizations of mathematics principles (Gelman & Gallistel, 1978; Gelman &

Greeno, 1989). Analogous to Gelman, our claim is that young children have principled knowledge about others' minds and that that knowledge sets the constraints for the principled knowledge that is its heir, that is, adults' models of the mind. We have no way of testing this idea at present and, truth be said, before doing work of that nature, we had better conduct more research in order to establish both the similarities and differences between children's and adults' models of the mind.

To sum up, the research described in this chapter is a beginning attempt to determine the developmental fate of young children's models of the mind. We made a very cautious claim that there seems to be a family resemblance between children's and adults' models. This has to be tested further to determine if our initial claim holds up under closer scrutiny. We also argued that this model seems to be resistant to instruction because the teachers were taught models other than the one they hold. In our view, this finding is intriguing because teachers seem to hold a common information processing model, university instruction to the contrary. We argued that one source of this common model may be the models they formed as youngsters. These early models set parameters and constraints on the models that get elaborated in their development, even when they become adults and are taught about how psychologists understand what minds are and how they work when learning occurs.

Appendix: Examples of teachers' sentences and their classification into categories and components

Teacher's statement: "The story is long for them."
    Category 1: Characteristics of subject matter
    Component: Size of the material

Teacher's statement: "First of all, I'd define things precisely."
    Category 2: Teacher as intermediary
    Component: Organizing the material

Teacher's statement: "For this age group, I wouldn't use frontal lessons."
    Category 3: Instruction
    Component: Frontal lessons

Teacher's statement: "There have to be experiences through the senses so that they'll understand the phenomenon."
    Category 6: Means
    Component: Physical experiences

Teacher's statement: "He can build analogies between the characters in the text and characters he knows."
    Category 9: Processes
    Component: Analogies

References

Ammon, P., & Hutcheson, B. P. (1989). Promoting the development of teachers' pedagogical conceptions. In A. Black (Ed.), *The genetic epistemologist* (pp. 23–89). Newark: College of Education, University of Delaware.

Argyris, C. J., & Schon, D. A. (1974). *Theory in practice: Increasing professional effectiveness.* San Francisco: Jossey-Bass.

Atkinson, R. C., & Shiffrin, R. M. (1968). Human memory: A proposed system and its control mechanisms. In K. W. Spence and J. T. Spence (Eds.), *The psychology of learning and motivation: Advances in research and theory*, Vol. 2. New York: Academic Press.

Atran, S., & Sperber, D. (1991). Learning without teaching: Its place in culture. In L. Tolchinsky Landsmann (Ed.), *Culture, schooling and psychological development* (pp. 39–55). Norwood: Ablex.

Benjamin, A. C. (1989). *Levels of expertise in early childhood teaching: An initial field test of a diagnostic instrument.* Unpublished dissertation, Tufts University.

Berliner, D. C. (1986). In pursuit of the expert pedagogue. *Educational Researcher, 15*, 5–13.

Berliner, D. C. (1987). Ways of thinking about students and classrooms by more and less experienced teachers. In J. Calderhead (Ed.), *Exploring teachers' thinking* (pp. 60–81). London: Cassell.

Black, A. (1989). Developmental teacher education: Preparing teachers to apply developmental principles across the curriculum. In A. Black (Ed.), *The genetic epistemologist* (pp. 5–22). Newark: College of Education, University of Delaware.

Carter, K. (1990). Teachers' knowledge and learning to teach. In R. W. Houston (Ed.), *Handbook of research on teacher education* (pp. 291–310). New York: Macmillan.

Carter, K., Cushing, K., Sabers, D., Stein, P., & Berliner, D. C. (1988). Expert–novice difference in perceiving and processing visual classroom information. *Journal of Teacher Education, 39*, 25–31.

Chi, M. T. H., Feltovich, H. A., & Glaser, R. (1981). Categorization and representation of physics problems by experts and novices. *Cognitive Science, 5*, 121–152.

Clark, C. M., & Peterson, P. L. (1986). Teachers' thought processes. In M. C. Wittrock (Ed.), *Handbook of research on teaching*, 3rd edition (pp. 255–296). New York: Macmillan.

diSessa, A. (1982). Unlearning Aristotelian physics: A study of knowledge-based learning. *Cognitive Science, 6*, 37–75.

diSessa, A. (in press). Speculations on the foundations of knowledge and intelligence. In D. Tirosh (Ed.), *Implicit and explicit knowledge: An educational approach.* Norwood: Ablex.

Dreyfus, H. L., & Dreyfus, S. H. (1986). Five steps from novice to expert. In H. L. Dreyfus, & S. H. Dreyfus (Eds.), *Mind over machine* (pp. 16–51). New York: Free Press.

Elbaz, F. (1983). *Teacher thinking: A study of practical knowledge.* London: Croom Heim.

Feiman-Nemser, S., & Buchmann, M. (1985). *The first year of teacher preparation: Transition to pedagogical thinking?* Institute for Research on Teaching, Research Series Number 156, Michigan State University.

Gelman, R., & Gallistel, C. R. (1978). *The child's understanding of number.* Cambridge, MA: Harvard University Press.

Gelman, R., & Greeno, J. C. (1989). On the nature of competence: Principles for understanding in a domain. In L. B. Resnick (Ed.), *Knowing and learning: Essays in honor of Robert Glaser* (pp. 125–186). Hillsdale, NJ: Erlbaum.

Lampert, M., & Clark, C. M. (1990). Expert knowledge and expert thinking in teaching: A response to Floden and Klinzing. *Educational Researcher, 19*, 21–23.

Leinhardt, G. (1989). Math lessons: A contrast of novice and expert competence. *Journal for Research in Mathematics Education, 20*, 52–75.

Leinhardt, G., & Fienberg, J. (1988). *Integration of lesson structure and teachers' subject matter knowledge.* University of Pittsburgh.

Livingston, C., & Borko, H. (1989). Expert–novice differences in teaching: A cognitive analysis and implications for teacher education. *Journal of Teacher Education, 40*, 36–42.

McCloskey, M. (1983). Naive theories of motion. In D. Gentner & A. L. Stevens (Eds.), *Mental models* (pp. 299–324). Hillsdale, NJ: Erlbaum.

McCloskey, M., & Kargon, R. (1988). The meaning and use of historical models in the study of intuitive physics. In S. Strauss (Ed.), *Ontogeny, phylogeny and historical development* (pp. 49–67). Norwood: Ablex.

Munby, H. (1983). *Metaphorical expressions of teachers' practical curriculum knowledge.* Paper presented at the Annual Meeting of the American Educational Research Association, Washington, D.C.

Peterson, P. L., Fennema, E., Carpenter, P. T., & Loef, M. (1989). Teachers' pedagogical content beliefs in mathematics. *Cognition and Instruction, 6*, 1–40.

Pintrich, P. R. (1990). Implications of psychological research on student learning and college teaching for teacher education. In R. W. Houston (Ed.), *Handbook of research on teacher education* (pp. 826–857). New York: Macmillan.

Reddy, M. (1979). The conduit metaphor. In A. Ortony (Ed.), *Metaphor and thought.* New York: Cambridge University Press.

Schon, D. A. (1983). *The reflective practitioner: How professionals think in action.* London: Temple Smith.

Schon, D. A. (1987). *Educating the reflective practitioner.* New York: Basic Books.

Shulman, L. S. (1986). Those who understand: Knowledge growth in teaching. *Educational Researcher, 15*, 4–14.

Strauss, S., & Shilony, T. (1992). *Teachers' pedagogical knowledge: A model of teachers' models of children's minds and learning.* Unpublished manuscript. Tel Aviv University.

Wellman, H. (1988). First steps in the child's theorizing about the mind. In J. W. Astingon, P. L. Harris, and D. L. Olson (Eds.), *Developing theories of mind* (pp. 64–92). New York: Cambridge University Press.

Wellman, H. (1990). *The child's theory of mind.* Cambridge: MIT Press.

Wilson, S. M., Shulman, L. S., & Richert, A. E. (1987). "150 different ways" of knowing: Representations of knowledge in teaching. In J. Calderhead (Ed.), *Exploring teachers' thinking* (pp. 104–124). London: Cassell Education.

Yaakobi, D., & Sharan, S. (1985). Teacher beliefs and practices: The discipline carries the message. *Journal of Education for Teaching, 11*, 197–199.

19   Situated rationalism: Biological and social preparation for learning

Lauren B. Resnick

The human sciences can be characterized as a working out of two sets of tensions in interpreting human experience: tensions between the biological and the social and between the particular and the general. In this chapter, I examine the relations between two lines of thinking, each commanding increasing attention among psychologists and social scientists, that appear to be contradictory. The first, a position I term *conceptual rationalism*, seeks biological foundations for specific concepts that are central and, perhaps, universal in human development. The second, a position that has come to be known as *situated cognition*, argues that knowledge is acquired in and attuned to specific social and historical situations and that conceptual development can be understood only in terms of the situational contexts of action. I argue here that the rationalist and situationist views, far from being contradictory, share important epistemological assumptions and can – perhaps must – be combined to provide a theory of cognitive development and functioning. I develop a view of learning and development that I call *situated rationalism*, illustrate it with some examples from mathematics and science learning, and consider its implications for education.

The conceptual rationalist argument: Biological preparedness

In recent years, there has been a reassertion of interest in the biological basis of human learning and thinking (e.g., Gelman & Carey, 1991; many chapters in the present volume). This new line of thinking grows out of recent research on language development, concept development in infancy and early childhood, and animal cognition and learning. The core proposal of those pursuing this line of thinking is that there exists a set of biological constraints on learning and cognitive development. This hypothesis leads to a search for evidence that certain aspects of knowledge, although learned in the sense that interaction with the environment over time is required, are nevertheless biologically preferred or "prepared." These highly specific *prepared schemas* or *skeletal structures* are the foundation for the development of mature knowledge by individuals. The argument is, roughly, that each species is specialized for certain forms of knowledge. This biologically preferred knowledge is tuned to the adaptive requirements of the species. It is, thus, situational in the sense that it prepares the young of the species to enter productively into the situations they are most likely to encounter as they grow and to learn from behaving in those situations. Most elaborated until recently as a theory of language acquisition, the argument for biological or "hard-wired" structures that guide and constrain infants as they interpret their earliest experience is now being put forth for basic mathematical, physical, and social concepts as well.

Following philosophical traditions, this can usefully be termed a *rationalist* position; it is reflected in the epistemologies of Plato and Kant, for example. Rationalists differ from associationists and other empiricists not only in postulating a biological basis for specific knowledge, but also in postulating wholes – sets of relationships that accumulate to something more than the sum of their parts – as the fundamental units of cognition. This is captured in the notion of a *schema* – an organizing "design" that superimposes a structure on the pieces. Among the great rationalists who had something to say about education and learning were Wertheimer, for whom the organizing designs were perceptual gestalts, and Piaget, for whom the organizing designs were logical structures.

I call today's rationalists *conceptual rationalists*, because they are more interested in conceptual than in either perceptual or purely logical foundations for thinking. Conceptual rationalists claim that biological preparation is highly domain specific, that infants are biologically prepared to take advantage of very specific *affording* features of the environment. They believe that the preparedness of the species reaches beyond perceptions (supposedly minimally processed recognitions – cf. Neisser, 1976) yet is more specific than the grand logical design of Piaget. They are interested in preparedness for reasoning about number and quantity; for concepts of causality; for notions of weightedness, movement, and rigidity; and for basic psychological and social ideas.

Today's conceptual rationalists do not claim that hard-wired concepts simply mature. Rather, for the biological endowment to be realized, particular environmental conditions must be met. Prepared structures do not substitute for learning but rather make learning possible by constraining and guiding attention, so that, from among the many stimuli children encounter, they select for attention those that will support the formation of particular concepts. Conceptual rationalism is a theory that says children *can teach themselves* if the right kinds of affordances are present in their environments. Children appear to choose for themselves the kind of stimuli to attend to and to engage in forms of practice that eventually establish a stable and useful concept. Learning and development occur when individuals prepared for certain concepts encounter environments with the kinds of affordances they need to elaborate these prepared structures.

Although conceptual rationalists search for biological foundations for specific concepts, they are, in another sense, generalists. The prepared concepts that they study are thought to be universal for the species. They give relatively little attention to social processes (although these are admitted as part of the environmental surround that allows children to elaborate their prepared schemas) or to variations in elaborated conceptual structures that may result from different kinds of experience. On the other hand, conceptual rationalists are individualists in the sense that biologically prepared structures are carried by each individual member of the species and each individual must interact with the environment to produce personal elaborations of the prepared structures. This is the essence of the constructivist argument, which is more or less assumed by the conceptual rationalists.

The situated cognition argument: Sociocultural preparedness

The term situated cognition has come to refer to a loose collection of theories and perspectives that propose a contextualized (and, therefore, particularist) and social view of the nature of thinking and learning. Students of situated cognition take as a starting point the *distributed* nature of cognitive activity – the fact that, under normal circumstances, mental activity involves social coordination. Getting a job done, figuring something out, are almost always done in coordination with others. What makes an individual competent is not just what he or she knows but also how his or her knowledge fits in with that of others with whom activity must be coordinated. Futhermore, activity is often shared with tools (e.g., Hutchins, 1991) and even with the everyday physical material about which people reason (Lave, 1988). There is, thus, a distribution of cognitive work not only among people but also between people and tools. Being competent means being able to use particular tools in particular ways. The tools themselves embody a portion of the intelligence that is needed to accomplish any particular task. The distributed nature of competent performance means that competence is highly situation specific. One must be good at behaving in a particular situation, with particular tools, and with particular other people. The situated cognition perspective, then, tends to lead away from a search for general structures of knowledge and toward the study of particular environments for cognitive activity and the knowledge attuned to those environments. At the same time, it stresses the social nature of cognitive activity and cognitive development.

In the situated cognition view, the social invisibly pervades even situations that appear to consist of individuals engaged in private cognitive activity. Social construals of the situation (e.g., What are the rules of the game? Who is in charge? What are the stakes?) influence the nature and course of thinking. And the tools of thought (ranging from external memory devices and measuring instruments to tables of arithmetic conversions and dictionaries, thesauruses, and maps) embody a culture's intellectual history. Tools have theories built into them, and users accept these theories – albeit often unknowingly – when they use these tools. This point is made dramatically by Latour (1987) in his constructed account of the process of challenging a scientific conclusion. Like biologically prepared structure, the tools that one uses not only enable thought and intellectual progress but also constrain and limit the range of what can be thought. In these invisible ways, the history of a culture, an inherently social history, is carried into each individual act of cognition (Cole, 1985).

Theories, implicit and explicit, both enable and constrain thinking, just as physical tools do. This observation has become commonplace in cognitive science. What individuals reason about, the knowledge they bring to a cognitive task, provides the interpretive frames of schemas that allow reasoning and problem solving to proceed. These beliefs, individuals' schemas for reasoning, are not purely individual constructions. Instead, they are heavily influenced by the kinds of beliefs and reasoning schemas available in the individuals' surrounding culture.

Not only theories but even ways of reasoning are themselves socially determined. Cognitive tools also include the forms of reasoning and argumentation that are accepted as normative in given cultures. Both Mead (1934) and Vygotsky (1978) proposed that mechanisms of thought are best conceived as internalizations of behaviors first engaged in externally, interacting with others. Mead called thought a "conversation with the generalized other," implying that, as we think individually, we attempt to respond – internally and vicariously – to the imagined responses of others to our ideas and arguments. Vygotsky's central claim was that, to understand individual psychological development, it is necessary to understand the system of social relations in which the individual lives and grows. This system is itself a product of generations of development over time, so that the individual is, in effect, historically situated, an heir to a long cultural development. Primary among the tools that, for Vygotsky, are each individual's patrimony is language, which mediates all thinking (cf. Wertsch, 1985).

Situated rationalism

Conceptual rationalists and situated learning theorists can each assemble convincing evidence in support of their views. Each appears, within its own terms, to offer a coherent account of human intellectual development. But each maintains its coherence by limiting the range of questions it is willing to address. Conceptual rationalists search for concepts that appear to be universal and focus their attention on the earliest emergence of these concepts. There is little attention to the varied forms that adult knowledge might take or to how more particular *cultural domains* of knowledge might develop out of biologically prepared structures.

Situationists, on the other hand, are interested in the ways that culture, history, and immediate social contexts shape cognitive activity. Although the language of domains rarely appears, there is much interest in different cultural systems of knowledge. They offer theories – such as Vygotsky's – of how participation in particular forms of social activity leads to personal cognitive competence. But these *sociohistorical* theories of cognition have little or nothing to say about the contributions that the individual might make to development. They do not consider the biological starting point of development, the constraints that biological endowment might place on the directions of socially shaped cognitive development. The issue generally is not discussed, but sociohistorical theories could just as well accept a tabula rasa basic theory of learning as a biologically constrained one – although there is no incompatibility with the idea of biological constraints, either.

The lack of attention to the individual's contribution by situationists is not limited to a failure to attend to biological constraints on learning and development. On the whole, today's students of situated cognition are more interested in mapping details of how people coordinate cognitive activity in particular social and tool situations than they are in accounting for personal structures of knowledge. A problem within situated cognition theory is that the individual seems to disappear. Individual competence is replaced by social and institutional forms of behavior. Individual knowledge and skill – characteristics of individuals that can be carried with them from one situation to another – are replaced by *emergent cognition* that belongs to no one and disappears when the moment of emergence has passed.

This contrast is meant to suggest how situated cognition and conceptual rationalism together might be able to do what neither appears able to do alone: provide an account of how individuals learn both the universal concepts for which they appear to be biologically prepared and the much greater variety of culturally specific knowledge and ways of acting that characterize mature people. The issue I address here is how to understand the relations between the prepared structures and the cultural domains. I assume that there are cultural elaborations of conceptions initially founded on the biologically prepared structures. Education – which I want to interpret broadly, not just in terms of institutionalized schooling – is clearly part of the cultural elaboration process.

The remainder of this chapter can be viewed as either reintroducing the individual into a radical theory of situated cognition or introducing the social into a theory of biological constraints on learning. Either way, my first task is to expand the notion of prepared structures beyond the biologically prepared, to include the socially prepared. Next, I suggest a theory of contextually specific learning that takes into account the idea of prepared structures brought into the situation by participating individuals.

Learning as tuning of prepared structures

The conceptual rationalists argue that learning occurs when prepared structures are elaborated in the course of interaction with the environment. The prepared structures direct and constrain attention to particular environmental features that will support elaborations of particular concepts. They render the individual sensitive to particular affordances of situations. With our view of socioculturally prepared structures, it is an easy extension to think of structures resulting from past engagements in culturally specific situations as similarly constraining the way in which individuals enter new situations. Once in a situation of engagement with the environment, prepared structures are modified and elaborated by that engagement. Engagement in a situation thus modifies the structures that prepare one for the next situation. It is this process of elaboration that we call learning.

The work of conceptual rationalists has focused on those elaborations that result in relatively permanent new structures, that is, those that will turn out to be tuned to the affordances of many future situations over an extended period of time. The situated rationalist argument calls for just a slight shift in perspective, one that in no way challenges the underlying argument of learning on the basis of elaborating prepared structures. It suggests that, in each situation of engagement, what is actually elaborated is only what is needed to act successfully in that particular situation. The new conceptual elaborations are "general" or permanent only to the extent that future situations afford their use. On any particular occasion, one tunes one's behavior and, thus, one's knowledge to the demands of the occasion.

Learning, for the situated rationalist, is a matter of tuning to one's immediate situation, of becoming good *in the situation* in which one practices. The situation is inclusively defined. It refers to everything in the physical surroundings and the material used; to the social, institutional, and personal purposes at play; to the other people engaged; and to the language used. In short, much of what is traditionally viewed as *context* for learning is viewed in a theory of situated practice as an essential part of learning and, thus, of what is learned.

The heart of the argument, then, is that learning is a matter of passing through successive situations in which the individual *becomes* competent. Individuals develop this situated competence in each situation on the basis of their prepared structures. These prepared structures have both biological and sociocultural roots, with the biological predominating in the earliest months and years and the sociocultural taking increasing control thereafter as each individual's personal history of situations grows and initial biologically prepared structures are successively modified. (See Gardner, 1991, and Johnson, 1987, for convincing arguments that earlier, more purely biologically based schemas do not wholly disappear from adults.)

The learning processes are the same, whether the prepared structures are, in a given instance, primarily biological or primarily sociocultural. In fact, because socialization into a culture begins at birth, there is probably no instance thereafter that can be categorized as purely biological or purely sociocultural in its preparation. In each new situation, learning is a matter of *beginning to act* in the environment on the basis of the particular affordances of that environment. One's initial actions are either successful or not. If they are dramatically unsuccessful, that is, if there is no match at all between one's prepared structures and the affordances of the environment, the most likely response is to leave the environment, either physically, if possible, or by "tuning out" when actual physical departure is not possible. If the match is complete, there is no learning to take place. One just acts.

But if the match is partial – enough to keep one engaged, but not enough to provide a ready-made set of actions – a process of tuning to the affordances of the environment sets in. This tuning is what I mean by learning. It produces an ability to act "perfectly" in the environment. But, because it is a tuning process, it results in a specifically situated competence. The competence developed will not be perfect for any other specific environment. An effort to specify the mechanisms of tuning would reach beyond what either situated cognition or conceptual rationalism has attempted to study until now. Connectionist models of cognition (Rumelhart, McClelland, & the PDP Research Group, 1986), however, suggest a metaphor, at least, for what the process might be like. In connectionist models, a cognitive system learns by spreading activation across multiple nodes simultaneously. No single node embodies meaning or knowledge; rather, meaning is *emergent*, the result of ongoing activity in the network. The state of the network (its nodes, the strength and directionality of its links) at the beginning of an episode interacts with new stimuli in the situation to produce a particular pattern of activity. This activity can be thought of as the tuning process. It produces a change in the network. The changed network will react somewhat differently – even to similar stimuli – at the start of the next episode and will again tune itself, in a more or less continuous cycle of situation-specific learning.

From skeletal structures to scientific concepts

I want to show how the idea of situated rationalism plays out in two well-studied knowledge domains. I will not explore personal histories or describe details of the tuning process, because the necessary research – macrolongitudinal and microlongitudinal combined – has not been much pursued until now. But it is possible, on the basis of an assembled body of research, to lay out some plausible hypotheses about the relations between biologically prepared and culturally elaborated knowledge structures in different domains.

There are, logically and empirically, at least two kinds of relations between biologically prepared and culturally elaborated structures of knowledge:

- The culturally accepted forms may be *coherent* with biologically prepared structures. For example, certain core concepts of number and algebra can be grown by elaboration of basic principles of counting, plus knowledge about physical material, that there is reason to believe are among the biologically prepared structures available to all human infants.
- Culturally accepted or scientific concepts may *contradict* beliefs that are rooted in biologically prepared structures. This appears to be the case for many concepts in physics, where the contradictions give rise to systematic "misconceptions" and difficulties in learning scientific concepts. It may also be the case for certain mathematical concepts, such as fractions or proportions.

The nature of learning can be expected to be quite different for cultural concepts that are coherent with biologically prepared structures than for those that are contradictory. At the very least, we should expect to find differences between the two in simple ease of learning. Such differences would be reflected in the ages at which children in a given society acquire the cultural concepts of interest; in the ways in which knowledge of and mastery of the concepts are distributed in the population; and in the extent to which mastery of the concepts appears to depend on formal instruction. For the concepts used as examples here, all three of these indicators distinguish well between the coherent and the contradictory. Non-Newtonian forms of thinking about the physical world predominate among all but the best educated; formal physics is learned relatively late, primarily in formal institutions of instruction, and with considerable difficulty by most students. By contrast, core mathematics concepts that are derivable from knowledge about counting and physical material are learned easily, at a young age, and by nearly everyone who participates in any kind of market economy.

The examples I have mentioned from physics and mathematics are prototype cases – instances in which enough research has been done to make it clear whether we are dealing with a coherent or a contradictory relationship between the prepared and the culturally elaborated. In other instances (e.g., religion, biology, discussed in this volume), it is not clear what kind of transformation – whether an elaboration of a biologically prepared concept or its replacement by a new idea – must take place to reach a culturally accepted concept. For many of the most important learned concepts, a mixture of coherent and contradictory relations with several different prepared structures is likely. To explore the question of relations between culturally elaborated and prepared structures, however, it is useful to focus attention first on these clean, prototypical domains.

Additive composition of positive integers: Origins of algebraic principles in biologically prepared structures

Much of elementary arithmetic has as its conceptual base the fact that all numbers are additive compositions of other numbers. This compositional character of numbers provides an intuitive basis for understanding fundamental properties of the number system. These properties include commutativity and associativity of addition, equivalence classes of addition pairs (additive composition), complementarity of addition and subtraction (additive inverse), and certain rules of distribution. Children appreciate these properties at a surprisingly young age, as shown primarily by studies of their invented arithmetic performances (see Resnick, 1986, for a summary of this research). Challenged to solve problems for which they have no ready algorithms, children invent procedures that can be shown to apply implicitly these principles. Similar reasoning takes place among minimally schooled adults carrying out arithmetic tasks as part of their daily work (e.g., Schliemann & Acioly, 1989). Together, these two lines of research point to a body of mathematical knowledge that appears to be easily and, probably, universally acquired. I want to show here how two algebraic principles might plausibly be clear elaborations of early biologically prepared structures.

Commutativity and associativity

Commutativity and associativity are distinct properties in number theory, but children appear to understand them as a single permission to combine numbers in any order. For example, here are the words of a child (7 years, 7 months) who considered this permission self-evident. He was asked to add 45 and 11 and then immediately afterward 11 and 45. He simply repeated his first answer and said, "They're the same numbers, so they have to equal the same thing" (Resnick, 1986: 166). A more sophisticated implicit application of commutativity and associativity was shown by Resnick and Omanson (1987) among second and third graders. Using a mixture of reaction time and interview data, they showed that several children added problems such as 23 + 8 by decomposing 23, yielding (20 + 3) + 8, and then reconfiguring the problem to (20 + 8) + 3. Because (20 + 8) could be recombined to 28 very quickly on the basis of place value knowledge, this allowed the children to apply a simple counting-on solution: "*twenty-eight . . . twenty-nine, thirty, thirty-one.*"

Two sets of skeletal structures seem to provide the biological foundations for learning commutativity and associativity. One of these, the structures underlying the rules for counting and numerical quantification, has been extensively analyzed by Rochel Gelman and her colleagues (Gelman & Gallistel, 1978). The second, a *protoquantitative part-whole* schema, is one of a set of structures for reasoning qualitatively about amounts of physical material that have been hypothesized by Resnick and Greeno (1992; Resnick, 1992). Although the necessary research on infants and very young children has not yet been done, we can plausibly hypothesize a skeletal structure that helps children develop understanding of how the physical material around them comes apart and recombines. Such a structure would specify that material amounts are *additive*. That is, one can cut a quantity into pieces that, taken together, equal the original quantity. Or, one can put two quantities together to make a bigger quantity and then join that bigger quantity with yet another in a form of hierarchical additivity. This protoquantitative knowledge allows children to make judgments about the relations between parts and wholes. Children know, for example, that a whole cake is bigger than any of its pieces. They also know that the order in which sets of candies of different colors are poured into a bag does not change the total amount of candy available (Irwin, 1990). This latter knowledge about order is the basis for an early understanding of commutativity and associativity that can be expressed in the form of protoquantitative equations:

(1) Part1 + Part2 = Part2 + Part1

(2) (Part1 + Part2) + Part3 = Part1 + (Part2 + Part3)

Knowledge of counting principles and of the protoquantitative part-whole schema appears initially to interact very little in children's thinking. That is, young children will count in order to determine how many are in a set, but they do not usually think spontaneously of using counting to solve problems involving compositions or decompositions of sets. It apparently requires some social provocation – informal teaching, if you will – to get children to combine their counting and their part-whole knowledge structures. When they do, however, a new prepared structure results, one that can be labeled a *quantified part-whole schema*. This schema allows children to use counting and numbers to reason more precisely about amounts of physical material. They can now specify by *how many* a set is *increased*, for example, or exactly *how much is left* when a set of 9 is broken up into parts and 3 items are removed.

All of the relationships between wholes and parts that were present in the protoquantitative schema are maintained in the new, quantified version. But now the relations apply to specific quantified amounts of material. As a result, children can now reason using quantified equations, such as:

(3) 4apples + 7apples = 7apples + 4apples

(4) (3apples + 5apples) + 4apples = 3apples + (5apples + 4apples)

Although numbers play a role in these quantified equations, they function at this stage essentially as *adjectives*, that is, as terms that describe the properties of the quantities of material being physically or mentally manipulated. Eventually, however, numbers begin to take on a life of their own. They become objects in their own right, mathematical entities that can be reasoned *about*. When this happens, the same basic part-whole schema can organize knowledge about relations among numbers themselves. The commutativity and associativity principles now apply not to physical material but to mentally constructed mathematical entities:

(5) $4 + 7 = 7 + 4$

(6) $(3 + 5) + 4 = 3 + (5 + 4)$

A final step in the elaboration of the part-whole schema is its extension to *numbers in general*, rather than specific numbers. At this point, children understand that commutativity and associativity are *always* true for addition, no matter what the numbers. Thus:

(7) $n + m = m + n$

(8) $(n + m) + p = n + (m + p)$

Equivalence classes of addition pairs

Another mathematical property that children learn easily is that there are many ways of composing a number. The number 9, for example, can be made of 1 and 8, 2 and 7, 3 and 6, or 4 and 5. Children further understand that these equivalences (e.g., of $[1 + 8]$ and $[2 + 7]$) are based on a set of compensating additions and subtractions to the parts that have the effect of maintaining the whole. To illustrate how children articulate this idea, here are the words of a $7\frac{1}{2}$-year-old who was asked how $23 + 41$ might be rewritten so it would still equal 64. He first said $24 + 40$ and then continued:

I'm going one less than 40 and this one more... 25 plus 39. Tell me what you're doing to get that. *I'm just having one go lower; take one away and put it on the 41 to make it 42. Like that, I was going lower, lower, higher, higher.* Okay... Now why do all those numbers equal the same amount? *Because this is taking some away from one number and putting it on the other number.* And that's okay to do?... Why not?... *Anyone can do that.... Because you still have the same amount. You're keeping that but putting that on something else.... You're not just taking it away.* (From Resnick, 1986: 165)

In a more systematic exploration, Putnam, deBettencourt, and Leinhardt (1990) asked third-grade children to watch puppets demonstrate "derived-fact strategies" for addition and subtraction, to complete the calculations, and then to justify them. Derived-fact strategies transform presented problems into problems that are easy to solve, because they use well-known addition and subtraction facts. The transformations in one number require compensating transformations in another. For example, $7 + 9$ can be transformed to $8 + 8$ to benefit from a well-known "doubles" fact. Putnam et al. found that 50% to 60% of third graders interviewed could explicitly justify addition derived-fact strategies with verbalizations expressing the compensation rules. Many more could complete the calculations and give partial explanations.

To account for this kind of understanding, we need to specify another schema that probably has biological roots, a *protoquantitative increase/decrease* schema. This is a structure that allows children to interpret increases and decreases in amounts of physical material. It allows children as young as

3 or 4 years old to reason that, if they have a certain amount of something and they get another amount of the same thing (perhaps mother adds another cookie to the two already on the child's plate), they have more than before. Young children also know that, if some of the original quantity is taken away, they have less than before; and, they know that, if nothing has been added or taken away, they have the same amount as before. For example, children show surprise and label as "magic" any change in the number of objects on a plate that occurs out of their sight (Gelman, 1972).

The protoquantitative part-whole and increase/decrease schemas jointly enable reasoning about equivalence classes of addition pairs by showing how the whole is maintained unchanged by compensating changes in the two parts. In protoquantitative terms, if an amount is taken from one part of a whole and the same amount is added to the other part, the amount of the whole is unchanged. In protoquantitative equation form, that is

$$(9) \ (Part1 + A) + (Part2 - A) = (Part1 + Part2) + (A - A) = (Part1 + Part2) = W$$

This early, protoquantitative structure can be elaborated in the same way as the protoquantitative commutativity and associativity structures:

$$(10) \ (4cakes + 2cakes) + (7cakes - 2\ cakes) = (4cakes + 7cakes) + (2cakes - 2cakes) = (4cakes + 7cakes) = 11\ cakes$$

$$(11) \ (4 + 2) + (7 - 2) = (4 + 7) + (2 - 2) = (4 + 7) = 11$$

$$(12) \ (m + a) + (n - a) = (m + n) + (a - a) = m + n$$

As for the commutativity and associativity sequence, the relational structure of the protoquantitative equation is maintained throughout, but the knowledge structure is elaborated by successive changes in the *objects* (first, unquantified stuff, then counted sets, then specific numbers, then numbers in general) that are related.

The Newtonian laws of motion: Cultural forms that contradict biologically prepared structures

In contrast to basic number concepts, certain scientific laws of physics seem to call on people to replace rather than elaborate their prepared structures for interpreting the motion of objects. A substantial body of research now documents the surprising difficulty that even well-educated people have in learning some of the basic Newtonian laws of motion (see, e.g., Halloun & Hestenes, 1985; McCloskey, 1983; Viennot, 1979). During the early years of research on naive conceptions, organized alternative theories – often thought to parallel those of classical and medieval physicists – were attributed to students. In the past few years, the dominant view has been that students' spontaneous conceptions should not be characterized as systematic theories but rather as collections of ad hoc explanations. In the most extensive and radical reanalysis, diSessa (in press) has claimed that there is no single organizing principle or set of principles that gives rise to naive physics explanations. Instead, these explanations are constructed out of a set of *phenomenological primitives* that are called on in response to specific situations. Some of diSessa's primitives are recognizable as the kinds of beliefs about objects and motion that students of infant cognition (e.g., Spelke and Carey, this volume) have been documenting for extremely young children. Presumably – although diSessa does not discuss their origin – they are rooted in skeletal structures that prepare infants to learn from interaction with the physical world. In this actual physical world, motions die away naturally, keeping an object in motion requires exertion of effort, and vertical and horizontal motions are experienced differently.

DiSessa argues that Newtonian physics is not discontinuous with these basic structures, but rather an elaboration of them based on increasingly fine-tuned recognition of when they do and do not appropriately apply. DiSessa supports his argument mostly from explanation protocols of MIT students learning physics. However, diSessa offers no account of why it has proven so difficult for most students – even many strong students at selective universities – to really assimilate Newtonian principles and use them in constructing explanations or predictions about the motion of objects.

Another kind of analysis (Nersessian & Resnick, 1989) suggests that although particular explanations may be local and ad hoc, as diSessa and others claim, certain fundamental presuppositions underlie and constrain naive physics explanations. People are not aware of having these commitments and do not normally articulate them, even under the kind of intensive probing that is often carried on in studies of physics conceptions. Indeed, precisely because they are *presuppositional*, taken for granted, they are powerful assimilators of new data and may create serious epistemological obstacles (Bachelard, 1980) to learning scientific concepts that require new ontologies (cf. Carey and Spelke, this volume).

I consider here two implicit presuppositions that could well be grounded in biologically prepared structures and that together can account for most of the evidence that has been collected on misconceptions about projectile and free fall motion. Nersessian and Resnick (1989) have mapped findings in the naive physics conceptions research literature to an epistemological analysis of the historical shift in physics to Newtonian intertial theory. Our analysis identifies two presuppositions shared by pre-Newtonian scientists and today's naive physics thinkers. One, which we term the *stasis* presupposition, selects some situations as requiring explanations and others as natural and, therefore, not needing to be explained. The second, which can be termed the *agency* presupposition, sets criteria for an acceptable explanation.

The stasis presupposition specifies that being at rest is a natural *state* of objects. This means that an object at rest does not require an explanation.

It just *is*. Motion, by contrast, is a *change in state* and, as such, requires an explanation. Our analysis suggests that typical naive conceptions of projectile and free fall motion are all based on an implicit presupposition that motion requires an explanation. In their presupposition that motion requires an explanation, naive thinkers about physics are like pre-Newtonian scientists. Aristotle, Burridan, and even Galileo, in the early part of his career, thought of motion as a *process*. It was distinct from rest, which they thought of as a *state*. Their ontology, like modern students', thus contained two separate categories: states and processes; rest and motion fell into different categories. In Newtonian inertial physics, however, uniform linear motion is incorporated into the state category. Change in motion (acceleration), but not motion itself, is considered a process. To construct a Newtonian explanation, then, requires overturning a fundamental, early belief, one that is plausibly rooted in bodily experience (cf. Johnson, 1987) of the difference between rest and exertion.

This basic physical experience would also give rise to the presupposition of agency. Naive physics thinkers appear to believe that explanations of physical events such as motion must include specification of a mechanism. They look for a causal agent that makes an event occur. This fits nicely with what we are learning about biologically prepared structures for causal reasoning. However, it contrasts sharply with the structure of scientific explanations in physics since Newton. Scientific physics accepts as primary explanations expressions of mathematical relations among formally defined entities. The constraint equations that express physical laws do not specify agencies. Force, for example, increases just because mass or acceleration increase and not because mass or acceleration is an agent of change.

The definition of motion as a change in state and the requirement that explanations include causal agents are not articulated by subjects; neither is the relationship between change and the need for explanation. These implicit definitions and presuppositions must be inferred from the general pattern of responses in preconceptions research. A brief summary of some of the major findings of that research follows, along with a discussion of how they might derive from the stasis and agency presuppositions.

Motion implies force. Every study of naive physics conceptions reports some variant of a belief that, if an object is in motion, there must be a force acting on the object. This belief fits naturally with the presupposition that motion requires explanation, together with the assumption than an explanation must specify a causal agent. If motion must be explained and if explanations require causal agents, then a limited number of possibilities exist.

If one believes that there must be an agent of change when there is motion, then one will probably look first for external agents – pushes, pulls, shoves, and all kinds of direct mechanical actions of one body on another. The situations typically posed to students in naive physics studies, however, are ones in which an object is moving without any *current* external force acting on it. In these situations, the only possibility is that the agent must be inside the object. This leads to the frequently expressed conception that a force of some kind is stored inside the moving object. This idea is expressed by subjects in various terms, some borrowed from scientific language (*energy, inertia, force,* even *potential force*) and some borrowed from distinctly everyday language (*oomph, power*).

Consider now the possible biologically prepared structures that might give rise to these beliefs. The infant's responsiveness to information about external agents of motion has been documented by Carey and Spelke (this volume) and others. Furthermore, the infant's experience of bodily expenditure of energy and observation of its relation to observed results in the world could plausibly be interpreted by skeletal structures that produce a concept of internal energy producing motion. Thus, the documented naive physics conceptions could well be elaborations of biologically prepared structures. These would have to be replaced in order to adopt a Newtonian scientific perspective.

Slowing down in the absence of external force. Virtually all naive thinkers about motion express the belief that objects will slow down and eventually stop if force is not applied externally. DiSessa treats this belief as a special case of a "dying away" primitive that expresses the belief that all events naturally come to an end. Naive physicists' belief in slowing down and dying away suggests that they have classified motion as a process rather than a state. States – stable conditions – do not die away; they are ended only by some kind of interference. Processes die away. They are time-bound; they have a beginning and an end.

Passive and active motions are different. Susan Hojnacki (1988) has probed a distinction between beliefs about active and passive motion. In Hojnacki's study, students without formal physics education were asked to predict and explain trajectories of objects in situations like those studied by psychologists (e.g., McCloskey, 1983) and physicists (e.g., Halloun & Hestenes, 1985). From a Newtonian perspective, all of the situations involved the combination of two motions. However, physics-naive subjects distinguished between two classes of situations, only one of which required the combination of motions.

For situations in which an object was moving actively, "on its own" (e.g., a ball rolling on a cliff, a spacecraft moving through space), before a new force came into play (e.g., the ball comes to the end of the cliff, an engine gives a new thrust to a spacecraft), Hojnacki's subjects all understood that the two motions had to be combined to predict the trajectory, although they often made errors in details of the combination. However, for situations in which an object was initially moving passively (e.g., a ball carried by a walking person and then dropped, garbage carried by a spacecraft and then ejected), many of Hojnacki's subjects made "straight down" predictions. That is, they assumed that the initial forward motion would not persist after the dropping. Students were unaware that they were making this active/passive distinction, as evidenced in a failure to sort active and passive problems into different categories or to verbalize the distinction.

This initially surprising pattern of responses is easily understandable if one accepts the idea that subjects are distinguishing between situations that do and do not require explanations in the way I have proposed here. The passive object's initial forward motion does not need an explanation. Because it is being carried, it does not, in effect, "own" its motion; it is, itself, in a state of rest. For this reason, no internal force or energy needs to be attributed to it. When the object is dropped or ejected, therefore, there is only one force acting on it, the new force just applied or the force of gravity. Thus, a "single vector" prediction will be made – straight down in the case of dropped objects, or perpendicular to the original motion in the case of ejected objects in space. But objects moving on their own must have internal agents causing the motion. Those internal agents – forces – will still be present when the object is dropped or ejected, and so the old and the new forces will combine to determine the direction of the object's motion.

Situated rationalism and education

The distinction between concepts that are coherent with biologically prepared structures and those that contradict them suggests the need for two different approaches to teaching and instruction. For coherent concepts, "teaching" is largely a process of helping children elaborate their initial, biologically guided concept into particular cultural forms. It is more a matter of guided exposure to new opportunities for using concepts than of directly telling them about new ideas, although experience with a culture's conceptual language and tools must be considered a key part of this exposure (cf. Resnick & Greeno, 1992). Most educators who espouse a "constructivist" philosophy – a clear majority today – are, I believe, acting on an implicit assumption that what children already know as they enter an instructional situation is coherent with the new concepts to be learned. On this assumption, it is reasonable to conclude that children's own cognitive constructions will move without much resistance toward the culturally accepted forms to which they are exposed.

In the case of cultural knowledge that contradicts biologically preferred concepts, however, education must follow a different path: still constructivist in the sense that simple telling will not work, but much less dependent on untutored discovery and exploration. For these contradictory concepts, ways of helping children replace rather than elaborate initial beliefs need to be found. We have not yet found very good ways of doing this. In physics education, for example, where the phenomenon of resistance to scientific concepts has been recognized for some time, an early idea was that confronting students empirically with the inadequacy of their initial concepts would stimulate rejection of the old and openness to new ideas. This has not worked very well. Students mostly find ways of reinterpreting the empirical data to fit their initial conceptions (Champagne, Klopfer, & Anderson, 1980; Johsua & Dupin, 1987). Even when they accept the inadequacy of their initial ideas, physical experience and data do not directly suggest new, scientific concepts.

Some researchers have experimented with the use of analogies – usually embodied in special physical models – as a way of teaching the new concepts. Their reported successes (e.g., Brown & Clement, 1989; Sayeki, Ueno, & Nagasaka, 1991; White, 1993) have always involved very large investments of time (for students and teachers alike) for learning very limited concepts. In another proposed approach (Chi, 1992; Chi & VanLehn, 1991; Ohlsson, 1992), students would be directly taught certain core scientific concepts and then guided through a process of applying those concepts to many cases. The idea is that students might at first apply the concepts rather mechanically but would eventually come to believe in them because they yielded intellectual power. At that point, but not earlier, it might be profitable to pit the new concepts against the initial, biologically rooted ones. This attractive idea still requires empirical testing.

Beyond the problems involved in teaching specific concepts, the situated rationalist view of learning and development suggests some new perspectives on traditional problems in education. In particular, *individual differences* and *transfer*, both central constructs in educational psychology, can be usefully reconstrued. Both of these constructs have been classically defined in terms of bundles of relatively stable skills. Over the decades, debate has focused on how to describe these skills and how they bundle together. The situated rationalist framework suggests that, instead of decontextualized skills, it would be helpful to think of *personal histories* as the important determinants of the way individuals will act in a particular situation.

When individuals move from situation to situation, they carry histories of prior experience with them. These are histories of ways of behaving. They include the elaborated knowledge structures, along with affective and social propensities, developed in the course of tuning to prior situations. The way one enters a new situation is influenced by one's history of past situations. Situations experienced as similar to a past situation will initially evoke – not necessarily consciously – ways of behaving that developed through practice and tuning in the previous situation. If these ways of behaving work – that is, if they result in successful behavior in the new situation – they will be further practiced and elaborated. On this analysis, "transfer" would be a case in which a prepared structure and the new situation's affordances interact to produce a situated performance in accordance with what educators have defined as the "right" response. Lack of transfer would be a case in which affordances and prepared structures produce a tuned performance not in accordance with educators' expectations.

Two features distinguish this notion of personal histories from traditional views of transfer of skills and knowledge. First, what one carries with one to a new situation is much more complex and organic than a collection of skills. It is a whole set of dispositions, interpretations, and representations that, together and interactively, produce an initial response. Second, one's personal history is determinative only as one enters the new situation. Thereafter, all of the people, tools, and material resources of the new situation shape a new situated practice. Cognition is emergent in the situation and specific to it. Yet the individual is not lost, for he or she leaves the encounter with a residue of preparation for the next situation.

The idea of personal histories as a way of thinking about individual differences and transfer suggests that we might profitably think of education as an effort to organize sequences of designed situations that are likely to prepare individuals to tune adaptively to the kinds of natural situations they will encounter outside designated institutions of learning. Current formal education does this very poorly (see Resnick, 1987). The special situation of the classroom – calling for private rather than socially shared work and isolating mental activity from engagement in the social and physical world – builds skills and knowledge that allow students to function in school, but often fail to transfer to the worlds of work, civic, and personal life. To change this thoughtfully and productively will require a form of theory that is now largely absent from psychological thinking and only loosely developed in other fields of social science, *a theory of situations*. Such a theory would define the dimensions – social, cognitive, and physical – of situations with an eye to how activity in one situation might prepare individuals to enter another. Developing such a theory, taking into account both biological and social constraints on learning, represents a major challenge for those who would apply the concepts of situated rationalism to education.

References

Bachelard, G. (1980). *La formation de l'esprit scientifique* [Development of the scientific mind]. Paris: Vrin.

Brown, D. E., & Clement, J. (1989, March). *Overcoming misconceptions via analogical reasoning: Abstract transfer versus explanatory model.* Paper presented at the American Educational Research Association, San Francisco.

Champagne, A. B., Klopfer, L. E., & Anderson, J. H. (1980). Factors influencing the learning of classical mechanics. *American Journal of Physics, 48,* 174.

Chi, M. T. H. (1992). Conceptual change within and across ontological categories: Examples from learning and discovery in science. In R. Giere (Ed.), *Cognitive models of science: Minnesota Studies in the Philosophy of Science* (pp. 129–160). Minneapolis: University of Minnesota Press.

Chi, M. T. H., & VanLehn, K. A. (1991). The content of physics self-explanations. *Journal of the Learning Sciences, 1,* 69–105.

Cole, M. (1985). The zone of proximal development: Where culture and cognition create each other. In J. V. Wertsch (Ed.), *Culture, communication, and cognition: Vygotskian perspectives* (pp. 146–161). Cambridge: Cambridge University Press.

diSessa, A. (1993). Toward an epistemology of physics. *Cognition and Instruction, 10,* 105–225.

Gardner, H. (1991). *The unschooled mind: How children learn, how schools should teach.* New York: Basic Books.

Gelman, R. (1972). Logical capacity of very young children: Number invariance rules. *Child Development, 43,* 75–90.

Gelman, R., & Carey, S. (Eds.). (1991). *The epigenesis of mind: Essays on biology and cognition.* Hillsdale, NJ: Erlbaum.

Gelman, R., & Gallistel, C. R. (1978). *The child's understanding of number.* Cambridge, MA: Harvard University Press.

Halloun, I. A., & Hestenes, D. (1985). Common sense concepts about motion. *American Journal of Physics, 53,* 1056–1065.

Hojnacki, S. K. (1988). *Consistency in naive physical reasoning.* Unpublished masters thesis, University of Pittsburgh.

Hutchins, E. (1991). The social organization of distributed cognition. In L. B. Resnick, J. M. Levine, & S. D. Teasley (Eds.), *Perspectives on socially shared cognition* (pp. 283–307). Washington, D.C.: American Psychological Association.

Irwin, K. (1990, July). *Children's understanding of compensation, addition, and subtraction.* Paper presented at the 14th meeting of Psychology of Mathematics Education, Mexico.

Johnson, M. (1987). *Body in the mind: The bodily basis of meaning, imagination, and reason.* Chicago: University of Chicago Press.

Johsua, S., & Dupin, J. J. (1987). Taking into account student conceptions in a didactic strategy: An example in physics. *Cognition and Instruction, 4,* 117–135.

Latour, B. (1987). *Science in action.* Cambridge, MA: Harvard University Press.

Lave, J. (1988). *Cognition in practice: Mind, mathematics and culture in everyday life.* Cambridge: Cambridge University Press.

McCloskey, M. (1983). Intuitive physics. *Scientific American,* April, 122–130.

Mead, G. H. (1934). *Mind, self, and society.* Chicago: University of Chicago Press.

Neisser, U. (1976). *Cognition and reality: Principles and implications of cognitive psychology.* San Francisco: W. H. Freeman.

Nersessian, N., & Resnick, L. B. (1989, August). *Comparing historical and intuitive explanations of motion: Does "naive physics" have a structure?* Paper presented at the 11th conference of the Cognitive Science Society. Ann Arbor, MI.

Ohlsson, S. (1992). The cognitive skill of theory articulation: A neglected aspect of science education? *Science and Education, 1,* 181–192.

Putnam, R. T., deBettencourt, L. U., & Leinhardt, G. (1990). Understanding of derived-fact strategies in addition and subtraction. *Cognition and Instruction, 7,* 245–285.

Resnick, L. B. (1986). The development of mathematical intuition. In M. Perlmutter (Ed.), *Perspectives on intellectual development: The Minnesota Symposia on Child Psychology* (Vol. 19, pp. 159–194). Hillsdale, NJ: Erlbaum.

Resnick, L. B. (1987). Learning in school and out. *Educational Researcher, 16*(9), 13–20.

Resnick, L. B. (1992). From protoquantities to operators: Building mathematical competence on a foundation of everyday knowledge. In G. Leinhardt, R. T. Putnam, & R. A. Hattrup (Eds.), *Analysis of arithmetic for mathematics teaching* (pp. 373–429). Hillsdale, NJ: Erlbaum.

Resnick, L. B., & Greeno, J. G. (1992). Conceptual growth of number and quantity. Unpublished manuscript, University of Pittsburgh, Learning Research and Development Center.

Resnick, L. B., & Omanson, S. (1987). Learning to understand arithmetic. In R. Glaser (Ed.), *Advances in instructional psychology* (Vol. 3, pp. 41–95). Hillsdale, NJ: Erlbaum.

Rumelhart, D. E., McClelland, J. L., & the PDP Research Group. (1986). *Parallel distributed processing: Explorations in the microstructure of cognition* (Vols. I and II). Cambridge, MA: Bradford Books/MIT Press.

Sayeki, Y., Ueno, N., & Nagasaka, T. (1991). Mediation as a generative model for obtaining an area. *Learning and Instruction, 1*, 229–242.

Schliemann, A. D., & Acioly, N. M. (1989). Mathematical knowledge developed at work: The contribution of practice versus the contribution of schooling. *Cognition and Instruction, 6*, 185–221.

Viennot, L. (1979). Spontaneous reasoning in elementary dynamics. *European Journal of Science Education, 1*, 105–221.

Vygotsky, L. S. (1978). *Mind in society.* Cambridge, MA: Harvard University Press.

Wertsch, J. V. (1985). *Vygotsky and the social formation of mind.* Cambridge, MA: Harvard University Press.

White, B. (1993). ThinkerTools: Causal models, conceptual change, and science education. *Cognition and Instruction, 10*, 1–100.

Author index

495

Subject index

abstract nouns, 82
abstractness, 260–261, 289n2
accessibility, 224
Ache, 109
action regulation, 92–94
active motion, 488–489
actual modular domain, 50–53
  cultural input, 53–59
  definition, 50–51
  proper domain relationship, 54
adaptation
  computational theory, 96–98
  domain-general explanations, weaknesses, 89–94
  in evolutionary theory, 85–89, 95–98
  research needs, 104–106
  statistical foundation in evolution, 93–94
  task analysis role, 88
adaptation, problems of, 87–96
addition tasks
  biological preparedness, 481–485
  infant responses, 373
adoptive parentage, 187–188
aesthetics, and morality, 153–154, 165
affordances, 475–476, 479–480, 490–491
Agency
  actional, 119, 122, 137–141
  attitudinal, 119, 122
  core architecture of, definition, 120; infant cognitive development, 123–125; overview, 121–123
Agency presupposition, 486–487
Agency theory, 119–146
Agents, 119–146
  actional properties, 137–141
  animate object distinction, 121
  and fictional circumstances, 137–138
  image schemas, 130–132
  infant's grasp, 130–137, 144n6, 145n7–8

intentional properties, 122, 137–143
  and motion, 132–137
  subsystems, 119, 122
  ToBy mechanisms, 119–137
  ToMM theory, 137–143
  as transmitters of information, 143
alarm calls, vervet monkeys, 89–90
algebraic principles (*see also* numerical understanding)
  and biological preparedness, 481–485
altruism, adaptive function, 96–97
American Sign Language, 8
analogical reasoning
  domain-specific issue, 224–225
  naturalization model, 204
  partial transfer, 205
  physical analogies, 181–183, 193
  social category acquisition, 201–227
  societal model, 205
  and totemism, 203–204
analogical transfer
  domain distinction, 23
  experimental failures, 225
  intuitive robustness, 225
  partial transfer in, 205
  in social category acquisition, 201–227
  use in teaching, 490
Anang, 383
ancestral-descendant lineage, 459, 469
ancestral model, 457–459
anger, 435–441, 443–444, 446
animacy
  animate object, 121, 145n7
  children's explanations, 356
  infant perceptions, 176
animal cognition
  constraints framing of, 16–17
  equipotentiality principle, 17
  theory-driven learning, 17–18

505